ADAM SMITH

I

An Inquiry into the Nature and Causes of the Wealth of Nations

THE GLASGOW EDITION OF THE WORKS AND CORRESPONDENCE OF ADAM SMITH

Commissioned by the University of Glasgow to celebrate the bicentenary of the Wealth of Nations

I
THE THEORY OF MORAL SENTIMENTS
Edited by D. D. RAPHAEL *and* A. L. MACFIE

II
AN INQUIRY INTO THE NATURE AND CAUSES OF THE WEALTH OF NATIONS
Edited by R. H. CAMPBELL *and* A. S. SKINNER; *textual editor* W. B. TODD

III
ESSAYS ON PHILOSOPHICAL SUBJECTS
(and Miscellaneous Pieces)
Edited by W. P. D. WIGHTMAN

IV
LECTURES ON RHETORIC AND BELLES LETTRES
Edited by J. C. BRYCE
This volume includes the *Considerations concerning the First Formation of Languages*

V
LECTURES ON JURISPRUDENCE
Edited by R. L. MEEK, D. D. RAPHAEL, *and* P. G. STEIN
This volume includes two reports of Smith's course together with the 'Early Draft' of the *Wealth of Nations*

VI
CORRESPONDENCE OF ADAM SMITH
Edited by E. C. MOSSNER *and* I. S. ROSS

Associated volumes:

ESSAYS ON ADAM SMITH
Edited by A. S. SKINNER *and* T. WILSON

LIFE OF ADAM SMITH
By I. S. ROSS

The Glasgow Edition of the Works and Correspondence of Adam Smith and the associated volumes are published in hardcover by Oxford University Press. The six titles of the Glasgow Edition, but not the associated volumes, are being published in paperback by Liberty Fund.

ADAM SMITH

An Inquiry into the Nature and Causes of the Wealth of Nations

GENERAL EDITORS

R. H. CAMPBELL
AND
A. S. SKINNER

TEXTUAL EDITOR

W. B. TODD

VOLUME 1

Liberty Fund

Indianapolis

1981

This book is published by Liberty Fund, Inc., a foundation established to encourage study of the ideal of a society of free and responsible individuals.

The cuneiform inscription that serves as our logo and as the design motif for our endpapers is the earliest-known written appearance of the word "freedom" (*amagi*), or "liberty." It is taken from a clay document written about 2300 B.C. in the Sumerian city-state of Lagash.

This Liberty Fund edition of 1981 is an exact photographic reproduction of the edition published by Oxford University Press in 1976 and reprinted here with minor corrections in 1979.

This reprint has been authorized by Oxford University Press.

97 98 99 00 P 12 11 10 9

Library of Congress Cataloging-in-Publication Data
Smith, Adam. 1723–1790.
 An inquiry into the nature and causes of the wealth of nations.

 Reprint. Originally published: Oxford : Clarendon Press, 1979.
(Glasgow edition of the works and correspondence of Adam Smith; 2)
 Includes indexes.
 I. Economics. I. Campbell, Roy Harold.   II. Skinner, Andrew S.
III. Title.   IV. Series: Smith, Adam, 1723–1790. Works. 1981.
AC7.S59 1981, vol. 2 [HB161] 330.15'3s 81-15578
ISBN 0-86597-006-8 (pbk. : v. 1)[330.15'3] AACR2
ISBN 0-86597-007-6 (pbk. : v. 2)
ISBN 0-86597-008-4 (pbk. : set)

Liberty Fund, Inc.
8335 Allison Pointe Trail, Suite 300
Indianapolis, IN 46250-1687
(317) 842-0880

Cover design by JMH Corporation, Indianapolis, Indiana
Printed & bound by Edwards Brothers, Inc., Ann Arbor, Michigan

Preface

WHILE this volume as a whole was prepared by the General Editors, the actual text of the *Wealth of Nations* was established by W. B. Todd following principles which are explained in a separate note.

As far as the general or non-textual editorial work is concerned, we have sought to provide a system of cross references within the WN, together with a comprehensive list of references from the WN to Smith's other works, including the Lecture Notes and Correspondence. In addition, Smith's own references have been traced and parallels with other writers indicated where it seems reasonably certain that he had actually used their works. Comment has been made on matters of historical fact where this might be of benefit to the modern reader.

In the introduction, we have tried to give some idea of the links which exist between Smith's economics and other parts of a wider system of social science, together with an account of the structure and scope of the WN itself. We have also sought to indicate the extent to which the WN was the reflection of the times in which Smith lived.

In executing a work of this kind we have incurred debts which are too numerous to mention. We should, however, like to acknowledge the great benefit which we have received from the work of Edwin Cannan, whose original index has been retained.

R.H.C.
A.S.S.

Contents

Key to Abbreviations and References

Corr.	*Correspondence*
ED	'Early Draft' of *The Wealth of Nations*
EPS	*Essays on Philosophical Subjects* (which include:)
Ancient Logics	'History of the Ancient Logics and Metaphysics'
Ancient Physics	'History of the Ancient Physics'
Astronomy	'History of Astronomy'
English and Italian Verses	'Of the Affinity between certain English and Italian Verses'
External Senses	'Of the External Senses'
Imitative Arts	'Of the Nature of that Imitation which takes place in what are called the Imitative Arts'
Music, Dancing, and Poetry	'Of the Affinity between Music, Dancing and Poetry'
Stewart	Dugald Stewart, 'Account of the Life and Writings of Adam Smith, LL.D.'
FA, FB	Two fragments on the division of labour, Buchan Papers, Glasgow University Library.
LJ(A)	*Lectures on Jurisprudence:* Report of 1762–63.
LJ(B)	*Lectures on Jurisprudence:* Report dated 1766.
LRBL	*Lectures on Rhetoric and Belles Lettres*
TMS	*The Theory of Moral Sentiments*
WN	*The Wealth of Nations*
Anderson Notes	From John Anderson's Commonplace Book, vol. i, Andersonian Library, University of Strathclyde.

References to Smith's published works are given according to the original divisions, together with the paragraph numbers added in the margin of the Glasgow edition. For example:

TMS I.iii.2.2 = *Theory of Moral Sentiments*, Part I, section iii, chapter 2, paragraph 2.

WN I.x.b.1 = *Wealth of Nations*, Book I, chapter x, section b, paragraph 1.

Astronomy, I.4 = 'History of Astronomy', Section I, paragraph 4.

The Table of Corresponding Passages appended to this volume identifies the sections into which the WN is divided and provides for each paragraph the page references in the Cannan editions of 1930 and 1937.

In the case of the lecture notes we have adopted the following practice: references to the LRBL are given in the form 'LRBL i.8' (=volume i, page 8 of the original manuscript), with references to the Lothian edition (London, 1963) in parenthesis. In the *Lectures on Jurisprudence* we have also cited the volume and page reference from the original manuscript (all of which will be included in the Glasgow edition) while retaining page references to the Cannan edition (Oxford, 1896) where appropriate. References to the *Correspondence* give date of letter and letter number from the Glasgow edition.

Postscript. The *Anderson Notes* are now published in R. L. Meek, *Smith, Marx and After* (London, 1977).

General Introduction

Scope and Method

ALTHOUGH it would be extravagant to claim that Adam Smith was the last of the great polymaths, it is nonetheless true that he wrote on a remarkable range of subjects including as it does economics and history; law and government; language and the arts, not to mention essays on astronomy, ancient logics and metaphysics. Indeed, the latter group of essays, apparently written in the 1750s, although not published until 1795, moved J. A. Schumpeter to remark that 'Nobody, I venture to say, can have an adequate idea of Smith's intellectual stature who does not know these essays' and to describe that on astronomy as the 'pearl of the collection'[1].

The Astronomy is especially valuable as an exercise in 'philosophical history'; a form of enquiry in which Smith was particularly interested, and which, in this case, led him to examine the first formation and subsequent development of those astronomical theories which had culminated in the work of Newton. But at the same time, the essay was designed to illustrate the principles which *lead* and *direct* philosophical enquiries. The essay was thus concerned with the question of *motivation*, and as such may tell us a good deal about Smith's own drives as a thinker, contributing in this way to our understanding of the form which his other works in fact assumed.

Smith's main purpose in the Astronomy was to consider the stimulus given to the exercise of the understanding by the sentiments of *surprise*, *wonder*, and *admiration*; sentiments which he did not necessarily consider to be the sole sources of stimuli to philosophical work, but which represented forces whose influence was, he believed, 'of far wider extent than we should be apt upon a careless view to imagine' (Intro., 7). In elaborating on this statement Smith made a number of simple assumptions: that man is endowed with certain faculties and propensities such as reason, reflection, and imagination, and that he is motivated by a desire to acquire the means of pleasure and to avoid pain, where in this context pleasure relates to a state of the imagination involving tranquility and composure; a state attained from the contemplation of relation, similarity, or customary connection. He went on to argue that we feel *surprise* when some object or relation does not fall into an expected pattern; a sentiment which is quickly followed by *wonder*, which is in turn associated with the

[1] *History of Economic Analysis* (London, 1954), 182.

perception of something like a gap or interval (i.e. a lack of known connection or failure to conform to an established classification) between the
object or objects of examination. For Smith, the essence of wonder was
that it gave rise to a feeling of pain (i.e. disutility) to which the normal
response is an act of attempted *explanation*, designed to restore the mind
to a state of equilibrium; a goal which can only be attained where an
explanation for the phenomena in question is found, and where that
explanation is coherent, capable of accounting for observed appearances,
and stated in terms of plausible (or familiar) principles.

Smith considered these feelings and responses to be typical of all men,
while suggesting that the philosopher or scientist was particularly subject to them, partly as a result of superior powers of observation and
partly because of that degree of curiosity which normally leads him to
examine problems (such as the conversion of flesh into bone) which are
to the ordinary man so 'familiar' as not to require any explanation at all
(II.11).

Nature as a whole, Smith argued, 'seems to abound with events which
appear solitary and incoherent' (II.12) so that the purpose of philosophy
emerges as being to find 'the connecting principles of nature' (II.12) with,
as its ultimate end, the 'repose and tranquility of the imagination' (IV.13).
It is here especially that the sentiment of *admiration* becomes relevant
in the sense that once an explanation has been offered for some particular
problem, the very existence of that explanation may heighten our appreciation of the 'appearances' themselves. Thus, for example, we may
learn to understand and thus to admire a complex economic structure
once its hidden 'springs' have been exposed, just as the theory of astronomy
leads us to admire the heavens by presenting 'the theatre of nature' as a
coherent and *therefore* as a more 'magnificent spectacle' (II.12). Scientific explanation is thus designed to restore the mind to a state of balance
and at the same time productive of a source of pleasure in this rather
indirect way. Smith also added, however, that men pursue the study of
philosophy for its own sake, 'as an original pleasure or good in itself,
without regarding its tendency to procure them the means of many other
pleasures' (III.3).

There are perhaps three features of this argument which are worth
emphasizing at this point. First, Smith's suggestion that the purpose of
philosophy is to explain the coherence of nature, allied to his recognition
of the interdependence of phenomena, leads directly to the idea of a
system which is designed to explain a *complex* of phenomena or 'appearances'. It is interesting to recall in this connection that the history of
astronomy unfolded in terms of four systems of this kind, and that Smith
should have likened such productions of the intellect to machines whose
function was to connect together 'in the fancy those different movements

and effects which are already in reality performed' (IV.19). Secondly, it is noteworthy that Smith should have associated intellectual effort, and the forms which the corresponding output may assume, with certain sources of pleasure. He himself often spoke of the *beauty* of 'systematical arrangement' (WN V.i.f.25) and his 'delight' in such arrangement was one of the qualities of his mind to which Dugald Stewart frequently drew attention. In the Imitative Arts (II.30) Smith likened the pleasure to be derived from the contemplation of a great system of thought to that felt when listening to 'a well composed concerto of instrumental Music' ascribing to both an almost sensual quality. Points such as these are relevant at least in the sense that a general preference for order or system may lead the thinker to work in certain ways and even to choose a particular method of organizing his arguments. Smith in fact considered the various ways of organizing scientific (or didactic) discourse in the LRBL where it is stated that the technique whereby we 'lay down certain principles, [primary?] or proved, in the beginning, from whence we account for the severall Phaenomena, connecting all together by the same chain' is 'vastly more ingenious' and *for that reason* 'more engaging' than any other. He added: 'It gives us a pleasure to see the phenomena which we reckoned the most unaccountable, all deduced from some principle (commonly, a wellknown one) and all united in one chain'. (LRBL ii.133–4, ed. Lothian, 140.) Elsewhere he referred to a *propensity*, common to all men, to account for 'all appearances from as few principles as possible' (TMS VII.ii.2.14).

However, while there is little doubt that Smith's major works (including of course the Astronomy itself) are dominated by such a choice, it would be as wrong to imply that such works are to be regarded as deductive exercises in practical aesthetics as it would be to ignore the latter element altogether. The fact is that the dangers as well as the delights of purely deductive reasoning were widely recognized at this time, and the choice of Newton rather than Descartes (who was also a proponent of the 'method' described above) as the model to be followed is indicative of the point. The distinctive feature of Newton's work was not, after all, to be found in the use of 'certain principles' in the explanation of complex phenomena, but rather in the fact that he (following the lead of others) sought to establish those principles *in a certain way*. Those interested in the scientific study of man at this time sought to apply the Newtonian vision of a law governed universe to a new sphere, and to employ the 'experimental method' as an aid to the discovery of those laws of nature which governed the behaviour of the machine and disclosed the intention of its Design.

Smith's contribution to what would now be defined as the 'social sciences' is contained in his work on ethics, jurisprudence, and economics,

which correspond in turn to the order in which he lectured on these subjects while Professor of Moral Philosophy at Glasgow. All are characterized by certain common features which are readily apparent on examination: in each case Smith sought to explain complex problems in terms of
a small number of basic principles, and each conforms to the requirements of the Newtonian method in the broad sense of that term. All three
make use of the typical hypothesis that the principles of human nature
can be taken as constant, and all employ the doctrine of 'unintended social
outcomes'—the thesis that man, in following the prompting of his nature,
unconsciously gives substantial expression to some parts of the [Divine?]
Plan. Again, each area of Smith's thought is marked by a keen sense of
the fact that manners and institutions may change through time and that
they may show striking variations in different communities at the same
point in time—a feature which was rapidly becoming quite common in
an age dominated by Montesquieu.

It is perhaps even more remarkable that not only were Smith's ethics,
jurisprudence, and economics, marked by a degree of systematic thought
of such a kind as to reveal a great capacity for model-building, but also by
an attempt to delineate the boundaries of a single system of thought, of
which these separate subjects were the component parts. For example,
the TMS may be seen to offer an explanation as to the way in which so
self-regarding a creature as man succeeds (by natural as distinct from artificial means) in erecting barriers against his own passions; an argument
which culminates in the proposition that some system of magistracy is
generally an essential condition of social stability. On the other hand, the
historical treatment of jurisprudence complements this argument by
showing the way in which government originates, together with the
sources of social and political change, the whole running in terms of a
four stage theory of economic development.[2] The economic analysis as
such may be seen to be connected with the other areas of Smith's thought
in the sense that it begins from a specific stage of historical development
and at the same time makes use of the psychological assumptions established by the TMS.

Before proceeding to the economics it may therefore be useful to review
the main elements of the other branches of Smith's work, and to elucidate
some of their interconnections. This may be an appropriate choice not
only because Smith himself taught the elements of economics against a
philosophical and historical background, but also because so much of that
background was formally incorporated in the WN itself—a book, after

---

[2] For comment, see R. L. Meek 'Smith, Turgot and the Four Stages Theory' in *History of Political Economy*, iii (1971), and his introduction to *Turgot on Progress, Sociology,
and Economics* (Cambridge, 1973).

all, which is concerned with much more than economics as that term is now commonly understood.

Social Theory

Smith's *Theory of Moral Sentiments* is, of course, an important contribution to moral philosophy in its own right, and one which attempted to answer the two main questions which Smith considered to be the proper province of this kind of philosopher:

First, wherein does virtue consist? Or what is the tone of temper, and tenour of conduct, which constitutes the excellent and praise-worthy character, the character which is the natural object of esteem, honour, and approbation? And, secondly, by what power or faculty in the mind is it, that this character, whatever it be, is recommended to us? Or in other words, how and by what means does it come to pass, that the mind prefers one tenour of conduct to another? (VII.i.2)

On Smith's argument, the process by which we distinguish between objects of approval or disapproval depends largely on our capacity for 'other-regarding' activities and involves a complex of abilities and propensities which include sympathy, imagination, reason and reflection. To begin with, he stated a basic principle in arguing that man is possessed of a certain fellow feeling which permits him to feel joy or sorrow according as the circumstances facing others contribute to their feelings of pleasure or pain. An expression of sympathy (broadly defined) for another person thus involves an act of reflection and imagination on the part of the observer in the sense that we can only form an opinion with regard to the mental state of another person by 'changing places in the fancy' with him. Smith was also careful to argue in this connection that our judgement with regard to others was always likely to be imperfect, at least in the sense that we can have 'no immediate experience of what other men feel' (I.i.1.2). Given these basic principles, Smith then proceeded to apply them in considering the two different 'aspects' or 'relations' under which we may judge an action taken by ourselves or others, 'first, in relation to the cause or object which excites it; and, secondly, in relation to the end which it proposes, or to the effect which it tends to produce' (II.i.2).

We may take these in turn:

In dealing with the first question we go beyond the consideration of the circumstances in which the subject of our judgement may find himself, and his *state* of mind (i.e. whether he is happy or sad) to consider the extent to which his actions or 'affections' (i.e. expressions of feeling) are *appropriate* to the conditions under which they take place or the objects which they seek to attain. In short, the purpose of judgement is to form an opinion as to the propriety or impropriety of an action, or expression of feeling, where these qualities are found to consist in 'the suitableness or unsuitableness, in the proportion or disproportion which the affection seems to bear to the cause or object which excites it' (I.i.3.6).

Given the principles so far established it will be evident that when the spectator of another man's conduct tries to form an opinion as to its propriety, he can only do so by 'bringing home to himself' *both* the circumstances and feelings of the subject. Smith went on to argue that exactly the same principles apply when we seek to form a judgement as to our own actions, the only difference being that we must do so indirectly rather than directly; by visualizing the manner in which the real or supposed spectator might react to them. Or, as Smith put it:

We can never survey our own sentiments and motives, we can never form any judgement concerning them; unless we remove ourselves, as it were, from our own natural station, and endeavour to view them as at a certain distance from us. But we can do this in no other way than by endeavouring to view them with the eyes of other people, or as other people are likely to view them. (III.1.2)

Given these points, we can now examine the second 'relation', that is, the propriety of action 'in relation to the end which it proposes, or the effect which it tends to produce'. Here, as far as the *agent* is concerned, Smith argued that the *spectator* can form a judgement as to whether or not an *action* is proper or improper in terms, for example, of motive as well as by reference to the propriety of the choice of means to attain a given end. In the same way, the spectator can form a judgement with regard to the propriety of the *reaction* of the subject (or person affected) to the circumstances created by the action of the agent.

Now while it is evident that the spectator can form these judgements when examining the actions of the two parties taken separately, it is an essential part of Smith's argument that a view with regard to the *merit* or *demerit* of a given action can be formed only by taking account of the activities of the two parties *simultaneously*. He was careful to argue in this connection, for example, that we might sympathize with the motives of the agent while recognizing that the action taken had had unintended consequences which might have either harmed or benefited some third party. Similarly, the spectator might sympathize with the reaction of the subject to a particular situation, while finding that sympathy qualified by recognition of the fact that the person acting had not intended another person either to gain or lose. It is only given a knowledge of the motives of the agent *and* the consequences of an action that we can form a judgement as to its merit or demerit, where that judgement is based on some perception of the propriety or impropriety of the activities of the two parties. Given these conditions Smith concluded that as our perception of the propriety of conduct 'arises from what I shall call a direct sympathy with the affections and motives of the person who acts, so our sense of its merit arises from what I shall call an indirect sympathy with the gratitude of the person who is, if I may say so, acted upon' (II.i.5.1).

Smith went on from this point to argue that where approval of motive is added to a perception of the beneficent tendency of the action taken, then such actions deserve *reward*; while those of the opposite kind 'seem then to deserve, and, if I may say so, to call aloud for, a proportionable punishment; and we entirely enter into, and thereby approve of, that resentment which prompts to inflict it' (II.i.4.4). As we shall see, this principle was to assume considerable importance in terms of Smith's discussion of *justice*.

Before going further there are perhaps three points which should be emphasized and which arise from Smith's discussion of the two different 'relations' in terms of which we can examine the actions of ourselves or other men.

First, Smith's argument is designed to suggest that judgement of our actions is always framed by the real or supposed spectator of our conduct. It is evident therefore that the accuracy of the judgement thus formed will be a function of the *information* available to the spectator with regard to action or motive, and the *impartiality* with which that information is interpreted.

Secondly, it follows from the above that wherever an action taken or a feeling expressed by one man is approved of by another, then an element of restraint (and therefore control of our 'affections') must be present. For example, it is evident that since we have no immediate experience of what other men feel, then we as spectators can 'enter into' their situation only to a limited degree. The person judged can therefore attain the agreement of the spectator only:

by lowering his passion to that pitch, in which the spectators are capable of going along with him. He must flatten, if I may be allowed to say so, the sharpness of its natural tone, in order to reduce it to harmony and concord with the emotions of those who are about him. (I.i.4.7)

Finally, it will be obvious that the individual *judged* will only make the effort to attain a certain 'mediocrity' of expression where he regards the opinion of the spectator as important. In fact Smith made this assumption explicit in remarking:

Nature when she formed man for society, endowed him with an original desire to please, and an original aversion to offend his brethren. She taught him to feel pleasure in their favourable, and pain in their unfavourable regard. She rendered their approbation most flattering . . . for its own sake; and their disapprobation most mortifying and most offensive. (III.2.6)

Given the desire to acquire the sources of pleasure and to avoid pain, this aspect of the psychology of man would appear to ensure that he *will* generally act in ways which will secure the approbation of his brethren, and that he is to this extent fitted for the society of other men. At the same time, however, Smith makes it clear that this general *disposition* may of itself be insufficient to ensure an adequate source of control over our actions and passions, and this for reasons which are at least in part connected with the spectator concept and the problem of self-interest.

We have already noted that the spectator can never be *entirely* informed with regard to the feelings of another person, and it will be evident therefore that it will always be particularly difficult to attain a knowledge of the motive which may prompt a given action. Smith noted this point in remarking that in fact the world judges by the event, and not by the design, classifying this tendency as one of a number of 'irregularities' in our moral sentiments. The difficulty is, of course, that such a situation must constitute something of a discouragement to virtue; a problem which was solved in Smith's model by employing an additional (and explicit) assumption with regard to the psychology of man. As Smith put it, a desire for approval and an aversion to the disapproval of his fellows would not alone have rendered man fit:

for that society for which he was made. Nature, accordingly, has endowed him not only with a desire of being approved of, but with a desire of being what ought to be approved of; or of being what he approves of in other men. The first desire could only have made him wish to appear to be fit for society. The second was necessary in order to render him anxious to be really fit. (III.2.7)

Hence the importance in Smith's argument of the ideal or supposed spectator, of the 'man within the breast', the abstract, ideal, spectator of our sentiments and conduct who is always well informed with respect to our *own* motives, and whose judgement would be that of the actual spectator where the latter was possessed of all the necessary information. It is this tribunal, the voice of principle and conscience, which, in Smith's argument, helps to ensure that we will in fact tread the path of virtue and which supports us in this path even when our due rewards are denied us or our sins unknown.

However, having made this point, Smith drew attention to another difficulty, namely that even where we have access to the *information* necessary to judge our own conduct, and even where we are generally disposed to judge ourselves as others might see us, if they knew all, yet there are at least two occasions on which we may be unlikely to regard our own actions with the required degree of *impartiality*: 'first, when we are about to act; and, secondly, after we have acted. Our views are apt to be very partial in both cases; but they are apt to be most partial when it is of most importance that they should be otherwise' (III.4.2). In this connection he went on to note that when 'we are about to act, the eagerness of passion will very seldom allow us to consider what we are doing with the candour of an indifferent person', while in addition a judgement formed in a cool hour may still be lacking in sufficient candour, because 'It is so disagreeable to think ill of ourselves, that we often purposely turn away our view from those circumstances which might render that judgement unfavourable' (III.4.4).

The solution to this particular logical problem is found in the idea of *general rules* of morality or accepted conduct; rules which we are disposed to obey by virtue of the claims of conscience, and of which we attain some knowledge by virtue of our ability to form judgements in particular cases. As Smith argued:

It is thus that the general rules of morality are formed. They are ultimately founded upon experience of what, in particular instances, our moral faculties, our natural sense of merit and propriety, approve, or disapprove of. We do not originally approve or condemn particular actions; because, upon examination, they appear to be agreeable or inconsistent with a certain general rule. The general rule, on the contrary, is formed, by finding from experience, that all actions of a certain kind, or circumstanced in a certain manner, are approved or disapproved of. (III.4.8)

It will be noted that such rules are based on our experience of what is fit and proper to be done or to be avoided, and that they become standards or yardsticks against which we can judge our conduct even in the heat of the moment, and which are therefore 'of great use in correcting the misrepresentations of self-love' (III.4.12).

Yet even here Smith does not claim that a knowledge of general rules will of itself be sufficient to ensure good conduct, and this for reasons which are not unconnected with (although not wholly explained by) yet a further facet of man's nature.

For Smith, man was an active being, disposed to pursue certain objectives which may be motivated by a desire to be thought well of by his fellows but which at the same time may lead him to take actions which have hurtful consequences as far as others are concerned. It is indeed one of Smith's more striking achievements to have recognized the social objective of many economic goals in remarking:

it is chiefly from this regard to the sentiments of mankind, that we pursue riches and avoid poverty. For to what purpose is all the toil and bustle of this world? what is the end of avarice and ambition, of the pursuit of wealth, of power and pre-eminence? ... what are the advantages we propose by that great purpose of human life which we call bettering our condition? To be observed, to be attended to, to be taken notice of with sympathy, complacency, and approbation, are all the advantages which we can propose to derive from it. (I.iii.2.1)

However, Smith was well aware that the pursuit of status, the desire to be well thought of in a public sense, could be associated with self-delusion, and with actions which could inflict damage on others either by accident or design. In this connection, he remarked that the individual:

In the race for wealth, and honours, and preferments ... may run as hard as he can, and strain every nerve and every muscle, in order to outstrip all his competitors. But if he should justle, or throw down any of them, the indulgence of the spectators is entirely at an end. It is a violation of fair play, which they cannot admit of. (II.ii.2.1)

Knowledge of the resentment of the spectators thus emerges as something of a deterrent as far as the agent is concerned, although Smith placed more emphasis on the fact that a feeling of *resentment* generated by some act of *injustice* produces a natural approval of punishment, just as the perception of the good consequences of some action leads, as we have seen, to a desire to see it rewarded. In this world at least, it is our disposition to punish and approval of punishment which restrains acts of injustice, and which thus helps to restrain the actions of individuals within due bounds. Justice in this sense of the term is of critical importance, and Smith went on to notice that while nature 'exhorts mankind to acts of beneficence, by the pleasing consciousness of deserved reward', beneficence is still the 'ornament which embellishes, not the foundation which supports the building'. He continued:

Justice, on the contrary, is the main pillar that upholds the whole edifice. If it is removed, the great, the immense fabric of human society ... must in a moment crumble into atoms. (II.ii.3.4)

In Smith's eyes, a fundamental pre-condition of social order was a system of positive law, embodying our conception of those rules of conduct which relate to justice. He added that these rules must be administered by some system of government or 'magistracy', on the ground that:

As the violation of justice is what men will never submit to from one another, the public magistrate is under a necessity of employing the power of the commonwealth to enforce the practice of this virtue. Without this precaution, civil society would become a scene of bloodshed and disorder, every man revenging himself at his own hand whenever he fancied he was injured. (VII.iv.36)

It now remains to be seen just how 'government' originates, to explain the sources of its authority, and the basis of obedience to that authority.

The Stages of Society

It was in the lectures on justice rather than the TMS that Smith set out to consider the grounds on which we were disposed to obey our 'magistrates', finding the basis of obedience in the principles of *utility* and *authority*. In practice, Smith placed most emphasis on the latter and identified four main sources: personal qualifications, age, fortune, and birth. Taking these four sources in turn, he argued that personal qualities such as wisdom, strength, or beauty, while important as sources of *individual* distinction, were yet of rather limited *political* value, since they are all qualities which are open to dispute. As a result, he suggests that *age*, provided there is no 'suspicion of dotage', represents a more important source of authority and of respect, since it is 'a plain and palpable quality' about which there can be no doubt'. Smith also observed that as a matter of fact age regulates rank among those who are in every other respect equal in both primitive and civilized societies, although its relative importance in the two cases is likely to vary.

The third source of authority, wealth, of all the sources of power is perhaps the most emphasized by Smith, and here again he cites two elements. First, he noted that through an 'irregularity' of our moral sentiments, men tend to admire and respect the rich (rather than the poor, who *may* be morally more worthy) as the possessors of all the imagined conveniences of wealth. Secondly, he argued that the possession of riches may also be associated with a degree of power which arises from the dependence of the poor for their subsistence. Thus, for example, the great chief who has no other way of spending his surpluses other than in the maintenance of men, acquires retainers and dependents who:

depending entirely upon him for their subsistence, must both obey his orders in war, and submit to his jurisdiction in peace. He is necessarily both their general and their judge, and his chieftainship is the necessary effect of the superiority of his fortune. (WN V.i.b.7)

Finally, Smith argues that the observed fact of our tendency to venerate antiquity of family, rather than the upstart or newly rich, also constitutes an important source of authority which may reinforce that of riches. He concluded that:

Birth and fortune are evidently the two circumstances which principally set one man above another. They are the two great sources of personal distinction, and are therefore the principal causes which naturally establish authority and subordination among men. (V.i.b.11)

Having made these points, Smith then went on to argue that just as wealth (and the *subsequent* distinction of birth) represents an important source of *authority*, so in turn it opens up an important source of *dispute*.

In this connection we find him arguing that where people are prompted by malice or resentment to hurt one another, and where they can be harmed only in respect of person or reputation, then men may live together with *some* degree of harmony; the point being that 'the greater part of men are not very frequently under the influence of those passions; and the very worst men are so only occasionally.' He went on to note:

As their gratification too, how agreeable soever it may be to certain characters, is not attended with any real or permanent advantage, it is in the greater part of men commonly restrained by prudential considerations. Men may live together in society with some tolerable degree of security, though there is no civil magistrate to protect them from the injustice of those passions. (V.i.b.2)

But in a situation where property can be acquired, Smith argued there could be an advantage to be gained by committing acts of injustice, in that here we find a situation which tends to give full rein to avarice and ambition.

The acquisition of valuable and extensive property, therefore, necessarily requires the establishment of civil government. Where there is no property, or at least none that exceeds the value of two or three days labour, civil government is not so necessary. (ibid.)

Elsewhere he remarked that 'Civil government, so far as it is instituted for the security of property, is in reality instituted for the defence of the rich against the poor, or of those who have some property against those who have none at all' (V.i.b.12). It is a government, on Smith's argument, which in some situations at least is supported by a perception of its utility, at least on the side of the 'rich', but which must gradually have evolved naturally and independently of any consideration of that necessity. In Smith's own words:

Civil government supposes a certain subordination. But as the necessity of civil government gradually grows up with the acquisition of valuable property, so the principal causes which naturally introduce subordination gradually grow up with the growth of that valuable property. (V.i.b.3)

In this way Smith stated the basic principles behind the origin of government and illustrated the four main sources of authority. In the subsequent part of the argument he then tried to show the way in which the outlines of society and government would vary, by reference to four broad socio-economic types: the stages of hunting, pasture, agriculture, and commerce.[3] One of the more striking features of Smith's argument is in fact the link which he succeeded in establishing between the form of economy prevailing (i.e. the mode of earning subsistence) and the source and

[3] LJ (B) 149, ed. Cannan 107. The socio-economic analysis appears chiefly in Books III and V of the WN.

distribution of power or dependence among the classes of men which make up a single 'society'.

The first stage of society was represented as the 'lowest and rudest' state, such 'as we find it among the native tribes of North America' (WN V.i.a.2). In this case, life is maintained through gathering the spontaneous fruits of the soil, and the dominant activities are taken to be hunting and fishing—a mode of acquiring subsistence which is antecedent to any social organization in production. As a result, Smith suggested that such communities would be small in size and characterized by a high degree of personal liberty—due of course to the absence of any form of economic dependence. Smith also observed that in the absence of private property which was also capable of accumulation, disputes between different members of the community would be minor 'so there is seldom any established magistrate or any regular administration of justice' (V.i.b.2) in such states. He added:

Universal poverty establishes there universal equality, and the superiority, either of age, or of personal qualities, are the feeble, but the sole foundations of authority and subordination. There is therefore little or no authority or subordination in this period of society. (V.i.b.7)

The second social stage is that of pasture, which Smith represented as a 'more advanced state of society, such as we find it among the Tartars and Arabs' (V.i.a.3). Here the use of cattle is the dominant economic activity and this mode of subsistence meant, as Smith duly noted, that life would tend to be nomadic and the communities larger in size than had been possible in the preceding stage. More dramatically, Smith observed that the appropriation of herds and flocks which introduced an inequality of fortune, was that which first gave rise to regular government. We also find here a form of property which can be accumulated and transmitted from one generation to another, thus explaining a change in the main sources of authority as compared to the previous period. As Smith put it:

The second period of society, that of shepherds, admits of very great inequalities of fortune, and there is no period in which the superiority of fortune gives so great authority to those who possess it. There is no period accordingly in which authority and subordination are more perfectly established. The authority of an Arabian scherif is very great; that of a Tartar khan altogether despotical. (V.i.b.7)

At the same time it is evident that the mode of subsistence involved will ensure a high degree of dependence on the part of those who must acquire the means of subsistence through the exchange of personal service, and those who, owning the means of subsistence, have no other means of expending it save on the maintenance of dependents, who also contribute to their military power. Smith added that while the distinction of birth, being subsequent to the inequality of fortune, can have no place in a nation of hunters, this distinction 'always does take place among nations of shepherds' (V.i.b.10). Since the great families lack, in this context, the means of dissipating wealth, it follows that 'there are no nations among whom wealth is likely to continue longer in the same families' (ibid.).

The third economic stage is perhaps the most complicated of Smith's four-fold classification at least in the sense that it seems to have a lower, middle and upper phase. Thus for example the initial stage may be seen to correspond to that situation which followed the overthrow of Rome by the barbarians; pastoral nations which had, however, acquired some idea of agriculture and of property in land. Smith argued that such peoples would naturally adapt existing institutions to their new situation and that their first act would be to divide the available territories, introducing by this means a settled abode and some form of rudimentary tillage; i.e. the beginnings of a new form of productive activity. Under the circumstances outlined, each estate or parcel of land would assume the character of a separate principality, while presenting many of the features of the second stage. As in the previous case, for example, the basis of power is property, and, as before, those who lack the means of subsistence can acquire it only through the exchange of personal service, thus becoming members of a group who 'having no equivalent to give in return for their maintenance' must obey their lord 'for the same reason that soldiers must obey the prince who pays them' (III.iv.5). Each *separate* estate could thus be regarded as stable in a political sense in that it was based on clear relations of power and dependence, although Smith did emphasize that there would be an element of instability in terms of the relations *between* the principalities; a degree of instability which remained even after the advent of the feudal period with its complex of rights and obligations. In Smith's words the authority possessed by the government of a whole country 'still continued to be, as before, too weak in the head and too strong in the inferior members' (III.iv.9), a problem basically created by the fact that:

In those disorderly times, every great landlord was a sort of petty prince. His tenants were his subjects. He was their judge, and in some respects their legislator in peace, and their leader in war. He made war according to his own discretion, frequently against his neighbours, and sometimes against his sovereign. (III.ii.3)

It was a situation which effectively prevented economic development, and one where the open country remained 'a scene of violence, rapine, and disorder' (III.iv.9).

The middle stage of this period may be represented as preserving the institutions of the previous stage (save with the substitution of the *feudal* for the *allodial* system of land-tenure), albeit with the significant addition of self-governing cities paying a 'rent certain' to the king. In this way, Smith suggested, the kings were able to acquire a source of power capable of offsetting that of the great lords, by way of a tactical alliance with the cities. Smith made exactly this point when remarking that mutual interest would lead the burghers to 'support the king, and the king to support them against the lords. They were the enemies of his enemies, and it was his interest to render them as secure and independent of those enemies as he could' (III.iii.8). Two significant developments were then traced from this situation, itself a response to the political instability of the agrarian period. First, the cities, as self-governing communities (a kind of independent republics Smith calls them) would create the essential conditions for economic development (personal security), while, secondly, their development would also generate an important shift in the balance of political power.

The upper stage of the period differs from the previous phase most obviously in that Smith here examines a situation where the trade and manufactures of the cities had had a significant impact on the power of the nobles, by providing them for the first time with a means of expending their surpluses. It was this trend, Smith suggested, which led the great proprietors to improve the form of leases (with a view to maximizing their exchangeable surpluses) and to the dismissal of the excess part of their tenants and retainers—all with consequent effects on the economic and thus the political power of this class. As Smith put it:

For a pair of diamond buckles perhaps, or for something as frivolous and useless, they exchanged the maintenance, or what is the same thing, the price of the maintenance of a thousand men for a year, and with it the whole weight and authority which it could give them. (III.iv.10)

The fourth and apparently final economic stage (commerce) may be simply described as one wherein all goods and services command a price, thus effectively eliminating the direct dependence of the feudal period and to this extent diminishing the power to be derived from the ownership of property. Thus for example Smith noted that in the present stage of Europe a man of ten thousand a year might maintain only a limited number of footmen, and that while tradesmen and artificers might be dependent on his custom, none the less 'they are all more or less independent of him, because generally they can all be maintained without him' (III.iv.11).

From the standpoint of the *economics* of the situation, the significant development was that of a two sector economy at the domestic level where

the constant drive to better our condition could provide the maximum
stimulus to economic growth within an institutional framework which
ensured that the pursuit of private interest was compatible with public
benefit. From the standpoint of the *politics* of the situation, the significant development was a new source of wealth which was more widely
distributed than previously, and which ultimately had the effect of limiting
the power of kings by shifting the balance of consideration away from the
old landed aristocracy and towards a new mercantile class. In the words
of John Millar, it was a general trend which served to propagate sentiments of personal independence, as a result of a change in the mode of
earning subsistence; a trend which must lead us to expect that 'the prero-
gatives of the monarch and of the ancient nobility will be gradually undermined, that the privileges of the people will be extended in the same
proportion, and that power, the usual attendant of wealth, will be in some
measure diffused over all the members of the community.'[4]

Once again we face a situation where a change in the mode of earning
subsistence has altered the balance and distribution of political power,
with consequent effects on the nature of government. Once again, we find
a situation where the basis of authority and obedience are found in the
principles of utility and authority, but where the significance of the latter
is diminished (and the former increased) by the change in the pattern of
dependence. It is also a situation where the ease with which fortunes may
be dissipated makes it increasingly unlikely that economic, and thus
political, power, will remain in the hands of particular families over
long periods of time.

The two areas of argument just considered disclose a number of interesting features.

The TMS for example can be seen to accept the proposition that mankind are always found in 'troops and companies' and to offer an explanation as to how it is that man is fitted for the society of his fellows. In
developing this argument Smith, as we have seen, makes much of the
importance of the rules of morality (including justice), while offering an
explanation of their origin of a kind which places him in the anti-rational-
ist tradition of Hutcheson and Hume. At the same time it is evident that
the form of argument used discloses Smith's awareness of the fact that
human experience may vary; a point which is made explicitly in the TMS,
and which is reflected in the fact that he did not seek to define the content
of general rules in any but the most general terms.

---

[4] John Millar, *The Origin of the Distinction of Ranks* (1771), ed. W. C. Lehmann and
included in his *John Millar of Glasgow* (Cambridge, 1960), 292.

The historical argument on the other hand, can be seen to offer an *explanation* for the origin of government (whose necessity was merely postulated in the TMS), and at the same time indirectly to throw some light on the causes of change in accepted patterns of behaviour as a result of the emphasis given to the four socio-economic stages of growth. This same argument may also throw into relief certain problems which the TMS does not formally handle; by drawing attention to the fact that societies are not homogeneous, and to the possibility of a conflict of values. Interestingly enough, exactly this point is made in the WN in the course of a discussion of religion: 'In every civilized society, in every society where the distinction of ranks has once been completely established, there have been always two different schemes or systems of morality current at the same time' (V.i.g.10).

But for the present purpose the most important connections are those which exist between the ethics and jurisprudence on the one hand, and the economics on the other.

The historical analysis, for example, has the benefit of showing that the commercial stage or exchange economy may be regarded as the product of certain historical processes, and of demonstrating that where such a form of economy prevails, a particular social structure or set of relations between classes is necessarily presupposed. At the same time the argument (developed especially in Book III of the WN) helps to demonstrate that a particular form of government will be associated with the same socio-economic institutions; a form of government which in the *particular* case of England had been perfected by the Revolution Settlement, and which reflected the growing importance of the 'middling' ranks.

But perhaps the links between the economic analysis and the TMS are even more readily apparent and possibly more important.

As we have seen, the whole point of the TMS is to show that society, like the individual men who make it up, represents something of a balance between opposing forces; a form of argument which gave due weight to our self-regarding propensities (much as Hutcheson had done) but which departs from the teaching of Hutcheson in denying that 'Self-love was a principle which could never be virtuous in any degree or in any direction' (TMS VII.ii.3.12). In much the same way Smith denied Mandeville's suggestion that the pursuit of 'whatever is agreeable in dress, furniture, or equipage' should be regarded as 'vicious' (VII.ii.4.12). To both he in effect replied that the 'condition of human nature were peculiarly hard, if those affections, which, by the very nature of our being, ought frequently to influence our conduct, could upon no occasion appear virtuous, or deserve esteem and commendation from any body' (VII.ii.3.18).

In many respects Smith was at his most successful in showing that the desire to be approved of by our fellows, which was so important in the discussion of moral judgement, was also relevant in the economic sphere. As we have seen, he argued that the whole object of bettering our condition was to find ourselves as objects of general esteem, and noted elsewhere that 'we cannot live long in the world without perceiving that the respect of our equals, our credit and rank in the society we live in, depend very much upon the degree in which we possess, or are supposed to possess', the advantages of external fortune (VI.i.3). While the pursuit of status and the imagined conveniences of wealth were important sources of dispute, Smith also emphasized their economic advantage even within the confines of the TMS. It is such drives, he asserted, which serve to rouse and keep in 'continual motion the industry of mankind' (IV.i.1.10) and he went on to note that those who have attained fortune are, in expending it,

led by an invisible hand to make nearly the same distribution of the necessaries of life, which would have been made, had the earth been divided into equal portions among all its inhabitants, and thus without intending it, without knowing it, advance the interest of the society, and afford means to the multiplication of the species. (ibid.)

Equally interesting is the fact that Smith should also have discussed at such length the means whereby the poor man may seek to attain the advantages of fortune, in emphasizing the importance of *prudence*, a virtue which, being uncommon, commands general admiration and explains that 'eminent esteem with which all men naturally regard a steady perseverance in the practice of frugality, industry, and application, though directed to no other purpose than the acquisition of fortune' (IV.i.2.8). It is indeed somewhat remarkable that it is the TMS, and in particular that portion of it (Part VI) which Smith wrote just before his death, that provides the most complete account of the psychology of Smith's public benefactor: the frugal man.

Economic Theory and the Exchange Economy

In terms of Smith's teaching, his work on economics was designed to follow on his treatment of ethics and jurisprudence, and therefore to add something to the sum total of our knowledge of the activities of man in society. To this extent, each of the three subjects can be seen to be interconnected, although it is also true to say that each component of the system contains material which distinguishes it from the others. One part of Smith's achievement was in fact to see all these different subjects as parts of a single whole, while at the same time differentiating economics from them. Looked at in this way, the economic analysis involves a high degree of abstraction which can be seen in a number of ways. For example, in his economic work, Smith was concerned only with some aspects of the psychology of man and in fact confined his attention to the self-regarding propensities; a fact which is neatly expressed in his famous statement that 'It is not from the benevolence of the butcher, the brewer, or the baker, that we expect our dinner, but from their regard to their own interest' (WN I.ii.2). Moreover, Smith was not concerned, at least in his *formal* analysis, with a level of moral or social experience other than that involved in a 'mercenary exchange of good offices according to an agreed valuation' (TMS II.ii.3.2); in short, all that the economic work requires is a situation where the minimum condition of justice obtains. Given this basic premiss, together with the hypothesis of self-interest, Smith then set out to explain the interdependence of economic phenomena. There are of course two types of account as to the way in which Smith fulfilled these purposes; one represented by the state of his knowledge when he left Glasgow in 1763, and the other by the WN itself.

We now have two versions of Smith's lecture course, together with the so called 'early draft' of the WN; sufficient at least to provide an adequate guide to the ground covered. There are differences between these documents: LJ (A), for example, while generally more elaborate, is less complete than LJ (B): it does not, for example, consider such topics as Law's Bank, interest, exchange, or the causes of the slow progress of opulence. The ED, on the other hand, contains a much more elaborate account of the division of labour than that provided in either of the lecture notes, although it has nothing to say regarding the link between the division of labour and the extent of the market. While the coverage of the ED is very similar to that found in LJ (B) it is also true to say that topics other than the division of labour are dealt with in note form. But these are basically differences in detail: the three documents are not marked by any major shifts of emphasis or of analytical perspective, and it is this fact which makes it quite appropriate to take LJ (B) as a reasonable guide to the state of Smith's thought on economics in the early 1760s.

Turning now to this version of the lectures, one cannot fail to be struck by the same quality of system which we have already had occasion to note elsewhere. The lectures begin with a discussion of the *natural wants* of man; a discussion already present in the ethics. Smith links this thesis to the development of the arts and of productive forces, before going on to remark on the material enjoyments available to the ordinary man in the modern state as compared to the chief of some savage nation. In both the lectures and the ED Smith continued to note that, while it cannot be difficult to explain the superior advantages of the rich man as compared to the savage, it seems at first sight more difficult to explain why the 'peasant should likewise be better provided' (ED 2.2), especially given the fact that he who 'bears, as it were, upon his shoulders the whole fabric of human society, seems himself to be pressed down below ground by the weight, and to be buried out of sight in the lowest foundations of the building' (ED 2.3).

The answer to this seeming paradox was found in the *division of labour*, which explained the great improvement in the productive powers of modern man. Smith continued to examine the sources of so great an increase in productivity, tracing the origin of the institution to the famous propensity to 'truck, barter and exchange', while observing that the scope of this development must be limited by the extent of the market.

Examination of the division of labour led directly to Smith's point that unlike the savage the modern man was largely dependent on the labour of others for the satisfaction of his full range of wants, thus directing attention to the importance of exchange. In the course of this discussion, Smith introduced the problem of *price* and the distinction between natural and market price.

In the *Lectures*, natural price (or supply price) was largely defined in terms of labour cost, the argument being that:

A man then has the natural price of his labour when it is sufficient to maintain him during the time of labour, to defray the expence of education, and to compensate the risk of not living long enough and of not succeeding in the business. When a man has this, there is sufficient encouragement to the labourer and the commodity will be cultivated in proportion to the demand. (LJ (B) 227, ed. Cannan 176)

Market price, on the other hand, was stated to be regulated by 'quite other circumstances', these being: the 'demand or need for the commodity', the 'abundance or scarcity of the commodity in proportion to the need of it' and the 'riches or poverty of those who demand' (LJ (B) 227–8, ed. Cannan 176–7). Smith then went on to argue that while distinct, these prices were 'necessarily connected' and to show that where the market exceeded the natural price, labour would crowd into this employment, thus expanding the supply, and *vice versa*, leading to the conclusion that in equilibrium the two prices would tend to coincide. Smith quite clearly understood that resources would tend to move between employments where there were differences in the available rates of return, thus showing a grasp of the interdependence of economic phenomena which led him to speak of a 'natural balance of industry' and of the 'natural connection of all trades in the stock' (LJ (B) 233–4, ed. Cannan 180–81).

Progressing logically from this point, Smith proceeded to show that any policy which prevented the market prices of goods from coinciding with their supply prices, such as monopolies or bounties, would tend to diminish public opulence and derange the distribution of stock between different employments.

The discussion of price led in turn to the treatment of money as the means of exchange; to a review of the qualities of the metals which made them so suitable as a means of exchange and to the discussion of coinage.[5] Smith also included an account of the problems of debasement at this stage of his analysis, making in the course of his argument a point with which he is not always associated, namely, that where the value of money is falling 'People are disposed to keep their goods from the market, as they know not what they will get for them' (LJ (B) 242, ed. Cannan 188).

It was in the course of this analysis that Smith defined money as merely the instrument of exchange, at least under normal circumstances, going on to suggest that it was essentially a 'dead stock in itself'; a point which helped to confirm 'the beneficial effects of the erection of banks and paper credit' (LJ (B) 246, ed. Cannan 191).

This argument led quite naturally to a critique of the prejudice that opulence consists in money and to Smith's argument that mercantile policy as currently understood was essentially self-contradictory, and that it hindered the division of labour by artificially restricting the extent of the market. It was a short step to the conclusion (stated with characteristic caution) that:

From the above considerations it appears that Brittain should by all means be made a free port, that there should be no interruptions of any kind made to forreign trade, that if it were possible to defray the expences of government by any other method, all duties, customs, and excise should be abolished, and that free commerce and liberty of exchange should be allowed with all nations and for all things. (LJ (B) 269, ed. Cannan 209)[6]

[5] It is a remarkable fact that Smith's systematic course of instruction on economic subjects closely follows the order used by his old teacher, Francis Hutcheson, in his *System of Moral Philosophy* (published posthumously in 1755). For Hutcheson, like Smith, begins with an account of the division of labour (II.iv) and having explained the sources of increase in 'skill and dexterity' proceeded to emphasize the interdependence of men which results from it. Having next examined the importance for exchange of the right to the property of one's own labour (II.vi) he then considered the determinants of value, using in the course of this discussion a distinction between demand and supply price and defining the latter in terms of labour cost (II.xii). The argument then proceeds to the discussion of money as a means of exchange and the analytical work is completed with an account of 'the principal contracts of a social life' such as interest and insurance (II.xiii). While Smith's own lectures were undoubtedly more complete, with the economic section developed as a single whole, the parallel is nonetheless worthy of note. For comment, see W. R. Scott, *Francis Hutcheson* (London, 1900).

[6] Hume had also drawn attention to the problems of trade regulation and shown a clear grasp of the interdependence of economic phenomena. There is certainly sufficient evidence to give some force to Dugald Stewart's claim that 'The Political Discourses of Mr. Hume were evidently of greater use to Mr. Smith, than any other book that had appeared prior to his Lectures' (Stewart, IV.24).

On the other hand, it would be wrong to imply that Smith may have taken an analytical structure established by Hutcheson and grafted on to it policy views, derived from Hume, regarding the freedom of trade (views which Hutcheson did not always share). To

It will be obvious that that section of the lectures which deals with 'cheapness and plenty' does in fact contain many of the subjects which were to figure in the WN. It also appears that many of his central ideas were already present in a relatively sophisticated form: ideas such as equilibrium price, the working of the allocative mechanism, and the associated concept of the 'natural balance' of industry. Smith also made allowance for the importance of 'stock' both in discussing the natural connection of all stocks in trade and with reference to the division of labour, while the distinction between employer and employed is surely implied in the discussion of the individual whose sole function is to contribute the eighteenth part of a pin.

Yet at the same time there is also a good deal missing from the lectures; there is, for example, no clear distinction between factors of production and categories of return,[7] not to mention the macro-economic analysis of the second Book of the WN with its model of the 'circular flow' and discussion of capital accumulation. While the distinction between rent, wages, and profits, may have come from James Oswald, or emerged as the natural consequence of Smith's own reflection on his lectures (which seems very probable), the macro-economic model which finally appeared in the WN may well have owed something, either directly or indirectly, to Smith's contact with the Physiocrats, and especially those who revised the system, such as Mercier de la Rivière, Baudeau and Turgot.[8]

qualify this position we have Smith's famous manifesto, dated 1755 and quoted by Dugald Stewart from a document, now lost, wherein Smith claimed some degree of originality with a good deal of 'honest and indignant warmth' apparently in respect of his main thesis of economic liberty. In this paper, which was read before one of Glasgow's literary societies, Smith rejected the common view that man could be regarded as the subject of a kind of political mechanics, and stated his belief that economic prosperity only required 'peace, easy taxes, and a tolerable administration of justice'. Such beliefs, he asserted, 'had all of them been the subject of lectures which I read at Edinburgh the winter before I left it, and I can adduce innumerable witnesses, both from that place and from this, who will ascertain them sufficiently to be mine.' (Stewart, IV.25.)

The possible links between Hutcheson, Hume, and Smith are explored in W. L. Taylor, *Frances Hutcheson and David Hume as Precursors of Adam Smith* (Duke, North Carolina, 1965). See also E. Rotwein's valuable introduction in *David Hume: Writings on Economics* (London, 1955).

[7] With regard to the separation of returns into wages, profits, and rent Dugald Stewart has stated that 'It appears from a manuscript of Mr. Smith's, now in my possession, that the foregoing analysis or division was suggested to him by Mr. Oswald of Dunnikier' (*Works*, ix (1856), 6). It is also stated in *Works* x (1858) that Oswald was 'well known to have possessed as a statesman and man of business, a taste for the more general and philosophical discussions of Political Economy. He lived in habits of great intimacy with Lord Kames and Mr. Hume, and was one of Mr. Smith's earliest and most confidential friends.' Memoir Note A

[8] Smith's initial stay in Paris as tutor to the Duke of Buccleuch, was for a period of only ten days, so that his real contact with the French thinkers came during the second visit (December 1765 to October 1766). By this time the School was well established: the *Tableau Economique* had been perfected in the late 1750s, and was followed in 1763

It is obviously difficult to the point of impossibility to establish the extent of Smith's debts to his predecessors, and Dugald Stewart probably had the right of it when he remarked that 'After all, perhaps the merit of such a work as Mr Smith's is to be estimated less from the novelty of the principles it contains, than from the reasonings employed to support these principles, and from the scientific manner in which they are unfolded in their proper order and connexion' (Stewart, IV.26). While Stewart duly noted that Smith had made an original contribution to the subject it need not surprise us to discover that the WN (like the TMS) may also represent a great synthetic performance whose real distinction was to exhibit a 'systematical view of the most important articles of Political Economy' (Stewart, IV.27); a systematical view whose content shows a clear development both from Smith's state of knowledge as it existed in the 1760s, and from that represented by the Physiocrats as a School.[9] While it would be inappropriate to review here the pattern

by the appearance of the *Philosophie Rurale*, the first text-book of the School and a joint production of Quesnay and Mirabeau.

Smith knew both men, while in addition his own commentary on the School (WN IV.ix) shows a close knowledge of its main doctrines. It is also known from the contents of Smith's library that he had a remarkably complete collection of the main literature, including copies of the *Journal de l'Agriculture* and a range of the *Epemèrides du Citoyen* which includes the first two (out of three) parts of Turgot's *Reflections on the Formation and Distribution of Riches*—a work which Turgot completed in 1766 when Smith was resident in Paris. See H. Mizuta, *Adam Smith's Library* (Cambridge, 1967).

In fact Turgot begins his account of the formation and distribution of riches in a way with which Smith would have immediately sympathized: with a discussion of the division of labour, exchange, and money, using this introductory section to confirm the importance of a prior accumulation of stock. The real advance, however, came from another source, and is the consequence of Turgot's reformulation of the basic Quesnay model in such a way as to permit him to employ a distinction between entrepreneurs and wage labour in both the agrarian and manufacturing sectors. This distinction led on to another in the sense that Turgot was able to offer a clear distinction between factors of production (land, labour, capital) and to point the way towards a theory of returns which included recognition of the point that profit could be regarded as a reward for the risks involved in combining the factors of production. At the same time, Turgot introduced a number of distinctions between the different employments of capital of a kind which is very close to that later used by Smith, before going on to show that the returns in different employments were necessarily interdependent and affected by the problems of 'net advantage'. While the account offered in the WN IV.ix of the agricultural system owes a good deal to Quesnay's work, it may not be unimportant to notice that the version which Smith expounded includes an allowance for wages, profit, and rent, distinctions which were not present in Quesnay's original model.

The most exhaustive modern commentary on the physiocrats as a school is R. L. Meek's *The Economics of Physiocracy* (London, 1962). This book includes translations of the main works: see also *Quesnay's Tableau Economique*, ed. M. Kuczynski and R. L. Meek (London, 1972). The possible links between Turgot and Smith are explored by P. D. Groenewegen in 'Turgot and Adam Smith', *Scottish Journal of Political Economy*, xvi (1969).

[9] The most comprehensive modern account of the content of Smith's work is by Samuel Hollander, *The Economics of Adam Smith* (Toronto, 1973).

of this development in detail (a task which we have attempted to fulfill in
the notes to the text) it may be useful to delineate at least some of the
elements of the reformulated system albeit in the broadest terms.

The first three chapters of the WN begin with an examination of the
division of labour which closely follows the elaborate account provided
in the ED.[10] The most obvious changes, as regards the latter document,
relate to the provision of a separate chapter linking the division of labour
to the extent of the market using an account which often parallels that
found in the two 'fragments', which W. R. Scott had thought to be
part of the Edinburgh Lectures.[11] It is also interesting to note that the
discussion of inequality is omitted from the WN and that the argument
as a whole is no longer prefaced by a statement of the thesis of 'natural
wants'. The following chapter is also recognizably a development of the
earlier work, and deals with the inconveniences of barter, the advantages of the metals as a medium of exchange, and the necessity for coinage; the only major difference relates to arrangement in that the discussion
of money now precedes that of price. Chapter v, which leads on from the
previous discussion, does however break new ground in discussing the
distinction between real and nominal price. In this place Smith was anxious
to establish the point that while the individual very naturally measures
the value of his receipts in money terms, the real measure of welfare is
to be established by the money's worth, where the latter is determined
by the quantity of products (i.e. labour commanded) which can be acquired. In this chapter Smith was not so directly concerned with the
problem of exchange value as normally understood, so much as with
finding an invariable measure of value which would permit him to compare levels of economic welfare at different periods of time. It was probably this particular perspective which led him to state but not to 'solve'
the so-called 'paradox of value'—a paradox which he had already explained in the *Lectures*.[12]

Chapter vi leads on to a discussion of the component parts of the price
of commodities and once more breaks new ground in formally isolating
the three main factors of production and the three associated forms of
monetary revenue: rent, wages and profit. These distinctions are, of

[10] In the WN, the division of labour was also associated with technical change, arising
from: improvements made by workmen as a consequence of their experience; inventions
introduced by the makers of machines, (once that has become a separate trade) and,
finally, inventions introduced by philosophers 'whose trade it is, not to do any thing, but
to observe every thing' (I.i.9). Of these, Smith considered that the first was likely to
be affected adversely by the consequences of the division of labour once it had attained
a certain level of development. See below, *39–40*.

[11] See R. L. Meek and A. S. Skinner, 'The Development of Adam Smith's Ideas on
the Division of Labour', *Economic Journal*, lxxxiii (1973).

[12] For a particularly helpful comment on Smith's treatment of value from this point
of view, see M. Blaug, *Economic Theory in Retrospect* (London, 1964), 48–52.

course, of critical importance, and perhaps Smith's acute awareness of
the fact is reflected in his anxiety to show how easily they may be confused. Chapter vii then proceeds to discuss the determinants of price,
developing ideas already present in the *Lectures* but in the more sophisticated form appropriate to the three-fold factor division. This section of
Smith's work is perhaps among the best from a purely analytical point
of view, and is quite remarkable for the formality with which the argument
unfolds. For example, the analysis is explicitly static in that Smith takes
as given certain rates of factor payment (the 'natural' rates), treating the
factors as stocks rather than flows. Smith's old concept of 'natural price'
is then redefined as obtaining when a commodity can be sold at a price
which covers the natural rates of rent, wages, and profits, i.e. its cost of
production. Market price, on the other hand, (the 'actual' price) is shown
to be determined by specific relations of demand and supply while both
prices are interconnected in that any divergence of the market from the
natural price must raise or lower the rates of factor payment in relation
to their natural rates, thus generating a flow of factors which has the effect
of bringing the market and natural prices to equality.[13]

The argument then proceeds to the discussion of those forces which
determine the 'natural' rates of return to factors. Chapter viii takes up the
problem of wages, and argues that this form of return is payable for the
use of a productive resource and normally arises where 'the labourer is
one person, and the owner of the stock which employs him another'
(I.viii.10). While making allowance for the relative importance of the

[13] There are perhaps four features of Smith's treatment of price which may be of particular interest to the modern reader:
1. While Smith succeeds in defining an equilibrium condition he was obviously more
interested in the nature of the processes by virtue of which it was attained. Natural price
thus emerged as the 'central price, to which the prices of all commodities are continually
gravitating', whatever be the obstacles which prevent its actual attainment (I.vii.15).
2. Smith gives a good deal of attention to what might be called 'natural' impediments;
i.e. impediments associated with the nature of the economy (as distinct from 'artificial'
obstacles which might be introduced by government action) in referring to such points
as the instability of agricultural output (I.vii.17), the importance of singularity of soil
or situation, spatial problems and secrets in manufacture.
3. Smith's account may be seen to suggest that before the whole system can be in equilibrium each commodity must be sold at its natural price and each factor paid in each
employment at its 'natural' rate. Any movement from this position can then be shown to
involve inter-related responses in the factor and commodity markets as a result of which
the trend towards equilibrium is sustained. Looked at from this point of view, Smith's
argument has a dynamic aspect at least in the sense that he handles the consequences of
a given change (say in demand) as a continuously unfolding process.
4. The discussion of price is linked to the analysis of the economy as a system in Book II
by throwing some light on the allocation of a given stock of resources amongst alternative
uses. At the same time, the analysis of Book II with its suggestion of a continuous cycle
of the purchase, consumption, and replacement of goods adds a further dimension to
the use of time in I.vii. For an interesting modern example of a problem of this kind
see W. J. Baumol, *Economic Dynamics* (2nd ed. New York, 1959), 6–7, where a time axis
is added to those dealing with price and quantity.

bargaining position of the two parties, Smith concluded that the wage rate would normally be determined by the size of the wages fund and the supply of labour, where both are affected by the price of wage goods.

Now this argument means that the wage rate actually payable in a given (annual) period may vary considerably (i.e. the prevailing or natural rate of the theory of price) as compared to other such time periods, and that it may be above, below, or equal to, the subsistence wage (where the latter must be sufficient to maintain the labourer and his family, including an allowance for customary expense). Smith illustrates these possibilities in terms of the examples of advancing, stationary, and declining economies, using this argument to suggest that whenever the prevailing wage rate sinks below, or rises above, the subsistence wage, then in the *long run* there will be a population adjustment.

Chapter ix shows the same basic features: that is, Smith sets out to show *why* profit accrues and in so doing differentiates it from interest as a category of return, while arguing that it is not a return for the work of 'inspection and direction' but rather for the risks involved in combining the factors of production. Again, there is a 'static' element in that Smith, while admitting the difficulty of finding an average rate of profit, argues that some indication will be given by the rate of interest, and that the rate of profit will be determined by the level of stock in relation to the business to be transacted together with the prevailing wage rate. Once more there is also a concern with the dynamics of the case, i.e. with the trend of profits over time, the conclusion being that profits, like wages, would tend to fall, as the number of capitals increases.

The following chapter is a direct development from the two which preceded it and is chiefly concerned with the 'static' aspects of the theory of allocation and returns. In dealing with the theory of 'net advantage', Smith provides a more elaborate account of the doctrine already found in the *Lectures*, and there confined to the discussion of labour. In the present context Smith dropped the assumption of given rates of factor payment (as made at the beginning of I.vii) in explaining that rates of monetary return may be expected to vary with the agreeableness or disagreeableness of the work, the cost of learning a trade, the constancy or inconstancy of employment, the great or small trust which may be involved, and the probability or improbability of success. Of these it is argued that only the first and the last affect profits, thus explaining the greater uniformity of rates of return (as compared to wages) in different employments. The whole purpose of the first section of this chapter is to elaborate on the above 'circumstances' and to show, at least where there is perfect liberty, that different rates of monetary return need occasion no difference in the 'whole of the advantages and disadvantages, real or imaginary' which affect different employments (I.x.b.39).

In terms of the discussion of the price mechanism, we now have a complex of rates of return in different employments and an equilibrium situation where the rate of return in each type of employment stands in such a relation to the others as to ensure that there is no tendency to enter or leave any one of them. The same argument adds a further dimension of difficulty to Smith's account of the allocative mechanism, by drawing attention to the problem of moving between employments which require different skills or levels of training.[14]

Mobility is in fact the theme of the second part of the chapter where (again elaborating on ideas present in the *Lectures*) Smith shows the various ways in which the policy of Europe prevented the equality of 'advantages and disadvantages' which would otherwise arise; citing such examples as the privileges of corporations, the statute of apprenticeship, public endowments and especially the poor law.

The closing chapter of Book I is concerned with the third and final form of return—rent—and is among the longest and most complex of the whole work. But perhaps the following points can be made when looking at the chapter from the standpoint of Smith's analytical system. First, and most obviously, the general structure of the chapter is similar to those which deal with wages and profit. That is, Smith initially tries to explain what rent *is* in suggesting that it is the price which must be paid for a scarce resource which is a part of the property of individuals, and in arguing that it must vary with the fertility and situation of the land. Unlike the other forms of revenue, Smith emphasized that rent was unique in that it accrued without necessarily requiring any effort from those to whom it was due, and that what was a cost to the individual farmer was really a surplus as far as society was concerned; a point which led Smith to the famous statement that rent 'enters into the composition of the price of commodities in a different way from wages and profit. High or low wages and profit, are the causes of high or low price; high or low rent is the effect of it.' (I.xi.a.8.)

Secondly, it is noteworthy that the analysis continues the 'static' theme already found in the theory of price, wages, and profits, by concentrating attention on the forces which determine the allocation of land between alternative uses (such as the production of corn and cattle) and in suggesting, at least in the general case, that rent payments would tend to equality in these different uses.

[14] While in general Smith seems to have considered that job mobility would be comparatively easy, it is evident that such movement might be difficult in cases where there is a considerable capital invested in learning—thus setting up distortions in the system (which could take time to resolve themselves) even in cases where there was perfect liberty. Smith also drew attention to the problems of status and geographical mobility. Citing as evidence the considerable differentials between London, Edinburgh, and their environs, in respect even of employments of a similar kind, he concluded that 'man is of all sorts of luggage the most difficult to be transported' (I.viii.31).

Thirdly, it is noteworthy that Smith should have included a dynamic perspective in the discussion of allocation, of such a kind as to make his historical sketch of the changing pattern of land use an important, if rather neglected, aspect of his general theory of economic development.

Finally, Smith continues the dynamic theme in the form in which it appears in the previous chapters by considering the long term trends as far as this form of return is concerned; the conclusion being that rent payments must increase as more land is brought into use under the pressure of a growing population, and that the real value of such payments must rise given that the real price of manufactures tends to fall in the long run.

If we look back over this Book from the (rather narrow) perspective of Smith's system, it will be evident that the argument is built up quite logically by dealing with a number of separate but inter-related subjects such as costs, price, and returns. At the same time two themes appear to run through the treatment of the different subjects: a static theme in that Smith is often concerned to explain the forces which determine the prevailing rates of return at particular points in time, together with the working of the allocative mechanisms, with factors treated as stocks rather than as flows; and, secondly, a dynamic aspect where Smith considers the general trends of factor payments over long periods, together with the pattern of land use and the probable changes in the real value of wage goods and manufactures. Both of these major themes were to find a place in the analysis of the following Books.

The Introduction to Book II sets the theme of the following chapters by taking the reader back to the division of labour and by re-iterating a point which had already been made in the *Lectures*, namely that the division of labour depends on the prior accumulation of stock. An important difference here, however, as compared to the *Lectures*, is to be found in the fact that the task of accumulation is now seen to face the employer of labour rather than the labourer himself. Chapter i then proceeds to elaborate on the nature of stock and its applications in suggesting that the individual may devote a part of his 'stock' to consumption purposes, and therefore earn no revenue or income from it, while a part may be devoted to the acquisition of income. In the latter case stock is divided, in the manner of the physiocrats, into circulating and fixed capital; it is also shown that different trades will require different combinations of the two types of stock and that no fixed capital can produce an income except when used in combination with a circulating capital.

Reasoning by analogy, Smith proceeded to argue that the stock of society taken as a whole could be divided into the same basic parts. In this connection he suggested that in any given period (such as a year) there would be a certain stock of goods, both perishable and durable reserved for immediate consumption, one characteristic being that such goods were used up at different rates. Secondly, he argued that society as a whole would possess a certain fixed capital, where the latter included such items as machines and useful instruments of trade, stocks of buildings which were used for productive purposes, improved lands, and the 'acquired and useful abilities' of the inhabitants (i.e. human capital). Finally, he identified the circulating capital of society as including the supply of money necessary to carry out circulation, the stocks of materials and goods in process held by the manufacturers or farmers, and the stocks of completed goods available for sale but still in the hands of producers or merchants as distinct from their 'proper' consumers.

Such an argument is interesting in that it provides an example of the ease with which Smith moved from the discussion of micro- to the discussion of macro-economic issues. At the same time it serves to introduce Smith's account of the 'circular flow', whereby he shows how, within a particular time period, goods available for sale are used up by the parties to exchange. In Smith's terminology, the pattern of events is such that the necessary purchases of goods by consumers and producers features a 'withdrawal' from the circulating capital of society, with the resulting purchases being used up during the current period or added to either the fixed capital or the stock of goods reserved for immediate consumption. As he pointed out, the constant withdrawal of goods requires replacement, and this can be done only through the production of additional raw materials and finished goods in both main sectors (agriculture and manufactures) thus exposing the 'real exchange which is annually made between those two orders of people' (II.i.28). The basic division into types of capital, and this particular way of visualizing the working of the process, may well owe a great deal to the Physiocrats, even if the basic sectoral division had already been suggested by Hume.

The remaining chapters of the Book are basically concerned to elaborate on the relations established in the first. For example, chapter ii makes the division into classes (proprietors, undertakers, wage-labour) explicit and establishes another connection with the analysis of Book I by reminding the reader that if the price of each commodity taken singly comprehends payments for rent, wages, and profits, then this must be true of all commodities taken 'complexly', so that in any given (annual) period aggregate income must be divided between the three factors of production in such a way as to reflect the prevailing levels of demand for, and supply of, them. Once again we find an implicit return to the 'static' analysis of Book I, save at a macro-economic level. The relationship between output and income adds something to Smith's general picture of the 'circular flow' and at the same time enabled him to expand on his account by drawing a distinction between gross and net aggregate output where the latter is established by deducting the cost of maintaining the fixed capital (together with the costs of maintaining the money supply) from the gross product. In this way Smith was able to indicate the desirability of reducing the maintenance costs of the fixed capital, and of the money supply (a part of society's circulating capital), introducing by this means the discussion of paper money (a cheaper instrument than coin) and of banks. The chapter goes on to provide a very long account of Scottish affairs in the 1760s and 1770s, together with a history of the Bank of England. Law's Bank is accorded a single paragraph, in contrast to the treatment in the *Lectures*, on the ground that its activities had already been adequately exposed by Messrs. DuVerney and DuTot. The Bank of Amsterdam, also mentioned in the conclusion of this chapter and in the *Lectures*, was accorded a separate digression in WN IV.iv.

The third chapter of the Book elaborates still further on the basic model by introducing a distinction between income in the aggregate and the proportion of that income devoted to consumption (revenue) or to savings. Smith also introduced the famous distinction between productive and unproductive labour at this point, where the former is involved in the creation of commodities and therefore of income while the latter is involved in the provision of services. Smith does not, of course, deny that services (such as defence or justice) are useful or even necessary, he merely wished to point out that the labour which is involved in the provision of a service is always maintained by the industry of other people and that it does not *directly* contribute to aggregate output. Smith's argument was of course that funds intended to function as a capital would always be devoted to the employment of productive labour, while those intended to act as a revenue might maintain *either* productive *or* unproductive labour. Two points arise from this argument: first, that the productive capacity of any society would depend on the proportion in which total income was distributed between revenue and capital; and, secondly, that capitals could only be increased through parsimony, i.e. through a willingness to forego present advantages with a view to attaining some greater future benefit. It was in fact Smith's view that net savings would always be possible during any given annual period, and that the effort would always be made through man's natural desire to better his condition. Moreover, he evidently believed that wherever savings were made they would be converted into investment virtually *sur le champ* (thus providing another parallel with Turgot) and that the rapid progress which had been made by England confirmed this general trend. In Book II economic dynamics begins to overshadow the static branch of the subject: an important reminder that Smith's version of the 'circular flow' is to be seen as a spiral of constantly expanding dimensions, rather than as a circle of constant size. It is also worth emphasizing in this connection that Smith's concern with economic growth takes us back in a sense to the oldest part of the edifice, namely his treatment of the division of labour, the point being that the increasing size of the market gives greater scope to this institution, thus enhancing the possibilities for expansion, which are further stimulated by technical change in the shape of the flow of invention (I.i.8).

The fourth and fifth chapters of this book offer further insights into the working of the 'flow' on the one hand, and the theory of economic growth on the other. II.iv, for example, contains not only an account of the determinants of interest, but confirms that interest is distinct from profit as a form of return, while introducing the monied interest as something separate from the manufacturing and agricultural interests.

The following chapter adds four additional uses for capitals (again providing a close parallel with Turgot) in stating that they may be used in the wholesale or retail trades in addition to all those above mentioned. Thus as far as our understanding of the circular flow is concerned, Smith argues that the retailer in purchasing from the wholesale merchant in effect replaces the capital which the latter had laid out in purchasing commodities for sale; purchases which had themselves contributed to replace the capitals advanced by the farmers or manufacturers in creating them. In the same way, the manufacturer, for example, in making purchases of the instruments of trade replaces the outlay of some fellow 'undertaker' while his purchases of raw materials contribute to restore the capitals laid out by the farmers on their production.[15] Smith's enumeration of the

---

[15] It may be useful to give a 'conjectural' picture of the 'circular flow', by drawing some of the elements of Smith's argument together.

Smith's theory of price has already established that since each commodity taken singly must comprehend payments for rent, wages, and profits, this must be true of all taken complexly (II.ii.2 and see above, p. 25 n. 13). He therefore suggests a relationship between aggregate output and income where the latter must be distributed between the three major forms of return. Taking the year as the time period within which the working of the system is to be examined, factors can be treated as stocks (as in the theory of price) whose ordinary or natural rates (i.e. natural within the framework of the year) are determined by current levels of demand and supply (a theme developed in the theory of distribution). This income can be used for the purchase of consumption goods, including services (thus generating a secondary source of income available for expenditure in the current period) or in the form of a fixed or circulating capital. If we examine the system from the standpoint of the beginning of the period in question, each group will have an accumulated stock of goods intended for consumption, together with a certain fixed capital representing acquired skills and useful abilities. The proprietors in addition possess a capital which is fixed in the land while the entrepreneurs engaged in manufacture, agriculture, or trade, own a fixed capital embodied in their machines, implements, etc. In addition, we can assume at the beginning of the period, that the undertakers and merchants have a stock of finished goods (consumption and investment goods) which are available for sale in the current period, together with raw materials and work in process—all of which make up a part of the circulating capital of *society*. Assume also the undertakers have a certain *net* income available for use in the current period. [continues]

different employments of capital is also relevant as far as his theory of growth is concerned, because each one can be shown to give employment to different quantities of productive labour. While he had already observed in the *Lectures* that agriculture was the most productive form of investment, the argument was here expanded to suggest that manufacture was the next most productive, followed by the wholesale and retail trades. He also argued with regard to the wholesale trade, that its contribution to the maintenance of productive labour varied, in declining order of importance, according as it was concerned with the home trade, the foreign trade of consumption, or the carrying trade, where the critical factor was the frequency of returns. A further dimension was added to this discussion in the opening chapter of Book III where it is suggested that, when left to their own devices, men would naturally choose to invest in agriculture, manufactures, and trade (in that order) thus contributing to maximize the rate of growth by choosing those forms of investment which generated the greatest level of output for a given injection of capital.

Smith's thesis concerning the different productivities of capital and the associated (although logically distinct) argument concerning the natural progress of opulence are sometimes regarded as being among the less successful parts of the edifice; a fact which makes it all the more important to observe the great burden which they are made to bear in the subsequent argument. In Book III, for example, Smith uses the history of Europe since the fall of the Roman Empire to confirm that the pattern of development had inverted the 'natural' order, in the sense that the stimulus to economic advance had initially come through the cities with

If the farmers transmit rent payments to the proprietors to secure the use of a productive resource, this gives the latter group an income with which they can make the necessary purchases of consumption and investment goods. The undertakers in both the main sectors may then transmit to wage-labour the content of the wages fund, thus generating an income which can be used to make purchases of consumption goods from each sector. Similarly, the undertakers will make purchases from each other, thus generating a series of flows of money and goods within and between the sectors—with the whole pattern carried on by the wholesale and retail trades. As a result of the complex of transactions, the content of the circulating capital of society (as represented, in part, by the stock of all goods available for sale) is withdrawn from the market and either *added* to the social stock of consumption goods, or fixed capital, or used to replace items which reached the end of their life during the present period, or used up within that period. On the other hand, these goods are replaced by current productive activity, so that the model taken as a whole admirably succeeds in its aim of elucidating the interconnections which exist between the parts of the machine. It is worth noting perhaps, here as in the theory of price, that the emphasis is on the processes involved, rather than on the formulation of equilibrium conditions. Indeed it would have been very difficult for Smith to formulate the conditions which would have to be met before the following period could open under identical conditions to those which obtained at the beginning of the period examined, (as for example Quesnay had done) if only because of the explicit allowance made for goods which have different life-spans and for stocks of goods which have different age structures.

their trade in surpluses. As we shall see in another context, (below, p. 55) the development of trade had given a stimulus to domestic manufactures based on the refinement of local goods or on imitation of the foreigner; a pattern of events which eventually impinged on the agrarian sector, and which is made to explain the transition to the final economic stage. Smith thus suggests that a process of development regarded as 'natural' from the standpoint of the theory of history, was essentially 'unnatural' from the standpoint of the analysis of the progress of opulence. However, the argument does explain the *position* of the third Book and the use there made of historical material which had been included in the *Lectures*, where it had been mainly intended to serve a very different purpose to that found in the WN.

The second main application of the thesis is in Book IV where Smith returns to a theme which had already figured prominently in the *Lectures*; the critique of mercantilism. Many of the points which had been made in the earlier work undoubtedly re-appear in this section of the WN. In the WN, the mercantile system, with its associated patterns of control over the import, export, and production of commodities, is again shown to be based on an erroneous notion of wealth. Smith also argues, as he had before, that the chief engines of mercantilism, such as monopoly powers, adversely affect the allocative mechanism and to this extent affect economic welfare. But the main burden of his argument concerning distortion in the use of resources runs in terms not of the static allocative mechanism, so much as the essentially dynamic theory of the natural progress of opulence, the argument being that mercantile policy had diverted stock to less productive uses, with slower returns, than would otherwise have been the case. This argument is particularly marked in Smith's treatment of the colonial relationship with America; a relationship which was central to the mercantile system as presented by Smith, and which sought to create a self-sufficient economic unit.[16] In this connection Smith argued that the mercantile system was essentially self-contradictory: that by encouraging the output of rude products in America, Great Britain had helped (unwittingly) only to accelerate an already rapid rate of growth to an extent which would inevitably make the restrictions imposed on American manufactures unduly burdensome. As far as Great Britain was concerned, Smith believed that her concentration on the American market had in effect drawn capital from trades carried on with European outlets and diverted it to the more distant one of America, while at the same time forcing a certain amount of capital from a direct to an indirect trade. Obviously, all of this must have had an adverse effect on the rate of economic growth in Great Britain; a matter of

[16] See D. N. Winch, *Classical Political Economy and the Colonies* (London, 1965), chapter 2.

some moment, in that, as Smith represents the case, a country with a sub-optimal rate of growth happened to face an increasing burden of costs from the colonies themselves. It is a plausible, powerful, thesis which may be defended on a variety of grounds other than those on which Smith relied. But, as one shrewd contemporary critic noted, Smith's view on the different productivities of investment was central to his case, and he begged leave to arrest his steps 'for a moment, while we examine the ground whereon we tread: and the more so, as I find these propositions used in the second part of your work as data; whence you endeavour to prove, that the monopoly of the colony trade is a disadvantageous . . . institution.'[17]

The Role of the State

While the immediately preceding sections have concentrated to a large extent on the *structure* and organization of Smith's thought, perhaps enough has also been said regarding its *content* to illustrate the existence of another kind of 'system'; an analytical system which treats the economy as a type of model analogous to some kind of machine whose parts are unconscious of their mutual connection, or of the end which their inter-action serves to promote, but where that interaction is governed by the laws of the machine. In economic terms, these law-governed *processes* refer, for example, to the working of the allocative mechanism, the theory of distribution, or of economic growth. The *components* of the 'model' are of course the sectors, the classes, and the individuals whose pursuit of gain contributes to the effective working of the whole. Thus, for example, the undertaker in pursuit of gain contributes to economic efficiency by endeavouring to make 'such a proper division and distribu-tion of stock' amongst his workmen as to enable them to 'produce the greatest quantity of work possible'. The individual workman or under-taker offers his services in the most lucrative employments and helps to ensure, by this means, that goods are sold at their cost of production, and all factors are paid at their 'natural' rates. Similarly, the constant desire to better one's condition contributes to the flow of savings and thus to the process of economic growth. In all these cases social benefit and economic order are the result of the self-interested actions of individuals rather than the consequences of some formal plan; indeed, Smith went further in insisting that public benefit would not and need not form any part of the normal motivation of the main actors in the drama. The famous doctrine of the invisible hand, already prefigured in the TMS in pre-

[17] *A Letter from Governor Pownall to Adam Smith, L.L.D. F.R.S.* (London, 1776), 23: cf. Winch, op. cit., 8–9.

cisely this connection, was designed to show that the individual, in pursuing his own objectives, contributed to the public benefit, thereby promoting an end 'which was no part of his intention' (WN IV.ii.9).[18]

Now this general view of the working of economic processes is important in that it helps to explain the functions which any government ought ideally to undertake, and the way in which these functions should be performed; broadly speaking, a subject which provides the focal point of Book V. In terms of the model itself, for example, governments have no strictly economic functions, at least in the sense that the sovereign should be discharged from 'the duty of superintending the industry of private people, and of directing it towards the employments most suitable to the interest of the society' (IV.ix.51). And yet, the functions of the state, if minimal, are quite indispensable in the sense that it must provide for such (unproductive) services as defence, justice, and those public works which are unlikely to be provided by the market because 'the profit could never repay the expence to any individual or small number of individuals' (IV.ix.51).

Smith's list of public services is a short one, but the discussion of the principles on which their provision should be organized is developed at some length and is interesting for two main reasons. First, Smith argued that public services should be provided only where the market has failed to do so; secondly, he suggested that the main problems with regard to such services were those of equity and efficiency. With regard to equity, Smith suggested, for example, that public services should always be paid for by those who use them (including roads and bridges). He also defended the principle of direct payment on the ground of efficiency in arguing that it is only in this way that we can avoid the building of roads through deserts for the sake of some private interest, or a situation where a great bridge is 'thrown over a river at a place where nobody passes, or merely to embellish the view from the windows of a neighbouring palace: things which sometimes happen, in countries where works of this kind are carried on by any other revenue than that which they themselves are capable of affording' (V.i.d.6). At the same time Smith insisted that all public ser-

---

[18] It is interesting to observe that the solitary example of the 'invisible hand' which occurs in the WN does so in the context of the thesis concerning the natural progress of opulence. It is remarked in IV.ii.9 that:

As every individual, therefore, endeavours as much as he can both to employ his capital in the support of domestick industry, and so to direct that industry that its produce may be of the greatest value; every individual necessarily labours to render the annual revenue of the society as great as he can. He generally, indeed, neither intends to promote the publick interest, nor knows how much he is promoting it. By preferring the support of domestick to that of foreign industry, he intends only his own security; and by directing that industry in such a manner as its produce may be of the greatest value, he intends only his own gain, and he is in this, as in many other cases, led by an invisible hand to promote an end which was no part of his intention.

vices should be provided by such bodies as found it in their interest to do so effectively, and that they should be organized in such a way as to take account of the self-interested nature of man. Smith stated his basic belief in remarking that 'Publick services are never better performed than when their reward comes only in consequence of their being performed, and is proportioned to the diligence employed in performing them' (V.i.b.20). He tirelessly emphasized this point, especially in reference to university teaching, while reminding his readers that the principle held good in all situations and in all trades.

Of course, Smith did recognise the limitations of this principle and the fact that it would not always be possible to fund or to maintain public services without recourse to general taxation. But here again the main features of the analytical system are relevant in that they affect the way in which taxation should, where possible, be handled. Thus Smith pointed out on welfare grounds that taxation should be imposed according to the famous canons of equality, certainty, convenience, and economy, and insisted that they should not be levied in ways which infringed the liberty of the subject—for example, through the 'odious visits' and examinations of the tax-gatherer (V.ii.b.3–7). Similarly he argued that ideally taxes ought not to interfere with the allocative mechanism (as for example, taxes on necessities) or constitute important disincentives to the individual effort on which the working of the whole system has been seen to depend (such as taxes on profits). In short, Smith's recommendations with regard to the functions of government are designed to ensure the freedom of the individual to pursue his own (socially beneficial) ends and merely require that the state should provide such services as facilitate the working of the system, while conforming to the constraints of human nature and the market mechanism. Looked at from this point of view, Smith's discussion of the role of the state is very much a part of his general model and confirms his view that the task of political economy, considered as a part of the science of the statesman or legislator, is 'to provide a plentiful revenue or subsistence for the people, or more properly to enable them to provide such a revenue or subsistence for themselves' (IV.Intro.1).

But Smith went much further than this in discussing the role of the state, and in ways which remind us of his essentially practical concerns, and of the importance of other branches of his general system such as the theory of history and the TMS.

To begin with, it will already be evident that one thread which runs through the WN involves criticism of those contemporary institutions which impeded the realization in its entirety of the system of natural liberty. Broadly speaking, these impediments can be reduced to four main categories each one of which Smith wished to see removed. First, there is the problem (already raised in terms of the historical analysis) that 'Laws frequently continue in force long after the circumstances, which first gave occasion to them, and which could alone render them reasonable, are no more' (III.ii.4). Secondly, Smith drew attention to certain institutions which had their origins in the past but which still commanded active support; institutions such as guilds and corporations, which could still regulate the government of trades. All such arrangements were, in Smith's view *impolitic* because they impeded the working of the allocative mechanism and *unjust* because they were a 'violation of this most sacred property' which 'every man has in his own labour' (I.x.c.12). In a very similar way Smith commented on the problems presented by the poor law and the laws of settlement and summarized his appeal to government in these terms: 'break down the exclusive privileges of corporations, and repeal the statute of apprenticeship, both which are real encroachments upon natural liberty, and add to these the repeal of the law of settlements . . .' (IV.ii.42). Thirdly, Smith criticised the continuing use of positions of privilege, such as monopoly powers, which did not necessarily have any particular link with the past. Here again the basic theme remains, that such institutions are impolitic and unjust: unjust because they *are* positions of privilege and impolitic because they again affect the working of the allocative mechanism, being besides, 'a great enemy to good management' (I.xi.b.5).

Finally, we have the main theme of Book IV which we have already had occasion to mention; that is Smith's call for a reform of national policy in so far as that was represented by the mercantile system.

All this amounts to a very considerable programme of reform, although, quite characteristically, Smith recognized that reality would fall a long way short of perfection, and that it could do so without damage to that fundamental drive to better our condition or to the capacity of that drive to overcome 'a hundred impertinent obstructions with which the folly of human laws too often encumbers its operations' (IV.v.b.43). Smith recognized the existence of many practical difficulties; that people are attached to old forms and institutions for example, quite as much as to old families and kings, and also that sectional economic pressures would always find some means of influencing the legislature in their favour, precisely because of those same economic forces which helped to explain the historical dominance of the House of Commons in England.[19] For such

[19] Smith's concern with sectional economic pressures is to be found throughout the WN; in the discussion of the regulation of wages, for example (I.x.c.61) and in his ascription of undue influence on colonial policy to mercantile groups (IV.vii.b.49). He referred frequently to the 'clamourous importunity of partial interests' and in speaking of the growth of monopoly pointed out that government policy 'has so much increased the number of some particular tribes of them, that, like an overgrown standing army, they have become formidable to the government, and upon many occasions intimidate the

reasons he concluded that 'To expect, indeed, that the freedom of trade
should ever be entirely restored in Great Britain, is as absurd as to expect
that an Oceana or Utopia should ever be established in it' (IV.ii.43).

If points such as these contribute to qualify the rather 'optimistic'
thesis with which Smith is generally associated, the impression is further
confirmed by those passages in the WN (occurring mainly in Book V)
which bear more directly on the analysis of the TMS. In the former
work, it will be remembered that welfare is typically defined in material
terms; in terms of the level of real income, i.e. the extent to which the
individual can command the produce (or labour) of others. On the other
hand, in the philosophical work welfare was defined more in terms of the
quality of life attainable, where 'quality' refers to a level of moral experience
greater than that involved in the 'mercenary exchange of good offices
according to an agreed valuation'. There is of course no inconsistency
between these two positions, since the two major books, while analytic-
ally linked, in fact refer to different areas of human experience. But at the
same time Smith made a number of points in the WN which establish
an important link between the philosophical and economic aspects of his
study of man in society, while constituting a reminder that welfare should
not be considered solely in economic terms. In this connection Smith
drew attention to the fact that the worker in a 'large manufactory' was
liable to the temptations of bad company with consequent effects on moral
standards (I.viii.48). In the same vein he also mentioned the problems
presented by large cities where, unlike the rich man who is noticed by
the public and who therefore has an incentive to attend to his own conduct,
the poor man is 'sunk in obscurity and darkness. His conduct is observed
and attended to by nobody, and he is therefore very likely to neglect it
himself, and to abandon himself to every sort of low profligacy and vice.'
(V.i.g.12.)

To this extent, the importance of the spectator is undermined, and so
too may be those faculties and propensities on which moral experience has
been seen to depend (a separate point). For Smith drew attention to the
'fact' that the division of labour which had contributed to economic growth
through the subdivision and simplification of productive processes, had
at the same time confined the activities of the worker to a few simple
operations which gave no stimulus to the exercise of his mind, thus widen-
ing the gulf between the philosopher and the ordinary man or his employer. Smith believed that the worker could lose the habit of mental
exertion, thus gradually becoming as 'stupid and ignorant as it is possible

legislature.' (IV.ii.43.) The point helps to explain Smith's recurring theme that legislative proposals emanating from members of this class 'ought never to be adopted till
after having been long and carefully examined, not only with the most scrupulous, but
with the most suspicious attention' (I.xi.p.10).

for a human creature to become' and he went on, in a famous passage, to remark:

The torpor of his mind renders him, not only incapable of relishing or bearing a part in any rational conversation, but of conceiving any generous, noble, or tender sentiment, and consequently of forming any just judgment concerning many even of the ordinary duties of private life. (V.i.f.50)

As Smith duly noted, this general trend could produce the apparently paradoxical result that while the inhabitants of the fourth economic stage enjoyed far greater material benefits than those available to the hunter or savage, yet the latter would be more likely to exercise his mental faculties and to this extent be 'better off' (V.i.f.51). Smith recognized that the occupations of the savage were unlikely to produce an 'improved and refined understanding', but his main point was that in the modern state this refinement can only be attained by the few who are able to reflect at large on a wide range of problems, including the social. As Smith put it, in a passage which once again reminds us of the importance of the Astronomy and of the problems of stratification in society:

The contemplation of so great a variety of objects necessarily exercises their minds in endless comparisons and combinations, and renders their understandings, in an extraordinary degree, both acute and comprehensive. Unless those few, however, happen to be placed in some very particular situations, their great abilities, though honourable to themselves, may contribute very little to the good government or happiness of their society. Notwithstanding the great abilities of those few, all the nobler parts of the human character may be, in a great measure, obliterated and extinguished in the great body of the people. (V.i.f.51)

Smith's belief that the 'labouring poor, that is, the great body of the people' (V.i.f.50) might suffer a kind of 'mental mutilation' led him directly to the discussion of education. To some extent he argued that market forces had proved themselves capable of the effective provision of this service, especially with regard to the education of women (V.i.f.47), and he also noted that it was the absence of such pressures which had enabled the ancient universities to become 'the sanctuaries in which exploded systems and obsolete prejudices' had found support and protection (V.i.f.34). Yet at the same time, he did not believe that the public could rely on the market, not least because the lower orders could scarce afford to maintain their children even in infancy, and he went on to note, with regard to the children of the relatively poor, that 'As soon as they are able to work, they must apply to some trade by which they can earn their subsistence' (V.i.f.53). Smith therefore advocated the provision of parish schools on the Scottish model wherein the young could be taught to read and to acquire the rudiments of geometry and mechanics—provided of course that their masters were 'partly, but not wholly paid by the publick' (V.i.f.55). Smith even went so far as to suggest that the public should *impose* 'upon almost the whole body of the people the necessity of acquiring those most essential parts of education, by obliging every man to undergo an examination or probation in them before he can obtain the freedom in any corporation, or be allowed to set up any trade' (V.i.f.57). Smith also advocated that the better off, despite their superior (economic) advantages in acquiring education, should be required to attain a rather higher standard of knowledge 'by instituting some sort of probation, even in the higher and more difficult sciences, to be undergone by every person before he was permitted to exercise any liberal profession, or before he could be received as a candidate for any honourable office of trust or profit' (V.i.g.14).

Such policies were defended on the ground of benefit to the individual, but also for more practical reasons. The labourer armed with a knowledge of the rudiments of geometry and mechanics was likely to be better placed to perform his tasks effectively and to continue to see how they could be improved. Similarly, Smith suggested that an educated people would be better placed to see through the interested claims of faction and sedition, while in addition an 'instructed and intelligent people . . . are always more decent and orderly than an ignorant and stupid one'. Such a people, he continued (in a strain which reminds us of the importance of the earlier discussion of political obligation) are also more likely to obtain the respect of their 'lawful superiors' and to reciprocate that respect. He concluded:

In free countries, where the safety of government depends very much upon the favourable judgment which the people may form of its conduct, it must surely be of the highest importance that they should not be disposed to judge rashly or capriciously concerning it. (V.i.f.61)

In this way Smith granted the state an important cultural purpose and at the same time introduced a significant qualification to the optimistic thesis with which he is often associated—both with regard to the efficacy of market forces and the benefits of economic growth.

The Institutional Relevance of the WN

The attractions of Smith's system, and of an analysis which stretched even beyond the WN to encompass his other works, was quickly recognized by contemporaries. A stream of tributes found their way to Smith. Hugh Blair, the erstwhile Minister of the High Kirk of Edinburgh and later Professor of Rhetoric and Belles Lettres at the University wrote:

I am Convinced that since Montesquieu's *Esprit des Lois*, Europe has not received any Publication which tends so much to Enlarge & Rectify the ideas of mankind.

Your Arrangement is excellent. One chapter paves the way for another; and your System gradually erects itself. Nothing was ever better suited than your Style is to the Subject; clear & distinct to the last degree, full without being too much so, and as tercly as the Subject could admit. Dry as some of the Subjects are, It carried me along.[20]

William Robertson was more to the point: 'You have formed into a regular and consistent system one of the most intricate and important parts of political science.'[21] In similar vein Joseph Black commended Smith for providing '. . . a comprehensive System composed with such just & liberal Sentiments'.[22] Lastly, some eighteen months later Edward Gibbon described the WN as 'the most profound and systematic treatise on the great objects of trade and revenue which had ever been published in any age or in any Country.'[23]

Unstinted admiration of Smith's system was accompanied by a fear, not always clearly expressed, that the work might not prove to have an immediate appeal, a fear based on an appreciation that the WN is not a simple but a difficult and involved book. With some feeling Hugh Blair pled for an index and a 'Syllabus of the whole', because, 'You travel thro' a great Variety of Subjects. One has frequently occasion to reflect & look back.' (Letter 151.) David Hume looked forward to a day which he, within months of his death, was not to see, when the book would be popular, but he was less sanguine about its immediate prospects:

. . . the Reading of it necessarily requires so much Attention, and the Public is disposed to give so little, that I shall still doubt for some time of its being at first very popular: But it has Depth and Solidity and Acuteness, and it is so much illustrated by curious Facts, that it must at last take the public Attention.[24]

A week later Hume offered a comparison with Gibbon's *Decline and Fall* to William Strahan, the publisher of both, a comparison not altogether in favour of the WN: 'Dr Smith's Performance is another excellent Work that has come from your Press this Winter; but I have ventured to tell him, that it requires too much thought to be as popular as Mr Gibbon's.'[25] Even on publication, there were signs that Hume was unduly pessimistic. In his reply Strahan, while concurring with Hume's comparison, admitted that the sales of the WN 'though not near so rapid, has been more than I

---

[20] Letter 151 addressed to Smith, dated 3 April 1776.
[21] Letter 153, 8 April 1776.   [22] Letter 152, April 1776.
[23] Letter 187, 26 November 1777.   [24] Letter 150, 1 April 1776.
[25] J. Y. T. Greig (ed.), *The Letters of David Hume* (Oxford, 1932), ii.314.

could have expected from a work that requires much thought and reflection'.[26] Adam Ferguson's more optimistic predictions were nearer the mark: 'You are not to expect the run of a novel, nor even of a true history; but you may venture to assure your booksellers of a steady and continual sale, as long as people wish for information on these subjects.'[27]

In the event the fears of lack of immediate success were ill-founded. The first edition of the WN, published on 9 March 1776, was sold out in six months. On 13 November 1776 Smith wrote to William Strahan acknowledging payment of a sum of £300, the balance of money due to him for the first edition, and proposed that the second edition 'be printed at your [Strahan's] expense, and that we should divide the profits'.[28] Strahan agreed and the second edition appeared early in 1778. Only minor amendments, though many of them, distinguished it from the first; but the third edition, published late in 1784, had such substantial additions that they were also published separately for the benefit of those who had purchased the earlier editions, under the title *Additions and Corrections to the First and Second Editions of Dr Adam Smith's Inquiry into the Nature and Causes of the Wealth of Nations*. The most notable changes were the introduction of Book IV, chapter viii (Conclusion of the Mercentile System); Book V, chapter i.e. (Of the Public Works and Institutions which are necessary for facilitating particular Branches of Commerce); passages on drawbacks (IV.iv.3–11), on the corn bounty (IV.v.8–9), on the herring bounty (IV.v.28–37) and the Appendix; and, particularly significant in view of Hugh Blair's early plea, the first index. The fourth edition of 1786 and the fifth of 1789, the last in Smith's lifetime, had only minor alterations. The English editions were not the only ones to appear in Smith's lifetime; by 1790 the book had been, or was being published in French, German, Danish and Italian.

The WN did not suffer the fate which befell the previous great treatise on economics, Sir James Steuart's *Principles of Political Oeconomy*, published only nine years earlier in 1767. Its success, judged even merely by its level of sales and the five editions in Smith's lifetime, hardly accorded with some of the fears for the book's popularity which tinged the otherwise unbounded admiration of Smith's friends. In welcoming the WN the members of Smith's intellectual circle faced a dilemma. They were attracted by the WN as the crown of Smith's system, but they feared that great achievement would not, perhaps even could not, be generally and immediately appreciated. There was, however, another side to the WN, a more pragmatic, down to earth side, which gave the work a practical

---

[26] Letter from William Strahan to David Hume, dated 12 April 1776 (Hume MSS. Royal Society of Edinburgh).

[27] Letter 154, 18 April 1776.

[28] Letter 179.

relevance in the eyes of many to whom the intellectual system was perhaps a mystery or merely irrelevant. Smith's friends did not always recognize that his 'proper attention to facts', even to Hume's 'curious facts', was to prove an immediate source of attraction. Having gained attention in this way, Smith then commanded respect because the practical conclusions which followed from the chief elements of his system were evidently related to the economic problems of the middle of the eighteenth century. These practical conclusions may be demonstrated by casting leading elements in Smith's system in the form of a series of practical prescriptions for economic growth. When the prescriptions are compared with the historical situation in Britain in the mid-eighteenth century, their immediate relevance is apparent. The various categories of Smith's system had thus an institutional content or background derived from the experience of his day, which many admired and followed even when the system and its categories remained difficult for them to understand.

The division of labour remained central to this institutional analysis. Even when Smith recognized the theoretical possibility of the operation of other factors—an increased labour force or mechanization—the division of labour remained in practice the fundamental cause of economic growth. The emphasis is clear in Book II where, as has already been pointed out (p. *30*), economic dynamics begins to overshadow economic statics, specifically in II.iii.*32*:

The annual produce of the land and labour of any nation can be increased in its value by no other means, but by increasing either the number of its productive labourers, or the productive powers of those labourers who had before been employed. The number of its productive labourers, it is evident, can never be much increased, but in consequence of an increase of capital, or of the funds destined for maintaining them. The productive powers of the same number of labourers cannot be increased, but in consequence either of some addition and improvement to those machines and instruments which facilitate and abridge labour; or of a more proper division and distribution of employment. In either case an additional capital is almost always required. It is by means of an additional capital only that the undertaker of any work can either provide his workmen with better machinery, or make a more proper distribution of employment among them.

Given that the division of labour remained the key to economic growth its full effectiveness was limited by an inadequate expansion of the market and by an inadequate supply of capital. An inadequate supply of capital also limited the effectiveness of those other influences—increased quantity of labour and mechanization—which Smith recognized as theoretical, if not practical causes of economic expansion. The distinction between productive and unproductive labour had led to the conclusion that growth

of capital depended on the most extensive use of funds in the employment of productive labour. Smith then developed his system to determine
those fields where productive labour was most effectively employed and
the conclusions, derived in this way from his analytical framework, had
highly institutional implications, for they indicated the areas where growth
was to be welcomed and encouraged. That was guidance for the practical
man.[29] Three propositions from II.v make the order of preference clear:

No equal capital puts into motion a greater quantity of productive labour than
that of the farmer. (12)

After agriculture, the capital employed in manufactures puts into motion the
greatest quantity of productive labour, and adds the greatest value to the annual produce. That which is employed in the trade of exportation, has the least
effect of any of the three. (19)

The capital, therefore, employed in the home-trade of any country will generally give encouragement and support to a greater quantity of productive labour
in that country, and increase the value of its annual produce more than an
equal capital employed in the foreign trade of consumption: and the capital
employed in this latter trade has in both these respects a still greater advantage
over an equal capital employed in the carrying trade. (31)

Such were the practical conclusions to which the theory led and, since
the desirable allocation was to be achieved through 'the uniform, constant,
and uninterrupted effort of every man to better his condition', the implication was obvious: government intervention had to be restrained,
especially when it was possible to demonstrate, as in Book IV, that intervention was usually exercised on behalf of those vested interests which
perverted the natural course of opulence. Well might Hugh Blair exclaim:

You have done great Service to the World by overturning all that interested
Sophistry of Merchants, with which they had Confounded the whole Subject

[29] Smith's friends recognized this aspect but were faintly worried by it. Hugh Blair
felt that some parts of the book, notably the discussion on the American colonies, might
well be left out because they made the book 'like a publication for the present moment'
(Letter 151), and Hume was aware that it had the attraction of offering 'curious facts'
(Letter 150). Whatever the estimates of Blair or Hume of the practical aspect of the WN,
it was a side which attracted a wider readership. A perceptive reviewer in an otherwise
uninformative and brief notice in the *Scots Magazine* (xxxviii (1776) 205–6) assessed
the twin attractions more equally and more fairly:
> Few writers . . . have united a proper attention to facts with a regular and scientific
> investigation of principles . . . [Smith] has taken an extensive and connected view of
> the several subjects in which the wealth of nations is concerned; and from an happy
> union of fact and theory has deduced a system, which, we apprehend, is on the whole
> more satisfactory, and rests on better grounds, than any which had before been offered
> to the public.

Hume, Blair, the reviewer in the *Scots Magazine*, each in his own and different way,
recognized both the intellectual attraction of a comprehensive and systematic analysis
and the additional attraction of a valid interpretation of contemporary events and problems.

of Commerce. Your work ought to be, and I am persuaded will in some degree become, the Commercial Code of Nations. (Letter 151)

Even a cursory survey of the major economic characteristics of Britain in the eighteenth century confirms the contemporary relevance of Smith's emphases. He advocated for example the desirability of encouraging agriculture because of the superior productivity of capital invested in it. To the practical man, whether he appreciated the full logic of Smith's analysis or not, the advocacy struck a responsive chord, since the main source of economic advance in Britain in the mid-eighteenth century lay in agriculture. Of that no one was unaware. Poor harvests and high prices benefited no one, obviously not industrial workers, and not the majority of farmers. Only a few specialist grain growers expected to reap the profits of scarcity and any potential gain was frequently eroded by the prohibitions on the use of grain for purposes other than the making of bread in times of scarcity and, more dramatically, by the activities of bread rioters. Hence a modern historian has described the period as one when 'the coming of dearth was sufficient in itself to halt, or reverse, an upward movement of activity'.[30] This restraint on increasing wealth was at last being tackled in the eighteenth century. Contemporaries, as well as later historians, disputed the significance and effectiveness of the specific agricultural improvements which brought the change to fruition, but, even when the method was disputed, the end was plain. The age-old spectre of famine was removed for the first time, and secure economic advance was possible. That was a dramatic change from the experience of many other countries.

A similar sympathetic response followed Smith's evaluation of the form and function of trade. Agriculture and commerce were the twin props of the economy in the eyes of many contemporaries and Smith's extensive treatment of the latter reflected its domination of economic thought and practice. More strikingly still, the pattern of foreign trade in the eighteenth century was changing and so drew attention to the relevance of Smith's attempt to assess the comparative contributions to economic growth of the different forms of trade. The relevance of the analysis is evident in the changes in the pattern of both commodities and markets.

Woollen exports had long been the traditional staple, particularly to European markets, which at the beginning of the eighteenth century took over 90 per cent of the woollen goods exported. Thereafter, though Spain and Portugal were taking more, other European countries were taking less; the future lay less with Europe than in the past. Later in the eighteenth century cotton assumed the role of leading export which wool had once held, but it was dependent on non-European markets. Between the two phases of domination by two different textile industries the

[30] T. S. Ashton, *Economic Fluctuations in England*, 1700–1800 (Oxford, 1959), 173.

buoyant trading sector lay in re-exports, which had not been of great significance until the second half of the seventeenth century, but by the beginning of the eighteenth century re-exports were equal to half the level of domestic exports. Sugar, tobacco, Indian calicos were the leading commodities, and their buoyancy reflected an economy which gained from a commerce based more on Britain's trading links than on the sale of domestic production overseas, an economy in which it was impossible to deny the paramount position, for good or ill, of overseas trade, and especially of the carrying trade. Nowhere in Britain was that situation more evident than in the economic structure of Glasgow in the third quarter of the eighteenth century. The foreign trade of Scotland had been turning from the continent of Europe to the New World even before the parliamentary union of 1707 confirmed the move, and the protection afforded by the Navigation Acts provided a firm and unfettered basis for Glasgow's success as an entrepot in the tobacco trade. Hence to read the practical discussion in Book IV of the WN, whether to accept or to reject its conclusions, was to read an account highly relevant to the contemporary economic scene. The Book discusses the stuff of which contemporary economic policy was made.

Though the problems of agriculture and of commerce were the economic issues which dominated the mind of the practical man of the eighteenth century, industrial production was increasing, and, when Smith wrote, its increase was bringing to an end a period of stability in the relative contributions to the national product of agriculture, manufacturing and commerce. Smith's emphasis on the growth, but not on the existing domination, of manufacturing industry, and particularly his exposition of the division of labour as the prime agent of change, accorded with contemporary experience. The increased industrial output was associated with a decline in the relative importance of the woollen industry and a marked growth in the relative contribution of metal manufactures, reflecting increased division of labour in small units and not the emergence of the larger and more modern units of industrial organisation which are associated with substantial capital formation and with joint-stock enterprise. The day of large-scale capital formation and extensive joint-stock enterprise came years after Smith. Though the problems of the industrial sector did not loom large in the minds of many contemporaries, when they did, they assumed the forms which Smith enunciated. The increasing capital intensity of production, and of its concentration, which was to begin with the appearance of the cotton industry, were yet to be, and the absence of any significant analysis of that sector in the WN should be cited less as a matter of regret and criticism and more as an indication of Smith's awareness of those aspects of the contemporary industrial scene which were of concern at the time he wrote.

The WN succeeded not only because its institutional emphasis made it thus so evidently, as Blair wrote, 'a publication for the present time' but also because it contained a stirring message. Its plea for liberty accorded with the intellectual presuppositions of the eighteenth century. The plea for liberty in the WN is a vital factor explaining the different reception accorded to Steuart and Smith within a decade of each other. Steuart may have suffered from additional handicaps. Apart from his personal handicap of Jacobitism, his work appealed less powerfully to the intellects of the eighteenth century, and above all Steuart's support for government intervention placed him in a different camp from Smith, and in one which was not popular among the increasingly influential elements in contemporary society.[31]

Smith provided a system with categories and elements which remain valid as parts of his analytical framework, but their institutional content, so pertinent to economic conditions in Britain in the eighteenth century, that it helped ensure the success of the WN, limits the acceptability and applicability of the system in other places and at other times. Whatever the intellectual attractiveness of Smith's writing on the continent of Europe, it was frequently institutionally irrelevant there when it was first published. For example, in contrast with Britain, ancient mercantilist and agrarian restrictions were acceptable on the continent. In Germany local monopolistic guilds still dominated economic life, and the advocacy of the new degree of economic freedom requisite for new forms of economic enterprise was not acceptable. Palyi suggests that the surprising aspect of the WN's reception in Germany was not that it was not readily received, but 'that the resistance against the WN did not last longer than some twenty years and did not take a more active form'.[32] In France, again as Palyi points out, the situation was confused because of the influence of the physiocrats. Smith gave sufficient recognition to the physiocratic point of view to lend some support to its claims, and that support was especially helpful since the acceptability of their

[31] Steuart's general position is perhaps adequately summarized in the statement that 'In treating every question of political œconomy, I constantly suppose a statesman at the head of government, systematically conducting every part of it, so as to prevent the vicissitudes of manners, and innovations, by their natural and immediate effects or consequences, from hurting any interest within the commonwealth.' (*An Inquiry into the Principles of Political Oeconomy: Being an Essay on the Science of Domestic Policy in Free Nations* (London, 1767) i. 120, ed. Skinner (Edinburgh 1966), i.122). Most of the contemporary reviews of Steuart's work commented on this aspect of it, in a way which throws an interesting light on the kind of reception Smith could expect. The *Critical Review*, xxiii (1767), commented for example: 'We have no idea of a statesman having any connection with the affair, and we believe that the superiority which England has at present over all the world, in point of commerce, is owing to her excluding statesmen from the executive part of all commercial concerns.' (412.)

[32] M. Palyi, 'The Introduction of Adam Smith on the Continent' in J. M. Clark *et al.*, *Adam Smith, 1776–1926* (1928, reprinted New York, 1966), 196.

doctrines was waning, partly because of the antagonism the physiocrats had engendered from the new and rising industrial groups, whose dislike of physiocracy grew from the support it provided to the large landowners. That confusion influenced the reception accorded to the WN.

Attempts to apply the WN to societies more advanced than Britain on the eve of the industrial revolution encounter similar, or even greater problems. The difficulty of doing so is demonstrated by contrasting Smith's emphasis on the division of labour as the central cause of economic growth and his neglect of other factors, such as increases in the supply of labour, particularly through the growth of population, and improvements in the productivity of labour through mechanization. Smith recognized that an increase in the labour force led to an increase in output, but he did not envisage unemployed labour resources being brought into use, and any increase in the supply of labour was likely to be a long-run consequence of an expansion of the national product.

The demand for those who live by wages, therefore, necessarily increases with the increase of the revenue and stock of every country, and cannot possibly increase without it. The increase of revenue and stock is the increase of national wealth. The demand for those who live by wages, therefore, naturally increases with the increase of national wealth, and cannot possibly increase without it. (I.viii.21)

Increasing population, whether a cause of economic growth, or as something to fear, was not highlighted. That may seem surprising. Others, among them Sir James Steuart, feared over-population, but it was possible to be as optimistic about the future in the mid-eighteenth century as at any time. The spectre of famine and of some diseases had been removed; the sharp rise in population and the problems of its concentration were yet to be. Hence it was easy to conceive the problem of economic growth as one of utilizing the labour force in ways which would most effectively meet the opportunities offered by the expansion of the market, either by improvements in the division of labour or by mechanization. Of the two possibilities Smith, with his analysis firmly rooted in the institutional structure of his day, stressed the former. Mechanization was recognized—as in his discussion of the steam engine—but it was conceived as a process accompanying the division of labour.

The owner of the stock which employs a great number of labourers, necessarily endeavours, for his own advantage, to make such a proper division and distribution of employment, that they may be enabled to produce the greatest quantity of work possible. For the same reason, he endeavours to supply them with the best machinery which either he or they can think of. (I.viii.57)

In consequence of better machinery, of greater dexterity, and of a more proper division and distribution of work, all of which are the natural effects of improvement, a much smaller quantity of labour becomes requisite for executing any particular piece of work. . . (I.xi.o.1)

Not only are the division of labour and mechanization closely interwoven, but invention itself was in Smith's opinion 'originally owing to the division of labour' (I.i.8).[33] Innovation is no more central to the analysis. Projectors pass through the pages of the WN, frequently to be dismissed as detrimental rather than helpful to economic growth. In spite of his stress on psychological propensities in other parts of his work, Smith did not extend his analysis in a serious way to evaluate the qualities which determined the ability to innovate successfully.

The dominance of the division of labour, and the comparative neglect of other categories in the analysis, notably mechanization, is, of course, a reflection of the institutional relevance of the WN to the British economy in the mid-eighteenth century. The penalty paid was the opening of a penetrating line of criticism for those who wished to stress Smith's comparative neglect of the other and ultimately more powerful agent of economic growth. Into that context can be placed the criticism of Lauderdale, who, though not distinguishing between capital and entrepreneurship, was anxious to remedy Smith's alleged failure to make adequate allowance for differences in knowledge and ability in different countries. Rae suggested even more forcefully that invention held the key to explaining the greater productivity of capital in some societies than in others. Smith's admirer, J. B. Say, developed the idea of entrepreneurship as a very special form of labour. Later Schumpeter placed the entrepreneur and his innovating ability at the heart of an explanation of economic growth. Lauderdale, Rae, Say, Schumpeter belong to later generations, which, unlike Smith's, had witnessed the effect of mechanization on industrial output. Smith was writing even before the large-scale application of mechanization to cotton-spinning. Hence, just as the WN did not seem so relevant to societies other than Britain in the later eighteenth century, so the institutional content of the WN was not applicable to the industrial state which Britain was beginning to be.

Nevertheless, discussion of Smith's institutional relevance can become almost pointless if it tries to prove either that Smith anticipated modern industrialization, or if it spends much time proving that he did not. Any evaluation must start from the obvious fact that Smith's thought was

---

[33] Even in the art of war, where the contribution of the 'state of the mechanical as well as of some other arts' is recognized in general, and the invention of fire-arms in particular (V.i.a.43), the division of labour is still the key to success: 'it is necessary that [the art of war] should become the sole or principal occupation of a particular class of citizens, and the division of labour is as necessary for the improvement of this, as of every other art.' (V.i.a.14).

formulated in the third quarter of the eighteenth century, and that many of his ideas had been formulated as early as the 1760s. To search the WN for examples of the institutional structure which was to emerge later in a more advanced industrial economy is to search for qualities which it cannot possess except fortuitously. The attraction of the WN was not that it was a tourist's guide to the subsequent course of industrialization, but that it had a command of the institutional structure of the time, sufficiently convincing to demonstrate its contemporary relevance.

The institutional features of the WN which date it also helped towards its immediate success. The modern reader may recognize the systematic analysis as the great intellectual achievement of the treatise and qualify the validity of Smith's views on public policy, or even adopt the extreme interpretation of dismissing them as totally irrelevant. No contemporary could have entertained such a view; obviously misleading or erroneous comments on the public policy of the age, or, worse still, irrelevant comments, would have detracted from the intellectual achievement in their eyes. The acceptance of the WN by contemporaries rested on its apparent relevance to the affairs of everyday life as much as on its systematic analysis. It became the authority to quote as much in public discussion as in parliamentary debate. But that was not all. Smith's relevance to his day and age insured such immediate acceptance for the WN that, even when its popularity as a guide to policy was waning, and was ultimately rejected, the work was so well established, and so generally established, that it was never neglected, and the systematic analysis was then recognized for the massive intellectual achievement which it is.

Smith's use of History

If Smith achieved the unusual distinction of being a prophet with honour in his own country, he did so partly because his work was firmly rooted in a historical situation. The WN may, therefore, be used as a historical source, in at least two distinctive senses. Since Smith frequently wrote as a historian—sometimes deliberately, sometimes otherwise—he may be judged accordingly by the common criteria of historical scholarship. In addition, Smith's account of events in the later eighteenth century may be assessed for its reliability as the report of a contemporary observer. In neither case is an account of Smith's writing a straightforward and uncomplicated matter. Just as anyone using Smith to illuminate later economic thought must make full allowance for the limitations of his institutional background on the general applicability of his theories, so those who use the WN as a historical source in whatever sense must make even greater allowances. In the former case the deficiencies are inevitable, as Smith could not have envisaged changes which were yet to be; in the latter case the omissions may even be deliberate and so misleading, especi-

ally if they are not obvious. As always, Smith's desire to devise a major
intellectual system determined the use he made of historical and factual
material. No one of his intellectual eminence would distort the facts,
even if only because refutation would thus have been infinitely easier,
but, even when facts were not distorted, they may still have been used
in such a subordinate and supporting role to the dominating systematic
model that their use for any other purpose needs qualification.

If parts of the WN are to be judged as straightforward pieces of historical writing, it is necessary to distinguish the different ways in which
Smith wrote as a historian. When he wrote as an orthodox historian, he
tried to assemble the best documentary and factual evidence for his case;
when he wrote as a philosopher of history, he tried to distil an ideal interpretation of an historical process ostensibly from the facts he had accumulated.

Smith, as any orthodox historian, may be assessed by a review of his
sources and his use of them. Their variety is striking, whether the impression be derived from those quoted in the WN itself, from the resources in Smith's personal library, or from the accounts of the Library
at Glasgow when he controlled its expenditure. The break with the tradition of Christian authority is obvious; even historical parts of the Bible
and its apparent relevance to the discussion of a nomadic life are virtually ignored, with only the most incidental of references to the Old Testa-
ment. By contrast, the classical tradition dominates and supplies many
illustrations of early times. Given the inevitable paucity of source material
for an account of an earlier age, and yet given the necessity of formulating
such an account as part of an essential background to the dynamic historical evolution which he was seeking, Smith—in common with others
who adopted his approach—was forced to use another group of source
materials: the travellers' tales and accounts of contemporary societies
which were at a much earlier and much more primitive stage of social
evolution. Travellers' tales bulk large in what is generally regarded as
Smith's historical writing, taking pride of place even over the classical
references. To a more orthodox historian the extensive use of travellers'
tales is even more suspect than the use of classical writers, whose
work can at least be subjected to a more critical appraisal of their
reliability. Travellers' tales, especially in an age when they were frequently rare, even unique, accounts of far off places, could not easily be
confirmed or refuted, and so the travellers tended to highlight the unusual
and the bizarre. A warning of Francis Hutcheson could well be taken to
heart:

The Entertainment therefore in these ingenious Studys consists chiefly in exciting
Horror, and making Men *stare* ... What is most surprizing in these Studys,

is the wondrous *Credulity* of some Gentlemen of great Pretentions in other Matters to Caution of Assent, for these *marvellous Memoirs* of Monks, Friars, Sea-Captains, Pirates; and for the *Historys, Annals, Chronologys*, received by oral Tradition, or Hieroglyphicks.[34]

Smith was not more culpable than many of his contemporaries in his use of such material. He was certainly less guilty than some others of falling into the trap against which Hutcheson warned, for he did not accept all his sources uncritically. Trade statistics were held perceptively and authoritatively to be unreliable:

Heavy duties being imposed upon almost all goods imported, our merchant importers smuggle as much, and make entry of as little as they can. Our merchant exporters, on the contrary, make entry of more than they export; sometimes out of vanity, and to pass for great dealers in goods which pay no duty; and sometimes to gain a bounty or a drawback. Our exports, in consequence of these different frauds, appear upon the customhouse books greatly to overbalance our imports; to the unspeakable comfort of those politicians who measure the national prosperity by what they call the balance of trade. (V.ii.k.29)

Hence it is not surprising that Smith, though ready to endorse Gregory King's skill in political arithmetic (I.viii.34), and willing to quote the calculations of Charles Smith on the corn trade (I.xi.g.18), had to admit that he himself had 'no great faith in political arithmetick' (IV.v.b.30). Quantitative sources were not the only ones treated with some reserve.

After all the wonderful tales which have been published concerning the splendid state of those countries [Mexico and Peru] in antient times, whoever reads, with any degree of sober judgment, the history of their first discovery and conquest, will evidently discern that, in arts, agriculture, and commerce, their inhabitants were much more ignorant than the Tartars of the Ukraine are at present. (I.xi.g.26)

Yet sometimes Smith's use of a source is less critical than it should be, especially when the source confirms an argument he is developing from other and more general, often speculative sources, so that the orthodox historian thus becomes the supporter of the philosophic historian. Instances range from the trivial to the substantial. At the most trivial level Smith's faults represent merely different standards of transcription between the eighteenth century and the present day. At times he seems to quote from memory, as when his quotations are not quite verbatim, or when he attributes a view to a source which it does not quite support, as for example, in his use of the works of Juan and Ulloa and of Frézier to support his condemnation of the mining of precious metals in the New World (I.xi.c.26–8). More serious still, in his use of statutes Smith falls

---

[34] F. Hutcheson, An Inquiry concerning Moral Good and Evil in *An Inquiry into the Original of our Ideas of Beauty and Virtue* (London, 4th ed., 1738), 207.

into the error, not unique among historians, of failing to distinguish between the intention of the statute and the manner and extent of its implementation. The error is surprising in Smith's case, because his experience at least after his appointment as Commissioner of Customs in 1778, enabled him to observe the gulf which could be fixed between intention and implementation in the case of some statutes, as in various attempts to suppress smuggling, and even more important because he himself sometimes provided the material for drawing such a distinction, as in his discussion of the laws relating to apprenticeship. A more serious example is his discussion of the settlement provisions of the poor law. In both cases Smith objected because of interference with the liberty he considered essential for the effective allocation of resources (above, *37*).

After castigating the generally restrictive effect of the Statute of Apprentices Smith proceeded to recognize the limitations on its application: to market towns and not in the country (I.x.c.8); to those trades which were established when the Act was passed and not to those which appeared subsequently, excluding—on Smith's own admission—'the manufactures of Manchester, Birmingham and Wolverhampton', or at least 'many of them' (I.x.c.9); and finally, not to soldiers and sea-men who, 'when discharged from the king's service, are at liberty to exercise any trade, within any town or place of Great Britain or Ireland' (IV.ii.42).

Smith's failure to make adequate allowance for the qualifications to the law of settlement is more serious. Smith objected to the legal restraints imposed on the right to obtain a settlement in a parish, with its entitlement to poor relief, as part of his general objection to artificial restraints on the free mobility of labour. He made his objection forcefully:

There is scarce a poor man in England of forty years of age ... who has not in some part of his life felt himself most cruelly oppressed by this ill-contrived law of settlements. (I.x.c.59)

The reasons had been as sweepingly advanced in the previous paragraph:

... in England, where it is often more difficult for a poor man to pass the artificial boundary of a parish, than an arm of the sea or a ridge of high mountains, natural boundaries which sometimes separate very distinctly different rates of wages in other countries. (I.x.c.58)

In addition Smith contrasted conditions in Scotland with those in England, alleging that in England the law of settlement ensured that 'The scarcity of hands in one parish ... cannot always be relieved by their super-abundance in another, as it is constantly in Scotland' (I.x.c.58). Once again Smith himself provided qualifications which should have led to the enunciation of his proposition in more moderate terms. He recognized the major mitigation of the restraints on the mobility of labour which followed the introduction of certificates, whereby a parish accepted liability for a potential pauper, though he promptly cast doubt on the effectiveness of the measure by commenting rather cynically, after quoting from a passage in Richard Burn's *Justice of the Peace*, that 'certificates ought always to be required by the parish where any poor man comes to reside, and that they ought very seldom to be granted by that which he proposes to leave' (I.x.c.56). Smith also provided a general explanation of differences of wage rates between Scotland and England; one dependent not on their different laws of settlement but on differences between their rates of development and between the levels of subsistence in the two countries (I.viii.33–4).

Other evidence reinforces the doubts Smith raises himself. Removals of potential paupers in England were probably less frequent than he implies, otherwise it is difficult to understand how the new developing areas ever obtained the labour force they required; in Scotland paupers were sometimes forcefully removed, though less frequently than in England. The issue was one of contemporary importance, and could have been investigated by a detailed examination of parochial administration, but of such investigation there is no evidence in the WN, so that in these matters Smith did not have knowledge comparable to that which he had about customs procedure, even before his appointment as a commissioner, and which enabled him to be more critical of evidence in that field. In his discussion of both the laws of apprenticeship and settlement Smith provides evidence which damages his own case against the restrictive legislation, and provides indications that investigations which might have been undertaken to confirm his case or otherwise were not carried out. The general principles, the opposition to restrictions damaging to the free allocation of resources, were held so strongly that there seemed no case to answer.

Criticism of Smith's use of sources becomes truly damaging only if he read into a source more serious evidence in support of a proposition than he was entitled to do. Even that criticism must not be pushed too far. All historians must choose the facts they judge relevant to their argument, and so their discussion is forced in one direction or another. Hence a significant distinction between the approaches of Smith and of orthodox historians can be drawn only if Smith's choice of evidence strayed beyond the limits set by human frailty in determining degrees of relevance towards a demonstrable distortion of historical evidence, whether deliberate or not. Then, even if Smith's use of his sources meets the requirements of the most refined critical apparatus of textual criticism, he would stand condemned by orthodox historians for his unacceptable choice of evidence.

Any such distinction, or even gulf, between the approaches of Smith and of orthodox historians appears only when Smith writes as a speculative or philosophical as well as an orthodox historian, and so a fundamental issue in any appreciation of the WN lies in determining how Smith deals with any tensions which emerge between the two approaches. Each strand of his historical reasoning, the orthodox and the speculative, is a logical entity, and each, if examined and judged by its own standards, is internally consistent. Problems emerge only when attempts are made to integrate the two in order to eliminate the tensions which seem to emerge between them. Smith does not recognize the tensions, he was probably unaware of them, because his grand design of a comprehensive system dominates every other approach. Yet tension between the two approaches appears at central parts of his analysis, most significantly in Book III, where the historical evidence is, of course, embedded at the centre of the exposition, not merely providing a peripheral part of the reasoning. The philosophical historian states unequivocally the course of the 'natural progress of opulence':

According to the natural course of things, therefore, the greater part of the capital of every growing society is, first, directed to agriculture, afterwards to manufactures, and last of all to foreign commerce. This order of things is so very natural, that in every society that had any territory, it has always, I believe, been in some degree observed. (III.i.8)

In the next paragraph the orthodox historian upsets 'the natural progress':

though this natural order of things must have taken place in some degree in every such society, it has, in all the modern states of Europe, been, in many respects, entirely inverted. The foreign commerce of some of their cities has introduced all their finer manufactures, or such as were fit for distant sale; and manufactures and foreign commerce together, have given birth to the principal improvements of agriculture. (III.i.9)

The last sentence of the chapter provides both an explanation and an accusation:

The manners and customs which the nature of their original government introduced, and which remained after that government was greatly altered, necessarily forced them into this unnatural and retrograde order. (III.i.9)

The three chapters which follow, to make up the shortest Book in the WN, then proceed to expound an orthodox historical progress of opulence in a way which differs from that outlined in 'the natural progress', of how, for example in III.iv, the commerce of the towns contributed to the improvement of the country.

This distinction between the speculative historical progress of opulence and the orthodox historical progress is the prime example of the tensions involved in the use of the WN as a historical source. Yet allegations of tension, of an uneasy relationship and even of contradictions between the two strands of thought, are evident only when Smith is judged by standards, and by a methodology, which he would not have accepted. Smith's objective was to delineate an ideal account of historical evolution, which did not need to conform to any actual historical situation, so historical evidence, while playing a central part in his thought, was supplementary evidence of secondary importance. If historical facts indicated a divergence from the ideal explanation, then Smith felt obliged to offer explanations of the divergence. He worked from the system to the facts not from the facts to the system, and in that context his protestation that he had 'no great faith in political arithmetic' is significant. If the historian or the political arithmetician demonstrated the divergence from the ideal that, for instance, the progress of opulence was from the town to the country and not the reverse, the interesting problem then lay in determining the reasons for the divergence—in the present example it lay in unwise and undesirable intervention from the government. H. T. Buckle, though given to overstating his case, made a vital point, and in a lively style:

Adam Smith . . .very properly rejected [statistical facts] as the basis of his science, and merely used them by way of illustration, when he could select what he liked. The same remark applies to other facts which he drew from the history of trade, and, indeed, from the general history of society. All of these are essentially subsequent to the argument. They make the argument more clear, but not more certain. For, it is no exaggeration to say, that, if all the commercial and historical facts in the *Wealth of Nations* were false, the book would still remain, and its conclusions would hold equally good, though they would be less attractive.[35]

Any tension between the speculative, or systematic, and the orthodox strands of Smith's thought is potentially even more misleading when the systematic thought is contrasted with, or used to illuminate aspects of contemporary policy. Then Smith's comments on the happenings of his time in the eighteenth century may be so coloured by his speculative approach that his accounts and views may have to be treated with some reserve and not used as reliable source material for historical studies of the period.

It was suggested earlier that the conclusion of greatest practical significance in Smith's analysis for the eighteenth century lay in his ordering of the productive use of capital, as in II.v.19: first, in agriculture; then in manufactures; last in 'the trade of exportation'. In the subsequent evaluation of the wholesale trade, the very practical conclusion was stated unequivocally:

[35] H. T. Buckle, *History of Civilization in England* (London, 1857–61). Reprinted as *On Scotland and the Scotch Intellect*, ed. H. J. Hanham (Chicago, 1970), 285.

... the great object of the political oeconomy of every country, is to encrease the riches and power of that country. It ought, therefore, to give no preference nor superior encouragement to the foreign trade of consumption above the home-trade, nor to the carrying trade above either of the other two. (II.v.31)

Just as Smith's orthodox historical work sometimes qualified the use that may be made of his speculative history, so his orthodox empirical studies cast doubt on some of the recommendations on contemporary policy derived directly from his analytical system. Examples can be given at both ends of his proposition concerning the desirable deployment of resources, from his comment on agriculture and on the colonial trade.

'In proportion as a greater share of [capital] is employed in agriculture, the greater will be the quantity of productive labour which it puts into motion within the country'. (II.v.19.) It was suggested above (p. 45) that the prospects for economic growth in Britain in the eighteenth century were greatest in agriculture, and Smith provides empirical evidence of the progress already made in that field in his own day and of further possible lines of progress, as, for example, in an accurate and perceptive account of the expansion of the Scottish cattle trade (I.xi.l.2–3). But another part of Smith's system, and the empirical content he gave to its operation in agriculture, casts doubt on the pre-eminence given to agriculture in economic progress. He asserts from empirical evidence that the division of labour, the great agent of change, is least applicable in agriculture (I.i.4). Once again the different strands of the argument are logically valid, but the relationship between the two is uneasy and unclear, and so too is the use which may be made of the evidence as reflecting economic conditions in the eighteenth century.

Smith's treatment of the colonial trade is even more significant, because it looms large in the WN and in contemporary discussion. Given his general analysis it is not surprising that Smith condemns the tobacco trade as an example of how undesirable government intervention had turned trade 'from a direction in which it would have maintained a greater quantity of productive labour, into one, in which it can maintain a much smaller quantity' and had 'rendered the whole state of that industry and commerce more precarious and less secure, than if their produce had been accommodated to a greater variety of markets'. (IV.vii.c.46 and 40.) It has already been suggested (p. 46) that Smith's account of the carrying trade, both of its dependence on current commercial policy and of its effect on the domestic economy, would have been recognized by his contemporaries as a realistic survey of the conditions of the time. The growth of re-exports, and the tobacco trade's domination, especially in Glasgow, owed much to the Navigation Acts, and the effect on the domestic economy was so limited that it is even possible to suggest that there existed two separate economies, each with its rate and extent of growth determined by different factors. But, once again, the WN itself provides the qualifications to the practical conclusion derived from the systematic analysis.

To begin with, it is not clear that commercial legislation was the critical cause of the growth of the colonial trade in general, and the tobacco trade in particular. 'There are no colonies of which the progress has been more rapid than that of the English in North America' (IV.vii.b.15), because 'Plenty of good land, and liberty to manage their own affairs their own way, seem to be the two great causes of the prosperity of all new colonies' (IV.vii.b.16). Even the exact influence of the monopoly is unclear: it 'raises the rate of mercantile profit, and therefore augments somewhat the gains of our merchants', but it also 'hinders the sum of profit from rising so high as it otherwise would do' (IV.vii.c.59). To determine the overall effect of the monopolistic restrictions, Smith is admitting in effect the necessity of a nice calculation of gain and loss. In the long-run even more necessary for that purpose is an evaluation of the use to which any profit is put: a smaller profit in the hands of those who use it in ways deemed appropriate may promote economic growth more rapidly than a larger profit in the hands of those who use it differently. Of that problem Smith was aware:

If the prodigality of some was not compensated by the frugality of others, the conduct of every prodigal, by feeding the idle with the bread of the industrious, tends not only to beggar himself, but to impoverish his country. (II.iii.20)

Smith's distinction between the prodigal and the frugal man raises immense difficulties for any attempt to use his systematic analysis as a final commentary on the effect of the colonial trade. The distinction can be highlighted in Smith's own words in II.iii:

The proportion between capital and revenue . . . seems every where to regulate the proportion between industry and idleness. Wherever capital predominates, industry prevails: wherever revenue, idleness. (13)
Capitals are increased by parsimony, and diminished by prodigality and misconduct. (14)
Parsimony, and not industry, is the immediate cause of the increase of capital. Industry, indeed, provides the subject which parsimony accumulates. But whatever industry might acquire, if parsimony did not save and store up, the capital would never be the greater. (16)

Hence, whatever the limitations, derived from Smith's systematic analysis, on the beneficial effects of the carrying trade, the colonial trade might still have made a major contribution to economic growth if the merchants were parsimonious and not prodigal, particularly if they then diverted their capital into agricultural enterprises at home. Smith recognized in general terms what was happening. 'Merchants are commonly ambitious of becoming country gentlemen, and when they do, they are generally the best of all improvers' (III.iv.3), certainly better than the great proprietors (III.ii.7). The experience of the eighteenth century confirms this aspect of Smith's discussion. Parsimony among the merchants, including colonial merchants, and their desire to become landed gentlemen, provided the capital which Smith recognized as essential for the exploitation of the agricultural resources of Scotland itself. The undesirability of concentration on the carrying trade which Smith's intellectual analysis demonstrated, was evidently much less in practice when a full study is made, and, once again as in the discussion of agriculture, for reasons which are embedded in the WN. The reasons are not stressed, because to do so would have required some qualification to conclusions derived from the central analysis of the desirable distribution of capital and to some of the allegedly harmful effects of the Navigation Acts.

Smith's historical writing has practical implications in the use of the WN. The historical writing is meaningful only if interpreted as part of the intellectual system which the historical material was used to illustrate and support. Similarly, Smith's discussion of contemporary problems and events, which can easily be assumed to be an example of unbiased reporting, must also be integrated into his entire system. The belief in the natural progress of opulence, almost in its inevitability, is so strong throughout the WN that, when dealing with a contemporary problem, Smith's main objective is to isolate those barriers which lay in the path of natural progress as he saw it, and to advocate their speedy removal. Hence on contemporary issues his writing verges on propaganda, he uses evidence in ways which are not wholly convincing to those not committed to his system, and he presses interpretations of contemporary events to more extreme conclusions than may well be warranted.

The defects of Smith's emphasis must not be stressed unduly, though they may seem to justify the suggestion that he was never noted for his consistency. Paradoxically the inconsistency was often consistent, because it rarely damaged the central analysis and was indeed usually introduced as a means of support for it. Nor can Smith easily be accused of inconsistency in the transfer of his analysis to policy, so long as his practical recommendations were confined to a general advocacy of the desirability of eliminating government intervention from many, if not from all aspects of economic life. The inconsistencies appear only in the detail. These are defects of greater consequence to those who read the WN today than to those who read the WN when it was first published. Then the analysis, both systematic and institutional, was largely applicable in Britain, and was a major cause of the work's popularity; it was excellent political propaganda and such stretching of empirical evidence as it contained was not such as could discredit the whole. The problem is for those readers of later generations who seek to use the WN as a source book of contemporary comment.

*

The Text and Apparatus

SINCE WN is a work of some magnitude and complexity, yet one inadequately described in the standard bibliographical references, it may be appropriate to define the various editions examined,[1] to indicate the circumstances of printing and issue,[2] and then to specify the relation of each edition to the present text.

1] 4° 1st edition. Published 9 March 1776 at £1.16.0 in blue-grey or marbled boards.

Vol. i: A⁴ a² B–L⁴ M⁴(±M3) N–P⁴ Q⁴(±Q1) R–T⁴ U⁴(±U3) X–2Y⁴ 2Z⁴(±2Z3) 3A⁴(±3A4) 3B–3N⁴ 3O⁴(±3O4) 3P–3T⁴. Pp. *i* title, *ii* advt for TMS 4th edn., *iii–xi* contents, *xii blank*. *12–510* text, *511–512 blank*. Vol. ii: A² B–C⁴ D⁴(±D1) E–3Y⁴ 3Z⁴(±3Z4) 4A⁴ 4B⁴ (–4B1.2 +4B1.2) 4C⁴(±4C2.3) 4D–4E⁴ 4F². Pp. *i* half-title, *iii* title, *iv* errata, *12–587* text, *588* advts. The substitute leaves, six in the first volume and six in the second, have been noted only in their cancelled state.[3]

The original edition, the first title of which serves as a frontispiece to this volume, properly serves as copy-text: the printing closest to original manuscript and thus ordinarily preserving in its 'accidentals', or spelling

---

[1] Altogether the survey has extended to forty-nine copies in seven institutions: British Library, editions *1–5* and separate issue *2A*; Bodleian Library, *1, 3, 4, 6*; University of Glasgow *1*(3 copies), *2, 2A, 4*(3), *5*(2); National Library of Australia, *1, 2, 2A*(bound in *2*), *3* (2), *4, 6*(2); New York Public Library, *1*(5), *2, 2A*(bound in *1*), *3, 4, 6*; Princeton University *1*(3), *2A*; University of Texas at Austin, *1*(2), *2–6*. Duplicate copies in each library were compared against each other and the unique register of press figures for every volume checked against every other comparable volume. The figures, as cited in subsequent notes, occasionally show some displacements or other disorders in press-work, but in no copy, as later inspection confirms, is there any textual variation within the edition.

[2] Issue date, for immediate reference listed first, is taken throughout from the *London Chronicle*, a journal which also carries preliminary advts. certifying the date: for first edition in the number 5–7 March 1776; for the third, 6–9 November 1784; for the fourth, 26–28 October 1786. The original preliminary notice wrongly gives the first-edition price as £2.2.0, a figure corrected on the date of publication. Rae (324), also cites the correct price but then curiously inflates the cost for the second to £2.2.0, though it still remains, as for the first, £1.16.0.

The printing ledgers maintained by William Strahan to 1785, and by his son Andrew thereafter, do not indicate any work for the first edition but thenceforth cite the data given, for editions 2–5, in British Library Add. MS. 48815 (ff. 9, 66, 85, 113) and for edition 6 in Add. MS. 48811 (f. 3).

[3] In several copies of volume ii there is no press figure p. 351 and, in all, p. 469 is figured either 6 or 8. Apparently (as noted in the *Times Literary Supplement*, 20 July 1940, 356) a few copies also exist with cancel titles having imprint extended to include W. Creech at Edinburgh.

and punctuation, the author's several idiosyncracies. Nonetheless, since the edition was printed not directly from the author's original script but, apparently like all his work, from a copy prepared by an amanuensis,[4] some of its peculiarities may be attributed to another hand and therefore discounted whenever the third edition, closely attended by the author, offers a less ambiguous reading.

2] 4° 2d edition. Published 28 February 1778 at £1.16.0 in boards.
Vol. i: A–G^4 H^4($\pm$ H4) I–2D^4 2E^4($\pm$ 2E2.3) 2F–2L^4 2M^4($\pm$ 2M2.3) 2N–3S^4 3T^4(– 3T4). Pp. *i* title, *iii–vii* contents, *viii* advt for TMS 4th edn. and errata, *12–510* text. Vol. ii: A^4 B–4E^4 4F^4(– F4). Pp. *i* half-title, *iii* title, *v–viii* contents, *12–589* text, *590 blank*. In Volume i the Texas copy still contains original leaf H4, first of the five cancelled in other specimens, but this is invariant from the cancellans.[5]
Strahan printing ledger: (Nov. 1777) 141$\frac{1}{2}$ sheets, 500 copies, @ 16s.=£113.4.0. Extra Corrections £4. This printing was done, it will be observed, three months before issue.
The second edition exhibits a number of alterations large and small, some providing new information, some correcting matters of fact, some perfecting the idiom, and a large number now documenting references in footnotes. All these substantive changes are incorporated in the text excepting only those further amended in the third edition.

2A] 4° 'Additions and Corrections.' Published 20 November 1784 at 2s. in blue-grey boards, 'to accommodate the purchasers of the former editions'.
Issue: B–L^4. Pp. *12–79* text, *80 blank*.
Strahan ledger: (Oct. 1784) 10 sheets, 500 copies, @ 16s. = £8.
As the collation would indicate, this is a very considerable supplement, representing in thirteen sections some 24,000 words. The 'Additions' were undertaken several years before when Smith first proposed a separate printing and his publisher, Thomas Cadell, agreed subject to a proviso— which could hardly be enforced—that the issue be sold only to those who had purchased the earlier editions.[6] Though many 'Corrections' doubt-

---

[4] As early as 1755 Smith refers to his Edinburgh lectures as 'written in the hand of a clerk who left my service six years ago' (Stewart IV.26) and his difficulty in writing a compact script doubtless led him to employ other clerks, one of whom, Alexander Gillies, has been identified as the amanuensis for WN. W. R. Scott, *Adam Smith as Student and Professor*, (Glasgow, 1937), 359–60.
[5] In several copies no figure appears, in volume i, at pp. 124, 386, 389, or 390 and none in ii at p. 24. Additionally in ii the figures for Texas copy gathering 4A (pp. 545–52) reveal this to be a stray sheet held over from the printing of the first edition.
[6] See Letter 222 addressed to Cadell dated 7 December 1782, and Cadell's answer, Letter 223, 12 December 1782.

less were then and thereafter also entered in Smith's copy of the Second Edition, and from the caption title would appear to be conveyed as well in this separate issue, a goodly number of lesser consequence could be accommodated expediently only in the edition next described.

3] 8° 3d edition. Published simultaneously with *2A* 20 November 1784 at 18*s.* in boards or one guinea bound.

Vol. i: A⁴ B–2I⁸ 2K². Pp. *i* title, *iii* Advertisement, *iv* errata, *v* vi–viii contents, *12–499* text, *500 blank*. Vol. ii: π² a² B–2K⁸ 2L⁶. Pp. *1–2 blank*, *i* title, *iii* iv–vi contents, *12–518* text, *519–523* Appendix, *524 blank*. Vol. iii: π² a² B–2K⁸ 2L². Pp. *1–2 blank*, *i* title, *iii* iv–v contents, *vi blank*, *12–465* text, *466 blank*, *467–515* index, *516* advt for TMS, 4th edn.[7]

Strahan ledger: (Oct. 1784) 97½ sheets, 1000 copies, @ £1.7.0 = £131.12.6. Extra for Index £3.5.0. Tables and Corrections £4.19.0.

In view of the author's later statement (see section 4 below) this issue must be accepted as representing his final version, one which incorporates with some further amendments all the additions issued in *2A*, further revises the text and, most significantly, supplies a lengthy index.[8] Moreover, as there is clear evidence that it was read several times in proof, with close attention to the pointing,[9] the third edition can be regarded as supervening even the first in many of its formal aspects, and thus now serves as printers' copy.

4] 8° 4th edition. Published 6 November 1786 at 18*s.* in boards.

Vol. i: A⁴ B–2I⁸ 2K². Pp. *i* title, *iii* Advt to 3d Ed., *iv* Advt to 4th Ed., *v* vi–viii contents, *12–499* text, *500* errata. Vol. ii: π² a² B–2K⁸ 2L⁶. Pp. *1–2 blank*, *i* title, *iii* iv–vi contents, *12–518* text, *519–523* Appendix, *524* errata. Vol. iii: A⁴ B–2K⁸ 2L². Pp. *1–2 blank*, *i* title, *iii* iv–v contents, *vi* errata, *12–465* text, *466 blank*, *467–515* index, *516* advt for TMS, 4th edn.[10]

Strahan ledger: (Oct. 1786) 98 sheets, 1250 copies, @ £1.11.0 = £151.18.0. Extra for Tables and Index £4.2.0.

If we accept Smith's own assurance, in the new 'Advertisement', that there are indeed 'no alterations of any kind' in this edition, then the 'few trifling alterations' which Cannan here observed, and accepted in his

---

[7] Volume ii page 422 is figured either 3 or 6.

[8] This may not have been by Smith (Cannan, xvi), but quite probably was done under his direction either by amanuensis Gillies or by someone else familiar with Scottish banking practices. In the New York Public Library copy index gathering 2K, as the figures indicate, has been greatly disordered in the original imposition.

[9] Letter 227 addressed to William Strahan, dated 22 May 1783, and Letter 237, 10 June 1784.

[10] In several copies no figure appears, in volume ii, at pp. 431 and 490.

own text, may be dismissed along with the others which he rightly perceived to be 'misreadings or unauthorized corrections of the printers'.[11] That there are no fewer than fourteen errata noted, some in each of the three volumes, attests however to the printer's continuing concern, a concern evidenced as late as the posthumous seventh edition of 1793, where F2 in the first volume is a cancel.

5] 8° 5th edition. Published 1789, possibly also, as for *4*, at 18*s*. in boards.
Vol. i: A⁶ B–2I⁸ 2K². Pp. *1–2 blank, i* title, *iii*–iv advt to 3d Edn., *v*–vi Advt to 4th Ed., *vii* viii–x contents, *12*–499 text, *500 blank*. Vol. ii: π² a² B–2K⁸ 2L⁶. Pp. *1–2 blank, i* title, *iii* iv–vi contents, *12*–5*18* text, *519–523* Appendix, *524 blank*. Vol. iii: A⁴ B–2K⁸ 2L². Pp. *1–2 blank, i* title, *iii* iv–v contents, *vi blank, 12*–465 text, *466 blank, 467–515* index, *516* advt for TMS 4th edn.[12]
Strahan ledger: (Feb. 1789) 98 sheets, 1500 copies, @ £1.14.0 = £166.12.0. Extra for Tables and Index £4.6.0.
From this edition the present text adopts one obvious correction only, the reading 'Hope' in the 'Advertisement to the Fourth Edition', but ordinarily, as with the Fourth, refuses any admittance to numerous adjustments (as well as many misprints) now again representing, apparently, only the work of the printer. It is certainly illogical to follow this text, as does Cannan, simply because it is 'the last published in Smith's Lifetime'.[13]

6] 8° 6th edition. Published 1791, possibly also, as for *4*, at 18*s*. in boards. Description as for *5*, except that final advt. is now for TMS 6th edn.[14]
Strahan ledger: (Dec. 1791) 98 sheets, 2000 copies, @ £2 = £196. Extra for Tables and Index £4.6.0.
Like the two preceding, this the first posthumous edition has been collated, and its variants also recorded below the text, as a matter of historical record. The account extends thus far to meet, and in this case to dismiss, any possibility that the author left some final revisions incorporated in the work only after his death.[15]

[11] Cannan, xvii. It may also be noted that, beginning with this edition, Strahan does not charge for any author's corrections.
[12] In a few copies, volume iii, no figure appears at pp. 137, 260 and, in all, p. 408 is figured 7 or 10.
[13] Cannan, xvii.
[14] Again in a few copies of volume iii, no figure appears at p. 32 and, in all, p. 287 is figured 7 or 9, p. 315 figured 6 or 7. Additionally in volume ii, gathering 2D, there are three figures, a circumstance which (when two is the maximum) is most extraordinary.
[15] The fourth, revised edition of Samuel Richardson's *Sir Charles Grandison* (1762), it will be recalled, began to appear seven months after his death, and yet another edition, differently revised, was issued as late as 1810. See R. C. Pierson's commentary in *Studies in Bibliography*, xxi (1968), 163–89.

Once the order and validity of readings was assessed, according to the rationale set out above, the preparation of this text then followed a set procedure. First at Texas the two available specimens of *1* (the copy-text) were read against all the later editions, including a photocopy of British Library *2A*, and every variant entered in a photocopy of Texas *3* (printer's copy), the substantive readings in one column, the accidentals in a second, and end-line hyphenations in a third. This record was then verified against the copies at Glasgow and printer's copy marked for the press. Thereafter the proofs were read independently by all three editors against *3*, any discrepancies again resolved at Glasgow, and revised proofs thereafter checked against the final record. As now prepared this edition contains a number of features all described below.

For the text proper the paragraphs within each section or part have been numbered both to facilitate cross reference in the annotations and to simplify later citation from this edition.[16] Within the text stars and daggers are the author's own devices for pointing a note, superscript figures the numbers entered by the present editors to signal their further commentary. Superscript letters, denoting substantive textual variants, are of two orders, e.g.:

shall [a] only   single indicator centered between two words, signifying, as noted below text, an additional reading once inserted at this point

[b]his capital[b]   double indicators abutting the word or words in question, both delimiting, as noted below text, a passage elsewhere in variant form or omitted.

Differences in spelling (ancient/antient, public/publick, &c) remain unaltered as representative of the variable orthography Smith himself continually allowed on the several occasions he revised his work. In general all accidentals, if necessarily introduced from some edition other than *3*, or in a few instances by the present editors, are listed in Schedule A; accidentals not admitted, along with misprinted substantives, are recorded in B; line-end hyphenation is registered in C. At the beginning of each original page in *3* the number of that page is entered in brackets.

Below the text page, as now printed, three kinds of data may appear. First are Smith's own references (together with appropriate indicators if these originally occur in some edition after the first or if they are later amended) followed immediately, within square brackets, by any extension of the reference the present editors consider necessary. Second are the

---

[16] To accomplish this numbering in an orderly manner some few adjustments have been made (all with due notice) in Smith's own keys to the arrangement of his sections and subsections.

substantive textual variants, all entered in a manner indicating the kind or extent of variation:

[a]not *2A*　　'not' inserted in *2A* 'Additions and Corrections' but not present in *1-2*, deleted in *3-6*, and therefore excluded from this text.

[b-b]*om. 4* ⟨corrected *4e-6*⟩　　passage first omitted in *4* but immediately corrected in *4* errata list and retained thereafter

[c-c]*om. 1*　　passage entered in all editions except *1*

[d-d]in this *1-2*　　words in *1-2* differing from phrase adopted in *3-6*

[e-e]*2-6* [includes the whole of this paragraph]
　　　　cautionary note for an extensive addition, where insertions [f] and [g] or other amendments [h-h] and [i-i] may intrude

Thirdly, below text page, as signalled by superscript numerals in the text, come the editors' own commentary. These number references are sequential only through each part.

Following the work, and the several editorial schedules, there are three indexes, each of which bears its own heading as to purpose and utility.

As an essential part of their own editorial work, the text and its variants have also been checked and scrutinized by the General Editors.

　　　　　　　　　　　　　　　　　　　　　　　　　　　　W.B.T.

A N

I N Q U I R Y

INTO THE

Nature and Caufes

OF THE

WEALTH OF NATIONS.

By ADAM SMITH, LL. D. and F. R. S.
Formerly Profeffor of Moral Philofophy in the Univerfity of GLASGOW.

IN TWO VOLUMES.
VOL. I.

LONDON:

PRINTED FOR W. STRAHAN; AND T. CADELL, IN THE STRAND.
MDCCLXXVI.

CONTENTS

BOOK II

6 Contents

ADVERTISEMENT*a*

THE first Edition of the following Work was printed in the end of the year 1775, and in the beginning of the year 1776. Through the greater part of the Book, therefore, whenever the present state of things is mentioned, it is to be understood of the state they were in, either about that time, or at some earlier period, during the time I was employed in writing the Book. To *b*this*b* third Edition, however, I have made several additions, particularly to the chapter upon Drawbacks, and to that upon Bounties; likewise a new chapter entitled, *The Conclusion of the Mercantile System*; and a new article to the chapter upon the expences of the sovereign. In all these additions, *the present state of things* means always the state in which they were during the year 1783 and the beginning of the *c*present*c* year 1784.[1]

a TO THE THIRD EDITION.· *4–6*   *b–b* the *4–6*   *c–c om. 4–6*

[1] The new material to be included in edition *3* is described by Smith in Letter 227 addressed to William Strahan, dated 22 May 1783 and in Letter 222, addressed to Thomas Cadell, dated 7 December 1782.

ADVERTISEMENT

TO THE

FOURTH EDITION

In this fourth Edition I have made no alterations of any kind. I now, however, find myself at liberty to acknowledge my very great obligations to Mr. Henry *a*Hope*a* of Amsterdam. To that Gentleman I owe the most distinct, as well as liberal information, concerning a very interesting and important subject, the Bank of Amsterdam; of which no printed account had ever appeared to me satisfactory, or even intelligible.[1] The name of that Gentleman is so well known in Europe, the information which comes from him must do so much honour to whoever has been favoured with it, and my vanity is so much interested in making this acknowledgement, that I can no longer refuse myself the pleasure of prefixing this Advertisement to this new Edition of my Book.

a-a Hop *4*

---

[1] Steuart's account of the Bank of Amsterdam can hardly be described as *unintelligible* (*Principles of Political Oeconomy* (London, 1767) IV.2, xxxvii–xxxix).

1   THE annual labour of every nation is the fund which originally supplies it with all the necessaries and conveniences of life which it annually consumes, and which consist always, either in the immediate produce of that labour, or in what is purchased with that produce from other nations.

2   According therefore, as this produce, or what is purchased with it, bears a greater or smaller proportion to the number of those who are to consume it, the nation will be better or worse supplied with all the necessaries and conveniences for which it has occasion.

3   But this proportion must in every nation be regulated by two different circumstances; first, by the skill, dexterity, and judgment with which [2] *its*ᵃ labour is generally applied ᵇ; and, secondly, by the proportion between the number of those who are employed in useful labour, and that of those who are not so employed. Whatever be the soil, climate, or extent of territory of any particular nation, the abundance or scantiness of its annual supply must, in that particular situation, depend upon those two circumstances.

4   The abundance or scantiness of this supply too seems to depend more upon the former of those two circumstances than upon the latter. Among the savage nations of hunters and fishers, every individual who is able to work, is more or less employed in useful labour, and endeavours to provide, as well as he can, the necessaries and conveniencies of life, for himself, ᶜorᶜ such of his family or tribe as are either too old, or too young, or too infirm to go a hunting and fishing. Such nations, however, are so miserably poor, that, from mere want, they are frequently reduced, or, at least, think themselves reduced, to the necessity sometimes of directly destroying, and sometimes of abandoning their infants, their old people, and those afflicted with lingering diseases, to perish with hunger, or to be devoured by wild beasts. Among civilized and thriving nations, on the contrary, though a great number of people do not labour at all, many of whom consume the produce of ten times, frequently of a hundred times more labour than the greater part of those who work; yet the produce of the whole labour of the society is so great, that all are often abundantly supplied, and a workman, even of the [3] lowest and poorest order, if he is frugal and industrious, may enjoy a greater share of the necessaries and conveniences of life than it is possible for any savage to acquire.

5   The causes of this improvement, in the productive powers of labour,

ᵃ⁻ᵃ 2–6   ᵇ in it *1*   ᶜ⁻ᶜ and *1*

and the order, according to which its produce is naturally distributed among the different ranks and conditions of men in the society, make the subject of the First Book of this Inquiry.

6   Whatever be the actual state of the skill, dexterity, and judgment with which labour is applied in any nation, the abundance or scantiness of its annual supply must depend, during the continuance of that state, upon the proportion between the number of those who are annually employed in useful labour, and that of those who are not so employed. The number of useful and productive labourers, it will hereafter appear, is every where in proportion to the quantity of capital stock which is employed in setting them to work, and to the particular way in which it is so employed. The Second Book, therefore, treats of the nature of capital stock, of the manner in which it is gradually accumulated, and of the different quantities of labour which it puts into motion, according to the different ways in which it is employed.

7   Nations tolerably well advanced as to skill, dexterity, and judgment, in the application of labour, have followed very different plans in the general conduct or direction of it; and those plans have not all been equally favourable to the [4] greatness of its produce. The policy of some nations has given extraordinary encouragement to the industry of the country; that of others to the industry of towns. Scarce any nation has dealt equally and impartially with every sort of industry. Since the downfal of the Roman empire, the policy of Europe has been more favourable to arts, manufactures, and commerce, the industry of towns; than to agriculture, the industry of the country. The circumstances which seem to have introduced and established this policy are explained in the Third Book.

8   Though those different plans were, perhaps, first introduced by the private interests and prejudices of particular orders of men, without any regard to, or foresight of, their consequences upon the general welfare of the society; yet they have given occasion to very different theories of political œconomy; of which some magnify the importance of that industry which is carried on in towns, others of that which is carried on in the country. Those theories have had a considerable influence, not only upon the opinions of men of learning, but upon the public conduct of princes and sovereign states. I have endeavoured, in the Fourth Book, to explain, as fully and distinctly as I can, those different theories, and the principal effects which they have produced in different ages and nations.

9   *d*To explain*d* in what has consisted the revenue of the great body of the people, or what *e*has been*e* the nature of those funds which, in different ages and nations, have supplied their annual consump-[5]tion, is *f*the object of*f* these Four first Books. The Fifth and last Book treats of

d-d 2–6   *e-e* is *1*   *f-f* treated of in *1* the revenue of the sovereign, or commonwealth. In this Book I have endeavoured to show; first, what are the necessary expences of the sovereign, or commonwealth; which of those expences ought to be defrayed by the general contribution of the whole society; and which of them, by that of some particular part only, or of some particular members of ^{g}it^g; secondly, what are the different methods in which the whole society may be made to contribute towards defraying the expences incumbent on the whole society, and what are the principal advantages and inconveniencies of each of those methods: and, thirdly and lastly, what are the reasons and causes which have induced almost all modern governments to mortgage some part of this revenue, or to contract debts, and what have been the effects of those debts upon the real wealth, the annual produce of the land and labour of the society.

$^{g-g}$ the society r

BOOK I

Of the Causes of Improvement in the productive Powers of Labour, and of the Order according to which its Produce is naturally distributed among the different Ranks of the People

CHAPTER I

Of the Division of Labour

1 THE greatest *improvement* in the productive powers of labour, and the greater part of the skill, dexterity, and judgment with which it is any where directed, or applied, seem to have been the effects of the division of labour.[1]

a-a improvements *1*

---

[1] The first considered exposition of the term division of labour by a modern writer was probably by Sir William Petty: 'Those who have the command of the Sea Trade, may Work at easier Freight with more profit, than others at greater: for as Cloth must be cheaper made, when one Cards, another Spins, another Weaves, another Draws, another Dresses, another Presses and Packs; than when all the Operations above-mentioned, were clumsily performed by the same hand; so those who command the Trade of Shipping, can build long slight Ships for carrying Masts, Fir-Timber, Boards, Balks, etc.' (*Political Arithmetick* (London, 1690), 19, in C. H. Hull, *The Economic Writings of Sir William Petty* (Cambridge, 1899), i. 260). 'For in so vast a City *Manufactures* will beget one another, and each *Manufacture* will be divided into as many parts as possible, whereby the work of each *Artisan* will be simple and easie: As for Example. In the making of a *Watch*, If one Man shall make the *Wheels*, another the *Spring*, another shall Engrave the *Dial-plate*, and another shall make the *Cases*, then the *Watch* will be better and cheaper, than if the whole Work be put upon any one Man.' (*Another Essay in Political Arithmetick, concerning the Growth of the City of London* (London, 1683), 36–7, in C. H. Hull, ii.473.)

Later use was by Mandeville and Harris: 'There are many Sets of Hands in the Nation, that, not wanting proper Materials, would be able in less than half a Year to produce, fit out, and navigate a First-Rate [Man of War]: yet it is certain, that this Task would be impracticable, if it was not divided and subdivided into a great Variety of different Labours; and it is as certain, that none of these Labours require any other, than working Men of ordinary Capacities.' (B. Mandeville, *The Fable of the Bees*, pt. ii.149, ed. F. B. Kaye (Oxford, 1924), ii.142.) 'No number of Men, when once they enjoy Quiet, and no Man needs to fear his Neighbour, will be long without learning to divide and subdivide their Labour.' (Ibid., pt. ii.335, ed. Kaye ii.284.) 'The advantages accruing to mankind from their betaking themselves severally to different occupations, are very great and

2   The effects of the division of labour, in the general business of society, will be more easily understood, by considering in what manner it operates in some particular manufactures. It is commonly supposed to be carried furthest in some very trifling ones; not perhaps that it really is carried further in them than in others of more importance: but in those trifling manufactures which are destined to supply the small wants of but a small number of people, the whole number of workmen must necessarily be small; and those employed in every different branch of the work can often be collected into the same [7] workhouse, and placed at once under the view of the spectator. In those great manufactures, on the contrary, which are destined to supply the great wants of the great body of the people, every different branch of the work employs so great a number of workmen, that it is impossible to collect them all into the same workhouse. We can seldom see more, at one time, than those employed in one single branch. Though *b*in such manufactures,*b* therefore, the work may really be divided into a much greater number of parts, than in those of a more trifling nature, the division is not near so obvious, and has accordingly been much less observed.

3   To take an example, therefore, from a very trifling manufacture; but one in which the division of labour has been very often taken notice of, the trade of the pin-maker; a workman not educated to this business (which the division of labour has rendered a distinct trade), nor acquainted with the use of the machinery employed in it (to the invention of which the same division of labour has probably given occasion), could scarce, perhaps, with his utmost industry, make one pin in a day, and certainly could not make twenty.[2] But in the way in which this business is now carried on, not only the whole work is a peculiar trade, but it is divided into a number of branches, of which the greater part are likewise peculiar

---

b–b in them *1*

obvious: For thereby, each becoming expert and skilful in his own particular art; they are enabled to furnish one another with the products of their respective labours, performed in a much better manner, and with much less toil, than any one of them could do of himself.' (J. Harris, *An Essay upon Money and Coins* (London, 1757), i. 16.)

    The advantages of the division of labour are also emphasized by Turgot in sections III and IV of his *Reflections on the Formation and Distribution of Riches* (1766). The translation used is by R. L. Meek and included in his *Turgot on Progress, Sociology and Economics* (Cambridge, 1973).

    [2] Cf. ED 2.4: 'to give a very frivolous instance, if all the parts of a pin were to be made by one man, if the same person was to dig the metall out of the mine, seperate it from the ore, forge it, split it into small rods, then spin these rods into wire, and last of all make that wire into pins, a man perhaps could with his utmost industry scarce make a pin in a year.' Smith added that even where the wire alone was furnished an unskilled man could probably make only about 20 pins a day. Similar examples occur in LJ (A) vi.29–30 and LJ (B) 213–14, ed. Cannan 163. It is remarked in LJ (A) vi.50 that the wire used in pin manufacture generally came from Sweden.

trades. One man draws out the wire, another straights it, a third cuts it, a fourth points it, a fifth grinds it at the top for receiving the head; to make the head requires [8] two or three distinct operations; to put it on, is a peculiar business, to whiten the pins is another; it is even a trade by itself to put them into the paper; and the important business of making a pin is, in this manner, divided into about eighteen distinct operations,[3] which, in some manufactories, are all performed by distinct hands, though in others the same man will sometimes perform two or three of them. I have seen a small manufactory of this kind where ten men only were employed, and where some of them consequently performed two or three distinct operations. But though they were very poor, and therefore but indifferently accommodated with the necessary machinery, they could, when they exerted themselves, make among them about twelve pounds of pins in a day.[4] There are in a pound upwards of four thousand pins of a middling size. Those ten persons, therefore, could make among them upwards of forty-eight thousand pins in a day. Each person, therefore, making a tenth part of forty-eight thousand pins, might be considered as making four thousand eight hundred pins in a day. But if they had all wrought separately and independently, and without any of them having been educated to this peculiar business, they certainly could not each of them have made twenty, perhaps not one pin in a day; that is, certainly, not the two hundred and fortieth, perhaps not the four thousand eight hundredth part of what they are at present capable of performing, in consequence of [9] a proper division and combination of their different operations.

4   In every other art and manufacture, the effects of the division of labour are similar to what they are in this very trifling one; though, in many of them, the labour can neither be so much subdivided, nor reduced to so great a simplicity of operation. The division of labour, however, so far as it can be introduced, occasions, in every art, a proportionable increase of the productive powers of labour. The separation of different trades and employments from one another, seems to have taken place, in consequence of this advantage. This separation too is generally carried furthest in those countries which enjoy the highest degree of industry and improvement; what is the work of one man, in a rude state of society, being generally that of several in an improved one. In every improved society, the

---

[3] Eighteen operations are described in the *Encyclopédie* (1755), v.804–7. See also *Chambers' Cyclopaedia* (4th ed. 1741), s.v. Pin.

[4] A very similar passage occurs in ED 2.4 which also concludes that where the processes of manufacture are divided among 18 persons, each should in effect be capable of producing 2,000 pins in a day. These figures are also cited in LJ (A) vi.30 and 51 and LJ (B) 214, ed. Cannan 163. In referring to the disadvantages of the division of labour in LJ (B) 329, ed. Cannan 255, the lecturer mentions the example of a person engaged on the 17th part of a pin or the 80th part of a button. See below, V.i.f.50.

farmer is generally nothing but a farmer; the manufacturer, nothing but a manufacturer.[5] The labour too which is necessary to produce any one complete manufacture, is almost always divided among a great number of hands. How many different trades are employed in each branch of the linen and woollen manufactures, from the growers of the flax and the wool, to the bleachers and smoothers of the linen, or to the dyers and dressers of the cloth! The nature of agriculture, indeed, does not admit of so many subdivisions of labour, nor of so complete a separation of one business from another, as manufactures.[6] It is impossible to separate so entirely, the business of [10] the grazier from that of the corn-farmer, as the trade of the carpenter is commonly separated from that of the smith. The spinner is almost always a distinct person from the weaver; but the ploughman, the harrower, the sower of the seed, and the reaper of the corn, are often the same.[7] The occasions for those different sorts of labour returning with the different seasons of the year, it is impossible that one man should be constantly employed in any one of them. This impossibility of making so complete and entire a separation of all the different branches of labour employed in agriculture, is perhaps the reason why the improvement of the productive powers of labour in this art, does not always keep pace with their improvement in manufactures. The most opulent nations, indeed, generally excel all their neighbours in agriculture as well as in manufactures; but they are commonly more distinguished by their superiority in the latter than in the former.[8] Their lands are in general better cultivated, and having more labour and expence bestowed upon them, produce more, in proportion to the extent and natural fertility of the ground. But ᶜthisᶜ superiority of produce is seldom much more than in proportion to the superiority of labour and expence. In agriculture, the labour of the rich country is not always much more productive than that of the poor; or, at least, it is never so much more productive, as it commonly is in manufactures. The corn of the rich country, therefore, will not always, in the same degree of goodness, come cheaper to [11] market than that of the poor. The corn of Poland, in the same degree of goodness, is as cheap as that of France, notwithstanding

ᶜ⁻ᶜ the *1*

---

[5] See below, I.x.b.52.

[6] The same point is made at IV.ix.35. The limitation imposed on the division of labour in agriculture is stated to require greater knowledge on the part of the workman at I.x.c.24. At the same time, agriculture was regarded by Smith as the most productive form of investment, II.v.12.

[7] LJ (A) vi.30–1 comments that: 'Agriculture however does not admit of this separation of employment in the same degree as the manufactures of wool or lint or iron work. The same man must often be the plougher of the land, sower, harrower, reaper and thresher of the corn (tho' here there may be some distinctions.)' Similar points are made in LJ (B) 214, ed. Cannan 164.

[8] The two preceding sentences follow the text of ED 2.5 very closely.

the superior opulence and improvement of the latter country. The corn
of France is, in the corn provinces, fully as good, and in most years nearly
about the same price with the corn of England, though, in opulence and
improvement, France is perhaps inferior to England. The ^{d}corn-lands^d
of England, however, are better cultivated than those of France, and the
^{e}corn-lands^e of France are said to be much better cultivated than those
of Poland. But though the poor country, notwithstanding the inferiority
of its cultivation, can, in some measure, rival the rich in the cheapness
and goodness of its corn, it can pretend to no such competition in its
manufactures; at least if those manufactures suit the soil, climate, and
situation of the rich country. The silks of France are better and cheaper
than those of England, because the silk manufacture, ^{f}at least under the
present high duties upon the importation of raw silk,^{f} does not ^{g}so well^g
suit the climate of England ^{h}as that of France.^{h} But the hard-ware and
the coarse woollens of England are beyond all comparison superior to
those of France, and much cheaper too in the same degree of goodness.[9]
In Poland there are said to be scarce any manufactures of any kind, a few
of those coarser household manufactures excepted, without which no
country can well subsist.

5   This great increase ^{i}of^i the quantity of work, which, ^{j}in consequence
of the division of labour,^{j} [12] the same number of people are capable
of performing, ^{k} is owing to three different circumstances; first, to the
increase of dexterity in every particular workman; secondly, to the saving
of the time which is commonly lost in passing from one species of work
to another; and lastly, to the invention of a great number of machines
which facilitate and abridge labour, and enable one man to do the work
of many.[10]

6   First, the improvement of the dexterity of the workman necessarily

---

$^{d-d}$ lands $_I$ $^{e-e}$ lands $_I$ $^{f-f}$ $_{2-6}$ $^{g-g}$ $_{2-6}$ $^{h-h}$ $_{2-6}$ $^{i-i}$ in 6
$^{j-j}$ $_{2-6}$ ^{k} in consequence of the division of labour, $_I$

[9] ED 2.5 ends with the statement that: 'The corn of France is fully as good and in the
provinces where it grows rather cheaper than that of England, at least during ordinary
seasons. But the toys of England, their watches, their cutlery ware, their locks & hinges
of doors, their buckles and buttons are in accuracy, solidity, and perfection of work out
of all comparison superior to those of France, and cheaper too in the same degree of
goodness.' A précis of this argument appears in LJ (A) vi.31–2, and LJ (B) 214, ed.
Cannan 164; and see below, I.xi.o.4, where Smith states that manufactures which use the
coarser metals have probably the greatest scope for the division of labour.

ED 2.6 and 7 are omitted from the WN. In these passages Smith elaborated on the
advantages of the division of labour in pin making and added that these advantages were
such as to suggest that any rich country which faced a loss of markets in international
trade to a poor one 'must have been guilty of some great error in its police.' There is
no corresponding passage in LJ (B), but a similar argument occurs in LJ (A) vi.34.

[10] This paragraph is evidently based on ED 2.8. Similar points appear in LJ (A)
vi.38; LJ (B) 215–16, ed. Cannan 166. The advantages are also cited in the *Encyclopédie*
(1755), i.713–17.

increases the quantity of the work he can perform, and the division of
labour, by reducing every man's business to some one simple operation,
and by making this operation the sole employment of his life, necessarily
increases very much the dexterity of the workman. A common smith,
who, though accustomed to handle the hammer, has never been used to
make nails, if upon some particular occasion he is obliged to attempt it,
will scarce, I am assured, be able to make above two or three hundred
nails in a day, and those too very bad ones. A smith who has been accustomed to make nails, but whose sole or principal business has not been
that of a nailer, can seldom with his utmost diligence make more than
eight hundred or a thousand nails in a day. I have seen several boys under
twenty years of age who had never exercised any other trade but that of
making nails, and who, when they exerted themselves, could make, each
of them, upwards of two thousand three hundred nails in a day. The
making of a nail, however, is by no means one [13] of the simplest operations. The same person blows the bellows, stirs or mends the fire as there
is occasion, heats the iron, and forges every part of the nail: In forging
the head too he is obliged to change his tools. The different operations
into which the making of a pin, or of a metal button, is subdivided, are
all of them much more simple, and the dexterity of the person, of whose
life it has been the sole business to perform them, is usually much greater.
The rapidity with which some of the operations of those manufactures
are performed, exceeds what the human hand could, by those who had
never seen them, be supposed capable of acquiring.[11]

7   Secondly, the advantage which is gained by saving the time commonly
lost in passing from one sort of work to another, is much greater than we
should at first view be apt to imagine it. It is impossible to pass very
quickly from one kind of work to another, that is carried on in a different
place, and with quite different tools. A country weaver, who cultivates
a small farm, must lose a good deal of time in passing from his loom
to the field, and from the field to his loom. When the two trades can

[11] This whole paragraph follows ED 2.9, save that the boy is there said to have been
19 years old. A similar argument occurs in LJ (A) vi.38, where a nailsmith of 15 is said
to be capable of producing 3,000–4,000 nails in a day. See also LJ (B) 216, ed. Cannan
166:

A country smith not accustomed to make nails will work very hard for 3 or 400 a day,
and these too very bad. But a boy used to it will easily make 2000 and these incomparably better; yet the improvement of dexterity in this very complex manufacture can
never be equal to that in others. A nail-maker changes postures, blows the bellows,
changes tools etca. and therefore the quantity produced cannot be so great as in manufactures of pins and buttons, where the work is reduced to simple operations.

(The manufacture of nails was common in central and east Scotland. In the village of
Pathhead and Gallatown near Kirkcaldy a number of nailers worked domestically, using
iron supplied by merchants from Dysart. The growth of the iron industry in central
Scotland provided local supplies later.)

be carried on in the same workhouse, the loss of time is no doubt much less. It is even in this case, however, very considerable. A man commonly saunters a little in turning his hand from one sort of employment to another. When he first begins the new work he is seldom very keen and hearty; his mind, as they say, does not go to it, and for some time he rather trifles than applies to good purpose.[12] The [14] habit of saunter- |
ing and of indolent careless application, which is naturally, or rather |
necessarily[13] acquired by every country workman who is obliged to change his work and his tools every half hour, and to apply his hand in twenty different ways almost every day of his life; renders him almost always slothful and lazy, and incapable of any vigorous application even on the most pressing occasions. Independent, therefore, of his deficiency in point of dexterity, this cause alone must always reduce considerably the quantity of work which he is capable of performing.[14]

8   Thirdly, and lastly, every body must be sensible how much labour is facilitated and abridged by the application of proper machinery. It is unnecessary to give any example.[15] I shall [1] only observe, [m]therefore,[m]

---

[1] therefore, *1*   [m-m] *2-6*

---

[12] Cf. ED 2.10: 'A man of great spirit and activity, when he is hard pushed upon some particular occasion, will pass with the greatest rapidity from one sort of work to another through a great variety of businesses. Even a man of spirit and activity, however, must be hard pushed before he can do this.'

[13] Smith often juxtaposes the terms 'naturally' and 'necessarily'. See, for example, I.viii.57, III.i.3, IV.i.30, IV.ii.4, 6, IV.vii.c.80, V.i.b.12, V.i.f.24, V.i.g.23.

[14] The preceding two sentences follow the concluding passages of ED 2.10 very closely. Similar arguments appear in LJ (A) vi.39–40 and LJ (B) 216–17, ed. Cannan 166–7.

[15] Smith cites three major improvements apart from the fire engines mentioned below, in I.xi.o.12, and see also II.ii.7. The 'condensing engine' and 'what is founded upon it, the wind gun' are cited as 'ingenious and expensive machines' in External Senses, 16. Cf. ED 2.11: 'By means of the *plough* two men, with the assistance of three horses, will cultivate more ground than twenty could do with the spade. A miller and his servant, with a wind *or* water mill, will at their ease, grind more corn than eight men could do, with the severest labour, by hand mills.' A similar example occurs in LJ (B) 217, ed. Cannan 167, save that it is said that the miller and his servant 'will do more with the water miln than a dozen men with the hand miln, tho' it too be a machine'. LJ (B) does not mention the windmill and it is also interesting to note that the example provided at LJ (A) vi.40 is exactly the same as that provided in ED. It is stated at I.xi.o.12 that neither wind nor water mills were known in England at the beginning of the sixteenth century.

Cf. Montesquieu, *Esprit des Lois*, trans. Thomas Nugent, ed. F. Neumann (New York, 1959), XXIII.xv.3, where it is stated that machines are not always useful, for example, in cases where their effect is to reduce employment. He added that 'if water-mills were not everywhere established, I should not have believed them so useful as is pretended'. In commenting on this remark Sir James Steuart confirmed that the advantages of using machines were 'so palpable that I need not insist upon them', especially in the current situation of Europe. He did, however, agree that the introduction of machines could cause problems of employment in the very short run, and that they might have adverse consequences in an economy incapable of further growth. See especially the *Principles of Political Oeconomy* (London, 1767), I.xix.

that the invention of all those machines by which labour is so much facilitated and abridged, seems to have been originally owing to the division
of labour. Men are much more likely to discover easier and readier methods
of attaining any object, when the whole attention of their minds is directed
towards that single object, than when it is dissipated among a great variety
of things. But in consequence of the division of labour, the whole of every
man's attention comes naturally to be directed towards some one very
simple object. It is naturally to be expected, therefore, that some one or
other of those who are employed in each particular branch of labour should
soon find out easier and readier methods of performing their own particular work, wherever the nature of it admits of such [15] improvement.[16]
A great part of the machines ⁿmade use ofⁿ in those manufactures in which
labour is most subdivided, were originally the inventions of common
workmen, who, being each of them employed in some very simple operation, naturally turned their thoughts towards finding out easier and
readier methods of performing it.[17] Whoever has been much accustomed
to visit such manufactures, must frequently have been shewn very pretty
machines, which were the inventions of ᵒsuchᵒ workmen, in order to
facilitate and quicken their own particular part of the work.[18] In the
first fire-engines,[19] a boy was constantly employed to open and shut
alternately the communication between the boiler and the cylinder,
according as the piston either ascended or descended. One of those boys,
who loved to play with his companions, observed that, by tying a string
from the handle of the valve, which opened this communication, to
another part of the machine, the valve would open and shut without his
assistance, and leave him at liberty to divert himself with his play-fellows.
One of the greatest improvements that has been made upon this machine,

ⁿ⁻ⁿ employed *1*   ᵒ⁻ᵒ common *1*

[16] Exactly these views are expressed in ED 2.11 and LJ (B) 217, ed. Cannan 167.
The brief statement in LJ (A) vi.41 reads that 'When one is employed constantly on one
thing his mind will naturally be employed in devising the most proper means of improving it.'
[17] It is stated at IV.ix.47 that invention of this kind is generally the work of freemen.
On the other hand Smith argues at V.i.f.50 that the mental faculties of the workers are
likely to be damaged by the division of labour, thus affecting the flow of invention from
this source.
[18] Cf. LJ (A) vi.54: 'if we go into the workhouse of any manufacturer in the new
works at Sheffield, Manchester, or Birmingham, or even some towns in Scotland, and
enquire concerning the machines, they will tell you that such or such an one was invented
by some common workman.' See also Astronomy, II.11: 'When we enter the work-houses
of the most common artizans; such as dyers, brewers, distillers; we observe a number
of appearances, which present themselves in an order that seems to us very strange and
wonderful.'
[19] In the Fourth Dialogue, Cleo refers to 'those Engines that raise Water by the Help
of Fire; the Steam you know, is that which forces it up.' Mandeville, *The Fable of the
Bees*, pt. ii.181–2, ed. Kaye ii.167. Fire engine was the name for the earliest steam
engines. The story that follows seems untrue. See T. K. Derry and T. I. Williams, *A
Short History of Technology* (Oxford, 1960), 316–19.

since it was first invented, was in this manner the discovery of a boy who wanted to save his own labour.[20]

9   All the improvements in machinery, however, have by no means been the inventions of those who had occasion to use the machines. Many improvements have been made by the ingenuity of the makers of the machines, when [16] to make them became the business of a peculiar trade;[21] and some by that of those who are called philosophers or men of speculation, whose trade it is, not to do any thing, but to observe every thing; and who, upon that account, are often capable of combining together the powers of the most distant and dissimilar objects.[22] In the progress of society, philosophy or speculation becomes, like every other employment, the principal or sole trade and occupation of a particular class of citizens. Like every other employment too, it is subdivided into a great number of different branches, each of which affords occupation

[20] In general, Smith concluded that machines would tend to become simpler as the result of improvement; a point made in Astronomy, IV.19 and First Formation of Languages, 41. He also commented in LRBL i.v.34, ed. Lothian 11, that 'machines are at first vastly complex but gradually the different parts are more connected and supplied by one another.' In ED 2.11 Smith ascribes the invention of the Drill Plow to the farmer while claiming that some 'miserable slave' probably produced the original hand-mill (cf. below, IV.ix.47). On the other hand, some improvements were ascribed to those who made the instruments involved, as distinct from using them, and to the 'successive discoveries of time and experience, and of the ingenuity of different artists'. This subject is briefly mentioned in LJ (B) 217–18, ed. Cannan 167. LJ (A) vi.42–3 provides a more elaborate illustration of the kind found in ED, while stating that the inventions of the mill and plough are so old that history gives no account of them (54).

[21] The 'fabrication of the instruments of trade' is described as a specialized function at IV.viii.1.

[22] Cf. ED. 2.11. Smith here suggests that it was probably a philosopher who first thought of harnessing both wind and water, especially the former, for the purposes of milling. Smith added that while the application of powers already known was not beyond the ability of the ingenious artist, innovation amounting to 'the application of new powers, which are altogether unknown' is the contribution of the philosopher (i.e. scientist):

> When an artist makes any such discovery he showes himself to be not a meer artist but a real philosopher, whatever may be his nominal profession. It was a real philosopher only who could invent the fire-engine, and first form the idea of producing so great an effect by a power in nature which had never before been thought of. Many inferior artists, employed in the fabric of this wonderful machine, may afterwards discover more happy methods of applying that power than those first made use of by its illustrious inventer.

In a note to the passage just cited W. R. Scott suggested that Smith was probably referring to James Watt. Similar points regarding the role of the philosopher are made in LJ (A) vi.42–3, and more briefly in LJ (B) 218, ed. Cannan 167–8.

Mandeville (*The Fable of the Bees*, pt. ii.152, ed. Kaye ii.144) was more sceptical with regard to the rôle of the philosopher: 'They are very seldom the same Sort of People, those that invent Arts, and Improvements in them, and those that enquire into the Reason of Things: this latter is most commonly practis'd by such, as are idle and indolent, that are fond of Retirement, hate Business, and take delight in Speculation: whereas none succeed oftener in the first, than active, stirring, and laborious Men, such as will put their Hand to the Plough, try Experiments, and give all their Attention to what they are about.'

to a peculiar tribe or class of philosophers; and this subdivision of employment in philosophy, as well as in every other business, improves dexterity,
and saves time. Each individual becomes more expert in his own peculiar
branch, more work is done upon the whole, and the quantity of science
is considerably increased by it.[23]

10   It is the great multiplication of the productions of all the different arts,
in consequence of the division of labour, which occasions, in a well-
governed society, that universal opulence which extends itself to the
lowest ranks of the people.[24] Every workman has a great quantity of his
own work to dispose of beyond what he himself has occasion for; and every
other workman being exactly in the same situation, he is enabled to exchange a great quantity of his own goods for a great quantity, or, what
comes to the same thing, for the price of a great quan-[17]tity of theirs.
He supplies them abundantly with what they have occasion for, and they
accommodate him as amply with what he has occasion for, and a general
plenty diffuses itself through all the different ranks of the society.

11   Observe the accommodation of the most common artificer or day-
labourer in a civilized and thriving country, and you will perceive that
the number of people of whose industry a part, though but a small part,
has been employed in procuring him this accommodation, exceeds all
computation. The woollen coat, for example, which covers the day-
labourer, as coarse and rough as it may appear, is the produce of the
joint labour of a great multitude of workmen.[25] The shepherd, the sorter
of the wool, the wool-comber or carder, the dyer, the scribbler, the
spinner, the weaver, the fuller, the dresser, with many others, must all
join their different arts in order to complete even this homely production.

[23] The last two paragraphs are considered in ED 2.11, but in a form which suggests
that this section of the WN was considerably redrafted, although the preceding three
sentences correspond very closely to the concluding sentences of ED 2.11. In the ED
Smith provides examples drawn from the separate trades of 'mechanical, chemical,
astronomical, physical, metaphysical, moral, political, commercial, and critical philosophers'. LJ (A) vi.43 includes a shorter list, but mentions 'ethical' and 'theological'
philosophers.

[24] This sentence corresponds to the opening sentence of ED 2.6 save that Smith there
refers to an 'immense multiplication' and 'all civilised societies'. He also alluded to 'the
great inequalities of property' in the modern state. See below, p. 24 n. 29.

[25] Related arguments occur in LJ (A) vi.16–17; LJ (B) 211–12, ed. Cannan 161–3.
The example of the 'coarse blue woolen coat' is cited in ED 2.1, LJ (A) vi.21 and LJ (B)
211, ed. Cannan 161. Cf. Mandeville (*The Fable of the Bees*, pt. i.182–3, ed. Kaye
i.169–70): 'A Man would be laugh'd at, that should discover Luxury in the plain Dress
of a poor Creature that walks along in a thick Parish Gown and a coarse Shirt under-
neath it; and yet what a number of People, how many different Trades, and what a variety
of Skill and Tools must be employed to have the most ordinary *Yorkshire* Cloth? What
depth of Thought and Ingenuity, what Toil and Labour, and what length of Time
must it have cost, before Man could learn from a Seed to raise and prepare so useful a
Product as Linen.' Cf. ibid., part i.411, ed. Kaye i.356: 'What a Bustle is there to be made
in several Parts of the World, before a fine Scarlet or crimson Cloth can be produced,
what Multiplicity of Trades and Artificers must be employ'd!'

How many merchants and carriers, besides, must have been employed in transporting the materials from some of those workmen to others who often live in a very distant part of the country! How much commerce and navigation in particular, how many ship-builders, sailors, sail-makers, rope-makers, must have been employed in order to bring together the different drugs made use of by the dyer, which often come from the remotest corners of the world! What a variety of labour too is necessary in order to produce the tools of the meanest of those workmen! To say nothing of such complicated ma-[18]chines as the ship of the sailor, the mill of the fuller, or even the loom of the weaver, let us consider only what a variety of labour is requisite in order to form that very simple machine, the shears with which the shepherd clips the wool.[26] The miner, the builder of the furnace for smelting the ore, the feller of the timber, the burner of the charcoal to be made use of in the smelting-house, the brick-maker, the brick-layer, the workmen who attend the furnace, the mill-wright, the forger, the smith, must all of them join their different arts in order to produce them. Were we to examine, in the same manner, all the different parts of his dress and household furniture, the coarse linen shirt which he wears next his skin, the shoes which cover his feet, the bed which he lies on, and all the different parts which compose it, the kitchen-grate at which he prepares his victuals, the coals which he makes use of for that purpose, dug from the bowels of the earth, and brought to him perhaps by a long sea and a long land carriage, all the other utensils of his kitchen, all the furniture of his table, the knives and forks, the earthen or pewter plates upon which he serves up and divides his victuals, the different hands employed in preparing his bread and his beer, the glass window which lets in the heat and the light, and keeps out the wind and the rain, with all the knowledge and art requisite for preparing that beautiful and happy invention, without which these northern parts of the world could scarce have afforded a very [19] comfortable habitation, together with the tools of all the different workmen employed in producing those different conveniencies; if we examine, I say, all these things, and consider what a variety of labour is employed about each of them, we shall be sensible that without the assistance and co-operation of many thousands, the very meanest person in a civilized country could not be provided, even according to, what we very falsely imagine, the easy and simple manner in which he is commonly accommodated.[27] Compared, indeed, with the more extravagant luxury of the

[26] ED 2.1 refers to the variety of labour needed to 'produce that very simple machine, the sheers of the clipper'.

[27] ' 'tis obvious that for the support of human life, to allay the painful cravings of the appetites, and to afford any of those agreeable external enjoyments which our nature is capable of, a great many external things are requisite; such as food, cloathing, habitations, many utensils, and various furniture, which cannot be obtained without a great

great, his accommodation must no doubt appear extremely simple and easy; and yet it may be true, perhaps, that the accommodation of an European prince does not always so much exceed that of an industrious and frugal peasant,²⁸ as the accommodation of the latter exceeds that of many an African king, the absolute master of the lives and liberties of ten thousand naked savages.²⁹

deal of art and labour, and the friendly aids of our fellows.' (Francis Hutcheson, *A System of Moral Philosophy* (London, 1755), i.287). John Locke (*Essay on Civil Government* (3rd ed. 1698), *Works* (London, 1823), v.363) also noted that:

> 'Twoud be a strange catalogue of things, that industry provided and made use of, about every loaf of bread, before it came to our use, if we could trace them; iron, wood, leather, bark timber, stone, bricks, coals, lime, cloth, dyeing, drugs, pitch, tar, masts, ropes, and all the materials made use of in the ship, that brought any of the commodities used by any of the workmen, to any part of the work: all which it would be almost impossible, at least too long, to reckon up. See also Thomas Mun, *England's Treasure by Forraigne Trade* (London, 1664), iii.12.

²⁸ Cf. Mandeville (*The Fable of the Bees*, pt. i.181, ed. Kaye i.169): 'If we trace the most flourishing Nations in their Origin, we shall find that in the remote Beginnings of every Society, the richest and most considerable Men among them were a great while destitute of a great many Comforts of Life that are now enjoy'd by the meanest and most humble Wretches.'

²⁹ The phrase 'absolute master' occurs in ED 2.1 in contrasting the luxury of the common day-labourer in England with that of 'many an Indian prince, the absolute master of the lives and liberties of a thousand naked savages'. The same paragraph also contains a contrast with the 'chief of a savage nation in North America'. LJ (A) vi.21, 23 repeats the former example. Cf. LJ (B) 212, ed. Cannan 162. It is also remarked at 287, ed. Cannan 223, that one explanation of the contrast is to be found in the fact that 'An Indian has not so much as a pick-ax, a spade, nor a shovel, or any thing else but his own labour.'

There is a considerable difference in the order in which the argument of ED and this part of the WN develops. For example, ED opens chapter 2 with an analysis which is very similar to that set out in the last two paragraphs of this chapter. It is then argued that while it cannot be difficult to explain the contrast between the poor savage and the modern rich (i.e. by reference to the division of labour), yet 'how it comes about that the labourer and the peasant should likewise be better provided is not perhaps so easily understood'. Smith further illustrates the difficulty by reference to the 'oppressive inequality' of the modern state; a theme which is developed at considerable length (mainly in 2.2,3) before the paradox is resolved by reference to arguments similar to those developed in the first nine paragraphs of this chapter. In LJ (A) and (B) the argument follows a similar order to that found in ED, save that the discussion opens in each case with an account of the 'natural wants of mankind', introducing by this means the general point that even the simplest wants require a multitude of hands before they can be satisfied. The 'natural wants' thesis would, presumably, have figured in the (missing) first chapter of ED. See LJ (A) vi.8–18; LJ (B) 206–13, ed. Cannan 157–63. The link between the development of productive forces and the natural wants of man also features in Hume's essays 'Of Commerce' and 'Of Refinement in the Arts'.

CHAPTER II

Of the Principle which gives occasion to the Division of Labour

1 THIS division of labour, from which so many advantages are derived, is not originally the effect of any human wisdom, which foresees and intends that general opulence to [20] which it gives occasion.[1] It is the necessary, though very slow and gradual consequence of a certain propensity in human nature which has in view no such extensive utility; the propensity to truck, barter, and exchange one thing for another.[2]

2 Whether this propensity be one of those original principles in human nature, of which no further account can be given; or whether, as seems more probable, it be the necessary consequence of the faculties of reason and speech, it belongs not to our present subject to enquire.[3] It is common to all men, and to be found in no other race of animals, which seem to know neither this nor any other species of contracts. Two greyhounds, in running down the same hare, have sometimes the appearance of acting in some sort of concert. Each turns her towards his companion, or endeavours to intercept her when his companion turns her towards himself. This, however, is not the effect of any contract, but of the accidental

---

[1] LJ (B) 218–19, ed. Cannan 168 reads: 'We cannot imagine this to have been an effect of human prudence. It was indeed made a law by Sesostratis that every man should follow the employment of his father. But this is by no means suitable to the dispositions of human nature and can never long take place. Everyone is fond of being a gentleman, be his father what he would.' The law is also mentioned in LJ (A) vi.54. See below, I.vii.31 and IV.ix.43.

[2] This paragraph closely follows the first three sentences in ED 2.12. The propensity to truck and barter is also mentioned in LJ (A) vi.44, 48 and LJ (B) 219 ff., ed. Cannan 169. Cf. LJ (B) 300–1, ed. Cannan 232: 'that principle in the mind which prompts to truck, barter and exchange, tho' it is the great foundation of arts, commerce and the division of labour, yet it is not marked with any thing amiable. To perform any thing, or to give any thing without a reward is always generous and noble, but to barter one thing for another is mean.' In a *Letter from Governor Pownall to Adam Smith, being an Examination of Several Points of Doctrine laid down in his Inquiry, into the Nature and Causes of the Wealth of Nations* (London, 1776), the author objected that the analysis of this chapter stopped short in ascribing the division of *labour directly* to a propensity to barter (4–5). Pownall, a former Governor of Massachusetts, also criticized Smith's views on labour as a measure of value, paper money, the employments of capital, colonies, etc. Smith acknowledged Pownall's work in Letter 182 addressed to Pownall, dated 19 January 1777. In Letter 208 addressed to Andreas Holt, dated 26 October 1780 Smith remarked that: 'In the second edition I flattered myself that I had obviated all the objections of Governor Pownal. I find however, he is by no means satisfied, and as Authors are not much disposed to alter the opinions they have once published, I am not much surprized at it.' There is very little evidence to suggest that Smith materially altered his views in response to Pownall, but see below, p. 50, n. 15.

[3] In LJ (B) 221, ed. Cannan 171, Smith argued in referring to the division of labour that 'The real foundation of it is that principle to persuade which so much prevails in human nature.' The same point is made in LJ (A) vi.56.

concurrence of their passions in the same object at that particular time.[4]
Nobody ever saw a dog make a fair and deliberate exchange of one bone
for another with another dog. Nobody ever saw one animal by its ges-
tures and natural cries signify to another, this is mine, that yours; I
am willing to give this for that. When an animal wants to obtain something either of a man or of another animal, it has no other means of
persuasion but to gain the favour of those whose service it requires. A
puppy fawns upon its dam, and a spaniel endea-[21]vours by a thousand
attractions to engage the attention of its master who is at dinner, when it
wants to be fed by him. Man sometimes uses the same arts with his brethren, and when he has no other means of engaging them to act according
to his inclinations, endeavours by every servile and fawning attention to
obtain their good will. He has not time, however, to do this upon every
occasion. In civilized society he stands at all times in need of the co-
operation and assistance of great multitudes, while his whole life is scarce
sufficient to gain the friendship of a few persons. In almost every other
race of animals each individual, when it is grown up to maturity, is intirely independent, and in its natural state has occasion for the assistance
of no other living creature.[5] But man has almost constant occasion for
the help of his brethren, and it is in vain for him to expect it from their
benevolence only.[6] He will be more likely to prevail if he can interest
their self-love in his favour, and shew them that it is for their own advantage to do for him what he requires of them. Whoever offers to another
a bargain of any kind, proposes to do this. Give me that which I want,
and you shall have this which you want, is the meaning of every such
offer; and it is in this manner that we obtain from one another the far
greater part of those good offices which we stand in need of. It is not from

---

[4] The example of the greyhounds occurs in LJ (B) 219, ed. Cannan 169. LJ (A) vi.44
uses the example of 'hounds in a chace' and again at 57. Cf. LJ (B) 222, ed. Cannan 171:
'Sometimes, indeed, animals seem to act in concert, but there is never any thing like a
bargain among them. Monkeys when they rob a garden throw the fruit from one to
another till they deposit it in the hoard, but there is always a scramble about the division of the booty, and usually some of them are killed.' In LJ (A) vi.57 a similar example
is based on the Cape of Good Hope.

[5] In ED 2.12 an additional sentence is added at this point: 'When any uncommon misfortune befals it, its piteous and doleful cries will sometimes engage its fellows, and
sometimes prevail even upon man, to relieve it.' With this exception, and the first sentence
of this paragraph, the whole of the preceding material follows ED 2.12 very closely and
in places verbatim. The remainder of the paragraph follows ED 2.12 to its close.

[6] 'To expect, that others should serve us for nothing, is unreasonable; therefore all
Commerce, that Men can have together, must be a continual bartering of one thing for
another. The Seller, who transfers the Property of a Thing, has his own Interest as much
at Heart as the Buyer, who purchases that Property; and, if you want or like a thing, the
Owner of it, whatever Stock of Provision he may have of the same, or how greatly soever
you may stand in need of it, will never part with it, but for a Consideration, which he
likes better, than he does the thing you want.' (Mandeville, *The Fable of the Bees*, pt. ii.
421–2, ed. Kaye, ii.349.)

the benevolence of the butcher, the brewer, or the baker, that we expect
our dinner, but from their [22] regard to their own interest. We address
ourselves, not to their humanity but to their self-love, and never talk
to them of our own necessities but of their advantages.[7] Nobody but a
beggar chuses to depend chiefly upon the benevolence of his fellow-
citizens. Even a beggar does not depend upon it entirely. The charity of
well-disposed people, indeed, supplies him with the whole fund of his
subsistence. But though this principle ultimately provides him with all
the necessaries of life which he has occasion for, it neither does nor can
provide him with them as he has occasion for them. The greater part of
his occasional wants are supplied in the same manner as those of other
people, by treaty, by barter, and by purchase. With the money which one
man gives him he purchases food. The old cloaths which another bestows
upon him he exchanges for other old cloaths which suit him better, or
for lodging, or for food, or for money, with which he can buy either
food, cloaths, or lodging, as he has occasion.

3   As it is by treaty, by barter, and by purchase, that we obtain from one
another the greater part of those mutual good offices which we stand in
need of, so it is this same trucking disposition which originally gives occasion to the division of labour. In a tribe of hunters or shepherds a particular
person makes bows and arrows, for example, with more readiness and
dexterity than any other. He frequently exchanges them for cattle or for
venison with his companions; and [23] he finds at last that he can in this
manner get more cattle and venison, than if he himself went to the field
to catch them. From a regard to his own interest, therefore, the making
of bows and arrows grows to be his chief business, and he becomes a sort
of armourer.[8] Another excels in making the frames and covers of their

---

[7] Cf. LJ (B) 220, ed. Cannan 169: 'The brewer and the baker serve us not from benevolence but from selflove. No man but a beggar depends on benevolence, and even they
would die in a week were their entire dependance upon it.' Also LJ (A) vi.46: 'You do
not adress his [the brewer's and baker's] humanity but his self-love. Beggars are the only
persons who depend on charity for their subsistence; neither do they do so alltogether.
For what by their supplications they have got from one, they exchange for something else
they more want. They give their old cloaths to a one for lodging, the mony they have
got to another for bread, and thus even they make use of bargain and exchange.'

[8] Cf. LJ (A) vi.46: 'This bartering and trucking spirit is the cause of the separation of
trades and the improvements in arts. A savage who supports himself by hunting, having
made some more arrows than he had occasion for, gives them in a present to some of his
companions, who in return give him some of the venison they have catched; and he at
last finding that by making arrows and giving them to his neighbour, as he happens to
make them better than ordinary, he can get more venison than by his own hunting, he
lays it aside unless it be for his diversion, and becomes an arrow-maker.' Similar points
are made in LJ (B) 220, ed. Cannan 169–70, and a similar passage occurs in ED 2.13.
Mandeville (*The Fable of the Bees*, pt. ii. 335–6, ed. Kaye ii.284) also noted that: 'Man',
as I have hinted before, naturally loves to imitate what he sees others do, which is the
reason that savage People all do the same thing: This hinders them from meliorating
their Condition, though they are always wishing for it: But if one will wholly apply himself to the making of Bows and Arrows, whilst another provides Food, a third builds

little huts or moveable houses. He is accustomed to be of use in this way to his neighbours, who reward him in the same manner with cattle and with venison, till at last he finds it his interest to dedicate himself entirely to this employment, and to become a sort of house-carpenter. In the same manner a third becomes a smith or a brazier, a fourth a tanner or dresser of hides or skins, the principal part of the clothing of savages.[9] And thus the certainty of being able to exchange all that surplus part of the produce of his own labour, which is over and above his own consumption, for such parts of the produce of other men's labour as he may have occasion for, encourages every man to apply himself to a particular occupation, and to cultivate and bring to perfection whatever talent or genius he may possess for that particular species of business.[10]

4   The difference of natural talents in different men is, in reality, much less than we are aware of; and the very different genius which appears to distinguish men of different professions, when grown up to maturity, is not upon many occasions so much the cause, as the effect of the division of labour.[11] The difference between the [24] most dissimilar characters, between a philosopher and a common street porter, for example,

Huts, a fourth makes Garments, and a fifth Utensils, they do not only become useful to one another, but the Callings and Employments themselves will in the same Number of Years receive much greater Improvements, than if all had been promiscously follow'd by every one of the Five.'

[9] Cf. Hutcheson (*System*, i.288–9): ''Nay 'tis well known that the produce of the labours of any given number, twenty, for instance, in providing the necessaries or conveniences of life, shall be much greater by assigning to one, a certain sort of work of one kind, in which he will soon acquire skill and dexterity, and to another assigning work of a different kind, than if each one of the twenty were obliged to employ himself, by turns, in all the different sorts of labour requisite for his subsistence, without sufficient dexterity in any. In the former method each procures a great quantity of goods of one kind, and can exchange a part of it for such goods obtained by the labours of others as he shall stand in need of. One grows expert in tillage, another in pasture and breeding cattle, a third in masonry, a fourth in the chace, a fifth in iron-works, a sixth in the arts of the loom, and so on throughout the rest. Thus all are supplied by means of barter with the work of complete artists. In the other method scarce any one could be dextrous and skilful in any one sort of labour.'

[10] This paragraph is based on ED 2.13, which it follows very closely.

[11] 'When we consider how nearly equal all men are in their bodily force, and even in their mental powers and faculties, till cultivated by education; we must necessarily allow, that nothing but their consent could, at first, associate them together, and subject them to any authority.' (D. Hume, 'Of the Original Contract', in *Political Discourses* (1752); *Essays Moral, Political and Literary*, ed. T. H. Green and T. H. Grose (London, 1882), i.444–5.) Cf. *Treatise of Human Nature*, III.i: 'The skin, pores, muscles, and nerves of a day-labourer, are different from those of a man of quality: so are his sentiments, actions, and manners. The different stations of life influence the whole fabric, external and internal; and these different stations arise necessarily, because uniformly, from the necessary and uniform principles of human nature.' On the other hand, Harris (*Essay*, i.15) believed that: 'Men are endued with various talents and propensities, which naturally dispose and fit them for different occupations; and are ... under a necessity of betaking themselves to particular arts and employments, from their inability of otherwise acquiring all the necessaries they want, with ease and comfort. This creates a dependance of one man upon another, and naturally unites men into societies.'

seems to arise not so much from nature, as from habit, custom, and education.[12] When they came into the world, and for the first six or eight years
of their existence, they were*a*, perhaps,*a* very much alike, and neither their
parents nor play-fellows could perceive any remarkable difference. About
that age, or soon after, they come to be employed in very different occupations. The difference of talents comes then to be taken notice of, and widens
by degrees, till at last the vanity of the philosopher is willing to acknowledge scarce any resemblance. But without the disposition to truck, barter,
and exchange, every man must have procured to himself every necessary
and conveniency of life which he wanted. All must have had the same
duties to perform, and the same work to do, and there could have been
no such difference of employment as could alone give occasion to any
great difference of talents.[13]

5   As it is this disposition which forms that difference of talents, so
remarkable among men of different professions, so it is this same disposition which renders that difference useful. Many tribes of animals acknowledged to be all of the same species, derive from nature a much more
remarkable distinction of genius, than what, antecedent to custom and

a-a *1, 4e–6*

---

[12] Cf. V.i.f 51. LJ (A) vi.47–8 reads: 'No two persons can be more different in their
genius as a philosopher and a porter, but there does not seem to have been any original
difference betwixt them. For the five or six first years of their lives there was hardly any
apparent difference: their companions looked upon them as persons of pretty much the
same stamp. No wisdom and ingenuity appeared in the one superior to that of the other.
From about that time a difference was thought to be perceived in them. Their manner
of life began to affect them, and without doubt had it not been for this they would have
continued the same.' Similar arguments appear in LJ (B) 220, ed. Cannan 170. There
is an interesting variant on this point in LJ (B) 327, ed. Cannan 253, where Smith commented on the fact that 'probity and punctuality' generally accompany the introduction
of commerce. He added that varying degrees of these qualities were 'not at all to be
imputed to national character as some pretend. There is no natural reason why an Englishman or a Scotchman should not be as punctual in performing agreements as a Dutchman.
It is far more reduceable to self interest, that general principle which regulates the
actions of every man . . .'

[13] The whole of the preceding paragraph follows ED 2.14 to this point. In ED, however, the sentence ends with '. . . any great difference in character' and goes on: 'It is
upon this account that a much greater uniformity of character is to be observed among
savages than among civilized nations. Among the former there is scarce any division
of labour and consequently no remarkable difference of employments; whereas among
the latter there is an almost infinite variety of occupations, of which the respective duties
bear scarce any resemblance to one another. What a perfect uniformity of character do
we find in all the heroes described by Ossian? And what a variety of manners, on the contrary, in those who are celebrated by Homer? Ossian plainly describes the exploits
of a nation of hunters, while Homer paints the actions of two nations, who, tho' far from
being perfectly civilised, were yet much advanced beyond the age of shepherds, who
cultivated lands, who built cities, and among whom he mentions many different trades
and occupations, such as masons, carpenters, smiths, merchants, soothsayers, priests,
physicians.' The texts then assume a similar form until the end of the following paragraph of the WN. The uniformity of character found among savages is also mentioned in
LJ (A) vi.48, LJ (B) 221, ed. Cannan 170.

education, appears to take place among men. By nature a philosopher is not in genius and disposition half so different from a street porter, as a mastiff is from a greyhound, or a greyhound from a spaniel, or this [25] last from a shepherd's dog. Those different tribes of animals, however, though all of the same species, are of scarce any use to one another. The strength of the mastiff is not, in the least, supported either by the swiftness of the greyhound, or by the sagacity of the spaniel, or by the docility of the shepherd's dog. The effects of those different geniuses and talents, for want of the power or disposition to barter and exchange, cannot be brought into a common stock, and do not in the least contribute to the better accommodation and conveniency of the species. Each animal is still obliged to support and defend itself, separately and independently, and derives no sort of advantage from that variety of talents with which nature has distinguished its fellows. Among men, on the contrary, the most dissimilar geniuses are of use to one another; the different produces of their respective talents, by the general disposition to truck, barter, and exchange, being brought, as it were, into a common stock, where every man may purchase whatever part of the produce of other men's talents he has occasion for.[14]

[14] The text of ED continues beyond this point to include an additional folio (N8) which elaborates on the interdependence between the philosopher and the porter and the advantages to be gained from these separate trades. This passage opens with the statement that 'Every thing would be dearer if before it was exposed to sale it had been carried packt and unpackt by hands less able and less dexterous, who for an equal quantity of work, would have taken more time, and must consequently have required more wages, which must have been charged upon the goods.' It is interesting to note that FA begins with the words '. . . who for an equal quantity of work' and then continues in parallel with ED for some 25 lines. The fragment then proceeds to elaborate on the link between the division of labour and the extent of the market (a subject which is not mentioned in ED) whereas ED continues with the preceding theme. It is possible that the fragments represent an alternative, and a later, rewriting of this section of Smith's work. The interdependence of philosopher and porter is briefly mentioned in LJ (A) vi.49, LJ (B) 221, ed. Cannan 171.

CHAPTER III

[26] *That the Division of Labour is limited by the Extent of the Market*[1]

1 As it is the power of exchanging that gives occasion to the division of labour, so the extent of this division must always be limited by the extent of that power, or, in other words, by the extent of the market.[2] When the market is very small, no person can have any encouragement to dedicate himself entirely to one employment, for want of the power to exchange all that surplus part of the produce of his own labour, which is over and above his own consumption, for such parts of the produce of other men's labour as he has occasion for. ✓

2 There are some sorts of industry, even of the lowest kind, which can be carried on no where but in a great town. A porter, for example, can find employment and subsistence in no other place. A village is by much too narrow a sphere for him; even an ordinary market town is scarce large enough to afford him constant occupation. In the lone houses and very small villages which are scattered about in so desert a country as the Highlands of Scotland, every farmer must be butcher, baker and brewer for his own family.[3] In such situations we can scarce expect to find even a smith, a carpenter, or a mason, within less than twenty miles of another of the same trade. The scattered families that [27] live at eight or ten miles distance from the nearest of them, must learn to perform themselves a great number of little pieces of work, for which, in more populous countries, they would call in the assistance of those workmen.[4] Country workmen

---

[1] The subjects of this chapter, as observed in the previous note, do not figure in ED. In LJ (A) vi Smith did develop the argument that the division of labour depends on the extent of the market, but did so in the course of offering a recapitulation of his treatment of price, i.e. outwith his main discussion of the division of labour. In LJ (B) the discussion of the extent of the market is brief, but integrated with the wider discussion of the division of labour. FA and FB thus provide the most elaborate examination of the subject; a fact which lends some support to the view that the fragments may have been written after ED. Paragraphs 1 and 2 of this chapter appear to be based on FA from the first complete paragraph of the latter 'As it is the power of exchanging . . .' while paragraphs 3–7 show the same close connection with the whole of FB.

[2] LJ (B) 222, ed. Cannan 172: 'From all that has been said we may observe that the division of labour must always be proportioned to the extent of commerce.' In LJ (A) vi.63 it is remarked that the division of labour 'is greater or less according to the market'.

[3] Cf. LJ (A) ii.40: 'It is found that society must be pretty far advanced before the different trades can all find subsistence: . . . And to this day in the remote and deserted parts of the country, a weaver or a smith, besides the exercise of his trade, cultivates a small farm, and in that manner exercises two trades; that of a farmer and that of a weaver.'

[4] The degree of correspondence between the preceding passages and FA ceases at this point and there is a long passage from the beginning of the following sentence, and ending 22 lines below ('a ship navigated by six') which has no counterpart in the fragment. This passage amounts to about three hundred words, which would make about one folio page in the hand of the amanuensis used. Smith may, therefore, have decided to omit the two final

are almost every where obliged to apply themselves to all the different branches of industry that have so much affinity to one another as to be employed about the same sort of materials.⁵ A country carpenter deals in every sort of work that is made of wood: a country smith in every sort of work that is made of iron. The former is not only a carpenter, but a joiner, a cabinet-maker, and even a carver in wood, as well as a wheel-wright, a plough-wright, a cart and waggon maker. The employments of the latter are still more various.⁶ It is impossible there should be such a trade as even that of a nailer in the remote and inland parts of the High-lands of Scotland. Such a workman at the rate of a thousand nails a day, and three hundred working days in the year, will make three hundred thousand nails in the year. But in such a situation it would be impossible to dispose of one thousand, that is, of one day's work in the year.⁷

3   As by means of water-carriage a more extensive market is opened to every sort of industry than what land-carriage alone can afford it, so it is upon the sea-coast, and along the banks of navigable rivers, that industry of every kind naturally begins to subdivide and improve itself, and it is frequently not till a long time after that [28] those improvements extend themselves to the inland parts of the country.⁸ A broad-wheeled waggon, attended by two men, and drawn by eight horses, in about six weeks time carries and brings back between London and Edinburgh near four ton

pages of FA and introduce a new page which is now lost. The passage from FA which is omitted from the WN had gone on to illustrate the link between the division of labour and the extent of the market by reference to primitive communities such as the North American Indians and the Hottentots, Arabs, and Tartars. In speaking of the Hottentots he pointed out that there was some separation of employments such as the tailor, physician, and smith, but that the people involved were *principally*, but not *entirely* supported by them. It was in this connection that Smith made the interesting point that 'The compleat division of labour however, is posteriour to the invention even of agriculture.'

⁵ See I.x.c.8 where it is stated that country labourers were excluded from the statute of apprenticeship by judicial interpretation, as a result of the nature of the employment.

⁶ LJ (A) vi.64 notes that 'A wright in the country is a cart-wright, a house carpenter, a square wright or cabinet maker and a carver in wood; each of which in a town makes a separate business. A merchant in Glasgow or Aberdeen who deals in linnen will have in his ware-house, Irish, Scots and Hamburg linnens, but at London there are separate dealers in each of these.'

⁷ Smith provides a further example, that of the shoemaker, at IV.ix.45.

⁸ 'Great Cities are usually built on the seacoast or on the banks of large Rivers for the convenience of transport; because water-carriage of the produce and merchandise neces-sary for the subsistence and comfort of the inhabitants is much cheaper than Carriages and Land Transport.' (R. Cantillon, *Essai sur la Nature du Commerce* (1755), 22–3; edited and translated by Henry Higgs (London, 1931), 19.) See below, II.v.33 and III.iii.20. While Smith gives a prominent place to navigation in explaining the historical origins of cities and manufactures in III.iii, he did not neglect the importance of land carriage. It is pointed out in LJ (B) 223, ed. Cannan 172, that 'Since the mending of large Rivers for the 40 or 50 years ago, its opulence has increased extremely.' In LJ (A) vi.65 he commented on the problem of bad roads and remarked that 'hence we see that the turnpikes of England have within these 30 or 40 years increased the opulence of the inland parts'. The advantages of good roads are also emphasized in I.xi.b.5 and V.i.d.17.

weight of goods. In about the same time a ship navigated by six or eight men, and sailing between the ports of London and Leith, frequently carries and brings back two hundred ton weight of goods. Six or eight men, therefore, by the help of water-carriage, can carry and bring back in the same time the same quantity of goods between London and Edinburgh, as fifty broad-wheeled waggons, attended by a hundred men, and drawn by four hundred horses.[9] Upon two hundred tons of goods, therefore, carried by the cheapest land-carriage from London to Edinburgh, there must be charged the maintenance of a hundred men for three weeks, and both the maintenance, and, what is nearly equal to the maintenance, the wear and tear of four hundred horses as well as of fifty great waggons. Whereas, upon the same quantity of goods carried by water, there is to be charged only the maintenance of six or eight men, and the wear and tear of a ship of two hundred tons burden, together with the value of the superior risk, or the difference of the insurance between land and water-carriage. Were there no other communication between those two places, therefore, but by land-carriage, as no goods could be transported from the one to the other, except such whose price was very consi-[29]derable in proportion to their weight, they could carry on but a small part of that commerce which ^a at present ^bsubsists^b between them, and consequently could give but a small part of that encouragement which they at present mutually afford to each other's industry.[10] There could be little or no commerce of any kind between the distant parts of the world. What goods could bear the expence of land-carriage between London and Calcutta? Or if there ^cwere^c any so precious as to be able to support this expence, with what

---

^a is *I*   ^{b–b} carried on *I*   ^{c–c} was *I*

---

[9] The remainder of this paragraph finds a close parallel in the opening passages of FB, save that 8 or 10 men sailing from the port of Leith can transport 200 tons between Edinburgh and London more cheaply than 'Sixty six narrow wheeled wagons drawn by three hundred & ninety horses & attended by a hundred & thirty two men; or than forty broad wheeled wagons drawn by three hundred & twenty horses & attended by eighty men.' Cf. LJ (B) 223, ed. Cannan 172: 'Water carriage is another convenience as by it 300 ton can be conveyed at the expence of the tare and wear of the vessel, and the wages of 5 or 6 men, and that too in a shorter time than by a 100 waggons which will take 6 horses and a man each.' In LJ (A) vi.66 Smith compares the expense of a ship of 200 tons navigated by four or five men with that incurred in the use of wagons.

[10] Smith may exaggerate the relative advantage of water-carriage, particularly in his example of the costs of carriage between London and Edinburgh. Carriage by sea had its own dangers: natural hazards; pilfering; privateering in time of war. Fine woollen goods were often sent by land in spite of its other disadvantages (cf. IV.viii.21). Smith was writing at the end of the first major phase of passing turnpike acts, but before the improvements which followed were fully evident. Coaching times, a fairly reliable indicator of improvement, show the change. Edinburgh and London were about four days apart in the mid-eighteenth century; only 60 hours by 1786. Smith's concern over the contribution of navigable rivers is more to the point. He was writing at the end of an age when rivers played a more important part in the economic life of Britain than they had ever done before or since.

safety could they be transported through the territories of so many barbarous nations? Those two cities, however, at present carry on [d] a very
considerable commerce [e]with each other[e], and by mutually affording a
market, give a good deal of encouragement to each other's industry.

4   Since such, therefore, are the advantages of water-carriage, it is natural
that the first improvements of art and industry should be made where this
conveniency opens the whole world for a market to the produce of every
sort of labour, and that they should always be much later in extending themselves into the inland parts of the country. The inland parts of the country
can for a long time have no other market for the greater part of their goods,
but the country which lies round about them, and separates them from the
sea-coast, and the great navigable rivers. The extent of their market,
therefore, must for a long time be in proportion to the riches and populousness of that country, and consequently their improvement must always be
pos-[30]terior to the improvement of that country. In our North American
colonies the plantations have constantly followed either the sea-coast or the
banks of the navigable rivers, and have scarce any where extended themselves to any considerable distance from both.[11]

5   The nations that, according to the best authenticated history, appear to
have been first civilized, were those that dwelt round the coast of the Mediterranean sea. That sea, by far the greatest inlet that is known in the world,
having no tides, nor consequently any waves except such as are caused by
the wind only, was, by the smoothness of its surface, as well as by the
multitude of its islands, and the proximity of its neighbouring shores,
extremely favourable to the infant navigation of the world; when, from their
ignorance of the compass, men were afraid to quit the view of the coast,
and from the imperfection of the art of ship-building, to abandon themselves to the boisterous waves of the ocean.[12] To pass beyond the pillars
of Hercules, that is, to sail out of the Streights of Gibraltar, was, in the
antient world, long considered as a most wonderful and dangerous exploit of navigation. It was late before even the Phenicians and Carthagin-
ians, the most skilful navigators and shipbuilders of those old times, attempted it, and they were for a long time the only nations that did attempt
it.

6   Of all the countries on the coast of the Mediterranean sea, Egypt seems
to have been the first in which either agriculture or manufactures were [31]

---

[d] together *1*   [e-e] *2–6*

> [11] This sentence appears verbatim in FB, which adds: 'What James the sixth of Scotland
> said of the county of Fife, of which the inland parts were at that time very ill while the sea
> coast was extremely well cultivated, that it was like a coarse woollen coat edged with gold
> lace, might still be said of the greater part of our North American colonies.' See below,
> I.ix.11.
> [12] The passage from the beginning of this paragraph follows FB very closely, and often
> verbatim, although there is nothing corresponding to the two following sentences.

cultivated and improved to any considerable degree.[13] Upper Egypt extends itself nowhere above a few miles from the Nile, and in Lower Egypt that great river breaks itself into many different canals, which, with the assistance of a little art, seem to have afforded a communication by water-carriage, not only between all the great towns, but between all the considerable villages, and even to many farm-houses in the country; nearly in the same manner as the Rhine and the Maese do in Holland at present. The extent and easiness of this inland navigation was probably one of the principal causes of the early improvement of Egypt.[14]

7   The improvements in agriculturè and manufactures seem likewise to have been of very great antiquity in the provinces of Bengal in the East Indies, and in some of the eastern provinces of China; though the great extent of this antiquity is not authenticated by any histories of whose authority we, in this part of the world, are well assured. In Bengal the Ganges and several other great rivers *'form a great number of navigable'* canals in the same manner as the Nile does in Egypt. In the Eastern provinces of China too, several great rivers form, by their different branches, a multitude of canals, and by communicating with one another afford an inland navigation much more extensive than that either of the Nile or the Ganges, or perhaps than both of them put together.[15] It is remarkable that neither the antient Egyptians, nor the Indians, nor the Chinese, encouraged foreign commerce, but [32] seem all to have derived their great opulence from this inland navigation.

8   All the inland parts of Africa, and all that part of Asia which lies any

'-' break themselves into many *I*

[13] In LJ (A) iv.60–2 and LJ (B) 31, ed. Cannan 22 the early economic development of Greece is attributed to its natural advantages including ease of communication. Smith added that 'Most of the European countries have most part of the same advantages. They are divided by rivers and branches of the sea, and are naturally fit for the cultivation of the soil and other arts.' The development of the arts and sciences in classical Greece was attributed to its early economic advance in LJ (A) iv.60, Astronomy, III.4 and, LRBL ii.117–9, ed. Lothian 132–3.

[14] This paragraph is evidently based on FB, which goes on, however, to conclude with the statement that 'Agriculture and manufactures too seem to have been of very great antiquity in some of the maritime provinces of China & in the province of Bengal in the East Indies. All these were countries very much of the same nature with Egypt, cut by innumerable canals which afford them an immense inland navigation.' LJ (A) iii.47 also remarks with regard to China, Egypt, and Bengal that 'These countries are all remarkably fruitful. The banks of the Nile and the Ganges are overflowed by . . . rivers and yield immense crops, 3 or 4 in a year. This as there must be plenty of food and subsistence for man must . . . promote population, as the number of men is proportion'd to the quantity of subsistence.'

[15] Smith comments on the inland navigation of China and Indostan at I.xi.g.28, and links the concern of these governments with canal and road improvement to their reliance on land-taxes at V.ii.d.5. He mentions that China was not eminent for foreign trade at II.v.22 and IV.iii.c.11, and comments on the limitations thereby imposed on her economic growth at I.ix.15, IV.ix.40,41. However, it is stated that at least some trade was carried on by foreigners at III.i.7 and IV.ix.45.

considerable way north of the Euxine and Caspian seas, the antient Scythia, the modern Tartary and Siberia, seem in all ages of the world to have been in the same barbarous and uncivilized state in which we find them at present.[16] The sea of Tartary is the frozen ocean which admits of no navigation, and though some of the greatest rivers in the world run through that country, they are at too great a distance from one another to carry commerce and communication through the greater part of it. There are in Africa none of those great inlets, such as the Baltic and Adriatic seas in Europe, the Mediterranean and Euxine seas in both Europe and Asia, and the gulphs of Arabia, Persia, India, Bengal, and Siam, in Asia, to carry maritime commerce into the interior parts of that great continent: and the great rivers of Africa are at too great a distance from one another to give occasion to any considerable inland navigation. The commerce besides which any nation can carry on by means of a river which does not break itself into any great number of branches or canals, and which runs into another territory before it reaches the sea, can never be very considerable; because it is always in the power of the nations who possess that other territory to obstruct the communication between the upper country and the sea. The navigation of the Danube is of very little use to the different [33] states of Bavaria, Austria and Hungary, in comparison of what it would be if any *9* of them possessed the whole of its course till it falls into the Black Sea.

9 one *I*

[16] Smith comments on the limited improvement in Arabia due to the poorness of the soil and difficulties of transport and uses this point to explain why the Arabs had not advanced beyond the shepherd state in LJ (A) iv.36, 56–62; see also LJ (B) 303, ed. Cannan 234: 'in Asia and other eastern countries; all inland commerce is carried on by great caravans, consisting of several thousands, for mutual defence, with waggons etca.' The passages from LJ (A) iv above cited make it plain that the preconditions for economic development include fertility of the soil, ease of defence, and of communication where the latter provides an opportunity for the export of surpluses. In LJ (A) iv.53 Smith also comments that the Tartars 'have indeed some of the largest rivers in the world' while adding that they 'have always been a state of shepherds, which they will always be from the nature of their country, which is dry and raised above the sea, with few rivers, tho' some very large ones, and the weather and the air is too cold for the produce of any grain.' See also 62, and cf. LJ (B) 30–1, ed. Cannan 22.

CHAPTER IV

Of the Origin and Use of Money[1]

1 WHEN the division of labour has been once thoroughly established, it is but a very small part of a man's wants which the produce of his own labour can supply. He supplies the far greater part of them by exchanging that surplus part of the produce of his own labour, which is over and above his own consumption, for such parts of the produce of other men's labour as he has occasion for. Every man thus lives by exchanging, or becomes in some measure a merchant, and the society itself grows to be what is properly a commercial society.

2 But when the division of labour first began to take place, this power of exchanging must frequently have been very much clogged and embarrassed in its operations.[2] One man, we shall suppose, has more of a certain commodity than he himself has occasion for, while another has less. The former consequently would be glad to dispose of, and the latter to purchase, a part of this superfluity. But if this latter should chance to have nothing that the former stands in need of, no exchange can be made between them. [34] The butcher has more meat in his shop than he himself can consume, and the brewer and the baker would each of them be willing to purchase a part of it. But they have nothing to offer in exchange, except the different productions of their respective trades, and the butcher is already provided with all the bread and beer which he has immediate occasion for. No exchange can, in this case, be made between them. He cannot be their merchant, nor they his customers; and they are all of them thus mutually less serviceable to one another. In order to avoid the inconveniency of such situations, every prudent man in every period of society, after the first

p. Locke

---

[1] In both sets of lectures and the ED Smith considers the analysis of money immediately after that of market and natural price (which forms the subjects of I.vii. below). The subjects of this chapter, e.g. with regard to the inconvenience of barter, the usefulness of the metals as a medium of exchange, the need for coinage, debasement, etc., are considered in LJ (A) vi.97–117, LJ (B) 235–44, ed. Cannan 182–90, ED 4.1–3. In ED 4, however, Smith planned to introduce at this point a discussion of banks and paper money (the subjects of II.ii below) before proceeding directly to the examination of the fallacy that opulence consists in money (the subjects of IV). The lectures also follow this order of argument, save that LJ (B) includes an account of John Law's scheme (see below, II.ii.78) and of the Bank of Amsterdam (below IV.iii.b). In ED Smith styled chapter 4 'Of money, its nature, origin and history, considered first, as the measure of value, and secondly as the instrument of commerce' and remarked that 'Under the first head I have little to say that is very new or particular; except a general history of the coins of France, England, & Scotland: the different changes they have undergone: their causes and effects.'

[2] It is remarked at I.xi.g.26 that the economy of Peru had been based on barter and that 'there was accordingly scarce any division of labour among them'. See also IV.vii.b.7. In LJ (A) ii.53 Smith cites the 'Negroes on the Coast of Guinea' as still operating a barter economy.

establishment of the division of labour, must naturally have endeavoured to manage his affairs in such a manner, as to have at all times by him, besides the peculiar produce of his own industry, a certain quantity of some one commodity or other, such as he imagined few people would be likely to refuse in exchange for the produce of their industry.[3]

3   Many different commodities, it is probable, were successively both thought of and employed for this purpose. In the rude ages of society, cattle are said to have been the common instrument of commerce; and, though they must have been a most inconvenient one, yet in old times we find things were frequently valued according to the number of cattle which had been given in exchange for them.[4] The armour of Diomede, says Homer, cost only nine oxen; but that of Glaucus cost *an* hundred oxen.[5] Salt is said to [35] be the common instrument of commerce and exchanges in Abyssinia;[6] a species of shells in some parts of the coast of India; dried cod at Newfoundland; tobacco in Virginia; sugar in some of our West India colonies; hides or dressed leather in some other countries; and there is at this day a village in Scotland where it is not uncommon, I am told, for a workman to carry nails instead of money to the baker's shop or the ale-house.[7]

4   In all countries, however, men seem at last to have been determined by irresistible reasons to give the preference, for this employment, to metals above every other commodity.[8] Metals can not only be kept with as little loss

a–a a *I*

---

[3] Cleomanes, In *The Fable of the Bees*, Sixth Dialogue (pt. ii.422, ed. Kaye ii.349), asks: 'Which way shall I persuade a Man to serve me, when the Service, I can repay him in, is such as he does not want or care for? . . . Money obviates and takes away all those Difficulties, by being an acceptable Reward for all the Services Men can do to one another.' See also Harris, *Essay*, i.34–6.

[4] See IV.i.2 where Smith comments on the Tartar economy and the use of cattle as a measure of value. The Greek economy at the time of the Trojan War is described as having just left the shepherd state, V.i.b.16.

[5] 'From Glaucus did Zeus, son of Cronos, take away his wits, seeing he made exchange of armour with Diomedes, son of Tydeus, giving golden for bronze, the worth of an hundred oxen for the worth of nine.'

(Homer, *Iliad*, vi.234–6, translated by A. T. Murray in Loeb Classical Library (1965) i.278–9.) The example of Glaucus and Diomede appears in LJ (A) vi.98 where Smith also adds a comment on the use of sheep as money in Italy and especially Tuscany. (Cf. LJ (B) 235, ed. Cannan 183 where the Greek cattle are said to have been black cattle.) Smith comments on the use of the metals as money in LJ (B) 238–9, ed. Cannan 185, and LJ (A) vi.99, 105, Montesquieu also noted that the Athenians made use of oxen and the Romans of sheep (*Esprit*, XXII.ii.2).

[6] The use of salt in Abyssinia is mentioned by Montesquieu, *Esprit*, XXII.i, note. He also suggests that it was used by the Moors in Africa in exchange for gold.

[7] Cantillon pointed out that 'Tobacco, Sugar, and Cocoa' had been used as money in the American colonies (*Essai*, 145, ed. Higgs 111). Harris also reviews the problems of barter, *Essay*, i.34–5, and goes on (42) to comment on the use of particular commodities such as salt or 'the small shells called by us *couries*' in barbarous countries such as Africa.

[8] Harris continued, *Essay*, i.43–4: 'For the purpose of universal commerce, metals seem the fittest materials for a standard measure, or *money*; as *copper*, *silver*, or *gold*; they having

as any other commodity, scarce any thing being less perishable that they are, but they can likewise, without any loss, be divided into any number of parts, as by fusion those parts can easily be re-united again; a quality ✓ which no other equally durable commodities possess, and which more than any other quality renders them fit to be the instruments of commerce and circulation. The man who wanted to buy salt, for example, and had nothing but cattle to give in exchange for it, must have been obliged to buy salt to the value of a whole ox, or a whole sheep at a time. He could seldom buy less than this, because what he was to give for it could seldom be divided without loss; and if he had a mind to buy more, he must, for the same reasons, have been obliged to buy double or triple the quantity, the value, to wit, of two or three oxen, or [36] of two or three sheep. If, on the contrary, instead of sheep or oxen, he had metals to give in exchange for it, he could easily proportion the quantity of the metal to the precise quantity of the commodity which he had immediate occasion for.

5   Different metals have been made use of by different nations for this purpose. Iron was the common instrument of commerce among the antient Spartans; copper among the antient Romans[9]; and gold and silver among all rich and commercial nations.[10]

6   Those metals seem originally to have been made use of for this purpose in rude bars, without any stamp or coinage. Thus we are told by Pliny*, upon the authority of *c*Timaeus*c*, an antient *d*historian*d*, that, till the time of Servius Tullius, the Romans had no coined money, but made use of unstamped bars of copper to purchase whatever they had occasion for. These rude bars, therefore, performed at this time the function of money.

7   The use of metals in this rude state was attended with two very considerable inconveniencies; first, with the trouble of weighing *e*; and, secondly, with *f*that*f* of assaying them. In the precious metals, where a small difference in the quantity makes a great difference in the value,

---

*b** Plin. Hist. Nat. lib. 33. cap. 3.*b* ['King Servius was the first to stamp a design on bronze; previously according to Timaeus, at Rome they used raw metal.' Pliny, *Natural History*, XXXIII. xiii translated by H. Rackham in Loeb Classical Library (1952), ix. 37.]

---

b-b 2–6   *c-c* one Remus *1*   *d-d* author *1*   *e* them *1*   *f-f* the trouble *1*

---

all the properties above required: They are moreover divisible into minute parts, which parts retain nevertheless an intrinsic value, in proportion to their quantity or weight; because those parts may, without injuring the metal, be again united together into a greater mass. These metals are durable, and also susceptible of any form, mark, or impression; and are convertible from money or coins, into utensils of various kinds; and from these, into money again.' See also Cantillon, *Essai*, I.xvii and II.i; Montesquieu, *Esprit*, XXII.ii, and John Law, *Money and Trade Considered* (Edinburgh, 1705), 8–9.

---

[9] See below, I.v.24.
[10] The examples of Rome and Sparta appear in LJ (A) vi.105 and similar points are made in LJ (B) 237, ed. Cannan 184–5. See also Cantillon, *Essai*, 143–4, ed. Higgs 109.

even the business of weighing, with proper exactness, requires at least
very accurate weights and scales. The weighing of gold in particular is an
[37] operation of some nicety. In the coarser metals, indeed, where a
small error would be of little consequence, less accuracy would, no doubt,
be necessary. Yet we should find it excessively troublesome, if every time
a poor man had occasion either to buy or sell a farthing's worth of goods,
he was obliged to weigh the farthing. The operation of assaying is still
more difficult, still more tedious, and, unless a part of the metal is fairly
melted in the crucible, with proper dissolvents, any conclusion that can be
drawn from it, is extremely uncertain. Before the institution of coined
money, however, unless they went through this tedious and difficult
operation, people must always have been liable to the grossest frauds and
impositions, and instead of a pound weight of pure silver, or pure copper,
might receive in exchange for their goods, an adulterated composition of
the coarsest and cheapest materials, which had, however, in their outward
appearance, been made to resemble those metals. To prevent such abuses,
to facilitate exchanges, and thereby to encourage all sorts of industry and
commerce, it has been found necessary, in all countries that have made any
considerable advances towards improvement, to affix a publick stamp upon
certain quantities of such particular metals, as were in those countries
commonly made use of to purchase goods. Hence the origin of coined
money, and of those publick offices called mints;[11] institutions exactly of
the same nature with those of the aulnagers and stampmasters of woollen
[38] and linen cloth.[12] All of them are equally meant to ascertain, by means

[11] Similar points are made by Harris, *Essay*, i.48. Pufendorf (citing the authority of
Aristotle) also comments on the advantages of coined money, *De Jure*, V.i.12. The same
arguments appear in his *De Officio*, I.xiv and cf. Grotius, *De Jure Belli*, II.xii.17. See
Aristotle, *Politics* I, 1372a (translated by William Ellis in Everyman Library (1912),
16): 'Barter introduced the use of money . . . for which reason they invented something
to exchange with each other which they should mutually give and take, that being really
valuable itself, should have the additional advantage of being of easy conveyance, for the
purposes of life, as iron and silver, or anything else of the same nature: and this at first
passed in value simply according to its weight or size, but in process of time it had a
certain stamp, to save the trouble of weighing, which stamp expressed its value.'
   Cf. '. . . as silver can be combined with Iron, Lead, Tin, Copper, etc. which are not
such scarce Metals and are mined at less expense, the exchange of Silver was subject to
much fraud, and this caused several Kingdoms to establish Mints in order to certify by a
public coinage the true quantity of silver that each coin contains and to return to individuals
who bring bars or ingots of Silver to it the same quantity in coins bearing a stamp or
certificate of the true quantity of Silver they contain.' Cantillon, *Essai*, 135–6, ed. Higgs
103: Hutcheson reviews the problems of barter, the advantages of the metals as an
acceptable equivalent in exchange, and the necessity of coinage (*System*, II.xii). Similar
arguments are developed in his *Short Introduction to Moral Philosophy* (Glasgow, 1747),
II.xii.
   [12] The aulanger sealed cloth which met prescribed standards and so ensured uniformity
of production. 10 Anne, c.23 (1711) in *Statutes of the Realm*, ix.682–4; 10 Anne, c.21 in
Ruffhead's edition provided for the stamping of linen in Scotland. 13 George I, c.26
(1726) detailed the standard length and breadth of cloth. See below, I.x.c.13.

of a publick stamp, the quantity and uniform goodness of those different commodities when brought to market.[13]

8   The first publick stamps of this kind that were affixed to the current metals, seem in many cases to have been intended to ascertain, what it was both most difficult and most important to ascertain, the goodness or fineness of the metal, and to have resembled the sterling mark which is at present affixed to plate and bars of silver, or the Spanish mark which is sometimes affixed to ingots of gold, and which being struck only upon one side of the piece, and not covering the whole surface, ascertains the fineness, but not the weight of the metal. Abraham weighs to Ephron the four hundred shekels of silver which he had agreed to pay for the field of Machpelah.[14] They are said however to be the current money of the merchant, and yet are received by weight and not by tale, in the same manner as ingots of gold and bars of silver are at present. The revenues of the antient Saxon kings of England are said to have been paid, not in money but in kind, that is, in victuals and provisions of all sorts.[15] William the Conqueror introduced the custom of paying them in money. This money, however, was, for a long time, received at the exchequer, by weight and not by tale.[16]

9   The inconveniency and difficulty of weighing those metals with exactness gave occasion to the institution of coins, of which the stamp, covering entirely both sides of the piece and sometimes [39] the edges too, was supposed to ascertain not only the fineness, but the weight of the metal. Such

[13] The subjects of the preceding paragraph are considered in LJ (A) vi.108–9 and LJ (B) 239, ed. Cannan 185. Cf. LJ (A) vi.114: 'It was necessary that the government should be at the trouble and expence of coinage; no other could find their interest in it. The stamp gives it no additionall value; it merely ascertains the value. The government found it in their interest to be at that expence, as money facilitated taxes and the intercourse by commerce, which as it enriched the people was beneficial to the government.' See below, I.v.38, where it is noted that the coinage was free in England.

[14] 'And Ephron answered Abraham . . . the land is worth four hundred shekels of silver . . . and Abraham weighed to Ephron the silver which he had named . . . four hundred shekels of silver, current money with the merchant. And the field of Ephron, which was in Machpelah . . . were made sure unto Abraham for a possession.' (Genesis 23: 14–18.)

[15] 'The revenues of the king seem to have consisted chiefly in his demesnes, which were large; and in the tolls and imports which he probably levied at discretion on the boroughs and sea-ports, that lay within his demesnes.' (D. Hume, *The History of England* (London, 1778), i.225.)

[16] '. . . when King *William* the First, for the better pay of his Warriors, caused the *Firmes*, which till his time, had for the most part been answered in Victuals, to be converted in *Pecuniam Numeratam* . . . the Money afterwards declining, and becoming worse, it was Ordained That the *Firmes* of Manors should not only be paid *ad Scalam*, but also *ad Pensam*, which latter was the paying as much money for a Pound *Sterling* as weighed Twelve Ounces *Troy*.' (W. Lowndes, *Report containing an Essay for the Amendment of the Silver Coins* (London, 1695), 4.) But as H. R. Loyn has pointed out, 'money was in general use for the last four centuries of Anglo-Saxon England' (*Anglo-Saxon England and the Norman Conquest* (London, 1962), 117).

coins, therefore, were received by tale as at present, without the trouble of
weighing.

10   The denominations of those coins seem originally to have expressed the
weight or quantity of metal contained in them. In the time of Servius
Tullius, who first coined money at Rome, the Roman As or Pondo contained a Roman pound of good copper.[17] It was divided in the same
manner as our Troyes pound, into twelve ounces, each of which contained
a real ounce of good copper. The English pound sterling, in the time of
Edward I., contained a pound, Tower weight, of silver of a known fineness.[18] The Tower pound seems to have been something more than the
Roman pound, and something less than the Troyes pound.[19] This last
was not introduced into the mint of England till the 18th of Henry VIII.[20]
The French livre contained in the time of Charlemagne a pound, Troyes
weight, of silver of a known fineness. The fair of Troyes in Champaign
was at that time frequented by all the nations of Europe, and the weights
and measures of so famous a market were generally known and esteemed.[21]
The Scots money pound contained, from the time of Alexander the First
to that of Robert Bruce, a pound of silver of the same weight and fineness
with the English pound sterling. English, French, and Scots pennies too,
contained all of them originally a real pennyweight of silver, the twentieth
part of an ounce, and the two-[40]hundred-and-fortieth part of a pound.
The shilling too seems originally to have been the denomination of a
weight. *When wheat is at twelve shillings the quarter*, says an antient statute
of Henry III. *then wastel bread of a farthing shall weigh eleven shillings and
four pence.*[22] The proportion, however, between the shilling and either
the penny on the one hand, or the pound on the other, seems not to have

---

[17] See IV.ix.47 where Smith comments on the price of the 'finer sort' of manufactures
in ancient Rome, and below I.v.24.

[18] These points appear in LJ (A) vi.111 and LJ (B) 239, ed. Cannan 186.

[19] A similar point is made in LJ (A) vi.112 and LJ (B) 240, ed. Cannan 187.

[20] '. . . the Tower weight does not seem to have been taken away before the 18th year of
the king's reign [Henry VIII]' (M. Folkes, *A Table of English Silver Coins* (London,
1745), 20). Harris commented that 'The *Tower weight* continued in use at the mint there,
from the conquest till the 18th year of the reign of Henry VIII; at which time it was laid
aside, and the *Troy weight* introduced in its stead' (*Essay*, i.50).

[21] The subjects of this sentence are considered in LJ (A) vi.111 and LJ (B) 240, ed.
Cannan 187. LJ (B) also adds at 304, ed. Cannan 234, that 'Till the sixteenth century all
commerce was carried on by fairs. The fairs of Bartholemew, of Leipsic, of Troy in Cham-
paigne, and even of Glasgow, are much talked of in antiquity.' In the latter passage from
LJ (B) Smith cited the use of fairs and staple towns as factors which contributed to the
slow progress of opulence in Europe.

[22] The statute is cited to the same end by Harris, *Essay*, i.50. Smith's library had a copy
of the *Statutes at Large from Magna Charta to the Twentieth Year of the Reign of King
George III*, 13 vols. (London, 1769–80). In the text (I.xi.e.20) Smith refers to this edition
of the Statutes by Ruffhead and takes his other references from it. In the present edition
statutes are cited according to the *Statutes of the Realm* for the period covered by that
edition, until the end of the reign of Queen Anne in 1713, and a cross-reference is given
to Ruffhead. Thereafter Ruffhead's edition is used. A 'Table of Variances' between the

been so constant and uniform as that between the penny and the pound. During the first race of the kings of France, the French sou or shilling appears upon different occasions to have contained five, twelve, twenty, ⁹and forty⁹ pennies. Among the antient Saxons a shilling appears at one time to have contained only five pennies,[23] and it is not improbable that it may have been as variable among them as among their neighbours, the antient Franks. From the time of Charlemagne among the French,[24] and from that of William the Conqueror among the English,[25] the proportion between the pound, the shilling, and the penny, seems to have been uniformly the same as at present, though the value of each has been very different. For in every country of the world, I believe, the avarice and injustice of princes and sovereign states, abusing the confidence of their subjects, have by degrees diminished the real quantity of metal, which had been originally contained in their coins. The Roman As, in the latter ages of the Republick, was reduced to the twenty-fourth part of its original value, and, instead of weighing a pound, came to weigh only [41] half an ounce.[26] The English pound and penny contain at present about a third only; the Scots pound and penny about a thirty-sixth; and the French pound and penny about a sixty-sixth part of their original value.[27] By means of those

⁹⁻⁹ forty, and forty-eight *1*

---

two editions is in *The Chronological Table of the Statutes* from which the dates of statutes are taken. The Assize of Bread and Ale, quoted here, is given various dates. *Statutes of the Realm*, i.199, n., gives the date as uncertain, but recognizes that the printed copies, including Ruffhead's, attributes it to 51 Henry III, which would make the date 1266–7. See also I.x.c.62, I.xi.e.6, 19–20.

[23] W. Fleetwood, *Chronicon Preciosum* (London, 1707), 30; Hume, *History of England* (1778), i.226.

[24] 'It is thought that the *livre*, or pound weight, of silver, was instituted as the *money integer*, by CHARLEMAGNE: And this he subdivided into *sols*, and *deniers*, which bore exactly the same proportion to the *pound*, as our *shillings* and *pence*, now do, to our *money pound*, or *pound sterling*.' (Harris, *Essay*, i.50.)

[25] 'It is thought that soon after the conquest a pound sterling was divided into twenty shillings.' Hume, *History of England* (1778), i.227.

[26] 'Next according to a law of Papirius *asses* weighing half an ounce were struck.' (Pliny, *Natural History*, XXXIII.xiii, translated by H. Rackham in Loeb Classical Library (1952), ix.39.) Also quoted in Montesquieu, *Esprit*, XXII.xi.3. See below, V.iii.61.

[27] Cf. 'Our money pound is at present . . . about one-third of what it was at the conquest . . . At the accession of King *James* I to this throne, the *Scotch money pound* was but equal to the $\frac{1}{12}$ of ours; and the *French livre* at present, only about half the value of the *Scotch pound*' (Harris, *Essay*, i.52n.). The problems of debasement are discussed at V.iii.59–64; in LJ (A) vi.114ff. and LJ (B) 240, ed. Cannan 186. The figures given in the text as regards the content of the English and Scots pound are cited at LJ (A) vi.116–17, and the French livre is said to have been reduced 'to less than one seventieth'. Smith also remarked with reference to Britain that 'still the coin is on a precarious footing, being under the management of the king and privy councill, as the parliament cannot legally intermeddle.' In LJ (A) ii.81 debasement is attributed to 'the difficulty of raising money' and the same point is made in LJ (B) 179–80, ed. Cannan 134, in the course of a discussion of the law of contract. In LJ (A) vi.114 and 118 debasement is attributed to the 'necessities or frauds of the government', cf. LJ (B) 241–2, ed. Cannan 187–8.

operations the princes and sovereign states which performed them were enabled, in appearance, to pay their debts and ʰtoʰ fulfil their engagements with a smaller quantity of silver than would otherwise have been requisite. It was indeed in appearance only; for their creditors were really defrauded of a part of what was due to them. All other debtors in the state were allowed the same privilege, and might pay with the same nominal sum of the new and debased coin whatever they had borrowed in the old.[28] Such operations, therefore, have always proved favourable to the debtor, and ruinous to the creditor, and have sometimes produced a greater and more universal revolution in the fortunes of private persons, than could have been occasioned by a very great publick calamity.[29]

11   It is in this manner that money has become in all civilized nations the universal instrument of commerce, by the intervention of which goods of all kinds are bought and sold, or exchanged for one another.[30]

12   What are the rules which men naturally observe in exchanging them either for money or for one another, I shall now proceed to examine. These rules determine what may be called the relative or exchangeable value of goods.

13   [42] The word VALUE, it is to be observed, has two different meanings, and sometimes expresses the utility of some particular object, and sometimes the power of purchasing other goods which the possession of that object conveys. The one may be called 'value in use;' the other, 'value in exchange.' The things which have the greatest value in use have frequently little or no value in exchange; and, on the contrary, those which have the greatest value in exchange have frequently little or no value in use. Nothing is more useful than water: but it will purchase scarce any thing; scarce any

ʰ⁻ʰ *om.* 6

---

[28] Cf. LJ (A) ii.80–1: 'Justice and equity plainly require that one should restore the same value as he received without regard to the nominal value of money . . . But the civil government in all countries have constituted the exact contrary of this.'

[29] Hutcheson develops a rather similar argument in the *System*, ii.60–1. Harris discusses the problem of debasement, and its impact on debtors and creditors, and those on fixed incomes, in the *Essay*, Part II, chapters 1, 10, 17, 18. See also Steuart *Principles*, III.2.vi and III.1.vi. The impact of debasement on creditors and debtors is considered in LJ (A) vi.119–20 where Smith also points out that a change in the coinage 'necessarily embarrasses commerce' since buyers and sellers will delay purchases and sales due to the prevailing state of uncertainty: 'And as both stand off in this manner, the merchant choosing rather to keep up his goods than to sell them too low, a stagnation must necessarily follow in the exchange of commodities; and money in some measure ceases to answer its end as a measure of value.' Cf. LJ (B) 242, ed. Cannan 188: 'People are disposed to keep their goods from the market, as they know not what they will get for them. Thus a stagnation of commerce is occasioned. Besides, the debasing of the coin takes away the public faith.' Montesquieu also noted that 'Trade is in its own nature extremely uncertain; and it is a great evil to add a new uncertainty to that which is founded on the nature of the thing' (*Esprit*, XXII.iii.4).

[30] In the lectures, the discussion of money proceeds from this point to the rejection of the view that opulence consists in money and to the examination of banks and paper money. The same order of argument is suggested in ED 4.1.

thing can be had in exchange for it. A diamond, on the contrary, has scarce any value in use; but a very great quantity of other goods may frequently be had in exchange for it.[31]

[31] Smith throws further light on the 'paradox of value' at I.xi.c.31, 32 and IV.vii.a.19. He also points out at I.xi.c.3 that under some circumstances goods which are of great value in use have little or no value in exchange. Cf. LJ (B) 205–6, ed. Cannan 157: 'Cheapness is in fact the same thing with plenty. It is only on account of the plenty of water that it is so cheap as to be got for the lifting, and on account of the scarcity of diamonds (for their real use seems not yet to be discovered) that they are so dear.'
  The so-called paradox of value figures in Smith's lectures on two occasions. In the first place, Smith set out to explain the grounds of preference 'which give occasion to pleasure and pain' (LJ (B) 209, ed. Cannan 159) in stating the general thesis that all the arts are subservient to the 'natural wants' of man. In this context Smith explained that men require basic necessities, but also that his delicacy of taste gives occasion to 'many insignificant demands'. For example he argued that qualities such as colour or variety constitute grounds of preference and thus help to explain why we place a value on commodities—including the precious stones. In LJ (A) vi.13–4 the 'paradox' is examined in exactly the same context and the grounds of preference summarized as 'colour, form, variety or rarity, and imitation' (LJ (A) vi.16). (It is interesting to note that Smith began the economic sections of his lectures in this way and that these passages should have been omitted from the WN.) The second example occurs in the course of a discussion of the determinants of price, which are stated to be (LJ (B) 227–8, ed. Cannan 176–7):

1st, The demand or need for the commodity. There is no demand for a thing of little use; it is not a rational object of desire.
2ndly, the abundance or scarcity of the commodity in proportion to the need of it. If the commodity be scarce, the price is raised, but if the quantity be more than is sufficient to supply the demand, the price falls. Thus it is that diamonds and other precious stones are dear, while iron, which is much more usefull, is so many times cheaper, tho' this depends principally on the last cause, viz:
3rdly, the riches or poverty of those who demand.

Smith was thus able to explain the paradox, while pointing out that in some conditions, such as the rich merchant lost in the deserts of Arabia, the price of water could be very high. The same examples occur in LJ (A) vi.70–5 where Smith also indicates that the price of diamonds would sink if 'by industry their quantity could be multiplied'. The determinants of market price are summarized in ED 3.1 and LJ (A) vi.70. See below I.vii.
  The contrast between the value of water and diamonds is stated and explained by Samuel von Pufendorf, who also cites Plato's *Euthydemus* 304B: 'Only what is rare is valuable, and water, which is the best of all things, . . . is also the cheapest.' *De Jure Naturae et Gentium*, V.i. 6, see generally V.i. and the same author's *De Officio Hominis et Civis Juxta Legem Naturalem*, I.xiv, 'On Value'. The latter work is an abridgement of the former. Cf. Grotius, *De Jure Belli ac Pacis*, II.xii, 14, and see below, I.xi. c.31–3. John Law, *Money and Trade Considered*, 4, also noted that:

Goods have a Value from the Uses they are apply'd to; And their Value is greater or Lesser, not so much from their more or less valuable, or necessary Uses: As from the greater or lesser Quantity of them in proportion to the Demand for them. Example Water is of great use, yet of little Value; Because the Quantity of Water is much greater than the Demand for it. Diamonds are of little use, yet of great Value, because the Demand for Diamonds is much greater, than the Quantity of them.

A similar example appears in Harris, *Essay* i.5., and cf. Cantillon, *Essai*, 36, ed. Higgs 29, and Mandeville, *The Fable of the Bees*, pt. ii.423, ed. Kaye ii.350. In his *System*, ii.53–4, Hutcheson remarked that:

14   In order to investigate the principles which regulate the exchangeable value of commodities, I shall endeavour to shew,

15   First, what is the real measure of this exchangeable value; or, wherein consists the real price of all commodities,

16   Secondly, what are the different parts of which this real price is composed or made up.

17   And, lastly, what are the different circumstances which sometimes raise some or all of these different parts of price above, and sometimes sink them below their natural or ordinary rate; or, what are the causes which sometimes hinder the market price, that is, the actual price of commodities, from coinciding exactly with what may be called their natural price.

18   [43] I shall endeavour to explain, as fully and distinctly as I can, those three subjects in the three following chapters, for which I must very earnestly entreat both the patience and attention of the reader: his patience in order to examine a detail which may perhaps in some places appear unnecessarily tedious; and his attention in order to understand what may, perhaps, after the fullest explication which I am capable of giving ⁱofⁱ it, appear still in some degree obscure. I am always willing to run some hazard of being tedious in order to be sure that I am perspicuous; and after taking the utmost pains that I can to be perspicuous, some obscurity may still appear to remain upon a subject ʲ in its own nature extremely abstracted.[32]

ⁱ⁻ⁱ *om. 6*   ʲ which is *1*

The natural ground of all value or price is some sort of use which goods afford in life; this is prerequisite to all estimation. But the prices or values in commerce do not at all follow the real use or importance of goods for the support, or natural pleasure of life. By the wisdom and goodness of Providence there is such plenty of the means of support, and of natural pleasures, that their prices are much lower than of many other things which to a wise man seem of little use. But when some aptitude to human use is presupposed, we shall find that the prices of goods depend on these two jointly, the *demand* on account of some use or other which many desire, and the *difficulty* of acquiring, or cultivating for human use.
A similar argument appears in his *Short Introduction*, 209–10.

[32] It is interesting that Steuart also found difficulty in dealing with the determinants of price, and that he too should have felt moved to confess that 'I feel a great want of language to express my ideas, and it is for this reason I employ so many examples, the better to communicate certain combinations of them, which otherwise would be inextricable' (*Principles*, i.197, ed. A. S. Skinner (Edinburgh and Chicago, 1966), i.172).

CHAPTER V

Of the real and nominal Price of Commodities, or of their Price in Labour, and their Price in Money

1 EVERY man is rich or poor according to the degree in which he can afford to enjoy the necessaries, conveniencies, and amusements of human life.[1] But after the division of labour has once thoroughly taken place, it is but a very small part of these with which a man's own labour can supply him. The far greater part of them he must derive from the labour of other [44] people, and he must be rich or poor according to the quantity of that labour which he can command, or which he can afford to purchase. The value of any commodity, therefore, to the person who possesses it, and who means not to use or consume it himself, but to exchange it for other commodities, is equal to the quantity of labour which it enables him to purchase or command.[2] Labour, therefore, is the real measure of the exchangeable value of all commodities.[3]

2 The real price of every thing, what every thing really costs to the man who wants to acquire it, is the toil and trouble of acquiring it.[4] What every thing is really worth to the man who has acquired it, and who wants to dispose of it or exchange it for something else, is the toil and trouble which it can save to himself, and which it can impose upon other people. What is bought with money or with goods is purchased by labour as much as what we acquire by the toil of our own body.[5] That money or those goods indeed save us this toil. They contain the value of a certain quantity of labour

[1] Cantillon, *Essai*, 1–2, ed. Higgs 1, states that 'The Land is the Source of Matter from whence all Wealth is produced. The Labour of man is the Form which produces it: and Wealth in itself is nothing but the Maintenance, Conveniences, and Superfluities of Life.' Harris, *Essay*, i.2, makes a similar point: '*wealth* or *riches* consist either in a propriety in land, or in the products of land and labour.' He also remarks at i.31 that 'labour, skill, and industry, are the true sources of wealth'.

[2] Cf. Harris, *Essay*, i.9: 'Men's various necessities and appetites, oblige them to part with their own commodities, at a rate proportionable to the labour and skill that had been bestowed upon those things, which they want in exchange.' Harris also stated that 'as in most productions, *labour* hath the greatest share; the value of labour is to be reckoned the chief standard that regulates the values of all commodities'.

[3] In commenting on this passage Pownall argued that labour cannot be the basis of exchangeable value: 'We must consider also the objects on which labour is employed; for it is not simply the *labour*, but the *labour mixed with these objects*, that is exchanged; it is *the composite article, the laboured article*; Some part of the exchangeable value is derived from the object itself, . . .' (*Letter*, 9). The discussion of value occurs mainly at pp. 9–13.

[4] Cf. LJ (A) i.59: 'One does not form such an attachment to a thing he has . . . acquired by little labour, as he does to what he has got by great pains and industry; . . .'

[5] 'Every thing in the world is purchased by labour; and our passions are the only causes of labour.' (D. Hume, 'Of Commerce', *Essays Moral, Political and Literary*, ed. Green and Grose, i.293.)

which we exchange for what is supposed at the time to contain the value of an equal quantity.[6] Labour was the first price, the original purchase-money that was paid for all things.[7] It was not by gold or by silver, but by labour, that all the wealth of the world was originally purchased;[8] and its value, to those who possess it and who want to exchange it for some new productions, is precisely equal to the quantity of labour which it can enable them to purchase or command.

3 [45] [a]Wealth, as Mr. Hobbes says, is power.[9] But the person who either acquires, or succeeds to a great fortune, does not necessarily acquire or succeed to any political power, either civil or military. His fortune may, perhaps, afford him the means of acquiring both, but the mere possession of that fortune does not necessarily convey to him either. The power which that possession immediately and directly conveys to him, is the power of purchasing; a certain command over all the labour, or over all the produce of labour which is then in the market. His fortune is greater or less, precisely in proportion to the extent of this power; or to the quantity either of other men's labour, or, what is the same thing, of the produce of other men's labour, which it enables him to purchase or command. The exchangeable value of every thing must always be precisely equal to the extent of this power which it conveys to its owner.[a]

4 But though labour be the real measure of the exchangeable value of all commodities, it is not that by which their value is commonly estimated. It is often difficult to ascertain the proportion between two different quantities of labour. The time spent in two different sorts of work will not always alone determine this proportion. The different degrees of hardship endured, and of ingenuity exercised, must likewise be taken into account.[10] There may be more labour in an hour's hard work than in two hours easy business; or in an hour's application to a trade which it cost ten years labour to learn, than in a [46] month's industry at an ordinary and obvious employment. But it is not easy to find any accurate measure either of hardship or ingenuity. In exchanging indeed the different pro-

---

[a-a] 2A–6

[6] In commenting on this passage, Pownall inquired (11): 'What then is to be the real standard or measure? Not labour itself. What is to give the respective estimation in which each holds his labour? ... value cannot be fixed by and in the nature of labour; it will depend upon the nature of the feelings and the activity of the persons estimating it.'

[7] See below, I.xi.e.34: 'Labour . . . is the ultimate price which is paid for everything.'

[8] 'It is . . . the Labour of the Poor, and not the high and low value that is set on Gold and Silver, which all the Comforts of Life must arise from.' (Mandeville, *The Fable of the Bees*, pt. i.345, ed. Kaye i.301.)

[9] 'Riches joined with liberality, is power; because it procureth friends, and servants; without liberality, not so; because in this case they defend not; but expose men to envy, as a prey'. (T. Hobbes, *Leviathan*, I.x.) See below II.v.31. Smith comments on the 'doctrine of Hobbes' in TMS VII.iii.2.

[10] The allowance for hardship is mentioned at I.vi.2 and, for example, at I.x.b.2,15.

ductions of different sorts of labour for one another, some allowance is commonly made for both. It is adjusted, however, not by any accurate measure, but by the higgling and bargaining of the market, according to that sort of rough equality which, though not exact, is sufficient for carrying on the business of common life.

5   Every commodity besides, is more frequently exchanged for, and thereby compared with, other commodities than with labour. It is more natural, therefore, to estimate its exchangeable value by the quantity of some other commodity than by that of the labour which it can purchase. The greater part of people too understand better what is meant by a quantity of a particular commodity, than by a quantity of labour. The one is a plain palpable object; the other an abstract notion, which, though it can be made sufficiently intelligible, is not altogether so natural and obvious.

6   But when barter ceases, and money has become the common instrument of commerce, every particular commodity is more frequently exchanged for money than for any other commodity. The butcher seldom carries his beef or his mutton to the baker, or the brewer, in order to exchange them for bread or for beer, but he carries them to the market, where he exchanges them for money, and afterwards exchanges that [47] money for bread and for beer. The quantity of money which he gets for them regulates too the quantity of bread and beer which he can afterwards purchase. It is more natural and obvious to him, therefore, to estimate their value by the quantity of money, the commodity for which he immediately exchanges them, than by that of bread and beer, the commodities for which he can exchange them only by the intervention of another commodity; and rather to say that his butcher's meat is worth threepence or fourpence a pound, than that it is worth three or four pounds of bread, or three or four quarts of small beer. Hence it comes to pass, that the exchangeable value of every commodity is more frequently estimated by the quantity of money, than by the quantity either of labour or of any other commodity which can be had in exchange for it.[11]

7   Gold and silver, however, like every other commodity, vary in their value, are sometimes cheaper and sometimes dearer, sometimes of easier and sometimes of more difficult purchase. The quantity of labour which any particular quantity of them can purchase or command, or the quantity of other goods which it will exchange for, depends always upon the fertility or barrenness of the mines which happen to be known about the time when such exchanges are made. The discovery of the abundant mines of America reduced, in the sixteenth century, the value of gold and silver in Europe to about a third of what it had been before.[12] As it cost less labour [48]

[11] Smith comments on the confusion between money and wealth at IV.i.1 in the course of developing his critique of the mercantile 'fallacy'.

[12] The reduction in the value of the metals consequent on the discovery of the American mines is discussed in I.xi.f.

to bring those metals from the mine to the market, so when they were brought *b*thither*b* they could purchase or command less labour; and this revolution in their value, though perhaps the greatest, is by no means the only one of which history gives some account.[13] But as a measure of quantity, such as the natural foot, fathom, or handful, which is continually varying in its own quantity, can never be an accurate measure of the quantity of other things; so a commodity which is itself continually varying in its own value, can never be an accurate measure of the value of other commodities.[14] Equal quantities of labour, *c* at all times and places, *d*may be to*d* be of equal value to the labourer. *e*In his ordinary state of health, strength and spirits; in the ordinary degree of his skill and dexterity,[15] he*e* must always lay down the same portion of his ease, his liberty, and his happiness.[16] The price which he pays must always be the same, whatever may be the quantity of goods which he receives in return for it. Of these, indeed, it may sometimes purchase a greater and sometimes a smaller quantity; but it is their value which varies, not that of the labour which purchases them. At all times and places that is dear which it is difficult to come at, or which it costs much labour to acquire; and that cheap

---

b–b there *1*   *c* must *1*   *d–d* 2–6   *e–e* He *1*

[13] Cantillon comments, *Essai*, 127–9, ed. Higgs 97: 'The real or intrinsic Value of Metals is like everything else proportionable to the Land and Labour that enters into their production. The outlay on the Land for this production is considerable only so far as the Owner of the Mine can obtain a profit from the work of the Miners when the veins are unusually rich. The Land needed for the subsistence of the Miners and Workers, that is the Mining Labour, is often the principal expense and the Ruin of the Proprietor. The Market Value of Metals, as of other Merchandise or Produce, is sometimes above, sometimes below, the intrinsic Value, and varies with their plenty or scarcity according to the demand.'

[14] LJ (A) vi.100 comments: 'All measures were originally taken from the human body; a fathom was measured by the stretch of a mans arms, a yard was the half of this . . . These natural measures could not long satisfy them, as they would vary greatly . . . Prudent men therefore contrived, and the publick established, artificiall yards, fathoms, feet, inches, etc. . . . For the same reason they converted the originall and naturall measures of value into others not so naturall, but more convenient . . .' Cf. LJ (B) 236, ed. Cannan 183.

[15] The passage 'In his ordinary state of health . . . dexterity' first appeared in ed. 2 and may reflect Smith's response to a comment which Pownall had made with regard to the original passage. Pownall had remarked that 'even the same person will, in different habits, relations and circumstances of life, estimate . . . his ease, liberty, and desire of happinness differently'. On this ground, Pownall questioned the validity of Smith's choice of labour as the ultimate standard of value (12). The complex meaning of the disutility of labour is discussed in I.x.b. It is pointed out at I.xi.p.8 that the proprietors of land are the only group in society who receive a revenue which costs them neither 'labour nor care'.

[16] Cf. Hutcheson, *System*, ii.58: 'a day's digging or ploughing was as uneasy to a man a thousand years ago as it is now, tho' he could not then get so much silver for it'. In his essay 'Of Money' Hume emphasized the disutility of work and also the point that wages could be regarded as the compensation for this disutility (*Essays Moral, Political and Literary*, ed. Green and Grose, i.313–14). In 'Of Refinement in the Arts', however, he made an additional point in stating that men frequently 'enjoy, as their reward, the occupation itself, as well as those pleasures which are the fruit of their labour' (ibid., i.301).

which is to be had easily, or with very little labour. Labour alone, therefore, never varying in its own value, is alone the ultimate and real standard
by which the value of all commodities can at all times and places be esti-   ?
mated and [49] compared. It is their real price; money is their nominal
price only.

8   But though equal quantities of labour are always of equal value to the
labourer, yet to the person who employs him they appear sometimes to be
of greater and sometimes of smaller value. He purchases them sometimes
with a greater and sometimes with a smaller quantity of goods, and to him
the price of labour seems to vary like that of all other things. It appears to
him dear in the one case, and cheap in the other. In reality, however, it is
the goods which are cheap in the one case, and dear in the other.

9   In this popular sense, therefore, labour, like commodities, may be said
to have a real and a nominal price. Its real price may be said to consist in
the quantity of the necessaries and conveniencies of life which are given
for it; its nominal price, in the quantity of money. The labourer is rich or   ?
poor, is well or ill rewarded, in proportion to the real, not to the nominal
price of his labour.[17]

10   The distinction between the real and the nominal price of commodities
and labour, is not a matter of mere speculation, but may sometimes be of
considerable use in practice. The same real price is always of the same value;
but on account of the variations in the value of gold and silver, the same
nominal price is sometimes of very different values. When a landed estate,
therefore, is sold with a reservation of a perpetual rent, if it is intended that
this rent should always be of the same value, it is of importance [50] to the
family in whose favour it is reserved, that it should not consist in a particular sum of money.[18] Its value would in this case be liable to variations of two different kinds; first, to those which arise from the different
quantities of gold and silver which are contained at different times in coin
of the same denomination; and, secondly, to those which arise from the
different values of equal quantities of gold and silver at different times.

11   Princes and sovereign states have frequently fancied that they had a

[17] LJ (A) vi.36 states that 'We are not to judge whether labour be cheap or dear by
the moneyd price of it, but by the quantity of the necessaries of life which may be got
by the fruits of it.' The same point is made at 52. Cf. Cantillon, *Essai*, 149–50, ed. Higgs
113:

> Gold and Silver, like other merchandise and raw produce, can only be produced at
> costs roughly proportionable to the value set upon them, and whatever Man produces
> by Labour, this Labour must furnish his maintenance. It is the great principle one hears
> from the mouths of the humble classes who have no part in our speculations, and who
> live by their Labour or their Undertakings. "Everybody must live".

[18] 'Be above all things careful how you are to make any composition or agreement for
any long space of years to receive a certain price of money for the corn that is due to you,
although for the present it may seem a tempting bargain.' (W. Fleetwood, *Chronicon
Preciosum*, 174.)

temporary interest to diminish the quantity of pure metal contained in their coins; but they seldom have fancied that they had any to augment it. The quantity of metal contained in the coins, I believe of all nations has, accordingly, been almost continually diminishing, and hardly ever augmenting.[19] Such variations therefore tend almost always to diminish the value of a money rent.

12   The discovery of the mines of America diminished the value of gold and silver in Europe. This diminution, it is commonly supposed, though, I apprehend, without any certain proof, is still going on gradually, and is likely to continue to do so for a long time.[20] Upon this supposition, therefore, such variations are more likely to diminish, than to augment the value of a money rent, even though it should be stipulated to be paid, not in such a quantity of coined money of such a denomination (in so many pounds sterling, for example), but in so many ounces either of pure silver, or of silver of a certain standard.

13   [51] The rents which have been reserved in corn have preserved their value much better than those which have been reserved in money, even where the denomination of the coin has not been altered.[21] By the 18th of Elizabeth[22] it was enacted, That a third of the rent of all college leases should be reserved in corn, to be paid, either in kind, or according to the current prices at the nearest publick market. The money arising from this corn rent, though originally but a third of the whole, is in the present times, according to Doctor Blackstone, commonly near double of what arises from the other two-thirds.[23] The old money rents of colleges must, according to this account, have sunk almost to a fourth part of their ancient value; or are worth little more than a fourth part of the corn which they were formerly worth. But since the reign of Philip and Mary the denomination of the English coin has undergone little or no alteration, and the same number of pounds, shillings and pence have contained very nearly the same quantity of pure silver. This degradation, therefore, in the value of the money rents of colleges, has arisen altogether from the degradation in the value of silver.

14   When the degradation in the value of silver is combined with the diminution of the quantity of it contained in the coin of the same denomination,

---

[19] See above, I.iv.10.   [20] But see below, I.xi.h.11.

[21] Hutcheson also remarked that it would be impossible to settle 'fixed salaries' in monetary terms, and added that 'The most invariable salary would be so many days labour of men, or a fixed quantity of goods produced by the plain inartificial labours, such goods as answer the ordinary purposes of life. Quantities of grain come nearest to such a standard.' (*System*, ii.62–3.)

[22] 18 Elizabeth I.c.6 (1575), applicable to Oxford, Cambridge, Winchester, and Eton.

[23] 'Though the rent so reserved in corn was at first but one third of the old rent, or half of what was still reserved in money, yet now the proportion is nearly inverted; and the money arising from corn rents is, *communibus annis*, almost double to the rents reserved in money.' (W. Blackstone, *Commentaries on the Laws of England* (Oxford, 1765–9), ii.322.)

the loss is frequently still greater. In Scotland, where the denomination of the coin has undergone much greater alterations than it ever did in England, and in France, where it has [52] undergone still greater than it ever did in Scotland,[24] some antient rents, originally of considerable value, have in this manner been reduced almost to nothing.

15   Equal quantities of labour will at distant times be purchased more nearly with equal quantities of corn, the subsistence of the labourer, than with equal quantities of gold and silver, or perhaps of any other commodity.[25] Equal quantities of corn, therefore, will, at distant times, be more nearly of the same real value, or enable the possessor to purchase or command more nearly the same quantity of the labour of other people. They will do this, I say, more nearly than equal quantities of almost any other commodity; for even equal quantities of corn will not do it exactly. The subsistence of the labourer, or the real price of labour, as I shall endeavour to show hereafter,[26] is very different upon different occasions; more liberal in a society advancing to opulence than in one that is standing still; and in one that is standing still than in one that is going backwards. Every other commodity, however, will at any particular time purchase a greater or smaller quantity of labour in proportion to the quantity of subsistence which it can purchase at that time. A rent therefore reserved in corn is liable only to the variations in the quantity of labour which a certain quantity of corn can purchase. But a rent reserved in any other commodity is liable, not only to the variations in the quantity of labour which any particular quantity of corn can [53] purchase, but to the variations in the quantity of corn which can be purchased by any particular quantity of that commodity.

16   Though the real value of a corn rent, it is to be observed however, varies much less from century to century than that of a money rent, it varies much more from year to year. The money price of labour, as I shall endeavour to show hereafter,[27] does not fluctuate from year to year with the money price of corn, but seems to be every where accommodated, not to the temporary or occasional, but to the average or ordinary price of that necessary of life. The average or ordinary price of corn again is regulated, as I shall likewise endeavour to show hereafter, by the value of silver, by the richness or barrenness of the mines which supply the market with that metal, or by the quantity of labour which must be employed, and consequently of corn which must be consumed, in order to bring any particular

[24] See above, I.iv.10.
[25] Cf. Hutcheson, *System*, ii.58: 'Properly, the value of labour, grain, and cattle, are always pretty much the same, as they afford the same uses in life, where no new inventions of tillage, or pasturage, cause a greater quantity in proportion to the demand. 'Tis the metal chiefly that has undergone the great change of value, since these metals have been in greater plenty . . .'
[26] In I.viii.
[27] See below I.viii.31 and cf. I.viii.52–7.

quantity of ⸀silver⸍ from the mine to the market. But the value of silver, though it sometimes varies greatly from century to century, seldom varies much from year to year, but frequently continues the same, or very nearly the same, for half a century or a century together.[28] The ordinary or average money price of corn, therefore, may, during so long a period, continue the same or very nearly the same too, and along with it the money price of labour, provided, at least, the society continues, in other respects, in the same or nearly in the same condition. In the mean time the temporary and [54] occasional price of corn may frequently be double, one year, of what it had been the year before, ōr fluctuate⸢, for example,⸣ from five and twenty to fifty shillings the quarter ⁱ . But when corn is at the latter price, not only the nominal, but the real value of a corn rent will be double of what it is when at the former, or will command double the quantity either of labour or of the greater part of other commodities; the money price of labour, and along with it that of most other things, continuing the same during all these fluctuations.

17 | Labour, therefore, it appears evidently, is the only universal, as well as the only accurate measure of value, or the only standard by which we can compare the values of different commodities at all times and at all places. We cannot estimate, it is allowed, the real value of different commodities from century to century by the quantities of silver which were given for them. We cannot estimate it from year to year by the quantities of corn. By the quantities of labour we can, with the greatest accuracy, estimate it both from century to century and from year to year. From century to century, corn is ⸀a⸍ better measure than silver, because, from century to century, equal quantities of corn will command the same quantity of labour more nearly than equal quantities of silver. From year to year, on the contrary, silver is a better measure than corn, because equal quantities of it will more nearly command the same quantity of labour.[29]

⸀⸍ it *1*   ⸢⸣ *2–6*   ⁱ for example *1*   ⸀⸍ om. *6*

[28] The relative stability of the value of the metals is discussed at I.xi.g.37.

[29] Locke (*Considerations of the lowering of Interest and raising the Value of Money* (1691), *Works* (London, 1823), v.47) commented: 'Wheat, therefore, in this part of the world, (and that grain, which is the constant general food of any other country) is the fittest measure to judge of the altered value of things, in any long tract of time: and therefore, wheat here, rice in Turkey, etc. is the fittest thing to reserve a rent in, which is designed to be constantly the same for all future ages. But money is the best measure of the altered value of things in a few years: because its vent is the same, and its quantity alters slowly. But wheat, or any other grain, cannot serve instead of money, because of its bulkiness, and too quick change of its quantity.' Harris, *Essay*, i.62,n., remarked on Locke:

> Mr Locke well observes, that that grain which is the most constant and general food of any country, as *wheat* in *England*, and *rice* in *Turkey*, is the most likely thing to keep the same proportion to its vent for a long course of time; and therefore the fittest thing to reserve a rent in, which is designed to be constantly the same in all future ages; and the fittest measure whereby to judge of the altered values of things in any long tract of time.

A similar point appears in Pufendorf, *De Jure*, V.i,15.

18   [55] But though in establishing perpetual rents, or even in letting very long leases, it may be of use to distinguish between real and nominal price, it is of none in buying and selling, the more common and ordinary transactions of human life.

19   At the same time and place the real and the nominal price of all commodities are exactly in proportion to one another. The more or less money you get for any commodity, in the London market, for example, the more or less labour it will at that time and place enable you to purchase or command. At the same time and place, therefore, money is the exact measure of the real exchangeable value of all commodities. It is so, however, at the same time and place only.

20   Though at distant places, there is no regular proportion between the real and the money price of commodities, yet the merchant who carries goods from the one to the other has nothing to consider but *their* money price, or the difference between the quantity of silver for which he buys them, and that for which he is likely to sell them. Half an ounce of silver at Canton in China may command a greater quantity both of labour and of the necessaries and conveniencies of life, than an ounce at London. A commodity, therefore, which sells for half an ounce of silver at Canton may there be really dearer, of more real importance to the man who possesses it there, than *a commodity* which sells for an ounce at London *is* to the man who possesses it at Lon-[56]don. If a London merchant, however, can buy at Canton for half an ounce of silver, a commodity which he can afterwards sell at London for an ounce, he gains a hundred per cent. by the bargain, just as much as if an ounce of silver was at London exactly of the same value as at Canton. It is of no importance to him that half an ounce of silver at Canton would have given him the command of more labour and of a greater quantity of the necessaries and conveniencies of life than an ounce can do at London. An ounce at London will always give him the command of double the quantity of all these which half an ounce could have done there, and this is precisely what he wants.

21   As it is the nominal or money price of goods, therefore, which finally determines the prudence or imprudence of all purchases and sales, and thereby regulates almost the whole business of common life in which price is concerned, we cannot wonder that it should have been so much more attended to than the real price.

22   In such *a* work as this, however, it may sometimes be of use to compare the different real values of a particular commodity at different times and places, or the different degrees of power over the labour of other people which it may, upon different occasions, have given to those who possessed it. We must in this case compare, not so much the different quantities of silver for which it was commonly sold, as the different quantities of labour

---

j–j the 6   *k–k* one *1*   *l–l* 2–6   *m–m* om. 4 ⟨corrected 4e–6.⟩

which those different quantities of silver could have purchased. [57] But the current prices of labour at distant times and places can scarce ever be known with any degree of exactness. Those of corn, though they have in few places been regularly recorded, are in general better known and have been more frequently taken notice of by historians and other writers.[30] We must generally, therefore, content ourselves with them, not as being always exactly in the same proportion as the current prices of labour, but as being the nearest approximation which can commonly be had to that proportion. I shall hereafter have occasion to make several comparisons of this kind.[31]

23   In the progress of industry, commercial nations have found it convenient to coin several different metals into money; gold for larger payments, silver for purchases of moderate value, and copper, or some other coarse metal, for those of still smaller consideration. They have always, however, considered one of those metals as more perculiarly the measure of value than any of the other two; and this preference seems generally to have been given to the metal which they happened first to make use of as the instrument of commerce. Having once begun to use it as their standard, which they must have done when they had no other money, they have generally continued to do so even when the necessity was not the same.

24   The Romans are said to have had nothing but copper money till within five years before the [58] first Punic war*, when they first began to coin silver. Copper, therefore, appears to have continued always the measure of value in that republick. At Rome all accounts appear to have been kept, and the value of all estates to have been computed either in *Asses* or in *Sestertii*. The *As* was always the denomination of a copper coin. The word *Sestertius* signifies two *Asses* and a half. Though the *Sestertius*, therefore, was °originally° a silver coin, its value was estimated in copper. At Rome, one who owed a great deal of money, was said to have a great deal of other people's copper.[32]

25   The northern nations who established themselves upon the ruins of the Roman empire, seem to have had silver money from the first beginning of their settlements, and not to have known either gold or copper coins for several ages thereafter. There were silver coins in England in the time of

---

ⁿ* Pliny, lib.xxxiii.c.3.ⁿ ['Silver was first coined in the 485th year of the city, in the consulship of Quintus Ogulnius and Gaius Fabius, five years before the first Punic War.' (Pliny, *Natural History*, XXXIII, xiii translated by H. Rackham in Loeb Classical Library (1952), ix.37.)]

ⁿ⁻ⁿ 2–6   °⁻° always 1–2

---

[30] Smith expressed doubts as to the accuracy of historians at I.xi.e.3,24.
[31] See below, I.xi, *passim*.
[32] See above I.iv.5,6. The silver *denarius* was first struck in 268 B.C. though there may have been Roman issues of silver coins of Greek denomination a little earlier. The Athenian coinage had silver, gold and bronze coins much earlier and influenced the Roman practice through Carthage. E. V. Morgan, *A History of Money* (London 1965), 15–16.

the Saxons;[33] but there was little gold coined till the time of Edward III. nor any copper till that of James I. of Great Britain. In England, therefore, and for the same reason, I believe, in all other modern nations of Europe, all accounts are kept, and the value of all goods and of all estates is generally computed in silver: and when we mean to express the amount of a person's fortune, we seldom mention the number of guineas, but the number of pounds *sterling* which we suppose would be given for it.[34]

26   [59] *Originally, in* all countries, I believe a legal tender of payment could *be made *only* in the coin of that metal, * which was peculiarly considered as the standard or measure of value. In England, gold was not considered as a legal tender for a long time after it was coined into money. The proportion between the values of gold and silver money was not fixed by any public law or proclamation; but was left to be settled by the market.[35] If a debtor offered payment in gold, the creditor might either reject such payment altogether, or accept of it at such a valuation of the gold as he and his debtor could agree upon. Copper is not at present a legal tender, except in the change of the smaller silver coins. In this state of things the distinction between the metal which was the standard, and that which was not the standard, was something more than a nominal distinction.

27   In process of time, and as people became gradually more familiar with the use of the different metals in coin, and consequently better acquainted with the proportion between their respective values, it has in most countries, I believe, been found convenient to ascertain this proportion, and to declare by a public law that a guinea, for example, of such a weight and fineness, should exchange for one-and-twenty shillings, or be a legal tender for a debt of that *amount*.[36] In this state of things, and during the continuance of any one regulated proportion of this kind, the distinction between the metal which is the standard and that which is not the [60] standard, becomes little more than a nominal distinction.

28   In consequence of any change, however, in this regulated proportion, this distinction becomes, or at least seems to become, something more than

---

p-p 2–6   q-q In *1*   r originally *1*   s-s 2–6   t only *1*   u-u sum *1*

[33] The *sceattas*, referred to as 'pennies' in the late seventh century. Morgan, *Money*, 18.

[34] A similar point is made in LJ (B) 239, ed. Cannan 186. Harris remarked in *Essay*, i.59–60: 'All nations having, for so many ages, made use of silver for the standard measure of the values of other things; that alone, seems to be a sufficient reason for continuing the same standard.'

[35] LJ (B) 243, ed. Cannan 189 stated that: 'The different coins are regulated not by the caprice of the government, but by the market price of gold and silver, and according to this the proportion of gold and silver is settled.' A similar point is made in LJ (A) vi.125.

[36] As A. Feaveryear has pointed out recently, the situation was not reached quite so easily as may be inferred. When the guinea was first issued in 1663, it was undervalued by the Mint. (*The Pound Sterling* (Oxford, 1963), 97–8, 120–1, 154.)

nominal again. If the regulated value of a guinea, for example, was either reduced to twenty, or raised to two-and-twenty shillings, all accounts being kept and almost all obligations for debt being expressed in silver money, the greater part of payments could in either case be made with the same quantity of silver money as before; but would require very different quantities of gold money; a greater in the one case, and a smaller in the other. Silver would appear to be more invariable in its value than gold. Silver would appear to measure the value of gold, and gold would not appear to measure the value of silver. The value of gold would seem to depend upon the quantity of silver which it would exchange for; and the value of silver would not seem to depend upon the quantity of gold which it would exchange for. This difference, however, would be altogether owing to the custom of keeping accounts, and of expressing the amount of all great and small sums rather in silver than in gold money. One of Mr Drummond's notes for five-and-twenty or fifty guineas would, after an alteration of this kind, be still payable with five-and-twenty or fifty guineas in the same manner as before. It would, after such an alteration, be payable with the same quantity of gold as before, but with [61] very different quantities of silver. In the payment of such a note, gold would appear to be more invariable in its value than silver. Gold would appear to measure the value of silver, and silver would not appear to measure the value of gold.[37] If the custom of keeping accounts, and of expressing promissory notes and other obligations for money in this manner, should ever become general, gold, and not silver, would be considered as the metal which was peculiarly the standard or measure of value.

29   In reality, during the continuance of any one regulated proportion between the respective values of the different metals in coin, the value of the most precious metal regulates the value of the whole coin. Twelve copper pence contain half a pound, avoirdupois, of copper, of not the best quality, which, before it is coined, is seldom worth sevenpence in silver. But as by the regulation twelve such pence are ordered to exchange for a shilling, they are in the market considered as worth a shilling, and a shilling can at any time be had for them. Even before the late reformation of the gold coin of Great Britain,[38] the gold, that part of it at least which circulated in London and its neighbourhood, was in general less degraded below its standard weight than the greater part of the silver. One-and-twenty worn and defaced shillings, however, were considered as equivalent to a guinea, which perhaps, indeed, was worn and defaced too, but seldom so much so. The

---

[37] 'It would be a ridiculous and vain attempt, to make a standard integer of gold, whose parts should be silver; or to make a motly standard, part gold and part silver. These different materials could not long agree in value; and silver being the most common and useful coin, would soon regain its antient place of a *standard measurer*.' (Harris, *Essay*, i.61.)

[38] In 1774 by 14 George III,c.70. The 'late recoinage' is considered below, I.xi.g.6 and IV.vi.18.

late regulations have brought the gold coin as near perhaps to its standard weight as it is possible to bring the cur-[62]rent coin of any nation; and the order, to receive no gold at the public offices but by weight, is likely to preserve it so *ᵛasᵛ* long as that order is enforced. The silver coin still continues in the same worn and degraded state as before the reformation of the gold coin. In the market, however, one-and-twenty shillings of this degraded silver coin are still considered as worth a guinea of this excellent gold coin.

30   The reformation of the gold coin has evidently raised the value of the silver coin which can be exchanged for it.

31   In the English mint a pound weight of gold is coined into forty-four guineas and a half, which, at one-and-twenty shillings the guinea, is equal to forty-six pounds fourteen shillings and six-pence. An ounce of such gold coin, therefore, is worth 3*l*.17*s*.10*d*. ½ in silver. In England no duty or seignorage is paid upon the coinage, and he who carries a pound weight or an ounce weight of standard gold bullion to the mint, gets back a pound weight or an ounce weight of gold in coin, without any deduction.[39] Three pounds seventeen shillings and ten-pence halfpenny an ounce, therefore is said to be the mint price of gold in England, or the quantity of gold coin which the mint gives in return for standard gold bullion.

32   Before the reformation of the gold coin, the price of standard gold bullion in the market had for many years been upwards of 3*l*.18*s*. sometimes 3*l*.19*s*. and very frequently 4*l*. an ounce; that sum, it is probable, in the worn and de-[63]graded gold coin, seldom containing more than an ounce of standard gold. Since the reformation of the gold coin, the market price of standard gold bullion seldom exceeds 3*l*.17*s*.7*d*. an ounce. Before the reformation of the gold coin, the market price was always more or less above the mint price.[40] Since that reformation, the market price has been constantly below the mint price. But that market price is the same whether it is paid in gold or in silver coin. The late reformation of the gold coin, therefore, has raised not only the value of the gold coin, but likewise that of the silver coin in proportion to gold bullion, and probably too in proportion to all other commodities; though the price of the greater part of other commodities being influenced by so many other causes, the rise in the value either of gold or silver coin in proportion to them, may not be so distinct and sensible.

ᵛ⁻ᵛ om. 4;   ,as 4e–6

[39] See II.ii.54 where Smith comments that government is 'properly at the expence of the coinage' and cf. IV.vi.18.

[40] See IV.iii.b.7 where Smith remarks that in Holland the market price of bullion is generally above the mint price for the same reason as it was in England before the reformation of the coinage.

33　　In the English mint a pound weight of standard silver bullion is coined into sixty-two shillings, containing, in the same manner, a pound weight of standard silver. Five shillings and two-pence an ounce, therefore, is said to be the mint price of silver in England, or the quantity of silver coin which the mint gives in return for standard silver bullion. Before the reformation of the gold coin, the market price of standard silver bullion was, upon different occasions, five shillings and four-pence, five shillings and five-pence, five shillings and six-pence, five shillings and seven-pence, and very often five shillings and eight-pence an ounce. Five shillings and seven-[64]pence, however, seems to have been the most common price. Since the reformation of the gold coin, the market price of standard silver bullion has fallen occasionally to five shillings and three-pence, five shillings and four-pence, and five shillings and five-pence an ounce, which last price it has scarce ever exceeded. Though the market price of silver bullion has fallen considerably since the reformation of the gold coin, it has not fallen so low as the mint price.

34　　In the proportion between the different metals in the English coin, as copper is rated very much above its real value, so silver is rated somewhat below it. In the market of Europe, in the French coin and in the Dutch coin, an ounce of fine gold exchanges for about fourteen ounces of fine silver. In the English coin, it exchanges for about fifteen ounces, that is, for more silver than it is worth according to the common estimation of Europe.[41] But as the price of copper in bars is not, even in England, raised by the high price of copper in English coin, so the price of silver in bullion is not sunk by the low rate of silver in English coin. Silver in bullion still preserves its proper proportion to gold; for the same reason that copper in bars preserves its proper proportion to silver.

35　　Upon the reformation of the silver coin in the reign of William III. the price of silver bullion still continued to be somewhat above the mint price.[42] Mr. Locke imputed this high price to the permission of exporting silver bullion, and to the prohibition of exporting silver coin.[43] This [65] permission of exporting, he said, rendered the demand for silver bullion greater than the demand for silver coin. But the number of people who want silver coin for the common uses of buying and selling at home, is surely much

---

[41] Gold to silver ratios: French coin, 1 to $14\frac{5803}{12279}$; Dutch coin, 1 to $14\frac{82550}{154425}$; English coin, 1 to $15\frac{14295}{68200}$. N. Magens, *The Universal Merchant*, ed. W. Horsley (London, 1753), 53–5.

[42] 7 and 8 William III,c.1 (1695) in *Statutes of the Realm*, vii.1–4; 7 William III,c.1 in Ruffhead's edition.

[43] 'Silver in standard bullion would not be in value one jot above the same silver in coin, if clipped money were not current by tale, and coined silver, . . . as well as bullion, had the liberty of exportation. For when we have no clipped money, but all our current coin is weight, according to the standard, all the odds of value that silver in bullion has to silver in coin, is only owing to the prohibition of its exportation in money.' (J. Locke, *Further Considerations concerning raising the Value of Money* (1695), *Works*, v.173.)

greater than that of those who want silver bullion either for the use of exportation or for any other use. There subsists at present a like permission of exporting gold bullion, and a like prohibition of exporting gold coin; and yet the price of gold bullion has fallen below the mint price. But in the English coin silver was then, in the same manner as now, under-rated in proportion to gold; and the gold coin (which at that time too was not supposed to require any reformation) regulated then, as well as now, the real value of the whole coin. As the reformation of the silver coin did not then reduce the price of silver bullion to the mint price, it is not very probable that a like reformation will do so now.

36   Were the silver coin brought back as near to its standard weight as the gold, a guinea, it is probable, would, according to the present proportion, exchange for more silver in coin than it would purchase in bullion. The silver *w*coin*w* containing its full standard weight, there would in this case be a profit in melting it down, in order, first, to sell the bullion for gold coin, and afterwards to exchange this gold coin for silver coin to be melted down in the same manner. Some alteration in the present proportion seems to be the only method of preventing this inconveniency.

37   [66] The inconveniency perhaps would be less if silver was rated in the coin as much above its proper proportion to gold as it is at present rated below it; provided it was at the same time enacted that silver should not be a legal tender for more than the change of a guinea; in the same manner as copper is not a legal tender for more than the change of a shilling. No creditor could in this case be cheated in consequence of the high valuation of silver in coin; as no creditor can at present be cheated in consequence of the high valuation of copper. The bankers only would suffer by this regulation. When a run comes upon them they sometimes endeavour to gain time by paying in sixpences,[44] and they would be precluded by this regulation from this discreditable method of evading immediate payment. They would be obliged in consequence to keep at all times in their coffers a greater quantity of cash than at present; and though this might no doubt be a considerable inconveniency to them, it would at the same time be a considerable security to their creditors.

38   Three pounds seventeen shillings and ten-pence halfpenny (the mint price of gold) certainly does not contain, even in our present excellent gold coin, more than an ounce of standard gold, and it may be thought, therefore, should not purchase more standard bullion. But gold in coin

---

w-w om. 5-6

[44] Cf. LJ (A) vi.124-5: 'It may even sometimes be a hardship to be obliged to take silver, as the banks have frequently endeavour'd to perplex by making payments in sixpences; but they ought not to be indulged in trifling in business.' It is stated at II.ii.85 that the Bank of England had been reduced to this expedient on occasion. The device was also used in Glasgow, and led to litigation in the Court of Session in the late 1750s.

is more convenient than gold in bullion, and though, in England, the coinage is free,[45] yet the gold which is carried in bullion to the mint, can seldom be returned in coin to the [67] owner till after a delay of several weeks. In the present hurry of the mint, it could not be returned till after a delay of several months. This delay is equivalent to a small duty, and renders gold in coin somewhat more valuable than an equal quantity of gold in bullion. If in the English coin silver was rated according to its proper proportion to gold, the price of silver bullion would probably fall below the mint price even without any reformation of the silver coin; the value even of the present worn and defaced silver coin being regulated by the value of the excellent gold coin for which it can be changed.

39   A small seignorage or duty upon the coinage of both gold and silver would probably increase still more the superiority of those metals in coin above an equal quantity of either of them in bullion. The coinage would in this case increase the value of the metal coined in proportion to the extent of this small duty; for the same reason that the fashion increases the value of plate in proportion to the price of that fashion. The superiority of coin above bullion would prevent the melting down of the coin, and would discourage its exportation.[46] If upon any public exigency it should become necessary to export the coin, the greater part of it would soon return again of its own accord. Abroad it could sell only for its weight in bullion. At home it would buy more than that weight. There would be a profit, therefore, in bringing it home again. In France a seignorage of about eight per cent. is [68] imposed upon the coinage,[47] and the French coin, when exported, is said to return home again of its own accord.

40   The occasional fluctuations in the market price of gold and silver bullion arise from the same causes as the like fluctuations in that of all other commodities. The frequent loss of those metals from various accidents by sea and by land, the continual waste of them in gilding and plating, in lace and embroidery, in the *x*wear and tear*x* of coin, and in *y*that*y* of plate;

---

x-x tear and wear *I*   *y-y* the tear and wear *I*

---

[45] The statutes governing coinage are mentioned at IV.vi.22.

[46] See below, IV.vi.18.

[47] See below IV.iii.a.10 and IV.vi.19. In Letter 150 addressed to Smith, dated 1 April 1776, Hume remarked that 'It appears to me impossible that the King of France can take a Seigniorage of 8 per cent. upon the Coinage. No-body would bring Bullion to the mint: It would all be sent to Holland or England, where it might be coined and sent back to France for less than two per cent. Accordingly Neckre says, that the French King takes only two per cent. of Seigniorage.' In fact the seigniorage was about 3 per cent. See Jacques Necker, *Sur la legislation et le commerce des grains* (1775), a work which Smith quotes below V.ii.k.78. Smith comments on the desirability of a charge for coinage in LJ (A) vi.150–1 calculated the costs incurred in England at £14,000. The same figure is given in LJ (B) 260. Cannan read it as £140,000 (p. 203). See below IV.vi.31. Sir James Steuart also cites 8 per cent as the seigniorage in France; *Principles*, i.552, ii.13,17. See especially III.2.ii.

require, in all countries which possess no mines of their own, a continual importation, in order to repair this loss and this waste. The merchant importers, like all other merchants, we may believe, endeavour, as well as they can, to suit their occasional importations to what, they judge, is likely to be the immediate demand. With all their attention, however, they sometimes over-do the business, and sometimes under-do it. When they import more bullion than is wanted, rather than incur the risk and trouble of exporting it again, they are sometimes willing to sell a part of it for something less than the ordinary or average price. When, on the other hand, they import less than is wanted, they get something more than this price. But when, under all those occasional fluctuations, the market price either of gold or silver bullion continues for several years together steadily and constantly, either more or less above, or more or less below the mint price; we may be assured that this steady and constant, either superiority or inferiority of price, is the [69] effect of something in the state of the coin, which, at that time, renders a certain quantity of coin either of more value or of less value than the precise quantity of bullion which it ought to contain. The constancy and steadiness of the effect, supposes a proportionable constancy and steadiness in the cause.

41   The money of any particular country is, at any particular time and place, more or less an accurate measure of value according as the current coin is more or less exactly agreeable to its standard, or contains more or less exactly the precise quantity of pure gold or pure silver which it ought to contain. If in England, for example, forty-four guineas and a half contained exactly a pound weight of standard gold, or eleven ounces of fine gold and one ounce of alloy, the gold coin of England would be as accurate a measure of the actual value of goods at any particular time and place as the nature of the thing would admit. But if, by rubbing and wearing, forty-four guineas and a half generally contain less than a pound weight of standard gold; the diminution, however, being greater in some pieces than in others; the measure of value comes to be liable to the same sort of uncertainty to which all other weights and measures are commonly exposed. As it rarely happens that these are exactly agreeable to their standard, the merchant adjusts the price of his goods, as well as he can, not to what those weights and measures ought to be, but to what, upon an average, he finds by experience they actually are. In conse-[70]quence of a like disorder in the coin the price of goods comes, in the same manner, to be adjusted, not to the quantity of pure gold or silver which the coin ought to contain, but to that which, upon an average, it is found by experience, it actually does contain.

42   By the money-price of goods, it is to be observed, I understand always the quantity of pure gold or silver for which they are sold, without any regard to the denomination of the coin. Six shillings and eight-pence, for

example, in the time of Edward I., I consider as the same money-price with a pound sterling in the present times; because it contained, as nearly as we can judge, the same quantity of pure silver.[48]

[48] The subjects of the latter part of this chapter are considered at some length in IV.vi, especially §§ 18–32 where Smith points out that this material might well have appeared 'in those chapters of the first book which treat of the origin and use of money' (32).

CHAPTER VI

Of the component Parts of the Price of Commodities

1 In that early and rude state of society which precedes both the accumulation of stock and the appropriation of land, the proportion between the quantities of labour necessary for acquiring different objects seems to be the only circumstance which can afford any rule for exchanging them for one another.[1] If among a nation of hunters, for example, it usually costs twice the labour to kill a beaver which it does to kill a deer, one beaver should naturally ex-[71]change for or be worth two deer. It is natural that what is usually the produce of two days or two hours labour, should be worth double of what is usually the produce of one day's or one hour's labour.

2 If the one species of labour should be more severe than the other, some allowance will naturally be made for this superior hardship;[2] and the produce of one hour's labour in the one way may frequently exchange for that of two hours labour in the other.

3 Or if the one species of labour requires an uncommon degree of dexterity and ingenuity, the esteem which men have for such talents, will naturally give a value to their produce, superior to what would be due to the time employed about it.[3] Such talents can seldom be acquired but in consequence of long application, and the superior value of their produce may frequently be no more than a reasonable compensation for the time and labour which must be spent in acquiring them. In the advanced state of society, allowances of this kind, for superior hardship and superior skill, are commonly made in the wages of labour; and something of the same kind must probably have taken place in its earliest and rudest period.

4 In this state of things*a*, the whole produce of labour belongs to the labourer; and*a* the quantity of labour commonly employed in acquiring or producing any commodity, is the only circumstance which can regulate the quantity of la-[72]bour which it ought commonly to purchase, command, or exchange for.

5 As soon as stock has accumulated in the hands of particular persons, some of them will naturally employ it in setting to work industrious people,

a-a 2–6

---

[1] There is an interesting discussion of property by occupation and its application to the hunting stage in LJ (A) i.27–46, ii.28. The problem is also mentioned in LJ (B) 150, ed. Cannan 108.

[2] Allowance for hardship is mentioned above I.v.4 and see also I.x.b.2,15.

[3] Cf. I.x.b.25 where it is pointed out that some talents of themselves admired are disapproved of when employed for gain, so that the rate of return must be sufficient to compensate the public discredit attending their use.

whom they will supply with materials and subsistence, in order to make a profit by the sale of their work, or by what their labour adds to the value of the materials. In exchanging the complete manufacture either for money, for labour, or for other goods, over and above what may be sufficient to pay the price of the materials, and the wages of the workmen, something must be given for the profits of the undertaker of the work who hazards his stock in this adventure.[4] The value which the workmen add to the materials, therefore, resolves itself in this case into two parts, of which the one pays their wages, the other the profits of their employer upon the whole stock of materials and wages which he advanced. He could have no interest to employ them, unless he expected from the sale of their work something more than what was sufficient to replace his stock to him; and he could have no interest to employ a great stock rather than a small one, unless his profits were to bear some proportion to the extent of his stock.

6   The profits of stock, it may perhaps be thought, are only a different name for the wages of a particular sort of labour, the labour of inspection and direction. They are, however, altogether different, are regulated by quite differ-[73]ent principles, and bear no proportion to the quantity, the hardship, or the ingenuity of this supposed labour of inspection and direction. They are regulated altogether by the value of the stock employed, and are greater or smaller in proportion to the extent of this stock. Let us suppose, for example, that in some particular place, where the common annual profits of manufacturing stock are ten per cent. there are two different manufactures, in each of which twenty workmen are employed at the rate of fifteen pounds a year each, or at the expence of three hundred a year in each manufactory. Let us suppose too, that the coarse materials annually wrought up in the one cost only seven hundred pounds, while the finer materials in the other cost seven thousand. The capital annually employed in the one will in this case amount only to one thousand pounds; whereas that employed in the other will amount to seven thousand three hundred pounds. At the rate of ten per cent. therefore, the undertaker of the one will expect an yearly profit of about one hundred pounds only; while that of the other will expect about seven hundred and thirty pounds. But though their profits are so very different, their labour of inspection and direction may be either altogether or very nearly the same. In many great works, almost the whole labour of this kind is [b] committed to some principal clerk. His wages properly express the value of this labour of inspection and direction. Though in settling them some regard is had commonly, not only to his [74] labour and skill, but to the trust which is reposed in him, yet they never bear any regular proportion to the capital of which he oversees the manage-

[b] frequently *1*

---

[4] The role of the undertaker is examined at some length in Cantillon, *Essai*, I.xiii. Cantillon particularly emphasized the issue of risk.

ment; and the owner of this capital, though he is thus discharged of almost all labour, still expects that his profits should bear a regular proportion to ᶜhis capitalᶜ. In the price of commodities, therefore, the profits of stock ᵈconstitute a component partᵈ altogether different from the wages of labour, and regulated by quite different principles.

7   In this state of things, ᵉthe whole produce of labour does not always belong to the labourer. He must in most cases share it with the owner of the stock which employs him. Neither isᵉ the quantity of labour commonly employed in acquiring or producing any commodity, ᶠ the only circumstance which can regulate the quantity which it ought commonly to pur-✓ chase, command, or exchange for. An additional quantity, it is evident, must be due for the profits of the stock which advanced the wages and furnished the materials of that labour.

8   As soon as the land of any country has all become private property, the landlords, like all other men, love to reap where they never sowed, and demand a rent even for its natural produce. The wood of the forest, the grass of the field, and all the natural fruits of the earth, which, when land was in common, cost ᵍthe labourerᵍ only the trouble of gathering them, comeʰ, even to him,ʰ to have an additional price fixed upon them. ⁱHeⁱ must then pay for the licence to gather [75] them; and ʲmust give up to the landlord a portion of what his labour either collects or produces. This portion, or, what comes to the same thing, the price of this portion, constitutes the rent of land, and in the price of the greater part of commodities makes a third component part.ʲ5

9   The real value of all the different component parts of priceᵏ, it must be observed, isᵏ measured by the quantity of labour which they can, each of them, purchase or command. Labour measures the value not only of that

ᶜ⁻ᶜ it *1–2*   ᵈ⁻ᵈ are a source of value *1*   ᵉ⁻ᵉ therefore, *1*   ᶠ is by no means *1*
ᵍ⁻ᵍ *2–6*   ʰ⁻ʰ *2–6*   ⁱ⁻ⁱ Men *1*

ʲ⁻ʲ in exchanging them either for money, for labour, or for other goods, over and above what is due, both for the labour of gathering them, and for the profits of the stock which employs that labour, some allowance must be made for the price of the licence, which constitutes the first rent of land. In the price, therefore, of the greater part of commodities the rent of land comes in this manner to constitute a third source of value.

In this state of things, neither the quantity of labour commonly employed in acquiring or producing any commodity, nor the profits of the stock which advanced the wages and furnished the materials of that labour, are the only circumstances which can regulate the quantity of labour which it ought commonly to purchase, command, or exchange for. A third circumstance must likewise be taken into consideration; the rent of the land; and the commodity must commonly purchase, command, or exchange for, an additional quantity of labour, in order to enable the person who brings it to market to pay this rent. *1*

ᵏ⁻ᵏ is in this manner *1*

---

⁵ But see below I.xi.a.8. Dugald Stewart indicated in his *Works*, (ed. Sir William Hamilton), ix (Edinburgh, 1856), 6, that the division of returns into rent, wages, and profits was first suggested to Smith by James Oswald of Dunnikier as 'appears from a manuscript of Mr. Smith's, now in my possession'. Cf. Stewart, III.2.

part of price which resolves itself into labour, but of that which resolves itself into rent, and of that which resolves itself into profit.⁶

10   In every society the price of every commodity finally resolves itself into
some one or other, or all of those three parts; and in every improved
society, all the three enter more or less, as component parts, into the price
of the far greater part of commodities.

11   In the price of corn, for example, one part pays the rent of the landlord,
another pays the wages or maintenance of the labourers and labouring
cattle employed in producing it, and the third pays the profit of the farmer.
These three parts seem either immediately or ultimately to make up the
whole price of corn. A fourth part, it may perhaps be thought, is necessary
for replacing the stock of the farmer, or for compensating the ᶦwear and
tearᶦ of his labouring cattle, and other instruments of husbandry. But it
must be considered that the price of any in-[76]strument of husbandry,
such as a labouring horse, is itself made up of the same three parts; the rent
of the land upon which he is reared, the labour of tending and rearing him,
and the profits of the farmer who advances both the rent of this land, and
the wages of this labour. Though the price of the corn, therefore, may pay
the price as well as the maintenance of the horse, the whole price still resolves itself either immediately or ultimately into the same three parts of
rent, labour, and profit.

12   In the price of flour or meal, we must add to the price of the corn, the
profits of the miller, and the wages of his servants; in the price of the bread,
the profits of the baker, and the wages of his servants; and in the price of
both, the labour of transporting the corn from the house of the farmer to
that of the miller, and from that of the miller to that of the baker, together
with the profits of those who advance the wages of that labour.

13   The price of flax resolves itself into the same three parts as that of corn.
In the price of linen we must add to this price the wages of the flax-dresser,
of the spinner, of the weaver, of the bleacher, &c. together with the profits
of their respective employers.

14   As any particular commodity comes to be more manufactured, that part
of the price which resolves itself into wages and profit, comes to be greater
in proportion to that which resolves itself into rent. In the progress of the
manufacture, not only the number of profits increase, [77] but every subsequent profit is greater than the foregoing; because the capital from which
it is derived must always be greater. The capital which employs the weavers,
for example, must be greater than that which employs the spinners; because it not only replaces that capital with its profits, but pays, besides, the
wages of the weavers; and the profits must always bear some proportion to
the capital.

ᶦ⁻ᶦ tear and wear *1*

---

⁶ The point is made with greater clarity at II.ii.20.

15   In the most improved societies, however, there are always a few commodities of which the price resolves itself into two parts only, the wages of labour, and the profits of stock; and a still smaller number in which it consists altogether in the wages of labour. In the price of sea-fish, for example, one part pays the labour of the fishermen, and the other the profits of the capital employed in the fishery. Rent very seldom makes any part of it, though it does sometimes, as I shall shew hereafter.[7] It is otherwise, at least through the greater part of Europe, in river fisheries. A salmon fishery pays a rent, and rent, though it cannot well be called the rent of land, makes a part of the price of a salmon as well as wages and profit. In some parts of Scotland a few poor people make a trade of gathering, along the sea-shore, those little variegated stones commonly known by the name of Scotch Pebbles. The price which is paid to them by the stone-cutter is altogether the wages of their labour; neither rent nor profit make any part of it.

16   [78] But the whole price of ᵐanyᵐ commodity must still finally resolve itself into some one or other, or all of those three parts; as whatever part of it remains after paying the rent of the land, and the price of the whole labour employed in raising, manufacturing, and bringing it to market, must necessarily be profit to somebody.

17   As the price or exchangeable value of every particular commodity, taken separately, resolves itself into some one or other or all of those three parts; so that of all the commodities which compose the whole annual produce of the labour of every country, taken complexly, must resolve itself into the same three parts, and be parcelled out among different inhabitants of the country, either as the wages of their labour, the profits of their stock, or the rent of their land.[8] The whole of what is annually either collected or produced by the labour of every society, or what comes to the same thing, the whole price of it, is in the manner originally distributed among some of its different members. Wages, profit, and rent, are the three original sources of all revenue as well as of all exchangeable value. All other revenue is ultimately derived from some one or other of these.

18   Whoever derives his revenue from a fund which is his own, must draw it either from his labour, from his stock, or from his land. The revenue derived from labour is called wages. That derived from stock, by the person who manages or employs it, is called profit. That derived from it by the person who does not em-[79]ploy it himself, but lends it to another, is called the interest or the use of money. It is the compensation which the borrower pays to the lender, for the profit which he has an opportunity of making by the use of the money. Part of that profit naturally belongs to the borrower, who runs the risk and takes the trouble of employing it; and part to the

ᵐ⁻ᵐ every *1–2*

[7] See below, I.xi.a.4.
[8] A similar passage occurs at I.xi.p.7 and II.ii.1.

lender, who affords him the opportunity of making this profit. The interest of money is always a derivative revenue, which, if it is not paid from the profit which is made by the use of the money, must be paid from some other source of revenue, unless perhaps the borrower is a spendthrift, who contracts a second debt in order to pay the interest of the first.[9] The revenue which proceeds altogether from land, is called rent, and belongs to the landlord. The revenue of the farmer is derived partly from his labour, and partly from his stock. To him, land is only the instrument which enables him to earn the wages of this labour, and to make the profits of this stock. All taxes, and all the revenue which is founded upon them, all salaries, pensions, and annuities of every kind, are ultimately derived from some one or other of those three original sources of revenue, and are paid either immediately or mediately from the wages of labour, the profits of stock, or the rent of land.

19   When those three different sorts of revenue belong to different persons, they are readily distinguished; but when they belong to the same [80] they are sometimes confounded with one another, at least in common language.[10]

20   A gentleman who farms a part of his own estate, after paying the expence of cultivation, should gain both the rent of the landlord and the profit of the farmer. He is apt to denominate, however, his whole gain, profit, and thus confounds rent with profit, at least in common language. The greater part of our North American and West Indian planters are in this situation. They farm, the greater part of them, their own estates, and accordingly we seldom hear of the rent of a plantation, but frequently of its profit.

21   Common farmers seldom employ any overseer to direct the general operations of the farm. They generally too work a good deal with their own hands, as ploughmen, harrowers, &c. What remains of the crop after paying the rent, therefore, should not only replace to them their stock employed in cultivation, together with its ordinary profits, but pay them the wages which are due to them, both as labourers and overseers. Whatever remains, however, after paying the rent and keeping up the stock, is called profit. But wages evidently make a part of it. The farmer, by saving these wages, must necessarily gain them. Wages, therefore, are in this case confounded with profit.

22   An independent manufacturer, who has stock enough both to purchase materials, and to maintain himself till he can carry his work to market, [81] should gain both the wages of a journeyman who works under a master, and the profit which that master makes by the sale of ⁿthe journeyman'sⁿ

ⁿ⁻ⁿ his *1*

---

[9] The rate of interest is discussed in II.iv.
[10] Examples of confusion between categories of return are given at I.viii.9, I.x.b.35 and 37.

work. His whole gains, however, are commonly called profit, and wages are, in this case too, confounded with profit.

23   A gardener who cultivates his own garden with his own hands, unites in his own person the three different characters, of landlord, farmer, and labourer. His produce, therefore, should pay him the rent of the first, the profit of the second, and the wages of the third. The whole, however, is commonly considered as the earnings of his labour. Both rent and profit are, in this case, confounded with wages.

24   As in a civilized country there are but few commodities of which the exchangeable value arises from labour only, rent and profit contributing largely to that of the far greater part of them, so the annual produce of its labour will always be sufficient to purchase or command a much greater quantity of labour than what was employed in raising, preparing, and bringing that produce to market. If the society °was° annually to employ all the labour which it can annually purchase, as the quantity of labour would increase greatly every year, so the produce of every succeeding year would be of vastly greater value than that of the foregoing. But there is no country in which the whole annual produce is employed in maintaining the industrious.[11] The idle every where consume a great part of it; and according to the different proportions in which [82] it is annually divided between those two different orders of people, its ordinary or average value must either annually increase, or diminish, or continue the same from one year to another.

°-° were 4-6

---

[11] See below, II.iii, where Smith examines the distinction between productive and unproductive labour.

CHAPTER VII

Of the natural and market Price of Commodities[1]

1 THERE is in every society or neighbourhood an ordinary or average rate both of wages and profit in every different employment of labour and stock. This rate is naturally regulated, as I shall show hereafter,[2] partly by the general circumstances of the society, their riches or poverty, their advancing, stationary, or declining condition; and partly by the particular nature of each employment.[3]

2 There is likewise in every society or neighbourhood an ordinary or average rate of rent, which is regulated too, as I shall show hereafter,[4] partly by the general circumstances of the society or neighbourhood in which the land is situated, and partly by the natural or improved fertility of the land.

3 These ordinary or average rates may be called the natural rates of wages, profit, and rent, at the time and place in which they commonly prevail.

4 When the price of any commodity is neither more nor less than what is sufficient to pay the [83] rent of the land, the wages of the labour, and the profits of the stock employed in raising, preparing, and bringing it to market, according to their natural rates, the commodity is then sold for what may be called its natural price.[5]

5 The commodity is then sold precisely for what it is worth, or for what it really costs the person who brings it to market; for though in common language what is called the prime cost of any commodity does not compre-

---

[1] In the lectures and ED, the analysis of price follows directly on the discussion of the division of labour and precedes that of money. The intervening chapters of the WN do not, therefore, have any counterpart in the older work. Moreover, in both lectures and ED, while the distinction between market and natural price is used, the latter is mainly defined in terms of the supply price of labour: 'When the wages are so proportion'd as that they are exactly sufficient to maintain the person, to recompense the expense of education, the risque of dying before this is made up, and the hazard that tho' one lives he shall never be able to become in any way serviceable, they are then at their naturall rate, and the temptation is great enough to induce anyone to apply to it' (LJ (A) vi.62–3). Much of the material with regard to the costs of education and of risk finds a place in I.x.b. See, for example, I.x.b.6 and II.i.17. The determinants of *market* price are discussed in LJ (A) vi.70, LJ (B) 227–8, ed. Cannan 176–7, and ED 3.2. This price is shown to be interrelated with natural price in LJ (A) vi.75–6, LJ (B) 229, ed. Cannan 178, and ED 3.3. In the lectures and ED Smith then proceeded directly to the discussion of policies which kept prices either above or below the equilibrium level; a theme which is also developed in the concluding paragraphs of this chapter.

[2] Below, I.viii and I.ix.

[3] Pownall comments on this passage, *Letter*, 13–15. He considered that Smith's distinction between market and natural price was ambiguous.

[4] Below, I.xi.b.

[5] Hume disagreed at least with regard to rent: 'I cannot think, that the Rent of Farms makes any part of the Price of the Produce, but that the Price is determined altogether by the Quantity and the Demand.' (Letter 150, addressed to Smith, dated 1 April 1776.)

hend the profit of the person who is to sell it again, yet if he sells it at a price which does not allow him the ordinary rate of profit in his neighbourhood, he is evidently a loser by the trade; since by employing his stock in some other way he might have made that profit. His profit, besides, is his revenue, the proper fund of his subsistence. As, while he is preparing and bringing the goods to market, he advances to his workmen their wages, or their subsistence; so he advances to himself, in the same manner, his own subsistence, which is generally suitable to the profit which he may reasonably expect from the sale of his goods. Unless they yield him this profit, therefore, they do not repay him what they may very properly be said to have really cost him.

6   Though the price, therefore, which leaves him this profit, is not always the lowest at which a dealer may sometimes sell his goods, it is the lowest at which he is likely to sell them for any considerable time; at least where there is perfect liberty,[6] or where he may change his trade as often as he pleases.

7   [84] The actual price at which any commodity is commonly sold is called its market price. It may either be above, or below, or exactly the same with its natural price.

8   The market price of every particular commodity is regulated by the proportion between the quantity which is actually brought to market, and the demand of those who are willing to pay the natural price of the commodity, or the whole value of the rent, labour, and profit, which must be paid in order to bring it thither. Such people may be called the effectual demanders, and their demand the effectual demand;[7] since it may be sufficient to effectuate the bringing of the commodity to market. It is different from the absolute demand. A very poor man may be said in some sense to have a demand for a coach and six; he might like to have it; but his demand is not an effectual demand, as the commodity can never be brought to market in order to satisfy it.[8]

9   When the quantity of any commodity which is brought to market falls short of the effectual demand, all those who are willing to pay the whole value of the rent, wages, and profit, which must be paid in order to bring it thither, cannot be supplied with the quantity which they want. Rather than want it altogether, some of them will be willing to give more. A competition will immediately begin among them, and the market price will rise

---

[6] The phrase 'perfect liberty' is used frequently; see for example I.vii.30, I.x.a.1, IV.vii.c.44. The term 'natural liberty' is used in the discussion of physiocracy at IV.ix.51.

[7] Cf. Turgot, *Reflections*, LXVI. Sir James Steuart used the term 'effectual demand' in the *Principles*, i. 115, ed. Skinner i. 117.

[8] 'If one, who is forced to walk on Foot envies a great Man for keeping a Coach and Six, it will never be with that Violence, or give him that Disturbance which it may to a Man, who keeps a Coach himself, but can only afford to drive with four Horses.' (Mandeville, *The Fable of the Bees*, pt. i. 141, ed. Kaye i. 136.)

more or less above the natural price, according as ^aeither^a the greatness of the deficiency^b, or the wealth and wanton luxury of the competitors, happen to animate^b more or less the eagerness of [85] ^cthe^c competition. ^dAmong competitors of equal wealth and luxury the^d same deficiency will generally occasion a more or less eager competition, according as the acquisition of the commodity happens to be of more or less importance to ^ethem^e. Hence the exorbitant price of the necessaries of life during the blockade of a town or in a famine.

10   When the quantity brought to market exceeds the effectual demand, it cannot be all sold to those who are willing to pay the whole value of the rent, wages and profit, which must be paid in order to bring it thither. Some part must be sold to those who are willing to pay less, and the low price which they give for it must reduce the price of the whole. The market price will sink more or less below the natural price, according as the greatness of the excess increases more or less the competition of the sellers, or according as it happens to be more or less important to them to get immediately rid of the commodity. The same excess in the importation of perishable, will occasion a much greater competition than in that of durable commodities; in the importation of oranges, for example, than ^fin^f that of old iron.[9]

11   When the quantity brought to market is just sufficient to supply the effectual demand and no more, the market price naturally comes to be either exactly, or as nearly as can be judged of, the same with the natural price. The whole quantity upon hand can be disposed of for this price, and cannot be disposed of for more. The [86] competition of the different dealers obliges them all to accept of this price, but does not oblige them to accept of less.

12   The quantity of every commodity brought to market naturally suits itself to the effectual demand. It is the interest of all those who employ their land, labour, or stock, in bringing any commodity to market, that the quantity never should exceed the effectual demand; and it is the interest of all other people that it never should fall short of ^gthat demand^g.

13   If at any time it exceeds the effectual demand, some of the component parts of its price must be paid below their natural rate. If it is rent, the

---

^{a–a} 2–6   ^{b–b} increases *1*   ^{c–c} this *1*   ^{d–d} The *1*   ^{e–e} the competitors *1*
^{f–f} om. 4 ⟨corrected 4e–6⟩   ^{g–g} it *1*

[9] See below, IV.i.18. Steuart particularly emphasized the importance of competition between buyers in order to procure stocks of a commodity, and competition between sellers in order to get rid of certain stocks. This form of argument enabled him to state one of the conditions for price stability in noting that 'In proportion . . . as the rising of price can stop demand, or the sinking of price can increase it, in the same proportion will competition prevent either the rise or fall from being carried beyond a certain length . . .' (*Principles*, i.203, ed. Skinner i.177). The discussion of the mechanics of price determination appears in II.iv, vii, viii, and x. The determinants of price are summarized in III.i.

interest of the landlords will immediately prompt them to withdraw a part of their land; and if it is wages or profit, the interest of the labourers in the one case, and of their employers in the other, will prompt them to withdraw a part of their labour or stock from this employment. The quantity brought to market will soon be no more than sufficient to supply the effectual demand. All the different parts of its price will rise to their natural rate, and the whole price to its natural price.

14   If, on the contrary, the quantity brought to market should at any time fall short of the effectual demand, some of the component parts of its price must rise above their natural rate. If it is rent, the interest of all other landlords will naturally prompt them to prepare more land for the raising of this commodity; if it is wages or profit, the interest of all other labourers and [87] dealers will soon prompt them to employ more labour and stock in preparing and bringing it to market. The quantity brought thither will soon be sufficient to supply the effectual demand. All the different parts of its price will soon sink to their natural rate, and the whole price to its natural price.

15   The natural price, therefore, is, as it were, the central price, to which the prices of all commodities are continually gravitating.[10] Different accidents may sometimes keep them suspended a good deal above it, and sometimes force them down even somewhat below it. But whatever may be the obstacles which hinder them from settling in this center of repose and continuance, they are constantly tending towards it.

16   The whole quantity of industry annually employed in order to bring any commodity to market, naturally suits itself in this manner to the effectual demand. It naturally aims at bringing always that precise quantity thither which may be sufficient to supply, and no more than supply, that demand.

17   But in some employments the same quantity of industry will in different years produce very different quantities of commodities; while in others it will produce always the same, or very nearly the same. The same number of labourers in husbandry will, in different years, produce very different quantities of corn, wine, oil, hops, &c. But the same number of spinners and weavers will every year produce the same or very nearly the same quantity of linen and woollen [88] cloth. It is only the average produce of the one species of industry which can be suited in any respect to the effectual demand; and as its actual produce is frequently much greater and frequently much less than its average produce, the quantity of the commodities brought to market will sometimes exceed a good deal, and sometimes fall short a good deal of the effectual demand. Even though that

---

[10] In Cantillon the distinction is between market price and intrinsic value, where the latter is taken to be constant, being the measure of the quantity of land and labour entering into the production of a commodity. Cantillon also refers to a 'perpetual ebb and flow' of market prices around this standard. See *Essai*, I.x.

demand therefore should continue always the same, their market price will be liable to great fluctuations, will sometimes fall a good deal below, and sometimes rise a good deal above their natural price. In the other species of industry, the produce of equal quantities of labour being always the same or very nearly the same, it can be more exactly suited to the effectual demand. While that demand continues the same, therefore, the market price of the commodities is likely to do so too, and to be either altogether, or as nearly as can be judged of, the same with the natural price. That the price of linen and woollen cloth is liable neither to such frequent nor to such great variations as the price of corn, every man's experience will inform him. The price of the one species of commodities varies only with the variations in the demand: That of the other varies, not only with the variations in the demand, but with the much greater and more frequent variations in the quantity of what is brought to market in order to supply that demand.

18   The occasional and temporary fluctuations in the market price of any commodity fall chiefly upon those parts of its price which resolve them-[89]selves into wages and profit. That part which resolves itself into rent is less affected by them. A rent certain in money is not in the least affected by them either in its rate or in its value. A rent which consists either in a certain proportion or in a certain quantity of the rude produce, is no doubt affected in its yearly value by all the occasional and temporary fluctuations in the market price of that rude produce: but it is seldom affected by them in its yearly rate. In settling the terms of the lease, the landlord and farmer endeavour, according to their best judgment, to adjust that rate, not to the temporary and occasional, but to the average and ordinary price of the produce.

19   Such fluctuations affect both the value and the rate either of wages or of profit, according as the market happens to be either over-stocked or under-stocked with commodities or with labour; with work done, or with work to be done. A publick mourning raises the price of black cloth[11] (with which the market is almost always under-stocked upon such occasions) and augments the profits of the merchants who possess any considerable quantity of it. It has no effect upon the wages of the weavers. The market is under-stocked with commodities, not with labour; with work done, not with work to be done. It raises the wages of journeymen taylors. The market is here under-stocked with labour. There is an effectual demand for *h*more*h* labour, for more work to be done than can be had. It sinks the price of coloured silks and cloths, and [90] thereby reduces the profits of the merchants who

h–h 2–6

---

[11] The example is used below, I.x.b.46 and see also I.x.c.43. It is pointed out at I.x.c.61 that the upper limits set by statute to the wages of master tailors in and around London were waived 'in the case of a general mourning'.

have any considerable quantity of them upon hand. It sinks too the wages of the workmen employed in preparing such commodities, for which all demand is stopped for six months, perhaps for a twelvemonth. The market is here over-stocked both with commodities and with labour.

20   But though the market price of every particular commodity is in this manner continually gravitating, if one may say so, towards the natural price, yet sometimes particular accidents, sometimes natural causes, and sometimes particular regulations of police, may, in many commodities, keep up the market price, for a long time together, a good deal above the natural price.[12]

21   When by an increase in the effectual demand, the market price of some particular commodity happens to rise a good deal above the natural price, those who employ their stocks in supplying that market are generally careful to conceal this change. If it was commonly known, their great profit would tempt so many new rivals to employ their stocks in the same way, that, the effectual demand being fully supplied, the market price would soon be reduced to the natural price, and perhaps for some time even below it. If the market is at a great distance from the residence of those who supply it, they may sometimes be able to keep the secret for several years together, and may so long enjoy their extraordinary profits without any new rivals.[13] Secrets of this kind, [91] however, it must be acknowledged, can seldom be long kept; and the extraordinary profit can last very little longer than they are kept.

22   Secrets in manufactures are capable of being longer kept than secrets in trade. A dyer who has found the means of producing a particular colour with materials which cost only half the price of those commonly made use of, may, with good management, enjoy the advantage of his discovery as long as he lives, and even leave it as a legacy to his posterity. His extraordinary gains arise from the high price which is paid for his private labour. They properly consist in the high wages of that labour. But as they are repeated upon every part of his stock, and as their whole amount bears, upon

[12] In discussing the forces which kept prices in excess of the natural or equilibrium level, Smith commented in LJ (B) 232–3, ed. Cannan 180: 'what raises the market price above the natural one diminishes public opulence . . .' and cited as examples taxes on necessaries, and monopolies. Cf. LJ (A) vi.84ff. He also objected to policies which kept the market price below the natural level (e.g. bounties) and endeavoured to show that both types of policy broke in effect 'what may be called the natural balance of industry' by artificially altering the distribution of stock between trades. See LJ (A) vi.92; LJ (B) 233, ed. Cannan 181, and ED 3.5 where it is stated that 'Whatever tends to break this balance tends to hurt the national or public opulence.' The argument is a feature of Smith's critique of mercantilism, see for example IV.ii.3 and IV.vii.c.89.

[13] In another connection Smith noted that spatial division could be an advantage, remarking that the dispersed situation of manufacturers and dealers militated against collusion and combination. The point was frequently made: see for example I.x.c.23, IV.ii.21, IV.v.b.4, IV.vii.b.24, IV.viii.4 and 34.

that account, a regular proportion to it, they are commonly considered as extraordinary profits of stock.

23   Such enhancements of the market price are evidently the effects of particular accidents, of which, however, the operation may sometimes last for many years together.

24   Some natural productions require such a singularity of soil and situation, that all the land in a great country, which is fit for producing them, may not be sufficient to supply the effectual demand. The whole quantity brought to market, therefore, may be disposed of to those who are willing to give more than what is sufficient to pay the rent of the land which produced them, together with the wages of the labour, and the profits of the stock which were employed in preparing and bringing them to market, ac-[92] cording to their natural rates. Such commodities may continue ⁱfor whole centuries togetherⁱ to be sold at this high price ʲ; and that part of it which resolves itself into the rent of land is in this case the part which is generally paid above its natural rate. The rent of the land which affords such singular and esteemed productions, like the rent of some vineyards in France of a peculiarly happy soil and situation, bears no regular proportion to the rent of other equally fertile and equally well-cultivated land in its neighbourhood.[14] The wages of the labour and the profits of the stock employed in bringing such commodities to market, on the contrary, are seldom out of their natural proportion to those of the other employments of labour and stock in their neighbourhood.

25   Such enhancements of the market price are evidently the effect of natural causes which may hinder the effectual demand from ever being fully supplied, and which may continue, therefore, to operate for ever.

26   A monopoly granted either to an individual or to a trading company has the same effect as a secret in trade or manufactures. The monopolists, by keeping the market constantly under-stocked, by never fully supplying the effectual demand, sell their commodities much above the natural price, and raise their emoluments, whether they consist in wages or profit, greatly above their natural rate.[15]

27   The price of monopoly is upon every occasion the highest which can be got. The natural price, [93] or the price of free competition, on the contrary, is the lowest which can be taken, not upon every occasion, indeed, but for

---

ⁱ⁻ⁱ 2–6   ʲ for whole centuries together, *1*

[14] See below, I.xi.b.31. Smith discusses taxes on the produce of rare vines at V.ii.k.54.
[15] It is suggested that monopoly powers destroy frugality by artificially raising the level of profit, IV.vii.c.61. Smith also argued that monopoly was an enemy to good management at I.xi.b.5, but did however admit the usefulness of temporary monopolies at V.i.e.30 and of exclusive privileges in particular cases. See for example, IV.vii.c.95 and V.i.e.5. He also said in LJ (A) ii.35 that all forms of monopoly are extremely detrimental and that 'Besides this, the goods are worse; as they know none can undersell them; so they keep up the price, and . . . care not what the quality be.'

any considerable time together. The one is upon every occasion the highest which can be squeezed out of the buyers, or which, it is supposed, they will consent to give: The other is the lowest which the sellers can commonly afford to take, and at the same time continue their business.

28   The exclusive privileges of corporations, statutes of apprenticeship, and all those laws which restrain, in particular employments, the competition to a smaller number than might otherwise go into them, have the same tendency, though in a less degree.[16] They are a sort of enlarged monopolies, and may frequently, for ages together and in whole classes of employments, keep up the market price of particular commodities above the natural price, and maintain both the wages of the labour and the profits of the stock employed about them somewhat above their natural rate.

29   Such enhancements of the market price may last as long as the regulations of police which give occasion to them.

30   The market price of any particular commodity, though it may continue long above, can seldom continue long below its natural price. Whatever part of it was paid below the natural rate, the persons whose interest it affected would immediately feel the loss, and would immediately withdraw either so much land, or so much labour, or so much stock, from being employed [94] about it, that the quantity brought to market would soon be no more than sufficient to supply the effectual demand. Its market price, therefore, would soon rise to the natural price. This at least would be the case where there was perfect liberty.[17]   *n.b.*

31   The same statutes of apprenticeship and other corporation laws indeed, which, when a manufacture is in prosperity, enable the workman to raise his wages a good deal above their natural rate, sometimes oblige him, when it decays, to let them down a good deal below it. As in the one case they exclude many people from his employment, so in the other they exclude him from many employments. The effect of such regulations, however, is not near so durable in sinking the workman's wages below, as in raising them above their natural rate. Their operation in the one way may endure for many centuries, but in the other it can last no longer than the lives of some of the workmen who were bred to the business in the time of its prosperity. When they are gone, the number of those who are afterwards

---

[16] Cf. LJ (B) 306, ed. Cannan 236 'All monopolies and exclusive privileges of corporations, for whatever good ends they were at first instituted, have the same bad effect. In like manner the statute of apprenticeship, which was originaly an imposition on government, has a bad tendencey.' Cf. LJ (A) vi.88. See also I.x.c.8 and 9 where Smith comments on the limitations to which the statute of apprenticeship was subject, and on the ease with which its restrictions could be avoided.

[17] Smith seems to have considered that the transfer of resources between employments would be quite easy, at least in the absence of institutional impediments. See for example I.x.c.43, but cf. I.viii.31 where it is stated that man is 'of all sorts of luggage the most difficult to be transported'.

educated to the trade will naturally suit itself to the effectual demand. The police must be as violent as that of Indostan or antient Egypt (where every man was bound by a principle of religion to follow the occupation of his father, and was supposed to commit the most horrid sacrilege if he changed it for another) which can in any particular employment, and for several generations together, sink either the wages of [95] labour or the profits of stock below their natural rate.[18]

32   This is all that I think necessary to be observed at present concerning the deviations, whether occasional or permanent, of the market price of commodities from the natural price.

33   The natural price itself varies with the natural rate of each of its component parts, of wages, profit, and rent; and in every society this rate varies according to their circumstances, according to their riches or poverty, their advancing, stationary, or declining condition. I shall, in the four following chapters, endeavour to explain, as fully and distinctly as I can, the causes of those different variations.

34   First, I shall endeavour to explain what are the circumstances which naturally determine the rate of wages, and in what manner those circumstances are affected by the riches or poverty, by the advancing, stationary, or declining state of the society.

35   Secondly, I shall endeavour to show what are the circumstances which naturally determine the rate of profit, and in what manner too those circumstances are affected by the like variations in the state of the society.

36   Though pecuniary wages and profit are very different in the different employments of labour and stock; yet a certain proportion seems commonly to take place between both the pecuniary wages in all the different employments of labour, and the pecuniary profits in all the different employments of stock. This proportion, it will [96] appear hereafter,[19] depends partly upon the nature of the different employments, and partly upon the different laws and policy of the society in which they are carried on. But though in many respects dependent upon the laws and policy, this proportion seems to be little affected by the riches or poverty of that society; by its advancing, stationary, or declining condition; but to remain the same or very nearly the same in all those different states. I shall, in the

---

[18] See IV.ix.43 and above, 25 n.1. It is pointed out in LJ (A) vi.54 that the law of Sesostris was designed to ensure that man's ambition to 'advance himself into what we call a gentlemanny character' did not leave the lower trades deserted. Cf. LJ (B) 218–19, ed. Cannan 168. Montesquieu remarks: 'Laws which oblige every one to continue in his profession, and to devolve it upon his children, neither are nor can be of use in any but despotic kingdoms; where nobody either can or ought to have emulation.' (*Esprit*, XX.xxii.2.)

[19] I.x.

third place, endeavour to explain all the different circumstances which regulate this proportion.

37   In the fourth and last place, I shall endeavour to show what are the circumstances which regulate the rent of land, and which either raise or lower the real price of all the different substances which it produces.

CHAPTER VIII

Of the Wages of Labour

1 THE produce of labour constitutes the natural recompence or wages of labour.

2 In that original state of things, which precedes both the appropriation of land and the accumulation of stock,[1] the whole produce of labour belongs to the labourer[2]. He has neither landlord nor master to share with him.

3 Had this state continued, the wages of labour would have augmented with all those improve-[97]ments in its productive powers, to which the division of labour gives occasion. All things would gradually have become cheaper. They would have been produced by a smaller quantity of labour; and as the commodities produced by equal quantities of labour would naturally in this state of things be exchanged for one another, they would have been purchased likewise with the produce of a smaller quantity.

4 But though all things would have become cheaper in reality, in appearance many things might have become dearer than before, or have been exchanged for a greater quantity of other goods. Let us suppose, for example, that in the greater part of employments the productive powers of labour had been improved to tenfold, or that a day's labour could produce ten times the quantity of work which it had done originally; but that in a particular employment they had been improved only to double, or that a day's labour could produce only twice the quantity of work which it had done before. In exchanging the produce of a day's labour in the greater part of employments, for that of a day's labour in this particular one, ten times the original quantity of work in them would purchase only twice the original quantity in it. Any particular quantity in it, therefore, a pound weight, for example, would appear to be five times dearer than before. In reality, however, it would be twice as cheap. Though it required five times the quantity of other goods to [98] purchase it, it would require only half the quantity of labour either to purchase or to produce it. The acquisition, therefore, would be twice as easy as before.

5 But this original state of things, in which the labourer enjoyed the whole produce of his own labour, could not last beyond the first introduction of the appropriation of land and the accumulation of stock. It was at an end, therefore, long before the most considerable improvements were made in the productive powers of labour, and it would be to no purpose to trace

---

[1] The same words are used, but in a different order, at I.vi.1.

[2] The same words are used above, I.vi.4.

^{a}farther^a what might have been its effects upon the recompence or wages of labour.

6   As soon as land becomes private property, the landlord demands a share of ^{b}almost all the^b produce ^{c}which^c the labourer can either raise, or collect from it. His rent makes the first deduction from the produce of the labour which is employed upon land.

7   It seldom happens that the person who tills the ground has wherewithal to maintain himself till he reaps the harvest. His maintenance is generally advanced to him from the stock of a master, the farmer who employs him, and who would have no interest to employ him, unless he was to share in the produce of his labour, or unless his stock was to be replaced to him with a profit. This profit makes a second deduction from the produce of the labour which is employed upon land.

8   The produce of almost all other labour is liable to the like deduction of profit. In all arts [99] and manufactures the greater part of the workmen stand in need of a master to advance them the materials of their work, and their wages and maintenance till it be compleated. He shares in the produce of their labour, or in the value which it adds to the materials upon which it is bestowed; and in this share consists his profit.[3]

9   It sometimes happens, indeed, that a single independent workman has stock sufficient both to purchase the materials of his work, and to maintain himself till it be compleated. He is both master and workman, and enjoys the whole produce of his own labour, or the whole value which it adds to the materials upon which it is bestowed. It includes what are usually two distinct revenues, belonging to two distinct persons, the profits of stock, and the wages of labour.[4]

10   Such cases, however, are not very frequent, and in every part of Europe, twenty workmen serve under a master for one that is independent; and the wages of labour are every where understood to be, what they usually are, when the labourer is one person, and the owner of the stock which employs him another.

11   What are the common wages of labour depends every where upon the contract usually made between those two parties, whose interests are by no means the same. The workmen desire to get as much, the masters to give as little as possible. The former are disposed to combine in order to raise, the latter in order to lower the wages of labour.

12   [100] It is not, however, difficult to foresee which of the two parties must, upon all ordinary occasions, have the advantage in the dispute, and force the other into a compliance with their terms. The masters, being fewer in

---

$^{a-a}$ further *1, 4–6* $^{b-b}$ whatever *1* $^{c-c}$ *2–6*

[3] See above, I.vi.5.
[4] Smith comments on the need to distinguish between types of return at I.vi.19.

number, ^dcan combine much more easily; and the law, besides, authorises, or at least does not prohibit their combinations,^d while it prohibits those of the workmen.[5] We have no acts of parliament against combining to lower the price of work; but many against combining to raise it. In all such disputes the masters can hold out much longer. A landlord, a farmer, a master manufacturer, or merchant, though they did not employ a single workman, could generally live a year or two upon the stocks which they have already acquired. Many workmen could not subsist a week, few could subsist a month, and scarce any a year without employment. In the long-run the workman may be as necessary to his master as his master is to him; but the necessity is not so immediate.

13   We rarely hear, it has been said, of the combinations of masters; though frequently of those of workmen. But whoever imagines, upon this account, that masters rarely combine, is as ignorant of the world as of the subject. Masters are always and every where in a sort of tacit, but constant and uniform combination, not to raise the wages of labour above their actual rate. To violate this combination is every where a most unpopular action, and a sort of reproach to a master among his neighbours and equals. We [101] seldom, indeed, hear of this combination, because it is the usual, and one may say, the natural state of things which nobody ever hears of.[6] Masters too sometimes enter into particular combinations to sink the wages of labour even below this rate. These are always conducted with the utmost silence and secrecy, till the moment of execution, and when the workmen yield, as they sometimes do, without resistance, though severely felt by them, they are never heard of by other people. Such combinations, however, are frequently resisted by a contrary defensive combination of the workmen; who sometimes too, without any provocation of this kind, combine of their own accord to raise the price of their labour. Their usual pretences are, sometimes the high price of provisions;[7] sometimes the great profit which their masters make by their work. But whether their combinations be offensive or defensive, they are always abundantly heard of. In order to bring the point to a speedy decision, they have always recourse to the loudest clamour, and sometimes to the most shocking violence and outrage. They

---

^{d-d} cannot only combine more easily, but the law authorizes their combinations, or at least does not prohibit them, *1*

---

[5] Smith comments on the role of government at I.x.c.34 and mentions statutes affecting wages at I.x.c.61. 7 George I, st.1, c.13 (1720) regulated journeymen tailors; 12 George I, c.34 (1725) regulated certain workmen in the woollen manufactures; 12 George I, c.35 (1725) regulated brickmakers; and 22 George II, c.27 (1748) extended the provisions to a wide range of industries.

[6] See below, I.x.c.61.

[7] Smith comments on the influence of the price of provisions on wages below, I.viii.46–57.

are desperate, and act with the folly and extravagance of desperate men, who must *either* starve, or frighten their masters into an immediate compliance with their demands. The masters upon these occasions are just as clamorous upon the other side, and never cease to call aloud for the assistance of the civil magistrate, and the rigorous execution of those laws which have been enacted with so much severity against the combinations of servants, labourers, [102] and journeymen. The workmen, accordingly, very seldom derive any advantage from the violence of those tumultuous combinations, which, partly from the interposition of the civil magistrate, partly from the superior steadiness of the masters, partly from the necessity which the greater part of the workmen are under of submitting for the sake of present subsistence, generally end in nothing, but the punishment or ruin of the ringleaders.[8]

But though in disputes with their workmen, masters must generally have the advantage, there is however a certain rate below which it seems impossible to reduce, for any considerable time, the ordinary wages even of the lowest species of labour.

15 A man must always live by his work, and his wages must at least be sufficient to maintain him. They must even upon most occasions be somewhat more; otherwise it would be impossible *for him* to bring up a family, and the race of such workmen could not last beyond the first generation. Mr. Cantillon seems, upon this account, to suppose that the lowest species of common labourers must every where earn at least double their own maintenance, in order that one with another they may be enabled to bring up two children; the labour of the wife, on account of her necessary attendance on the children, being supposed no more than sufficient to provide for herself. But one-half the children born, it is computed, die before the age of manhood.[9] The poorest labourers, therefore, ac-[103]cording to this account, must, one with another, attempt to rear at least four children, in order that two may have an equal chance of living to that age. But the necessary maintenance of four children, it is supposed, may be nearly equal to that of one man. The labour of an able-bodied slave, the same author adds, is computed to be worth double his maintenance; and that of the meanest labourer, he thinks, cannot be worth less than that of an able-bodied slave. Thus far at least seems certain, that, in order to bring up a family, the labour of the husband and wife together must, even in the lowest species of common labour, be able to earn something more than what is precisely necessary

---

e-e 2–6   *f-f* 2–6

---

[8] It is noted in the index under the article 'Labourers' that they 'are seldom successful in their outrageous combinations'. The same point is made under the article 'Wages'.

[9] 'According to the calculations and observations of the celebrated Dr. Halley' (Cantillon, *Essai*, 42–3, ed. Higgs 33). Examples of child mortality are given at I.viii.38.

for their own maintenance;[10] but in what proportion, whether in that above-mentioned, or in any other, I shall not take upon me to determine.[11]

16   There are certain circumstances, however, which sometimes give the labourers an advantage, and enable them to raise their wages considerably above this rate; evidently the lowest which is consistent with common humanity.

17   When in any country the demand for those who live by wages; labourers, journeymen, servants of every kind, is continually increasing; when every year furnishes employment for a greater number than had been employed the year before, the workmen have no occasion to combine in order to raise their wages. The scarcity of hands occasions a competition among masters, who bid against one another, in order to get *g*workmen*g*, and thus voluntarily break [104] through the natural combination of masters not to raise wages.

18   The demand for those who live by wages, it is evident, cannot increase but in proportion to the increase of the funds which are destined for the payment of wages. These funds are of two kinds; first, the revenue which is over and above what is necessary for the maintenance; and, secondly, the stock which is over and above what is necessary for the employment of their masters.

19   When the landlord, annuitant, or monied man, has a greater revenue than what he judges sufficient to maintain his own family, he employs either the whole or a part of the surplus in maintaining one or more menial servants. Increase this surplus, and he will naturally increase the number of those servants.

20   When an independent workman, such as a weaver or shoe-maker, has got more stock than what is sufficient to purchase the materials of his own work, and to maintain himself till he can dispose of it, he naturally employs one or more journeymen with the surplus, in order to make a profit by their work. Increase this surplus, and he will naturally increase the number of his journeymen.

21   The demand for those who live by wages, therefore, necessarily increases with the increase of the revenue and stock of every country, and

---

g-g them *1*

[10] Cf. Harris, *Essay*, i.9–10: 'It may be reasonably allowed, that a labouring man ought to earn at least, twice as much as will maintain himself in ordinary food and cloathing; that he may be enabled to breed up children, pay rent for a small dwelling, find himself in necessary utensils, &c. So much at least the labourer must be allowed, that the community may be perpetuated.'

[11] Cantillon holds that the problem 'does not admit of exact calculation, and exactitude is not very necessary; it suffices to be near enough to the truth' (*Essai*, 44, ed. Higgs 35). It is noteworthy, in this connection, that in speaking of the subsistence wage, Smith made allowance for customary expense and for 'those things which the established rules of decency have rendered necessary to the lowest rank of people'. See, for example, V.ii.k.3 and 15.

cannot possibly increase without it. The increase of revenue and stock is the increase of national wealth. The demand for those who live [105] by wages, therefore, naturally increases with the increase of national wealth, and cannot possibly increase without it.

22   It is not the actual greatness of national wealth, but its continual increase, which occasions a rise in the wages of labour. It is not, accordingly, in the richest countries, but in the most thriving, or in those which are growing rich the fastest, that the wages of labour are highest. England is certainly, in the present times, a much richer country than any part of North America. The wages of labour, however, are much higher in North America than in any part of England.[12] In the province of New York, common labourers earn* three shillings and sixpence currency, equal to two shillings sterling, a day; ship carpenters, ten shillings and sixpence currency, with a pint of rum worth sixpence sterling, equal in all to six shillings and sixpence sterling; house carpenters and bricklayers, eight shillings currency, equal to four shillings and sixpence sterling; journeymen taylors, five shillings currency, equal to about two shillings and ten pence sterling. These prices are all above the London price; and wages are said to be as high in the other colonies as in New York. The price of provisions is every where in North America much lower than in England. A dearth has never been known there. In the worst seasons, they have always had a sufficiency [106] for themselves, though less for exportation. If the money price of labour, therefore, be higher than it is any where in the mother country, its real price, the real command of the necessaries and conveniencies of life which it conveys to the labourer, must be higher in a still greater proportion.

23   But though North America is not yet so rich as England, it is much more thriving, and advancing with much greater rapidity to the further acquisition of riches.[13] The most decisive mark of the prosperity of any country

ʰ* This was written in 1773, before the commencement of the ʲpresentʲ disturbances.ʰ

ʰ⁻ʰ 2–6   ʲ⁻ʲ late 4–6

---

[12] In commenting on Smith's doctrine that the highest wages would be found in those countries which had the highest rates of growth Pownall pointed out that the rate of increase in the price of commodities might outstrip the rate of increase in the 'price' of wages, so that in the 'triumph of prosperity' the lower orders could find themselves in 'a constant state of helpless oppression'. *Letter*, 15–16. He makes a similar point at p. 7, suggesting that commodity prices 'do *forerun*, and must, during the progress of improvement, *always forerun*' both wages and rent. Pownall made the additional point at pp. 32–3 that in a country enjoying a rapid rate of improvement, the rate of change in the prices of manufactured goods would tend to outstrip that of corn, thus placing both landlords and wage-labour in a relatively unfavourable position. Pownall argued that 'the landed men and labourers must be in a continual state of oppression and distress: that they are so in fact, the invariable and universal experience of all improving countries.' For a modern examination of a similar problem, see H. J. Habakkuk, *American and British Technology in the Nineteenth Century* (Cambridge, 1962).

[13] See below, II.v.21, where the rapid rate of growth in America is ascribed to the predominance of investment in agriculture, and *cf.* IV.vii.c.79.

is the increase of the number of its inhabitants. In Great Britain, and most other European countries, they are not supposed to double in less than five hundred years.[14] In the British colonies in North America, it has been found, that they double in twenty or five-and-twenty years.[15] Nor in the present times is this increase principally owing to the continual importation of new inhabitants, but to the great multiplication of the species. Those who live to old age, it is said, frequently see there from fifty to a hundred, and sometimes many more, descendants from their own body. Labour is there so well rewarded that a numerous family of children, instead of being a burthen is a source of opulence and prosperity to the parents. The labour of each child, before it can leave their house, is computed to be worth a hundred pounds clear gain to them. A young widow with four or five young children, who, among the middling or inferior ranks of people in Europe, would have so little chance for a [107] second husband, is there frequently courted as a sort of fortune. The value of children is the greatest of all encouragements to marriage. We cannot, therefore, wonder that the people in North America should generally marry very young. Notwithstanding the great increase occasioned by such early marriages, there is a continual complaint of the scarcity of hands in North America.[16] The demand for labourers, the funds destined for maintaining them, increase, it seems, still faster than they can find labourers to employ.[17]

[14] Sir William Petty calculated '360 Years for the time of doubling (including some Allowance for *Wars, Plagues*, and *Famine*, the Effects thereof, though they be *Terrible* at the Times and Places where they happen, yet in a period of 360 Years, is no great Matter in the whole Nation.)' (*Another Essay in Political Arithmetick concerning the Growth of the City of London* (London, 1683), 15, ed. C. H. Hull, ii.463.) Cf. Gregory King: 'That, Anno 1260, or about 200 years after the Norman Conquest, the kingdom had 2,750,000 people, or half the present number; so that the people of England have doubled in about 435 years last past; That in probability the next doubling of the people of England will be in about 600 years to come.' (*Natural and Political Observations and Conclusions upon the State and Condition of England, 1688*, in G. Chalmers, *Comparative Strength of Great Britain to 1803* (London, 1804), 41; quoted in C. D'avenant, *Political and Commercial Works*, ed. C. Whitworth (London, 1771), ii.176.)

[15] The same figures are cited below, III.iv.19. It is stated at IV.iii.c.12 that the population of France was 24, and that of America, 3 millions. The same figure for America is cited at V.iii.76 where it is also stated that Britain had less than 8 and Ireland more than 2 million inhabitants. Richard Price also remarked, on the authority of Dr. Heberden, that: 'in Madeira, the inhabitants double their own number in 84 years. But this . . . is a very slow increase, compared with that which takes place among our colonies in AMERICA. In the back settlements, where the inhabitants apply themselves entirely to agriculture, and luxury is not known, they double their own number in 15 years; and all thro' the northern colonies, in 25 years.' (*Observations on Reversionary Payments* (London, 1772), 203.) Evidently Smith did not admire Price. Letter 251 addressed to George Chalmers, dated 22 December 1785 reads: 'Price's speculations cannot fail to sink into the neglect that they always deserved. I have always considered him as a factious citizen, a most superficial Philosopher and by no means an able calculator.'

[16] The profitability of children is mentioned at IV.vii.b.2.

[17] It is pointed out in LJ (B) 329–30, ed. Cannan 256, that in Scotland there is relatively little demand for the labour of the very young, owing to prevailing economic conditions:

24   Though the wealth of a country should be very great, yet if it has been
long stationary, we must not expect to find the wages of labour very high
in it. The funds destined for the payment of wages, the revenue and stock
of its inhabitants, may be of the greatest extent, but if they have continued
for several centuries of the same, or very nearly of the same extent, the
number of labourers employed every year could easily supply, and even
more than supply, the number wanted the following year. There could
seldom be any scarcity of hands, nor could the masters be obliged to bid
against one another in order to get them. The hands, on the contrary,
would, in this case, naturally multiply beyond their employment. There
would be a constant scarcity of employment, and the labourers would be
obliged to bid against one another in order to get it. If in such a country
the wages of labour had ever been more than sufficient to maintain the
labourer, and to enable him to bring up a [108] family, the competition of
the labourers and the interest of the masters would soon reduce them to
this lowest rate which is consistent with common humanity. China has
been long one of the richest, that is, one of the most fertile, best cultivated,
most industrious, and most populous countries in the world. It seems, however, to have been long stationary. Marco Polo, who visited it more than
five hundred years ago,[18] describes its cultivation, industry, and populousness, almost in the same terms in which they are described by travellers in
the present times. It had perhaps, even long before his time, acquired that
full complement of riches which the nature of its laws and institutions permits it to acquire.[19] The accounts of all travellers, inconsistent in many
other respects, agree in the low wages of labour, and in the difficulty which
a labourer finds in bringing up a family in China. If by digging the ground
a whole day he can get what will purchase a small quantity of rice in the
evening, he is contented. The condition of artificers is, if possible, still
worse. Instead of waiting indolently in their work-houses, for the calls of
their customers, as in Europe, they are continually running about the streets
with the tools of their respective trades, offering their service, and as it were
begging employment.[20] The poverty of the lower ranks of people in China
far surpasses that of the most beggarly nations in Europe. In the neighbourhood of Canton many hundred, it is commonly said, many thousand
families have no habitation on [109] the land, but live constantly in little
fishing boats upon the rivers and canals. The subsistence which they find
there is so scanty that they are eager to fish up the nastiest garbage thrown

'This however is not the case in the commercial parts of England. A boy of 6 or 7 years of
age at Birmingham can gain his 3 pence or sixpence a day, and parents find it to be their
interest to set them soon to work.' See below, V.i.f.53.

[18] In 1275. Marco Polo is also mentioned below, IV.vii.a.8.
[19] See below, I.ix.15.
[20] 'Les artisans courent les villes du matin au soir pour chercher pratique.' (F. Quesnay,
Oeuvres économiques et philosophiques, ed. A. Oncken (Paris, 1888), 581.)

overboard from any European ship. Any carrion, the carcase of a dead dog or cat, for example, though half putrid and stinking, is as welcome to them as the most wholesome food to the people of other countries. Marriage is encouraged in China, not by the profitableness of children, but by the liberty of destroying them. In all great towns several are every night exposed in the street, or drowned like puppies in the water. The performance of this horrid office is even said to be the avowed business by which some people earn their subsistence.[21]

25 China, however, though it may perhaps stand still, does not seem to go backwards. Its towns are no-where deserted by their inhabitants. The lands which had once been cultivated are no-where neglected. The same or very nearly the same annual labour must therefore continue to be performed, and the funds destined for maintaining it must not, consequently, be sensibly diminished. The lowest class of labourers, therefore, notwithstanding their scanty subsistence, must some way or another make shift to continue their race so far as to keep up their usual numbers.

26 But it would be otherwise in a country where the funds destined for the maintenance of labour were sensibly decaying. Every year the demand for servants and labourers would, in all the dif-[110]ferent classes of employments, be less than it had been the year before. Many who had been bred in the superior classes, not being able to find employment in their own business, would be glad to seek it in the lowest. The lowest class being not only overstocked with its own workmen, but with the overflowings of all the other classes, the competition for employment would be so great in it, as

[21] The authority is probably J. B. Du Halde, *Description geographique, historique, chronologique, politique, et physique de l'Empire de la Chine et de la Tartarie Chinoise* (Paris, 1735), ii.73–4. See also Cantillon, *Essai*, 88–90, ed. Higgs 67–9. TMS V.i.2.15 refers to the barbarous custom of exposing children and observes that the practice was followed by civilized nations such as the Greeks, and condoned by philosophers such as Plato and Aristotle. Smith added: 'We find, at this day, that this practice prevails among all savage nations; and in that rudest and lowest state of society it is undoubtedly more pardonable than in any other.' He makes the same points in LJ (A) iii.80–1 and also refers to the practice in China where women were said to go from house to house collecting children to be thrown into the river: 'as we would send a parcell of puppies or kittens to be drowned. The fathers [i.e. of the Church] make a great merit of their conduct on this occasion. They converted to Christianity two of these women, and took their promise that they should bring them to be baptised before they drowned them. And in this they glory as having saved a vast number of souls.' In LJ (A) iii.79 Smith mentioned the exposure of children in Rome, and Athens, and that it was also 'practised in most early nations' and in many countries where polygamy took place. He also pointed out in LJ (B) 146, ed. Cannan 104, that 'Even in the times of exposition, when an infant was some time kept it was thought cruel to put him to death.' The Anderson Notes contain the comment that exposure 'took place among the Greeks and Romans, but if the child lived several weeks the father had no right to expose it' (28). In his essay 'Of the Populousness of Ancient Nations' Hume refers to the modern Chinese practice of exposing children and makes the point that in ancient times it was so common that it was 'not spoken of by any author of those times with the horror it deserves, or scarcely even with dissapprobation' (*Essays Moral, Political and Literary*, ed. Green and Grose, i.396). See also Montesquieu, *Esprit*, VIII.xxi.13, XXIII.xvi.1 and xxii.

to reduce the wages of labour to the most miserable and scanty subsistence of the labourer. Many would not be able to find employment even upon these hard terms, but would either starve, or be driven to seek a subsistence either by begging, or by the perpetration perhaps of the greatest enormities. Want, famine, and mortality would immediately prevail in that class, and from thence extend themselves to all the superior classes, till the number of inhabitants in the country was reduced to what could easily be maintained by the revenue and stock which remained in it, and which had escaped either the tyranny or calamity which had destroyed the rest. This perhaps is nearly the present state of Bengal, and of some other of the English settlements in the East Indies.[22] In a fertile country which had before been much depopulated, where subsistence, consequently, should not be very difficult, and where, notwithstanding, three or four hundred thousand people die of hunger in one year, we may be assured that the funds destined for the maintenance of the labouring poor are fast decaying. The difference between the genius of [111] the British constitution which protects and governs North America, and that of the mercantile company which oppresses and domineers in the East Indies, cannot perhaps be better illustrated than by the different state of those countries.[23]

27   The liberal reward of labour, therefore, as it is the necessary effect, so it is the natural symptom of increasing national wealth. The scanty maintenance of the labouring poor, on the other hand, is the natural symptom that things are at a stand, and their starving condition that they are going fast backwards.

28   In Great Britain the wages of labour seem, in the present times, to be evidently more than what is precisely necessary to enable the labourer to bring up a family. In order to satisfy ourselves upon this point it will not be necessary to enter into any tedious or doubtful calculation of what may be the lowest sum upon which it is possible to do this. There are many plain symptoms that the wages of labour are no-where in this country regulated by this lowest rate which is consistent with common humanity.

29   First, in almost every part of Great Britain there is a distinction, even in the lowest species of labour, between summer and winter wages. Summer wages are always highest. But on account of the extraordinary expence of fewel, the maintenance of a family is most expensive in winter. Wages, therefore, being highest when this expence is lowest, it seems evident that they are not regulated by what is necessary for this expence; but by the quantity and supposed [112] value of the work. A labourer, it may be said indeed, ought to save part of his summer wages in order to defray his winter

[22] It is stated at I.xi.g.25 that Spain and Portugal, alone among the European nations, seem to have gone 'backwards' since the discovery of America.

[23] The influence of British institutions on the development of America is considered at IV.vii.b.17–21 and IV.vii.b.51. The government of the East India Company is described at IV.vii.c.101–7.

expence; and that through the whole year they do not exceed what is necessary to maintain his family through the whole year. A slave, however, or one absolutely dependent on us for immediate subsistence, would not be treated in this manner. His daily subsistence would be proportioned to his daily necessities.

30   Secondly, the wages of labour do not in Great Britain fluctuate with the price of provisions. These vary every-where from year to year, frequently from month to month. But in many places the money price of labour remains uniformly the same sometimes for half a century together. If in these places, therefore, the labouring poor can maintain their families in dear years, they must be at their ease in times of moderate plenty, and in affluence in those of extraordinary cheapness. The high price of provisions during these ten years past has not in many parts of the kingdom been accompanied with any sensible rise in the money price of labour. It has, indeed, in some; owing probably more to the increase of the demand for labour, than to that of the price of provisions.

31   Thirdly, as the price of provisions varies more from year to year than the wages of labour, so, on the other hand, the wages of labour vary more from place to place than the price of provisions. The prices of bread and butcher's meat are generally the same or very nearly the same [113] through the greater part of the united kingdom. These and most other things which are sold by retail, the way in which the labouring poor buy all things, are generally fully as cheap or cheaper in great towns than in the remoter parts of the country, for reasons which I shall have occasion to explain hereafter.[24] But the wages of labour in a great town and its neighbourhood are frequently a fourth or a fifth part, twenty or five-and-twenty per cent. higher than at a few miles distance. Eighteen pence a day may be reckoned the common price of labour in London and its neighbourhood. At a few miles distance it falls to fourteen and fifteen pence. Ten pence may may be reckoned its price in Edinburgh and its neighbourhood.[25] At a few miles distance it falls to eight pence, the usual price of common labour through the greater part of the low country of Scotland, where it varies a good deal less than in England.[26] Such a difference of prices, which it seems is not always sufficient to transport a man from one parish to another, would necessarily occasion so great a transportation of the most bulky commodities, not only from one parish to another, but from one end of the kingdom, almost from one end of the world to the other, as would soon reduce them more nearly to a level. After all that has been said of the levity

[24] See below, I.x.b.37.

[25] Smith may overestimate the wage rates slightly. At Whittinghame in East Lothian a day labourer earned 4*d*. to 6*d*. in 1760 and 10*d* to 1*s*. in 1790. *Old Statistical Account*, ii.354. See also below, I.x.b.31.

[26] Smith mentioned the law of settlement in England as part of the explanation for the relatively wide differences in wage rates at I.x.c.58.

and inconstancy of human nature, it appears evidently from experience that a man is of all sorts of luggage the most difficult to be transported. If the labouring poor, therefore, can maintain their families in those parts of the kingdom where the [114] price of labour is lowest, they must be in affluence where it is highest.

32   Fourthly, the variations in the price of labour not only do not correspond either in place or time with those in the price of provisions, but they are frequently quite opposite.

33   Grain, the food of the common people, is dearer in Scotland than in England, whence Scotland receives almost every year very large supplies. But English corn must be sold dearer in Scotland, the country to which it is brought, than in England, the country from which it comes; and in proportion to its quality it cannot be sold dearer in Scotland than the Scotch corn that comes to the same market in competition with it.[27] The quality of grain depends chiefly upon the quantity of flour or meal which it yields at the mill, and in this respect English grain is so much superior to the Scotch, that, though often dearer in appearance, or in proportion to the measure of its bulk, it is generally cheaper in reality, or in proportion to its quality, or even to the measure of its weight. The price of labour, on the contrary, is dearer in England than in Scotland. If the labouring poor, therefore, can maintain their families in the one part of the united kingdom, they must be in affluence in the other. Oatmeal indeed supplies the common people in Scotland with the greatest and the best part of their food, which is in general much inferior to that of their neighbours of the same rank in England.[28] This difference, however, in the mode of their subsistence is not the cause, [115] but the effect of the difference in their wages; though, by a strange misapprehension, I have frequently heard it represented as the cause. It is not because one man keeps a coach while his neighbour walks a-foot, that the one is rich and the other poor; but because the one is rich he keeps a coach, and because the other is poor he walks a-foot.

34   During the course of the last century, taking one year with another, grain was dearer in both parts of the united kingdom than during that of the present. This is a matter of fact which cannot now admit of any reasonable doubt; and the proof of it is, if possible, still more decisive with regard to Scotland than with regard to England. It is in Scotland supported by the

---

[27] The same point is made in similar words at I.xi.e.34.

[28] Smith judges by contemporary social conventions and not by modern nutritional standards. R. H. Campbell, 'Diet in Scotland: An Example of Regional Variation', in T. C. Barker, J. C. McKenzie, and J. Yudkin, *Our Changing Fare* (London, 1966), 48. A. H. Kitchen and R. Passmore, *The Scotsman's Food* (Edinburgh, 1949), 6–13. See below, I.xi.b.41. Smith later points out that 'it is not more than a century ago that in many parts of the highlands of Scotland, butcher's-meat was as cheap or cheaper than even bread made of oatmeal' (I.xi.b.8). But contemporary livestock husbandry was inefficient because of the low price (see below, I.xi.l.2).

evidence of the publick fiars,[29] annual valuations made upon oath, according to the actual state of the markets, of all the different sorts of grain in every different county of Scotland. If such direct proof could require any collateral evidence to confirm it, I would observe that this has likewise been the case in France, and probably in most other parts of Europe. With regard to France there is the clearest proof.[30] But though it is certain that in both parts of the united kingdom grain was somewhat dearer in the last century than in the present, it is equally certain that labour was much cheaper. If the labouring poor, therefore, could bring up their families then, they must be much more at their ease now. In the last century, the most usual day-wages of common labour through the greater part of Scotland [116] were sixpence in summer and five-pence in winter. Three shillings a week, the same price very nearly, still continues to be paid in some parts of the Highlands and Western Islands. Through the greater part of the low country the most usual wages of common labour are now eight-pence a day; ten-pence, sometimes a shilling about Edinburgh, in the counties which border upon England, probably on account of that neighbourhood, and in a few other places where there has lately been a considerable rise in the demand for labour, about Glasgow, Carron, Ayrshire, &c. In England the improvements of agriculture, manufactures and commerce began much earlier than in Scotland. The demand for labour, and consequently its price, must necessarily have increased with those improvements. In the last century, accordingly, as well as in the present, the wages of labour were higher in England than in Scotland. They have risen too considerably since that time, though, on account of the greater variety of wages paid there in different places, it is more difficult to ascertain how much. In 1614, the pay of a foot soldier was the same as in the present times, eight pence a day. When it was first established it would naturally be regulated by the usual wages of common labourers, the rank of people from which foot soldiers are commonly drawn.[31] Lord Chief

---

[29] The fiars' prices do not necessarily prove Smith's point. Prices were lower in the early eighteenth century. R. Mitchison, 'The Movements of Scottish Corn Prices in the Seventeenth and Eighteenth Centuries', *Economic History Review* xviii (1965), 278. Prices were certainly higher during the years of scarcity in the later seventeenth century. For further discussion of fiars' prices see below I.xi.n.5.

[30] See below I.xi.n.5.

[31] 'The common pay of a private man in the infantry was eight pence a-day, a lieutenant two shillings, an ensign eighteen pence.' (D. Hume, *History of England*, (1778), vi.178, quoting Rymer, xvi.717.) In LJ (A) vi.138 a soldier's pay is calculated at £9 per year, 'and he has besides this kept as his arrears nearly £3 for cloathes and lodging'. Cf. LJ (A) iii.134: 'A man according to the ordinary computation may make a shift to support himself and perhaps a wife and family on ten pounds a year.' Steuart remarked that 'If a foot soldier have eight pence per diem, he is in a higher class than a Scots labourer who gains eight pence per diem; because he is paid for Sundays, as well as days of sickness and interruption from labour.' *Principles*, ed. Skinner ii.399 (this passage did not appear in the 1767 edition).

Justice Hales, who wrote in the time of Charles II. computes the necessary expence of a labourer's family, consisting of six persons, the father and mother, two children able [117] to do something, and two not able, at ten shillings a week, or twenty-six pounds a year. If they cannot earn this by their labour, they must make it up, he supposes, either by begging or stealing.³² He appears to have enquired very carefully into this subject*. In 1688, Mr. Gregory King, whose skill in political arithmetick is so much extolled by Doctor Davenant,³³ computed the ordinary income of labourers and out-servants to be fifteen pounds a year to a family, which he supposed to consist, one with another, of three and a half persons. His calculation, therefore, though different in appearance, corresponds very nearly at bottom with that of judge Hales. Both suppose the weekly expence of such families to be about twenty pence a head. Both the pecuniary income and expence of such families have increased considerably since that time through the greater part of the kingdom; in some places more, and in some less; though perhaps scarce any where so much as some exaggerated accounts of the present wages of labour have lately represented them to the publick. The price of labour, it must be observed, cannot be ascertained very accurately any where, different prices being often paid at the same place and for the same sort of labour, not only according to the different abilities of the workmen, but according to the easiness or hardness of the masters. Where wages are not regulated by law, all that we can [118] pretend to determine is what are the most usual; and experience seems to show that law can never regulate them properly, though it has often pretended to do so.

35   The real recompence of labour, the real quantity of the necessaries and conveniencies of life which it can procure to the labourer, has, during the course of the present century, increased perhaps in a still greater proportion than its money price. Not only grain has become somewhat cheaper, but many other things from which the industrious poor derive an agreeable and wholesome variety of food, have become a great deal cheaper. Potatoes, for example, do not at present, through the greater part of the kingdom, cost half the price which they used to do thirty or forty years ago. The same

---

ʲ* See his scheme for the maintenance of the Poor, in Burn's History of the Poor-laws.ʲ
[R. Burn, *History of the Poor Laws* (London, 1764), 135–60.]

ʲ⁻ʲ 2–6

---

³² '. . . a Poor Man and his Wife though able to work, may have four Children, two of them possibly able to work, two not able: The Father and Mother are not able to maintain themselves and their Family in Meat, Drink, Cloathing and House-rent under ten Shillings *per* Week, and so much they might probably get if imployed; This amounts to £26 *per Annum* . . . without a supply Equivalent to this they must live by Begging or Stealing, or Starve.' (M. Hale, *Discourse touching Provision for the Poor* (London 1683), 16–17.)

³³ Gregory King, *State and Condition of England*, in G. Chalmers, *Comparative Strength of Great Britain to 1803*, 49; quoted in C. D'avenant, *Political and Commercial Works*, ed. Whitworth, ii.175. Gregory King is also mentioned at I.xi.g.9. Smith comments on his own lack of faith in 'political arithmetic' at IV.v.b.30.

thing may be said of turnips, carrots, cabbages; things which were formerly never raised but by the spade, but which are now commonly raised
by the plough.[34] All sort of garden stuff too has become cheaper. The greater
part of the apples and even of the onions consumed in Great Britain were
in the last century imported from Flanders. The great improvements in the
coarser manufactures of both linen and woollen cloth furnish the labourers
with cheaper and better cloathing; and those in the manufactures of the
coarser metals, with cheaper and better instruments of trade, as well as
with many agreeable and convenient pieces of houshold furniture. Soap,
salt, candles, leather, and fermented liquors have, indeed, become a good
deal dearer; chiefly from the taxes which [119] have been laid upon them.
The quantity of these, however, which the labouring poor are under any
necessity of consuming, is so very small, that the increase in their price
does not compensate the diminution in that of so many other things.[35]
The common complaint that luxury extends itself even to the lowest ranks
of the people, and that the labouring poor will not now be contented with the
same food, cloathing and lodging which satisfied them in former times, may
convince us that it is not the money price of labour only, but its real recompence, which has augumented.

36   Is this improvement in the circumstances of the lower ranks of the people
to be regarded as an advantage or as an inconveniency to the society? The
answer seems at first sight abundantly plain. Servants, labourers and workmen of different kinds, make up the far greater part of every great political
society. But what improves the circumstances of the greater part can never
be regarded as an inconveniency to the whole. No society can surely be
✓ flourishing and happy, of which the far greater part of the members are
poor and miserable. It is but equity, besides, that they who feed, cloath
and lodge the whole body of the people, should have such a share of the
produce of their own labour as to be themselves tolerably well fed, cloathed
and lodged.

37   Poverty, though it no doubt discourages, does not always prevent marriage. It seems even to be favourable to generation.[36] A half-starved [120]
Highland woman frequently bears more than twenty children, while
a pampered fine lady is often incapable of bearing any, and is generally

---

[34] See below, I.xi.n.10.

[35] It is remarked in LJ (B) 231, ed. Cannan 179, that taxes keep up the price of commodities and thus diminish public opulence, such as 'all taxes upon industry, upon leather and
upon shoes, which people grudge most, upon salt, beer, or whatever is the strong drink of
the country, for no country wants some kind of it'. Similar points are made in LJ (A)
vi.85 and see below, I.xi.n.11, IV.ii.33, and V.ii.k.4–13 where it is stated that salt, leather,
soap, and candles may be regarded as necessaries so that taxes on them must raise the price
of subsistence and therefore wages. Spirits are stated to be a luxury at V.ii.k.3 and Smith
went on to argue that taxes on this commodity would not therefore raise wages but rather
have the desirable effect of reducing consumption, V.ii.k.50.

[36] See below, V.ii.k.7.

exhausted by two or three. Barrenness, so frequent among women of fashion, is very rare among those of inferior station. Luxury in the fair sex, while it enflames perhaps the passion for enjoyment, seems always to weaken, and frequently to destroy altogether, the powers of generation.

38   But poverty, though it does not prevent the generation, is extremely unfavourable to the rearing of children. The tender plant is produced, but in so cold a soil and so severe a climate, soon withers and dies. It is not uncommon, I have been frequently told, in the Highlands of Scotland for a mother who has borne twenty children not to have two alive. Several officers of great experience have assured me, that so far from recruiting their regiment, they have never been able to supply it with drums and fifes from all the soldiers children that were born in it. A greater number of fine children, however, is seldom seen anywhere than about a barrack of soldiers. Very few of them, it seems, arrive at the age of thirteen or fourteen. In some places one half the children born die before they are four years of age; in many places before they are seven; and in almost all places before they are nine or ten.[37] This great mortality, however, will every where be found chiefly among the children of the common people, who cannot afford to tend them with the same care as those [121] of better station. Though their marriages are generally more fruitful than those of people of fashion, a smaller proportion of their children arrive at maturity. In foundling hospitals, and among the children brought up by parish charities, the mortality is still greater than among those of the common people.

39   Every species of animals naturally multiplies in proportion to the means of their subsistence, and no species can ever multiply beyond it.[38] But in civilized society it is only among the inferior ranks of people that the scantiness of subsistence can set limits to the further multiplication of the

[37] LJ (A) iii.133 comments: 'It is generally reckon'd that half of mankind die before 5 years of age. But this is the case only with the meaner and poorer sort, whose children are neglected and exposed to many hardships from the inclemencies of the weather and other dangers. The better sort, who can afford attendance and attention to their children, seldom lose near so many. Few women of middling rank who have borne 8 children have lost 4 by the time they are 5 years old, and frequently none of them at all. It is therefore neglect alone that is the cause of this great mortality.' See also I.viii.15. Cf. Anderson Notes, 36: 'Of mankind the half die under 7, and of these the children of the vulgar most commonly. It is not unusual in Wales, Ireland, and the Highlands to see women without a child who have borne half a dozen, which is owing to their poverty which renders them unfit to bring up the most tender of all animals, viz infants.'

[38] LJ (A) iii.47 comments that: 'the number of men is proportion'd to the quantity of subsistence'. The same point is made below, I.xi.b.1. With regard to the link between population and the food supply, see also I.xi.c.7, IV.ii.22, and IV.v.a.8. Cf. Cantillon, *Essai*, 110, ed. Higgs 83: 'Men multiply like Mice in a barn if they have unlimited Means of Subsistence.' In speaking of the relationship between population and the food supply, Steuart remarked that 'the generative faculty resembles a spring loaded with a weight, which always exerts itself in proportion to the diminution of resistance' (*Principles*, i.20, ed. Skinner i.32.

human species; and it can do so in no other way than by destroying a great part of the children which their fruitful marriages produce.

40   The liberal reward of labour, by enabling them to provide better for their children, and consequently to bring up a greater number, naturally tends to widen and extend those limits. It deserves to be remarked too, that it necessarily does this as nearly as possible in the proportion which the demand for labour requires. If this demand is continually increasing, the reward of labour must necessarily encourage in such a manner the marriage and multiplication of labourers, as may enable them to supply that continually increasing demand by a continually increasing population. If *k*the reward*k* should at any time be less than what was requisite for this purpose, the deficiency of hands would soon raise it; and if it should at any time be more, their excessive multiplication would soon lower it to [122] this necessary rate. The market would be so much under-stocked with labour in the one case, and so much over-stocked in the other, as would soon force back its price to that proper rate which the circumstances of the society required. It is in this manner that the demand for men, like that for any other commodity, necessarily regulates the production of men; quickens it when it goes on too slowly, and stops it when it advances too fast. It is this demand which regulates and determines the state of propagation in all the different countries of the world, in North America, in Europe, and in China; which renders it rapidly progressive in the first, slow and gradual in the second, and altogether stationary in the last.

41   The *l*wear and tear*l* of a slave, it has been said, is at the expence of his master; but that of a free servant is at his own expence. The *m*wear and tear*m* of the latter, however, is, in reality, as much at the expence of his master as that of the former. The wages paid to journeymen and servants of every kind must be such as may enable them, one with another, to continue the race of journeymen and servants, according as the increasing, diminishing, or stationary demand of the society may happen to require. But though the *n*wear and tear*n* of a free servant be equally at the expence of his master, it generally costs him much less than that of a slave. The fund destined for replacing or repairing, if I may say so, the *o*wear and tear*o* of the slave, is commonly managed by a negligent master or careless overseer. That destined for performing the [123] same office with regard to the free man, is managed by the free man himself. The disorders which generally prevail in the œconomy of the rich, naturally introduce themselves into the management of the former: The strict frugality and parsimonious attention of the poor as naturally establish themselves in that of the latter. Under such different management, the same purpose must require very different

---

k-k it *I*   *l-l* tear and wear *I*   *m-m* tear and wear *I*   *n-n* tear and wear *I*
o-o tear and wear *I*

degrees of expence to execute it. It appears, accordingly, from the experience of all ages and nations, I believe, that the work done by freemen comes cheaper in the end than that performed by slaves.[39] It is found to do so even at Boston, New York, and Philadelphia, where the wages of common labour are so very high.

42   The liberal reward of labour, therefore, as it is the effect of increasing wealth, so it is the cause of increasing population. To complain of it is to lament over the necessary effect and cause of the greatest publick prosperity.

43   It deserves to be remarked, perhaps, that it is in the progressive state, while the society is advancing to the further acquisition, rather than when it has acquired its full complement of riches, that the condition of the labouring poor, of the great body of the people, seems to be the happiest and the most comfortable. It is hard in the stationary, and miserable in the declining state. The progressive state is in reality the chearful and the hearty state to all the different orders of the society. The stationary is dull; the declining, melancholy.

44   [124] The liberal reward of labour, as it encourages the propagation, so it increases the industry of the common people. The wages of labour are the encouragement of industry, which, like every other human quality, improves in proportion to the encouragement it receives. A plentiful subsistence increases the bodily strength of the labourer, and the comfortable hope of bettering his condition,[40] and of ending his days perhaps in ease and plenty, animates him to exert that strength to the utmost. Where wages are high, accordingly, we shall always find the workmen more active, diligent, and expeditious, than where they are low; in England, for example, than in Scotland; in the neighbourhood of great towns, than in remote country places. Some workmen, indeed, when they can earn in four days what will maintain them through the week, will be idle the other three.[41] This, however, is by no means the case with the greater part.[42]

---

[39] ED 5.6 remarks that 'the work which is done by slaves always [comes] dearer than that which is done by freemen'. The same point is made in LJ (B) 290,299, ed. Cannan 225,231. Cf. LJ (A) iii.111: 'the advantage gained by the labours of the slaves, if we deduce their originall cost and the expence of their maintenance, will not be so great as that which is gain'd from free tenants.' The labour of freemen is stated to be cheaper than that of slaves at III.ii.9 and IV.ix.47; cf. IV.vii.b.54.

[40] See below, II.iii.31, where Smith refers to the 'uniform, constant, and uninterrupted effort of every man to better his condition'.

[41] LJ (B) 330, ed. Cannan 257, comments that 'their work thro' half the week is sufficient to maintain them, and thro' want of education they have no amusement for the other but riot and debauchery.' Cf. Mandeville (*The Fable of the Bees*, pt.i.211, ed. Kaye, i.192.) 'Every Body knows that there is a vast number of Journey-men Weavers, Tailors, Clothworkers, and twenty other Handicrafts; who, if by four Days Labour in a Week they can maintain themselves, will hardly be persuaded to work the fifth; . . .'

[42] Cf. I.x.c.14 where it is stated that in the inferior employments, the sweets of labour consist entirely in its recompense.

Workmen, on the contrary, when they are liberally paid by the piece, are very apt to over-work themselves, and to ruin their health and constitution in a few years. A carpenter in London, and in some other places, is not supposed to last in his utmost vigour above eight years. Something of the same kind happens in many other trades, in which the workmen are paid by the piece; as they generally are in manufactures, and even in country labour, wherever wages are higher than ordinary. Almost every class of artificers is subject to some peculiar infirmity occasioned by excessive application [125] to their peculiar species of work. Ramuzzini, an eminent Italian physician, has written a particular book concerning such diseases.[43] We do not reckon our soldiers the most industrious set of people among us. Yet when soldiers have been employed in some particular sorts of work, and liberally paid by the piece, their officers have frequently been obliged to stipulate with the undertaker, that they should not be allowed to earn above a certain sum every day, according to the rate at which they were paid.[44] Till this stipulation was made, mutual emulation and the desire of greater gain, frequently prompted them to over-work themselves, and to hurt their health by excessive labour. Excessive application during four days of the week, is frequently the real cause of the idleness of the other three, so much and so loudly complained of. Great labour, either of mind or body, continued for several days together, is in most men naturally followed by a great desire of relaxation, which, if not restrained by force or by some strong necessity, is almost irresistible. It is the call of nature, which requires to be relieved by some indulgence, sometimes of ease only, but sometimes too of dissipation and diversion. If it is not complied with, the consequences are often dangerous, and sometimes fatal, and such as almost always, sooner or later, bring on the peculiar infirmity of the trade. If masters would always listen to the dictates of reason and humanity, they have frequently occasion rather to moderate, than to animate the application of many of [126] their workmen. It will be found, I believe, in every sort of trade, that the man who works so moderately, as to be able to work constantly, not only preserves his health the longest, but, in the course of the year, executes the greatest quantity of work.

45   In cheap years, it is pretended, workmen are generally more idle, and in dear ones more industrious than ordinary. A plentiful subsistence, therefore, it has been concluded, relaxes, and a scanty one quickens their industry. That a little more plenty than ordinary may render some workmen idle, cannot well be doubted; but that it should have this effect upon the greater part, or that men in general should work better when they are ill fed than when they are well fed, when they are disheartened than when they are in

---

[43] B. Ramazzini, *De morbis artificum diatriba*, translated into English as *A Treatise of the Diseases of Tradesmen* (London, 1705).

[44] See below, V.i.d.10 and note. Smith also comments on the use of piece rates at I.x.c.14.

good spirits, when they are frequently sick than when they are generally in good health, seems not very probable. Years of dearth, it is to be observed, are generally among the common people years of sickness and mortality, which cannot fail to diminish the produce of their industry.

46   In years of plenty, servants frequently leave their masters, and trust their subsistence to what they can make by their own industry. But the same cheapness of provisions, by increasing the fund which is destined for the maintenance of servants, encourages masters, farmers especially, to employ a greater number. Farmers upon such occasions expect more profit from their corn by maintaining a few more labouring servants, than [127] by selling it at a low price in the market. The demand for servants increases, while the number of those who offer to supply that demand diminishes. The price of labour, therefore, frequently rises in cheap years.[45]

47   In years of scarcity, the difficulty and uncertainty of subsistence make all such people eager to return to service. But the high price of provisions, by diminishing the funds destined for the maintenance of servants, disposes masters rather to diminish than to increase the number of those they have. In dear years too, poor independent workmen frequently consume the little stocks with which they had used to supply themselves with the materials of their work, and are obliged to become journeymen for subsistence. More people want employment than can easily get it; many are willing to take it upon lower terms than ordinary, and the wages of both servants and journeymen frequently sink in dear years.

48   Masters of all sorts, therefore, frequently make better bargains with their servants in dear than in cheap years, and find them more humble and dependent in the former than in the latter. They naturally, therefore, commend the former as more favourable to industry. Landlords and farmers, besides, two of the largest classes of masters, have another reason for being pleased with dear years. The rents of the one and the profits of the other depend very much upon the price of provisions. Nothing can be more absurd, however, than to imagine that men in ge-[128]neral should work less when they work for themselves, than when they work for other people. A poor independent workman will generally be more industrious than even a journeyman who works by the piece. The one enjoys the whole produce of his own industry; the other shares it with his master. The one, in his separate independent state, is less liable to the temptations of bad company, which in large manufactories so frequently ruin the morals of the other.[46] The superiority of the independent workman over those servants who are hired by the month or by the year, and whose wages and maintenance are the same whether they do much or do little, is likely to be still greater.

    [45] This example is extensively examined in LJ (A) vi.78–80 and see also LJ (B) 230, ed. Cannan 178.
    [46] See below, V.i.g.12, where Smith comments on the additional problems presented by the quality of life in large cities.

Cheap years tend to increase the proportion of independent workmen to
journeymen and servants of all kinds, and dear years to diminish it.

49   A French author of great knowledge and ingenuity, Mr. Messance,
receiver of the *ᵖtailles*ᵖ in the election of St. Etienne, endeavours to show
that the poor do more work in cheap than in dear years, by comparing the
quantity and value of the goods made upon those different occasions in
three different manufactures; one of coarse woollens carried on at Elbeuf;
one of linen, and another of silk, both which extend through the whole
generality of Rouen.⁴⁷ It appears from his account, which is copied from
the registers of the publick offices, that the quantity and value of the goods
made in all those three manufactures has generally been greater in cheap
than in dear years; and that it has always [129] been greatest in the cheapest,
and least in the dearest years. All the three seem to be stationary manufactures, or which, though their produce may vary somewhat from year to
year, are upon the whole neither going backwards nor forwards.

50   The manufacture of linen in Scotland, and that of coarse woollens in the
west riding of Yorkshire, are growing manufactures, of which the produce
is generally, though with some variations, increasing both in quantity and
value. Upon examining, however, the accounts which have been published
of their annual produce, I have not been able to observe that its variations
have had any sensible connection with the dearness or cheapness of the
seasons. In 1740, a year of great scarcity, both manufactures, indeed,
appear to have declined very considerably.⁴⁸ But in 1756, another year of
great scarcity, the Scotch manufacture made more than ordinary advances.⁴⁹
The Yorkshire manufacture, indeed, declined, and its produce did
not rise to what it had been in 1755 till 1766, after the repeal of the
American stamp act.⁵⁰ In that and the following year it greatly exceeded

---

ᵖ⁻ᵖ taillies 3–6

⁴⁷ Messance, *Recherches sur la population des généralites d'Auvergne, de Lyon, de Rouen
et de quelques provinces et villes du royaume, avec des réflexions sur la valeur du bled taut en
France qu'en Angleterre, depuis 1674, jusqu'en 1764* (Paris 1766). Messance is one of the
authorities cited in I.xi.n.5.

⁴⁸ Smith overstates his case.

Output	1738	1739	1740	1741	1742
Broad cloth (thousand pieces)	42·4	43·1	41·4	46·4	45·0
Scottish linen (thousand yards)	4,666	4,802	4,610	4,858	4,432

(B. R. Mitchell, *Abstract of British Historical Statistics* (Cambridge, 1962), 189 and 200.)

⁴⁹ The increase in output of Scottish linen was more probably the result of the restoration of export bounties, which were first granted in 1742 and withdrawn for two years in
1754. R. H. Campbell, *States of the Annual Progress of the Linen Manufacture, 1727–54*
(Edinburgh, 1964), vi.

⁵⁰ The increase in output of West Riding cloth in 1766 may have followed improved
methods of supervision. H. Heaton, *The Yorkshire Woollen and Worsted Industries* (Oxford,
1920), 414–16. The stamp act is mentioned below, IV.vii.c.43.

what it had ever been before, and it has continued to �q advance �q ever since.

51   The produce of all great manufactures for distant sale must necessarily depend, not so much upon the dearness or cheapness of the seasons in the countries where they are carried on, as upon the circumstances which affect the demand in the countries where they are consumed; upon peace or war, upon the prosperity or declension of [130] other rival manufactures, and upon the good or bad humour of their principal customers. A great part of the extraordinary work, besides, which is probably done in cheap years, never enters the publick registers of manufactures. The men servants who leave their masters become independent labourers. The women return to their parents, and commonly spin in order to make cloaths for themselves and their families. Even the independent workmen do not always work for publick sale, but are employed by some of their neighbours in manufactures for family use. The produce of their labour, therefore, frequently makes no figure in those publick registers of which the records are sometimes published with so much parade, and from which our merchants and manufacturers would often vainly pretend to announce the prosperity or declension of the greatest empires.

52   Though the variations in the price of labour, not only do not always correspond with those in the price of provisions, but are frequently quite opposite, we must not, upon this account, imagine that the price of provisions has no influence upon that of labour.[51] The money price of labour is necessarily regulated by two circumstances; the demand for labour, and the price of the necessaries and conveniencies of life.[52] The demand for labour, according as it happens to be increasing, stationary, or declining, or to require an increasing, stationary, or declining population, determines the quantity of the necessaries and conveniencies of life which must be [131] given to the labourer; and the money price of labour is determined by what is requisite for purchasing this quantity. Though the money price of labour, therefore, is sometimes high where the price of provisions is low, it would be still higher, the demand continuing the same, if the price of provisions was high.

53   It is because the demand for labour increases in years of sudden and extraordinary plenty, and diminishes in those of sudden and extraordinary scarcity, that the money price of labour sometimes rises ᵃ the one, and sinks in the other.

54   In a year of sudden and extraordinary plenty, there are funds in the hands of many of the employers of industry, sufficient to maintain and employ a greater number of industrious people than had been employed the year before; and this extraordinary number cannot always be had.

�q⁻�q do so *1*

[51] See below, IV.v.a.12.   [52] See below, V.ii.k.4.

Those masters, therefore, who want more workmen, bid against one another, in order to get them, which sometimes raises both the real and the money price of their labour.

55   The contrary of this happens in a year of sudden and extraordinary scarcity. The funds destined for employing industry are less than they had been the year before. A considerable number of people are thrown out of employment, who bid 'against one' another, in order to get it, which sometimes lowers both the real and the money price of labour. In 1740, a year of extraordinary scarcity, many people were willing to work for bare subsistence. In the succeeding [132] years of plenty, it was more difficult to get labourers and servants.

56   The scarcity of a dear year, by diminishing the demand for labour, tends to lower its price, as the high price of ˢprovisionsˢ tends to raise it. The plenty of a cheap year, on the contrary, by increasing the demand, tends to raise the price of labour, as the cheapness of provisions tends to lower it. In the ordinary variations of the price of provisions, those two opposite causes seem to counterbalance one another; which is probably in part the reason why the wages of labour are every-where so much more steady and permanent than the price of provisions.

57   The increase in the wages of labour necessarily increases the price of many commodities, by increasing that part of it which resolves itself into wages, and so far tends to diminish their consumption both at home and abroad. The same cause, however, which raises the wages of labour, the increase of stock, tends to increase its productive powers, and to make a smaller quantity of labour produce a greater quantity of work. The owner of the stock which employs a great number of labourers, necessarily endeavours, for his own advantage, to make such a proper division and distribution of employment, that they may be enabled to produce the greatest quantity of work possible. For the same reason, he endeavours to supply them with the best machinery which either he or they can think of.[53] What takes place among the labourers in a particular [133] workhouse, takes place, for the same reason, among those of a great society. The greater their number, the more they naturally divide themselves into different classes and subdivisions of employment. More heads are occupied in inventing the most proper machinery for executing the work of each, and it is, therefore, more likely to be invented. There are many commodities, therefore, which, in consequence of these improvements, come to be produced by so much less labour than before, that the increase of its price ᵗis more than compensated byᵗ the diminution of its quantity.[54]

ʳ⁻ʳ one against 6   ˢ⁻ˢ provision 6   ᵗ⁻ᵗ does not compensate *1*

[53] A similar point is made in the introduction to II.

[54] See below, I.xi.o. and V.i.e.26 (p. 748), where it is pointed out with regard to an increase in the level of demand for manufactured goods, that 'though in the beginning it may sometimes raise the price of goods, never fails to lower it in the long run'.

CHAPTER IX

Of the Profits of Stock

1 THE rise and fall in the profits of stock depend upon the same causes with the rise and fall in the wages of labour, the increasing or declining state of the wealth of the society; but those causes affect the one and the other very differently.

2 The increase of stock, which raises wages, tends to lower profit. When the stocks of many rich merchants are turned into the same trade, their mutual competition naturally tends to lower its profit; and when there is a like increase of stock in all the different trades carried [134] on in the same society, the same competition must produce the same effect in them all.[1]

3 It is not easy, it has already been observed, to ascertain what are the average wages of labour even in a particular place, and at a particular time.[2] We can, even in this case, seldom determine more than what are the most usual wages. But even this can seldom be done with regard to the profits of stock. Profit is so very fluctuating, that the person who carries on a particular trade cannot always tell you himself what is the average of his annual profit. It is affected, not only by every variation of price in the commodities which he deals in, but by the good or bad fortune both of his rivals and of his customers, and by a thousand other accidents to which goods when carried either by sea or by land, or even when stored in a warehouse, are liable. It varies, therefore, not only from year to year, but from day to day, and almost from hour to hour.[3] To ascertain what is the average profit of all the different trades carried on in a great kingdom, must be much more difficult; and to judge of what it may have been formerly, or in remote periods of time, with any degree of precision, must be altogether impossible.

4 But though it may be impossible to determine, with any degree of precision, what are or were the average profits of stock, either in the present, or in antient times, some notion may be formed of them from the interest of money.[4] It may be laid down as a maxim, that wherever a great deal can be made by the use of money, [135] a great deal will commonly be given for the use of it; and that wherever little can be made by it, less will commonly be given for it.[5] According, therefore, as the usual market rate of interest varies in any country, we may be assured that the ordinary profits of stock must vary with it, must sink as it sinks, and rise as it rises. The progress of

---

[1] See below, I.x.c.26 and II.iv.8.
[2] See above, I.viii.34.
[3] Cf. above, I.vii.1.
[4] Defined above, I.vi.18, and examined in II.iv.
[5] Cf. II.iv.13.

interest, therefore, may lead us to form some notion of the progress of profit.[6]

5   By the 37th of Henry VIII. all interest above ten per cent. was declared unlawful.[7] More, it seems, had sometimes been taken before that. In the reign of Edward VI. religious zeal prohibited all interest.[8] This prohibition, however, like all others of the same kind, is said to have produced no effect, and probably rather increased than diminished the evil of usury.[9] The statute of Henry VIII. was revived by the 13th of Elizabeth, cap. 8.[10] and ten per cent. continued to be the legal rate of interest till the 21st of James I. when it was restricted to eight per cent.[11] It was reduced to six per cent. soon after the restoration,[12] and by the 12th of Queen Anne, to five per cent.[13] All these different statutory regulations seem to have been made with great propriety. They seem to have followed and not to have gone before the market rate of interest, or the rate at which people of good credit usually borrowed.[14] Since the time of Queen Anne, five per cent. seems to have been rather above than below the market rate. Before the late war, the government borrowed at three per cent.;[15] and people of good credit in the capital, and in [136] many other parts of the kingdom, at three and a half, four, and four and a half per cent.

6   Since the time of Henry VIII. the wealth and revenue of the country have been continually advancing, and, in the course of their progress, their pace seems rather to have been gradually accelerated than retarded. They seem, not only to have been going on, but to have been going on faster and faster. The wages of labour have been continually increasing during the same period, and in the greater part of the different branches of trade and manufactures the profits of stock have been diminishing.

7   It generally requires a greater stock to carry on any sort of trade in a great town than in a country village. The great stocks employed in every branch of trade, and the number of rich competitors, generally reduce the

---

[6] Cantillon remarked, with regard to interest, that 'its constant usage in States seems based upon the Profits which the Undertakers can make out of it' (*Essai*, 265, ed. Higgs 201).

[7] 37 Henry VIII, c.9 (1545).

[8] 5 and 6 Edward VI, c.20 (1551).

[9] 'Nothing is more amusing than the multitude of Laws and Canons made in every age on the subject of the Interest of Money, always by Wiseacres who were hardly acquainted with Trade and always without effect.' (Cantillon, *Essai*, 278–9, ed. Higgs, 211.)

[10] Of 1571.

[11] 21 James I, c.17 (1623).

[12] 12 Charles II, c.13 (1660).

[13] 13 Anne, c.15 (1713), in *Statutes of the Realm*, ix.928; 12 Anne, st.2, c.16, in Ruffhead's edition. See also V.ii.f.8 and V.iii.27.

[14] The relationship between the market and legal rates of interest is discussed below, II.iv.15.

[15] The approximate yield on 3 per cent Funds was 3 per cent or below from 1750 to 1755. The yield increased during the war years from 1756 to a peak of 4·2 per cent in 1762.

rate of profit in the former below what it is in the latter. But the wages of labour are generally higher in a great town than in a country village. In a thriving town the people who have great stocks to employ, frequently cannot get the number of workmen they want, and therefore bid against one another in order to get as many as they can, which raises the wages of labour, and lowers the profits of stock. In the remote parts of the country there is frequently not stock sufficient to employ all the people, who therefore bid against one another in order to get employment, which lowers the wages of labour, and raises the profits of stock.

8   [137] In Scotland, though the legal rate of interest is the same as in England, the market rate is rather higher. People of the best credit there seldom borrow under five per cent. Even private bankers in Edinburgh give four per cent. upon their promissory notes, of which payment either in whole or in part may be demanded at pleasure. Private bankers in London give no interest for the money which is deposited with them. There are few trades which cannot be carried on with a smaller stock in Scotland than in England. The common rate of profit, therefore, must be somewhat greater. The wages of labour, it has already been observed, are lower in Scotland than in England.[16] The country too is not only much poorer, but the steps by which it advances to a better condition, for it is evidently advancing, seem to be much slower and more tardy.[17]

9   The legal rate of interest in France has not, during the course of the present century, been always regulated by the market rate*. In 1720 interest was reduced from the twentieth to the fiftieth penny, or from five to two per cent. In 1724 it was raised to the thirtieth penny, or to 3⅓ per cent. In 1725 it was again raised to the twentieth penny, or to five per cent. In 1766, during the administration of Mr. Laverdy, it was reduced to the twenty-fifth penny, or to four per cent. The Abbe Terray raised it afterwards to the old rate of five per cent. The sup-[138]posed purpose of many of those violent reductions of interest was to prepare the way for reducing that of the publick debts; a purpose which has sometimes been executed. France is perhaps in the present times not so rich a country as England; and though the legal rate of interest has in France frequently been lower than in England, the market rate has generally been higher; for there, as in other countries, they have several very safe and easy methods of evading the law.[18] The profits of trade, I have been assured by British merchants who had traded in both countries, are higher in France than in England;

ᵃ* See Denisart, Article Taux de Terres, tom.iii. p. 18.ᵃ [J. B. Denisart, *Collection de décisions nouvelles et de notions relatives à la jurisprudence actuelle* (Paris, 7th ed., 1771).]

ᵃ⁻ᵃ 2–6

---

[16] See above, I.viii.31,33.
[17] See below, I.xi.e.35.
[18] See below, II.iv.16. In England the usury laws were generally respected.

and it is no doubt upon this account that many British subjects chuse
rather to employ their capitals in a country where trade is in disgrace, than
in one where it is highly respected. The wages of labour are lower in France
than in England. When you go from Scotland to England, the difference
which you may remark between the dress and countenance of the common
people in the one country and in the other, sufficiently indicates the difference in their condition. The contrast is still greater when you return
from France.[19] France, though no doubt a richer country than Scotland,
seems not to be going forward so fast. It is a common and even a popular
opinion in the country that it is going backwards; an opinion which, I
apprehend, is ill founded even with regard to France, but which nobody can
possibly entertain with regard to Scotland, who sees the country now and
who saw it twenty or thirty years ago.

10   [139] The province of Holland, on the other hand, in proportion to the
extent of its territory and the number of its people, is a richer country than
England. The government there borrow at two per cent., and private
people of good credit at three. The wages of labour are said to be higher in
Holland than in England, and the Dutch, it is well known, trade upon
lower profits than any people in Europe.[20] The trade of Holland, it has
been pretended by some people, is decaying, and it may perhaps be true
that some particular branches of it are so. But these symptoms seem to
indicate sufficiently that there is no general decay. When profit diminishes,
merchants are very apt to complain that trade decays; though the diminution of profit is the natural effect of its prosperity, or of a greater stock being
employed in it than before. During the late war the Dutch gained the whole
carrying trade of France, of which they still retain a very large share. The
great property which they possess both in the French and English funds,[21]
about forty millions, it is said, in the latter (in which I suspect, however,
there is a considerable exaggeration);[22] the great sums which they lend to

[19] Cf. Imitative Arts, I.14: 'In France, the condition of the inferior ranks of people is
seldom so happy as it frequently is in England.'
[20] See below, V.ii.f.13 and V.ii.k.80.
[21] It is stated at V.ii.a.9 that the policy of lending to foreign states was peculiar to the
Canton of Berne.
[22] There were differences of opinion. According to Postlethwayt, 'The annuity we are
constantly obliged to pay to foreigners, for the proportion of the principal money debt,
which has been estimated by some at $\frac{1}{5}$, and by others at $\frac{1}{4}$, of the whole debt.' (M. Postlethwayt, *Dictionary of Commerce* (London, 1774).) By contrast, 'It is more than probable,
that Foreigners are not concerned in any Thing like One-fourth of the national Debt;
the Dutch, who are the principal Creditors, however engaged before, not advancing an equal
Proportion of the last accumulated Debt of 30,000,000. I have been informed, that most of
the Money which the Dutch have here, is in Bank, *East India*, and *South Sea* Stocks, and that
their Interest in them might account to One-third of the Whole.' (N. Magens, *The
Universal Merchant*, ed. Horsley 13.) In *The Present State of the Nation* (1768), 30, the
author states that 'the interest of the debt due to foreigners amounts to £1,560,000, which
must be paid out of the profits of our trade'. Foreigners would hold about one-quarter on
his computation.

private people in countries where the rate of interest is higher than in their own, are circumstances which no doubt demonstrate the redundancy of their stock, or that it has increased beyond what they can employ with tolerable profit in the proper business of their own country: but they do not demonstrate that that business has decreased. As the capital of a [140] private man, though acquired by a particular trade, may increase beyond what he can employ in it, and yet that trade continue to increase too; so may likewise the capital of a great nation.

11   In our North American and West Indian colonies, not only the wages of labour, but the interest of money, and consequently the profits of stock, are higher than in England. In the different colonies both the legal and the market rate of interest run from six to eight per cent. High wages of labour and high profits of stock, however, are things, perhaps, which scarce ever go together, except in the peculiar circumstances of new colonies.[23] A new colony must always for some time be more under-stocked in proportion to the extent of its territory, and more under-peopled in proportion to the extent of its stock, than the greater part of other countries.[24] They have more land than they have stock to cultivate. What they have, therefore, is applied to the cultivation only of what is most fertile and most favourably situated, the *b*lands*b* near the sea shore, and along the banks of navigable rivers.[25] Such land too is frequently purchased at a price below the value even of its natural produce.[26] Stock employed in the purchase and improvement of such lands must yield a very large profit, and consequently afford to pay a very large interest. Its rapid accumulation in so profitable an employment enables the planter to increase the number of his hands faster than he can find them in a new settlement. Those whom he can find, therefore, are very liberally rewarded. [141] As the colony increases, the profits of stock gradually diminish. When the most fertile and best situated lands have been all occupied, less profit can be made by the cultivation of what is inferior both in soil and situation, and less interest can be afforded for the stock which is so employed. In the greater part of our colonies, accordingly, both the legal and the market rate of interest have been considerably reduced during the course of the present century. As riches, improvement, and population have increased, interest has declined. The wages of labour do not sink with the profits of stock. The demand for labour increases with the increase of stock whatever be its profits; and after these are diminished, stock may not only continue to increase, but to increase much faster than before. It is with industrious nations who are advancing

b–b land 4–6

---

[23] See above, I.ix.23.   [24] See below, IV.vii.c.38.
[25] See above, I.iii.4, and below, II.v.21, where Smith comments on the importance of investment in agriculture, as explaining the rapid growth rate of the American colonies.
[26] See below, III.i.5 and IV.vii.b.2.

in the acquisition of riches, as with industrious individuals. A great stock, though with small profits, generally increases faster than a small stock with great profits. Money, says the proverb, makes money. When you have got a little, it is often easy to get more. The great difficulty is to get that little. The connection between the increase of stock and that of industry, or of the demand for useful labour, has partly been explained already,[27] but will be explained more fully hereafter in treating of the accumulation of stock.[28]

12   The acquisition of new territory, or of new branches of trade, may sometimes raise the profits of stock,[29] and with them the interest of money, [142] even in a country which is fast advancing in the acquisition of riches. The stock of the country not being sufficient for the whole accession of business, which such acquisitions present to the different people among whom it is divided, is applied to those particular branches only which afford the greatest profit. Part of what had before been employed in other trades, is necessarily withdrawn from them, and turned into some of the new and more profitable ones. In all those old trades, therefore, the competition comes to be less than before. The market comes to be less fully supplied with many different sorts of goods. Their price necessarily rises more or less, and yields a greater profit to those who deal in them, who can, therefore, afford to borrow at a higher interest. For some time after the conclusion of the late war, not only private people of the best credit, but some of the greatest companies in London, commonly borrowed at five per cent. who before that had not been used to pay more than four, and four and a half per cent. The great accession both of territory and trade, by our acquisitions in North America and the West Indies, will sufficiently account for this, without supposing any diminution in the capital stock of the society. So great an accession of new business to be carried on by the old stock, must necessarily have diminished the quantity employed in a great number of particular branches, in which the competition being less, the profits must have been greater. I shall hereafter have occasion to mention the reasons which [143] dispose me to believe that the capital stock of Great Britain was not diminished even by the enormous expence of the late war.[30]

13   The diminution of the capital stock of the society, or of the funds destined for the maintenance of industry, however, as it lowers the wages of labour, so it raises the profits of stock, and consequently the interest of money. By the wages of labour being lowered, the owners of what stock remains in the society can bring their goods ᶜat less expenceᶜ to market

ᶜ⁻ᶜ cheaper *1–2*

[27] See above, I.viii.   [28] See below, II.iii.
[29] See below, especially IV.vii.c.19–25. This argument was to be a feature of Smith's critique of colonial policy in IV.vii.c.
[30] See below, II.iii.35 and V.iii.58

than before, and less stock being employed in supplying the market than before, they can sell them dearer. Their goods cost them less, and they get more for them. Their profits, therefore, being augmented at both ends, can well afford a large interest. The great fortunes so suddenly and so easily acquired in Bengal and the other British settlements in the East Indies, may satisfy us that, as the wages of labour are very low, so the profits of stock are very high in those ruined countries. The interest of money is proportionably so. In Bengal, money is frequently lent to the farmers at forty, fifty, and sixty per cent. and the succeeding crop is mortgaged for the payment. As the profits which can afford such an interest must eat up almost the whole rent of the landlord, so such enormous usury must in its turn eat up the greater part of those profits. Before the fall of the Roman republick, a usury of the same kind seems to have been common in the provinces, under the ruinous administration of their proconsuls. The virtuous Brutus lent [144] money in Cyprus at ^deight-and-forty^d per cent. as we learn from the letters of Cicero.[31]

14   In a country which had acquired that full complement of riches which the nature of its soil and climate, and its situation with respect to other countries allowed it to acquire; which could, therefore, advance no further, and which was not going backwards, both the wages of labour and the profits of stock would probably be very low. In a country fully peopled in proportion to what either its territory could maintain or its stock employ, the competition for employment would necessarily be so great as to reduce the wages of labour to what was barely sufficient to keep up the number of labourers, and, the country being already fully peopled, that number could never be augmented. In a country fully stocked in proportion to all the business it had to transact, as great a quantity of stock would be employed in every particular branch as the nature and extent of the trade would admit. The competition, therefore, would everywhere be as great, and consequently the ordinary profit as low as possible.

15   But perhaps no country has ever yet arrived at this degree of opulence. China seems to have been long stationary, and had probably long ago acquired that full complement of riches which is consistent with the nature of its laws and institutions.[32] But this complement may be much inferior

^{d-d} five and forty *I*

---

[31] 'If Brutus thinks that I ought to have allowed 48 per cent, when throughout my province I have recognized only 12 per cent, and have fixed this rate in my edict, with the approval of the most grasping userers; . . . I shall be sorry that he is angry with me, but I shall be far sorrier at discovering that he is not the man I imagined he was.' (Cicero, *Letters to Atticus*, VI, i.5–6, translated by E. O. Winstedt in Loeb Classical Library (1912), i.422–3.)
[32] See above, I.viii.24. Smith comments on China's neglect of foreign commerce, for example, at I.iii.7, II.v.22, III.i.7, and IV.iii.c.11, arguing at IV.ix.40 and 41 that any relaxation of the laws governing her trade would give a considerable stimulus to growth.

to what, with other laws and institutions, the nature of its soil, climate, and situation might admit of. A country which neglects [145] or despises foreign commerce, and which admits the vessels of foreign nations into one or two of its ports only, cannot transact the same quantity of business which it might do with different laws and institutions.[33] In a country too, where, though the rich or the owners of large capitals enjoy a good deal of security, the poor or the owners of small capitals enjoy scarce any, but are liable, under the pretence of justice, to be pillaged and plundered at any time by the inferior mandarines, the quantity of stock employed in all the different branches of business transacted within it, can never be equal to what the nature and extent of that business might admit. In every different branch, the oppression of the poor must establish the monopoly of the rich, who, by engrossing the whole trade to themselves, will be able to make very large profits. Twelve per cent. accordingly is said to be the common interest of money in China, and the ordinary profits of stock must be sufficient to afford this large interest.[34]

16   A defect in the law may sometimes raise the rate of interest considerably above what the condition of the country, as to wealth or poverty, would require. When the law does not enforce the performance of contracts,[35] it puts all borrowers nearly upon the same footing with bankrupts or people of doubtful credit in better regulated countries. The uncertainty of recovering his money makes the lender exact the same usurious interest which is usually required from bankrupts. Among the barbarous nations who [146] over-run the western provinces of the Roman empire, the performance of contracts was left for many ages to the faith of the contracting parties. The courts of justice of their kings seldom intermeddled in it. The high rate of interest which took place in those antient times may perhaps be partly accounted for from this cause.

17   When the law prohibits interest altogether, it does not prevent it. Many people must borrow, and nobody will lend without such a consideration for the use of their money as is suitable, not only to what can be made by the use of it, but to the difficulty and danger of evading the law. The high rate of interest among all Mahometan nations is accounted for by Mr.

[33] Montesquieu attributed the lack of trade to the character of the Chinese, whose precarious subsistence inspired them with such 'an excessive desire of gain, that no trading nation can confide in them. This acknowledged infedility has secured them the possession of the trade to Japan.' *Esprit*, XIX.x.3. In XIX.xx.1 the Chinese are described as the 'greatest cheats upon earth'.

[34] Cantillon held that in China the large number of small undertakers 'keep up the rate of Interest in the highest class at 30 per cent, while it hardly exceeds 5 per cent in our Europe. At Athens in the time of Solon interest was at 18 per cent. In the Roman Republic it was most commonly 12 per cent, but has been known to be 48, 20, 8, 6 and the lowest 4 per cent.' (*Essai*, 281–2, ed. Higgs 213.)

[35] For a discussion of contract, see LJ (B) 175–80, ed. Cannan 130–4.

Montesquieu, not from their poverty, but partly from this, and partly from the difficulty of recovering the money.[36]

18   The lowest ordinary rate of profit must always be something more than what is sufficient to compensate the occasional losses to which every employment of stock is exposed.[37] It is this surplus only which is neat or clear profit. What is called gross profit comprehends frequently, not only this surplus, but what is retained for compensating such extraordinary losses. ✓ The interest which the borrower can afford to pay is in proportion to the clear profit only.

19   The lowest ordinary rate of interest must, in the same manner, be something more than sufficient to compensate the occasional losses to which lending, even with tolerable prudence, is ex-[147]posed. Were it not more, charity or friendship could be the only motives for lending.

20   In a country which had acquired its full complement of riches, where in every particular branch of business there was the greatest quantity of stock that could be employed in it, as the ordinary rate of clear profit would be very small, so that usual market rate of interest which could be afforded out of it, would be so low as to render it impossible for any but the very wealthiest people to live upon the interest of their money. All people of small or middling fortunes would be obliged to superintend themselves the employment of their own stocks. It would be necessary that almost every man should be a man of business, or engage in some sort of trade. The province of Holland seems to be approaching near to this state. It is there unfashionable not to be a man of business. Necessity makes it usual for almost every man to be so, and custom every where regulates fashion. As it is ridiculous not to dress, so is it, in some measure, not to be employed, like other people. As a man of a civil profession seems aukward in a camp or a garrison, and is even in some danger of being despised there, so does an idle man among men of business.

21   The highest ordinary rate of profit may be such as, in the price of the greater part of commodities, eats up the whole of what should go to the rent of the land, and leaves only what is sufficient to pay the labour of preparing and bring-[148]ing them to market, according to the lowest rate at which labour can any-where be paid, the bare subsistence of the labourer. The workman must always have been fed in some way or other while he was about the work; but the landlord may not always have been paid. The

---

[36] 'The laws of Mahomet confound usury with lending upon interest. Usury increases in Mahommedan countries in proportion to the severity of the prohibition. The lender indemnifies himself for the danger he undergoes of suffering the penalty.

In those Eastern countries, the greater part of the people are secure in nothing; there is hardly any proportion between the actual possession of a sum and the hopes of receiving it again after having lent it: usury, then, must be raised in proportion to the danger of insolvency.' (Montesquieu, *Esprit*, XXII.xix.5–6.)

[37] See below, V.ii.f, where Smith discusses taxes on profits.

profits of the trade which the servants of the East India Company carry on in Bengal may not perhaps be very far from this state.[38]

22   The proportion which the usual market rate of interest ought to bear to the ordinary rate of clear profit, necessarily varies as profit rises or falls. Double interest is in Great Britain reckoned, what the merchants call, a good, moderate, reasonable profit;[39] terms which I apprehend mean no more than a common and usual profit. In a country where the ordinary rate of clear profit is eight or ten per cent., it may be reasonable that one half of it should go to interest, wherever business is carried on with borrowed money. The stock is at the risk of the borrower, who, as it were, insures it to the lender; and four or five per cent. may, in the greater part of trades, be both a sufficient profit upon the risk of this insurance, and a sufficient recompence for the trouble of employing the stock. But the proportion between interest and clear profit might not be the same in countries where the ordinary rate of profit was either a good deal lower, or a good deal higher. If it were a good deal lower, one half of it perhaps could not be afforded for interest; and [149] more might be afforded if it were a good deal higher.

23   In countries which are fast advancing to riches, the low rate of profit may, in the price of many commodities, compensate the high wages of labour, and enable those countries to sell as cheap as their less thriving neighbours, among whom the wages of labour may be lower.

24   ᵉIn reality high profits tend much more to raise the price of work than high wages. If in the linen manufacture, for example, the wages of the different working people; the flax-dressers, the spinners, the weavers, &c. should, all of them, be advanced two pence a day: it would be necessary to heighten the price of a piece of linen only by a number of two pences equal to the number of people that had been employed about it, multiplied by the number of days during which they had been so employed. That part of the price of the commodity which resolved itself into wages would, through all the different stages of the manufacture, rise only in arithmetical proportion to this rise of wages. But if the profits of all the different employers of those working people should be raised five per cent. that part of the price of the commodity which resolved itself into profit, would, through all the different stages of the manufacture, rise in geometrical proportion to this rise of profit. The employer of the flax-dressers would in selling his flax require an additional five per cent. upon the whole value of the materials and wages which he advanced to his workmen. The employer of [150] the spinners would require an additional five per cent. both upon the ad-

ᵉ⁻ᵉ 2–6 [includes the whole of this paragraph]

[38] See below, IV.vii.c.101–5.
[39] See below, V.ii.e.2, where Smith discusses profits on house-building.

vanced price of the flax and upon the wages of the spinners. And the employer of the weavers would require a like five per cent. both upon the advanced price of the linen yarn and upon the wages of the weavers. In raising the price of commodities the rise of wages operates in the same manner as simple interest does in the accumulation of debt. The rise of profit operates like compound interest. Our merchants and master-manufacturers complain much of the bad effects of high wages in raising the price, and thereby lessening the sale of their goods both at home and abroad. They say nothing concerning the bad effects of high profits. They are silent with regard to the pernicious effects of their own gains. They complain only of those of other people.^{e40}

⁴⁰ Similar sentiments are expressed below, IV.vii.c.29. Smith also states that high profits destroy parsimony, at IV.vii.c.61.

CHAPTER X

Of Wages and Profit in the different Employments of Labour and Stock

1 THE whole of the advantages and disadvantages of the different employments of labour and stock must, in the same neighbourhood, be either perfectly equal or continually tending to equality. If in the same neighbourhood, there was any employment *a*evidently either*a* more or less advantageous than the rest, so many people would crowd into it in the one case, and so many would desert it in the other, that its advantages would soon return to the level of other employments.[1] This at least would be the case in a society where things were left to follow their natural course, where there was perfect liberty,[2] and where every man was perfectly free both to chuse what occupation he thought proper, and to change it as often as he thought proper. Every man's interest would prompt him to seek the advantageous, and to shun the disadvantageous employment.

2 Pecuniary wages and profit, indeed, are every-where in Europe extremely different according to the different employments of labour and stock. But this difference arises partly from certain circumstances in the employments themselves, which, either really, or at least in the imaginations of men, make up for a small pecuniary gain in some, and counter-balance a great one in others; and partly from the policy of [152] Europe, which nowhere leaves things at perfect liberty.

3 The particular consideration of those circumstances and of that policy will divide this chapter into two parts.

PART I

Inequalities arising from the Nature of the Employments themselves

1 The five following are the principal circumstances which, so far as I have been able to observe, make up for a small pecuniary gain in some employments, and counter-balance a great one in others: first, the agreeableness or disagreeableness of the employments themselves; secondly, the easiness and cheapness, or the difficulty and expence of learning them; thirdly, the constancy or inconstancy of employment in them; fourthly, the

---

a-a either evidently *1-2*

[1] Smith uses the doctrine of net advantages in discussing taxes on particular employments, below, V.ii.i.6.
[2] This term is used, for example, at I.vii.6 and 30, IV.vii.c.44.

small or great trust which must be reposed in those who exercise them; and, fiftly, the probability or improbability of success in them.[3]

2   First, The wages of labour vary with the ease or hardship, the cleanliness or dirtiness, the honourableness or dishonourableness of the employment. Thus in most places, take the year round, a journeyman taylor earns less than a journeyman weaver. His work is much easier. A journeyman weaver earns less than a journeyman smith. His work is not always easier, but it is much cleanlier. A journeyman blacksmith, though an artificer, seldom earns so much in [153] twelve hours as a collier, who is only a labourer, does in eight. His work is not quite so dirty, is less dangerous, and is carried on in day-light, and above ground. Honour makes a great part of the reward of all honourable professions. In point of pecuniary gain, all things considered, they are generally under-recompensed, as I shall endeavour to show by and by.[4] Disgrace has the contrary effect. The trade of a butcher is a brutal and an odious business; but it is in most places more profitable than the greater part of common trades. The most detestable of all employments, that of public executioner, is in proportion to the quantity of work done, better paid than any common trade whatever.

3   Hunting and fishing, the most important employments of mankind in the rude state of society, become in its advanced state their most agreeable amusements, and they pursue for pleasure what they once followed from

---

[3] Cf. Cantillon, *Essai*, 24, 26–7, ed. Higgs 19, 21–3:

Those who employ Artisans or Craftsmen must needs therefore pay for their labour at a higher rate than for that of a Husbandman or common Labourer; and their labour will necessarily be dear in proportion to the time lost in learning the trade and the cost and risk incurred in becoming proficient.
The Crafts which require the most Time in training or most Ingenuity and Industry must necessarily be the best paid. A skilful Cabinet-maker must receive a higher price for his work than an ordinary Carpenter, and a good Watchmaker more than a Farrier. The Arts and Crafts which are accompanied by risks and dangers like those of Founders, Mariners, Silver miners, etc. ought to be paid in proportion to the risks. When over and above the dangers skill is needed they ought to be paid still more, e.g. Pilots, Divers, Engineers, etc. When Capacity and trustworthiness are needed the labour is paid still more highly, as in the case of Jewellers, Bookkeepers, Cashiers and others.

Also Harris, *Essay*, i.13: 'And as any given trade is attended with greater risques of any sort, requires more skill, more trust, more expence in setting up, *etc.* the artificer will be entitled to still better wages. In like manner, those professions that require genius, great confidence, a liberal education, *etc.* have a right to be rewarded proportionably.' Hutcheson also points out that wages and profits may be affected by the costs of maintaining the 'dignity of station in which, according to the custom of a country, the men must live who provide us with certain goods, or works of art' (*System*, ii.55; Cf. ii.63 and below, V.ii.k.3). Smith discusses the different considerations which will induce a man 'to apply all his art and industry to some particular branch of business' in LJ (A) vi.58–63, 67–9, LJ (B) 224–7, ed. Cannan 173–6. See also ED 3.1: the returns from any employment must be sufficient '1st to maintain him; 2ndly to indemnify him for the expence of his education to that particular business; 3dly to compensate him for the risk he may run, either of not living long enough to receive this indemnification, or of not succeding in the trade, let him live ever so long.'

[4] See below, I.x.b.24.

necessity.[5] In the advanced state of society, therefore, they are all very poor people who follow as a trade, what other people pursue as a pastime.[6] Fishermen have been so since the time of *Theocritus. A poacher is everywhere a very poor man in Great Britain. In countries where the rigour of the law suffers no poachers, the licensed hunter is not in a much better condition. The natural taste for those employments makes more people follow them than can live comfortably by them, and the produce of their labour, in proportion to its quantity, comes always too cheap to mar-[154]ket to afford any thing but the most scanty subsistence to the labourers.

4   Disagreeableness and disgrace affect the profits of stock in the same manner as the wages of labour. The keeper of an inn or tavern, who is never master of his own house, and who is exposed to the brutality of every drunkard, exercises neither a very agreeable nor a very creditable business. But there is scarce any common trade in which a small stock yields so great a profit.

5   Secondly, the wages of labour vary with the easiness and cheapness, or the difficulty and expence of learning the business.[7]

6   When any expensive machine is erected, the extraordinary work to be performed by it before it is worn out, it must be expected, will replace the capital laid out upon it, with at least ᵇtheᵇ ordinary profits.[8] A man educated at the expence of much labour and time to any of those employments which require extraordinary dexterity and skill, may be compared to one of those expensive machines.[9] The work which he learns to perform, it must be expected, over and above the usual wages of common labour, will replace to him the whole expence of his education, with at least the ordinary profits of an ᶜequallyᶜ valuable capital. It must do this too in a reasonable time,

---

ᵃ* See Idyllium xxi.ᵃ [Idyll xxi, 'The Fishermen', begins, 'It is Poverty . . . that alone can rouse the crafts', translated by R. C. Trevelyan, *The Idylls of Theocritus* (Cambridge, 1947), 66–8.]

ᵃ⁻ᵃ *3–6*   ᵇ⁻ᵇ its *1–2*   ᶜ⁻ᶜ equal *4* ⟨corrected *4e–6*⟩

---

[5] LJ (A) i.56 refers to the 'delight the great take in hunting and the great inclination they have to screw all they can out of their hands.'

[6] Cf. I.xi.b.25.

[7] 'Nothing can be dear, of which there is great Plenty, how beneficial soever it may be to Man; and Scarcity inhances the Price of Things much oftener than the Usefulness of them. Hence it is evident why those Arts and Sciences will always be the most lucrative that cannot be attain'd to, but in great length of Time, by tedious Study and close Application; or else require a particular Genius, not often to be met with. It is likewise evident, to whose Lot, in all Societies, the hard and dirty Labour, which no Body would meddle with, if he could help it, will ever fall.' (Mandeville, *The Fable of the Bees*, pt. ii. 423, ed. Kaye ii.350–1.)

[8] See below, II.ii.7.

[9] See below, II.i.17, where Smith includes the 'acquired and useful abilities' of the inhabitants in the nation's fixed capital, and cf. IV.viii.44, where the artificer is described as a 'living instrument' of trade.

regard being had to the very uncertain duration of human life, in the same manner as to the more certain duration of the machine.[10]

7   The difference between the wages of skilled [155] labour and those of common labour, is founded upon this principle.

8   The policy of Europe considers the labour of all mechanicks, artificers, and manufacturers, as skilled labour; and that of all country labourers as common labour. It seems to suppose that of the former to be of a more nice and delicate nature than that of the latter. It is so perhaps in some cases; but in the greater part it is quite otherwise, as I shall endeavour to shew by and by.[11] The laws and customs of Europe, therefore, in order to qualify any person for exercising the one species of labour, impose the necessity of an apprenticeship,[12] though with different degrees of rigour in different places. They leave the other free and open to every body. During the continuance of the apprenticeship, the whole labour of the apprentice belongs to his master. In the mean time he must, in many cases, be maintained by his parents or relations, and in almost all cases must be cloathed by them.[13] Some money too is commonly given to the master for teaching him his trade. They who cannot give money, give time, or become bound for more than the usual number of years; a consideration which, though it is not always advantageous to the master, on account of the usual idleness of apprentices, is always disadvantageous to the apprentice. In country labour, on the contrary, the labourer, while he is employed about the easier, learns the more difficult parts of his business, and his own labour maintains him through all the different stages of his employ-[156]ment. It is reasonable, therefore, that in Europe the wages of mechanicks, artificers, and manufacturers, should be somewhat higher than those of common labourers. They are so accordingly, and their superior gains make them in most places be considered as a superior rank of people. This superiority, however, is generally very small; the daily or weekly earnings of journeymen in the more common sorts of manufactures, such as those of plain linen and woollen cloth, computed at an average, are, in most places, very little more than the day wages of common labourers. Their employment, indeed, is more steady and uniform, and the superiority of their earnings, taking the whole year together, may be somewhat greater. It seems evidently, however, to be no greater than what is sufficient to compensate the superior expence of their education.

9   Education in the ingenious arts and in the liberal professions, is still more tedious and expensive. The pecuniary recompence, therefore, of painters and sculptors, of lawyers and physicians, ought to be much more liberal: and it is so accordingly.

[10] In LJ (A) vi.60 the life of a man, after completing his apprenticeship, is estimated at 10 or 12 years' purchase. The same figure is cited in LJ (B) 225, ed. Cannan 174, and in Cantillon, *Essai*, 24, ed. Higgs 19.

[11] See below, I.x.c.23.   [12] See below, I.x.c.14.   [13] See LJ (A) vi.59.

10 The profits of stock seem to be very little affected by the easiness or difficulty of learning the trade in which it is employed. All the different ways in which stock is commonly employed in great towns seem, in reality, to be almost equally easy and equally difficult to learn. One branch either of foreign or domestick trade, cannot well [157] be a much more intricate business than another.

11 Thirdly, The wages of labour in different occupations vary with the constancy or inconstancy of employment.

12 Employment is much more constant in some trades than in others. In the greater part of manufactures, a journeyman may be pretty sure of employment almost every day in the year that he is able to work. A mason or bricklayer, on the contrary, can work neither in hard frost nor in foul weather, and his employment at all other times depends upon the occasional calls of his customers. He is liable, in consequence, to be frequently without any. What he earns, therefore, while he is employed, must not only maintain him while he is idle, but make him some compensation for those anxious and desponding moments which the thought of so precarious a situation must sometimes occasion. Where the computed earnings of the greater part of manufacturers, accordingly, are nearly upon a level with the day wages of common labourers, those of masons and bricklayers are generally from one-half more to double those wages. Where common labourers earn four and five shillings a week, masons and bricklayers frequently earn seven and eight; where the former earn six, the latter often earn nine and ten; and where the former earn nine and ten, as in London, the latter commonly earn fifteen and eighteen. No species of skilled labour, however, seems more easy to learn than that of masons and bricklayers. [158] Chairmen in London, during the summer season, are said sometimes to be employed as bricklayers. The high wages of those workmen, therefore, are not so much the recompence of their skill, as the compensation for the inconstancy of their employment.

13 A house carpenter seems to exercise rather a nicer and [d] more ingenious trade than a mason. In most places, however, for it is not universally so, his day-wages are somewhat lower. His employment, though it depends much, does not depend so entirely upon the occasional calls of his customers; and it is not liable to be interrupted by the weather.

14 When the trades which generally afford constant employment, happen in a particular place not to do so, the wages of the workmen always rise a good deal above their ordinary proportion to those of common labour. In London almost all journeymen artificers are liable to be called upon and dismissed by their masters from day to day, and from week to week, in the same manner as day-labourers in other places. The lowest order of artifi-

[d] a 6

cers, journeymen taylors, accordingly, earn there half a crown a-day,[14] though eighteen-pence may be reckoned the wages of common labour. In small towns and country-villages, the wages of journeymen taylors frequently scarce equal those of common labour; but in London they are often many weeks without employment, particularly during the summer.

15   [159] When the inconstancy of employment is combined with the hardship, disagreeableness and dirtiness of the work, it sometimes raises the wages of the most common labour above those of the most skilful artificers. A collier working by the piece is supposed, at Newcastle, to earn commonly about double, and in many parts of Scotland about three times the wages of common labour.[15] His high wages arise altogether from the hardship, disagreeableness, and dirtiness of his work. His employment may, upon most occasions, be as constant as he pleases. The coal-heavers in London exercise a trade which in hardship, dirtiness, and disagreeableness, almost equals that of colliers; and from the unavoidable irregularity in the arrivals of coal-ships, the employment of the greater part of them is necessarily very inconstant. If colliers, therefore, commonly earn double and triple the wages of common labour, it ought not to seem unreasonable that coal-heavers should sometimes earn four and five times those wages. In the enquiry made into their condition a few years ago, it was found that at the rate at which they were then paid, they could earn from six to ten shillings a day. Six shillings are about four times the wages of common labour in London, and in every particular trade, the lowest common earnings may always be considered as those of the far greater number. How extravagant

[14] See below, I.x.c.61.
[15] In LJ (B) 139, ed. Cannan 100, the wages of labour are given as between 6 and 8 pence, and as not exceeding 10 pence or a shilling for Newcastle colliers. In LJ (A) iii.129–30 it is stated that these colliers will not earn in excess of 13 or 14 pence a day and that 6 pence is the mean rate for other classes of labour, with agricultural rates varying between 8 and 5 pence. In contrast, wages in the Scottish collieries, which used a form of slave labour, were stated in LJ (B) 139, ed. Cannan 100, to be of the order of 2s. 6d. and in LJ (A) iii.129 to vary between 2s. and 3s. In referring to the differential between Scottish and Newcastle rates in the mines, Smith comments that colliers still left Scottish coal works . . . 'and run there tho' they have less wages, where they have liberty' (LJ (B) 139).
   With regard to the differential between wages in the Scottish collieries and other employments in the same country Smith says in LJ (A) iii.129–30 that the collier has 'about four times the wages he would have were the work open to all men', many of whom were deterred from entering into the trade, since 'it is a rule that one who works a year and a day in the coal pit becomes a slave as the rest and may be claimed by the owner, unless he has bargain'd not to take advantage of this.' Cf. Anderson, *Notes*, 34:

Were our salters and colliers put upon the same footing with other labourers, it would be much better for their masters. When men are constrained to work for another they will not work so hard as if at liberty—this is manifest in quarrying and other mines. In the Newcastle mines work is done cheaper than in this country. In this country a collier and salter can earn more than a quarrier or any other labourer who works as hard.

Smith comments on the high cost of slave labour, above, I.viii.41, and contrasts its use with that of free men in mining at IV.ix.47.

soever those earnings may appear, if they were more than sufficient to compensate all the disagreeable circumstances of the business, there [160] would soon be so great a number of competitors as, in a trade which has no exclusive privilege, would quickly reduce them to a lower rate.

16   The constancy or inconstancy of employment cannot ^eaffect^e the ordinary profits of stock in any particular trade. Whether the stock is or is not constantly employed depends, not upon the trade, but the trader.

17   Fourthly, The wages of labour vary according to the small or great trust which must be reposed in the workmen.[16]

18   The wages of goldsmiths and jewellers are every-where superior to those of many other workmen, not only of equal, but of much superior ingenuity; on account of the precious materials with which they are intrusted.

19   We trust our health to the physician; our fortune and sometimes our life and reputation to the lawyer and attorney. Such confidence could not safely be reposed in people of a very mean or low condition. Their reward must be such, therefore, as may give them that rank in the society which so important a trust requires. The long time and the great expence which must be laid out in their education, when combined with this circumstance, necessarily enhance still further the price of their labour.[17]

20   When a person employs only his own stock in trade, there is no trust; and the credit which he may get from other people, depends, not upon the nature of his trade, but upon their opinion of his fortune, probity, and prudence. The dif-[161]ferent rates of profit, therefore, in the different branches of trade, cannot arise from the different degrees of trust reposed in the traders.

21   Fifthly, the wages of labour in different employments vary according to the probability or improbability of success in them.

22   The probability that any particular person shall ever be qualified for the employment to which he is educated, is very different in different occupations. In the greater part of mechanick trades, success is almost certain; but very uncertain in the liberal professions. Put your son apprentice to a shoemaker, there is little doubt of his learning to make a pair of shoes: But send him to study the law, it is at least twenty to one if ever he makes such proficiency as will enable him to live by the business. In a perfectly fair lottery, those who draw the prizes ought to gain all that is lost by those who draw the blanks. In a profession where twenty fail for one that succeeds,

---

^{e-e} effect 5

[16] 'It is a familiar rule in all business, that every man should be payed, in proportion to the trust reposed in him, and to the power, which he enjoys.' (Hume, *History of England* (1778), viii.325.)

[17] Cf. Letter 143 addressed to Cullen, dated 20 September 1774: 'There never was, and I will venture to say there never will be, a University from which a degree could give any tolerable security, that the person upon whom it had been conferred, was fit to practice physic.' See below, V.i.f.11.

that one ought to gain all that should have been gained by the unsuccessful twenty.[18] The counsellor at law who, perhaps, at near forty years of age, begins to make something by his profession, ought to receive the retribution, not only of his own so tedious and expensive education, but of that of more than twenty others who are never likely to make any thing by it. How extravagant soever the fees of counsellors at law may sometimes appear, their real retribution is never equal to this. Compute in any particular place, what is likely to be annually gained, and what is likely to be an-[162] nually spent, by all the different workmen in any common trade, such as that of shoemakers or weavers, and you will find that the former sum will generally exceed the latter. But make the same computation with regard to all the counsellors and students of law, in all the different inns of court, and you will find that their annual gains bear but a very small proportion to their annual expence, even though you rate the former as high, and the latter as low, as can well be done. The lottery of the law, therefore, is very far from being a perfectly fair lottery; and that, as well as many other liberal and honourable professions, *are*, in point of pecuniary gain, evidently under-recompenced.

23   Those professions keep their level, however, with other occupations, and, notwithstanding these discouragements, all the most generous and liberal spirits are eager to crowd into them. Two different causes contribute to recommend them. First, the desire of the reputation which attends upon superior excellence in any of them; and, secondly, the natural confidence which every man has more or less, not only in his own abilities, but in his own good fortune.

24   To excel in any profession, in which but few arrive at mediocrity, is the most decisive mark of what is called genius or superior talents. The publick ✓ admiration which attends upon such distinguished abilities, makes always a part of their reward; a greater or smaller in proportion as it is higher or lower in degree. It makes a considerable part of *that reward* in the profession of [163] physick; a still greater perhaps in that of law; in poetry and philosophy it makes almost the whole.[19]

f-f is 5–6   *g-g* it *1*

---

[18] Smith makes a similar point in LJ (A) vi.68–9 in the course of discussing the relative merits of raising corn and mining for the precious metals; cf. LJ (B) 226, ed. Cannan 176.

[19] The point is further illustrated at V.i.b.19, and V.ii.k.80. Cf. LJ (A) vi.62, with regard to the profession of law: 'The temptation to engage in this or any other of the liberall arts is rather the respect, credit, and eminence it gives one, than the profit of it.' Cf. LJ (B) 226, ed. Cannan 175. In LJ (A) v.37, Smith commented that judges were usually men of 'great integrity and knowledge' and often one of 'the first men in the kingdom'. However, LJ (A) v.5 refers to the humbler office of sheriff as one which was not 'attended with great dignity and . . . profit, so that many pay a fine of £500 to be excused from it'. TMS III.i.2.20 points out that some philosophers, for example mathematicians such as Sir Isaac Newton, 'are frequently very indifferent about the reception they meet with from

25   There are some very agreeable and beautiful talents of which the possession commands a certain sort of admiration; but of which the exercise
for the sake of gain is considered, whether from reason or prejudice, as a
sort of publick prostitution. The pecuniary recompence, therefore, of
those who exercise them in this manner, must be sufficient, not only to
pay for the time, labour, and expence of acquiring the talents, but for the
discredit which attends the employment of them as the means of subsistence.[20] The exorbitant rewards of players, opera-singers, opera-
dancers, &c. are founded upon those two principles; the rarity and beauty
of the talents, and the discredit of employing them in this manner.[21] It
seems absurd at first sight that we should despise their persons, and yet
reward their talents with the most profuse liberality. While we do the one,
however, we must of necessity do the other. Should the publick opinion or
prejudice ever alter with regard to such occupations, their pecuniary recompence would quickly diminish. More people would apply to them, and
the competition would quickly reduce the price of their labour. Such
talents, though far from being common, are by no means so rare as is
imagined. Many people possess them in great perfection, who disdain to
make this use of them; and many more are capable of acquiring [164] them,
if any thing could be made honourably by them.

26   The over-weening conceit which the greater part of men have of their
own abilities, is an antient evil remarked by the philosophers and moralists
of all ages. Their absurd presumption in their own good fortune, has been
less taken notice of.[22] It is, however, if possible, still more universal. There
is no man living who, when in tolerable health and spirits, has not some

the public', being assured of the truth of their discoveries. He added that in this respect
natural philosophers 'approach nearly to mathematicians'.
    Mandeville took note of a related problem in observing that 'There are abundance of
Men of a *Genteel* Education, that have but very small *Revenues*, and yet are forced, by their
Reputable *Callings*, to make a greater *Figure* than ordinary People of twice their *Income*.'
(*The Fable of the Bees*, pt.i.46, ed. Kaye, i.59.)
    [20] This concept of concern with the public opinion of our conduct is further illustrated
at II.iii.40, V.i.g.12, and V.ii.k.3.
    [21] These employments are described as unproductive at II.iii.2. LRBL ii.230, ed. Lothian
183, refers to Aeschines 'who was bred a player, an employment as creditable at that time
as it is discreditable now'. In TMS I.iii.2.1 Smith argues that men naturally seek the approval of their fellows, a point which may explain why certain levels of monetary return are
required in order to compensate the kind of public disapprobation incurred by the opera
singer or dancer. By the same token, public approbation may help to explain why in some
cases, monetary returns should be relatively low.
    [22] Hutcheson, however, had commented on the 'vain hopes of multitudes, and a sort of
self-flattery in their good fortune' in discussing the disadvantages of lotteries (*System*, ii.75).
In the same vein, he stated in the *Short Introduction*, 221, with regard to lotteries, that 'as
men thro' some vain opinions of their own good luck are generally very prone to them;
they should be every where under the restraint of laws'. Smith comments on man's absurd
presumption of success for example at I.x.b.33, I.xi.c.26, and V.iii.33. Cf. Montesquieu:
'Mankind are generally fond of gaming; and even the most prudent have no aversion to it'
(*Esprit*, XX.vi.3).

share of it. The chance of gain is by every man more or less over-valued, and the chance of loss is by most men under-valued, and by scarce any man, who is in tolerable health and spirits, valued more than it is worth.

27   That the chance of gain is naturally over-valued, we may learn from the universal success of lotteries. The world neither ever saw, nor ever will see, a perfectly fair lottery; or one in which the whole gain compensated the whole loss; because the undertaker could make nothing by it. In the state lotteries the tickets are really not worth the price which is paid by the original subscribers, and yet commonly sell in the market for twenty, thirty, and sometimes forty per cent. advance. The vain hope of gaining some of the great prizes is the sole cause of this demand. The soberest people scarce look upon it as a folly to pay a small sum for the chance of gaining ten or twenty thousand pounds; though they know that even that small sum is perhaps twenty or thirty per cent. more than the chance is worth. In a lottery in which no prize exceeded [165] twenty pounds, though in other respects it approached much nearer to a perfectly fair one than the common state lotteries, there would not be the same demand for tickets. In order to have a better chance for some of the great prizes, some people purchase several tickets, and others, small shares in a still greater number. There is not, however, a more certain proposition in mathematicks, than that the more tickets you adventure upon, the more likely you are to be a loser. Adventure upon all the tickets in the lottery, and you lose for certain; and the greater the number of your tickets the nearer you approach to this certainty.

28   That the chance of loss is frequently under-valued, and scarce ever valued more than it is worth, we may learn from the very moderate profit of insurers.[23] In order to make insurance, either from fire or sea-risk, a trade at all, the common premium must be sufficient to compensate the common losses, to pay the expence of management, and to afford such a profit as might have been drawn from an equal capital employed in any common trade. The person who pays no more than this, evidently pays no more than the real value of the risk, or the lowest price at which he can reasonably expect to insure it. But though many people have made a little money by insurance, very few have made a great fortune; and from this consideration alone, it seems evident enough, that the ordinary balance of profit and loss is not more advantageous in this, than in other common trades by [166] which so many people make fortunes. Moderate, however, as the premium of insurance commonly is, many people despise the risk too much to care to pay it. Taking the whole kingdom at an average, nineteen houses in twenty, or rather perhaps ninety-nine in a hundred, are not

---

[23] The trade of insurance is described as suitable for a joint stock company, being reducible to strict rule and method, at V.i.e.32. Smith describes the attraction of the joint stock organization in terms of the exemption provided from risk at V.i.e.18.

insured from fire. Sea risk is more alarming to the greater part of people, and the proportion of ships insured to those not insured is much greater. Many sail, however, at all seasons, and even in time of war, without any insurance. This may sometimes perhaps be done without any imprudence. When a great company, or even a great merchant, has twenty or thirty ships at sea, they may, as it were, insure one another. The premium saved upon them all, may more than compensate such losses as they are likely to meet with in the common course of chances. The neglect of insurance upon shipping, however, in the same manner as upon houses, is, in most cases, the effect of no such nice calculation, but of mere thoughtless rashness and presumptuous contempt of the risk.

29   The contempt of risk and the presumptuous hope of success, are in no period of life more active than at the age at which young people chuse their professions. How little the fear of misfortune is then capable of balancing the hope of good luck, appears still more evidently in the readiness of the common people to enlist as soldiers,[24] or to go to sea, than in the eagerness of those of better fashion to enter into what are called the liberal professions.

30   [167] What a common soldier may lose is obvious enough. Without regarding the danger, however, young volunteers never enlist so readily as at the beginning of a new war; and though they have scarce any chance of preferment, they figure to themselves, in their youthful fancies, a thousand occasions of acquiring honour and distinction which never occur. These romantick hopes make the whole price of their blood. Their pay is less than that of common labourers, and in actual service their fatigues are much greater.[25]

31   The lottery of the sea is not altogether so disadvantageous as that of the army. The son of a creditable labourer or artificer may frequently go to sea with his father's consent; but if he enlists as a soldier, it is always without it. Other people see some chance of his making something by the one trade: nobody but himself sees any of his making any thing by the other. The great admiral is less the object of publick admiration than the great general, and the highest success in the sea service promises a less brilliant fortune and reputation than equal success in the land. The same difference runs through all the inferior degrees of preferment in both. By the rules of precedency a captain in the navy ranks with a colonel in the army: but he does not rank with him in the common estimation. As the great prizes in the lottery are less, the smaller ones must be more numerous. Common

---

[24] See below, V.i.a.14.

[25] Cf. Mandeville, *The Fable of the Bees*, pt. i.366, ed. Kaye i.319: 'When it is taken for granted that a Soldier, whose Strength and Vigour is to be kept up at least as much as any Body's, can live upon Six-Pence a Day, I can't conceive the Necessity of giving the greatest part of the Year Sixteen and Eighteen Pence to a Day-Labourer.'

sailors, therefore, more frequently get some fortune and preferment than common soldiers; and the hope of those prizes is what principally recommends [168] the trade. Though their skill and dexterity are much superior to that of almost any artificers, and though their whole life is one continual scene of hardship and danger, yet for all this dexterity and skill, for all those hardships and dangers, while they remain in the condition of common sailors, they receive scarce any other recompence but the pleasure of exercising the one and of surmounting the other. Their wages are not greater than those of common labourers at the port which regulates the rate of seamens wages. As they are continually going from port to port, the monthly pay of those who sail from all the different ports of Great Britain, is more nearly upon a level than that of any other workmen in those different places; and the rate of the port to and from which the greatest number sail, that is the port of London, regulates that of all the rest. At London the wages of the greater part of the different classes of workmen are about double those of the same classes at Edinburgh.[26] But the sailors who sail from the port of London seldom earn above three or four shillings a month more than those who sail from the port of Leith, and the difference is frequently not so great. In time of peace, and in the merchant service, the London price is from a guinea to about seven-and-twenty shillings the calendar month. A common labourer in London, at the rate of nine or ten shillings a week, may earn in the calendar month from forty to five-and-forty shillings. The sailor, indeed, over and above his pay, is supplied with provi-[169]sions. Their value, however, may not perhaps always exceed the difference between his pay and that of the common labourer; and though it sometimes should, the excess will not be clear gain to the sailor, because he cannot share it with his wife and family, whom he must maintain out of his wages at home.

32　　The dangers and hair-breadth escapes of a life of adventures, instead of disheartening young people, seem frequently to recommend a trade to them. A tender mother, among the inferior ranks of people, is often afraid to send her son to school at a sea-port town, lest the sight of the ships and the conversation and adventures of the sailors should entice him to go to sea. The distant prospect of hazards, from which we can hope to extricate ourselves by courage and address, is not disagreeable to us, and does not raise the wages of labour in any employment. It is otherwise with those in which courage and address can be of no avail. In trades which are known to be very unwholesome, the wages of labour are always remarkably high. Unwholesomeness is a species of disagreeableness, and its effects upon the wages of labour are to be ranked under that general head.

33　　In all the different employments of stock, the ordinary rate of profit varies more or less with the certainty or uncertainty of the returns. These

[26] See above, I.viii.31.

are in general less uncertain in the inland than in the foreign trade, and in some branches of foreign trade than in others; in the trade to North America, for example, than in that to Jamaica.[27] [170] The ordinary rate of profit always rises more or less with the risk.[28] It does not, however, seem to rise in proportion to it, or so as to compensate it compleately. Bankruptcies are most frequent in the most hazardous trades. The most hazardous of all trades, that of a smuggler, though when the adventure succeeds it is likewise the most profitable, is the infallible road to bankruptcy. The presumptuous hope of success seems to act here as upon all other occasions, and to entice so many adventurers into those hazardous trades, that their competition reduces ʰtheʰ profit below what is sufficient to compensate the risk. To compensate it compleatly, the common returns ought, over and above the ordinary profits of stock, not only to make up for all occasional losses, but to afford a surplus profit to the adventurers of the same nature with the profit of insurers. But if the common returns were sufficient for all this, bankruptcies would not be more frequent in these than in other trades.

34   Of the five circumstances, therefore, which vary the wages of labour, two only affect the profits of stock; the agreeableness or disagreeableness of the business, and the risk or security with which it is attended.[29] In point of agreeableness or disagreeableness, there is little or no difference in the far greater part of the different employments of stock; but a great deal in those of labour; and the ordinary profit of stock, though it rises with the risk, does not always seem to rise in proportion to it. It should follow from all this, that, in the same society or [171] neighbourhood, the average and ordinary rates of profit in the different employments of stock should be more nearly upon a level than the pecuniary wages of the different sorts of labour. They are so accordingly. The difference between the earnings of a common labourer and those of a well employed lawyer or physician, is evidently much greater, than that, between the ordinary profits in any two different branches of trade. The apparent difference, besides, in the profits of different trades, is generally a deception arising from our not always distinguishing what ought to be considered as wages, from what ought to be considered as profit.[30]

35   Apothecaries profit is become a bye-word, denoting something uncommonly extravagant. This great apparent profit, however, is frequently

ʰ⁻ʰ their 5–6

---

[27] See below, III.ii.10, where Smith admits that the profits on sugar plantations in the West Indian colonies were 'generally much greater than those of any other cultivation that is known either in Europe or America'.
[28] See above, I.ix.18.
[29] See IV.v.b.8 regarding the corn trade, and II.iv.17 with reference to investment in land.
[30] Smith comments on the need to distinguish categories of return at I.vi.19.

no more than the reasonable wages of labour. The skill of an apothecary is a much nicer and more delicate matter than that of any artificer whatever; and the trust which is reposed in him is of much greater importance. He is the physician of the poor in all cases, and of the rich when the distress or danger is not very great. His reward, therefore, ought to be suitable to his skill and his trust, and it arises generally from the price at which he sells his drugs. But the whole drugs which the best employed apothecary, in a large market town, will sell in a year, may not perhaps cost him above thirty or forty pounds. Though he should sell them, therefore, for three or four hundred, or at a thousand per cent. profit, this may frequently be [172] no more than the reasonable wages of his labour charged, in the only way in which he can charge them, upon the price of his drugs. The greater part of the apparent profit is real wages disguised in the garb of profit.

36   In a small sea-port town, a little grocer will make forty or fifty per cent. upon a stock of a single hundred pounds, while a considerable wholesale merchant in the same place will scarce make eight or ten per cent. upon a stock of ten thousand. The trade of the grocer may be necessary for the conveniency of the inhabitants, and the narrowness of the market may not admit the employment of a larger capital in the business. The man, however, must not only live by his trade, but live by it suitably to the qualifications which it requires. Besides possessing a little capital, he must be able to read, write, and account, and must be a tolerable judge too of, perhaps, fifty or sixty different sorts of goods, their prices, qualities, and the markets where they are to be had cheapest. He must have all the knowledge, in short, that is necessary for a great merchant, which nothing hinders him from becoming but the want of a sufficient capital. Thirty or forty pounds a year cannot be considered as too great a recompence for the labour of a person so accomplished. Deduct this from the seemingly great profits of his capital, and little more will remain, perhaps, than the ordinary profits of stock. The greater part of the apparent profit is, in this case too, real wages.

37   [173] The difference between the apparent profit of the retail and that of the wholesale trade, is much less in the capital than in small towns and country villages.[31] Where ten thousand pounds can be employed in the grocery trade, the wages of the grocer's labour ᶦmake butᶦ a very trifling addition to the real profits of so great a stock. The apparent profits of the wealthy retailer, therefore, are there more nearly upon a level with those of the wholesale merchant. It is upon this account that goods sold by retail are generally as cheap and frequently much cheaper in the capital than in small towns and country villages. Grocery goods, for example, are generally much cheaper; bread and butcher's meat frequently as cheap. It costs no

---

ᶦ⁻ᶦ must be 6

---

[31] See above, I.viii.31.

more to bring grocery goods to the great town than to the country village; but it costs a great deal more to bring corn and cattle, as the greater part of them must be brought from a much greater distance. The prime cost of grocery goods, therefore, being the same in both places, they are cheapest where the least profit is charged upon them. The prime cost of bread and butcher's-meat is greater in the great town than in the country village; and though the profit is less, therefore, they are not always cheaper there, but often equally cheap. In such articles as bread and butcher's meat, the same cause, which diminishes apparent profit, increases prime cost. The extent of the market, by giving employment to greater stocks, diminishes apparent profit; but by requiring supplies from a greater distance, it [174] increases prime cost. This diminution of the one and increase of the other seem, in most cases, nearly to counter-balance one another; which is probably the reason that, though the prices of corn and cattle are commonly very different in different parts of the kingdom, those of bread and butcher's-meat are generally very nearly the same through the greater part of it.

38   Though the profits of stock both in the wholesale and retail trade are generally less in the capital than in small towns and country villages, yet great fortunes are frequently acquired from small beginnings in the former, and scarce ever in the latter. In small towns and country villages, on account of the narrowness of the market, trade cannot always be extended as stock extends. In such places, therefore, though the rate of a particular person's profits may be very high, the sum or amount of them can never be very great, nor consequently that of his annual accumulation. In great towns, on the contrary, trade can be extended as stock increases, and the credit of a frugal and thriving man increases much faster than his stock. His trade is extended in proportion to the amount of both, and the sum or amount of his profits is in proportion to the extent of his trade, and his annual accumulation in proportion to the amount of his profits. It seldom happens, however, that great fortunes are made even in great towns by any one regular, established, and well-known branch of business, but in consequence of a long life of industry, frugality, and attention. Sudden fortunes, indeed, are some-[175]times made in such places by what is called the trade of speculation. The speculative merchant exercises no one regular, established, or well-known branch of business. He is a corn merchant this year, and a wine merchant the next, and a sugar, tobacco, or tea merchant the year after. He enters into every trade when he foresees that it is likely to be more than commonly profitable, and he quits it when he foresees that its profits are likely to return to the level of other trades. His profits and losses, therefore, can bear no regular proportion to those of any one established and well-known branch of business. A bold adventurer may sometimes acquire a considerable fortune by two or three successful speculations; but ¹ is

¹ it 3 *om.* 1–2 ⟨corrected 3e–6⟩

just as likely to lose one by two or three unsuccessful ones. This trade can be carried on no where but in great towns. It is only in places of the most extensive commerce and correspondence that the intelligence requisite for it can be had.

39   The five circumstances above mentioned, though they occasion considerable inequalities in the wages of labour and profits of stock, occasion none in the whole of the advantages and disadvantages, real or imaginary, of the different employments of either. The nature of those circumstances is such, that they make up for a small pecuniary gain in some, and counter-balance a great one in others.

40   In order, however, that this equality may take place in the whole of their advantages or disadvantages, three things are requisite even [176] where there is the most perfect freedom. First, the employments must be well known and long established in the neighbourhood; secondly, they must be in their ordinary, or what may be called their natural state; and, thirdly, they must be the sole or principal employments of those who occupy them.

41   First, this equality can take place only in those employments which are well known, and have been long established in the neighbourhood.

42   Where all other circumstances are equal, wages are generally higher in new than in old trades. When a projector attempts to establish a new manufacture, he must at first entice his workmen from other employments by higher wages than they can either earn in their own trades, or than the nature of his work would otherwise require, and a considerable time must pass away before he can venture to reduce them to the common level. Manufactures for which the demand arises altogether from fashion and fancy, are continually changing, and seldom last long enough to be considered as old established manufactures. Those, on the contrary, for which the demand arises chiefly from use or necessity, are less liable to change, and the same form or fabrick may continue in demand for whole centuries together. The wages of labour, therefore, are likely to be higher in manufactures of the former, than in those of the latter kind. Birmingham deals chiefly in manufactures of the former kind; Sheffield in those of the latter; [177] and the wages of labour in those two different places, are said to be suitable to this difference in the nature of their manufactures.[32]

43   The establishment of any new manufacture, of any new branch of commerce, or of any new practice in agriculture, is always a speculation, from which the projector promises himself extraordinary profits.[33] These profits sometimes are very great, and sometimes, more frequently, perhaps, they

---

[32] See below, III.iii.20, where the manufactures of Sheffield and Birmingham are stated to have developed as a result of the refinement of domestic output, as distinct from having been introduced as a consequence of foreign contacts.

[33] Smith argues below, II.iii.26, that unsuccessful projects diminish the funds available for investment. This argument is linked to Smith's willingness to regulate the rate of interest. See below, II.iv.15.

are quite otherwise; but in general they bear no regular proportion to those of other old trades in the neighbourhood. If the project succeeds, they are commonly at first very high. When the trade or practice becomes thoroughly established and well known, the competition reduces them to the level of other trades.

44   Secondly, this equality in the whole of the advantages and disadvantages of the different employments of labour and stock, can take place only in the ordinary, or what may be called the natural state of those employments.

45   The demand for almost every different species of labour, is sometimes greater and sometimes less than usual. In the one case the advantages of the employment rise above, in the other they fall below the common level. The demand for country labour is greater at hay-time and harvest, than during the greater part of the year; and wages rise with the demand. In time of war, when forty or fifty thousand sailors are forced from the merchant service into that of the king, the demand for sailors to merchant ships necessarily rises with their scarcity, and their wages [178] upon such occasions commonly rise from a guinea and seven-and-twenty-shillings, to forty shillings and three pounds a month.[34] In a decaying manufacture, on the contrary, many workmen, rather than quit their old trade, are contented with smaller wages than would otherwise be suitable to the nature of their employment.

46   The profits of stock vary with the price of the commodities in which it is employed. As the price of any commodity rises above the ordinary or average rate, the profits of at least some part of the stock that is employed in bringing it to market, rise above their proper level, and as it falls they sink below it. All commodities are more or less liable to variations of price, but some are much more so than others. In all commodities which are produced by human industry, the quantity of industry annually employed is necessarily regulated by the annual demand, in such a manner that the average annual produce may, as nearly as possible, be equal to the average annual consumption. In some employments, it has already been observed,[35] the same quantity of industry will always produce the same, or very nearly the same quantity of commodities. In the linen or woollen manufactures, for example, the same number of hands will annually work up very nearly the same quantity of linen and woollen cloth. The variations in the market price of such commodities, therefore, can arise only from some accidental variation in the demand. A publick mourning raises the price of black cloth.[36] But as the demand [179] for most sorts of plain linen and woollen cloth is pretty uniform, so is likewise the price. But there are other employments in which the same quantity of industry will not always produce the same quantity of commodities. The same quantity of industry, for example, will, in different years, produce very different quantities of corn, wine,

[34] See below, IV.ii.42.   [35] See above, I.vii.17.   [36] See above, I.vii.19.

hops, sugar, tobacco, &c. The price of such commodities, therefore, varies not only with the variations of demand, but with the much greater and more frequent variations of quantity, and is consequently extremely fluctuating. But the profit of some of the dealers must necessarily fluctuate with the price of the commodities. The operations of the speculative merchant are principally employed about such commodities. He endeavours to buy them up when he foresees that their price is likely to rise, and to sell them when it is likely to fall.

47   Thirdly, This equality in the whole of the advantages and disadvantages of the different employments of labour and stock; can take place only in such as are the sole or principal employments of those who occupy them.

48   When a person derives his subsistence from one employment, which does not occupy the greater part of his time; in the intervals of his leisure he is often willing to work at another for less wages than would otherwise suit the nature of the employment.[37]

49   There still subsists in many parts of Scotland a set of people called Cotters or Cottagers,[38] though they were more frequent some years ago [180] than they are now. They are a sort of out-servants of the landlords and farmers. The usual reward which they receive from their masters is a house, a small garden for pot-herbs, as much grass as will feed a cow, and, perhaps, an acre or two of bad arable land. When their master has occasion for their labour, he gives them, besides, two pecks of oatmeal a week, worth about sixteen-pence sterling. During a great part of the year he has little or no occasion for their labour, and the cultivation of their own little possession is not sufficient to occupy the time which is left at their own disposal. When such occupiers were more numerous than they are at present, they are said to have been willing to give their spare time for a very small recompence to any body, and to have wrought for less wages than other labourers. In antient times they seem to have been common all over Europe. In countries ill cultivated and worse inhabited, the greater part of landlords and farmers could not otherwise provide themselves with the extraordinary number of hands, which country labour requires at certain seasons. The daily or weekly recompence which such labourers occasionally received from their masters, was evidently not the whole price of their labour. Their small tenement made a considerable part of it. This daily or weekly recompence, however, seems to have been considered as the whole of it, by many writers

---

[37] See below, V.i.d.10, where Smith discusses a proposal to employ soldiers on the roads.

[38] For a description of this set of people, see M. Gray, *The Highland Economy* (Edinburgh, 1957), 201–4. Cf. Sir James Steuart: 'In some countries you find every farm-house surrounded with small huts, possessed by numbers of people, supposed to be useful to the farmer. These in Scotland are called cottars, (cottagers).' He added that he imagined this sort of subsistence farming 'to be, less or more, the picture of Europe 400 years ago' (*Principles*, i.103, ed. Skinner, i.105–6).

who have collected the prices of labour and provisions in antient times, and who have taken pleasure in representing both as wonderfully low.

50   [181] The produce of such labour comes frequently cheaper to market than would otherwise be suitable to its nature.[39] Stockings in many parts of Scotland are knit much cheaper than they can any-where be wrought upon the loom. They are the work of servants and labourers, who derive the principal part of their subsistence from some other employment. More than a thousand pair of Shetland stockings are annually imported into Leith, of which the price is from five-pence to seven-pence a pair. At Lear-wick,[40] the small capital of the Shetland islands, ten-pence a day, I have been assured, is a common price of common labour. In the same islands they knit worsted stockings to the value of a guinea a pair and upwards.

51   The spinning of linen yarn is carried on in Scotland nearly in the same way as the knitting of stockings, by servants who are chiefly hired for other purposes. They earn but a very scanty subsistence, who endeavour to get their whole livelihood by either of those trades. In most parts of Scotland she is a good spinner who can earn twenty-pence a week.[41]

52   In opulent countries the market is generally so extensive, that any one trade is sufficient to employ the whole labour and stock of those who occupy it. Instances of people's living by one employment, and at the same time deriving some little advantage from another, occur chiefly in poor countries. The following instance, however, of something of the same kind is to be found in the capital of a very rich one. There [182] is no city in Europe, I believe, in which house-rent is dearer than in London, and yet I know no capital in which a furnished apartment can be hired so cheap.[42] Lodging is not only much cheaper in London than in Paris; it is much cheaper than in Edinburgh of the same degree of goodness; and what may seem extra-ordinary, the dearness of house-rent is the cause of the cheapness of lodg-ing. The dearness of house-rent in London arises, not only from those causes which render it dear in all great capitals, the dearness of labour, the dearness of all the materials of building, which must generally be brought from a great distance, and above all the dearness of ground-rent, every landlord acting the part of a monopolist, and frequently exacting a higher rent for a single acre of bad land in a town, than can be had for a hundred of the best in the country; but it arises in part from the peculiar manners and customs of the people, which oblige every master of a family to hire a whole house from top to bottom. A dwelling-house in England means every thing

---

[39] A similar point is made below, I.xi.o.14.   [40] Lerwick.   [41] Cf. IV.viii.4.
[42] James Boswell lived for £22 a year in comfortable lodgings in London in 1762. J. Boswell, *London Journal*, 1762–3, (ed. F. A. Pottle and C. Marley, Harmondsworth, 1966), 85. In a letter dated London, 11 March 1766, Professor Rouet informed Baron Mure that Sir James Steuart had rented 'a parlour and two pair of stair rooms to sleep in, at one guinea per week' (*Caldwell Papers* (Maitland Club, 1854), ii.81), Skinner, xlv.

that is contained under the same roof. In France, Scotland, and many other parts of Europe, it frequently means no more than a single story. A trades- man in London is obliged to hire a whole house in that part of the town where his customers live. His shop is upon the ground-floor, and he and his family sleep in the garret; and he endeavours to pay a part of his house- rent by letting the two middle stories to lodgers. He expects to maintain his family by his trade, and [183] not by his lodgers. Whereas, at Paris and Edinburgh, the people who let lodgings, have commonly no other means of subsistence; and the price of the lodging must pay, not only the rent of the house, but the whole expence of the family.

PART II
Inequalities occasioned by the Policy of Europe

1   Such are the inequalities in the whole of the advantages and disadvan- tages of the different employments of labour and stock, which the defect of any of the three requisites above-mentioned must occasion, even where there is the most perfect liberty. But the policy of Europe, by not leaving things at perfect liberty, occasions other inequalities of much greater im- portance.

2   It does this chiefly in the three following ways. First, by restraining the competition in some employments to a smaller number than would other- wise be disposed to enter into them; secondly, by increasing it in others beyond what it naturally would be; and, thirdly, by obstructing the free circulation of labour and stock, both from employment to employment and from place to place.[1]

3   First, The policy of Europe occasions a very important inequality in the whole of the advantages and disadvantages of the different employments of labour and stock, by restraining the [184] competition in some employ- ments to a smaller number than might otherwise be disposed to enter into them.

4   The exclusive privileges of corporations are the principal means it makes use of for this purpose.[2]

5   The exclusive privilege of an incorporated trade necessarily restrains the competition, in the town where it is established, to those who are free of the trade. To have served an apprenticeship in the town, under a master pro- perly qualified, is commonly the necessary requisite for obtaining this freedom. The bye-laws of the corporation regulate sometimes the number of apprentices which any master is allowed to have, and almost always the number of years which each apprentice is obliged to serve. The intention of

---

[1] Smith comments at IV.viii.44 on the restrictions imposed on the movement of artificers between countries.

[2] At V.i.e.7 Smith maintains that regulated companies resemble 'in every respect, the corporations of trades'.

both regulations is to restrain the competition to a much smaller number than might otherwise be disposed to enter into the trade. The limitation of the number of apprentices restrains it directly. A long term of apprenticeship restrains it more indirectly, but as effectually, by increasing the expence of education.[3]

6   In Sheffield no master cutler can have more than one apprentice at a time, by a bye-law of the corporation. In Norfolk and Norwich no master weaver can have more than two apprentices, under pain of forfeiting five pounds a month to the king.[4] No master hatter can have more than two apprentices any-where in England, or in the English plantations, under pain of forfeiting five pounds a month, half to the [185] king, and half to him who shall sue in any court of record.[5] Both these regulations, though they have been confirmed by a publick law of the kingdom, are evidently dictated by the same corporation spirit which enacted the bye-law of Sheffield. The silk weavers in London had scarce been incorporated a year when they enacted a bye-law, restraining any master from having more than two apprentices at a time. It required a particular act of parliament to rescind this bye-law.[6]

7   Seven years seem antiently to have been, all over Europe, the usual term established for the duration of apprenticeships in the greater part of incorporated trades. All such incorporations were antiently called universities; which indeed is the proper Latin name for any incorporation whatever. The university of smiths, the university of taylors, &c. are expressions which we commonly meet with in the old charters of antient towns.[7] When those particular incorporations which are now peculiarly called universities were first established, the term of years which it was necessary to study, in order to obtain the degree of master of arts, appears evidently to have been copied from the term of apprenticeship in common trades, of which the incorporations were much more antient. As to have wrought seven years under a master properly qualified, was necessary, in order to intitle any person to become a master, and to have himself apprentices in a common trade; so to have studied seven years under a master properly qua-[186]lified, was necessary to entitle him to become a master,

[3] Smith called for the abolition of such privileges, including the law of settlements and the statute of apprenticeship, at IV.ii.42.

[4] 14 Charles II, c.5 (1662) in *Statutes of the Realm*, v.370–4; 13 and 14 Charles II, c.5 in Ruffhead's edition.

[5] 8 Elizabeth I, c.11 (1566), further enforced by 1 James I, c.17 (1603), in *Statutes of the Realm*, iv(2) 1035; 2 (vulgo 1) James I, c.17 in Ruffhead's edition and extended to the American colonies by 5 George II, c.22 (1731).

[6] 19 and 20 Charles II, c.11 (1670) in *Statutes of the Realm*, v.640; 20 Charles II, c.6 in Ruffhead's edition; s.3 states 'no By-law already made or hereafter to be made by the said Company shall or may limit or confine any Freeman of the said Company to take a lesse number than three Apprentices at any time'.

[7] Thomas Madox, *Firma Burgi* (London, 1726), 32.

teacher, or doctor (words antiently synonimous) in the liberal arts, and to have scholars or apprentices (words likewise originally synonimous) to study under him.[8]

8   By the 5th of Elizabeth, commonly called the Statute of Apprenticeship,[9] it was enacted, that no person should for the future exercise any trade, craft, or mystery at that time exercised in England, unless he had previously served to it an apprenticeship of seven years at least; and what before had been the bye-law of many particular corporations, became in England the general and publick law of all trades carried on in market towns. For though the words of the statute are very general, and seem plainly to include the whole kingdom, by interpretation its operation has been limited to market towns, it having been held that in country villages a person may exercise several different trades, though he has not served a seven years apprenticeship to each, they being necessary for the conveniency of the inhabitants, and the number of people frequently not being sufficient to supply each with a particular sett of hands.[10]

9   By a strict interpretation of the words too the operation of this statute has been limited to those trades which were established in England before the 5th of Elizabeth, and has never been extended to such as have been introduced since that time.[11] This limitation has given occasion to several distinctions which, considered as rules of police, appear as foolish as can well be ima-[187]gined. It has been adjudged, for example, that a coach-maker can neither himself make nor employ journeymen to make his coach-wheels, but must buy them of a master wheel-wright; this latter trade having been exercised in England before the 5th of Elizabeth. But a wheel-wright, though he has never served an apprenticeship to a coach-maker, may either himself make or employ journeymen to make coaches; the trade of a coach-maker not being within the statute, because not exercised in England at the time when it was made. The manufactures of Manchester, Birmingham, and Wolverhampton, are many of them, upon this account, not within the statute; not having been exercised in England before the 5th of Elizabeth.[12]

10   In France, the duration of apprenticeships is different in different towns

[8] In Letter 143 addressed to Cullen, dated 20 September 1774 Smith remarked that the Universities required 5 and 7 years for a Master of Arts, 11 and 16 for a Doctor of Law, Physic, or Divinity. He added that the real motive behind such long periods of study was commercial, and they were simply designed so that 'the student may spend more money among them, and that they may make more profit by him'. See below, V.i.e.7, and V.i.f.11.

[9] 5 Elizabeth I, c.4 (1562). See below, I.x.c.42.

[10] See above, I.iii.2.

[11] Discharged soldiers and sailors were allowed to exercise any trade even against 5 Elizabeth I, c.4 by 12 Charles II, c.16 (1660). Similar provisions were made by 12 Anne, c.14 (1712) in *Statutes of the Realm*, ix.791–3; 12 Anne, st.1, c.13 in Ruffhead's edition, and by 3 George III, c.8 (1762). See below, IV.ii.42.

[12] A brief discussion of the legal and other qualifications in the operation of the Act is in J. H. Clapham *A Concise Economic History of Britain* (Cambridge, 1949), 256–7.

and in different trades. In Paris, five years is the term required in a great number; but before any person can be qualified to exercise the trade as a master, he must, in many of them, serve five years more as a journeyman. During this latter term he is called the companion of his master, and the term itself is called his companionship.[13]

11   In Scotland there is no general law which regulates universally the duration of apprenticeships. The term is different in different corporations. Where it is long, a part of it may generally be redeemed by paying a small fine. In most towns too a very small fine is sufficient to purchase the freedom of any corporation. The weavers of linen and hempen cloth, the principal [188] manufactures of the country, as well as all other artificers subservient to them, wheel-makers, reel-makers, &c. may exercise their trades in any town corporate without paying any fine. In all towns corporate all persons are free to sell butcher's-meat upon any lawful day of the week. Three years is in Scotland a common term of apprenticeship, even in some very nice trades; and in general I know of no country in Europe in which corporation laws are so little oppressive.[14]

12   The property which every man has in his own labour, as it is the original foundation of all other property, so it is the most sacred and inviolable. The patrimony of a poor man lies in the strength and dexterity of his hands; and to hinder him from employing this strength and dexterity in what manner he thinks proper without injury to his neighbour, is a plain violation of this most sacred property. It is a manifest encroachment upon the just liberty both of the workman, and of those who might be disposed to employ him. As it hinders the one from working at what he thinks proper, so it hinders the *others* from employing whom they think proper. To judge whether he is fit to be employed, may surely be trusted to the discretion of the employers whose interest it so much concerns. The affected anxiety of the law-giver lest they should employ an improper person, is evidently as impertinent as it is oppressive.

13   The institution of long apprenticeships can give no security that insufficient workmanship shall not frequently be exposed to publick sale. When this [189] is done it is generally the effect of fraud, and not of inability; and the longest apprenticeship can give no security against fraud. Quite different regulations are necessary to prevent this abuse. The sterling

---

a–a other *I*

---

[13] 'Compagnon' and 'compagnonnage'.

[14] There were considerable local variations in Scotland, and the prescribed period of three years was not necessarily so general as Smith implies. I. F. Grant, *Social and Economic Development of Scotland before 1603* (Edinburgh, 1930), 422–3. Miss Grant also holds that 'the object of the craftsmen was rather to limit their privileges to those who were willing to pay for them than to exclude as many people as possible' (420).

mark upon plate,[15] and the stamps upon linen[16] and woollen cloth,[17] give the purchaser much greater security than any statute of apprenticeship.[18] He generally looks at these, but never thinks it worth while to enquire whether the *b*workman*b* had served a seven years apprenticeship.

14   The institution of long apprenticeships has no tendency to form young people to industry. A journeyman who works by the piece is likely to be industrious, because he derives a benefit from every exertion of his industry.[19] An apprentice is likely to be idle, and almost always is so, because he has no immediate interest to be otherwise.[20] In the inferior employments, the sweets of labour consist altogether in the recompence of labour. They who are soonest in a condition to enjoy the sweets of it, are likely soonest to conceive a relish for it, and to acquire the early habit of industry. A young man naturally conceives an aversion to labour, when for a long time he receives no benefit from it. The boys who are put out apprentices from publick charities are generally bound for more than the usual number of years, and they generally turn out very idle and worthless.

15   Apprenticeships were altogether unknown to the antients. The reciprocal duties of master and apprentice make a considerable article in [190] every modern code. The Roman law is perfectly silent with regard to them. I know no Greek or Latin word (I might venture, I believe, to assert that there is none) which expresses the idea we now annex to the word Apprentice, a servant bound to work at a particular trade for the benefit of a master, during a term of years, upon condition that the master shall teach him that trade.

16   Long apprenticeships are altogether unnecessary. The arts, which are much superior to common trades, such as those of making clocks and watches, contain no such mystery as to require a long course of instruction.[21] The first invention of such beautiful machines, indeed, and even that of some of the instruments employed in making them, must, no doubt,

---

b-b workmen 5–6

[15] 28 Edward I, c.20 (1300).

[16] 10 Anne, c.23 (1711) in *Statutes of the Realm*, ix.682–4; 10 Anne, c.21 in Ruffhead's edition provided for the stamping of linen in Scotland. 13 George I, c.26 (1726) detailed the standard length and breadth of cloth.

[17] 39 Elizabeth I, c.20 (1597), confirmed by 43 Elizabeth I, c.10 (1601). See above, I.iv.7.

[18] LJ (B) 306–7, ed. Cannan 236, comments that a seven-year apprenticeship was no security against bad cloth, and added that: 'You yourself cannot inspect a large piece of cloth, this must be left to the stampmaster, whose credit must be depended upon.'

[19] Cantillon remarked, *Essai*, 52, ed. Higgs 41, that where piece rates are used, journeymen will 'work for their own interest as hard as they can without further inspection'. See also Steuart, *Principles*, i.193, ed. Skinner, i.169. See above, I.viii.44, where payment by the piece is also discussed.

[20] See above, I.x.b.8, on the idleness of apprentices.

[21] Smith was rather more generous in LJ (B) 225, ed. Cannan 175:

a watchmaker must be acquainted with several sciences in order to understand his business well, such as arithmetic, geometry, and astronomy with regard to the equation of time, and their wages must be high in order to compensate the additional expence. [*continues*]

have been the work of deep thought and long time, and may justly be considered as among the happiest efforts of human ingenuity. But when both have been fairly invented and are well understood, to explain to any young man, in the compleatest manner, how to apply the instruments and how to construct the machines, cannot well require more than the lessons of a few weeks: perhaps those of a few days might be sufficient. In the common mechanick trades, those of a few days might certainly be sufficient. The dexterity of hand, indeed, even in common trades, cannot be acquired without much practice and experience. But a young man would practise with much more diligence and attention, if from the beginning he wrought as a journey-[191]man, being paid in proportion to the little work which he could execute, and paying in his turn for the materials which he might sometimes spoil through awkwardness and inexperience. His education would generally in this way be more effectual, and always less tedious and expensive. The master, indeed, would be a loser. He would lose all the wages of the apprentice, which he now saves, for seven years together. In the end, perhaps, the apprentice himself would be a loser. In a trade so easily learnt he would have more competitors, and his wages, when he came to be a compleat workman, would be much less than at present. The same increase of competition would reduce the profits of the masters as well as the wages of the workmen. The trades, the crafts, the mysteries, would all be losers. But the publick would be a gainer, the work of all artificers coming in this way much cheaper to market.

17   It is to prevent this reduction of price, and consequently of wages and profit, by restraining that free competition which would most certainly ocasion it, that all corporations, and the greater part of corporation laws, have been established. In order to erect a corporation, no other authority in antient times was requisite in many parts of Europe, but that of the town corporate in which it was established.[22] In England, indeed, a charter from the king was likewise necessary. But this prerogative of the crown seems to have been reserved rather for extorting money from the subject, than for the defence of the common [192] liberty against such oppressive monopolies. Upon paying a fine to the king, the charter seems generally to have

Cf. LJ (A) vi.61:

> a watchmaker must read and write, must understand arithmetick, a little of geometry, triginometry, and astronomy. A weaver may in this manner by the time he is 16 or 17 be a proficient in his trade, whereas a watchmaker will be 22 or 23 before he can be any way skilled in his art.

It is interesting that in Letter 125 addressed to John Davidson, dated 11 March 1771 Smith complained of a repair he had sent to Cowan the watchmaker: 'I suppose he had given her to some of his apprentices. I must now beg that he will take the trouble to look at her with some care himself.'

[22] For the practice in Scotland see W. M. Mackenzie, *The Scottish Burghs* (Edinburgh, 1949), 117–19. A seal of cause from the burghs was treated as a charter of incorporation by the crafts.

been readily granted; and when any particular class of artificers or traders thought proper to act as a corporation without a charter, such adulterine guilds, as they were called, were not always disfranchised upon that account, but obliged to fine annually to the king for permission to exercise their usurped privileges*. The immediate inspection of all corporations, and of the bye-laws which they might think proper to enact for their own government, belonged to the town corporate in which they were established; and whatever discipline was exercised over them, proceeded commonly, not from the king, but from that greater incorporation of which those subordinate ones were only parts or members.

18   The government of towns corporate was altogether in the hands of traders and artificers; and it was the manifest interest of every particular class of them, to prevent the market from being over-stocked, as they commonly express it, with their own particular species of industry; which is in reality to keep it always under-stocked. Each class was eager to establish regulations proper for this purpose, and, provided it was allowed to do so, was willing to consent that every other class should do the same. In consequence of such regulations, indeed, each class was obliged to buy the goods they had occasion for [193] from every other within the town, somewhat dearer than they otherwise might have done. But in recompence, they were enabled to sell their own just as much dearer; so that so far it was as broad as long, as they say; and in the dealings of the different classes within the town with one another, none of them were losers by these regulations. But in their dealings with the country they were all great gainers; and in these latter dealings consists the whole trade which supports and enriches every town.

19   Every town draws its whole subsistence, and all the materials of its industry, from the country.[23] It pays for these chiefly in two ways: first, by sending back to the country a part of those materials wrought up and manufactured; in which case their price is augmented by the wages of the workmen, and the profits of their masters or immediate employers: secondly, by sending to it a part both of the rude and manufactured produce, either of other countries, or of distant parts of the same country, imported into the town; in which case too the original price of those goods is augmented by the wages of the carriers or sailors, and by the profits of the merchants who employ them. In what is gained upon the first of those two branches of

---

^c* See Madox Firma Burgi, p. 26, &c.^c ['Anciently, a Gild either Religious or Secular could not legally be set-up without the King's Licence. If any Persons erected a Gild without warrant, that is, without the King's Leave, it was a Trespass, and they were lyable to be punished for it.' Madox, *Firma Burgi*, 26.]

---

^{c–c} 2–6

---

[23] See below, I.xi.c.7, II.i.28, and III.i.1.

commerce, consists the advantage which the town makes by its manufactures; in what is gained upon the second, the advantage of its inland and foreign trade. The wages of the workmen, and the profits of their different employers, make up the whole of what is gained upon both. What-[194]ever regulations, therefore, tend to increase those wages and profits beyond what they otherwise would be, tend to enable the town to purchase, with a smaller quantity of its labour, the produce of a greater quantity of the labour of the country. They give the traders and artificers in the town an advantage over the landlords, farmers, and labourers in the country, and break down that natural equality which would otherwise take place in the commerce which is carried on between them. The whole annual produce of the labour of the society is annually divided between those two different sets of people. By means of those regulations a greater share of it is given to the inhabitants of the town than would otherwise fall to them; and a less to those of the country.

20   The price which the town really pays for the provisions and materials annually imported into it, is the quantity of manufactures and other goods annually exported from it. The dearer the latter are sold, the cheaper the former are bought. The industry of the town becomes more, and that of the country less advantageous.

21   That the industry which is carried on in towns is, every-where in Europe, more advantageous than that which is carried on in the country, without entering into any very nice computations, we may satisfy ourselves by one very simple and obvious observation. In every country of Europe we find, at least, a hundred people who have acquired great fortunes from [195] small beginnings by trade and manufactures, the industry which properly belongs to towns, for one who has done so by that which properly belongs to the country, the raising of rude produce by the improvement and cultivation of land.[24] Industry, therefore, must be better rewarded, the wages of labour and the profits of stock must evidently be greater in the one situation than in the other. But stock and labour naturally seek the most advantageous employment. They naturally, therefore, resort as much as they can to the town, and desert the country.

22   The inhabitants of a town, being collected into one place, can easily combine together. The most insignificant trades carried on in towns have accordingly, in some place or other, been incorporated; and even where they have never been incorporated, yet the corporation spirit, the jealousy of strangers, the aversion to take apprentices, or to communicate the secret of their trade, generally prevail in them, and often teach them, by voluntary associations and agreements, to prevent that free competition which they cannot prohibit by bye-laws. The trades which employ but a small

[24] It is pointed out at II.v.37 that agriculture in Europe was capable of absorbing a much greater capital.

number of hands, run most easily into such combinations. Half a dozen
wool-combers, perhaps, are necessary to keep a thousand spinners and
weavers at work. By combining not to take apprentices they can not only
engross the employment, but reduce the whole manufacture into a sort of
slavery to themselves, and raise the price of their labour much above what
is due to the nature of their work.

23   [196] The inhabitants of the country, dispersed in distant places, cannot easily combine together.[25] They have not only never been incorporated,
but the corporation spirit never has prevailed among them. No apprenticeship has ever been thought necessary to qualify for husbandry, the great
trade of the country. After what are called the fine arts, and the liberal
professions, however, there is perhaps no trade which requires so great a
variety of knowledge and experience.[26] The innumerable volumes which
have been written upon it in all languages, may satisfy us, that among the
wisest and most learned nations, it has never been regarded as a matter
very easily understood. And from all those volumes we shall in vain attempt
to collect that knowledge of its various and complicated operations, which
is commonly possessed even by the common farmer; how contemptuously
soever the very contemptible authors of some of them may sometimes
affect to speak of him. There is scarce any common mechanick trade, on the
contrary, of which all the operations may not be as compleatly and distinctly explained in a pamphlet of a very few pages, as it is possible for
words illustrated by figures to explain them. In the history of the arts, now
publishing by the French academy of sciences,[27] several of them are
actually explained in this manner. The direction of operations, besides,
which must be varied with every change of the weather, as well as with
many other accidents, requires much more judgment and discretion, than
that of [197] those which are always the same or very nearly the same.

24   Not only the art of the farmer, the general direction of the operations of
husbandry, but many inferior branches of country labour require much
more skill and experience than the greater part of mechanick trades. The
man who works upon brass and iron, works with instruments and upon
materials of which the temper is always the same, or very nearly the same.
But the man who ploughs the ground with a team of horses or oxen, works
with instruments of which the health, strength, and temper are very different upon different occasions. The condition of the materials which he
works upon too is as variable as that of the instruments which he works
with, and both require to be managed with much judgment and discretion.
The common ploughman, though generally regarded as the pattern of

[25] Cf. IV.ii.21, IV.v.b.4, IV.vii.b.24, IV.viii.34.
[26] The limitation on the division of labour in agriculture is discussed above, I.i.4.
[27] *Descriptions des Arts et Métiers faites ou approuvées par Messieurs de l'Académie Royale des Sciences* (1761–88).

stupidity and ignorance, is seldom defective in this judgment and discretion. He is less accustomed, indeed, to social intercourse than the mechanick who lives in a town. His voice and language are more uncouth and more difficult to be understood by those who are not used to them. His understanding, however, being accustomed to consider a greater variety of objects, is generally much superior to that of the other, whose whole attention from morning till night is commonly occupied in performing one or two very simple operations.[28] How much the lower ranks of people in the country are really superior to those of the town, is well known to every man whom either [198] business or curiosity has led to converse much with both. In China and Indostan accordingly both the rank and the wages of country labourers are said to be superior to those of the greater part of artificers and manufacturers. They would probably be so every where, if corporation laws and the corporation spirit did not prevent it.

25   The superiority which the industry of the towns has every where in Europe over that of the country, is not altogether owing to corporations and corporation laws. It is supported by many other regulations. The high duties upon foreign manufactures and upon all goods imported by alien merchants, all tend to the same purpose.[29] Corporation laws enable the inhabitants of towns to raise their prices, without fearing to be under-sold by the ᵈfreeᵈ competition of their own countrymen. Those other regulations secure them equally against that of foreigners. The enhancement of price occasioned by both is every where finally paid by the landlords, farmers, and labourers of the country, who have seldom opposed the establishment of such monopolies. They have commonly neither inclination nor fitness to enter into combinations; and the clamour and sophistry of merchants and manufacturers easily persuade them that the private interest of a part, and of a subordinate part of the society, is the general interest of the whole.

26   In Great Britain the superiority of the industry of the towns over that of the country, seems to have been greater formerly than in the present times. The wages of country labour approach [199] nearer to those of manufacturing labour, and the profits of stock employed in agriculture to those of trading and manufacturing stock, than they are said to have done in the last century, or in the beginning of the present. This change may be regarded as the necessary, though very late consequence of the extraordinary encouragement given to the industry of the towns. The stock accumulated in them comes in time to be so great, that it can no longer be employed with the antient profit in that species of industry which is peculiar to them. That

---

ᵈ⁻ᵈ *1-5*

[28] Cf. LJ (B) 328, ed. Cannan 255: 'When the mind is employed about a variety of objects, it is somehow expanded and enlarged, and on this account a country artist is generally acknowledged to have a range of thoughts much above a city one.' See below, V.i.f.50.

[29] The tax on alien merchants is mentioned below, IV.ii.30, IV.iii.c.10, and V.ii.k.21.

industry has its limits like every other; and the increase of stock, by increasing the competition, necessarily reduces the profit.[30] The lowering of profit in the town forces out stock to the country, where, by creating a new demand for country labour, it necessarily raises its wages. It then spreads itself, if I may say so, over the face of the land, and by being employed in agriculture is in part restored to the country, at the expence of which, in a great measure, it had originally been accumulated in the town. That every where in Europe the greatest improvements of the country have been owing to such overflowings of the stock originally accumulated in the towns, I shall endeavour to show hereafter;[31] and at the same time to demonstrate, that though some countries have by this course attained to a considerable degree of opulence, it is in itself necessarily slow, uncertain, liable to be disturbed and interrupted by innumerable accidents, and in every respect contrary to the order of nature [200] and of reason. The interests, prejudices, laws and customs which have given occasion to it, I shall endeavour to explain as fully and distinctly as I can in the third and fourth books of this enquiry.

27   People of the same trade seldom meet together, even for merriment and diversion, but the conversation ends in a conspiracy against the publick, or in some contrivance to raise prices. It is impossible indeed to prevent such meetings, by any law which either could be executed, or would be consistent with liberty and justice. But though the law cannot hinder people of the same trade from sometimes assembling together, it ought to do nothing to facilitate such assemblies; much less to render them necessary.

28   A regulation which obliges all those of the same trade in a particular town to enter their names and places of abode in a publick register, facilitates such assemblies. It connects individuals who might never otherwise be known to one another, and gives every man of the trade a direction where to find every other man of it.

29   A regulation which enables those of the same trade to tax themselves in order to provide for their poor, their sick, their widows and orphans, by giving them a common interest to manage, renders such assemblies necessary.

30   An incorporation not only renders them necessary, but makes the act of the majority binding upon the whole. In a free trade an effectual combination cannot be established but by the unanimous consent of every single *trader*[e], and it [201] cannot last longer than every single *trader*[f] continues of the same mind. The majority of a corporation can enact a bye-law with proper penalties, which will limit the competition more effectually and more durably than any voluntary combination whatever.

[e-e] member of it *I*   [f-f] member of it *I*

---

[30] See above, I.ix.2 and II.iv.8.   [31] See below, III.iv.

31   The pretence that corporations are necessary for the better government
of the trade, is without any foundation. The real and effectual discipline
which is exercised over a workman, is not that of his corporation, but that
of his customers. It is the fear of losing their employment which restrains
his frauds and corrects his negligence. An exclusive corporation necessarily weakens the force of this discipline. A particular set of workmen must
then be employed, let them behave well or ill. It is upon this account that
in many large incorporated towns no tolerable workmen are to be found,
even in some of the most necessary trades. If you would have your work
tolerably executed, it must be done in the suburbs, where the workmen
having no exclusive privilege, have nothing but their character to depend
upon, and you must then smuggle it into the town as well as you can.

32   It is in this manner that the policy of Europe, by restraining the competition in some employments to a smaller number than would otherwise be
disposed to enter into them, occasions a very important inequality in the
whole of the advantages and disadvantages of the different employments of
labour and stock.

33   [202] Secondly, The policy of Europe, by increasing the competition in
some employments beyond what it naturally would be, occasions another
inequality of an opposite kind in the whole of the advantages and disadvantages of the different employments of labour and stock.

34   It has been considered as of so much importance that a proper number of
young people should be educated for certain professions, that, sometimes
the publick, and sometimes the piety of private founders have established
many pensions, scholarships, exhibitions, bursaries, &c.[32] for this purpose,
which draw many more people into those trades than could otherwise pretend to follow them. In all christian countries, I believe, the education of
the greater part of churchmen is paid for in this manner. Very few of them
are educated altogether at their own expence. The long, tedious and expensive education, therefore, of those who are, will not always procure
them a suitable reward, the church being crowded with people who, in
order to get employment, are willing to accept of a much smaller recompence than what such an education would otherwise have entitled them to;
and in this manner the competition of the poor takes away the reward of
the rich. It would be indecent, no doubt, to compare either a curate or a
chaplain with a journeyman in any common trade. The pay of a curate or
chaplain, however, may very properly be considered as of the same nature
with the wages of a journeyman. They are, all three, paid for their work
according to the con-[203]tract which they may happen to make with their
respective superiors. Till after the middle of the fourteenth century, five
merks, containing about as much silver as ten pounds of our present money,

[32] See below, V.i.f.12.

was in England the usual pay of a curate or ^{g} stipendiary parish priest, as we find it regulated by the decrees of several different national councils.[33] At the same period four-pence a day, containing the same quantity of silver as a shilling of our present money, was declared to be the pay of a master mason, and three-pence a day, equal to nine-pence of our present money, that of a journeyman mason*. The wages of both these labourers, therefore, supposing them to have been constantly employed, were much superior to those of the curate. The wages of the master mason, supposing him to have been without employment one-third of the year, would have fully equalled them. By the 12th of Queen Anne, c.12,[34] it is declared, "That whereas for want of sufficient maintenance and encouragement to curates, the cures have in several places been meanly supplied, the bishop is, therefore, empowered to appoint by writing under his hand and seal a sufficient certain stipend or allowance, not exceeding fifty and not less than twenty pounds a year". Forty pounds a year is reckoned at present very good pay for a curate, and notwithstanding this act of parliament, there are many curacies under twenty pounds a year. There are [204] journeymen shoe-makers in London who earn forty pounds a year, and there is scarce an industrious workman of any kind in that metropolis who does not earn more than twenty. This last sum indeed does not exceed what is frequently earned by common labourers in many country parishes. Whenever the law has attempted to regulate the wages of workmen, it has always been rather to lower them than to raise them.[35] But the law has upon many occasions attempted to raise the wages of curates, and for the dignity of the church, to oblige the rectors of parishes to give them more than the wretched maintenance which they themselves might be willing to accept of. And in both cases the law seems to have been equally ineffectual, and has never either been able to raise the wages of curates or to sink those of labourers to the degree that was intended; because it has never been able to hinder either the one from being willing to accept of less than the legal allowance, on account of the indigence of their situation and the multitude of their competitors; or the other from receiving more, on account of the contrary competition of those who expected to derive either profit or pleasure from employing them.

---

^{h*} See the Statute of labourers, 25 Ed.III.^{h} [25 Edward III, 2 (1350) in *Statutes of the Realm*, i.311; 25 Edward II, st.1 in Ruffhead's edition. See below, I.xi.e.2.]

---

^{g} a 5 $^{h-h}$ 2–6

---

[33] In 1378 the stipend of curates was raised from five marks to eight marks a year. The intention, according to Burn, was to give the curate 'double of what would reasonably pay for his board'. R. Burn, *Ecclesiastical Law* (London, 1763), i.434.

[34] 13 Anne, c.11 (1713) in *Statutes of the Realm*, ix.922; 12 Anne, st.2, c.12 in Ruffhead's edition. The quotation which follows is not verbatim.

[35] Cf. I.viii.13.

35   The great benefices and other ecclesiastical dignities support the honour of the church, notwithstanding the mean circumstances of some of its inferior members. The respect paid to the profession too makes some compensation even to them for the meanness of their pecuniary recom-[205]pence. In England, and in all Roman Catholick countries, the lottery of the church is in reality much more advantageous than is necessary. The example of the churches of Scotland, of Geneva, and of several other protestant churches, may satisfy us that in so creditable a profession, in which education is so easily procured, the hopes of much more moderate benefices will draw a sufficient number of learned, decent, and respectable men into holy orders.

36   In professions in which there are no benefices, such as law and physick, if an equal proportion of people were educated at the publick expence, the competition would soon be so great, as to sink very much their pecuniary reward. It might then not be worth any man's while to educate his son to either of those professions at his own expence. They would be entirely abandoned to such as had been educated by those publick charities, whose numbers and necessities would oblige them in general to content themselves with a very miserable recompence, to the entire degradation of the now respectable professions of law and physick.

37   That unprosperous race of men commonly called men of letters, are pretty much in the situation which lawyers and physicians probably would be in upon the foregoing supposition. In every part of Europe the greater part of them have been educated for the church, but have been hindered by different reasons from entering into holy orders.[36] They have generally, therefore, been educated at the publick expence, and [206] their numbers are every-where so great as commonly to reduce the price of their labour to a very paultry recompence.

38   Before the invention of the art of printing, the only employment by which a man of letters could make any thing by his talents, was that of a publick ⁱor privateⁱ teacher, or by communicating to other people the curious and useful knowledge which he had acquired himself: And this is still surely a more honourable, a more useful, and in general even a more profitable employment than that other of writing for a bookseller, to which the art of printing has given occasion. The time and study, the genius, knowledge, and application requisite to qualify an eminent teacher of the

---

ⁱ⁻ⁱ 2–6

---

[36] The Snell Exhibition, which enabled Smith to attend Balliol College, Oxford, between 1740 and 1746, included among its provisions the condition that the holder be bound, under penalty of £500, to enter orders of the Church of England 'but in noe case to come back into England, nor to goe into any other place but onely into the Kingdome of Scotland for his or their preferrment'. From the will of John Snell in W.I. Addison, *Snell Exhibitions* (Glasgow, 1901), 199–200.

sciences, are at least equal to what is necessary for the greatest practitioners in law and physick. But the usual reward of the eminent teacher bears no proportion to that of the lawyer or physician; because the trade of the one is crowded with indigent people who have been brought up to it at the publick expence; whereas those of the other two are incumbered with very ✓ few who have not been educated at their own. The usual recompence, however, of publick and private teachers, small as it may appear, would undoubtedly be less than it is, if the competition of those yet more indigent men of letters who write for bread was not taken out of the market.[37] Before the invention of the art of printing, a scholar and a beggar seem to have been terms very nearly synonymous. The different governors of the universities before that [207] time appear to have often granted licences to their scholars to beg.[38]

39   In antient times, before any charities of this kind had been established for the education of indigent people to the learned professions, the rewards of eminent teachers appear to have been much more considerable. Isocrates, in what is called his discourse against the sophists, reproaches the teachers of his own times with inconsistency. "They make the most magnificent promises to their scholars", says he, "and undertake to teach to be wise, to be happy, and to be just, and in return for so important a service they stipulate the paultry reward of four or five minae. They who teach wisdom", continues he, "ought certainly to be wise themselves; but if any man *jwasj* to sell such a bargain for such a price, he would be convicted of the most evident folly."[39] He certainly does not mean here to exaggerate the reward, and we may be assured that it was not less than he represents it. Four minae were equal to thirteen pounds six shillings and eight pence: five minae to sixteen pounds thirteen shillings and four pence. Something not less than the largest of those two sums, therefore, must at that time have been usually paid to the most eminent teachers at Athens. Isocrates

j–j were 4–6

---

[37] In LJ (A) vi.67 Smith refers to the trade of a 'hackney writer' and states that an individual would not apply to this trade 'unless he had a prospect of maintaining himself and recompensing the expense of education'.

[38] The practice was followed in Scotland. Cf. 'All vagaboundis scollaris of the universiteis of Sanctandrois, Glasgow and Abirdene not licencit be the rector and dene of faculte of the universitie to ask almous . . . salbe takein, adjugeit, demed and puneist as strang beggaris and vagaboundis . . .' (*Acts of the Parliaments of Scotland*, iii.86–9, 1574).

[39] 'But these professors have gone so far in their lack of scruple that they attempt to persuade our young men that if they will only study under them they will know what to do in life and through this knowledge will become happy and prosperous. More than that, although they set themselves up as masters and dispensers of goods so precious, they are not ashamed of asking for them a price of three or four minae! Why, if they were to sell any other commodity for so trifling a fraction of its worth they would not deny their folly.' (Isocrates, *Against the Sophists*, 3–4, translated by G. Norlin, *Isocrates* (Loeb Classical Library, 1929), ii.165; also mentioned in C. Arbuthnot, *Table of Ancient Coins Weights and Measures* (London, 1727), 198.)

himself demanded ten minae, or thirty-three pounds six shillings and eight pence, from each scholar.[40] When he taught at Athens, he is said to have had an hundred scholars. I understand this to be the number whom he taught at one time, or who attended what we would call [208] one course of lectures, a number which will not appear extraordinary from so great a city to so famous a teacher, who taught too what was at that time the most fashionable of all sciences, rhetorick. He must have made, therefore, by each course of lectures, a thousand minae, or 3,333 *l*. 6*s*. 8*d*. A thousand minae, accordingly, is said by Plutarch in another place, to have been his Didactron, or usual price of teaching.[41] Many other eminent teachers in those times appear to have acquired great fortunes. Gorgias made a present to the temple of Delphi of his own statue in solid gold.[42] We must not, I presume, suppose that it was as large as the life. His way of living, as well as that of Hippias and Protagoras, two other eminent teachers of those times, is represented by Plato as splendid even to ostentation. Plato himself is said to have lived with a good deal of magnificence. Aristotle, after having been tutor to Alexander and most munificently rewarded,[43] as it is universally agreed, both by him and his father Phillip, thought it worth while, notwithstanding, to return to Athens, in order to resume the teaching of his school. Teachers of the sciences were probably in those times less common than they came to be in an age or two afterwards, when the competition had probably somewhat reduced both the price of their labour and the admiration for their persons. The most eminent of them, however, appear always to have enjoyed a degree of consideration much superior to any of the like profession in the present times. The Athenians [209] sent Carneades the academick, and Diogenes the stoick, upon a solemn embassy to Rome; and though their city had then declined from its former grandeur, it was still an independent and considerable republick. Carneades too was a Babylonian by birth, and as there never was a people more jealous of admitting foreigners to publick offices than the Athenians, their consideration for him must have been very great.[44]

[40] Plutarch, *Demosthenes*, v.4, translated by B. Perrin in *Plutarch's Lives* (Loeb Classical Library, 1928), vii.13.

[41] Also quoted in C. Arbuthnot, *Table of Ancient Coins, Weights and Measures*, 198. For further comment on teaching in classical times see below V.i.g.40.

[42] 'The first solid gold statue of a human being was one of himself set up by Gorgias of Leontini in the temple at Delphi about the 70th Olympiad. So great were the profits to be made by teaching the art of oratory.' (Pliny, *Natural History*, XXXIII, xxiv, translated by H. Rackham (Loeb Classical Library, 1952), ix.65.)

[43] Philip 'sent for the most famous and learned of philosophers, Aristotle, and paid him a noble and appropriate tuition-fee' (Plutarch, *Alexander*, vii.2, translated by B. Perrin in *Plutarch's Lives* (Loeb Classical Library, 1928), vii.241).

[44] Carneades was a native of Cyrene; Diogenes was a Babylonian. Cf. LJ (B) 41, 86, ed. Cannan 28, 62. LJ (A) iv.92–3 points out that 'the Athenians were very chary and scrupulous in admitting anyone into the freedom of their city.' In contrast to the situation in Rome, 'the citizenship of Athens was attended with some profit . . . and for that reason was

40   This inequality is upon the whole, perhaps, rather advantageous than hurtful to the publick. It may somewhat degrade the profession of a publick teacher; but the cheapness of literary education is surely an advantage which greatly over-balances this trifling inconveniency. The publick too might derive still greater benefit from it, if the constitution of those schools and colleges, in which education is carried on, was more reasonable than it is at present through the greater part of Europe.[45]

41   Thirdly, The policy of Europe, by obstructing the free circulation of labour and stock both from employment to employment, and from place to place, occasions in some cases a very inconvenient inequality in the whole of the advantages and disadvantages of their different employments.

42   The statute of apprenticeship obstructs the free circulation of labour from one employment to another, even in the same place.[46] The exclusive privileges of corporations obstruct it from one place to another, even in the same employment.

43   [210] It frequently happens that while high wages are given to the workmen in one manufacture, those in another are obliged to content themselves with bare subsistence. The one is in an advancing state, and has, therefore, a continual demand for new hands: The other is in a declining state, and the super-abundance of hands is continually increasing. Those two manufactures may sometimes be in the same town, and sometimes in the same neighbourhood, without being able to lend the least assistance to one another. The statute of apprenticeship may oppose it in the one case, and both that and an exclusive corporation in the other. In many different manufactures, however, the operations are so much alike, that the workmen could easily change trades with one another, if those absurd laws did not hinder them.[47] The arts of weaving plain linen and plain silk, for example, are almost entirely the same. That of weaving plain woollen is somewhat different; but the difference is so insignificant, that either a linen or a silk weaver might become a tolerable workman in a *k*very*k* few days.[48] If any of those three capital manufactures, therefore, were decaying, the

k-k *1-5*

---

a defalcation from the fortunes of the rest of the citizens, who would therefore never consent to the admission of new members.' Cf. LJ (A) v.87–8. See below, IV.vii.c.77, where Smith discusses the problems faced by Rome after having adopted a less restrictive policy.

[45] This topic is examined at some length in V.i.f.

[46] In I.x.c.9 Smith recognised that the Statute of Apprenticeship could be circumvented, but J. H. Clapham has pointed out that it was more likely to be enforced if backed by the 'coercive power of a company' (*Concise Economic History of Britain to 1750*, 256).

[47] See below, IV.ii.42.

[48] In his essay 'Of the Jealousy of Trade' Hume made a similar point: 'If the spirit of industry be preserved, it may easily be diverted from one branch to another; and the manufacturers of wool, for instance, be employed in linen, silk, iron, or any other commodities, for which there appears to be a demand.' (*Essays Moral, Political and Literary*, ed. Green and Grose, i.347.)

workmen might find a resource in one of the other two which was in a more prosperous condition; and their wages would neither rise too high in the thriving, nor sink too low in the decaying manufacture. The linen manufacture indeed is, in England, by a particular statute,[49] open to every body; but, as it is not much cultivated through the greater part of the country, [211] it can afford no general resource to the workmen of other decaying manufactures, who, wherever the statute of apprenticeship takes place, have no other choice but either to come upon the parish, or to work as common labourers, for which, by their habits, they are much worse qualified than for any sort of manufacture that bears any resemblance to their own. They generally, therefore, chuse to come upon the parish.

44   Whatever obstructs the free circulation of labour from one employment to another, obstructs that of stock likewise; the quantity of stock which can be employed in any branch of business depending very much upon that of ᶦtheᶦ labour which can be employed in it. Corporation laws, however, give less obstruction to the free circulation of stock from one place to another than to that of labour. It is every-where much easier for a wealthy merchant to obtain the privilege of trading in a town corporate, than for a poor artificer to obtain that of working in it.

45   The obstruction which corporation laws give to the free circulation of labour is common, I believe, to every part of Europe. That which is given to it by the poor laws ᵐis, so far as I know,ᵐ peculiar to England. It consists in the difficulty which a poor man finds in obtaining a settlement, or even in being allowed to exercise his industry in any parish but that to which he belongs. It is the labour of artificers and manufacturers only of which the free circulation is obstructed by corporation laws. The difficulty [212] of obtaining settlements obstructs even that of common labour. It may be worth while to give some account of the rise, progress, and present state of this disorder, the greatest perhaps of any in the police of England.[50]

46   When by the destruction of monasteries the poor had been deprived of the charity[51] of those religious houses, after some other ineffectual attempts for their relief, it was enacted by the 43d of Elizabeth, c.2.[52] that every parish should be bound to provide for its own poor; and that overseers

---

ᶦ⁻ᶦ 2–6   ᵐ⁻ᵐ, so far as I know, is *1*

---

[49] 15 Charles II, c.15 (1663).

[50] Even more than in his discussion of the Statute of Apprenticeship Smith concentrates on the statutory basis of the law of settlement and not on its operation. Interference with the mobility of labour was probably much less in practice than he believed. D. Marshall, 'The Old Poor Law, 1662–1795', *Economic History Review*, viii (1937), 1.

[51] See below, V.i.g.22, where Smith comments on the historical role of the clergy with regard to charity.

[52] 43 Elizabeth I, c.2 (1601), An Act for the Relief of the Poor.

of the poor should be annually appointed, who, with the churchwardens, should raise by a parish rate, competent sums for this purpose.

47   By this statute the necessity of providing for their own poor was indispensably imposed upon every parish. Who were to be considered as the poor of each parish, ⁿbecame, therefore,ⁿ a question of some importance. *church* This question, after some variation, was at last determined by the 13th and 14th of Charles II.[53] when it was enacted, that forty days undisturbed residence should gain any person a settlement in any parish; but that within that time it should be lawful for two justices of the peace, upon complaint made by the churchwardens or overseers of the poor, to remove any new inhabitant to the parish where he was last legally settled; unless he either rented a tenement of ten pounds a year, or could give such security for the discharge of the parish where he was then living, as those justices should judge sufficient.

48   [213] Some frauds, it is said, were committed in consequence of this statute; parish officers sometimes bribing their own poor to go clandestinely to another parish, and by keeping themselves concealed for forty days to gain a settlement there, to the discharge of that to which they properly belonged. It was enacted, therefore, by the 1st of James II.[54] that the forty days undisturbed residence of any person necessary to gain a settlement, should be accounted only from the time of his delivering notice in writing, of the place of his abode and the number of his family, to one of the churchwardens or overseers of the parish where he came to dwell.

49   But parish officers, it seems, were not always more honest with regard to their own, than they had been with regard to other parishes, and sometimes connived at such intrusions, receiving the notice, and taking no proper steps in consequence of it. As every person in a parish, therefore, was supposed to have an interest to prevent as much as possible their being burdened by such intruders, it was further enacted by the 3d of William III.[55] that the forty days residence should be accounted only from the publication of such notice in writing on Sunday in the church, immediately after divine service.

50   "After all," says Doctor Burn, "this kind of settlement, by continuing forty days after publication of notice in writing, is very seldom obtained; and the design of the acts is not so much for gaining of settlements, as for the avoiding of them, by persons coming into [214] a parish clandestinely: for the giving of notice is only putting a force upon the parish to remove. But if a person's situation is such, that it is doubtful whether he is actually removeable or not, he shall by giving of notice compel the parish either to

---

ⁿ⁻ⁿ therefore, became *1*

[53] 14 Charles II, c.12 (1662) in *Statutes of the Realm*, v. 401–5; 13 and 14 Charles II, c.12 in Ruffhead's edition.

[54] 1 James II, c.17 (1685).   [55] 3 William and Mary, c.11, s.2. (1691).

allow him a settlement uncontested, by suffering him to continue forty days; or, by removing him, to try the right".[56]

51   This statute, therefore, rendered it almost impracticable for a poor man to gain a new settlement in the old way, by forty days inhabitancy. But that it might not appear to preclude altogether the common people of one parish from ever establishing themselves with security in another, it appointed four other ways by which a settlement might be gained without any notice delivered or published. The first was, by being taxed to parish rates and paying them; the second, by being elected into an annual parish office and serving in it a year; the third, by serving an apprenticeship in the parish; the fourth, by being hired into service there for a year, and continuing in the same service during the whole of it.[57]

52   Nobody can gain a settlement by either of the two first ways, but by the publick deed of the whole parish, who are too well aware of the consequences to adopt any new-comer who has nothing but his labour to support him, either by taxing him to parish rates, or by electing him into a parish office.

53   [215] No married man can well gain any settlement in either of the two last ways. An apprentice is scarce ever married; and it is expressly enacted, that no married servant shall gain any settlement by being hired for a year.[58] The principal effect of introducing settlement by service, has been to put out in a great measure the old fashion of hiring for a year, which before had been so customary in England, that even at this day, if no particular term is agreed upon, the law intends that every servant is hired for a year. But masters are not always willing to give their servants a settlement by hiring them in this manner; and servants are not always willing to be so hired, because as every last settlement discharges all the foregoing, they might thereby lose their original settlement in the places of their nativity, the habitation of their parents and relations.

54   No independent workman, it is evident, whether labourer or artificer, is likely to gain any new settlement either by apprenticeship or by service. When such a person, therefore, carried his industry to a new parish, he was liable to be removed, how healthy and industrious soever, at the caprice of any churchwarden or overseer, unless he either rented a tenement of ten pounds a year, a thing impossible for one who has nothing but his labour to live by; or could give such security for the discharge of the parish as two justices of the peace should judge sufficient. What security they shall require, indeed, is left altogether to their discretion; but they cannot well require less than thirty pounds, it having [216] been enacted, that the purchase even of a free-hold estate of less than thirty pounds value, shall not

[56] R. Burn, *Justice of the Peace* (London, 13th ed., 1776), iii.413.
[57] 3 William and Mary, c.11, ss.5–7 (1691).
[58] 3 William and Mary, c.11 does not expressly prohibit a married servant from gaining a settlement but confines settlement to the unmarried.

gain any person a settlement, as not being sufficient for the discharge of the parish.[59] But this is a security which scarce any man who lives by labour can give; and much greater security is frequently demanded.

55   In order to restore in some measure that free circulation of labour which those different statutes had almost entirely taken away, the invention of certificates was fallen upon. By the 8th and 9th of William III.[60] it was enacted, that if any person should bring a certificate from the parish where he was last legally settled, subscribed by the churchwardens and overseers of the poor, and allowed by two justices of the peace, that every other parish should be obliged to receive him; that he should not be removeable merely upon account of his being likely to become chargeable, but only upon his becoming actually chargeable, and that then the parish which granted the certificate should be obliged to pay the expence both of his maintenance and of his removal. And in order to give the most perfect security to the parish where such certificated man should come to reside, it was further enacted by the same statute,[61] that he should gain no settlement there by any means whatever, except either by renting a tenement of ten pounds a year, or by serving upon his own account in an annual parish office for one whole year; and consequently neither by notice, nor by service, nor by apprenticeship, nor by paying parish rates. By [217] the 12th of Queen Anne too, stat. I. c. 18.[62] it was further enacted, that neither the servants nor apprentices of such certificated man should gain any settlement in the parish where he resided under such certificate.

56   How far this invention has restored that free circulation of labour which the preceding statutes had almost entirely taken away, we may learn from the following very judicious observation of Doctor Burn. "It is obvious," says he, "that there are divers good reasons for requiring certificates with persons coming to settle in any place; namely, that persons residing under them can gain no settlement, neither by apprenticeship, nor by service, nor by giving notice, nor by paying parish rates; that they can settle neither apprentices nor servants; that if they become chargeable, it is certainly known whither to remove them, and the parish shall be paid for the re- moval, and for their maintenance in the mean time; and that if they fall sick, and cannot be removed, the parish which gave the certificate must maintain them: none of all which can be without a certificate. Which

---

[59] 9 George I, c.7, s.5 (1722).
[60] The original Act of Settlement of 1662 (14 Charles II, c.12; 13 and 14 Charles II, c.12 in Ruffhead's edition) exempted harvest and other temporary workers from removal, if they produced certificates accepting liability from their parish of settlement. 8 and 9 William III, c.30 (1696) extended the provision. See 9 William III, c.11 (1697); 9 and 10 William III, c.11 in Ruffhead's edition for details of the grounds on which settlement could be obtained.
[61] By 9 William III, c.11 (1697) in *Statutes of the Realm*, vii. 364–5; 9 and 10 William III c.11 in Ruffhead's edition.
[62] 12 Anne, c.18 (1712) in *Statutes of the Realm*, ix.796–7. 12 Anne, st.1, c.18 in Ruff- head's edition.

reasons will hold proportionably for parishes not granting certificates in ordinary cases; for it is far more than an equal chance, but that they will have the certificated persons again, and in a worse condition".[63] The moral of this observation seems to be, that certificates ought always to be required by the parish where any poor man comes to reside, and that they ought very seldom [218] to be granted by that which he proposes to leave. "There is somewhat of hardship in this matter of certificates" says the same very intelligent author in his History of the Poor Laws, "by putting it in the power of a parish officer, to imprison a man as it were for life; however inconvenient it may be for him to continue at that place where he has had the misfortune to acquire what is called a settlement, or whatever advantage he may propose to himself by living elsewhere".[64]

57   Though a certificate carries along with it no testimonial of good behaviour, and certifies nothing but that the person belongs to the parish to which he really does belong, it is altogether discretionary in the parish officers either to grant or to refuse it. A mandamus was once moved for, says Doctor Burn, to compel the church-wardens and overseers to sign a certificate; but the court of King's Bench rejected the motion as a very strange attempt.[65]

58   The very unequal price of labour which we frequently find in England in places at no great distance from one another, is probably owing to the obstruction which the law of settlements gives to a poor man who would carry his industry from one parish to another without a certificate.[66] A single man, indeed, who is healthy and industrious, may sometimes reside by sufferance without one; but a man with a wife and family who should attempt to do so, would in most parishes be sure of being removed, and if the single man should afterwards marry, he would generally be [219] removed likewise. The scarcity of hands in one parish, therefore, cannot always be relieved by their super-abundance in another, as it is constantly in Scotland,[67] and, I believe, in all other countries where there is no difficulty of settlement. In such countries, though wages may sometimes rise a little in the neighbourhood of a great town, or wherever else there is an extraordinary demand for labour, and sink gradually as the distance from such places increases, till they fall back to the common rate of the country; yet we never meet with those sudden and unaccountable differences in the wages of neighbouring places which we sometimes find in England, where

---

[63] R. Burn, *Justice of the Peace* (1764), ii.274.

[64] R. Burn, *History of the Poor* , 235–6. The quotation is not quite verbatim.

[65] 'In the case of K. and St. Ives, H. 3 G. 2. a *mandamus* was moved for, to compel the churchwardens and overseers to sign a certificate; but the court rejected the motion as a very strange attempt.' (R. Burn, *Justice of the Peace*, iii.310.)

[66] See above, I.viii.31.

[67] The evidence is scanty, but there is little reason to believe that wages were more uniform in Scotland than in England. See above, I.viii.33.

it is often more difficult for a poor man to pass the artificial boundary of a parish, than an arm of the sea or a ridge of high mountains, natural boundaries which sometimes separate very distinctly different rates of wages in other countries.

59   To remove a man who has committed no misdemeanour from the parish where he chuses to reside, is an evident violation of natural liberty and justice. The common people of England, however, so jealous of their liberty, but like the common people of most other countries never rightly understanding wherein it consists, have now for more than a century together suffered themselves to be exposed to this oppression without a remedy. Though men of reflection too have sometimes complained of the law of settlements as a publick grievance; yet it has never been the object of any general popular clamour, [220] such as that against general warrants, an abusive practice undoubtedly, but such a one as was not likely to occasion any general oppression. There is scarce a poor man in England of forty years of age, I will venture to say, who has not in some part of his life felt himself most cruelly oppressed by this ill-contrived law of settlements.

60   I shall conclude this long chapter with observing,[68] that though antiently it was usual to rate wages, first by general laws extending over the whole kingdom, and afterwards by particular orders of the justices of peace in every particular county, both these practices have now gone entirely into disuse. "By the experience of above four hundred years," says Doctor Burn, "it seems time to lay aside all endeavours to bring under strict regulations, what in its own nature seems incapable of minute limitation: for if all persons in the same kind of work were to receive equal wages, there would be no emulation, and no room left for industry or ingenuity".[69]

61   Particular acts of parliament, however, still attempt sometimes to regulate wages in particular trades and in particular places. Thus the 8th of George III.[70] prohibits under heavy penalties all master taylors in London, and five miles round it, from giving, and their workmen from accepting, more than two shillings and seven-pence halfpenny a day, except in the case of a general mourning.[71] Whenever the legislature attempts to regulate the differences between masters and their workmen, its counsellors are [221] always the masters.[72] When the regulation, therefore, is in favour of

---

[68] A similar usage occurs below, I.xi.p.1.

[69] 'By the experience of above 400 years, it seems time to lay aside all endeavours to bring under strict regulations, what in its own nature seems incapable of minute limitation: As thereby it leaves no room for industry or ingenuity; for if all persons, in the same kind of work, were to receive equal wages, there would be no emulation'. (R. Burn, *History of the Poor Laws*, 130.)

[70] 8 George III, c.17 (1768).

[71] See above, I.vii.19 and I.x.b.14, where journeymen tailors are said to earn 2s.6d. a day.

[72] See above, I.viii.13.

the workmen, it is always just and equitable; but it is sometimes otherwise when in favour of the masters. Thus the law which obliges the masters in several different trades to pay their workmen in money and not in goods, is quite just and equitable. It imposes no real hardship upon the masters. It only obliges them to pay that value in money, which they pretended to pay, but did not always really pay, in goods.[73] This law is in favour of the workmen; but the 8th of George III. is in favour of the masters.[74] When masters combine together in order to reduce the wages of their workmen, they commonly enter into a private bond or agreement, not to give more than a certain wage under a certain penalty. Were the workmen to enter into a contrary combination of the same kind, not to accept of a certain wage under a certain penalty, the law would punish them very severely; and if it dealt impartially, it would treat the masters in the same manner. But the 8th of George III. enforces by law that very regulation which masters sometimes attempt to establish by such combinations. The complaint of the workmen, that it puts the ablest and most industrious upon the same footing with an ordinary workman, seems perfectly well founded.

62   In antient times too it was usual to attempt to regulate the profits of merchants and other dealers, by rating the price both of provisions and other goods. The assize of bread is, so far as I know, the only remnant of this ancient [222] usage.[75] Where there is an exclusive corporation, it may perhaps be proper to regulate the price of the first necessary of life. But where there is none, the competition will regulate it much better than any assize. The method of fixing the assize of bread established by the 31st of George II.[76] could not be put in practice in Scotland, on account of a defect in the law; its execution depending upon the office of clerk of the market, which does not exist there. This defect was not remedied till the 3d of George III.[77] The want of an assize occasioned no sensible inconveniency, and the establishment of one, in the few places where it has yet taken place, has produced no sensible advantage. In the greater part of the towns of Scotland, however, there is an incorporation of bakers who claim exclusive privileges, though they are not very strictly guarded.

63   The proportion between the different rates both of wages and profit in

---

[73] 1 Anne, st.2, c.22 (1702) in *Statutes of the Realm*, viii.220–1; 1 Anne, st.2, c.18 in Ruffhead's edition provided for workmen in woollen, linen, fustian, cotton, and iron manufacture; 13 George II, c.8 (1739) for those engaged in the manufacture of gloves, breeches, boots, shoes, and slippers.

[74] 8 George III, c.17 (1768) developed the restrictions of 7 George I, st.1, c.13 (1720), the terms of which Smith condemned above. See I.viii.12.

[75] LJ (A) vi.89 comments that the assize of bread, 'tho' necessary where corporations are allowed, does not answer the end of a plentifull market in any shape so well as that of allowing a free concurrence'. See also LJ (B) 232, ed. Cannan 180.

[76] 31 George II, c.29 (1757).

[77] Magistrates and justices of the peace were empowered to act in place of the clerk of the market by 3 George III, c.6 (1762).

the different employments of labour and stock, seems not to be much affected, as has already been observed,[78] by the riches or poverty, the advancing, stationary, or declining state of the society. Such revolutions in the publick welfare, though they affect the general rates both of wages and profit, must in the end affect them equally in all different employments. The proportion between them, therefore, must remain the same, and cannot well be altered, at least for any considerable time, by any such revolutions.

[78] See above, I.vii.36.

CHAPTER XI
Of the Rent of Land

1 RENT, considered as the price paid for the use of land, is naturally the highest which the tenant can afford to pay in the actual circumstances of the land. In adjusting the terms of the lease, the landlord endeavours to leave him no greater share of the produce than what is sufficient to keep up the stock from which he furnishes the seed, pays the labour, and purchases and maintains the cattle and other instruments of husbandry, together with the ordinary profits of farming stock in the neighbourhood.[1] This is evidently the smallest share with which the tenant can content himself without being a loser, and the landlord seldom means to leave him any more. Whatever part of the produce, or, what is the same thing, whatever part of its price, is over and above this share, he naturally endeavours to reserve to himself as the rent of his land, which is evidently the highest the tenant can afford to pay in the actual circumstances of the land. Sometimes, indeed, the liberality, more frequently the ignorance, of the landlord,[2] makes him accept of somewhat less than this portion; and sometimes too, though more rarely, the ignorance of the tenant makes him undertake to pay somewhat more, or to content himself with somewhat less than the ordinary profits of farming stock in the neighbourhood. This portion, [224] however, may still be considered as the natural rent of land, or the rent for which it is naturally meant that land should for the most part be let.

2 The rent of land, it may be thought, is frequently no more than a reasonable profit or interest for the stock laid out by the landlord upon its improvement. This, no doubt, may be partly the case upon some occasions; for it can scarce ever be more than partly the case.[3] The landlord demands a rent even for unimproved land, and the supposed interest or profit upon the expence of improvement is generally an addition to this original rent. Those improvements, besides, are not always made by the stock of the landlord, but sometimes by that of the tenant. When the lease comes to be renewed, however, the landlord commonly demands the same augmentation of rent, as if they had been all made by his own.

---

[1] 'The Farmer who conducts the working of it [the land] has generally two thirds of the produce, one third pays his expenses and upkeep, the other remains for the profit of his enterprise.' (Cantillon, *Essai*, 266, ed. Higgs 201.)

[2] Cf. V.ii.c.12.

[3] Smith distinguishes between the gross and net rent of the landlords at II.ii.4 and describes their responsibilities with regard to the land at V.iii.54. Smith recommends that landlords *should* cultivate their ground at V.ii.ç.15 since this group, he argued, have the capital and can afford experiments. However, he did not think highly of this class as improvers. See, for example, III.ii.7 and III.iv.3.

3   He sometimes demands rent for what is altogether incapable of human improvement. Kelp is a species of sea-weed, which, when burnt, yields an alkaline salt, useful for making glass, soap, and for several other purposes. It grows in several parts of Great Britain, particularly in Scotland, upon such rocks only as lie within the high water mark, which are twice every day covered with the sea, and of which the produce, therefore, was never augmented by human industry.[4] The landlord, however, whose estate is bounded by a kelp shore of this kind, demands a rent for it as much as for his corn fields.[5]

4   The sea in the neighbourhood of the islands of Shetland is more than commonly abundant in [225] fish, which make a great part of the subsistence of their inhabitants. But in order to profit by the produce of the water, they must have a habitation upon the neighbouring land. The rent of the landlord is in proportion, not to what the farmer can make by the land, but to what he can make both by the land and *by* the water. It is partly paid in sea-fish; and one of the very few instances in which rent makes a part of the price of that commodity, is to be found in that country.

5   The rent of land, therefore, considered as the price paid for the use of the land, is naturally a monopoly price.[6] It is not at all proportioned to what the landlord may have laid out upon the improvement of the land, or to what he can afford to take; but to what the farmer can afford to give.[7]

6   Such parts only of the produce of land can commonly be brought to market of which the ordinary price is sufficient to replace the stock which must be employed in bringing them thither, together with its ordinary profits. If the ordinary price is more than this, the surplus part of it will naturally go to the rent of the land. If it is not more, though the commodity

a–a 3–6

---

[4] LJ (A) i.61 makes an interesting and related point:

The sea coast . . . seems to be common to the whole community, and accession to it to belong to the whole body, but the king has usurped this to himself, insomuch that in Lincoln shire, where frequent accessions and diminutions happen, a certain person having 100 acres added by the sea could not take possession of it tho' his charter comprehended all the land betwixt that coast and Denmark . . .

Cf. LJ (A) i.69.

[5] In October 1797 the Chamberlain of Mull reported to the Duke of Argyll that he 'has always had it in view . . . to calculate thirty shillings per ton upon the highest quantity of kelp that their shores were known to produce, which was thought to be as much as the price given for this article before the war would enable the tenants to pay' (*Argyll Estate Instructions, 1771–1805*, ed. E. R. Cregeen (Edinburgh, 1964), 187–90). The great rise in kelp prices and in income for both tenant and landlord came immediately after the publication of *The Wealth of Nations*.

[6] It is pointed out at IV.ii.21 that country gentlemen are the least subject to the 'wretched spirit of monopoly'.

[7] Smith uses this argument at V.ii.e.10 where it is suggested that taxes on the rent of land will not have disincentive effects.

may be brought to market, it can afford no rent to the landlord. Whether the price is, or is not more, depends upon the demand.

7　　There are some parts of the produce of land for which the demand must always be such as to afford a greater price than what is sufficient to bring them to market; and there are others for [226]which it either may or may not be such as to afford this greater price. The former must always afford a rent to the landlord. The latter sometimes may, and sometimes may not, according to different circumstances.[8]

8　　Rent, it is to be observed, therefore, enters into the composition of the price of commodities in a different way from wages and profit. High or low wages and profit, are the causes of high or low price; high or low rent is the effect of it.[9] It is because high or low wages and profit must be paid, in order to bring a particular commodity to market, that its price is high or low. But it is because its price is high or low; a great deal more, or very little more, or no more, than what is sufficient to pay those wages and profit, that it affords a high rent, or a low rent, or no rent at all.

9　　The particular consideration, first, of those parts of the produce of land which always afford some rent; secondly, of those which sometimes may and sometimes may not afford rent; and, thirdly, of the variations which, in the different periods of improvement, naturally take place, in the relative value of those two different sorts of rude produce, when compared both with one another and with manufactured commodities, will divide this chapter into three parts.

PART I

Of the Produce of Land which always affords Rent

[227]

1　　As men, like all other animals, naturally multiply in proportion to the means of their subsistence, food is always, more or less, in demand.[1] It can always purchase or command a greater or smaller quantity of labour, and somebody can always be found who is willing to do something, in order to obtain it. The quantity of labour, indeed, which it can purchase, is not always equal to what it could maintain, if managed in the most œconomical manner, on account of the high wages which are sometimes given to labour. But it can always purchase such a quantity of labour as it can maintain, according to the rate at which that sort of labour is commonly maintained in the neighbourhood.

2　　But land, in almost any situation, produces a greater quantity of food than what is sufficient to maintain all the labour necessary for bringing

---

[8] Smith examines the case of coalmines which yield no rent at I.xi.c.13.

[9] Cf. I.vi.8. The doctrine that rent is a residual is applied in the discussion of the incidence of taxation, for example, at V.ii.d, V.ii.g.8, and V.ii.i.2.

[1] The same point is made at I.viii.39.

it to market, in the most liberal way in which that labour is ever maintained. The surplus too is always more than sufficient to replace the stock
which employed that labour, together with its profits. Something, therefore, always remains for a rent to the landlord.²

3   The most desart moors in Norway and Scotland produce some sort of
pasture for cattle, of which the milk and the increase are always more [228]
than sufficient, not only to maintain all the labour necessary for tending
them, and to pay the ordinary profit to the farmer or owner of the herd
or flock; but to afford some small rent to the landlord. The rent increases
in proportion to the goodness of the pasture. The same extent of ground
not only maintains a greater number of cattle, but as they are brought
within a smaller compass, less labour becomes requisite to tend them, and
to collect their produce. The landlord gains both ways; by the increase
of the produce, and by the diminution of the labour which must be
maintained out of it.

4   The rent of land ᵃnot onlyᵃ varies with its fertility, whatever be its
produce, ᵇbutᵇ with its situation, whatever be its fertility.³ Land in the
neighbourhood of a town, gives a greater rent than land equally fertile
in a distant part of the country. Though it may cost no more labour to
cultivate the one than the other, it must always cost more to bring the
produce of the distant land to market. A greater quantity of labour, therefore, must be maintained out of it; and the surplus, from which are
drawn both the profit of the farmer and the rent of the landlord, must
be diminished. But in remote parts of the country the rate of ᶜprofitᶜ,
as has already been shown,⁴ is generally higher than in the neighbourhood
of a large town. A smaller proportion of this diminished surplus, therefore, must belong to the landlord.

5   Good roads, canals, and navigable rivers, by diminishing the expence
of carriage, put the re-[229]mote parts of the country more nearly upon
a level with those in the neighbourhood of the town.⁵ They are upon that
account the greatest of all improvements. They encourage the cultivation
of the remote, which must always be the most extensive circle of the
country. They are advantageous to the town, by breaking down the
monopoly of the country in its neighbourhood. They are advantageous
even to that part of the country. Though they introduce some rival commodities into the old market, they open many new markets to its produce.
Monopoly, besides, is a great enemy to good management, which can never

ᵃ⁻ᵃ *3–6*   ᵇ⁻ᵇ and *1–2*   ᶜ⁻ᶜ profits *4–6*

² The thesis that agriculture is the most productive form of investment is considered
at II.v.12 where Smith also comments on the relationship between fertility and rent.
³ The same point is made concerning mines at I.xi.c.10. The advantage of situation
with regard to house-rents is mentioned at V.ii.e.3.
⁴ See above, I.ix.7.
⁵ Smith considers public works which facilitate commerce in V.i.d.

be universally established but in consequence of that free and universal competition which forces every body to have recourse to it for the sake of self-defence. It is not more than fifty years ago that some of the counties in the neighbourhood of London, petitioned the parliament against the extension of the turnpike roads into the remoter counties. Those remoter counties, they pretended, from the cheapness of labour, would be able to sell their grass and corn cheaper in the London market than themselves, and would thereby reduce their rents, and ruin their cultivation. Their rents, however, have risen, and their cultivation has been improved since that time.

6   A corn field of moderate fertility produces a much greater quantity of food for man, than the best pasture of equal extent. Though its cultivation requires much more labour, yet the surplus which remains after replacing the seed and [230] maintaining all that labour, is likewise much greater. If a pound of butcher's-meat, therefore, was never supposed to be worth more than a pound of bread, this greater surplus would everywhere be of greater value, and constitute a greater fund both for the profit of the farmer and the rent of the landlord. It seems to have done so universally in the rude beginnings of agriculture.

7   But the relative values of those two different species of food, bread and butcher's-meat, are very different in the different periods of agriculture. In its rude beginnings, the unimproved wilds, which then occupy the far greater part of the country, are all abandoned to cattle. There is more butcher's-meat than bread, and bread, therefore, is the food for which there is the greatest competition, and which consequently brings the greatest price.[6] At Buenos Ayres, we are told by Ulloa, four reals, one-and-twenty pence halfpenny sterling, was, forty or fifty years ago, the ordinary price of an ox, chosen from a herd of two or three hundred.[7] He says nothing of the price of bread, probably because he found nothing remarkable about it. An ox there, he says, costs little more than the labour of catching him. But corn can no-where be raised without a great deal of labour, and in a country which lies upon the river Plate, at that time the direct road from Europe to the silver mines of Potosi, the money price of labour could not be very cheap. It is otherwise when cultivation is extended over the greater part of the country. [231] There is then more bread than butcher's-meat. The competition changes its direction, and the price of butcher's-meat becomes greater than the price of bread.

---

[6] See below, IV.vii.b.29.

[7] A similar statement occurs at I.xi.e.25. Juan and Ulloa commented: 'The country to the W. S. and N. of Buenos Ayres, lately abounded so greatly in cattle and horses, that the whole cost consisted in taking them; and even then a horse was sold for a dollar of that money, and the usual price of a beast, chosen out of a herd of two or three hundred, only four rials.' (*Voyage historique de l'Amérique méridionale* (1752), i.552, translated by John Adams, *A Voyage to South America* (London, 1807), ii.187.)

8   By the extension besides of cultivation, the unimproved wilds become insufficient to supply the demand for butcher's-meat.[8] A great part of the cultivated lands must be employed in rearing and fattening cattle, of which the price, therefore, must be sufficient to pay, not only the labour necessary for tending them, but the rent which the landlord and the profit which the farmer could have drawn from such land employed in tillage. The cattle bred upon the most uncultivated moors, when brought to the same market, are, in proportion to their weight or goodness, sold at the same price as those which are reared upon the most improved land. The proprietors of those moors profit by it, and raise the rent of their land in proportion to the price of their cattle. It is not more than a century ago that in many parts of the highlands of Scotland, butcher's-meat was as cheap or cheaper than even bread made of oatmeal.[9] The union opened the market of England to the highland cattle. Their ordinary price is at present about three times greater than at the beginning of the century, and the rents of many highland estates have been tripled and quadrupled in the same time. In almost every part of Great Britain a pound of the best butcher's-meat is, in the present times, generally worth more than two pounds of the best white bread; and in [232] plentiful years it is sometimes worth three or four pounds.

9   It is thus that in the progress of improvement the rent and profit of unimproved pasture come to be regulated in some measure by the rent and profit of what is improved, and these again by the rent and profit of corn.[10] Corn is an annual crop, butcher's-meat, a crop which requires four or five years to grow. As an acre of land, therefore, will produce a much smaller quantity of the one species of food than of the other, the inferiority of the quantity must be compensated by the superiority of the price. If it was more than compensated, more corn land would be turned into pasture; and if it was not compensated, part of what was in pasture would be brought back into corn.

10   This equality, however, between the rent and profit of grass and those of corn; of the land of which the immediate produce is food for cattle, and of that of which the immediate produce is food for men; must be understood to take place only through the greater part of the improved lands of a great country. In some particular local situations it is quite otherwise, and the rent and profit of grass are much superior to what can be made by corn.

11   Thus in the neighbourhood of a great town, the demand for milk and for forage to horses, frequently contribute, *d*together*d* with the high price of butcher's-meat, to raise the value of grass above what may be called

d–d along *I*

---

[8] See below, I.xi.l.2.   [9] See below, I.xi.c.4 and I.xi.l.2.
[10] See below, I.xi.b.35, I.xi.l.12, and V.ii.k.54.

its natural proportion to that of corn. This local advantage, [233] it is evident, cannot be communicated to the lands at a distance.

12   Particular circumstances have sometimes rendered some countries so populous, that the whole territory, like the lands in the neighbourhood of a great town, has not been sufficient to produce both the grass and the corn necessary for the subsistence of their inhabitants. Their lands, therefore, have been principally employed in the production of grass, the more bulky commodity, and which cannot be so easily brought from a great distance; and corn, the food of the great body of the people, has been chiefly imported from foreign countries.[11] Holland is at present in this situation,[12] and a considerable part of antient Italy, seems to have been so during the prosperity of the Romans. To feed well, old Cato said, as we are told by Cicero, was the first and most profitable thing in the management of a private estate; to feed tolerably well, the second; and to feed ill, the third.[13] To plough, he ranked only in the fourth place of profit and advantage. Tillage, indeed, in that part of antient Italy which lay in the neighbourhood of Rome, must have been very much discouraged by the distributions of corn which were frequently made to the people, either gratuitously, or at a very low price. This corn was brought from the conquered provinces, of which several, instead of taxes, were obliged to furnish a tenth part of their produce at a stated price, about sixpence a peck, to the republick. The low price at which this corn was distributed to [234] the people, must necessarily have sunk the price of what could be brought to the Roman market from Latium, or the antient territory of Rome, and must have discouraged its cultivation in that country.[14]

13   In an open country too, of which the principal produce is corn, a well-enclosed piece of grass will frequently rent higher than any corn field in

---

[11] Cf. IV.ii.20, where Smith comments on the small quantity of corn imported into Britain even in times of scarcity.

[12] See below, I.xi.e.38, where Smith comments further on the high price of corn in Holland, and also IV.ix.37.

[13] 'When he [old Cato] was asked what was the most profitable feature of an estate, he replied: 'Raising cattle successfully'. What next to that? 'Raising cattle with fair success'. And next? 'Raising cattle with but slight success'. And fourth? 'Raising crops'. And when his questioner said, 'How about money-lending? Cato replied: 'How about murder?' (Cicero, *De Officiis*, ii.xxv, translated by W. Miller in Loeb Classical Library (1921), 266–7.) Cicero's authority is also cited in this connection in LJ (B) 297, ed. Cannan 229.

[14] See below, I.xi.k.1. Smith comments on the Roman distributions of corn and on the discouragement thereby given to agriculture at III.ii.21 and IV.vii.a.3. LRBL ii.157, ed. Lothian 150, refers to the method used by those men 'who from their attachment to the populace were called Populares', which was 'to propose laws for the equall division of lands and the distributing of corn at the publick charge'. He cited Marius and Clodius as examples. Smith refers to the discouragement thus given to corn production in Rome in LJ (B) 296–7, ed. Cannan 229–30, and in ED 5.10 where the low level of corn output is attributed to the prohibition on its export, together with 'the distributions which were annually made by the government of Sicilian, Egyptian, and African corn at a very low price to the people'.

its neighbourhood. It is convenient for the maintenance of the cattle employed in the cultivation of the corn, and its high rent is, in this case,
not so properly paid from the value of its own produce, as from that of
the corn lands which are cultivated by means of it. It is likely to fall, if
ever the neighbouring lands are compleatly inclosed. The present high
rent of enclosed land in Scotland seems owing to the scarcity of enclosure,
and will probably last no longer than that scarcity.[15] The advantage of
enclosure is greater for pasture than for corn. It saves the labour of guarding the cattle, which feed better too when they are not liable to be disturbed by their keeper or his dog.

14   But where there is no local advantage of this kind, the rent and profit of
corn, or whatever else is the common vegetable food of the people, must
naturally regulate, upon the land which is fit for producing it, the rent
and profit of pasture.

15   The use of the artificial grasses, of turnips, carrots, cabbages, and the
other expedients which have been fallen upon to make an equal quantity
of land feed a greater number of cattle [235] than when in natural grass,
should somewhat reduce, it might be expected, the superiority which,
in an improved country, the price of butcher's-meat naturally has over
that of bread. It seems accordingly to have done so; and there is some
reason for believing that, at least in the London market, the price of
butcher's-meat in proportion to the price of bread is a good deal lower in
the present times than it was in the beginning of the last century.[16]

16   In the appendix to the Life of prince Henry, Doctor Birch has given us
an account of the prices of butcher's-meat as commonly paid by that
prince. It is there said, that the four quarters of an ox weighing six hundred pounds usually cost him nine pounds ten shillings, or thereabouts;
that is, thirty-one shillings and eight pence per hundred pounds weight.[17]
Prince Henry died on the 6th of November, 1612, in the nineteenth year
of his age.

17   In March, 1764, there was a parliamentary enquiry into the causes of

---

[15] The high rent of enclosed land also reflected the considerable costs of enclosure.
[16] The same point is made at I.xi.l.9. It is doubtful if the relationship was so clear cut.
T. S. Ashton summarised the position (*An Economic History of England: the Eighteenth
Century* (London, 1955), 54–5):

After 1700 the price of meat fell sharply and that of bread even more so, until 1708.
In 1709–10 both bread and meat rose to famine levels, but from this time to 1740 there
seems to have been relative stability of the ratio between the two. For the next quarter
of a century, however, the price of meat was high compared with that of bread, for the
losses of sheep in the early 'forties and middle 'fifties were serious, and—more important—the prolonged cattle plague forced up the price of beef. The years from 1766
to 1780 showed little alteration in the ratio.

[17] T. S. Birch, *The Life of Henry Prince of Wales* (London, 1760), 449.

the high price of provisions at that time.[18] It was then, among other proof to the same purpose, given in evidence by a Virginia merchant, that in March, 1763, he had victualled his ships for twenty-four or twenty-five shillings the hundred weight of beef, which he considered as the ordinary price; whereas, in that dear year, he had paid twenty-seven shillings for the same weight and sort.[19] This high price in 1764, is, however, four shillings and eight-pence cheaper than the ordinary price paid by [236] prince Henry; and it is the best beef only, it must be observed, which is fit to be salted for those distant voyages.

18   The price paid by prince Henry amounts to 3 $\frac{4}{5}$th *d*. per pound weight of the whole carcase, coarse and choice pieces taken together; and at that rate the choice pieces could not have been sold by retail for less than 4$\frac{1}{2}$*d*. or 5*d*. the pound.

19   In the parliamentary enquiry in 1764, the witnesses stated the price of the choice pieces of the best beef to be to the consumer 4*d*. and 4$\frac{1}{4}$*d*. the pound; and the coarse pieces in general to be from seven farthings to 2$\frac{1}{2}$*d*. and 2$\frac{3}{4}$*d*.; and this they said was in general one half-penny dearer than the same sort of pieces had usually been sold in the month of March. But even this high price is still a good deal cheaper than what we can well suppose the ordinary retail price to have been in the time of prince Henry.

20   During the twelve first years of the last century, the average price of the best wheat at the Windsor market was 1 *l*. 18*s*. 3 1/6*d*. the quarter of nine Winchester bushels.

21   But in the twelve years preceding 1764, including that year, the average price of the same measure of the best wheat at the same market was 2 *l*. 1*s*. 9$\frac{1}{2}$*d*.[20]

22   In the twelve first years of the last century, therefore, wheat appears to have been a good deal cheaper, and butcher's-meat a good deal dearer than in the twelve years preceding 1764, including that year.

23   [237] In all great countries the greater part of the cultivated lands are employed in producing either food for men or food for cattle. The rent and profit of these regulate the rent and profit of all other cultivated land. If any particular produce afforded less, the land would soon be turned into corn or pasture; and if any afforded more, some part of the lands in corn or pasture would soon be turned to that produce.

---

[18] *A Report from the Committee who, upon the 8th day of February, 1764, were appointed to inquire into the Causes of the High Price of Provisions with the proceedings of the House thereupon. House of Commons Journals*, 29 (1761–64), 1046.

[19] Ibid. Mr. Capel Hanbury 'confirmed this Evidence by the comparative Prices of his own Charge, in victualing his ships for *Virginia*, which he said he victualed in March, last year, at the Rate of 24 or 25 Shillings *per* Hundred Weight, Beef: Whereas he last Year gave 27 Shillings for the same Weight and Sort'.

[20] These prices are from the tables at the end of this chapter.

24   Those productions, indeed, which require either a greater original
expence of improvement, or a greater annual expence of cultivation, in
order to fit the land for them, appear commonly to afford, the one a
greater rent, the other a greater profit than corn or pasture. This superiority, however, will seldom be found to amount to more than a reasonable interest or compensation for this superior expence.

25   In a hop garden, a fruit garden, a kitchen garden, both the rent of the
landlord, and the profit of the farmer, are generally greater than in a corn
or grass field. But to bring the ground into this condition requires more
expence. Hence a greater rent becomes due to the landlord. It requires
too a more attentive and skilful management. Hence a greater profit becomes due to the farmer. The crop too, at least in the hop and fruit garden, is more precarious. Its price, therefore, besides compensating all
occasional losses, must afford something like the profit of insurance. The
circumstances of gardeners, generally mean, and always moderate, may
satisfy us that their great ingenuity is not [238] commonly over-recom-
pensed. Their delightful art is practised by so many rich people for
amusement, that little advantage is to be made by those who practise it
for profit; because the persons who should naturally be their best customers, supply themselves with all their most precious productions.[21]

26   The advantage which the landlord derives from such improvements
seems at no time to have been greater than what was sufficient to compensate the original expence of making them. In the antient husbandry,
after the vineyard, a well-watered kitchen garden seems to have been the
part of the farm which was supposed to yield the most valuable produce.
But Democritus, who wrote upon husbandry about two thousand years
ago, and who was regarded by the antients as one of the fathers of the art,
thought they did not act wisely who enclosed a kitchen garden. The profit,
he said, would not compensate the expence of a stone wall; and bricks (he
meant, I suppose, bricks baked in the sun) mouldered with the rain, and
the winter storm, and required continual repairs. Columella, who reports this judgment of Democritus, does not controvert it, but proposes
a very frugal method of enclosing with a hedge of *ᵉbrambles*ᵉ and briars,
which, he says, he had found by experience to be both a lasting and an
impenetrable fence;[22] but which, it seems, was not commonly known in
the time of Democritus. Palladius adopts the opinion of Columella, which

---

ᵉ⁻ᵉ thorns *1*

---

[21] It is pointed out at I.x.b.3 that as society advances 'they are all very poor people who
follow as a trade, what other people pursue as a pastime'.

[22] 'This thorn-hedge cannot be destroyed unless you care to dig it up by the roots.'
(Columella, *De Re Rustica*, xi.3, translated by E. S. Forster and E. H. Heffner in Loeb
Classical Library (1955), xi.1–8.)

had before been recommended by [239] Varro.[23] In the judgment of those antient improvers, the produce of a kitchen garden had, it seems, been little more than sufficient to pay the extraordinary culture and the expence of watering; for in countries so near the sun, it was thought proper, in those times as in the present, to have the command of a stream of water, which could be conducted to every bed in the garden. Through the greater part of Europe, a kitchen garden is not at present supposed to deserve a better inclosure than that recommended by Columella. In Great Britain, and some other northern countries, the finer fruits cannot be brought to perfection but by the assistance of a wall. Their price, therefore, in such countries must be sufficient to pay the expence of building and maintaining what they cannot be had without. The fruit-wall frequently surrounds the kitchen garden, which thus enjoys the benefit of an enclosure which its own produce could seldom pay for.

27   That the vineyard, when properly planted and brought to perfection, was the most valuable part of the farm, seems to have been an undoubted maxim in the antient agriculture, as it is in the modern through all the wine countries. But whether it was advantageous to plant a new vineyard, was a matter of dispute among the antient Italian husbandmen, as we learn from Columella.[24] He decides, like a true lover of all curious cultivation, in favour of the vineyard, and endeavours to show, by a comparison of the profit and expence, that it was a most advan-[240]tageous improvement. Such comparisons, however, between the profit and expence of new projects, are commonly very fallacious; and in nothing more so than in agriculture. Had the gain actually made by such plantations been commonly as great as he imagined it might have been, there could have been no dispute about it. The same point is frequently at this day a matter of controversy in the wine countries. Their writers on agriculture, indeed, the lovers and promoters of high cultivation, seem generally disposed to decide with Columella in favour of the vineyard. In France the anxiety

[23] 'Now I shall speak of the enclosures which are constructed for the protection of the farm as a whole, or its divisions. There are four types of such defences: . . . The first type, the natural, is a hedge, usually planted with brush or thorn, having roots and being alive, and so with nothing to fear from the flaming torch of a mischievous passer-by.' (Varro, *De Re Rustica*, i.xiv, translated by W. D. Hooper, and revised by H. B. Ash in Loeb Classical Library (1934), 216–17.) Cannan observes: 'Gesnerus' edition of Columella in *Scriptores rei rusticae* in Adam Smith's library (see Bonar's *Catalogue*, s.v. Gesnerus), commenting on the passage referred to above, quotes the opinions of Varro, *De Re rustica*, i.14, and Palladius, *De Re rustica*, i.34'.

[24] 'Most people would be doubtful [whether vines should be kept at all], to such an extent that many would avoid and dread such an ordering of their land, and would consider it preferable to own meadows and pastures, or woodland for cutting; for in the matter of ground planted with trees for the support of vines there has been no little dispute even among authorities.' And later: 'for like a careful accountant, he sees, when his calculations are made, that this kind of husbandry is of the greatest advantage to the estate.' (Columella, *De Re Rustica*, iii.3 and 7, translated by H. B. Ash in Loeb Classical Library (1941), i.253 and 259.)

of the proprietors of the old vineyards to prevent the planting of any
new ones, seems to favour their opinion, and to indicate a consciousness
in those who must have the experience, that this species of cultivation is
at present in that country more profitable than any other. It seems at
the same time, however, to indicate another opinion, that this superior
profit can last no longer than the laws which at present restrain the free
cultivation of the vine.[25] In 1731, they obtained an order of council,
prohibiting both the planting of new vineyards, and the renewal of those
old ones, of which the cultivation had been interrupted for two years;
without a particular permission from the king, to be granted only in
consequence of an information from the intendant of the province, certifying that he had examined the land, and that it was incapable of any
other culture.[26] The pretence of this order was the scarcity of corn and
pasture, and the [241] super-abundance of wine. But had this super-
abundance been real, it would, without any order of council, have effectually prevented the plantation of new vineyards, by reducing the profits
of this species of cultivation below their natural proportion to those of
corn and pasture. With regard to the supposed scarcity of corn occasioned
by the multiplication of vineyards,[27] corn is no where in France more carefully cultivated than in the wine provinces, where the land is fit for producing it; as in Burgundy, Guienne, and the Upper Languedoc.[28] The
numerous hands employed in the one species of cultivation necessarily
encourage the other, by affording a ready market for its produce. To
diminish the number of those who are capable of paying for it, is surely
a most unpromising expedient for encouraging the cultivation of corn.
It is like the policy which would promote agriculture by discouraging
manufactures.

28　　　The rent and profit of those productions, therefore, which require
either a greater original expence of improvement in order to fit the land
for them, or a greater annual expence of cultivation, though often much
superior to those of corn and pasture, yet when they do no more than

---

[25] Cf. V.ii.g.8.

[26] The Conseil du Roi passed a decree (arrêt) on 5 June 1731 at Fontainebleau. M. An-
toine, *Le Conseil du Roi sous le règne de Louis XV* (Geneva, 1970), 479, n. In ED 3.5
Smith refers to the 'French kings edict against planting new vineyards, and of some equally
absurd laws of other nations'. Cf. Hume's remarks on this policy in his essay 'Of the
Balance of Trade', *Essays Moral, Political and Literary*, ed. Green and Grose, i.336.

[27] There was considerable alarm at the time through the loss of agricultural land to
vineyards, especially since wheat prices in France rose for about half a century after 1730.
Even a small deficiency in the crop could lead to a sharp rise in price and to bread riots.

[28] Smith had first-hand experience of Languedoc; a province which had attained such
a degree of prosperity at the time of Smith's visit that it was said to have enjoyed a superior
credit rating to that of the central government of France. Rae, *Life*, 184. In Letter 83 addressed to Hume, dated 21 October 1764, Smith indicated that he proposed to 'go to see
the meeting of the States of Longuedoc, at Montpelier' and asked for an introduction
to the Intendant there. See below, I.xi.e.13n.

compensate such extraordinary expence, are in reality regulated by the rent and profit of those common crops.

29   It sometimes happens, indeed, that the quantity of land which can be fitted for some particular produce, is too small to supply the effectual demand. The whole produce can be disposed [242] of to those who are willing to give somewhat more than what is sufficient to pay the whole rent, wages and profit necessary for raising and bringing it to market, according to their natural rates, or according to the rates at which they are paid in the greater part of other cultivated land. The surplus part of the price which remains after defraying the whole expence of improvement and cultivation may commonly, in this case, and in this case only, bear no regular proportion to the like surplus in corn or pasture, but may exceed it in almost any degree; and the greater part of this excess naturally goes to the rent of the landlord.

30   The usual and natural proportion, for example, between the rent and profit of wine and those of corn and pasture, must be understood to take place only with regard to those vineyards which produce nothing but good common wine, such as can be raised almost any where, upon any light, gravelly, or sandy soil, and which has nothing to recommend it but its strength and wholesomeness. It is with such vineyards only that the common land of the country can be brought into competition; for with those of a peculiar quality it is evident that it cannot.

31   The vine is more affected by the difference of soils than any other fruit tree. From some it derives a flavour which no culture or management can equal, it is supposed, upon any other. This flavour, real or imaginary, is sometimes peculiar to the produce of a few vineyards; sometimes it extends through the greater part of [243] a small district, and sometimes through a considerable part of a large province. The whole quantity of such wines that is brought to market falls short of the effectual demand, or the demand of those who would be willing to pay the whole rent, profit and wages necessary for preparing and bringing them thither, according to the ordinary rate, or according to the rate at which they are paid in common vineyards.[29] The whole quantity, therefore, can be disposed of to those who are willing to pay more, which necessarily raises the price above that of common wine. The difference is greater or less, according as the fashionableness and scarcity of the wine render the competition of the buyers more or less eager. Whatever it be, the greater part of it goes to the rent of the landlord. For though such vineyards are in general more carefully cultivated than most others, the high price of the wine seems to be, not so much the effect, as the cause of this careful cultivation. In so valuable a produce the loss occasioned by negligence is so great as to

[29] The term 'effectual demand' is defined above, I.vii.8. Smith discusses the demand for the products of particularly favoured vineyards at I.vii.24 and V.ii.k.54.

force even the most careless to attention. A small part of this high price, therefore, is sufficient to pay the wages of the extraordinary labour bestowed upon their cultivation, and the profits of the extraordinary stock which puts that labour into motion.

32   The sugar colonies possessed by the European nations in the West Indies, may be compared to those precious vineyards. Their whole produce falls short of the effectual demand of Europe, and can be disposed of to those who are willing to [244] give more than what is sufficient to pay the whole rent, profit and wages necessary for preparing and bringing it to market, according to the rate at which they are commonly paid by any other produce.[30] In Cochin-china the finest white sugar commonly sells for three piasters the quintal, about thirteen shillings and sixpence of our money, as we are told by* Mr. Poivre, a very careful observer of the agriculture of that country. What is there called the quintal weighs from a hundred and fifty to two hundred Paris pounds, or a hundred and seventy-five Paris pounds at a medium, which reduces the price of the hundred weight English to about eight shillings sterling, not a fourth part of what is commonly paid for the brown or muskavada sugars imported from our colonies, and not a sixth part of what is paid for the finest white sugar.[31] The greater part of the cultivated lands in Cochin-china are employed in producing corn and rice, the food of the great body of the people. The respective prices of corn, rice, and sugar, are there probably in the natural proportion, or in that which naturally takes place in the different crops of the greater part of cultivated land, and which recompences the landlord and farmer, as nearly as can be computed, according to what is usually the original expence of improvement and the annual expence of cultivation. But in our sugar colonies the price of sugar bears no such proportion to that of the produce of a rice or corn field either in Europe or *⁹in⁹* America. It is commonly [245] said, that a sugar planter expects that the rum and the molasses should defray the whole expence of his cultivation, and that his sugar should be all clear profit.

---

*⁑*Voyages d'un Philosophe.*ᶠ* ['The white sugar of the best quality is generally sold at the port of Faifo, in exchange for other merchandize, at the rate of three piastres (about fourteen shillings) the Cochin-china quintal, which weighs from one hundred and fifty to two hundred pounds French.' Translated as P. Poivre, *Travels of a Philosopher, or, Observations on the Manners and Arts of Various Nations in Africa and Asia* (Glasgow, 1790), 121–2.]

ᶠ⁻ᶠ 2–6   *⁹⁻⁹ om.* 6

---

[30] See below, III.ii.10, regarding the high profits of sugar plantations, and also IV.vii. b.31.
[31] In Letter 258 addressed to Sir John Sinclair, dated 11 April 1786, Smith stated that when he lived in Glasgow 'a hoghead of Muscovado Sugar' was valued at 30 to 36 shillings per cwt. and that his usual purchase was 'breakfast sugar' at 8–9*d*. per lb.

If this be true, for I pretend not to affirm it, it is as if a corn farmer expected to defray the expence of his cultivation with the chaff and the straw, and that the grain should be all clear profit. We see frequently societies of merchants in London and other trading towns, purchase waste lands in our sugar colonies, which they expect to improve and cultivate with profit by means of factors and agents; notwithstanding the great distance and the uncertain returns, from the defective administration of justice in those countries. Nobody will attempt to improve and cultivate in the same manner the most fertile lands of Scotland, Ireland, or the corn provinces of North America, though from the more exact administration of justice in these countries, more regular returns might be expected.

33   In Virginia and Maryland, the cultivation of tobacco is preferred, as *more* profitable, to that of corn.[32] Tobacco might be cultivated with advantage through the greater part of Europe; but in almost every part of Europe it has become a principal subject of taxation, and to collect a tax from every different farm in the country where this plant might happen to be cultivated, would be more difficult, it has been supposed, than to levy one upon its importation at the custom-house. The cultivation of tobacco has upon this account been most absurdly prohibited [246] through the greater part of Europe,[33] which necessarily gives a sort of monopoly to the countries where it is allowed; and as Virginia and Maryland produce the greatest quantity of it, they share largely, though with some competitors, in the advantage of this monopoly. The cultivation of tobacco, however, seems not to be so advantageous as that of sugar. I have never even heard of any tobacco plantation that was improved and cultivated by the capital of merchants who resided in Great Britain, and our tobacco colonies send us home no such wealthy planters as we see frequently arrive from our sugar islands. Though from the preference given in those colonies to the cultivation of tobacco above that of corn, it would appear that the effectual demand of Europe for tobacco is not compleatly supplied, it probably is more nearly so than that for sugar: And though the present price of tobacco is probably more than sufficient to pay the whole rent, wages and profit necessary for preparing and bringing it to market, according to the rate at which they are commonly paid in corn land; it must not be so much more as the present price of sugar. Our tobacco planters, accordingly, have shewn the same fear of the super-abundance of tobacco, which the proprietors of the old vineyards in France have of the super-abundance of wine. By act of assembly they have restrained its cultivation to six thousand plants, supposed to yield

---

h-h most 6

[32] See below, IV.vii.c.17.
[33] Prohibited in England, Ireland, and the Channel Islands by 12 Charles II, c. 34 (1660) and in Scotland by 22 George III ― ― (1782). See below, IV.vii.b.45.

a thousand weight of tobacco, for every negro between sixteen and sixty years of age.[34] Such a negro, over and above this quantity of [247] tobacco, can manage, they reckon, four acres of Indian corn. To prevent the market from being overstocked too, they have sometimes, in plentiful years, we are told by Dr. Douglas, (I suspect he has been ill informed)* burnt a certain quantity of tobacco for every negro, in the same manner as the Dutch are said to do of spices.[35] If such violent methods are necessary to keep up the present price of tobacco, the superior advantage of its culture over that of corn, if it still has any, will not probably be of long continuance.

34   It is in this manner that the rent of the cultivated land, of which the produce is human food, regulates the rent of the greater part of other cultivated land. No particular produce can long afford less; because the land would immediately be turned to another use: And if any particular produce commonly affords more, it is because the quantity of land which can be fitted for it is too small to supply the effectual demand.

35   In Europe corn is the principal produce of land which serves immediately for human food. Except in particular situations, therefore, the rent of corn land regulates in Europe that of all other cultivated land.[36] Britain need envy neither the vineyards of France nor the olive plantations of Italy. Except in particular situations, the value of these is regulated by that of corn, in which the fertility of Britain is not much inferior to that of either of those two countries.

36   [248] If in any country the common and favourite vegetable food of the people should be drawn from a plant of which the most common land, with the same or nearly the same culture, produced a much greater quantity than the most fertile does of corn, the rent of the landlord, or the surplus quantity of food which would remain to him, after paying the labour and replacing the stock of the farmer together with its ordinary profits, would necessarily be much greater. Whatever was the rate at

---

*ᶦ*Douglas's Summary, vol. ii., p. 372, 373.ᶦ [Virginia and Maryland sometimes produce more tobacco than they can vent to advantage, by glutting the markets. (Note: This is sometimes the case with the Dutch East-India spices, and the West-India sugars.) William Douglass, *A Summary*, ii.372–3.]

ᶦ⁻ᶦ 2–6

---

[34] William Douglass, *A Summary, Historical and Political, of the First Planting, Progressive Improvements and Present State of the British Settlements in North America* (London, 1760), ii.360.

[35] This example is also given at IV.v.b.4 and IV.vii.c.101. Pufendorf also cites the example of the modern Dutch who were said to 'destroy the clove and nutmeg plants in many sections of India in order to prevent an over-supply of those spices.' Pufendorf also pointed out that the Egyptians had kept up the price of papyrus in the same way. *De Jure*, V.i.6, translated by C. H. and W. A. Oldfather, *Classics of International Law* (Oxford, 1934).

[36] Below, I.xi.l.12, and above, I.xi.b.9.

which labour was commonly maintained in that country, this greater surplus could always maintain a greater quantity of it, and consequently enable the landlord to purchase or command a greater quantity of it. The real value of his rent, his real power and authority, his command of the necessaries and conveniencies of life with which the labour of other people could supply him, would necessarily be much greater.

37   A rice field produces a much greater quantity of food than the most fertile corn field.[37] Two crops in the year from thirty to sixty bushels each, are said to be the ordinary produce of an acre. Though its cultivation, therefore, requires more labour, a much greater surplus remains after maintaining all that labour. In those rice countries, therefore, where rice is the common and favourite vegetable food of the people, and where the cultivators are chiefly maintained with it, a greater share of this greater surplus should belong to the landlord than in corn countries. In Carolina, where the [249] planters, as in other British colonies, are generally both farmers and landlords, and where rent consequently is confounded with profit,[38] the cultivation of rice is found to be more profitable than that of corn, though their fields produce only one crop in the year, and though, from the prevalence of the customs of Europe, rice is not there the common and favourite vegetable food of the people.

38   A good rice field is a bog at all seasons, and at one season a bog covered with water. It is unfit either for corn, or pasture, or vineyard, or, indeed, for any other vegetable produce that is very useful to men: And the lands which are fit for those purposes, are not fit for rice. Even in the rice countries, therefore, the rent of rice lands cannot regulate the rent of the other cultivated land which can never be turned to that produce.

39   The food produced by a field of potatoes is not inferior in quantity to that produced by a field of rice, and much superior to what is produced by a field of wheat. Twelve thousand weight of potatoes from an acre of land is not a greater produce than two thousand weight of wheat. The food or solid nourishment, indeed, which can be drawn from each of those two plants, is not altogether in proportion to their weight, on account of the watery nature of potatoes. Allowing, however, half the weight of this root to go to water, a very large allowance, such an acre of potatoes will still produce six thousand weight of solid nourishment, three [250] times the quantity produced by the acre of wheat. An acre of potatoes is cultivated with less expence than an acre of wheat; the fallow, which generally precedes the sowing of wheat, more than compensating the hoeing and other extraordinary culture which is always given to potatoes. Should this root ever become in any part of Europe, like rice in some rice countries, the common and favourite vegetable food of the people, so as to occupy the same proportion of the lands in tillage which wheat and other

[37] See below, I.xi.g.28.   [38] See above, I.vi.19.

sorts of grain for human food do at present, the same quantity of cultivated land would maintain a much greater number of people, and the labourers being generally fed with potatoes, a greater surplus would remain after replacing all the stock and maintaining all the labour employed in cultivation. A greater share of this surplus too would belong to the landlord. Population would increase, and rents would rise much beyond what they are at present.

40   The land which is fit for potatoes, is fit for almost every other useful vegetable. If they occupied the same proportion of cultivated land which corn does at present, they would regulate, in the same manner, the rent of the greater part of other cultivated land.

41   In some parts of Lancashire it is pretended, I have been told, that bread of oatmeal is a heartier food for labouring people than wheaten bread, and I have frequently heard the same doctrine held in Scotland. I am, however, somewhat doubtful of the truth of it. The com-[251]mon people in Scotland, who are fed with oatmeal, are in general neither so strong, nor so handsome as the same rank of people in England, who are fed with wheaten bread. They neither work, so well nor look so well; and as there is not the same difference between the people of fashion in the two countries, experience would seem to show, that the food of the common people in Scotland is not so suitable to the human constitution as that of their neighbours of the same rank in England.[39] But it seems to be otherwise with potatoes. The chairmen, porters, and coalheavers in London, and those unfortunate women who live by prostitution, the strongest men and the most beautiful women perhaps in the British dominions, are said to be, the greater part of them, from the lowest rank of people in Ireland, who are generally fed with this root. No food can afford a more decisive proof of its nourishing quality, or of its being peculiarly suitable to the health of the human constitution.[40]

42   It is difficult to preserve potatoes through the year, and impossible to store them, like corn, for two or three years together. The fear of not being able to sell them before they rot, discourages their cultivation, and is, perhaps, the chief obstacle to their ever becoming in any great country, like bread, the principal vegetable food of all the different ranks of the people.[41]

[39] See above, I.viii.33.

[40] Potatoes are described as not 'very much esteemed' in Europe at IV.vii.a.12, but as one of the most important improvements in European agriculture at I.xi.n.10.

[41] Smith suggests that meat is not strictly speaking a necessity at V.ii.k.15. He believed that grain supplemented by vegetables could afford a most 'invigorating diet'. See also I.xi.e.29 and I.xi.n.10.

[252]   PART II

Of the Produce of Land which sometimes does, and
sometimes does not, afford Rent

1   Human food seems to be the only produce of land which always and necessarily affords some rent to the landlord. Other sorts of produce sometimes may and sometimes may not, according to different circumstances.

2   After food, cloathing and lodging are the two great wants of mankind.[1]

3   Land in its original rude state can afford the materials of cloathing and lodging to a much greater number of people than it can feed. In its improved state it can sometimes feed a greater number of people than it can supply with those materials; at least in the way in which they require them, and are willing to pay for them. In the one state, therefore, there is always a super-abundance of those materials, which are frequently, upon that account, of little or no value. In the other there is often a scarcity, which necessarily augments their value. In the one state a great part of them is thrown away as useless, and the price of what is used is considered as equal only to the labour and expence of fitting it for use, and can, therefore, afford no rent to the landlord. In the other they are all made use of, and there is frequently a demand for more than can be had. Somebody is always willing to give more for every part of them than [253] what is sufficient to pay the expence of bringing them to market. Their price, therefore, can always afford some rent to the landlord.

4   The skins of the larger animals were the original materials of cloathing. Among nations of hunters and shepherds, therefore, whose food consists chiefly in the flesh of those animals, every man, by providing himself with food, provides himself with the materials of more cloathing than he can wear. If there was no foreign commerce, the greater part of them would be thrown away as things of no value. This was probably the case among the hunting nations of North America, before their country was discovered by the Europeans, with whom they now exchange their surplus peltry, for blankets, fire-arms, and brandy, which gives it some value. In the present commercial state of the known world, the most barbarous nations, I believe, among whom land property is established, have some foreign commerce of this kind, and find among their wealthier neighbours such a demand for all the materials of cloathing, which their land produces, and which can neither be wrought up nor consumed at home, as raises their price above[a] what it costs to send them [a]to those wealthier neighbours[a].

[a-a] thither *1*

[1] Smith considers the effect of 'improvement' on the prices of such commodities as provide clothing in I.xi.m.

It affords, therefore, some rent to the landlord. When the greater part of the highland cattle were consumed on their own hills, the exportation of their hides made the most considerable article of the commerce of that country, and what they were exchanged for afforded some addition to the rent [254] of the highland estates.[2] The wool of England, which in old times could neither be consumed nor wrought up at home, found a market in the then wealthier and more industrious country of Flanders, and its price afforded something to the rent of the land which produced it. In countries not better cultivated than England was then, or than the highlands of Scotland are now, and which had no foreign commerce, the materials of cloathing would evidently be so super-abundant, that a great part of them would be thrown away as useless, and no part could afford any rent to the landlord.[3]

5   The materials of lodging cannot always be transported to so great a distance as those of cloathing, and do not so readily become an object of foreign commerce. When they are super-abundant in the country which produces them, it frequently happens, even in the present commercial state of the world, that they are of no value to the landlord. A good stone quarry in the neighbourhood of London would afford a considerable rent. In many parts of Scotland and Wales it affords none. Barren timber for building is of great value in a populous and well-cultivated country, and the land which produces it, affords a considerable rent. But in many parts of North America the landlord would be much obliged to any body who would carry away the greater part of his large trees.[4] In some parts of the highlands of Scotland the bark is the only part of the wood which, for want of roads and water-carriage, can be sent to [255] market.[5] The timber is left to rot upon the ground. When the materials of lodging are so super-abundant, the part made use of is worth only the labour and expence of fitting it for that use.[6] It affords no rent to the landlord, who generally grants the use of it to whoever takes the trouble of asking it. The demand of wealthier nations, however, sometimes enables him to get a rent for it. The paving of the streets of London has enabled the owners of some barren rocks on the coast of Scotland to draw a rent from

[2] See above, I.xi.b.8 and below, I.xi.l.2.
[3] The argument of this paragraph anticipated the 'vent for surplus' doctrine, as stated for example at III.i.1, IV.i.31, and IV.iii.c.4.
[4] Smith examines the policies which had helped to raise the price of timber in America at IV.vii.b.28, 38.
[5] Improvements in water-carriage were already proving vitally important to the Highlands. The search for supplies of charcoal led ironmasters to examine the possibilities of using the area's supplies of timber.
[6] Samuel Johnson's frequent references to the absence of trees and timber in the Highlands provides a different interpretation. At Fort Augustus 'the country is totally denuded of its wood'. S. Johnson, *Journey to the Western Islands of Scotland* (1775), Oxford Standard Author ed., 30.

what never afforded any before. The woods of Norway and of the coasts of the Baltick, find a market in many parts of Great Britain which they could not find at home, and thereby afford some rent to their proprietors.

6　　Countries are populous, not in proportion to the number of people whom their produce can cloath and lodge, but in proportion to that of those whom it can feed. When food is provided, it is easy to find the necessary cloathing and lodging. But though these are at hand, it may often be difficult to find food. In some parts *even* of the British dominions what is called A House, may be built by one day's labour of one man. The simplest species of cloathing, the skins of animals, requires somewhat more labour to dress and prepare them for use. They do not, however, require a great deal. Among savage *and* barbarous nations, a hundredth or little more than *a* hundredth part of the labour of the whole year, will be sufficient to provide them with such cloathing and lodging as satisfy the [256] greater part of the people. All the other ninety-nine parts are frequently no more than enough to provide them with food.

7　　But when by the improvement and cultivation of land the labour of one family can provide food for two, the labour of half the society becomes sufficient to provide food for the whole. The other half, therefore, or at least the greater part of them, can be employed in providing other things, or in satisfying the other wants and fancies of mankind.[7] Cloathing and lodging, houshold furniture, and what is called Equipage, are the principal objects of the greater part of those wants and fancies. The rich man consumes no more food than his poor neighbour.[8] In quality it may be very different, and to select and prepare it may require more labour and art; but in quantity it is very nearly the same. But compare the spacious palace and great wardrobe of the one, with the hovel and the few rags of

---

b-b om. 6　　　　*c-c* or 6　　　　*d-d* the 6

---

[7] Cf. I.x.c.19, II.i.28, and III.i.1, and for further elaboration, I.xi.c.36 and I.xi.g.28. Cf. Pufendorf, *De Jure*, V.i.15: 'in the more civilised states there are in general two classes of men, that which devotes itself to cultivating the soil, and that which in different occupations looks after the conveniences of life.' And cf. Cantillon, *Essai*, 57, ed. Higgs 45: 'It is generally calculated that one half of the Inhabitants of a kingdom subsist and make their Abode in Cities, and the other half live in the Country.' Hume in 'Of Commerce' remarks that the bulk of every state 'may be divided into *husbandmen* and *manufacturers*'. He went on to point out, 'As soon as men quit their savage state, where they live chiefly by hunting and fishing, they must fall into these two classes; though the arts of agriculture employ *at first* the most numerous part of the society.' (*Essays Moral, Political, and Literary*, ed. Green and Grose, i.289.)

[8] Cf. LJ (A) iii.135:

A man who consumes 10,000 pounds appears to destroy what ought to give maintenance to 1,000 men. He therefore appears to be the most destructive member of society we can possible conceive. But if we observe this man we shall find that he is no way prejudiciall to society, but rather of advantage to it. In the 1st place, he eats no more than what any other man does; he has not a larger stomach than any ordinary ploughman . . . [*continues*]

the other, and you will be sensible that the difference between their cloathing, lodging and houshold furniture, is almost as great in quantity as it is in quality. The desire of food is limited in every man by the narrow capacity of the human stomach; but the desire of the conveniencies and ornaments of building, dress, equipage, and houshold furniture, seems to have no limit or certain boundary.[9] Those, therefore, who have the command of more food than they themselves can consume, are always willing to exchange the surplus, or, what is the same thing, the price of it, for gratifications of [257] this other kind. What is over and above satisfying the limited desire, is given for the amusement of those desires which cannot be satisfied, but seem to be altogether endless.[10] The poor, in order to obtain food, exert themselves to gratify those fancies of the rich, and to obtain it more certainly, they vie with one another in the cheapness and perfection of their work. The number of workmen increases with the increasing quantity of food, or with the growing improvement and cultivation of the lands; and as the nature of their business admits of the utmost subdivisions of labour, the quantity of materials which they can work up, increases in a much greater proportion than their numbers. Hence arises a demand for every sort of material which human invention can employ, either usefully or ornamentally, in building, dress,

Smith went on to point out that the expenditures of the rich gave employment to the poor and concluded at p. 139 that:

> in the present state of things a man of great fortune is rather of advantage than dissadvantage to the state, providing that there is a graduall descent of fortunes betwixt these great ones and others of the least and lowest fortunes.—

—as in the case of England. Similar points are made in LJ (B) 139, ed. Cannan 100; and see below, II.iii.39, III.iv.11, IV.ii.9. In TMS IV.i.1.10 Smith comments with regard to the rich man that 'The homely and vulgar proverb, that the eye is larger than the belly, never was more fully verified than with regard to him.' He added that the rich:

> consume little more than the poor, and in spite of their natural selfishness and rapacity, though they mean only their own conveniency, though the sole end which they propose from the labours of all the thousands whom they employ, be the gratification of their own vain and insatiable desires, they divide with the poor the produce of all their improvements. They are led by an invisible hand to make nearly the same distribution of the necessaries of life, which would have been made, had the earth been divided into equal portions among all its inhabitants, and thus without intending it, without knowing it, advance the interest of the society, and afford means to the multiplication of the species.

Cf. TMS VII.ii.4.12.

[9] Cf. Steuart (*Principles*, i.144, ed. Skinner, i.139) 'there is no bounds to the consumption of *work;* but as for articles of nourishment, the case is quite different. The most delicate liver in Paris will not put more of the earth's productions into his belly, than another.'

[10] See below, I.xi.c.36, I.xi.g.28. The argument is also applied in Book III in discussing the historical process of growth. See, for example, III.iii.12 and III.iv.11.

equipage, or houshold furniture; for the fossils and minerals contained in the bowels of the earth; the precious metals, and the precious stones.

8   Food is in this manner, not only the original source of rent, but every other part of the produce of land which afterwards affords rent, derives that part of its value from the improvement of the powers of labour in producing food by means of the improvement and cultivation of land.

9   Those other parts of the produce of land, however, which afterwards afford rent, do not afford it always. Even in improved and cultivated countries, the demand for them is not always such as to afford a greater price than what [258] is sufficient to pay the labour, and replace, together with its ordinary profits, the stock which must be employed in bringing them to market. Whether it is or is not such, depends upon different circumstances.

10   Whether a coal-mine, for example, can afford any rent, depends partly upon its fertility, and partly upon its situation.[11]

11   A mine of any kind may be said to be either fertile or barren, according as the quantity of mineral which can be brought from it by a certain quantity of labour, is greater or less than what can be brought by an equal quantity from the greater part of other mines of the same kind.

12   Some coal-mines advantageously situated, cannot be wrought on account of their barrenness. The produce does not pay the expence. They can afford neither profit nor rent.

13   There are some of which the produce is barely sufficient to pay the ᵉlabourᵉ, and replace, together with its ordinary profits, the stock employed in working them. They afford some profit to the undertaker of the work, but no rent to the landlord. They can be wrought advantageously by nobody but the landlord, who being himself undertaker of the work, gets the ordinary profit of the capital which he employs in it. Many coal-mines in Scotland are wrought in this manner, and can be wrought in no other. The landlord will allow nobody else to work them without paying some rent, and nobody can afford to pay any.[12]

14   [259] Other coal-mines in the same country sufficiently fertile, cannot be wrought on account of their situation. A quantity of mineral sufficient to defray the expence of working, could be brought from the mine by the ordinary, or even less than the ordinary quantity of labour: But in an inland country, thinly inhabited, and without either good roads or water-carriage, this quantity could not be sold.

15   Coals are a less agreeable fewel than wood: they are said too to be less

ᵉ⁻ᵉ labourer 5

[11] See above, I.xi.b.4, where a similar point is made with regard to the land.

[12] Landowners may have worked their own coalmines because only they had the capital resources to do so. T. C. Smout, 'Scottish Landowners and Economic Growth, 1650-1850', *Scottish Journal of Political Economy*, xi (1964), 220-1.

wholesome. The expence of coals, therefore, at the place where they are consumed, must generally be somewhat less than that of wood.

16   The price of wood again varies with the state of agriculture, nearly in the same manner, and exactly for the same reason, as the price of cattle. In its rude beginnings the greater part of every country is covered with wood, which is then a mere incumbrance of no value to the landlord, who would gladly give it to any body for the cutting. As agriculture advances, the woods are partly cleared by the progress of tillage, and partly go to decay in consequence of the increased number of cattle. These, though they do not increase in the same proportion as corn, which is altogether the acquisition of human industry, yet multiply under the care and protection of men; who store up in the season of plenty what may maintain them in that of scarcity, who through the whole year furnish them with a greater quantity of food than uncultivated nature provides for them, and who by de-[260]stroying and extirpating their enemies, secure them in the free enjoyment of all that she provides. Numerous herds of cattle, when allowed to wander through the woods, though they do not destroy the old trees, hinder any young ones from coming up, so that in the course of a century or two the whole forest goes to ruin. The scarcity of wood then raises its price. It affords a good rent, and the landlord sometimes finds that he can scarce employ his best lands more advantageously than in growing barren timber, of which the greatness of the profit often compensates the lateness of the returns. This seems in the present times to be nearly the state of things in several parts of Great Britain, where the profit of planting is found to be equal to that of either corn or pasture. The advantage which the landlord derives from planting, can no-where exceed, at least for any considerable time, the rent which these could afford him; and in an inland country which is highly cultivated, it will frequently not fall much short of this rent. Upon the sea-coast of a well-improved country, indeed, if *f*coals*f* can conveniently *g*be had*g* for fewel, it may sometimes be cheaper to bring barren timber for building from less cultivated foreign countries, than to raise it at home. In the new town of Edinburgh, built within these few years, there is not, perhaps, a single stick of Scotch timber.[13]

17   Whatever may be the price of wood, if that of coals is such that the expence of a coal-fire is nearly equal to that of a wood one, we may be

f-f it *I*   *g-g* get coals *I*

[13] The building of the New Town was only starting. The North Bridge, providing access from the Old to the New Town, was in full use from 1772. Other buildings to the south of the old Town, notably George Square, dated from earlier in the century. It is difficult to accept Smith's sweeping assertion that Scotch timber was not used. A. J. Youngson, *The Making of Classical Edinburgh* (Edinburgh, 1966), esp. chs. 3 and 4, pp. 52–110.

[261] assured, that at that place, and in these circumstances, the price of coals is as high as it can be. It seems to be so in some of the inland parts of England, particularly in Oxfordshire, where it is usual, even in the fires of the common people, to mix coals and wood together, and where the difference in the expence of those two sorts of fewel cannot, therefore, be very great.

18   Coals, in the coal countries, are every-where much below this highest price. If they were not, they could not bear the expence of a distant carriage, either by land or by water. A small quantity only could be sold, and the coal masters and coal proprietors find it more for their interest to sell a great quantity at a price somewhat above the lowest, than a small quantity at the highest. The most fertile coal mine too, regulates the price of coals at all the other mines in its neighbourhood. Both the proprietor and the undertaker of the work find, the one that he can get a greater rent, the other that he can get a greater profit, by somewhat under-selling all their neighbours. Their neighbours are soon obliged to sell at the same price, though they cannot so well afford it, and though it always diminishes, and sometimes takes away altogether both their rent and their profit. Some works are abandoned altogether; others can afford no rent, and can be wrought only by the proprietor.

19   The lowest price at which coals can be sold for any considerable time, is, like that of all other commodities, the price which is barely sufficient [262] to replace, together with its ordinary profits, the stock which must be employed in bringing them to market. At a coal-mine for which the landlord can get no rent, but which he must either work himself or let it alone altogether, the price of coals must generally be nearly about this price.

20   Rent, even where coals afford one, has generally a smaller share in their price than in that of most other parts of the rude produce of land. The rent of an estate above ground, commonly amounts to what is supposed to be a third of the gross produce; and it is generally a rent certain and independent of the occasional variations in the crop.[14] In coal-mines a fifth of the gross produce is a very great rent; a tenth the common rent,

---

[14] The same point is made at II.iii.9, II.v.12, and V.ii.a.16, where it is stated that the value of rents in Britain was of the order of £20 millions. In LJ (B) 289, ed. Cannan 224, rent is stated to be 'generally about a third of the produce'. In LJ (A) vi.140, however, this proportion is said to be probably more typical of Scotland than England since 'as England is a more opulent country the reward of the farmer must be higher'. In LJ (A) iii.112 it is stated that 'in the fruitfull countries of Greece and Italy' rent was about one sixth part of the produce, compared to such relatively 'barren and cold' countries as Scotland and England, where rent was generally about one third. Smith attributes this difference to the use of slave labour in Italy and Greece. A similar point is made in LJ (B) 138, ed. Cannan 99. See below, III.ii.8, 9, on the use of slave labour on the land and cf. Cantillon's *Essai*, 62, ed. Higgs 49, where it is stated that the rent paid by the undertaker engaged in farming is 'generally supposed to be equal in value to the third of the produce'. A similar point is made at 56, 160, 267, ed. Higgs 43, 121, 201.

and it is seldom a rent certain, but depends upon the occasional variations in the produce. These are so great, that in a country where thirty years purchase is considered as a moderate price for the property of a landed estate, ten years purchase is regarded as a good price for that of a coal-mine.

21   The value of a coal-mine to the proprietor *frequently depends* as much upon its situation as upon its fertility.[15] That of a metallick mine depends more upon its fertility, and less upon its situation. The coarse, and still more the precious metals, when separated from the ore, are so valuable that they can generally bear the expence of a very long land, and of the most distant sea carriage. Their market is not confined to the countries in the neighbourhood of [263] the mine, but extends to the whole world. The copper of Japan makes an article *of commerce in* Europe; the iron of Spain in that of Chili and Peru. The silver of Peru finds its way, not only to Europe, but from Europe to China.

22   The price of coals in Westmorland or Shropshire can have little effect on their price at Newcastle; and their price in the Lionnois can have none at all. The productions of such distant coal-mines can never be brought into competition with one another. But the productions of the most distant metallick mines frequently may, and in fact commonly are. The price, therefore, of the coarse, and still more that of the precious metals, at the most fertile mines in the world, must necessarily more or less affect their price at every other in it. The price of copper in Japan must have some influence upon its price at the copper mines in Europe. The price of silver in Peru, or the quantity either of labour or of other goods which it will purchase there, must have some influence on its price, not only at the silver mines of Europe, but at those of China. After the discovery of the mines of Peru, the silver mines of Europe were, the greater part of them, abandoned. The value of silver was so much reduced that their produce could no longer pay the expence of working them, or replace, with a profit, the food, cloaths, lodging and other necessaries which were consumed in that operation. This was the case too with the mines of Cuba and St. Domingo, and [264] even with the antient mines of Peru, after the discovery of those of Potosi.

23   The price of every metal at every mine, therefore, being regulated in some measure by its price at the most fertile mine in the world that is actually wrought, it can at the greater part of mines do very little more than pay the expence of working, and can seldom afford a very high rent of the landlord. Rent, accordingly, seems at the greater part of mines to

---

h–h depends frequently *1*   *i–i* in the commerce of *1*

[15] See below, V.ii.k.12, where Smith defends the use of bounties or subsidies with regard to the transport of coal.

have but a small share in the price of the coarse, and a still smaller in that of the precious metals. Labour and profit make up the greater part of both.

24   A sixth part of the gross produce may be reckoned the average rent of the tin mines of Cornwall, the most fertile that are known in the world, as we are told by the Reverend Mr. Borlace, vice-warden of the stannaries. Some, he says, afford more, and some do not afford so much.[16] A sixth part of the gross produce is the rent too of several very fertile lead mines in Scotland.[17]

25   In the silver mines of Peru, we are told by Frezier and Ulloa,[18] the proprietor frequently exacts no other acknowledgement from the under-taker of the mine, but that he will grind the ore at his mill, paying him the ordinary multure or price of grinding. *ʲTill 1736, indeed, the tax of the king of Spain amountedʲ* to one-fifth of the standard silver, which *ᵏtill then mightᵏ* be considered as the real rent of the greater part of the silver

ʲ⁻ʲ The tax of the king of Spain, indeed, amounts *1*   *ᵏ⁻ᵏ* may *1*

[16] 'The tin-ore being raised out of the mine, is then divided into as many shares, as there are Lords and adventurers. The Lord usually hath a sixth-part clear of cost, but in consideration of draining the mine, and otherwise encouraging the adventure, is often-times content with an eighth, and sometimes a tenth.' (W. Borlase, *The Natural History of Cornwall* (Oxford, 1758), 175.)

[17] One bar in six was a traditional rent when the mine was fully operative. It was usually less in the early stages of development. T. C. Smout, 'Lead-Mining in Scotland, 1650–1850', in P. L. Payne ed., *Studies in Scottish Business History* (London, 1967), 113.

[18] Much of the information about Peru in this and the following three paragraphs is based on A. F. Frézier, *A Voyage to the South Sea* (London, 1717), 108–9:

[The] Sport of Nature makes the Miners live in hopes of finding what they call the Purse, being the Ends of Veins, so rich that they have sometimes made a Man wealthy at once; and this same Inequality sometimes ruins [marginal note: Gold hath been the Ruin of many, and their Destruction was present, Eccl. xxxi, 6] them, which is the Reason, that it is more rare to see a Gold Miner rich than a Silver Miner, or of any other Metal, tho' there be less Expence in drawing it from the Mineral, as shall be said hereafter: For this Reason also the Miners have particular Privileges; for they cannot be sued to Execution on Civil Accounts, and Gold pays only a 20th Part to the King, which is called *Covo*, from the Name of a private Person, to whom the King made that Grant, because they used before to pay the Fifth, as they do of silver. The Gold Mines, like all others of what Metal soever, belong to him who first discovers them. There needs nothing but presenting a Petition to the Magistrates to have them adjudg'd to him. They measure on the Vein 80 *Vara's* or *Spanish* Yards in length, that is, 246 Foot and 40 in breadth, for him it is adjudg'd to, who chooses that Space as he thinks fit. Then they measure 80 more, which belong to the King; the rest goes to the first Claimer, according to the same Measure, who disposes of it as he pleases. That which belongs to the King, is sold to the highest Bidder, who is willing to pur-chase an unknown and uncertain Treasure. Furthermore, those who are willing to labour themselves, easily obtain of the Miner a Vein to work on: What they get out of it is their own, paying him the King's Duty, and the Hire of the Mill, which is so considerable, that some are satisfied with the Profit it yields, without employing any to work for them in the Mines.

For Ulloa see below, I.xi.c.28.

mines of Peru, the richest which [l]have been[l] known in the world. If there [m]had been[m] [265] no tax this fifth would naturally [n]have belonged[n] to the landlord, and many mines might [o]have been[o] wrought which [p]could not then be wrought[p], because they [q]could not[q] afford this tax. The tax of the duke of Cornwall upon tin is supposed to amount to more than five per cent. or one-twentieth part of the value;[19] and whatever may be his proportion, it would naturally too belong to the proprietor of the mine, if tin was duty free. But if you add one-twentieth to one-sixth, you will find that the whole average rent of the tin mines of Cornwall, [r]was[r] to the whole average rent of the silver mines of Peru, as thirteen to twelve. [s]But the silver mines of Peru are not now able to pay even this low rent, and the tax upon silver was, in 1736, reduced from one-fifth to one-tenth.[20] Even this tax upon silver too gives more temptation to smuggling than the tax of one-twentieth upon tin;[s] and smuggling must be much easier in the precious than in the bulky commodity. The tax of the king of Spain accordingly is said to be very ill paid, and that of the duke of Cornwall very well. Rent, therefore, it is probable, makes a greater part of the price of tin at the most fertile tin mines, than it does of silver at the most fertile silver mines in the world. After replacing the stock employed in working those different mines, together with its ordinary profits, the residue which remains to the proprietor, is greater it seems in the coarse, than in the precious metal.

26 Neither are the profits of the undertakers of silver mines commonly very great in Peru. The [266] same most respectable and well informed authors acquaint us, that when any person undertakes to work a new mine in Peru, he is universally looked upon as a man destined to bankruptcy and ruin, and is upon that account shunned and avoided by every body. Mining, it seems, is considered there in the same light as here, as a lottery, in which the prizes do not compensate the blanks, though the greatness of some tempts many adventurers to throw away their fortunes in such unprosperous projects.[21]

[l–l] are *I* [m–m] was *I* [n–n] belong *I* [o–o] be *I*
[p–p] cannot be wrought at present *I* [q–q] cannot *I* [r–r] is *I*
[s–s] The high tax upon silver too, gives much greater temptation to smuggling than the low tax upon tin, *I*

---

[19] The Duke of Cornwall was paid 4*s*. duty on every cwt. of white tin. Before it could be sold tin had to be stamped by an officer appointed by the Duke of Cornwall to assay it in one of the five coinage towns, Liskeard, Losthwithiel, Truro, Helston, and Penzance.

[20] See below, I.xi.g.21, I.xi.h.8, IV.vii.a.16.

[21] See above, I.x.b.27, and below, IV.vii.a.18, where mining for the precious metals is described as 'perhaps the most disadvantageous lottery in the world'. The example of mining as being a kind of lottery is also used in LJ (A) vi.68; LJ (B) 226, ed. Cannan 176. Cf. Juan and Ulloa (*Voyage historique*, i.379, trans. John Adams, i.457):

> . . . when a person expresses his intention of working in some mine, others look upon him as a man running headlong to his destruction, and who risks certain ruin for

27   As the sovereign, however, derives a considerable part of his revenue
from the produce of silver mines, the law in Peru gives every possible
encouragement to the discovery and working of new ones. Whoever discovers a new mine, is entitled to measure off two hundred and forty-six
feet in length, according to what he supposes to be the direction of the
vein, and half as much in breadth. He becomes proprietor of this portion
of the mine, and can work it without paying any acknowledgement to
the landlord. The interest of the duke of Cornwall has given occasion to
a regulation nearly of the same kind in that antient dutchy. In waste and
uninclosed lands any person who discovers a tin mine, may mark out its
limits to a certain extent, which is called bounding a mine. The bounder
becomes the real proprietor of the mine, and may either work it himself,
or give it in lease to another, without the consent of the owner of the
land, to whom, however, a very small acknowledgement must be paid
upon working it.[22] In both regula-[267]tions the sacred rights of private
property are sacrificed to the supposed interests of publick revenue.

28   The same encouragement is given in Peru to the discovery and working
of new gold mines; and in gold the king's tax amounts only to a twentieth
part of the standard metal. It was once a fifth, *and afterwards a tenth,*
as in silver; but it was found that the work could not bear *even the
lowest of these two taxes*. If it is rare, however, say the same authors,
Frezier and Ulloa, to find a person who has made his fortune by a silver,
it is still much rarer to find one who has done so by a gold mine.[23] This

t–t 2–6   *u–u* it *1*

---

remote and uncertain hopes. They endeavour therefore to divert him from his purpose; and if they cannot succeed in this, they fly from him as if they were afraid he
should communicate the information to them.

[22] Borlase (*The Natural History of Cornwall*, 169 and 175) described the system:

No one in Cornwall can search for tin in this or any other manner, where and when
he pleases. If the land where the shode is found is inclosed and not *bounded*, the leave
of the Lord of the Soil must be first obtained; if the land is bounded, then is the
bounder's consent only necessary; but if the land is neither bounded nor inclosed, but
a wastrel or common, then may any one mark out *bounds* there, (observing the legal
forms) and search for tin.
If the lands are bounded, then the bounder has the right of *setting*, or giving authority
to search and work, and has the sixth clear, or as he agrees, and the Lord of the soil
has only a fifteenth. The adventurers have in proportion to the part of the work which
they carry on.

[23] Smith goes further than Juan and de Ulloa, who wrote (*Voyage historique*, i.371,
trans. John Adams, i.447–8):

contrary to the nature of things, the name of rich is bestowed on that province where
most mines are worked, though so entirely destitute of the other more necessary products, that the great number of the people, employed in the mines, are under a necessity of being supplied from other parts; and those provinces, whose pastures are
covered with flocks, and herds, whose fields yield plentiful harvests, and their trees
bend beneath rich fruits, under the fertilizing influence of a benign climate, but destitute

twentieth part seems to be the whole rent which is paid by the greater part of the gold mines in Chili and Peru. Gold too is much more liable to be smuggled than even silver; not only on account of the superior value of the metal in proportion to its bulk, but on account of the peculiar way in which nature produces it. Silver is very seldom found virgin, but, like most other metals, is generally mineralized with some other body, from which it is impossible to separate it in such quantities as will pay for the expence, but by a very laborious and tedious operation, which cannot well be carried on but in workhouses erected for the purpose, and therefore exposed to the inspection of the king's officers. Gold, on the contrary, is almost always found virgin. It is sometimes found in pieces of some bulk; and even when mixed in small and almost insensible particles with sand, earth, and other extra-[268]neous bodies, it can be separated from them by a very short and simple operation, which can be carried on in any private house by any body who is possessed of a small quantity of mercury. If the king's tax, therefore, is but ill paid upon silver, it is likely to be much worse paid upon gold; and rent must make a much smaller part of the price of gold, than even of that of silver.

29   The lowest price at which the precious metals can be sold, or the smallest quantity of other goods for which they can be exchanged during any considerable time, is regulated by the same principles which fix the lowest ordinary price of all other goods. The stock which must commonly be employed, the food, cloaths and lodging which must commonly be consumed in bringing them from the mine to the market, determine it. It must at least be sufficient to replace that stock, with the ordinary profits.

30   Their highest price, however, seems not to be necessarily determined by any thing but the actual scarcity or plenty of those metals themselves. It is not determined by that of any other commodity, in the same manner as the price of coals is by that of wood, beyond which no scarcity can ever raise it. Increase the scarcity of gold to a certain degree, and the smallest bit of it may become more precious than a diamond, and exchange for a greater quantity of other goods.[24]

31   The demand for those metals arises partly from their utility, and partly from their beauty.[25] If you except iron, they are more useful than, perhaps,

of mines, or forgotten through neglect, are looked upon as poor: and, indeed, except in the plentiful surface of the earth, make no wealthy appearance.

[24] See above, I.iv.13. The link between value and scarcity is also established below, IV.vii.a.19.
[25] Smith remarks in LJ (A) vi.106 with regard to the metals that 'Their value is not as Mr Locke imagines founded on an agreement of men to put it upon them; they have what we may call a naturall value, and would bear a high one considered merely as a commodity, tho' not used as the instrument of exchange.' Cf. Cantillon, *Essai*, 148, ed. Higgs 113.

any other metal. As they are less [269] liable to rust and impurity, they can more easily be kept clean; and the utensils either of the table or the kitchen are often upon that account more agreeable when made of them. A silver boiler is more cleanly than a lead, copper, or tin one; and the same quality would render a gold boiler still better than a silver one.[26] Their principal merit, however, arises from their beauty, which renders them peculiarly fit for the ornaments of dress and furniture. No paint or dye can give so splendid a colour as gilding. The merit of their beauty is greatly enhanced by their scarcity.[27] With the greater part of rich people, the chief enjoyment of riches consists in the parade of riches, which in their *eyes* is never so compleat as when they appear to possess those decisive marks of opulence which nobody can possess but themselves.[28] In their eyes the merit of an object which is in any degree either useful or beautiful, is greatly enhanced by its scarcity, or by the great labour which it requires to collect any considerable quantity of it, a labour which nobody can afford to pay but themselves.[29] Such objects

---

v–v eye 4–6

---

[26] Cf. LJ (A) vi.106: 'all houshould utensils, as plates, spoons, kettles, etc., etc. all with a few exceptions, would be the better if made of gold or silver.' Also LJ (B) 238, ed. Cannan 185: 'Gold and silver however do not derive their whole utility from being the medium of exchange. Tho' they never had been used as money, they are more valuable than any other mettals. They have a superiour beauty, are capable of a finer polish, and are more proper for making any instrument except those with an edge.'

[27] It is stated in LRBL ii.237, ed. Lothian 187, that 'novelty generally inhances the value of a thing'. In LJ (A) vi.13 the value of the precious stones is linked with their colour and rarity.

[28] Cf. Imitative Arts, I.13:

In arts which address themselves, not to the prudent and the wise, but to the rich and the great, to the proud and the vain, we ought not to wonder if the appearance of great expence, of being what few people can purchase, of being one of the surest characteristics of great fortune, should often stand in the way of exquisite beauty, and contribute equally to recommend their productions. As the idea of expence seems often to embellish, so that of cheapness seems as frequently to tarnish the lustre even of very agreeable objects.

Also TMS I.iii.2.1:

It is the vanity, not the ease, or the pleasure, which interests us. But vanity is always founded upon the belief of our being the object of attention and approbation. The rich man glories in his riches, because he feels that they naturally draw upon him the attention of the world . . .

See below, II.iii.39 and IV.ix.47, where Smith points out that variety rather than expense may be a source of distinction, and also V.ii.e.6, where it is stated that the 'luxuries and vanities of life occasion the principal expence of the rich'.

[29] The sources of merit or utility are discussed in the essay on the Imitative Arts and in the TMS IV, 'Of the Effect of Utility upon the Sentiment of Approbation'. See also TMS V.i.1, 'Of the Influence of Custom and Fashion upon our notions of Beauty and Deformity'. See also LJ (A) vi.13–16; LJ (B) 206–9, ed. Cannan 158–9, where Smith discusses the 'natural wants' of man.

they are willing to purchase at a higher price than things much more beautiful and useful, but more common. These qualities of utility, beauty, and scarcity, are the original foundation of the high price of those metals, or of the great quantity of other goods for which they can every where be exchanged. This value was antecedent to and independent of their being employed as coin, and was the quality which fitted them for that employment. That [270] employment, however, by occasioning a new demand, and by diminishing the quantity which could be employed in any other way, may have afterwards contributed to keep up or increase their value.

32   The demand for the precious stones arises altogether from their beauty. They are of no use, but as ornaments; and the merit of their beauty is greatly enhanced by their scarcity, or by the difficulty and expence of getting them from the mine.[30] Wages and profit accordingly make up, upon most occasions, almost the whole of their high price. Rent comes in but for a very small share; frequently for no share; and the most fertile mines only afford any considerable rent. When Tavernier, a jeweller, visited the diamond mines of Golconda and Visiapour, he was informed that the sovereign of the country, for whose benefit they were wrought, had ordered all of them to be shut up, except those which [w]yielded[w] the largest and finest stones.[31] The others, it seems, were to the proprietor not worth the working.

33   As the price both of the precious metals and of the precious stones is regulated all over the world by their price at the most fertile mine in it, the rent which a mine of either can afford to its proprietor is in proportion, not to its absolute, but to what may [x]be[x] called its relative fertility, or to its superiority over other mines of the same kind. If new mines were discovered as much superior to those of Potosi as they were superior to those of Europe, the value of silver might be [271] so much degraded as to render even the mines of Potosi not worth the working. Before the discovery of the Spanish West Indies, the most fertile mines in Europe may have afforded as great a rent to their proprietor as the richest mines in Peru do at present. Though the quantity of silver was much less, it might have exchanged for an equal quantity of other goods, and the proprietor's share might have enabled him to purchase or command an

---

[w-w] yield 4-6   [x-x] om. 3

[30] See above I.iv.13 and below IV.vii.a.19.

[31] Tavernier's account (1676) is not quite as Smith suggests (*Travels in India*, translated by V. Ball (London, 1889), ii.78–9):

About thirty or forty years ago a mine situated between Kollur and Ramulkota was discovered, but the King ordered it to be closed on account of fraud . . . Stones were found in it which had this green crust, beautiful and transparent, they were even more beautiful than the others, but when one attempted to grind them they broke in pieces . . . It is . . . on account of the deceptions which have been practiced with these stones that the King ordered the mine to be closed.

There is a general account of the diamond mines in ii.53–99.

equal quantity either of labour or of commodities. The value both of the
produce and of the rent, the real revenue which they afforded both to the
publick and to the proprietor, might have been the same.

34   The most abundant mines either of the precious metals or of the precious stones could add little to the wealth of the world. A produce of
which the value is principally derived from its scarcity, is necessarily degraded by its abundance. A service of plate, and the other frivolous ornaments of dress and furniture, could be purchased for a smaller quantity of
labour, or for a smaller quantity of commodities; and in this would consist
the sole advantage which the world could derive from that abundance.

35   It is otherwise in estates above ground. The value both of their produce
and of their rent is in proportion to their absolute, and not to their relative fertility. The land which produces a certain quantity of food, cloaths,
and lodging, can always feed, cloath, and lodge a certain number of
people; and whatever may be the proportion of the landlord, it will always
give [272] him a proportionable command of the labour of those people,
and of the commodities with which that labour can supply him. The value
of the most barren lands is not diminished by the neighbourhood of the
most fertile. On the contrary, it is generally increased by it. The great
number of people maintained by the fertile lands afford a market to
many parts of the produce of the barren, which they could never have
found among those whom their own produce could maintain.

36   Whatever increases the fertility of land in producing food, increases
not only the value of the lands upon which the improvement is bestowed,
but contributes likewise to increase that of many other lands, by creating
a new demand for their produce. That abundance of food, of which, in
consequence of the improvement of land, many people have the disposal beyond what they themselves can consume, is the great cause of the
demand both for the precious metals and the precious stones, as well as
for every other conveniency and ornament of dress, lodging, houshold
furniture, and equipage.[32] Food not only constitutes the principal part
of the riches of the world, but it is the abundance of food which gives
the principal part of their value to many other sorts of riches. The poor
inhabitants of Cuba and St. Domingo, when they were first discovered
by the Spaniards, used to wear little bits of gold as ornaments in their
hair and other parts of their dress. They seemed to value them as we would
do any little pebbles of [273] somewhat more than ordinary beauty, and to
consider them as just worth the picking up, but not worth the refusing
to any body who asked them. They gave them to their new guests at the
first request, without seeming to think that they had made them any

[32] See above, I.xi.c.7, and below, I.xi.g.28. Smith argues at III.iii.20 that cheap provisions helped historically to develop manufactures through the encouragement given to
artificers to settle in particular places.

very valuable present.[33] They were astonished to observe the rage of the Spaniards to obtain them; and had no notion that there could any where be a country in which many people had the disposal of so great a superfluity of food, so scanty always among themselves, that for a very small quantity of those glittering baubles they would willingly give as much as might maintain a whole family for many years. Could they have been made to understand this, the passion of the Spaniards would not have surprised them.

PART III
Of the Variations in the Proportion between the respective Values of that Sort of Produce which always affords Rent, and of that which sometimes does, and sometimes does not, afford Rent

1   The increasing abundance of food, in consequence of increasing improvement and cultivation, must necessarily increase the demand for every part of the produce of land which is not food, and which can be applied either to use or to ornament. In the whole progress of improvement, it might therefore be expected, there should be only one variation in the comparative [274] values of those two different sorts of produce. The value of that sort which sometimes does and sometimes does not afford rent, should constantly rise in proportion to that which always affords some rent. As art and industry advance, the materials of cloathing and lodging, the useful fossils and minerals of the earth, the precious metals and the precious stones should gradually come to be more and more in demand, should gradually exchange for a greater and a greater quantity of food, or in other words, should gradually become dearer and dearer. This accordingly has been the case with most of these things upon most occasions, and would have been the case with all of them upon all occasions, if particular accidents had not upon some occasions increased the supply of some of them in a still greater proportion than the demand.

2   The value of a free-stone quarry, for example, will necessarily increase with the increasing improvement and population of the country round about it; especially if it should be the only one in the neighbourhood. But the value of a silver mine, even though there should not be another within a thousand miles of it, will not necessarily increase with the im-

[33] Cf. LJ (B) 209, ed. Cannan 159:

What we are every day accustomed to does but very indifferently affect us. Gems and diamonds are on this account much esteemed by us. In like manner our pinchbeck and many of our toys were so much valued by the Indians, that in bartering their jewels and diamonds for them they thought they had made much the better bargain.

A similar argument appears in LJ (A) vi.15. See below, IV.i.2, where the Spanish view of wealth is compared unfavourably with the Tartar. It is stated at IV.vii.a.17 that Spanish colonization was generally motivated by a desire for gold.

provement of the country in which it is situated. The market for the produce of a free-stone quarry can seldom extend more than a few miles round about it, and the demand must generally be in proportion to the improvement and population of that small district. But the market for the produce of a [275] silver mine may extend over the whole known world. Unless the world in general, therefore, be advancing in improvement and population, the demand for silver might not be at all increased by the improvement even of a large country in the neighbourhood of the mine. Even though the world in general were improving, yet, if, in the course of its improvement new mines should be discovered, much more fertile than any which had been known before, though the demand for silver would necessarily increase, yet the supply might increase in so much a greater proportion, that the real price of that metal might gradually fall; that is, any given quantity, a pound weight of it, for example, might gradually purchase or command a smaller and a smaller quantity of labour, or exchange for a smaller and a smaller quantity of corn, the principal part of the subsistence of the labourer.

3   The great market for silver is the commercial and civilized part of the world.

4   If by the general progress of improvement the demand of this market should increase, while at the same time the supply did not increase in the same proportion, the value of silver would gradually rise in proportion to that of corn. Any given quantity of silver would exchange for a greater and a greater quantity of corn; or, in other words, the average money price of corn would gradually become cheaper and cheaper.

5   If, on the contrary, the supply by some accident should increase for many years together in a [276] greater proportion than the demand, that metal would gradually become cheaper and cheaper; or, in other words, the average money price of corn would, in spite of all improvements, gradually become dearer and dearer.[1]

6   But if, on the other hand, the supply of the metal should increase nearly in the same proportion as the demand, it would continue to purchase or exchange for nearly the same quantity of corn, and the average money price of corn would, in spite of all improvements, continue very nearly the same.

7   These three seem to exhaust all the possible combinations of events which can happen in the progress of improvement; and during the course of the four centuries preceding the present, if we may judge by what has happened both in France and Great Britain, each of those three different

[1] Cf. J. Law, *Money and Trade*, 43–4: 'There is no way Silver can be made more valuable, but by lessening the Quantity, or encreasing the Demand for it. If the Export and Consumption of Silver be greater than the Import, or the Demand be encreas'd; Silver will be of more Value. If the Quantity Imported be greater than the Quantity Exported or Consumed, or the Demand lessen'd; Silver will be of less Value.'

combinations seem to have taken place in the European market, and nearly in the same order too in which I have here set them down.

Digression concerning the Variations in the Value of Silver during the Course of the Four last Centuries

FIRST PERIOD

1   In 1350, and for some time before, the average price of the quarter of wheat in England seems not to have been estimated lower than four ounces of silver, Tower-weight, equal to about twenty shillings of our present money. From [277] this price it seems to have fallen gradually to two ounces of silver, equal to about ten shillings of our present money, the price at which we find it estimated in the beginning of the sixteenth century, and at which it seems to have continued to be estimated till about 1570.

2   In 1350, being the 25th of Edward III, was enacted what is called, The statute of labourers.[1] In the preamble it complains much of the insolence of servants, who endeavoured to raise their wages upon their masters.[2] It therefore ordains, that all servants and labourers should for the future be contented with the same wages and liveries (liveries in those times signified, not only cloaths, but provisions) which they had been accustomed to receive in the 20th year of the king, and the four preceding years; that upon this account their livery wheat should no where be estimated higher than ten-pence a bushel, and that it should always be in the option of the master to deliver them either the wheat or the money. Ten-pence a bushel, therefore, had in the 25th of Edward III, been reckoned a very moderate price of wheat, since it required a particular statute to oblige servants to accept of it in exchange for their usual livery of provisions; and it had been reckoned a reasonable price ten years before that, or in the 16th year of the king, the term to which the statute refers. But in the 16th year of Edward III, ten-pence contained about half an ounce of silver, Tower-weight, and was nearly equal to half a crown of our present money.[3] Four ounces of silver, Tower-weight, [278] therefore, equal to six shillings and eight-pence of the money of those times, and to near twenty shillings of that of the present, must have been reckoned a moderate price for the quarter of eight bushels.

3   This statute is surely a better evidence of what was reckoned in those times a moderate price of grain, than the prices of some particular years which have generally been recorded by historians and other writers on

---

[1] 25 Edward III, st. 2 (1350) in *Statutes of the Realm*, i.311; 25 Edward III, st. 1 in Ruffhead's edition. See also I.x.c.34n.

[2] See above, I.viii.13.

[3] Smith seems to have made most conversions to contemporary values from the conversion table in M. Folkes, *A Table of English Silver Coins* (London, 1745), 142, though

account of their extraordinary dearness or cheapness, and from which, therefore, it is difficult to form any judgment concerning what may have been the ordinary price.[4] There are, besides, other reasons for believing that in the beginning of the fourteenth century, and for some time before, the common price of wheat was not less than four ounces of silver the quarter, and that of other grain in proportion.

4   In 1309, Ralph de Born, prior of St. Augustine's, Canterbury, gave a feast upon his installation-day, of which William Thorn has preserved, not only the bill of fare, but the prices of many particulars. In that feast were consumed, 1st, fifty-three quarters of wheat, which cost nineteen pounds, or seven shillings and two-pence a quarter, equal to about one-and-twenty shillings and six-pence of our present money: 2dly, Fifty-eight quarters of malt, which cost seventeen pounds ten shillings, or six shillings a quarter, equal to about eighteen shillings of our present money: 3dly, Twenty quarters of oats, which cost four pounds, or four shillings a quar-[279]ter, equal to about twelve shillings of our present money.[5] The prices of malt and oats seem here to be higher than their ordinary proportion to the price of wheat.

5   These prices are not recorded on account of their extraordinary dearness or cheapness, but are mentioned accidentally as the prices actually paid for large quantities of grain consumed at a feast which was famous for its magnificence.

6   In 1262, being the 51st of Henry III, was revived an ancient statute called, *The Assize of Bread and Ale*,[6] which, the king says in the preamble, had been made in the times of his progenitors sometime kings of England.

he did not always use the exact conversion ratio. Folkes gives the following proportions of ancient to contemporary values for particular coins.

Year of reign	Calendar year	Proportion
Conquest	1066	2·906
28 Edward I	1300	2·871
18 Edward III	1344	2·622
20 Edward III	1346	2·583
27 Edward III	1353	2·325
13 Henry IV	1412	1·937
4 Edward IV	1464	1·55
18 Henry VIII	1527	1·378
34 Henry VIII	1543	1·163
36 Henry VIII	1545	0·466
5 Edward VI	1551	0·232
6 Edward VI	1552	1·028
1 Mary	1553	1·024
2 Elizabeth	1560	1·033
43 Elizabeth	1601	1·000

[4] See above, I.v.22.   [5] W. Fleetwood, *Chronicon Preciosum*, 83–5.

[6] The date of the statute is uncertain. If it were during the 51st of Henry III, the date should be 1266–7. *Statutes of the Realm*, i.199, n., discusses the uncertainty. See above, I.iv.10, I.x.c.62, and below, I.xi.e.20.

It is probably, therefore, as old at least as the time of his grandfather Henry II, and may have been as old as the conquest. It regulates the price of bread according as the prices of wheat may happen to be, from one shilling to twenty shillings the quarter of the money of those times. But statutes of this kind are generally presumed to provide with equal care for all deviations from the middle price, for those below it as well as for those above it. Ten shillings, therefore, containing six ounces of silver, Tower-weight, and equal to about thirty shillings of our present money, must, upon this supposition, have been reckoned the middle price of the quarter of wheat when this statute was first enacted, and must have continued to be so in the 51st of Henry III. We cannot therefore be very *a* wrong in supposing that the middle price was not less than one-third of the highest price at which this [280] statute regulates the price of bread, or than six shillings and eight-pence of the money of those times, containing four ounces of silver, Tower-weight.

7   From these different facts, therefore, we seem to have some reason to conclude, that about the middle of the fourteenth century, and for a considerable time before, the average or ordinary price of the quarter of wheat was not supposed to be less than four ounces of silver, Tower-weight.[7]

8   From about the middle of the fourteenth to the beginning of the sixteenth century, what was reckoned the reasonable and moderate, that is the ordinary or average price of wheat, seems to have sunk gradually to about one-half of this price; so as at last to have fallen to about two ounces of silver, Tower-weight, equal to about ten shillings of our present money. It continued to be estimated at this price till about 1570.

9   In the houshold book of Henry, the fifth earl of Northumberland, drawn up in 1512, there are two different estimations of wheat. In one of them it is computed at six-shillings and eight-pence the quarter, in the other at five shillings and eight-pence only.[8] In 1512, six shillings and eight-pence contained only two ounces of silver Tower-weight, and were equal to about ten shillings of our present money.

10   From the 25th of Edward III, to the beginning of the reign of Elizabeth, during the space of more than two hundred years, six shillings and

---

a far *1*

---

[7] Prices of agricultural products remained fairly stable, though with a slow secular rise, from the turn of the twelfth and thirteenth centuries to the mid-fourteenth century. Fluctuations were considerable, particularly because of poor harvests, and so can affect statistical averages.

[8] Two separate quotations are given, but that of 5s. 8d. is probably a misprint since 118 quarters 2 bushels are reckoned to have cost £39. 8s. 4d. *The Regulations and Establishment of the Household of Henry Algernon Percy, the Fifth Earl of Northumberland, at his castles of Wresill and Lekinfield in Yorkshire, begun A.D. MDXII* (London, 1827), 2 and 4.

eight-pence, it appears from several different statutes, had continued to be considered as what [281] is called the moderate and reasonable, that is the ordinary or average price of wheat. The quantity of silver, however, contained in that nominal sum was, during the course of this period, continually diminishing, in consequence of some alterations which were made in the coin. But the increase of the value of silver had, it seems, so far compensated the diminution of the quantity of it contained in the same nominal sum, that the legislature did not think it worth while to attend to this circumstance.

11   Thus in 1436 it was enacted, that wheat might be exported without a licence when the price was so low as six shillings and eight-pence:[9] And in 1463 it was enacted, that no wheat should be imported if the price was not above six shillings and eight-pence the quarter.[10] The legislature had imagined, that when the price was so low, there could be no inconveniency in exportation, but that when it rose higher, it became prudent to allow of importation. Six shillings and eight-pence, therefore, containing about the same quantity of silver as thirteen shillings and four-pence of our present money (one third part less than the same nominal sum contained in the time of Edward III.), had in those times been considered as what is called the moderate and reasonable price of wheat.

12   In 1554, by the 1st and 2d of Philip and Mary;[11] and in 1558, by the 1st of Elizabeth, the exportation of wheat was in the same manner prohibited, whenever the price of the quarter should exceed six shillings and eight-pence,[12] [282] which did not then contain two penny worth more silver than the same nominal sum does at present. But it had soon been found that to restrain the exportation of wheat till the price was so very low, was, in reality, to prohibit it altogether. In 1562, therefore, by the 5th of Elizabeth, the exportation of wheat was allowed from certain ports whenever the price of the quarter should not exceed ten shillings,[13] containing nearly the same quantity of silver as the like nominal sum does at present. This price had at this time, therefore, been considered as what is called the moderate and reasonable price of wheat. It agrees nearly with the estimation of the Northumberland book in 1512.

13   That in France the average price of grain was, in the same manner, much lower in the end of the fifteenth and beginning of the sixteenth century, than in the two centuries preceding, has been observed both by

---

[9] 15 Henry VI, c. 2 (1436).
[10] 3 Edward IV, c. 2 (1463).
[11] 1 and 2 Philip and Mary, c. 5 (1554).
[12] 1 Elizabeth I, c. 11 (1558). Smith does not qualify his use of this and the previous statute. Both prohibited the export of wheat at the price he states, but 1 and 2 Philip and Mary, c. 5 allowed exports under licence and 1 Elizabeth I, c. 11 allowed exports from Norfolk and Suffolk under certain circumstances.
[13] 5 Elizabeth, c. 5 (1562).

Mr. Duprè de St. Maur,[14] and by the elegant author of the Essay on the police of grain.[15] Its price, during the same period, had probably sunk in the same manner through the greater part of Europe.

14   This rise in the value of silver in proportion to that of corn, may either have been owing altogether to the increase of the demand for that metal, in consequence of increasing improvement and cultivation, the supply in the mean time continuing the same as before: Or, the demand continuing the same as before, it may have been owing altogether to the gradual diminution of the supply; the greater part of the mines [283] which were then known in the world, being much exhausted, and consequently the expence of working them much increased: Or it may have been owing partly to the one and partly to the other of those two circumstances. In the end of the fifteenth and beginning of the sixteenth centuries, the greater part of Europe was approaching towards a more settled form of government than it had enjoyed for several ages before. The increase of security would naturally increase industry and improvement; and the demand for the precious metals, as well as for every other luxury and ornament, would naturally increase with the increase of riches. A greater annual produce would require a greater quantity of coin to circulate it; and a greater number of rich people would require a greater quantity of plate and other ornaments of silver. It is natural to suppose too, that the greater part of the mines which then supplied the European market with silver, might be a good deal exhausted, and have become more expensive in the working. They had been wrought many of them from the time of the Romans.

15   It has been the opinion, however, of the greater part of those who have written upon the prices of commodities in antient times, that, from the Conquest, perhaps from the invasion of Julius Caesar till the discovery of the mines of America, the value of silver was continually diminishing.[16] This opinion they seem to have been led into, partly by the observations

[14] Presumably Smith based his statement on an examination of the detailed examples of prices given in F. Dupré de Saint Maur's *Variations arrivées dans le prix de divers choses pendant le cours des cinq derniers siècles*, printed in his *Essai sur les Monnoies ou réflexions sur le rapport entre l'argent et les denrées* (Paris, 1746) but separately paginated, 1–188. Dupré de Saint Maur was at one time Intendant of Basse-Guienne and also wrote the *Recherches sur la valeur des Monnoies et sur le prix de grains avant et après le concile de Francfort* (Paris, 1762).

[15] *Essai sur la police générale des grains, sur leur prix et sur les effets de l'agriculture* (Berlin, 1755), by C. J. Herbert. Smith mentions the *Essai* and Dupré's work in Letter 115 addressed to Lord Hailes, dated 15 January 1769. The authorities cited in this letter include: William Fleetwood, *Chronicum Preciosum*, Messance, *Recherches sur la population*, Charles Smith, *Three Tracts on the Corn Trade and Corn Laws* (2nd ed., London, 1766) and Thomas Madox, *History and Antiquities of the Exchequer of the Kings of England. From the Norman Conquest to Edward II* (London, 1711).

[16] Smith states the contrary view at V.ii.c.5.

which they had occasion to make upon the prices both [284] of corn and of some other parts of the rude produce of land; and partly by the popular notion, that as the quantity of silver naturally increases in every country with the increase of wealth, so its value diminishes as its quantity increases.

16   In their observations upon the prices of corn, three different circumstances seem frequently to have misled them.

17   First, In antient times almost all rents were paid in kind; in a certain quantity of corn, cattle, poultry, &c. It sometimes happened, however, that the landlord would stipulate ^{b}, that he should be at liberty to demand ^{c}of the tenant,^{c} either the annual payment in kind, or a certain sum of money instead of it. The price at which the payment in kind was in this manner exchanged for a certain sum of money, is in Scotland called the conversion price. As the option is always in the landlord to take either the substance or the price, it is necessary for the safety of the tenant, that the conversion price should rather be below than above the average market price. In many places, accordingly, it is not much above one-half of this price. Through the greater part of Scotland this custom still continues with regard to poultry, and in some places with regard to cattle. It might probably have continued to take place too with regard to corn, had not the institution of the publick fiars put an end to it. These are annual valuations, according to the judgment of an assize, of the average price of all the different sorts of grain, and of all the different qualities of each, accord-[285]ing to the actual market price in every different county.[17] This institution rendered it sufficiently safe for the tenant, and much more convenient for the landlord, to convert, as they call it, the corn rent^d, rather at what should happen to be^d the price of the fiars of each year, ^{e} than at any certain fixed price.[18] But the writers who have collected the

----

^{b} with the tenant 1 $^{c-c}$ 2–6 $^{d-d}$ at 1 ^{e} rather 1

----

[17] See above, I.viii.34.

[18] In Letter 115 addressed to Lord Hailes, dated 15 January 1769, Smith wrote that he would be obliged for a sight of Hailes's paper upon prices as 'I have no papers upon this subject' apart from 'an account of the fiars of Midlothian from 1626 & this was copied too from a printed Paper produced in a process before the Court of Session some years ago'. Smith added that he hoped to get additional information, and in particular an account from the Victualling Office, and also mentions that he had made use of certain English Acts of Parliament and some 'Ordonnances of the french Kings'. In Letter 116 addressed to Hailes, dated 5 March 1769, Smith wrote to say that he had not yet received the paper and offered to send his servant for it. Hailes despatched the manuscript on the following day and in his accompanying letter (Letter 117) referred to 'a Book lately published as to the prices of Corn &c. in England since the Conquest' which he had not as yet seen. In Letter 118 addressed to Hailes, dated 12 March 1769, Smith acknowledged that the papers which he had received 'will be of very great use to me'. On 23 May he returned the material 'having taken a copy of that upon prices, as your Lordship permitted me to do it'. Hailes's paper is included in the Corr. and entitled

prices of corn in antient times, seem frequently to have mistaken what is called in Scotland the conversion price for the actual market price.[19] Fleetwood acknowledges, upon one occasion, that he had made this mistake. As he wrote his book, however, for a particular purpose, he does not think proper to make this acknowledgment till after transcribing this conversion price fifteen times.[20] The price is eight shillings the quarter of wheat. This sum in 1423, the year at which he begins with it, contained the same quantity of silver as sixteen shillings of our present money. But in 1562, the year at which he ends with it, it contained no more than the same nominal sum does at present.

18   Secondly, They have been misled by the slovenly manner in which some antient statutes of assize had been sometimes transcribed by lazy copiers; and sometimes perhaps actually composed by the legislature.

19   The antient statutes of assize seem to have begun always with determining what ought to be the price of bread and ale when the price of wheat and barley were at the lowest, and to have proceeded gradually to determine what it ought [286] to be, according as the prices of those

---

'Prices of Corn, Cattle &c. in Scotland from the earliest accounts to the death of James V'. It would appear from this correspondence with Hailes that Smith must have embarked on the analysis of what was to form part of the 'Digression on Silver' quite early.

[19] Examples of the conversion price are given in Hailes's paper, for example with regard to deeds made by the Bishop of Murray (*sic*) for the years 1540, 1544, 1554, 1561. In 1544 it appears that the conversion price for 'poultrie' was 3*d.*, and for salmon (per barrel) £2. 10*s.* Smith discussed the issue in Letter 118 addressed to Hailes, dated 12 March 1769, in the course of which he commented that 'In this neighbourhood the price of good fowl, a hen, has been for many years from ten pence, to a Shilling and fifteen pence. Several years ago a friend of mine converted all the Poultry upon his estate at a Shilling. Five pence, however, is a common conversion price in a lease, the option being in the Landlord. Leases of this kind have been let within [these] two or three years.' In this letter, Smith also adverted to the 'extremely loose and inaccurate' notions of our ancestors with regard to grain prices, pointing out that 'the same nominal sum was frequently considered as the Average price both of grain and of other things' in periods where there had been substantial alterations in the intrinsic value of the coin. See above, I.v.

[20] Smith is not quite accurate. Fleetwood wrote (*Chronicon Preciosum*, 121–2):

I would not have been weary of transcribing such Accounts as these, if I had judged the knowledge of them, any thing to your Purpose; but I perceive the Way was now, and had been so for some Years before, as well as many that follow, to settle the Price of Corn betwixt the Landlord and Tenant, without regard to what it truly was. Wheat was generally fix'd to 8s. the Quarter, and Malt and Oats at 5s. But finding it so for 20, 30, or 40 years together, you may reasonably conclude, that was not the true Market-Price, because it is not in the nature of the Thing possible, that Corn should be so long at the same stand. But yet if you take Things for 20 Years together, 'tis likely that such a Price might be equal enough, betwixt the Landlord and the Tenant, and therefore well agreed upon.

Smith accepts fiars prices elsewhere, in I.viii.34. Though fiars prices were not market prices, they were based on them.

two sorts of grain should gradually rise above this lowest price. But the transcribers of those statutes seem frequently to have thought it sufficient, to copy the regulation as far as the three or four first and lowest prices; saving in this manner their own labour, and judging, I suppose, that this was enough to show what proportion ought to be observed in all higher prices.

20   Thus in the assize of bread and ale, of the 51st of Henry III. the price of bread was regulated according to the different prices of wheat, from one shilling to twenty shillings the quarter, of the money of those times. But in the manuscripts from which all the different editions of the statutes, preceding that of Mr. Ruffhead, were printed, the copiers had never transcribed this regulation beyond the price of twelve shillings.[21] Several writers, therefore, being misled by this faulty transcription, very naturally concluded that the middle price, or six shillings the quarter, equal to about eighteen shillings of our present money, was the ordinary or average price of wheat at that time.

21   In the statute of Tumbrel and Pillory, enacted nearly about the same time,[22] the price of ale is regulated according to every sixpence rise in the price of barley, from two shillings to four shillings the quarter. That four shillings, however, was not considered as the highest price to which barley might frequently rise in those times, and that these prices were only given as an example of the proportion which ought to be observed in [287] all other prices, whether higher or lower, we may infer from the last words of the statute; "et sic deinceps crescetur vel diminuetur per sex denarios". The expression is very slovenly, but the meaning is plain enough; "That the price of ale is in this manner to be increased or diminished according to every six-pence rise or fall in the price of barley". In the composition of this statute the legislature itself seems to have been as negligent as the copiers were in the transcription of the other.[23]

22   In an antient manuscript of the Regiam Majestatem,[24] an old Scotch law book, there is a statute of assize, in which the price of bread is regulated according to all the different prices of wheat, from ten-pence to three shillings the Scotch boll, equal to about half an English quarter. Three shillings Scotch, at the time when this assize is supposed to have been enacted, were equal to about nine shillings sterling of our present

[21] *Statutes of the Realm*, i.199, n. does not confirm Smith's view of the editions before Ruffhead. See above, I.iv.10, I.x.c.62, and I.xi.e.6.

[22] *Statutes of the Realm*, i.201, gives date as uncertain. Ruffhead attributes to 51 Henry III, st. 6. The problem is similar to that over the Assize of Bread and Ale. See above, I.iv.10.

[23] *Statutes of the Realm*, i.202, translates as, 'And so from henceforth the Prices shall increase and decrease after the Rate of Sixpence.'

[24] In Letter 119, addressed to Lord Hailes, dated 16 May 1769, Smith agreed that the *Regiam Majestatem* had probably been written at a time 'posterior to Richard 2nd.' and

money. Mr. Ruddiman seems* to conclude from this, that three shillings
was the highest price to which wheat ever rose in those times, and that
ten-pence, a shilling, or at most two shillings, were the ordinary prices.
Upon consulting the manuscript, however, it appears evidently, that all
these prices are only set down as examples of the proportion which
ought to be observed between the respective prices of wheat and bread.
The last words of the statute are, "reliqua judicabis secundum prae-
scripta habendo respectum [288] ad pretium bladi." "You shall judge
of the remaining cases according to what is above written having a respect
to the price of corn."

23   Thirdly, They seem to have been misled too by the very low price at
which wheat was sometimes sold in very antient times; and to have
imagined, that as its lowest price was then much lower than in later times,
its ordinary price must likewise have been much lower. They might have
found, however, that in those antient times, its highest price was fully
as much above, as its lowest price was below any thing that had ever
been known in later times. Thus in 1270, Fleetwood gives us two prices
of the quarter of wheat.²⁵ The one is four pounds sixteen shillings of the
money of those times, equal to fourteen pounds eight shillings of that
of the present; the other is six pounds eight shillings, equal to nineteen
pounds four shillings of our present money. No price can be found in
the end of the fifteenth, or beginning of the sixteenth century, which
approaches to the extravagance of these. The price of corn, though at

---

ᶠ* See his preface to Anderson's *Diplomata Scotiae*.ᶠ [James Anderson, *Selectus
diplomatum et numismatum Scotiae thesaurus*, ed. T. Ruddiman (Edinburgh, 1739), 82.
In translation, T. Ruddiman, *An Introduction to Mr. James Anderson's Diplomata Scotiae*
(Edinburgh, 1782), 228, though Ruddiman records, 174, that a boll of corn sold for 18s.
Scots in 1435 and for 30s. Scots in 1438.]

ᶠ⁻ᶠ 2–6

---

that the work was not intended to be a record of original statutes, being rather 'the
composition of some private man, who meant to describe the great outlines of the Laws
and customs of his Country, which he supposed, or had been told by tradition, were first
introduced by some antient and famous king of the name of Malcolm; either Malcolm
McKenneth or Malcolm Canmore; the former just as probably as the latter.' Hailes's
position had been established in *An Examination of Some of the Arguments for the High
Antiquity of Regiam Majestatem* (Edinburgh, 1769).
    In Letter 120, addressed to Hailes, dated 23 May 1769, Smith also showed that he was
familiar with Sir John Skene's translation from the Latin: *Regiam Majestatem. The
Auld Laws and Constitutions of Scotland. Faithfullie collected furth of the Register, and
other auld authentick Bukes, from the Dayes of King Malcolme the Second untill the Time
of King James the First* (Edinburgh, 1609). Smith refers to the *Regiam Majestatem* in
LJ (A) i.137 in connection with the Scots Law on inheritance. In LJ (A) ii.48 Smith also
cites 'our old book, the *Regiam majestatem*' in considering the law of contract.
    ²⁵ Fleetwood was aware of this danger. He quoted from *Antiq. Britan* in *Vita Joh.
Pecham* that 'provisions were so scarce that parents did eat their own children', but adds
he hopes he need not be believed ''tis only an Expression of the greatest Want imagin-
able' (*Chronicon Preciosum*, 78–9).

all times liable to ⁹variations⁹, varies most in those turbulent and disorderly societies, in which the interruption of all commerce and communication hinders the plenty of one part of the country from relieving the scarcity of another.²⁶ In the disorderly state of England under the Plantagenets, who governed it from about the middle of the twelfth, till towards the end of the fifteenth century, one district might be in plenty, while another at no great distance, by having its crop destroyed [289] either by some accident of the seasons, or by the incursion of some neighbouring baron, might be suffering all the horrors of a famine; and yet if the lands of some hostile lord were interposed between them, the one might not be able to give the least assistance to the other. Under the vigorous administration of the Tudors, who governed England during the latter part of the fifteenth, and through the whole of the sixteenth century, no baron was powerful enough to dare to disturb the publick security.²⁷

24   The reader will find at the end of this chapter all the prices of wheat which have been collected by Fleetwood from 1202 to 1597, both inclusive, reduced to the money of the present times, and digested according to the order of time, into seven divisions of twelve years each. At the end of each division too, he will find the average price of the twelve years of which it consists. In that long period of time, Fleetwood has been able to collect the prices of no more than eighty years, so that four years are wanting to make out the last twelve years. I have added, therefore, from the accounts of Eton college, the prices of 1598, 1599, 1600, and 1601. It is the only addition which I have made. The reader will see that from the beginning of the thirteenth, till after the middle of the sixteenth century, the average price of each twelve years grows gradually lower and lower; and that towards the end of the sixteenth century it begins to rise again. The prices, indeed, which Fleetwood has been able to collect, seem to have been those chiefly which were [290] remarkable for extraordinary dearness or cheapness; and I do not pretend that any very certain conclusion can be drawn from them. So far, however, as they prove any thing at all, they confirm the account which I have been endeavouring to give. Fleetwood himself, however, seems, with most other writers, to have believed, that during all this period the value of silver, in consequence of its increasing abundance, was continually diminishing. The prices of corn which he himself has collected, certainly do not agree with this opinion. They agree perfectly with that of Mr. Duprè de St. Maur, and with that which I have been endeavouring to explain. Bishop Fleetwood and Mr. Duprè de St. Maur are the two

⁹⁻⁹ variation 4–6

²⁶ Smith comments on feudal anarchy at III.ii.7, III.iv.9; cf. III.i.3 and V.iii.1.

²⁷ Regional variations in prices in England were declining in the thirteenth and fourteenth centuries. N. S. B. Gras, *The Evolution of the English Corn Market from the Twelfth to the Eighteenth Century* (London, 1915).

authors who seem to have collected, with the greatest diligence and
fidelity, the prices of things in antient times. It is somewhat curious that,
though their opinions are so very different, their facts, so far as they
relate to the price of corn at least, should coincide so very exactly.[28]

25   It is not, however, so much from the low price of corn, as from that of
some other parts of the rude produce of land, that the most judicious
writers have inferred the great value of silver in those very antient times.
Corn, it has been said, being a sort of manufacture, was, in those rude
ages, much dearer in proportion than the greater part of other commodities; it is meant, I suppose, than the greater part of unmanufactured
commodities; such as cattle, poultry, game of all kinds, &c. That in those
times of poverty and barbarism these were proportion-[291]ably much
cheaper than corn, is undoubtedly true. But this cheapness was not the
effect of the high value of silver, but of the low value of those commodities.
It was not *h*because*h* silver would in such times purchase or represent a
greater quantity of labour, but *i*because*i* such commodities would purchase or represent a much smaller quantity than in times of more opulence and improvement. Silver must certainly be cheaper in Spanish
America than in Europe; in the country where it is produced, than in the
country to which it is brought, at the expence of a long carriage both by
land and by sea, of a freight and an insurance. One-and-twenty pence
halfpenny sterling, however, we are told by Ulloa, was, not many years
ago, at Buenos Ayres, the price of an ox chosen from a herd of three or
four hundred. Sixteen shillings sterling, we are told by Mr. Byron, was
the price of a good horse in the capital of Chili.[29] In a country naturally
fertile, but of which the far greater part is altogether uncultivated, cattle,
poultry, game of all kinds, &c. as they can be acquired with a very small
quantity of labour, so they will purchase or command but a very small

---

h-h that *1*   *i-i* that *1*

[28] Inaccuracy and the variety of conclusions reached on the basis of the same information may help to explain Smith's lack of faith in political arithmetic as stated at IV.v.b.30.
In his section on 'Prix des grains en Angleterre', Dupré de Saint Maur uses Fleetwood's
figures (*Essai sur les monnoies*, 183–8). His statistics, and those of Smith in the Appendix
to Book I, are normally identical. In Letter 119, addressed to Hailes, dated 16 May 1769,
Smith commented on 'The Discrepancies which your Lordship has taken notice of in
the prices of several different things' as being similar to those which 'occur in the antient
Coutumes of many different provinces of france. Mr Du Pré de Saint Maur has tortured
his brain to reconcile them and make them all consistent.'

[29] 'Without doubt the wheat of Chili is the finest in the world, and the fruits are all
excellent in their kinds. Beef and Mutton are so cheap, that you may have a good cow
for three dollars, and a fat sheep for two shillings. Their horses are extraordinary good;
and though some of them go at a great price, you may have a very good one for four dollars, or about eighteen shillings of our money.' (J. Byron, *Narrative of the Hon. John
Byron, containing an Account of the Great Distresses suffered by himself and his companions
on the Coast of Patagonia from the Year 1740 until their Arrival in England 1746* (London,
1780), 226.)

quantity.³⁰ The low money price for which they may be sold, is no proof that the real value of silver is there very high, but that the real value of those commodities is very low.

26   Labour, it must always be remembered, and not any particular commodity or sett of commodities, is the real measure of the value both of silver and of all other commodities.³¹

27   [292] But in countries almost waste, or but thinly inhabited, cattle, poultry, game of all kinds, &c. as they are the spontaneous productions of nature, so she frequently produces them in much greater quantities than the consumption of the inhabitants requires. In such a state of things the supply commonly exceeds the demand. In different states of society, in different stages of improvement, therefore, such commodities will represent, or be equivalent to, very different quantities of labour.

28   In every state of society, in every stage of improvement, corn is the production of human industry. But the average produce of every sort of industry is always suited, more or less exactly, to the average consumption; the average supply to the average demand. In every different stage of improvement, besides, the raising of equal quantities of corn in the same soil and climate, will, at an average, require nearly equal quantities of labour; or what comes to the same thing, the price of nearly equal quantities; the continual increase of the productive powers of labour in an ʲimprovingʲ state of cultivation, being more or less counter-balanced by the continually increasing price of cattle, the principal instruments of agriculture.³² Upon all these accounts, therefore, we may rest assured, that equal quantities of corn will, in every state of society, in every stage of improvement, more nearly represent, or be equivalent to, equal quantities of labour, than equal quantities of any other part of the rude produce of land. Corn, accordingly, [293] it has already been observed,³³ is, in all the different stages of wealth and improvement, a more accurate measure of value than any other commodity or sett of commodities. In all those different stages, therefore, we can judge better of the real value of silver, by comparing it with corn, than by comparing it with any other commodity, or sett of commodities.

29   Corn, besides, or whatever else is the common and favourite vegetable food of the people, constitutes, in every civilized country, the principal part of the subsistence of the labourer. In consequence of the extension of agriculture, the land of every country produces a much greater quantity

ʲ⁻ʲ improved 5–6

---

³⁰ See above, I.xi.b.7. Smith comments on the long-run trends in prices of this kind in I.xi.l.
³¹ See above, I.v.i.
³² Smith comments on the falling price of *meat* at I.xi.b.19 and I.xi.l.8.
³³ See above, I.v.15.

of vegetable than of animal food, and the labourer every where lives chiefly upon the wholesome food that is cheapest and most abundant. Butcher's-meat, except in the most thriving countries, or where labour is most highly rewarded, makes but an insignificant part of his subsistence:[34] poultry makes a still smaller part of it, and game no part of it. In France, and even in Scotland, where labour is somewhat better rewarded than in France, the labouring poor seldom eat butcher's-meat, except upon holidays, and other extraordinary occasions. The money price of labour, therefore, depends much more upon the average money price of corn, the subsistence of the labourer, than upon that of butcher's-meat, or of any other part of the rude produce of land. The real value of gold and silver, therefore, the real quantity of labour which they can purchase or command, depends much more upon the quantity of corn which [294] they can purchase or command, than upon that of butcher's-meat, or any other part of the rude produce of land.

30   Such slight observations, however, upon the prices either of corn or of other commodities, would not probably have misled so many intelligent authors, had they not been ᵏinfluenced, at the same time, byᵏ the popular notion, that as the quantity of silver naturally increases in every country with the increase of wealth, so its value diminishes as its quantity increases. This notion, however, seems to be altogether groundless.

31   The quantity of the precious metals may increase in any country from two different causes: either, first, from the increased abundance of the mines which supply it; or, secondly, from the increased wealth of the people, from the increased produce of their annual labour. The first of these causes is no doubt necessarily connected with the diminution of the value of the precious metals; but the second is not.

32   When more abundant mines are discovered, a greater quantity of the precious metals is brought to market, and the quantity of the necessaries and conveniencies of life for which they must be exchanged being the same as before, equal quantities of the metals must be exchanged for smaller quantities of commodities. So far, therefore, as the increase of the quantity of the precious metals in any country arises from the increased abundance of the mines, it is necessarily connected with some diminution of their value.[35]

33   When, on the contrary, the wealth of any country increases, when the

ᵏ⁻ᵏ agreeable to *1*

---

[34] It is stated below, V.ii.k.15, that butcher's meat is nowhere a necessary of life; Cf. I.xi.b.41. Smith discusses the relationship between wages and the price of corn in I.viii.

[35] Cf. Harris, *Essay*, i.68: '. . . the value of a given quantity or sum of money, in any country, will be less or more, according as the sum total, or the whole quantity of money in currency, is greater or less, in proportion to the whole of the commodities of that country, exchangeable for money.'

annual produce of [295] its labour becomes gradually greater and greater, a greater quantity of coin becomes necessary in order to circulate a greater quantity of commodities; and the people, as they can afford it, as they have more commodities to give for it, will naturally purchase a greater and a greater quantity of plate. The quantity of their coin will increase from necessity; the quantity of their plate from vanity and ostentation, or from the same reason that the quantity of fine statues, pictures, and of every other luxury and curiosity, is likely to increase among them. But as statuaries and painters are not likely to be worse rewarded in times of wealth and prosperity, than in times of poverty and depression, so gold and silver are not likely to be worse paid for.

34   The price of gold and silver, when the accidental discovery of more abundant mines does not keep it down, as it naturally rises with the wealth of every country, so, whatever be the state of the mines, it is at all times naturally higher in a rich than in a poor country. Gold and silver, like all other commodities, naturally seek the market where the best price is given for them, and the best price is commonly given for every thing in the country which can best afford it. Labour, it must be remembered, is the ultimate price which is paid for every thing,[36] and in countries where labour is equally well rewarded, the money price of labour will be in proportion to that of the subsistence of the labourer. But gold and silver will naturally exchange for a greater quantity of subsistence in a rich than in a [296] poor country, in a country which abounds with subsistence, than in one which is but indifferently supplied with it. If the two countries are at a great distance, the difference may be very great; because though the metals naturally fly from the worse to the better market, yet it may be difficult to transport them in such quantities as to bring their price nearly to a level in both. If the countries are near, the difference will be smaller, and may sometimes be scarce perceptible; because in this case the transportation will be easy. China is a much richer country than any part of Europe,[37] and the difference between the price of subsistence in China and in Europe is very great. Rice in China is much cheaper than wheat is any where in Europe. England is a much richer country than Scotland; but the difference between the money-price of corn in those two countries is much smaller, and is but just perceptible. In proportion to the quantity or measure, Scotch corn generally appears to be a good deal cheaper than English; but in proportion to its quality, it is certainly somewhat dearer. Scotland receives almost every year very large supplies from England, and every commodity must commonly be somewhat dearer in the country to which it is brought than in that from which it comes. English corn, therefore, must be dearer in Scotland than in England, and yet in

[36] See above, I.v.i.
[37] The same point is made below, I.xi.n.1, and above, I.viii.24.

proportion to its quality, or to the quantity and goodness of the flour or meal which can be made from it, it cannot commonly be sold higher there than the [297] Scotch corn which comes to market in competition with it.[38]

35   The difference between the money price of labour in China and in Europe, is still greater than that between the money price of subsistence; because the real recompence of labour is higher in Europe, than in China, the greater part of Europe being in an improving state, while China seems to be standing still. The money price of labour is lower in Scotland than in England because the real recompence of labour is much lower; Scotland, though advancing to greater wealth, *advances* much more slowly than England.[39] *The frequency of emigration from Scotland, and the rarity of it from England, sufficiently prove that the demand for labour is very different in the two countries.* The proportion between the real recompence of labour in different countries, it must be remembered, is naturally regulated, not by their actual wealth or poverty, but by their advancing, stationary, or declining condition.[40]

36   Gold and silver, as they are naturally of the greatest value among the richest, so they are naturally of *the* least value among the poorest nations. Among savages, the poorest of all nations, they are of scarce any value.

37   In great towns corn is always dearer than in remote parts of the country. This, however, is the effect, not of the real cheapness of silver, but of the real dearness of corn. It does not cost less labour to bring silver to the great town than to the remote parts of the country; but it costs a great deal more to bring corn.

38   [298] In some very rich and commercial countries, such as Holland and the territory of Genoa, corn is dear for the same reason that it is dear in great towns.[41] They do not produce enough to maintain their inhabitants. They are rich in the industry and skill of their artificers and manufacturers; in every sort of machinery which can facilitate and abridge labour; in shipping, and in all the other instruments and means of carriage and commerce: but they are poor in corn, which, as it must be brought to them from distant countries, must, by an addition to its price, pay for the carriage from those countries. It does not cost less labour to bring silver to Amsterdam than to Dantzick; but it costs a great deal more to bring corn. The real cost of silver must be nearly the same in both places; but that of corn must be very different. Diminish the real opulence either of Holland or of the territory of Genoa, while the number of their inhabitants *remains* the same: diminish their power of supplying themselves from distant countries; and the price of corn, instead of sinking with that diminution in the quantity of their silver, which must necessarily

---

l-l advancing *1–5*   *m-m* 2–6   *n-n* 2–6   *o-o* remain 2

[38] The same point is made at I.viii.33.   [39] The same point is made at I.ix.8.
[40] See above, I.viii.   [41] See above, I.xi.b.12 and IV.ix.37.

accompany this declension either as its cause or as its effect, will rise to the price of a famine. When we are in want of necessaries we must part with all superfluities, of which the value, as it rises in times of opulence and prosperity, so it sinks in times of poverty and distress. It is otherwise with necessaries. Their real price, the quantity of labour which they can purchase or command, rises in times of poverty and distress, and sinks in times of opulence and [299] prosperity, which are always times of great abundance; for they could not otherwise be times of opulence and prosperity. Corn is a necessary, silver is only a superfluity.

39   Whatever, therefore, may have been the increase in the quantity of the precious metals, which, during the period between the middle of the fourteenth and that of the sixteenth century, arose from the increase of wealth and improvement, it could have no tendency to diminish their value either in Great Britain, or in any other part of Europe. If those who have collected the prices of things in ancient times, therefore, had, during this period, no reason to infer the diminution of the value of silver, from any observations which they had made upon the prices either of corn or of other commodities, they had still less reason to infer it from any supposed increase of wealth and improvement.

SECOND PERIOD

1   But how various soever may have been the opinions of the learned concerning the progress of the value of silver during *this* first period, they are unanimous concerning it during the second.[1]

2   From about 1570 to about 1640, during a period of about seventy years, the variation in the proportion between the value of silver and that of corn, held a quite opposite course. Sil-[300]ver sunk in its real value, or would exchange for a smaller quantity of labour than before; and corn rose in its nominal price, and instead of being commonly sold for about two ounces of silver the quarter, or about ten shillings of our present money, came to be sold for six and eight ounces of silver the quarter, or about thirty and forty shillings of our present money.

3   The discovery of the abundant mines of America, seems to have been the sole cause of this diminution in the value of silver in proportion to that of corn.[2] It is accounted for accordingly in the same manner by every body; and there never has been any dispute either about the fact, or about

---

a-a the 6

---

[1] 'Everybody agrees that the abundance of money or its increase in exchange, raises the price of everything. The quantity of money brought from America to Europe for the last two centuries justifies this truth by experience.' (Cantillon, *Essai*, 212, ed. Higgs 161.)

[2] See above, I.v.7, and below, IV.i.32 and V.ii.c.5.

the cause of it. The greater part of Europe was, during this period, advancing in industry and improvement, and the demand for silver must consequently have been increasing. But the increase of the supply had, it seems, so far exceeded that of the demand, that the value of that metal sunk considerably. The discovery of the mines of America, it is to be observed, does not seem to have had any very sensible effect upon the prices of things in England till after 1570; though even the mines of Potosi had been discovered more than *b*twenty*b* years before.[3]

4   From 1595 to 1620, both inclusive, the average price of the quarter of nine bushels of the best wheat at Windsor market, appears from the accounts of Eton College, to have been 2*l*. 1*s*. 6*d*. $\frac{9}{13}$. From which sum, neglecting the fraction, and deducting a ninth.[4] or 4*s*. 7*d*. $\frac{1}{3}$, [301] the price of the quarter of eight bushels comes out to have been 1*l*. 16*s*. 10*d*.$\frac{2}{3}$. And from this sum, neglecting likewise the fraction, and deducting a ninth, or 4*s*. 1*d*. $\frac{1}{9}$, for the difference between the price of the best wheat and that of the middle wheat, the price of the middle wheat comes out to have been about 1*l*. 12*s*. 8*d*. $\frac{8}{9}$, or about six ounces and one-third of an ounce of silver.

5   From 1621 to 1636, both inclusive, the average price of the same measure of the best wheat at the same market, appears, from the same accounts, to have been 2*l*. 10*s*.; from which making the like deductions as in the foregoing case, the average price of the quarter of eight bushels of middle wheat comes out to have been 1*l*. 19*s*. 6*d*. or about seven ounces and two-thirds of an ounce of silver.

THIRD PERIOD

1   Between 1630 and 1640, or about 1636, the effect of the discovery of the mines of America in reducing the value of silver, appears to have been compleated, and the value of that metal seems never to have sunk lower in proportion to that of corn than it was about that time. It seems to have risen somewhat in the course of the present century, and it had probably begun to do so even some time before the end of the last.

2   From 1637 to 1700, both inclusive, being the sixty-four last years of the last century, the ave-[302]rage price of the quarter of nine bushels of the best wheat at Windsor market, appears, from the same accounts, to have

---

b-b thirty *1-2* (twenty *2e-6*)

[3] LJ (A) vi.134–5 comments that 'From the fall of the Roman empire till the discovery of the Span. West Indies prices continually rose, since which they have fallen, unless at the Revolution when they rose for some time.' Cf. LJ (B) 254, ed. Cannan 198.

[4] 'It hath been found that the value of all the Wheat fit for bread, if mixed together, would be eight ninths of the value of the best Wheat, and the same proportion may reasonable be supposed in Barley'. (C. Smith, *Three Tracts on the Corn Trade and Corn Laws* (2nd ed., London, 1766), 104.)

been 2*l*. 11*s*. 0*d*. $\frac{1}{3}$; which is only 1*s*. 0*d*. $\frac{1}{3}$ dearer than it had been during the sixteen years before. But in the course of these sixty-four years there happened two events which must have produced a much greater scarcity of corn than what the course of the seasons would otherwise have occasioned, and which, therefore, without supposing any further reduction in the value of silver, will much more than account for this very small enhancement of price.

3   The first of these events was the civil war, which, by discouraging tillage and interrupting commerce, must have raised the price of corn much above what the course of the seasons would otherwise have occasioned. It must have had this effect more or less at all the different markets in the kingdom, but particularly at those in the neighbourhood of London, which require to be supplied from the greatest distance. In 1648, accordingly, the price of the best wheat at Windsor market, appears, from the same accounts, to have been 4*l*. 5*s*. and in 1649 to have been 4*l*. the quarter of nine bushels. The excess of those two years above 2*l*. 10*s*. (the average price of the sixteen years preceding 1637) is 3*l*. 5*s*.; which divided among the sixty-four last years of the last century, will alone very nearly account for that small enhancement of price which seems to have taken place in them. These, however, though the highest, are by no [303] means the only high prices which seem to have been occasioned by the civil wars.

4   The second event was the bounty upon the exportation of corn, granted in 1688.[1] The bounty, it has been thought by many people, by encouraging tillage,[2] may, in a long course of years, have occasioned a greater abundance, and consequently a greater cheapness of corn in the home-market, than what would otherwise have taken place there. *a*How far the bounty could produce this effect at any time,[3] I shall examine hereafter;[4] I shall only observe at present, that*a* between 1688 and 1700, it had *b*not*b* time to produce *c*any such*c* effect. During this short period its only effect must have been, by encouraging the exportation of the surplus produce of every year, and thereby hindering the abundance of one year from compensating the scarcity of another, to raise the price in the home-market. The scarcity which prevailed in England from 1693 to 1699, both inclusive, though no doubt principally owing to the badness of the seasons, and, therefore, extending through a considerable part of Europe, must have been some-

---

a-a But *1*   *b-b* no *1*   *c-c* this *1*

[1] 1 William and Mary, c. 12 (1688). When malt or barley did not exceed 24*s*. per Winchester quarter, rye, 32*s*., wheat 48*s*., the bounties per quarter were 2*s*. 6*d*. for malt or barley, 3*s*. 6*d*. for rye, and 5*s*. for wheat. See below, III.iv.20, IV.v.a.5, IV.v.b.37, V.ii.k.13.

[2] See below, IV.v.a.7.

[3] The impact of the bounty on the state of tillage is considered in LJ (A) vi.95; cf. LJ (B) 233, ed. Cannan 180.

[4] Below, IV.v.

what enhanced by the bounty. In 1699, accordingly, the further exportation of corn was prohibited for nine months.[5]

5   There was a third event which occurred in the course of the same
period, and which, though it could not occasion any scarcity of corn, nor,
perhaps, any augmentation in the real quantity of silver which was usually
paid for it, must necessarily have occasioned some augmentation in
[304] the nominal sum. This event was the great ᵈdebasementᵈ of the silver
coin, by clipping and wearing. This evil had begun in the reign of Charles
II. and had gone on continually increasing till 1695;[6] at which time, as we
may learn from Mr. Lowndes, the current silver coin was, at an average,
near five-and-twenty per cent. below its standard value.[7] But the nominal
sum which constitutes the market-price of every commodity is necessarily
regulated, not so much by the quantity of silver, which, according to the
standard, ought to be contained in it, as by that which, it is found by
experience, actually is contained in it. This nominal sum, therefore, is
necessarily higher when the coin is much ᵉdebasedᵉ by clipping and wearing, than when near to its standard value.

6   In the course of the present century, the silver coin has not at any time
been more below its standard weight than it is at present. But though very
much defaced, its value has been kept up by that of the gold coin for which
it is exchanged. For though before the late re-coinage,[8] the gold coin was
a good deal defaced too, it was less so than the silver. In 1695, on the contrary, the value of the silver coin was not kept up by the gold coin; a
guinea then commonly exchanging for thirty shillings of the worn and
clipt silver.[9] Before the late re-coinage of the gold, the price of silver
bullion was seldom higher than five shillings and seven-pence an ounce,
which is but five-pence above the mint price. But in 1695, the common
price of silver bullion was six shil-[305]lings and five-pence an ounce*,
which is fifteen-pence above the mint price. Even before the late recoinage of the gold, therefore, the coin, gold and silver together, when
compared with silver bullion, was not supposed to be more than eight per

---

ᶠ* Lowndes's Essay on the Silver Coin, p. 68.ᶠ

ᵈ⁻ᵈ degradation *1*   ᵉ⁻ᵉ degraded *1*   ᶠ⁻ᶠ 2–6

⁵ 10 William III, c.3. The prohibition was for one year from 10 February 1699.
⁶ Though clipping had been reducing the weight of coins for a century, the price of
silver bullion began to rise only in 1694, and very sharply only in 1695. J. K. Horsefield,
British Monetary Experiments 1650–1710 (Cambridge Mass., 1960), 11 and 27.
⁷ 'I infer, *First*, That the Moneys commonly Currant are Diminished near one Half,
to wit, in a Proportion something greater than that of Ten to Twenty two.' (W. Lowndes,
Report, 107.) Lowndes is mentioned below, IV.iii.a.9.
⁸ The recoinage of 1774 is considered at I.v.29 and IV.vi.18.
⁹ 'The value of the Silver in the Coin ought to be Raised to the Foot of Six Shillings
Three Pence in every Crown, because the Price of Standard Silver in Bullion is Risen
(from divers necessary and unnecessary Causes, producing at length a great scarcity
thereof in *England*) to Six Shillings Five Pence an Ounce.' (W. Lowndes, *Report*, 68.)

cent. below its standard value. In 1695, on the contrary, it had been supposed to be near five-and-twenty per cent. below that value. But in the beginning of the present century, that is, immediately after the great recoinage in King William's time, the greater part of the current silver coin must have been still nearer to its standard weight than it is at present. In the course of the present century too there has been no great publick calamity, such as the civil war, which could either discourage tillage, or interrupt the interior commerce of the country. And though the bounty, which has taken place through the greater part of this century, must always raise the price of corn somewhat higher than it otherwise would be in the actual state of tillage; yet as, in the course of this century, the bounty has had full time to produce all the good effects commonly imputed to it, to encourage tillage, and thereby to increase the quantity of corn in the home market, it may^g, upon the principles of a system which I shall explain and examine hereafter,^{g10} be supposed to have done something to lower the price of that commodity the one way, as well as to raise it the other. It is by many people supposed to have done more ^{h} . [306] In the sixty-four ^{i}first^i years of the present century accordingly, the average price of the quarter of nine bushels of the best wheat at Windsor market, appears, by the accounts of Eton College, to have been 2*l*. 0*s*. 6$d\frac{19}{32}$,^{11} which is about ten shillings and sixpence, or more than five-and-twenty per cent.^{12} cheaper than it had been during the sixty-four last years of the last century; and about nine shillings and six-pence cheaper than it had been during the sixteen years preceding 1636, when the discovery of the abundant mines of America may be supposed to have produced its full effect; and about one shilling cheaper than it had been in the twenty-six years preceding 1620, before that discovery can well be supposed to have produced its full effect. According to this account, the average price of middle wheat, during these sixty-four first years of the present century, comes out to have been about thirty-two shillings the quarter of eight bushels.

7   The value of silver, therefore, seems to have risen somewhat in proportion to that of corn during the course of the present century, and it had probably begun to do so even some time before the end of the last.

8   In 1687, the price of the quarter of nine bushels of the best wheat at Windsor market was 1*l*. 5*s*. 2*d*. the lowest price at which it had ever been from 1595.

$^{g-g}$ 2–6 ^{h}; a notion which I shall examine hereafter $_I$ $^{i-i}$ *om.* 5–6

---

^{10} See below, IV.v.a. ^{11} A mistake. $\frac{19}{32}$ should read $\frac{9}{32}$. See below (274).
^{12} A mistake. The reduction is about 21·5 per cent. The fall has been calculated on the average of £2. 0*s*. 6 $\frac{19}{32}$*d*. for 1701 to 1764 instead of on the average of £2. 11*s*. 0$\frac{1}{2}$*d*. for 1637 to 1700.

9   In 1688, Mr. Gregory King, a man famous for his knowledge in matters
of this kind, estimated the average price of wheat in years of [307] moderate
plenty to be to the grower 3*s*. 6*d*. the bushel, or eight-and-twenty shillings
the quarter.[13] The grower's price I understand to be the same with what is
sometimes called the contract price, or the price at which a farmer contracts for a certain number of years to deliver a certain quantity of corn to a
dealer. As a contract of this kind saves the farmer the expence and trouble
of marketing, the contract price is generally lower than what is supposed
to be the average market price. Mr. King had judged eight-and-twenty
shillings the quarter to be at that time the ordinary contract price in years
of moderate plenty. Before the scarcity occasioned by the late extraordinary course of bad seasons, it was*ʲ*, I have been assured,*ʲ* the ordinary
contract price in all common years.

10   In 1688 was granted the parliamentary bounty upon the exportation
of corn.[14] The country gentlemen, who then composed a still greater
proportion of the legislature than they do at present,[15] had felt that the
money price of corn was falling. The bounty was an expedient to raise it
artificially to the high price at which it had frequently been sold in the
times of Charles I. and II. It was to take place, therefore, till wheat was so
high as forty-eight shillings the quarter; that is twenty shillings, or $\frac{5}{7}$ths
dearer than Mr. King had in that very year estimated the grower's price
to be in times of moderate plenty. If his calculations deserve any part of
the reputation which they have obtained very universally, eight-and-forty
shillings the quarter, [308] was a price which, without some such expedient
as the bounty, could not at that time be expected, except in years of extraordinary scarcity. But the government of King William was not then fully
settled. It was in no condition to refuse any thing to the country gentlemen,
from whom it was at that very time soliciting the first establishment of the
annual land-tax.[16]

11   The value of silver, therefore, in proportion to that of corn, had probably
risen somewhat before the end of the last century; and it seems to have
continued to do so during the course of the greater part of the present;[17]
though the necessary operation of the bounty must have hindered that

ʲ⁻ʲ 2–6

[13] Gregory King, *State and Condition of England, 1688*, in G. Chalmers, *Comparative
Strength of Great Britain to 1803*, 53; quoted in C. D'avenant, *Political and Commercial
Works*, ed. C. Whitworth, ii.217, who adds 'this value is what the same is worth upon the
spot where the corn grew; but this value is increased by the carriage to the place where it
is at last spent, at least ¼ part more.' King is mentioned above, I.viii.34.
[14] 1 William and Mary, c.12 (1688). See I.xi.g.4.
[15] See below, IV.v.a.23, where Smith comments on the futility of this policy.
[16] In LJ (A) vi.139 the yield of the land tax in King William's time, calculated at 4*s*.
in the pound, is stated to have been £2·5 million in England. See also LJ (B) 234, ed.
Cannan 181.
[17] Cf. IV.i.14 and IV.v.a.5.

rise from being so sensible as it otherwise would have been in the actual state of tillage.

12   In plentiful years the bounty, by occasioning an extraordinary exportation, necessarily raises the price of corn above what it otherwise would be in those years. To encourage tillage, by keeping up the price of corn even in the most plentiful years, was the avowed end of the institution.

13   In years of great scarcity, indeed, the bounty has generally been suspended. It must, however, have had some effect ᵏevenᵏ upon the prices of many of those years. By the extraordinary exportation which it occasions in years of plenty, it must frequently hinder the plenty of one year from compensating the scarcity of another.

14   Both in years of plenty and in years of scarcity, therefore, the bounty raises the price of corn above what it naturally would be in the [309] actual state of tillage. If, during the sixty-four first years of the present century, therefore, the average price has been lower than during the sixty-four last years of the last century, it must, in the same state of tillage, have been much more so, had it not been for this operation of the bounty.[18]

15   But without the bounty, it may be said, the state of tillage would not have been the same. What may have been the effects of this institution upon the agriculture of the country, I shall endeavour to explain hereafter, when I come to treat particularly of bounties. I shall only observe at present, that this rise in the value of silver, in proportion to that of corn, has not been peculiar to England. It has been observed to have taken place in France during the same period, and nearly in the same proportion too, by three very faithful, diligent, and laborious collectors of the prices of corn, Mr. Duprè de St. Maur, Mr. Messance, and the author of the Essay on the police of grain.[19] But in France, till 1764, the exportation of grain was by law prohibited;[20] and it is somewhat difficult to suppose, that nearly the same diminution of price which took place in one country, notwithstanding this prohibition, should in another be owing to the extraordinary encouragement given to exportation.

16   It would be more proper, perhaps, to consider this variation in the average money price of corn as the effect rather of some gradual rise in the real value of silver in the European market, [310] than of any fall in the real average value of corn. Corn, it has already been observed,[21] is at distant periods of time a more accurate measure of value than either silver, or perhaps any other commodity. When, after the discovery of the abundant

ᵏ⁻ᵏ *om. 5–6*

---

[18] Below, IV.v.a.7.

[19] Smith refers to Messance above, I.viii.49, as an author of 'great knowledge and ingenuity'. In Letter 115 addressed to Hailes, dated 15 January 1769, wherein Smith reviewed a number of printed authorities, Messance was described as 'the most judicious author of them all'. See also I.xi.n.5.

[20] Below, IV.v.a.5 and IV.ix.38.   [21] Above, I.v.15.

mines of America, corn rose to three and four times its former money price, this change was universally ascribed, not to any rise in the real value of corn, but to a fall in the real value of silver. If during the sixty-four first years of the present century, therefore, the average money price of corn has fallen somewhat below what it had been during the greater part of the last century, we should in the same manner impute this change, not to any fall in the real value of corn, but to some rise in the real value of silver in the European market.

17   The high price of corn during these ten or twelve years past, indeed, has occasioned a suspicion that the real value of silver still continues to fall in the European market. This high price of corn, however, seems evidently to have been the effect of the extraordinary unfavourableness of the seasons, and ought therefore to be regarded, not as a permanent, but as a transitory and occasional event. The seasons for these ten or twelve years past have been unfavourable through the greater part of Europe;[22] and the disorders of Poland have very much increased the scarcity in all those countries, which, in dear years, used to be supplied from that market.[23] So long a course of bad seasons, though not a very common event, is by no means a singular one; and whoever [311] has enquired much into the history of the prices of corn in former times, will be at no loss to recollect several other examples of the same kind. Ten years of extraordinary scarcity, besides, are not more wonderful than ten years of extraordinary plenty. The low price of corn from 1741 to 1750, both inclusive, may very well be set in opposition to its high price during these last eight or ten years. From 1741 to 1750, the average price of the quarter of nine bushels of the best wheat at Windsor market, it appears from the accounts of Eton College, was only 1*l.* 13*s.* 9*d.*$\frac{4}{5}$, which is nearly 6*s.* 3*d.* below the average price of the sixty-four first years of the present century. The average price of the quarter of eight bushels of middle wheat, comes out, according to this account, to have been, during these ten years, only 1*l.* 6*s.* 8*d.*[24]

18   Between 1741 and 1750, however, the bounty must have hindered the price of corn from falling so low in the home market as it naturally would have done. During these ten years the quantity of all sorts of grain exported, it appears from the custom-house books, amounted to no less than eight millions twenty-nine thousand one hundred and fifty-six quarters one bushel. The bounty paid for this amounted to 1,514,962*l.* 17*s.* 4*d.*$\frac{1}{2}$.[25] In 1749 accordingly, Mr. Pelham, at that time prime minister,

---

[22] A view which is supported by recent investigations. The weather in the early 1770s seems to have been unfavourable. E. L. Jones, *Seasons and Prices* (London, 1964), 144–6.

[23] See below, I.xi.n.1.

[24] The sum of £1. 6*s.* 8*d.* is obtained by deducting one-ninth from £1 13*s.* 9$\frac{4}{5}$*d.* to allow for the difference in measure, and then by deducting one-ninth from the remainder to take account of the difference in quality. See above, I.xi.f.4.

[25] The amounts said to have been paid in bounties in this paragraph were derived by multiplying the figures for grain exported given in C. Smith, *Three Tracts on the Corn*

observed to the House of Commons,[26] that for the three years preceding, a very extraordinary sum had been paid as bounty for the exportation of corn. [312] He had good reason to make this observation, and in the following year he might have had still better. In that single year the bounty paid amounted to no less than 324,176*l.* 10*s.* 6*d.*[*27] It is unnecessary to observe how much this forced exportation must have raised the price of corn above what it otherwise would have been in the home market.

19   At the end of the accounts annexed to this chapter the reader will find the particular account of those ten years separated from the rest. He will find there too the particular account of the preceding ten years, of which the average is likewise below, though not so much below, the general average of the sixty-four first years of the century. The year 1740, however, was a year of extraordinary scarcity. These twenty years preceding 1750, may very well be set in opposition to the twenty preceding 1770. As the former were a good deal below the general average of the century, notwithstanding the intervention of one or two dear years; so the latter have been a good deal above it, notwithstanding the intervention of one or two cheap ones, of 1759, for example.[28] If the former have not been as much below the general average, as the latter have been above it, we ought probably to impute it to the bounty. The change has evidently been too sudden to be ascribed to any change in the value of silver, which is always slow and gradual. The suddenness of the effect can be [313] accounted for only by a cause which can operate suddenly, the accidental variation of the seasons.

20   The money price of labour in Great Britain has, indeed, risen during the course of the present century.[29] This, however, seems to be the effect,

---

[*] See Tracts on the Corn Trade; Tract 3d.[1]

[1-1] 2–6

Trade and Corn Laws (London, 1766), 110–11, by the bounties quoted ibid., 81 n. See above, 212, n. 1.

[26] 'It is hardly possible to suppose, that the provisions necessary for the poor can be dear in this country, where there is such a superabundance of corn, that incredible quantities have been lately exported. I should be afraid to mention what quantities have been exported, if it did not appear upon our custom-house books; but from them it appears, that lately there was in three months' time above £220,000 paid for bounties upon corn exported; and all our other exports have, since the peace, been more considerable than they had ever been for many years before.' (Cobbett's *Parliamentary History*, xiv (1747–53), col. 589 (1749).)

[27] See below, IV.v.a.39, where it is stated that the bounty had sometimes cost more than £300,000. Cf. V.ii.k.29.

[28] Smith's figures at the end of the chapter do not continue to 1770 but stop in 1764. It is difficult to see why he cites 1759 as a cheap year, since the price he gives for 1761 is 9*s.* 7*d.* lower.

[29] There were regional variations. The index of money wages in London rose from 100 in 1700 to 118 in 1776; in Lancashire from 100 to 200. The comparable indices of real wages were 100 to 98 and 100 to 167. E. W. Gilboy, 'The Cost of Living and Real Wages in Eighteenth Century England', *Review of Economic Statistics*, xviii (1936), 134–43.

not so much of any diminution in the value of silver in the European market, as of an increase in the demand for labour in Great Britain, arising from the great, and almost universal prosperity of the country. In France, a country not altogether so prosperous, the money price of labour has, since the middle of the last century, been observed to sink gradually with the average money price of corn. Both in the last century and in the present, the day-wages of common labour are there said to have been pretty uniformly about the twentieth part of the average price of the septier of wheat, a measure which contains a little more than four Winchester bushels. In Great Britain the real recompence of labour, it has already been shown,[30] the real *m*quantities*m* of the necessaries and conveniencies of life which are given to the labourer, has increased considerably during the course of the present century. The rise in its money price seems to have been the effect, not of any diminution of the value of silver in the general market of Europe, but of a rise in the real price of labour in the particular market of Great Britain, owing to the peculiarly happy circumstances of the country.

21   For some time after the first discovery of America, silver would continue to sell at its [314] former, or not much below its former price. The profits of mining would for some time be very great, and much above their natural rate. Those who imported that metal into Europe, however, would soon find that the whole annual importation could not be disposed of at this high price. Silver would gradually exchange for a smaller and a smaller quantity of goods. Its price would sink gradually lower and lower till it fell to its natural price; or to what was just sufficient to pay, according to their natural rates, the wages of the labour, the profits of the stock, and the rent of the land, which must be paid in order to bring it from the mine to the market. In the greater part of the silver mines of Peru, the tax of the king of Spain, amounting to a *n*tenth*n* of the gross produce, eats up, it has already been observed,[31] the whole rent of the land. This tax was originally a half; it soon afterwards fell to a third, *o* then to a fifth, *p*and at last to a tenth,*p* at which rate it still continues. In the greater part of the silver mines of Peru this, it seems, is all that remains after replacing the stock of the undertaker of the work, together with its ordinary profits; and it seems to be universally acknowledged that these profits, which were once very high, are now as low as they can well be, consistently with carrying on *q*the*q* works.

22   The tax of the king of Spain was reduced to a fifth *r*part*r* of the registered silver in 1504*, one-[315] and-*t*forty*t* years before *u*1545*u*, the date of the

*s** Solorzano, vol. ii.*s* [Solorzano-Pereira, *De Indiarum Jure* (Madrid, 1777), ii.883.]

m–m quantity *1*.   *n–n* fifth *1*   *o* and *1*   *p–p* 2–6   *q–q* their 5–6
r–r om. 6   *s–s* 2–6   *t–t* thirty *1*   *u–u* 1535 *1*

[30] Above, I.viii.35.   [31] Above, I.xi.c.25.

discovery of the mines of Potosi.[32] In the course of *ᵛninety yearsᵛ*, or before 1636, these mines, the most fertile in all America, had time sufficient to produce their full effect, or to reduce the value of silver in the European market as low as it could well fall, while it continued to pay this tax to the king of Spain. *ᵂNinetyᵂ* years is time sufficient to reduce any commodity, of which there is no monopoly, to its natural price, or to the lowest price at which, while it pays a particular tax, it can continue to be sold for any considerable time together.[33]

23   The price of silver in the European market might perhaps have fallen still lower, and it might have become necessary either to *ˣreduceˣ* the tax upon it, *ʸnot only to one tenth, as in 1736, but to one twentieth,ʸ* in the same manner as that upon gold, or to give up working the greater part of the American mines which are now wrought. The gradual increase of the demand for silver, or the gradual enlargement of the market for the produce of the silver mines of America, is probably the cause which has prevented this from happening, and which has not only kept up the value of silver in the European market, but has perhaps even raised it somewhat higher than it was about the middle of the last century.

24   Since the first discovery of America, the market for the produce of its silver mines has been growing gradually more and more extensive.

25   [316] First, The market of Europe has become gradually more and more extensive. Since the discovery of America, the greater part of Europe has been much improved. England, Holland, France, and Germany; even Sweden, Denmark, and Russia, have all advanced considerably both in agriculture and in manufactures. Italy seems not to have gone backwards. The fall of Italy preceded the conquest of Peru. Since that time it seems rather to have recovered a little. Spain and Portugal, indeed, are supposed to have gone backwards. Portugal, however, is but a very small part of Europe, and the declension of Spain is not, perhaps, so great as is commonly imagined. In the beginning of the sixteenth century, Spain was a very poor country, even in comparison with France, which has been so much improved since that time. It was the well-known remark of the Emperor Charles V. who had travelled so frequently through both countries, that every thing abounded in France, but that every thing was wanting in Spain. The increasing produce of the agriculture and manufactures of Europe must necessarily have required a gradual increase in the quantity of silver coin to circulate it; and the increasing number of wealthy individuals must have required the like increase in the quantity of their plate and other ornaments of silver.

ᵛ⁻ᵛ a century *1*   *ᵂ⁻ᵂ* A hundred *1*   *ˣ⁻ˣ* lower *1*   *ʸ⁻ʸ* 2⁻6

[32] Date given in Juan and Ulloa, *Voyage historique*, i.521–2, trans. John Adams, ii.146–7.
[33] See above, I.vii.6.

26   Secondly, America is itself a new market for the produce of its own silver
mines; and as its advances in agriculture, industry, and population, are
much more rapid than those of the most [317] thriving countries in Europe,
its demand must increase much more rapidly. The English colonies are
altogether a new market, which, partly for coin and partly for plate, requires a continually augmenting supply of silver through a great continent
where there never was any demand before. The greater part too of the
Spanish and Portuguese colonies are altogether new markets. New
Granada, the Yucatan, Paraguay, and the Brazils were, before discovered
by the Europeans, inhabited by savage nations, who had neither arts nor
agriculture. A considerable degree of both has now been introduced into
all of them. Even Mexico and Peru, though they cannot be considered
as altogether new markets, are certainly much more extensive ones than
they ever were before. After all the wonderful tales which have been
published concerning the splendid state of those countries in antient times,
whoever reads, with any degree of sober judgment, the history of their
first discovery and conquest, will evidently discern that, in arts, agriculture,
and commerce, their inhabitants were much more ignorant than the Tartars of the Ukraine are at present. Even the Peruvians, the more civilized
nation of the two, though they made use of gold and silver as ornaments,
had no coined money of any kind. Their whole commerce was carried on by
barter, and there was accordingly scarce any division of labour among
them.[34] Those who cultivated the ground were obliged to build their own
houses, to make their own houshold furniture, their own [318] clothes,
shoes, and instruments of agriculture. The few artificers among them are
said to have been all maintained by the sovereign, the nobles, and the
priests, and were probably their servants or slaves. All the ancient arts
of Mexico and Peru have never furnished one single manufacture to
Europe. The Spanish armies, though they scarce ever exceeded five
hundred men, and frequently did not amount to half that number, found
almost every where great difficulty in procuring subsistence. The famines
which they are said to have occasioned almost wherever they went, in
countries too which at the same time are represented as very populous and
well-cultivated, sufficiently demonstrate that the story of this populousness
and high cultivation is in a great measure fabulous. The Spanish colonies
are under a government in many respects less favourable to agriculture,
improvement and population, than that of the English colonies.[35] They

[34] See above, I.iv.2, where Smith discusses the inconveniences of barter, and below,
IV.vii.b.7, where Mexico is cited in addition to Peru as an example of such an economy.
See, however, LJ (A) vi.117–18: 'The Europeans, on their first going into China, Mexico,
Peru, and all the eastern countries, found metalls used as the instruments of commerce,
and they had the publick stamp upon them . . .'
[35] See below, IV.vii.b.7–9. Smith comments on the advantage of English institutions
to the colonies at IV.vii.b.16–25.

seem, however, to be advancing in all these much more rapidly than any country in Europe. In a fertile soil and happy climate, the great abundance and cheapness of land, a circumstance common to all new colonies,[36] is, it seems, so great an advantage as to compensate many defects in civil government. Frezier, who visited Peru in 1713, represents Lima as containing between twenty-five and twenty-eight thousand inhabitants.[37] Ulloa, who resided in the same country between 1740 and 1746, represents it as containing more than fifty thousand.[38] The difference in their accounts of the populous-[319]ness of several other principal towns in Chili and Peru is nearly the same;[39] and as there seems to be no reason to doubt of the good information of either, it marks an increase which is scarce inferior to that of the English colonies. America, therefore, is a new market for the produce of its own silver mines, of which the demand must increase much more rapidly than that of the most thriving country in Europe.

27   Thirdly, The East Indies is another market for the produce of the silver mines of America, and a market which, from the time of the first discovery of those mines, has been continually taking off a greater and a greater quantity of silver. Since that time, the direct trade between America and the East Indies, which is carried on by means of the Acapulco ships,[40] has been continually augmenting, and the indirect intercourse by the way of Europe has been augmenting in a still greater proportion. During the sixteenth century, the Portuguese were the only European nation who carried on any regular trade to the East Indies. In the last years of that century the Dutch began to encroach upon this monopoly, and in a few years expelled them from their principal settlements in India. During the greater part of the last century those two nations divided the most considerable part of the East India trade between them; the trade of the Dutch

[36] This point is made at I.ix.11, IV.vii.b.2 and 6.

[37] 'The number of *Spanish* Families in Lima may make up about 8 or 9,000 Whites; the rest are only Mestizo's, Mulatto's, Blacks and some Indians; tho' in the whole, there are about 25 or 30,000 Souls, including the Friers and Nuns, who take up at least a Quarter of the City.' (A. F. Frézier, *A Voyage to the South Sea*, 218.)

[38] The same figure is cited below, IV.vii.b.7. Juan and Ulloa do not quote an exact figure but state: 'the inhabitants of Lima are composed of whites, or Spaniards, Negroes, Indians, Mestizos and other casts proceeding from the mixture of all three.' Of Spanish families there were 'sixteen or eighteen thousand whites'; 'the Negroes, Mulattoes, and their descendants, form the greatest number of the inhabitants'; the Indians and Mestizos 'are very small in proportion to the largeness of the city, and the multitudes of the second class'. (*Voyage historique*, i.443–5, trans. John Adams, ii.52–5.)

[39] Juan and Ulloa (*Voyage historique*, i.468 and ii.49, trans. John Adams, ii.84 and 258) gave Callao as having a population of 4,000 and Santiago 'at about four thousand families'. Frézier (*A Voyage to the South Sea*, 102 and 202) suggests the number of inhabitants in Callao does not exceed 400 'tho' they reckon 600'; in Santiago, 2,000 white, with the rest about three times as great without including 'Friendly Indians', whom he puts at 15,000.

[40] One ship, and after 1720 two ships, were to sail from Acapulco to the Philippines. Details of the trade, particularly of what could be carried are in G. de Uztariz, *The Theory and Practice of Commerce*, translated by John Kippax (London, 1751), i.206–8.

continually augmenting in a still greater proportion than that of the Portuguese declined. The English and French carried on some trade [320] with India in the last century, but it has been greatly augmented in the course of the present. The East India trade of the Swedes and Danes began in the course of the present century. Even the Muscovites now trade regularly with China by a sort of caravans which go over land through Siberia and Tartary to Pekin. The East India trade of all these nations, if we except that of the French, which the last war had well nigh annihilated, has been almost continually augmenting. The increasing consumption of East India goods in Europe is, it seems, so great, as to afford a gradual increase of employment to them all. Tea, for example, was a drug very little used in Europe before the middle of the last century. At present the value of the tea annually imported by the English East India Company, for the use of their own countrymen, amounts to more than a million and a half a year; and even this is not enough; a great deal more being constantly smuggled into the country from the ports of Holland, from Gottenburg in Sweden, and from the coast of France too, as long as the French East India Company was in prosperity. The consumption of the porcelain of China, of the spiceries of the Moluccas, of the piece goods of Bengal, and of innumerable other articles, has increased very nearly in a like proportion. The tonnage accordingly of all the European shipping employed in the East India trade, at any one time during the last century, was not, perhaps, much greater than [321] that of the English East India Company before the late reduction of their shipping.[41]

28   But in the East Indies, particularly in China and Indostan, the value of the precious metals, when the Europeans first began to trade to those countries, was much higher than in Europe; and it still continues to be so. In rice countries, which generally yield two, sometimes three crops in the year, each of them more plentiful than any common crop of corn, the abundance of food must be much greater than in any corn country of equal extent.[42] Such countries are accordingly much more populous. In them too the rich, having a greater super-abundance of food to dispose of beyond what they themselves can consume, have the means of purchasing a much greater quantity of the labour of other people. The retinue of a grandee in China or Indostan accordingly is, by all accounts, much more numerous and splendid than that of the richest subjects in Europe. The same super-abundance of food, of which they have the disposal, enables them to give a greater quantity of it for all those singular and rare productions which nature furnishes but in very small quantities; such as the

----

[41] 12 George III, c.54 (1772) prohibited the East India Company from building ships at home until its total tonnage in service was below 45,000 tons and from employing ships constructed after March 1772. The objective was to conserve supplies of timber.

[42] See above, I.xi.b.37.

precious metals and the precious stones, the great objects of the competition of the rich.[43] Though the mines, therefore, which supplied the Indian
market had been as abundant as those which supplied the European, such
commodities would naturally exchange for a greater quantity of food in
India than in Europe. But the mines which supplied the Indian [322]
market with the precious metals seem to have been a good deal less abundant, and those which supplied it with the precious stones a good deal more
so, than the mines which supplied the European. The precious metals,
therefore, would naturally exchange ²in India² for somewhat a greater
quantity of the precious stones, and for a much greater quantity of food
ᵃ than in Europe.[44] The money price of diamonds, the greatest of all superfluities, would be somewhat lower, and that of food, the first of all necessaries, a great deal lower in the one country than in the other. But the real
price of labour, the real quantity of the necessaries of life which is given
to the labourer, it has already been observed,[45] is lower both in China and
Indostan, the two great markets of India, than it is through the greater part
of Europe. The wages of the labourer will there purchase a smaller quantity
of food; and as the money price of food is much lower in India than in
Europe, the money price of labour is there lower upon a double account;
upon account both of the small quantity of food which it will purchase,
and of the low price of that food. But in countries of equal art and industry,
the money price of the greater part of manufactures will be in proportion
to the money price of labour; and in manufacturing art and industry,
China and Indostan, though inferior, seem not to be much inferior to any
part of Europe. The money price of the greater part of manufactures,
therefore, will naturally be much lower in those great empires than it is
any-where in Europe. Through the greater part of Europe too the expence
of [323] land-carriage increases very much both the real and nominal
price of most manufactures. It costs more labour, and therefore more
money, to bring first the materials, and afterwards the compleat manufacture to market. In China and Indostan the extent and variety of inland
navigations[46] save the greater part of this labour, and consequently of this
money, and thereby reduce still lower both the real and the nominal price
of the greater part of their manufactures. Upon all these accounts, the
precious metals are a commodity which it always has been, and still continues to be, extremely advantageous to carry from Europe to India. There
is scarce any commodity which brings a better price there; or which, in
proportion to the quantity of labour and commodities which it costs in
Europe, will purchase or command a greater quantity of labour and
commodities in India. It is more advantageous too to carry silver thither

²⁻² 2–6   ᵃ in India 1

[43] A similar point is made above, I.xi.c.36.   [44] See below, I.xi.h.2.
[45] Above, I.viii.24.   [46] See above, I.iii.7.

than gold; because in China, and the greater part of the other markets of India, the proportion between fine silver and fine gold is but as ten[b], or at most as twelve,[b] to one; whereas in Europe it is as fourteen or fifteen to one.[47] In China, and the greater part of the other markets of India, ten[c], or at most twelve,[c] ounces of silver will purchase an ounce of gold: in Europe it requires from fourteen to fifteen ounces. In the cargoes, therefore, of the greater part of European ships which sail to India, silver has generally been one of the most valuable articles. It is the most valuable article in the Acapulco ships which [324] sail to Manilla. The silver of the new continent seems in this manner to be [d]one of the principal commodities[d] by which the commerce between the two extremities of the old one is carried on, and it is by means of it[e], in a great measure,[e] that those distant parts of the world are connected with one another.

29   In order to supply so very widely extended a market, the quantity of silver annually brought from the mines must not only be sufficient to support that continual increase both of coin and of plate which is required in all thriving countries; but to repair that continual waste and consumption of silver which takes place in all countries where that metal is used.

30   The continual consumption of the precious metals in coin by wearing, and in plate both by wearing and cleaning, is very sensible; and in commodities of which the use is so very widely extended, would alone require a very great annual supply. The consumption of those metals in some particular manufactures, though it may not perhaps be greater upon the whole than this gradual consumption, is, however, much more sensible, as it is much more rapid. In the manufactures of Birmingham alone, the quantity of gold and siver annually employed in gilding and plating, and thereby disqualified from ever afterwards appearing in the shape of those metals, is said to amount to more than fifty thousand pounds sterling. We may from thence form some notion how great must be the annual

---

[b]-[b] 2–6   [c]-[c] 2–6   [d]-[d] the principal commodity *1*   [e]-[e] chiefly *1*

---

[47] 'In Japan where there are a good many silver mines the ratio of gold to silver is today 1 to 8: in China 1 to 10: in the other countries of the Indies on this side 1 to 11, 1 to 12, 1 to 13, and 1 to 14, as we get nearer to the West and to Europe.' (Cantillon, *Essai*, 365, ed. Higgs 275.) 'In Japan, the proportion of gold to silver, is as one to eight; in China, as one to ten; in other parts of India, as one to eleven, twelve, thirteen or fourteen, as we advance further west. The like variations are to be met in with Europe . . . When Columbus penetrated into America, the proportion was less than one to twelve. The quantity of these metals which was then brought from Mexico and Peru, not only made them more common, but still increased the value of gold above silver, as there were greater plenty of the latter in those parts. Spain, that was of course the best judge of the proportion, settled it at one to fifteen in the coin of the kingdom; and this system, with some slight variations, was adopted throughout Europe.' (G. T. F. Raynal, *Histoire philosophique et politique des établissemens et du commerce des Européens dans les deux Indes* (Amsterdam, 1775), iii.381, translated by J. Justamond, *A Philosophical and Political History of the Settlements and Trade of the Europeans in the East and West Indies* (Edinburgh, 1777), ii.423–4.)

consumption in all the different parts of the world, [325] either in manufactures of the same kind with those of Birmingham, or in laces, embroideries, gold and silver stuffs, the gilding of books, furniture, &c. A considerable quantity too must be annually lost in transporting those metals from one place to another both by sea and by land. In the greater part of the governments of Asia, besides, the almost universal custom of concealing treasures in the bowels of the earth, of which the knowledge frequently dies with the person who makes the concealment, must occasion the loss of a still greater quantity.

31   The quantity of gold and silver imported at both Cadiz and Lisbon (including not only what comes under register, but what may be supposed to be smuggled) amounts, according to the best accounts, to about six millions sterling a year.

32   According to Mr. Meggens* the annual importation of the precious metals into Spain, at an average of six years; viz. from 1748 to 1753, both inclusive; and into Portugal, at an average of seven years; viz. from 1747 to 1753, both inclusive; amounted in silver to 1,101,107 pounds weight; and in gold to 49,940 pounds weight. The silver, at sixty-two shillings the pound Troy, amounts to 3,413,431*l.* 10*s.* sterling. The gold, at forty-four guineas and a [326] half the pound Troy, amounts to 2,333,446*l.* 14*s.* sterling.[48] Both together amount to 5,746,878*l.* 4*s.* sterling. The account of what was imported under register, he assures us is exact. He gives us the detail of the particular places from which the gold and silver were brought, and of the particular quantity of each metal, which, according to the register, each of them afforded. He makes an allowance too for the quantity of each metal which he supposes may have been smuggled. The great experience of this judicious merchant renders his opinion of considerable weight.

33   According to the eloquent and, sometimes, well-informed Author of the Philosophical and Political History of the establishment of the Europeans in the two Indies, the annual importation of registered gold and silver into Spain, at an average of eleven years; viz. from 1754 to 1764, both inclusive; amounted to 13,984,185 $\frac{939}{5}$ piastres of ten reals. On account of what may have been smuggled, however, the whole annual importation, he supposes, may have amounted to seventeen millions of piastres; which, at 4*s.* 6*d.* the piastre, is equal to 3,825,000 *l.* sterling. He gives the detail too of the

⸍ Postscript to the Universal Merchant, p. 15 and 16. This Postscript was not printed till 1756, three years after the publication of the book, which has never had a second edition. The postscript is, therefore, to be found in few copies. It corrects several errors in the book.⸍

⸍⁻⸍ 2–6   ᵍ⁻ᵍ $\frac{3}{4}$ 1

[48] It is stated below that the annual imports into Spain and Portugal does not much exceed six millions sterling, IV.i.28.

particular places from which the gold and silver were brought, and of the particular quantities of each metal which, according to the register, each of them afforded.[49] He informs us too, that if we were to judge of the quantity of gold annually imported from the Brazils into Lisbon by the amount of the tax paid to the [327] king of Portugal, which it seems is one-fifth of the standard metal, we might value it at eighteen millions of cruzadoes, or forty-five millions of French livres, equal to about two millions sterling. On account of what may have been smuggled, however, we may safely, he says, add to this sum an eighth more, or 250,000 *l.* sterling, so that the whole will amount to 2,250,000 *l.* sterling. According to this account, therefore, the whole annual importation of the precious metals into both Spain and Portugal, amounts to about 6,075,000 *l.* sterling.[50]

34   Several other very well authenticated*ʰ*, though manuscript,*ʰ* accounts, I have been assured, agree, in making this whole annual importation amount at an average to about six millions sterling, sometimes a little more, sometimes a little less.

35   The annual importation of the precious metals into Cadiz and Lisbon, indeed, is not equal to the whole annual produce of the mines of America. Some part is sent annually by the Acapulco ships to Manilla; some part is employed in the contraband trade which the Spanish colonies carry on with those of other European nations; and some part, no doubt, remains in the country. The mines of America, besides, are by no means the only gold and silver mines in the world. They are, however, by far the most abundant. The produce of all the other mines which are known, is insignificant, it is acknowledged, in comparison with theirs; and the far greater part of their produce, it is likewise acknowledged, is annually imported into Cadiz [328] and Lisbon. But the consumption of Birmingham alone, at the rate of fifty thousand pounds a year, is equal to the hundred-and-twentieth part of this annual importation at the rate of six millions a year. The whole annual consumption of gold and silver, therefore, in all the different countries of the world where those metals are used, may perhaps

ʰ⁻ʰ 2–6

---

[49] G. T. F. Raynal, *Histoire philosophique*, iii.307–8, trans. J. Justamond, ii.368–9.
[50] The same point is made below, I.xi.h.6. Cf. G. T. F. Raynal, *Histoire philosophique*, iii.380, trans. J. Justamond, ii.423:

> If we were to estimate the gold that Brazil annually yields, by the fifth that the king of Portugal receives, it would appear to be forty-five millions of livres [£1,968,750 according to Justamond]; but we shall not be taxed with exaggeration, if we suppose, that one-eighth of the duty is kept back, notwithstanding all the vigilance of government. To this account must be added the silver drawn from the illicit trade with Buenos Ayres, which was formerly immense; but the measures lately taken by Spain, have reduced it to about three millions [about £131,000 according to Justamond] a year.

Smith should have added to the total an amount for the illicit trade in silver.

be nearly equal to the whole annual produce. The remainder may be no more than sufficient to supply the increasing demand of all thriving countries. It may even have fallen so far short of this demand as somewhat to raise the price of those metals in the European market.

36   The quantity of brass and iron annually brought from the mine to the market is out of all proportion greater than that of gold and silver. We do not, however, upon this account, imagine that those coarse metals are likely to multiply beyond the demand, or to become gradually cheaper and cheaper. Why should we imagine that the precious metals are likely to do so? The coarse metals, indeed, though harder, are put to much harder uses, and, as they are of less value, less care is employed in their preservation. The precious metals, however, are not necessarily immortal any more than they, but are liable too to be lost, wasted, and consumed in a great variety of ways.

37   The price of all metals, though liable to slow and gradual variations, varies less from year to year than that of almost any other part of the rude produce of land;[51] and the price of the pre-[329]cious metals is even less liable to sudden variations than that of the coarse ones. The durableness of metals is the foundation of this extraordinary steadiness of price. The corn which was brought to market last year, will be all or almost all consumed long before the end of this year. But some part of the iron which was brought from the mine two or three hundred years ago, may be still in use, and perhaps some part of the gold which was brought from it two or three thousand years ago. The different masses of corn which in different years must supply the consumption of the world, will always be nearly in proportion to the respective produce of those different years. But the proportion between the different masses of iron which may be in use in two different years, will be very little affected by any accidental difference in the produce of the iron mines of those two years; and the proportion between the masses of gold will be still less affected by any such difference in the produce of the gold mines. Though the produce of the greater part of metallick mines, therefore, varies, perhaps, still more from year to year than that of the greater part of cornfields, those variations have not the same effect upon the price of the one species of commodities, as upon that of the other.

[330] *Variations in the Proportion between the respective Values of Gold and Silver*

1   Before the discovery of the mines of America, the value of fine gold to fine silver was regulated in the different mints of Europe, between the proportions of one to ten and one to twelve; that is, an ounce of fine gold was supposed to be worth from ten to twelve ounces of fine silver. About

[51] See above, I.v.16.

the middle of the last century it came to be regulated, between the proportions of one to fourteen and one to fifteen; that is, an ounce of fine gold came to be supposed worth between fourteen and fifteen ounces of fine silver. Gold rose in its nominal value, or in the quantity of silver which was given for it. Both metals sunk in their real value, or in the quantity of labour which they could purchase; but silver sunk more than gold. Though both the gold and silver mines of America exceeded in fertility all those which had ever been known before, the fertility of the silver mines had, it seems, been proportionably still greater than that of the gold ones.

2   The great quantities of silver carried annually from Europe to India, have, in some of the English settlements, gradually reduced the value of that metal in proportion to gold. In the mint of Calcutta, an ounce of fine gold is supposed to be worth fifteen ounces of fine silver, in the same manner as in Europe. It is in the mint perhaps rated too high for the value which it bears in the [331] market of Bengal. In China, the proportion of gold to silver still continues as one to ten[a], or one to twelve[a]. In Japan, it is said to be as one to eight.

3   The proportion between the quantities of gold and silver annually imported into Europe, according to Mr. Meggens's account, is as one to twenty-two nearly; that is, for one ounce of gold there are imported a little more than twenty-two ounces of silver. The great quantity of silver sent annually to the East Indies, reduces, he supposes, the quantities of those metals which remain in Europe to the proportion of one to fourteen or fifteen, the proportion of their values. The proportion between their values, he seems to think, must necessarily be the same as that between their quantities, and would therefore be as one to twenty-two, were it not for this greater exportation of silver.[1]

4   But the ordinary proportion between the respective values of two commodities is not necessarily the same as that between the quantities of them which are commonly in the market. The price of an ox, reckoned at ten guineas, is about threescore times the price of a lamb, reckoned at 3s. 6d.

[a-a] 2-6

[1] N. Magens, *The Universal Merchant*, ed. Horsley, 207, reprints Isaac Newton's *Representation to the Lords of the Treasury* and quotes: 'In China and Japan, 1 Pound Weight of fine Gold is worth but 9 or 10 Pounds Weight of fine Silver; and in East-India it may be worth 12. And this low Price of Gold in Proportion to Silver carries away the Silver from all *Europe*'. Magens adds in a note: 'Till about the Year 1732, we know of great Quantities of Silver going from *Europe* to *China*, to fetch Gold back, which has caused the Price of Gold in *China* to rise so much, that it is now not worth sending farther any Silver there.' Cantillon was less sure of the attractiveness of the trade in gold and silver 'Taking the ratio at 1 to 15 in England and 1 to 8 in Japan there would be more than 87 per cent. to gain by carrying silver from England to Japan and bringing back gold. But this difference is not enough in the ordinary course to pay the costs of so long and difficult a voyage.' (Cantillon, *Essai*, 370, ed. Higgs 279.)

It would be absurd, however, to infer from thence, that there are commonly in the market threescore lambs for one ox: and it would be just as absurd to infer, because an ounce of gold will commonly purchase from fourteen to fifteen ounces of silver, that there are commonly in the market only fourteen or fifteen ounces of silver for one ounce of gold.

5 [332] The quantity of silver commonly in the market, it is probable, is much greater in proportion to that of gold, than the value of a certain quantity of gold is to that of an equal quantity of silver. The whole quantity of a cheap commodity brought to market, is commonly not only greater, but of greater value, than the whole quantity of a dear one. The whole quantity of bread annually brought to market, is not only greater, but of greater value than the whole quantity of butcher's-meat; the whole quantity of butcher's-meat, than the whole quantity of poultry; and the whole quantity of poultry, than the whole quantity of wild fowl. There are so many more purchasers for the cheap than for the dear commodity, that, not only a greater quantity of it, but a greater value can commonly be disposed of. The whole quantity, therefore, of the cheap commodity must commonly be greater in proportion to the whole quantity of the dear one, than the value of a certain quantity of the dear one, is to the value of an equal quantity of the cheap one. When we compare the precious metals with one another, silver is a cheap, and gold a dear commodity. We ought naturally to expect, therefore, that there should always be in the market, not only a greater quantity, but a greater value of silver than of gold. Let any man, who has a little of both, compare his own silver with his gold plate, and he will probably find, that, not only the quantity, but the value of the former greatly exceeds that of the latter. Many people, besides, [333] have a good deal of silver who have no gold plate, which, even with those who have it, is generally confined to watch-cases, snuff-boxes, and such like trinkets, of which the whole amount is seldom of great value. In the British coin, indeed, the value of the gold preponderates greatly, but it is not so in that of all countries. In the coin of some countries the value of the two metals is nearly equal. In the Scotch coin, before the union with England, the gold preponderated very little, though it did somewhat*, as it appears by the accounts of the mint. In the coin of many countries the silver preponderates. In France, the largest sums are commonly paid in that metal, and it is there difficult to get more gold than what *c* is necessary to carry about in your pocket. The superior value, however, of the silver plate above that of the gold, which takes place in all countries, will much more

*b** See Ruddiman's Preface to Anderson's Diplomata &c. Scotiæ.* [James Anderson, *Selectus diplomatum et numismatum Scotiæ thesaurus*, ed. T. Ruddiman (Edinburgh, 1739), 84–5; and see below, II.ii.42.]

b–b 2–6   *c* it *1*

than compensate the preponderancy of the gold coin above the silver, which takes place only in some countries.

6   Though, in one sense of the word, silver always has been, and probably always will be, much cheaper than gold; yet in another sense, gold may, perhaps, in the present state of the *d*Spanish*d* market, be said to be somewhat cheaper than silver. A commodity may be said to be dear or cheap, not only according to the absolute greatness or smallness of its usual price, but [334] according as that price is more or less above the lowest for which it is possible to bring it to market for any considerable time together. This lowest price is that which barely replaces, with a moderate profit, the stock which must be employed in bringing the commodity thither. It is the price which affords nothing to the landlord, of which rent makes not any component part, but which resolves itself altogether into wages and profit. But, in the present state of the *e*Spanish*e* market, gold is certainly somewhat nearer to this lowest price than silver. The tax of the King of Spain upon gold is only one-twentieth part of the standard metal, or five per cent.; whereas his tax upon silver amounts to *f*one-tenth*f* part of it, or to *g*ten*g* per cent. In these taxes too, it has already been observed,[2] consists the whole rent of the greater part of the gold and silver mines of Spanish America; and that upon gold is still worse paid than that upon silver. The profits of the undertakers of gold mines too, as they more rarely make a fortune, must, in general, be still more moderate than those of the undertakers of silver mines.[3] The price of Spanish gold, therefore, as it affords both less rent and less profit, must, in the *h*Spanish*h* market, be somewhat nearer to the lowest price for which it is possible to bring it thither, than the price of Spanish silver. *i*When all expences are computed, the whole quantity of the one metal, it would seem, cannot, in the Spanish market, be disposed of so advantageously as the whole quantity of the other. The tax, [335] indeed, of the King of Portugal upon the gold of the Brazils, is the same with the ancient tax of the King of Spain upon the silver of Mexico and Peru; or one-fifth part of the standard metal.[4] It may, therefore, be uncertain whether to the general market of Europe the whole mass of American gold comes at a price nearer to the lowest for which it is possible to bring it thither, than the whole mass of American silver.*i*

7   The price of diamonds and other precious stones may, perhaps, be still

---

d-d European *1*   *e-e* European *1*   *f-f* one-fifth *1*   *g-g* twenty *1*   *h-h* European *1*
i-i The tax of the king of Portugal, indeed, upon the gold of the Brazils, is the same with that of the king of Spain, upon the silver of Mexico and Peru; or one fifth part of the standard metal. It must still be true, however, that the whole mass of American gold comes to the European market, at a price nearer to the lowest for which it is possible to bring it thither, than the whole mass of American silver. When all expences are computed, it would seem, the whole quantity of the one metal cannot be disposed of so advantageously as the whole quantity of the other. *1*

---

[2] Above, I.xi.c.25 and I.xi.g.21.   [3] Above, I.xi.c.28.   [4] Above, I.xi.g.33.

nearer to the lowest price at which it is possible to bring them to market, than even the price of gold.

8   ʲThough it is not very probable, that any part of a tax, which is not only imposed upon one of the most proper subjects of taxation, a mere luxury and superfluity, but which affords so very important a revenue, as the tax upon silver, will ever be given up as long as it is possible to pay it; yet the same impossibility of paying it, which in 1736 made it necessary to reduce it from one-fifth to one-tenth, may in time make it necessary to reduce it still further; in the same manner as it made it necessary to reduce the tax upon gold to one-twentiethʲ.[5] That the silver mines of Spanish America, like all other mines, become gradually more expensive in the working, on account of the greater depths at which it is necessary to carry on the works, and of the greater expence of drawing out the water and of supplying them with fresh air at those depths, is acknowledged by every body who has enquired into the state of those mines.

9   [336] These causes, which are equivalent to a growing scarcity of silver (for a commodity may be said to grow scarcer when it becomes more difficult and expensive to collect a certain quantity of it) must, in time, produce one or other of the three following events. The increase of the expence must either, first, be compensated altogether by a proportionable increase in the price of the metal; or, secondly, it must be compensated altogether by a proportionable diminution of the tax upon silver; or, thirdly, it must be compensated partly by the one, and partly by the other of those two expedients. This third event is very possible. As gold rose in its price in proportion to silver, notwithstanding a great diminution of the tax upon gold; so silver might rise in its price in proportion to labour and commodities, notwithstanding an equal diminution of the tax upon silver.

10   ᵏSuch successive reductions of the tax, however, though they may not prevent altogether, must certainly retard, more or less, the rise of the

---

ʲ⁻ʲ Were the king of Spain to give up his tax upon silver, the price of that metal might not, upon that account, sink immediately in the European market. As long as the quantity brought thither continued the same as before, it would still continue to sell at the same price. The first and immediate effect of this change, would be to increase the profits of mining, the undertaker of the mine now gaining all that he had been used to pay to the king. These great profits would soon tempt a greater number of people to undertake the working of new mines. Many mines would be wrought which cannot be wrought at present, because they cannot afford to pay this tax, and the quantity of silver brought to market would, in a few years, be so much augmented, probably, as to sink its price about one-fifth below its present standard. This diminution in the value of silver would again reduce the profits of mining nearly to their present rate.

It is not indeed very probable, that any part of a tax which affords so important a revenue, and which is imposed too upon one of the most proper subjects of taxation, will ever be given up as long as it is possible to pay it. The impossibility of paying it, however, may in time make it necessary to diminish it, in the same manner as made it necessary to diminish the tax upon gold. *1*

ᵏ⁻ᵏ 2–6 [includes the whole of this paragraph]

---

[5] Above, I.xi.c.25 and I.xi.g.21.

value of silver in the European market. In consequence of such reductions, many mines may be wrought which could not be wrought before, because they could not afford to pay the old tax; and the quantity of silver annually brought to market must always be somewhat greater, and, therefore, the value of any given quantity somewhat less, than it otherwise would have been. In consequence of the reduction in 1736, the value of silver in the European market, though it may not at this day be lower than before that [337] reduction, is, probably, at least ten per cent. lower than it would have been, had the Court of Spain continued to exact the old tax.[k]

11   [l]That, notwithstanding this reduction, the value of silver has, during the course of the present century, begun to rise somewhat in the European market, the facts and arguments which have been alleged above, dispose me to believe, or more properly to suspect and conjecture; for the best opinion which I can form upon this subject scarce, perhaps, deserves the name of belief.[l] The rise, indeed, [m]supposing there has been any,[m] has hitherto been so very small, that after all that has been said, it may, perhaps, appear to many people uncertain, not only whether this event has actually taken place; but whether the contrary may not have taken place, or whether the value of silver may not still continue to fall in the European market.[6]

12   [n]It must be observed, however, that whatever may be the supposed annual importation of gold and silver, there must be a certain period, at which the annual consumption of those metals will be equal to that annual importation. Their consumption must increase as their mass increases, or rather in a much greater proportion. As their mass increases, their value diminishes. They are more used, and less cared for, and their consumption consequently increases in a greater proportion than their mass. After a certain period, therefore, the annual consumption of those metals must, in this manner become equal to their annual importation, provided that importation [338] is not continually increasing; which, in the present times, is not supposed to be the case.

13   If, when the annual consumption has become equal to the annual importation, the annual importation should gradually diminish, the annual consumption, may, for some time, exceed the annual importation. The mass of those metals may gradually and insensibly diminish, and their value gradually and insensibly rise, till the annual importation becoming again stationary, the annual consumption will gradually and insensibly accommodate itself to what that annual importation can maintain.[n][7]

[l-l] That the first of these three events has already begun to take place, or that silver has during the course of the present century, begun to rise somewhat in its value in the European market, the facts and arguments which have been alledged above dispose me to believe. *1*   [m-m] *2-6*   [n-n] *2A-6* [includes § 12 and 13]

[6] See above, I.v.12.
[7] 'If the annual consumption of bullion in *Europe*, both by the *East-India* trade, and by

Grounds of the Suspicion that the Value of Silver still continues to decrease

1   The increase of the wealth of Europe, and the popular notion that, as the quantity of the precious metals naturally increases with the increase of wealth, so their value diminishes as their quantity increases, may, *ᵃperhapsᵃ*, dispose many people to believe that their value still continues to fall in the European market; and the still gradually increasing price of many parts of the rude produce of land may *ᵇ* confirm them still further in this opinion.

2   That that increase *ᶜinᶜ* the quantity of the precious metals *ᵈ*, which arises *ᵉin any countryᵉ* from the increase of wealth, has no tendency to diminish their value, I have endeavoured to show already.[1] Gold and silver naturally resort to a [339] rich country, for the same reason that all sorts of luxuries and curiosities resort to it; not because they are cheaper there than in poorer countries, but because they are dearer, or because a better price is given for them. It is the superiority of price which attracts them, and as soon as that superiority ceases, they necessarily cease to go thither.

3   If you except corn and such other vegetables as are raised altogether by human industry, that all other sorts of rude produce, cattle, poultry, game of all kinds, the useful fossils and minerals of the earth, &c. naturally grow dearer as the society advances in wealth and improvement, I have endeavoured to show already.[2] Though such commodities, therefore, come to exchange for a greater quantity of silver than before, it will not from thence follow that silver has become really cheaper, or will purchase less labour than before, but that such commodities have become really dearer, or will purchase more labour than before. It is not their nominal price only, but their real price which rises in the progress of improvement. The rise of their nominal price is the effect, not of any degradation of the value of silver, but of the rise in their real price.

Different Effects of the Progress of Improvement upon the real price of three different Sorts of rude Produce

1   These different sorts of rude produce may be divided into three classes. The first comprehends those which it is scarce in the [340] power of human industry to multiply at all. The second, those which it can multiply in

---

ᵃ⁻ᵃ besides *1*   ᵇ , perhaps, *1*   ᶜ⁻ᶜ of *1*   ᵈ in any country *1*   ᵉ⁻ᵉ *2–6*

---

the conversion of it into plate, be equal to what the *American* mines annually supply; the value of money taken abstractly, or without referring it to commodities, will remain invariable: But if the said consumption be less, or more, than the said produce of the mines; the whole quantity of money will be accordingly increased, or diminished; and the value of a given part or sum, will be lessened, or increased, in that proportion.' (J. Harris, *Essay*, i.79.)

[1] Above, I.xi.e.30.   [2] Above, I.xi.d.

proportion to the demand. The third, those in which the efficacy of industry is either limited or uncertain. In the progress of wealth and improvement, the real price of the first may rise to any degree of extravagance, and seems not to be limited by any certain boundary. That of the second, though it may rise greatly, has, however, a certain boundary beyond which it cannot well pass for any considerable time together. That of the third, though its natural tendency is to rise in the progress of improvement, yet in the same degree of improvement it may sometimes happen even to fall, sometimes to continue the same, and sometimes to rise more or less, according as different accidents render the efforts of human industry, in multiplying this sort of rude produce, more or less successful.

First Sort

1   The first sort of rude produce of which the price rises in the progress of improvement, is that which it is scarce in the power of human industry to multiply at all. It consists in those things which nature produces only in certain quantities, and which being of a very perishable nature, it is impossible to accumulate together the produce of many different seasons. Such are the greater part of rare and singular birds and fishes, many different sorts of game, almost all wild-fowl, all birds of passage in particular, as well as many other things. When wealth and [341] the luxury which accompanies it increase, the demand for these is likely to increase with them, and no effort of human industry may be able to increase the supply much beyond what it was before this increase of the demand. The quantity of such commodities, therefore, remaining the same, or nearly the same, while the competition to purchase them is continually increasing, their price may rise to any degree of extravagance, and seems not to be limited by any certain boundary. If woodcocks should become so fashionable as to sell for twenty guineas a-piece, no effort of human industry could increase the number of those brought to market, much beyond what it is at present. The high price paid by the Romans, in the time of their greatest grandeur, for rare birds and fishes, may in this manner easily be accounted for. These prices were not the effects of the low value of silver in those times, but of the high value of such rarities and curiosities as human industry could not multiply at pleasure. The real value of silver was higher at Rome, for some time before and after the fall of the republick, than it is through the greater part of Europe at present. Three sestertii, equal to about sixpence sterling, was the price which the republick paid for the modius or peck of the tithe wheat of Sicily.[1] This price, however, was probably below the average market price, the obligation to deliver their wheat at this rate being considered as a tax upon the Sicilian farmers. When the Romans, therefore,

[1] The same figures are cited above, I.xi.b.12. cf. Steuart, *Principles*, II.xxx. 'Quest. 3'.

had occasion to order more corn than the tithe of [342] wheat amounted
to, they were bound by capitulation to pay for the surplus at the rate of
four sestertii, or eight-pence sterling the peck;[2] and this had probably
been reckoned the moderate and reasonable, that is, the ordinary or average
contract price of those times; it is equal to about one-and-twenty shillings
the quarter. Eight-and-twenty shillings the quarter was, before the late
years of scarcity,[3] the ordinary contract price of English wheat, which in
quality is inferior to the Sicilian, and generally sells for a lower price in the
European market. The value of silver, therefore, in those antient times,
must have been to its value in the present, as three to four inversely, that
is, three ounces of silver would then have purchased the same quantity
of labour and commodities which four ounces will do at present.[4] When
we read in Pliny, therefore, that Seius*[5] bought a white nightingale, as
a present for the empress Agrippina, at the price of six thousand sestertii,
equal to about fifty pounds of our present money; and that Asinius Celer†[6]
purchased a surmullet at the price of eight thousand sestertii equal to
about sixty-six pounds thirteen shillings and four-pence of our present
money; the extravagance of those prices, how much soever it may surprise
us, is apt, notwithstanding, to appear to us about one-third less than it
really was. Their real price, the quantity of labour and subsistence which
was given away for them, was about one-third more than their nominal
price is apt to express to us [343] in the present times. Seius gave for the
nightingale the command of a quantity of labour and subsistence, equal to
what 66*l.* 13*s.* 4*d.* would purchase in the present times; and Asinius Celer
gave for the surmullet the command of a quantity equal to what 88*l.*
17*s.* 9⅓*d.* would purchase. What occasioned the extravagance of those
high prices was, not so much the abundance of silver, as the abundance of
labour and subsistence, of which those Romans had the disposal, beyond
what was necessary for their own use. The quantity of silver, of which

---

a* Lib.x.c.29.a   b† Lib.ix.c.17.b

---

a–a 2–6   b–b 2–6

---

[2] 'There were two kinds of purchase to be carried out, the first of a tithe, the second an
additional purchase to be distributed fairly among the various communities. . . . The price
fixed was 3 sesterces a peck for the tithe corn and 3½ sesterces a peck for the requisitioned
corn'. (Cicero, *Verrine Orations*, iii.70, translated by L. H. G. Greenwood in Loeb Classical
Library (1935), ii.200–1.)

[3] See above, I.xi.g.17.

[4] Further examples are provided below, IV.ix.47.

[5] 'I know of one bird, a white one it is true, which is nearly unprecedented, that was
sold for 600,000 sesterces to be given as a present to the emperor Claudius's consort
Agrippina.' (Pliny, *Natural History*, X.xliii, translated by H. Rackham in Loeb Classical
Library (1950), iii.347.)

[6] 'With a fish of this kind one of the proconsulur body, Asinius Celer, in the principate
of Gaius, issued a challenge—it is not so easy to say who won the match—to all the spendthrifts by giving 8,000 sesterces for a mullet.' (Ibid. IX.xxxi, trans. Rackham, iii.207.)

they had the disposal, was a good deal less than what the command of the same quantity of labour and subsistence would have procured to them in the present times.

Second Sort

1   The second sort of rude produce of which the price rises in the progress of improvement, is that which human industry can multiply in proportion to the demand. It consists in those useful plants and animals, which, in uncultivated countries, nature produces with such profuse abundance,[1] that they are of little or no value, and which, as cultivation advances, are therefore forced to give place to some more profitable produce.[2] During a long period in the progress of improvement, the quantity of these is continually diminishing, while at the same time the demand for them is continually increasing. Their real value, therefore, the real quantity of labour which they will purchase or [344] command, gradually rises, till at last it gets so high as to render them as profitable a produce as any thing else which human industry can raise upon the most fertile and best cultivated land. When it has got so high it cannot well go higher. If it did, more land and more industry would soon be employed to increase their quantity.

2   When the price of cattle, for example, rises so high that it is as profitable to cultivate land in order to raise food for them, as in order to raise food for man, it cannot well go higher. If it did, more corn land would soon be turned into pasture. The extension of tillage, by diminishing the quantity of wild pasture, diminishes the quantity of butcher's-meat which the country naturally produces without labour or cultivation, and by increasing the number of those who have either corn, or, what comes to the same thing, the price of corn, to give in exchange for it, increases the demand. The price of butcher's meat, therefore, and consequently of cattle, must gradually rise till it gets so high, that it becomes as profitable to employ the most fertile and best cultivated lands in raising food for them as in raising corn.[3] But it must always be late in the progress of improvement before tillage can be so far extended as to raise the price of cattle to this height; and till it has got to this height, if the country is advancing at all, their price must be continually rising. There are, perhaps, some parts of Europe in which the price of cattle has not yet got to this height. [345] It had not got to this height in any part of Scotland before the union.[4] Had the Scotch cattle been always confined to the market of Scotland, in a country in which the quantity of land, which can be applied to no other purpose but the feeding of cattle, is so great in proportion to what can be applied to

---

[1] Above, I.xi.e.27.   [2] See above, I.xi.b.7, for an analysis of this issue.
[3] See I.xi.b.8.
[4] Not till almost a century after the Union. The difficulties of wintering cattle proved a major hurdle in the expansion of the Scottish cattle trade.

other purposes, it is scarce possible, perhaps, that their price could ever have risen so high as to render it profitable to cultivate land for the sake of feeding them. In England, the price of cattle, it has already been observed,[5] seems, in the neighbourhood of London, to have got to this height about the beginning of the last century; but it was much later probably before it got to it through the greater part of the remoter counties; in some of which, perhaps, it may scarce yet have got to it. Of all the different substances, however, which compose this second sort of rude produce, cattle is, perhaps, that of which the price, in the progress of improvement, *a*first rises*a* to this height.

3   Till the price of cattle, indeed, has got to this height, it seems scarce possible that the greater part, even of those lands which are capable of the highest cultivation, can be completely cultivated. In all farms too distant from any town to carry manure from it, that is, in the far greater part of those of every extensive country, the quantity of well-cultivated land must be in proportion to the quantity of manure which the farm itself produces; and this again must be in proportion to the stock of cattle which are maintained upon it. The land is [346] manured either by pasturing the cattle upon it, or by feeding them in the stable, and from thence carrying out their dung to it. But unless the price of the cattle be sufficient to pay both the rent and profit of cultivated land, the farmer cannot afford to pasture them upon it; and he can still less afford to feed them in the stable. It is with the produce of improved and cultivated land only, that cattle can be fed in the stable; because to collect the scanty and scattered produce of waste and unimproved lands would require too much labour and be too expensive. If the price of the cattle, therefore, is not sufficient to pay for the produce of improved and cultivated land, when they are allowed to pasture it, that price will be still less sufficient to pay for that produce when it must be collected with a good deal of additional labour, and brought into the stable to them. In these circumstances, therefore, no more cattle can, with profit, be fed in the stable than what are necessary for tillage. But these can never afford manure enough for keeping constantly in good condition, all the lands which they are capable of cultivating. What they afford being insufficient for the whole farm, will naturally be reserved for the lands to which it can be most advantageously or conveniently applied; the most fertile, or those, perhaps, in the neighbourhood of the farm-yard. These, therefore, will be kept constantly in good condition and fit for tillage. The rest will, the greater part of them, be allowed to lie waste, producing scarce any thing but some miserable [347] pasture, just sufficient to keep alive a few straggling, half-starved cattle; the farm, though much understocked

a-a rises first *I*

---

[5] See above, I.xi.b.15 and I.xi.l.8.

in proportion to what would be necessary for its complete cultivation, being very frequently overstocked in proportion to its actual produce. A portion of this waste land, however, after having been pastured in this wretched manner for six or seven years together, may be ploughed up, when it will yield, perhaps, a poor crop or two of bad oats, or of some other coarse grain, and then, being entirely exhausted, it must be rested and pastured again as before and another portion ploughed up to be in the same manner exhausted and rested again in its turn. Such accordingly was the general system of management all over the low country of Scotland before the union. The lands which were kept constantly well manured and in good condition, seldom exceeded a third or a fourth part of the whole farm, and sometimes did not amount to a fifth or a sixth part of it. The rest were never manured, but a certain portion of them was in its turn, notwithstanding, regularly cultivated and exhausted. Under this system of management, it is evident, even that part of the lands of Scotland which is capable of good cultivation, could produce but little in comparison of what it may be capable of producing. But how disadvantageous soever this system may appear, yet before the union the low price of cattle seems to have rendered it almost unavoidable. If, notwithstanding a great rise in their price, it still continues to prevail through a considerable part of the country, it is owing, in [348] many places, no doubt, to ignorance and attachment to old customs, but in most places to the unavoidable obstructions which the natural course of things opposes to the immediate or speedy establishment of a better system: first, to the poverty of the tenants, to their not having yet had time to acquire a stock of cattle sufficient to cultivate their lands more compleatly, the same rise of price which would render it advantageous for them to maintain a greater stock, rendering it more difficult for them to acquire it; and, secondly, to their not having yet had time to put their lands in condition to maintain this greater stock properly, supposing they were capable of acquiring it. The increase of stock and the improvement of land are two events which must go hand in hand, and of which the one can no where much out-run the other. Without some increase of stock, there can be scarce any improvement of land, but there can be no considerable increase of stock but in consequence of a considerable improvement of land; because otherwise the land could not maintain it. These natural obstructions to the establishment of a better system, cannot be removed but by a long course of frugality and industry; and half a century or a century more, perhaps, must pass away before the old system, which is wearing out gradually, can be compleatly abolished through all the different parts of the country. Of all *b*the*b* commercial advantages, however, which Scotland has derived from the union with

b–b 3e–b

England, this rise in the price of cattle is, perhaps, the greatest.[6] It has not only raised the value of all highland estates, [349] but it has, perhaps, been the principal cause of the improvement of the low country.

4   In all new colonies the great quantity of waste land, which can for many years be applied to no other purpose but the feeding of cattle, soon renders them extremely abundant, and in every thing great cheapness is the necessary consequence of great abundance. Though all the cattle of the European colonies in America were originally carried from Europe, they soon multiplied so much there, and became of so little value, that even horses were allowed to run wild in the woods without any owner thinking it worth while to claim them.[7] It must be a long time after the first establishment of such colonies, before it can become profitable to feed cattle upon the produce of cultivated land. The same causes, therefore, the want of manure, and the disproportion between the stock employed in cultivation, and the land which it is destined to cultivate, are likely to introduce there a system of husbandry not unlike that which still continues to take place in so many parts of Scotland. Mr. Kalm, the Swedish traveller, when he gives an account of the husbandry of some of the English colonies in North America, as he found it in 1749, observes, accordingly, that he can with difficulty discover there the character of the English nation, so well skilled in all the different branches of agriculture.[8] They make scarce any manure for their corn fields, he says; but when one piece of ground has been exhausted by continual cropping, they clear and cultivate another [350] piece of fresh land; and when that is exhausted, proceed to a third.

---

[6] Smith argued that this particular advantage was less likely to accrue to Ireland at IV.ii.17. He describes some of the political advantages arising from union at V.iii.89. In Letter 50 addressed to Strahan, dated 4 April 1760, Smith commented with regard to Scotland that in the short run, Union with England had depressed the dignity of the nobility, gentry, clerical, and even the merchant classes. He added: 'Nothing, however, appears to me more excusable than the disaffection of Scotland at that time. The Union was a measure from which infinite Good had been derived to this country. The Prospect of that good, however, must then have appeared very remote and very uncertain. . . . The dignity of the nobility was undone by it . . . Even the merchants seemed to suffer at first.' In connection with the latter point, Smith argued that although the colonial trade was opened as a result of union, Scottish merchants were less familiar with the new trade patterns than they were with the more traditional continental routes, now 'laid under new embaressments'.

[7] See above, I.xi.b.7.

[8] 'Aoke Helm . . . upwards of seventy years of age . . . told us, that in his youth there was grass in the woods, which grew very close, and was every where two feet high; but that it was so much lessened at present, that the cattle hardly find food enough, and that therefore four cows now give no more milk than one at that time; but the causes of this alteration are easy to find. In the younger years of old *Helm*, the country was little inhabited, and hardly the tenth part of the cattle kept which is at present; a cow had therefore as much food at that time, as ten now have. Further, most kinds of grass here are annual . . . they must sow themselves every year . . . The great numbers of cattle hinder this sowing, as the grass is eaten before it can produce flowers and fruit.' (P. Kalm, *Travels into North America*, translated by J. R. Forster (Warrington, 1770), i.343–4.)

Their cattle are allowed to wander through the woods and other uncultivated grounds, where they are half-starved; having long ago extirpated
almost all the annual grasses by cropping them too early in the spring,
before they had time to form their flowers, or to shed their seeds*. The
annual grasses were, it seems, the best natural grasses in that part of North
America; and when the Europeans first settled there, they used to grow
very thick, and to rise three or four feet high. A piece of ground which,
when he wrote, could not maintain one cow, would in former times, he
was assured, have maintained four, each of which would have given four
times the quantity of milk, which that one was capable of giving. The poorness of the pasture had, in his opinion, occasioned the degradation of their
cattle, which degenerated sensibly from one generation to another. They
were probably not unlike that stunted breed which was common all over
Scotland thirty or forty years ago, and which is now so much mended
through the greater part of the low country, not so much by a change of
the breed, though that expedient has been employed in some places, as by
a more plentiful method of feeding them.

5   Though it is late, therefore, in the progress of improvement before cattle
can bring such a price as to render it profitable to cultivate land for the
[351] sake of feeding them; yet of all the different parts which compose
this second sort of rude produce, they are perhaps the first which bring
this price; because till they bring it, it seems impossible that improvement
can be brought near even to that degree of perfection to which it has arrived
in many parts of Europe.

6   As cattle are among the first, so perhaps venison is among the last
parts of this sort of rude produce which bring this price. The price of
venison in Great Britain, how extravagant soever it may appear, is not
near sufficient to compensate the expence of a deer park, as is well known
to all those who have had any experience in the feeding of deer. If it was
otherwise, the feeding of deer would soon become an article of common
farming; in the same manner as the feeding of those small birds called
Turdi was among the antient Romans. Varro and Columella assure us
that it was a most profitable article.[9] The fattening of Ortolans, birds of

---

ᶜ* Kalm's Travels, vol. i. p.343, 344.ᶜ

ᶜ⁻ᶜ 2–6

---

[9] 'Thanks to the expenditure in this way of money and care, so Marcus Terentius
[Varro] informs us, these birds were often bought for three *denarii* a piece in our grandfather's time, when those who celebrated triumphs gave a feast to the people. But at the
present day luxury has made this their everyday price; wherefore this source of income
must not be despised even by farmers.' (Columella, *De Re Rustica*, viii.10, translated by
E. S. Forster and E. H. Heffner in Loeb Classical Library (1954), ii.373–5.) 'From the
aviary alone which is in that villa I happen to know that there were sold 5,000 fieldfares,
for three denarii apiece, so that that department of the villa in that year brought in sixty
thousand sesterces—twice as much as your farm of 200 iugera at Reate brings in'. (Varro,

passage which arrive lean in the country, is said to be so in some parts of France. If venison continues in fashion, and the wealth and luxury of Great Britain increase as they have done for some time past, its price may very probably rise still higher than it is at present.

7   Between that period in the progress of improvement which brings to its height the price of so necessary an article as cattle, and that which brings to it the price of such a superfluity as venison, there is a very long interval, in the course of which many other sorts of rude produce [352] gradually arrive at their highest price, some sooner and some later, according to different circumstances.

8   Thus in every farm the offals of the barn and stables will maintain a certain number of poultry. These, as they are fed with what would otherwise be lost, are a mere save-all; and as they cost the farmer scarce any thing, so he can afford to sell them for very little. Almost all that he gets is pure gain, and their price can scarce be so low as to discourage him from feeding this number. But in countries ill cultivated, and, therefore, but thinly inhabited, the poultry, which are thus raised without expence, are often fully sufficient to supply the whole demand. In this state of things, therefore, they are often as cheap as butcher's-meat, or any other sort of animal food. But the whole quantity of poultry, which the farm in this manner produces without expence, must always be much smaller than the whole quantity of butcher's-meat which is reared upon it; and in times of wealth and luxury what is rare, with only nearly equal merit, is always preferred to what is common.[10] As wealth and luxury increase, therefore, in consequence of improvement and cultivation, the price of poultry gradually rises above that of butcher's-meat, till at last it gets so high that it becomes profitable to cultivate land for the sake of feeding them. When it has got to this height, it cannot well go higher. If it did, more land would soon be turned to this purpose. In several provinces of France, the feeding of poultry is [353] considered as a very important article in rural œconomy, and sufficiently profitable to encourage the farmer to raise a considerable quantity of Indian corn and buck-wheat for this purpose. A middling farmer will there sometimes have four hundred fowls in his yard. The feeding of poultry seems scarce yet to be generally considered as a matter of so much importance in England. They are certainly, however, dearer in England than in France, as England receives considerable supplies from France. In the progress of improvement, the period at which every particular sort of animal food is dearest, must naturally be that which immediately precedes the general practice of cultivating land for the sake of raising it. For some time before this practice becomes general, the

De Re Rustica, iii.2, translated by W. D. Hooper, revised by H. B. Ash in the Loeb Classical Library (1934), 436–7.)

   [10] See above, I.xi.c.31.

scarcity must necessarily raise the price. After it has become general, new methods of feeding are commonly fallen upon, which enable the farmer to raise upon the same quantity of ground a much greater quantity of that particular sort of animal food. The plenty not only obliges him to sell cheaper, but in consequence of these improvements he can afford to sell cheaper; for if he could not afford it, the plenty would not be of long continuance. It has been probably in this manner that the introduction of clover, turnips, carrots, cabbages, &c. has contributed to sink the common price of butcher's-meat in the London market somewhat below what it was about the beginning of the last century.[11]

9   [354] The hog, that finds his food among ordure, and greedily devours many things rejected by every other useful animal, is, like poultry, originally kept as a save-all. As long as the number of such animals, which can thus be reared at little or no expence, is fully sufficient to supply the demand, this sort of butcher's-meat comes to market at a much lower price than any other. But when the demand rises beyond what this quantity can supply, when it becomes necessary to raise food on purpose for feeding and fattening hogs, in the same manner as for feeding and fattening other cattle, the price necessarily rises, and becomes proportionably either higher or lower than that of other butcher's-meat, according as the nature of the country, and the state of its agriculture, happen to render the feeding of hogs more or less expensive than that of other cattle. In France, according to Mr. Buffon,[12] the price of pork is nearly equal to that of beef. In most parts of Great Britain it is at present somewhat higher.

10   The great rise in the price both of hogs and poultry has in Great Britain been frequently imputed to the diminution of the number of cottagers and other small occupiers of land; an event which has in every part of Europe been the immediate fore-runner of improvement and better cultivation, but which at the same time may have contributed to raise the price of those articles, both somewhat sooner and somewhat faster than it would otherwise have risen.[13] As the [355] poorest family can often maintain a cat or a dog, without any expence; so the poorest occupiers of land can commonly maintain a few poultry, or a sow and a few pigs, at very little. The little offals of their own table, their whey, skimmed milk, and butter-milk, supply those animals with a part of their food, and they find the rest in the neighbouring fields without doing any sensible damage to

---

[11] See above, I.xi.b.15 and I.xi.l.2.

[12] 'No one who lives in the country is ignorant of the profits arising from the hog; his flesh sells for more than that of the ox.' (Buffon, *Histoire naturelle*, translated as *Barr's Buffon's Natural History* (London, 1797), v.299.) In his *Edinburgh Review* article of 1755, Smith referred to Buffon as a gentleman of 'the most universally acknowledged merit' and as being connected with the writing of 'a compleat system of natural history'.

[13] It is remarked above, I.x.b.49, that cottagers still subsist in Scotland, although in smaller numbers than formerly.

any body. By diminishing the number of those small occupiers, therefore, the quantity of this sort of provisions which is thus produced at little or no expence, must certainly have been a good deal diminished, and their price must consequently have been raised both sooner and faster than it would otherwise have risen. Sooner or later, however, in the progress of improvement, it must at any rate have risen to the utmost height to which it is capable of rising; or to the price which pays the labour and expence of cultivating the land which furnishes them with food as well as these are paid upon the greater part of ᵈotherᵈ cultivated land.

11   The business of the dairy, like the feeding of hogs and poultry, is originally carried on as a save-all. The cattle necessarily kept upon the farm, produce more milk than either the rearing of their own young, or the consumption of the farmer's family requires; and they produce most at one particular season. But of all the productions of land, milk is perhaps the most perishable. In the warm season, when it is most abundant, it will scarce keep four-and-twenty hours. The farmer, by making it into fresh [356] butter, stores a small part of it for a week: by making it into salt butter, for a year: and by making it into cheese, he stores a much greater part of it for several years. Part of all these is reserved for the use of his own family. The rest goes to market, in order to find the best price which is to be had, and which can scarce be so low as to discourage him from sending thither whatever is over and above the use of his own family. If it is very low, indeed, he will be likely to manage his dairy in a very slovenly and dirty manner, and will scarce perhaps think it worth while to have a particular room or building on purpose for it, but will suffer the business to be carried on amidst the smoke, filth, and nastiness of his own kitchen; as was the case of almost all the farmers dairies in Scotland thirty or forty years ago, and as is the case of many of them still. The same causes which gradually raise the price of butcher's-meat, the increase of the demand, and, in consequence of the improvement of the country, the diminution of the quantity which can be fed at little or no expence, raise, in the same manner, that of the produce of the dairy, of which the price naturally connects with that of butcher's-meat, or with the expence of feeding cattle. The increase of price pays for more labour, care, and cleanliness. The dairy becomes more worthy of the farmer's attention, and the quality of its produce gradually improves. The price at last gets so high that it becomes worth while to employ some of the most fertile and best cultivated [357] lands in feeding cattle merely for the purpose of the dairy; and when it has got to this height, it cannot well go higher. If it did, more land would soon be turned to this purpose. It seems to have got to this height through the greater part of England, where much good land is commonly employed

ᵈ⁻ᵈ their 4 ⟨corrected 4e–6⟩

in this manner. If you except the neighbourhood of a few considerable towns, it seems not yet to have got to this height any where in Scotland, where common farmers seldom employ much good land in raising food for cattle merely for the purpose of the dairy. The price of the produce, though it has risen very considerably within these few years, is probably still too low to admit of it. The inferiority of the quality, indeed, compared with that of the produce of English dairies, is fully equal to that of the price. But this inferiority of quality is, perhaps, rather the effect of this lowness of price than the cause of it. Though the quality was much better, the greater part of what is brought to market could not, I apprehend, in the present circumstances of the country, be disposed of at a much better price; and the present price, it is probable, would not pay the expence of the land and labour necessary for producing a much better quality. Through the greater part of England, notwithstanding the superiority of price, the dairy is not reckoned a more profitable employment of land than the raising of corn, or the fattening of cattle, the two great objects of agriculture. Through the greater part of Scotland, therefore, it cannot yet be ^{e}even so^e profitable.

12   [358] The lands of no country, it is evident, can ever be compleatly cultivated and improved, till once the price of every produce, which human industry is obliged to raise upon them, has got so high as to pay for the expence of compleat improvement and cultivation. In order to do this, the price of each particular produce must be sufficient, first, to pay the rent of good corn land, as it is that which regulates the rent of the greater part of other cultivated land;[14] and, secondly, to pay the labour and expence of the farmer as well as they are commonly paid upon good corn-land; or, in other words, to replace with the ordinary profits the stock which he employs about it. This rise in the price of each particular produce, must evidently be previous to the improvement and cultivation of the land which is destined for raising it. Gain is the end of all improvement, and nothing could deserve that name of which loss was to be the necessary consequence. But loss must be the necessary consequence of improving land for the sake of a produce of which the price could never bring back the expence. If the compleat improvement and cultivation of the country be, as it most certainly is, the greatest of all publick advantages, this rise in the price of all those different sorts of rude produce, instead of being considered as a publick calamity, ought to be regarded as the necessary forerunner and attendant of the greatest of all publick advantages.

13   This rise too in the nominal or money-price of all those different sorts of rude produce has [359] been the effect, not of any degradation in the value of silver, but of a rise in their real price. They have become worth,

$^{e-e}$ equally $\mathit{1}$

---

[14] See above, I.xi.b.35.

not only a greater quantity of silver, but a greater quantity of labour and subsistence than before. As it costs a greater quantity of labour and subsistence to bring them to market, so when they are brought thither, they represent or are equivalent to a greater quantity.

Third Sort

1   The third and last sort of rude produce, of which the price naturally rises in the progress of improvement, is that in which the efficacy of human industry, in augmenting the quantity, is either limited or uncertain. Though the real price of this sort of rude produce, therefore, naturally tends to rise in the progress of improvement, yet, according as different accidents happen to render the efforts of human industry more or less successful in augmenting the quantity, it may happen sometimes even to fall, sometimes to continue the same in very different periods of improvement, and sometimes to rise more or less in the same period.

2   There are some sorts of rude produce which nature has rendered a kind of appendages to other sorts; so that the quantity of the one which any country can afford, is necessarily limited by that of the other. The quantity of wool or of raw hides, for example, which any [360] country can afford, is necessarily limited by the number of great and small cattle that are kept in it. The state of its improvement, and the nature of its agriculture, again necessarily determine this number.

3   The same causes, which, in the progress of improvement, gradually raise the price of butcher's-meat, should have the same effect, it may be thought, upon the prices of wool and raw hides, and raise them too nearly in the same proportion. It probably would be so, if in the rude beginnings of improvement the market for the latter commodities was confined within as narrow bounds as that for the former. But the extent of their respective markets is commonly extremely different.

4   The market for butcher's-meat is almost every-where confined to the country which produces it. Ireland, and some part of British America indeed, carry on a considerable trade in salt provisions; but they are, I believe, the only countries in the commercial world which do so, or which export to other countries any considerable part of their butcher's-meat.

5   The market for wool and raw hides, on the contrary, is in the rude beginnings of improvement very seldom confined to the country which produces them. They can easily be transported to distant countries, wool without any preparation, and raw hides with very little: and as they are the materials of many manufactures, the industry of other countries may occasion a demand [361] for them, though that of the country which produces them might not occasion any.

6   In countries ill cultivated, and therefore but thinly inhabited, the price

of the wool and the hide bears always a much greater proportion to that of the whole beast, than in countries where, improvement and population being further advanced, there is more demand for butcher's-meat. Mr. Hume observes, that in the Saxon times, the fleece was estimated at two-fifths of the value of the whole sheep, and that this was much above the proportion of its present estimation.[1] In some provinces of Spain, I have been assured, the sheep is frequently killed merely for the sake of the fleece and the tallow. The carcase is often left to rot upon the ground, or to be devoured by beasts and birds of prey. If this sometimes happens even in Spain, it happens almost constantly in Chili, at Buenos Ayres, and in many other parts of Spanish America, where the horned cattle are almost constantly killed merely for the sake of the hide and the tallow.[2] This too used to happen almost constantly in Hispaniola, while it was infested by the Buccaneers, and before the settlement, improvement, and populousness of the French plantations (which now extend round the coast of almost the whole western half of the island) had given some value to the cattle of the Spaniards, who still continue to possess, not only the eastern part of the coast, but the whole inland and mountainous part of the country.

7   [362] Though in the progress of improvement and population, the price of the whole beast necessarily rises, yet the price of the carcase is likely to be much more affected by this rise than that of the wool and the hide. The market for the carcase, being in the rude state of society confined always to the country which produces it, must necessarily be extended in proportion to the improvement and population of that country. But the market for the wool and the hides even of a barbarous country often extending to the whole commercial world, it can very seldom be enlarged in the same proportion. The state of the whole commercial world can seldom be much affected by the improvement of any particular country; and the market for such commodities may remain the same or very nearly the same, after such improvements, as before. It should, however, in the natural course of things rather upon the whole be somewhat extended in consequence of them. If the manufactures, especially, of which those commodities are the materials, should ever come to flourish in the country, the market, though it might not be much enlarged, would at least be brought much nearer to the place of growth than before; and the price of those materials might at least be increased by what had usually been the expence of transporting

---

[1] 'A sheep by the laws of Athelstan was estimated at a shilling; that is, fifteen-pence of our money. The fleece was two-fifths of the value of the whole sheep; much above its present estimation; and the reason probably was, that the Saxons, like the ancients, were little acquainted with any clothing but what was made of wool.' (D. Hume, *The History of England* (1778), i.226.)

[2] 'It is the usual custom to buy the hides of the beast, the carcase being in some measure a gratuitous addition; and the meat is always fat and very palateable.' (Juan and Ulloa, *Voyage historique*, i.552, trans. John Adams, ii.187.)

them to distant countries. Though it might not rise therefore in the same proportion as that of butcher's-meat, it ought naturally to rise somewhat, and it ought certainly not to fall.

8   [363] In England, however, notwithstanding the flourishing state of its woollen manufacture, the price of English wool has fallen very considerably since the time of Edward III. There are many authentick records which demonstrate that during the reign of that prince (towards the middle of the fourteenth century, or about 1339) what was reckoned the moderate and reasonable price of the tod or twenty-eight pounds of English wool was not less than ten shillings of the money of those times*,[3] containing, at the rate of twenty-pence the ounce, six ounces of silver Tower-weight, equal to about thirty shillings of our present money. In the present times, one-and-twenty shillings the tod may be reckoned a good price for very good English wool. The money-price of wool, therefore, in the time of Edward III, was to its money-price in the present times as ten to seven. The superiority of its real price was still greater. At the rate of six shillings and eight-pence the quarter, ten shillings was in those antient times the price of twelve bushels of wheat. At the rate of twenty-eight shillings the quarter, one-and-twenty shillings is in the present times the price of six bushels only. The proportion between the real prices of antient and modern times, therefore, is as twelve to six, or as two to one. In those antient times a tod of wool would have purchased twice the quantity of subsistence which it will purchase at present; and consequently twice [364] the quantity of labour, if the real recompence of labour had been the same in both periods.

9   This degradation both in the real and nominal value of wool, could never have happened in consequence of the natural course of things. It has accordingly been the effect of violence and artifice: First, of the absolute prohibition of exporting wool from England;[4] Secondly, of the permission of importing it from *ᵇSpainᵇ* duty free;[5] Thirdly, of the prohibition of exporting it from Ireland to any other country but England.[6] In conse-

---

* See Smith's Memoirs of Wool,ᵃ vol.i.c.5, 6, and 7; also, vol.ii.c.176.ᵃ [In the Parliament of 1339, 'the Laity granted the King one half of all their Wool for the next Summer. At the same time he took the whole from the Clergy, making them pay nine Marks for every Sack of the best Wool. *Which nine Marks* per *Sack was equal to 14s.* per *Stone of our present Money.*' John Smith, *Chronicon Rusticum Commerciale; or Memoirs of Wool, etc.* (London, 1747), i.25, n.]

ᵃ⁻ᵃ 2–6   ᵇ⁻ᵇ all other countries *1–2*

---

³ See below, IV.viii.25, where Smith is described as the 'very accurate and intelligent author of the Memoirs of Wool'.
⁴ 14 Charles II, c.18 (1662) in *Statutes of the Realm*, v.410–412; 13 and 14 Charles II, c.18 in Ruffhead's edition. See below, IV.viii.18, IV.viii.33, IV.viii.35, V.ii.k.23.
⁵ H. Saxby, *The British Customs* (London, 1757), 263, states that Spanish wool for clothing and Spanish felt-wool was duty free.
⁶ 10 William III, c.16 (1698) in *Statutes of the Realm*, vii.524–8; 10 and 11 William III, c.10 in Ruffhead's edition.

quence of these regulations, the market for English wool, instead of being
somewhat extended in consequence of the improvement of England, has
been confined to the home market, where the wool of ᶜseveralᶜ other
countries is allowed to come into competition with it, and where that of
Ireland is forced into competition with it. As the woollen manufactures
too of Ireland are fully as much discouraged as is consistent with justice
and fair dealing, the Irish can work up but a small part of their own wool
at home, and are, therefore, obliged to send a greater proportion of it to
Great Britain, the only market they are allowed.[7]

10   I have not been able to find any such authentick records concerning
the price of raw hides in antient times. Wool was commonly paid as a
subsidy to the king, and its valuation in that subsidy ascertains, at least
in some degree, what was its ordinary price. But this seems not to have been
the case with raw hides. Fleetwood, however, from an account in 1425,
between the prior [365] of Burcester Oxford and one of his canons, gives
us their price, at least as it was stated, upon that particular occasion; viz.
five ox hides at twelve shillings; five cow hides at seven shillings and three
pence; thirty-six ᵈsheepᵈ skins of two years old at nine shillings; sixteen
ᵉcalvesᵉ skins at two shillings.[8] In 1425, twelve shillings contained about the
same quantity of silver as four-and-twenty shillings of our present money.
An ox hide, therefore, was in this account valued at the same quantity of
silver as 4s. ⅘ths of our present money. Its nominal price was a good deal
lower than at present. But at the rate of six shillings and eight-pence the
quarter, twelve shillings would in those times have purchased fourteen
bushels and four-fifths of a bushel of wheat, which, at three and six-pence
the bushel, would in the present times cost 51s. 4d. An ox hide, therefore,
would in those times have purchased as much corn as ten shillings and

---

ᶜ⁻ᶜ all *1–2*   ᵈ⁻ᵈ sheeps *1–2*   ᵉ⁻ᵉ calf *6*

---

[7] In Letter 201 addressed to Henry Dundas, dated 1 November 1779, and in Letter 202
addressed to Lord Carlisle, dated 8 November 1779, Smith referred to the restraints which
had been placed on the Irish woollen industry. He wrote to Carlisle that:

At present they can export Glass, tho' of their own manufacture, to no country whatever. Raw Silk, a forreign commodity, is under the same restraint. Wool they can export
only to Great Britain. Woollen manufactures they can export only from certain Ports
in Ireland to certain Ports in Great Britain. A very slender interest of our own Manufactures is the foundation of all these unjust and oppressive restraints. The watchful
jealousy of those Gentlemen is alarmed, least the Irish, who have never be able to supply
compleatly even their own market with Glass or Woollen manufactures, should be
able to rival them in forreign Markets.

Smith had been asked his opinion as to the consequences of free trade with Ireland, and
took the view in these letters that Britain had nothing to fear from it. Smith refers to the
restraints imposed on trade with Ireland at V.iii.72 and to the advantages of union at
V.iii.89.

[8] W. Fleetwood, *Chronicon Preciosum*, 100.

three-pence would purchase at present. Its real value was equal to ten shillings and three-pence of our present money. In those antient times, when the cattle were half starved during the greater part of the winter, we cannot suppose that they were of a very large size. An ox hide which weighs four stone of sixteen pounds averdupois, is not in the present times reckoned a bad one; and in those antient times would probably have been reckoned a very good one. But at half a crown the stone, which at this moment (February, 1773) I understand to be the common price, such a hide would at present cost only ten [366] shillings. Though its nominal price, therefore, is higher in the present than it was in those antient times, its real price, the real quantity of subsistence which it will purchase or command, is rather somewhat lower. The price of cow hides, as stated in the above account, is nearly in the common proportion to that of ox hides. That of sheep skins is a good deal above it. They had probably been sold with the wool. That of calves skins, on the contrary, is greatly below it. In countries where the price of cattle is very low, the calves, which are not intended to be reared in order to keep up the stock, are generally killed very young; as was the case in Scotland twenty or thirty years ago. It saves the milk, which their price would not pay for. Their skins, therefore, are commonly good for little.

11   The price of raw hides is a good deal lower at present than it was a few years ago; owing probably to the taking off the duty upon seal skins, and to the allowing, for a limited time, the importation of raw hides from Ireland and from the plantations duty free, which was done in 1769.[9] Take the whole of the present century at an average, their real price has probably been somewhat higher than it was in those antient times. The nature of the commodity renders it not quite so proper for being transported to distant markets as wool. It suffers more by keeping. A salted hide is reckoned inferior to a fresh one, and sells for a lower price. This circumstance must necessarily have some tendency to sink the price of raw hides produced [367] in a country which does not manufacture them, but is obliged to export them; and comparatively to raise that of those produced in a country which does manufacture them. It must have some tendency to sink their price in a barbarous, and to raise it in an improved and manufacturing country. It must have had some tendency therefore to sink it in antient, and to raise it in modern times. Our tanners besides have not been quite so successful as our clothiers, in convincing the wisdom of the nation, that the safety of the commonwealth depends upon the prosperity of their particular manufacture.[10] They have accordingly been much less favoured.

[9] 9 George III, c.39 (1769), extended by 14 George III, c.86 (1774) and 21 George III, c.29 (1781). See below, IV.viii.3.

[10] It is stated at IV.viii.17 that the manufacturers of woollen goods had been 'more successful than any other class of workmen' in persuading the legislature to give protection to the trade. See generally I.xi.p.10.

The exportation of raw hides has, indeed, been prohibited, and declared a nuisance:[11] but their importation from foreign countries has been subjected to a duty;[12] and though this duty has been taken off from those of Ireland and the plantations (for the limited time of five years only), yet Ireland has not been confined to the market of Great Britain for the sale of its surplus hides, or of those which are not manufactured at home. The hides of common cattle have but within these few years been put among the enumerated commodities which the plantations can send nowhere but to the mother country; neither has the commerce of Ireland been in this case oppressed hitherto, in order to support the manufactures of Great Britain.

12   Whatever regulations tend to sink the price either of wool or of raw hides below what it naturally would be, must, in an improved and [368] cultivated country, have some tendency to raise the price of butcher's-meat. The price both of the great and small cattle, which are fed on improved and cultivated land, must be sufficient to pay the rent which the landlord, and the profit which the farmer has reason to expect from improved and cultivated land. If it is not, they will soon cease to feed them. Whatever part of this price, therefore, is not paid by the wool and the hide, must be paid by the carcase. The less there is paid for the one, the more must be paid for the other. In what manner this price is to be divided upon the different parts of the beast, is indifferent to the landlords and farmers, provided it is all paid to them. In an improved and cultivated country, therefore, their interest as landlords and farmers cannot be much affected by such regulations, though their interest as consumers may, by the rise in the price of provisions.[13] It would be quite otherwise, however, in an unimproved and uncultivated country, where the greater part of the lands could be applied to no other purpose but the feeding of cattle, and where the wool and the hide made the principal part of the value of those cattle. Their interest as landlords and farmers would in this case be very deeply affected by such regulations, and their interest as consumers very little. The fall in the price of the wool and the hide, would not in this case raise the price of the carcase; because the greater part of the lands of the country being applicable to no other purpose but the feeding of cattle, the same number would [369] still continue to be fed. The same quantity of butcher's-meat would still come to market. The demand for it would be no greater than before. Its price, therefore, would be the same as before.

---

[11] By 5 Elizabeth I, c.22 (1562), amended and confirmed by 8 Elizabeth I, c.14 (1566), and 18 Elizabeth I, c.9 (1575). 14 Charles II, c.7 (1662) in *Statutes of the Realm*, v. 397; 13 and 14 Charles II, c.7 in Ruffhead's edition declares that 'all such Exportation and Transportation of any Hides or Leather contrary to this Act is hereby adjudged and declared to be a common and publick Nusance'. See below, IV.viii.34.

[12] 9 Anne, c.12 (1710) in *Statutes of the Realm*, ix.405-17; 9 Anne, c.11 in Ruffhead's edition.

[13] This passage, from the beginning of the paragraph, is quoted below at IV.viii.26.

The whole price of cattle would fall, and along with it both the rent and the profit of all those lands of which cattle was the principal produce, that is, of the greater part of the lands of the country. The perpetual prohibition of the exportation of wool, which is commonly, but very falsely, ascribed to Edward III,[14] would, in the then circumstances of the country, have been the most destructive regulation which could well have been thought of. It would not only have reduced the actual value of the greater part of the lands of the kingdom, but by reducing the price of the most important species of small cattle, it would have retarded very much its subsequent improvement.

13   The wool of Scotland fell very considerably in its price in consequence of the union with England, by which it was excluded from the great market of Europe, and confined to the narrow one of Great Britain.[15] The value of the greater part of the lands in the southern counties of Scotland, which are chiefly a sheep country, would have been very deeply affected by this event, had not the rise in the price of butcher's-meat fully compensated the fall in the price of wool.

14   As the efficacy of human industry, in increasing the quantity either of wool or of raw hides, is limited, so far as it depends upon the [370] produce of the country where it is exerted; so it is uncertain so far as it depends upon the produce of other countries. It so far depends, not so much upon the quantity which they produce, as upon that which they do not manufacture; and upon the restraints which they may or may not think proper to impose upon the exportation of this sort of rude produce. These circumstances, as they are altogether independent of domestick industry, so they necessarily render the efficacy of its efforts more or less uncertain. In multiplying this sort of rude produce, therefore, the efficacy of human industry is not only limited, but uncertain.

15   In multiplying another very important sort of rude produce, the quantity of fish that is brought to market, it is likewise both limited and uncertain. It is limited by the local situation of the country, by the proximity or distance of its different provinces from the sea, by the number of its lakes

---

[14] John Smith (*Memoirs of Wool*, i.25) commented that the words of the statute 'are far from implying a fixed Resolution of prohibiting absolutely, for ever, the Exportation of Wool; on the contrary, they only denote at the most a temporary Expedient or Revulsion in Favour of the Woolen Manufacture, then about to be enlarged in *England*.'

[15] An Act of 1704 permitted the export of wool (Acts of the Parliament of Scotland, xi.190) to meet the claims of the politically powerful woolmasters. The wider market gave better prices for Scottish wool, though the removal of cheaper wool was a factor in the collapse of the Scottish woollen industry which had been encouraged by a policy of protection. W. R. Scott, *The New Mills Cloth Manufactory* (Edinburgh, 1905), lxxix–lxxxiii. The woolmasters suffered by the Union but the major benefit of the Union to the English woollen trade was that of closing an illicit outlet for their wool through Scotland to foreign producers. C. Gulvin, 'The Union and the Scottish Woollen Industry 1707–1760', *Scottish Historical Review*, l (1971), 122–3. In general the Scottish clip was not of interest to the English producers. See also IV.viii.25.

and rivers, and by what may be called the fertility or barrenness of those seas, lakes and rivers, as to this sort of rude produce. As population increases, as the annual produce of the land and labour of the country grows greater and greater, there come to be more buyers of fish, and those buyers too have a greater quantity and variety of other goods, or, what is the same thing, the price of a greater quantity and variety of other goods, to buy with. But it will generally be impossible to supply the great and extended market without employing a quantity of labour greater than in proportion to [371] what had been requisite for supplying the narrow and confined one. A market which, from requiring only one thousand, comes to require annually ten thousand ton of fish, can seldom be supplied without employing more than ten times the quantity of labour which had before been sufficient to supply it. The fish must generally be sought for at a greater distance, larger vessels must be employed, and more expensive machinery of every kind made use of. The real price of this commodity, therefore, naturally rises in the progress of improvement. It has accordingly done so, I believe, more or less in every country.

16　　Though the success of a particular day's fishing may be a very uncertain matter, yet, the local situation of the country being supposed, the general efficacy of industry in bringing a certain quantity of fish to market, taking the course of a year, or of several years together, it may perhaps be thought, is certain enough; and it, no doubt, is so. As it depends more, however, upon the local situation of the country, than upon the state of its wealth and industry; as upon this account it may in different countries be the same in very different periods of improvement, and very different in the same period; its connection with the state of improvement is uncertain, and it is of this sort of uncertainty that I am here speaking.

17　　In increasing the quantity of the different minerals and metals which are drawn from the bowels of the earth, that of the more precious [372] ones particularly, the efficacy of human industry seems not to be limited, but to be altogether uncertain.

18　　The quantity of the precious metals which is to be found in any country is not limited by any thing in its local situation, such as the fertility or barrenness of its own mines. Those metals frequently abound in countries which possess no mines. Their quantity in every particular country seems to depend upon two different circumstances; first, upon its power of purchasing, upon the state of its industry, upon the annual produce of its land and labour, in consequence of which it can afford to employ a greater or a smaller quantity of labour and subsistence in bringing or purchasing such superfluities as gold and silver, either from its own mines or from those of other countries; and, secondly, upon the fertility or barrenness of the mines which may happen at any particular time to supply the commercial world with those metals. The quantity of those metals in the countries most remote from the mines, must be more or less affected by this fertility or barrenness, on account of the easy and cheap transportation of those metals, of their small bulk and great value. Their quantity in China and Indostan must have been more or less affected by the abundance of the mines of America.

19   So far as their quantity in any particular country depends upon the former of those two circumstances (the power of purchasing), their real price, like that of all other luxuries and superfluities, is likely to rise with the wealth and im-[373]provement of the country, and to fall with its poverty and depression. Countries which have a great quantity of labour and subsistence to spare, can afford to purchase any particular quantity of those metals at the expence of a greater quantity of labour and subsistence, than countries which have less to spare.

20   So far as their quantity in any particular country depends upon the latter of those two circumstances (the fertility or barrenness of the mines which happen to supply the commercial world) their real price, the real quantity of labour and subsistence which they will purchase or exchange for, will, no doubt, sink more or less in proportion to the fertility, and rise in proportion to the barrenness of those mines.

21   The fertility or barrenness of the mines, however, which may happen at any particular time to supply the commercial world, is a circumstance which, it is evident, may have no sort of connection with the state of industry in a particular country. It seems even to have no very necessary connection with that of the world in general. As arts and commerce, indeed, gradually spread themselves over a greater and a greater part of the earth, the search for new mines, being extended over a wider surface, may have somewhat a better chance for being successful, than when confined within narrower bounds. The discovery of new mines, however, as the old ones come to be gradually exhausted, is a matter of the greatest uncertainty, and such as no human skill or industry can ensure. All [374] indications, it is acknowledged, are doubtful, and the actual discovery and successful working of a new mine can alone ascertain the reality of its value, or even of its existence. In this search there seem to be no certain limits either to the possible success, or to the possible disappointment of human industry. In the course of a century or two, it is possible that new mines may be discovered more fertile than any that have ever yet been known; and it is just equally possible that the most fertile mine then known may be more barren than any that was wrought before the discovery of the mines of America. Whether the one or the other of those two events may happen to take place, is of very little importance to the real wealth and prosperity of the world, to the real value of the annual produce of the land and labour of mankind. Its nominal value, the quantity of gold and silver by which this annual produce could be expressed or represented, would, no doubt, be

very different; but its real value, the real quantity of labour which it could purchase or command, would be precisely the same. A shilling might in the one case represent no more labour than a penny does at present; and a penny in the other might represent as much as a shilling does now. But in the one case he who had a shilling in his pocket, would be no richer than he who has a penny at present; and in the other he who had a penny would be just as rich as he who has a shilling now. The cheapness and abundance of gold and silver plate, would be the sole advantage [375] which the world could derive from the one event, and the dearness and scarcity of those trifling superfluities the only inconveniency it could suffer from the other.

Conclusion of the Digression concerning the Variations in the Value of Silver

1   The greater part of the writers who have collected the money prices of things in antient times, seem to have considered the low money price of corn, and of goods in general, or, in other words, the high value of gold and silver, as a proof, not only of the scarcity of those metals, but of the poverty and barbarism of the country at the time when it took place. This notion is connected with the system of political œconomy which represents national wealth as consisting in the abundance, and national poverty in the scarcity of gold and silver; a system which I shall endeavour to explain and examine at great length in the fourth book of this enquiry. I shall only observe at present, that the high value of the precious metals can be no proof of the poverty or barbarism of any particular country at the time when it took place. It is a proof only of the barrenness of the mines which happened at that time to supply the commercial world. A poor country, as it cannot afford to buy more, so it can as little afford to pay dearer for gold and silver than a rich one; and the value of those metals, therefore, is not likely to be higher in the former than in the latter. In China, a coun-[376] try much richer than any part of Europe,[1] the value of the precious metals is much higher than in any part of Europe. As the wealth of Europe, indeed, has increased greatly since the discovery of the mines of America, so the value of gold and silver has gradually diminished. This diminution of their value, however, has not been owing to the increase of the real wealth of Europe, of the annual produce of its land and labour, but to the accidental discovery of more abundant mines than any that were known before. The increase of the quantity of gold and silver in Europe, and the increase of its manufactures and agriculture, are two events which, though they have happened nearly about the same time, yet have arisen from very different causes, and have scarce any natural connection with one another. The one

[1] See above, I.viii.24 and I.xi.e.34.

has arisen from a mere accident, in which neither prudence nor policy either had or could have any share: The other from the fall of the feudal system, and from the establishment of a government which afforded to industry, the only encouragement which it requires, some tolerable security that it shall enjoy the fruits of its own labour.[2] Poland, where the feudal system still continues to take place, is at this day as beggarly a country as it was before the discovery of America.[3] The money price of corn, however, has risen; the real value of the precious metals has fallen in Poland, in the same manner as in other parts of Europe. Their quantity, therefore, must have increased there as in other places, and nearly in [377] the same proportion to the annual produce of its land and labour. This increase of the quantity of those metals, however, has not, it seems, increased that annual produce, has neither improved the manufactures and agriculture of the country, nor mended the circumstances of its inhabitants. Spain and Portugal, the countries which possess the mines, are, after Poland, perhaps, the two most beggarly countries in Europe. The value of the precious metals, however, must be lower in Spain and Portugal than in any other part of Europe; as they come from those countries to all other parts of Europe, loaded, not only with a freight and an insurance, but with the expence of smuggling, their exportation being either prohibited, or subjected to a duty. In proportion to the annual produce of the land and labour, therefore, their quantity must be greater in those countries than in any other part of Europe: Those countries, however, are poorer than the greater part of Europe. Though the feudal system has been abolished in Spain and Portugal, it has not been succeeded by a much better.[4]

2 As the low value of gold and silver, therefore, is no proof of the wealth and flourishing state of the country where it takes place; so neither is their high value, or the low money price either of goods in general, or of corn in particular, any proof of its poverty and barbarism.[5]

3 But though the low money price either of goods in general, or of corn in particular, be no proof of the poverty or barbarism of the times, [378] the low money price of some particular sorts of goods, such as cattle, poultry, game of all kinds, *&c.*ᵃ in proportion to that of corn, is a most

a–a 2–6

---

[2] See below, III.iv.4. The decline of the feudal system is examined in III.

[3] The 'disorders' in Poland are mentioned at I.xi.g.17, and its feudal structure at III.ii.8.

[4] Cf. III.iv.22. The causes of the slow progress of Spain and Portugal are summarized at IV.vii.c.53.

[5] 'Let the Value of Gold and Silver either rise or fall, the Enjoyment of all Societies will ever depend upon the Fruits of the Earth, and the Labour of the People; both which joined together are a more certain, a more inexhaustible, and a more real Treasure, than the Gold of *Brazil*, or the Silver of *Potosi*.' (Mandeville, *The Fable of the Bees*, pt. i.216, ed. Kaye i.197–8.)

decisive one. It clearly demonstrates, first, their great abundance in proportion to that of corn, and consequently the great extent of the land which they occupied in proportion to what was occupied by corn; and, secondly, the low value of this land in proportion to that of corn land, and consequently the uncultivated and unimproved state of the far greater part of the lands of the country. It clearly demonstrates that the stock and population of the country did not bear the same proportion to the extent of its territory, which they commonly do in civilized countries, and that society was at that time, and in that country, but in its infancy. From the high or low money price either of goods in general, or of corn in particular, we can infer only that the mines which at that time happened to supply the commercial world with gold and silver, were fertile or barren, not that the country was rich or poor. But from the high or low money-price of some sorts of goods in proportion to that of others, we can infer with a degree of probability that approaches almost to certainty, that it was rich or poor, that the greater part of its lands were improved or unimproved, and that it was either in a more or less barbarous state, or in a more or less civilized one.

4   Any rise in the money price of goods which proceeded altogether from the degradation of the value of silver, would affect all sorts of goods [379] equally, and raise their price universally a third, or a fourth, or a fifth part higher, according as silver happened to lose a third, or a fourth, or a fifth part of its former value.[6] But the rise in the price of provisions, which has been the subject of so much reasoning and conversation, does not affect all sorts of provisions equally. Taking the course of the present century at an average, the price of corn, it is acknowledged, even by those who account for this rise by the degradation of the value of silver, has risen much less than that of some other sorts of provisions. The rise in the price of those other sorts of provisions, therefore, cannot be owing altogether to the degradation of the value of silver. Some other causes must be taken into the account, and those which have been above assigned, will, perhaps, without having recourse to the supposed degradation of the value of silver, sufficiently explain this rise in those particular sorts of provisions of which the price has actually risen in proportion to that of corn.

5   As to the price of corn itself, it has, during the sixty-four first years of the present century, and before the late extraordinary course of bad seasons, been somewhat lower than it was during the sixty-four last years of the preceding century. This fact is attested, not only by the accounts of Windsor market, but by the publick fiars[7] of all the different counties of Scotland, and by the accounts of several different markets in France, which have been collected with great diligence and fidelity by Mr. Messance, and

---

[6] Strictly silver should lose a fourth, a fifth, or a sixth part of its value.
[7] Public fiars are mentioned above, I.viii.34.

by Mr. Dupré [380] de St. Maur.⁸ The evidence is more compleat than could well have been expected in a matter which is naturally so very difficult to be ascertained.

6   As to the high price of corn during these last ten or twelve years, it can be sufficiently accounted for from the badness of the seasons, without supposing any degradation in the value of silver.

7   The opinion, therefore, that silver is continually sinking in its value, seems not to be founded upon any good observations, either upon the prices of corn, or upon those of other provisions.

8   The same quantity of silver, it may, perhaps, be said, will in the present times, even according to the account which has been here given, purchase a much smaller quantity of several sorts of provisions than it would have done during some part of the last century; and to ascertain whether this change be owing to a rise in the value of those goods, or to a fall in the value of silver, is only to establish a vain and useless distinction, which can be of no sort of service to the man who has only a certain quantity of silver to go to market with, or a certain fixed revenue in money. I certainly do not pretend that the knowledge of this distinction will enable him to buy cheaper. It may not, however, upon that account be altogether useless.

9   It may be of some use to the publick by affording an easy proof of the prosperous condition of the country. If the rise in the price of some [381] sorts of provisions be owing altogether to a fall in the value of silver, it is owing to a circumstance from which nothing can be inferred but the fertility of the American mines. The real wealth of the country, the annual produce of its land and labour, may, notwithstanding this circumstance, be either gradually declining, as in Portugal and Poland; or gradually advancing, as in most other parts of Europe. But if this rise in the price of some sorts of provisions be owing to a rise in the real value of the land which produces them, to its increased fertility; or, in consequence of more extended improvement and good cultivation, to its having been rendered fit for producing corn; it is owing to a circumstance which indicates in the clearest manner the prosperous and advancing state of the country. The land constitutes by far the greatest, the most important, and the most durable part of the wealth of every extensive country. It may surely be of some use, or, at least, it may give some satisfaction to the Publick, to have so decisive a proof of the increasing value of by far the greatest, the most important, and the most durable part of its wealth.

10   It may too be of some use to the Publick in regulating the pecuniary reward of some of its inferior servants. If this rise in the price of some sorts of provisions be owing to a fall in the value of silver, their pecuniary reward,

⁸ See above, I.xi.g.15.

provided it was not too large before, ought certainly to be augmented in proportion to the extent of this fall. If it is not augmented, their real re-[382]compence will evidently be so much diminished. But if this rise of price is owing to the increased value, in consequence of the improved fertility of the land which produces such provisions, it becomes a much nicer matter to judge either in what proportion any pecuniary reward ought to be augmented, or whether it ought to be augmented at all. The extension of improvement and cultivation, as it necessarily raises more or less, in proportion to the price of corn, that of every sort of animal food, so it as necessarily lowers that of, I believe, every sort of vegetable food. It raises the price of animal food; because a great part of the land which produces it, being rendered fit for producing corn, must afford to the land-lord and farmer the rent and profit of corn-land. It lowers the price of vegetable food; because, by increasing the fertility of the land, it increases its abundance. The improvements of agriculture too introduce many sorts of vegetable food, which, requiring less land and not more labour than corn, come much cheaper to market. Such are potatoes[9] and maize, or what is called Indian corn, the two most important improvements which the agriculture of Europe, perhaps, which Europe itself, has received from the great extension of its commerce and navigation. Many sorts of vegetable food, besides, which in the rude state of agriculture are confined to the kitchen-garden, and raised only by the spade, come in its improved state to be introduced into common fields, and to be raised by the plough: such as turnips, carrots, cab-[383]bages, &c. If in the progress of improvement, therefore, the real price of one species of food necessarily rises, that of another as necessarily falls, and it becomes a matter of more nicety to judge how far the rise in the one may be compensated by the fall in the other.[10] When the real price of butcher's-meat has once got to its height (which, with regard to every sort, except, perhaps, that of hogs flesh, it seems to have done through a great part of England, more than a century ago), any rise which can afterwards happen in that of any other sort of animal food, cannot much affect the circumstances of the inferior ranks of people. The circumstances of the poor through a great part of England cannot surely be so much distressed by any rise in the price of poultry, fish, wild-fowl, or venison, as they must be relieved by the fall in that of potatoes.

11   In the present season of scarcity the high price of corn no doubt dis-tresses the poor. But in times of moderate plenty, when corn is at its ordinary or average price, the natural rise in the price of any other sort of rude produce cannot much affect them. They suffer more, perhaps, by the artificial rise which has been occasioned by taxes in the price of some

[9] See above, I.xi.b.41, where Smith comments on the nourishing qualities of the potato.
[10] See above, I.viii.35.

manufactured commodities; as of salt, soap, leather, candles, malt, beer, and ale, &c.[11]

[384]   *Effects of the Progress of Improvement upon the real*
Price of Manufactures

1   It is the natural effect of improvement, however, to diminish gradually the real price of almost all manufactures. That of the manufacturing workmanship diminishes, perhaps, in all of them without exception. In consequence of better machinery, of greater dexterity, and of a more proper division and distribution of work, all of which are the natural effects of improvement, a much smaller quantity of labour becomes requisite for executing any particular piece of work; and though, in consequence of the flourishing circumstances of the society, the real price of labour should rise very considerably, yet the great diminution of the quantity will generally much more than compensate the greatest rise which can happen in the price.[1]

2   There are, indeed, a few manufactures, in which the necessary rise in the real price of the rude materials will more than compensate all the advantages which improvement can introduce into the execution of the work. In carpenters and joiners work, and in the coarser sort of cabinet work, the necessary rise in the real price of barren timber, in consequence of the improvement of land, will more than compensate all the advantages which can be derived from the best machinery, the greatest dexterity, and the most proper division and distribution of work.

3   [385] But in all cases in which the real price of the rude materials either does not rise at all, or does not rise very much, that of the manufactured commodity sinks very considerably.

4   This diminution of price has, in the course of the present and preceding century, been most remarkable in those manufactures of which the materials are the coarser metals. A better movement of a watch, than about the middle of the last century could have been bought for twenty pounds, may now perhaps be had for twenty shillings. In the work of cutlers and locksmiths, in all the toys[2] which are made of the coarser metals, and in all those goods which are commonly known by the name of Birmingham and Sheffield ware, there has been, during the same period, a very great reduction of price, though not altogether so great as in watch-work. It has, however, been sufficient to astonish the workmen of every other part of Europe, who in many cases acknowledge that they can produce no work of equal goodness for double, or even for triple the price. There are perhaps no manufactures in which the division of labour can be carried further, or

---

[11] See above, I.viii.35, and below, IV.ii.33, V.ii.k.11.
[1] The same point is made above, I.viii.57.
[2] See LJ (B) 209, 214, ed. Cannan 159, 164.

in which the machinery employed admits of a greater variety of improvements, than those of which the materials are the coarser metals.

5   In the clothing manufacture there has, during the same period, been no such sensible reduction of price. The price of superfine cloth, I have been assured, on the contrary, has, within these five-and-twenty or thirty years, risen somewhat [386] in proportion to its quality; owing, it was said, to a considerable rise in the price of material, which consists altogether of Spanish wool. That of the Yorkshire cloth, which is made altogether of English wool, is said indeed, during the course of the present century, to have fallen a good deal in proportion to its quality. Quality, however, is so very disputable a matter, that I look upon all *information* of this kind as somewhat uncertain. In the clothing manufacture, the division of labour is nearly the same now as it was a century ago, and the machinery employed is not very different. There may, however, have been some small improvements in both, which may have occasioned some reduction of price.[3]

6   *But the reduction* will appear much more sensible and undeniable, if we compare the price of this manufacture in the present times with what it was in a much remoter period, towards the end of the fifteenth century, when the labour was probably much less subdivided, and the machinery employed much more imperfect than it is at present.

7   In 1487, being the 4th of Henry VII.[4] it was enacted, that "whosoever shall sell by retail a broad yard of the finest scarlet grained, or of other grained cloth of the finest making, above sixteen shillings, shall forfeit forty shillings for every yard so sold." Sixteen shillings, therefore, containing about the same quantity of silver as four-and-twenty shillings of our present money, was, at that time, reckoned [387] not an unreasonable price for a yard of the finest cloth; and as this is a sumptuary law, such cloth, it is probable, had usually been sold somewhat dearer. A guinea may be reckoned the highest price in the present times. Even though the quality of the cloths, therefore, should be supposed equal, and that of the present times is most probably much superior, yet, even upon this supposition, the money price of the finest cloth appears to have been considerably reduced since the end of the fifteenth century. But its real price has been much more reduced. Six shillings and eight-pence was then, and long afterwards, reckoned the average price of a quarter of wheat. Sixteen shillings, therefore, was the price of two quarters and more than three

---

a-a informations *1*   *b-b* The reduction, however, *1*

---

[3] Cf. I.xi.o.12.

[4] 4 Henry VII, c.8 (1488). The parliament of 4 Henry III which began on 13 January 1488/9 was on 23 February prorogued to 14 October of 5 Henry VII, 1489, in which session were passed the Acts numbered c.1 to c.7. On 14 October Parliament met until 14 December and was then prorogued until 25 January following and in that session were passed Acts numbered c.8 and c.9. *Statutes of the Realm*, ii.524, n. The quotation is not verbatim.

bushels of wheat. Valuing a quarter of wheat in the present times at eight-and-twenty shillings, the real price of a yard of fine cloth must, in those times, have been equal to at least three pounds six shillings and sixpence of our present money. The man who bought it must have parted with the command of a quantity of labour and subsistence equal to what that sum would purchase in the present times.

8   The reduction in the real price of the coarse manufacture, though considerable, has not been so great as in that of the fine.

9   In 1463, being the 3d of Edward IV.[5] it was enacted, that "no servant in husbandry, nor common labourer, nor servant to any artificer inhabiting out of a city or burgh, shall use or wear in their cloathing any cloth above two [388] shillings the broad yard." In the 3d of Edward IV. two shillings contained very nearly the same quantity of silver as four of our present money. But the Yorkshire cloth which is now sold at four shillings the yard, is probably much superior to any that was then made for the wearing of the very poorest order of common servants. Even the money price of their cloathing, therefore, may, in proportion to the quality, be somewhat cheaper in the present than it was in those antient times. The real price is certainly a good deal cheaper. Ten pence was then reckoned what is called the moderate and reasonable price of a bushel of wheat. Two shillings, therefore, was the price of two bushels and near two pecks of wheat, which in the present times, at three shillings and sixpence the bushel, would be worth eight shillings and nine-pence. For a yard of this cloth the poor servant must have parted with the power of purchasing a quantity of subsistence equal to what eight shillings and nine-pence would purchase in the present times. This is a sumptuary law too, restraining the luxury and extravagance of the poor. Their cloathing, therefore, had commonly been much more expensive.

10   The same order of people are, by the same law, prohibited from wearing hose, of which the price should exceed fourteen-pence the pair, equal to about eight-and-twenty pence of our present money. But fourteen-pence was in those times the price of a bushel and near two pecks of wheat; which, in the present times, at three and [389] sixpence the bushel, would cost five shillings and three-pence. We should in the present times consider this as a very high price for a pair of stockings to a servant of the poorest and lowest order. He must, however, in those times have paid what was really equivalent to this price for them.

11   In the time of Edward IV. the art of knitting stockings was probably not known in any part of Europe. Their hose were made of common cloth, which may have been one of the causes of their dearness. The first person that wore stockings in England is said to have been Queen Elizabeth. She received them as a present from the Spanish ambassador.

[5] 3 Edward IV, c.5 (1463) The quotation is not verbatim.

12   Both in the coarse and in the fine woollen manufacture, the machinery
employed was much more imperfect in those antient, than it is in the present
times.[6] It has since received three very capital improvements, besides,
probably, many smaller ones of which it may be difficult to ascertain either
the number or the importance. The three capital improvements are; first,
The exchange of the rock and spindle for the spinning-wheel, which, with
the same quantity of labour, will perform more than double the quantity of
work. Secondly, the use of several very ᶜvery ᶜingenious machines which
facilitate and abridge in a still greater proportion the winding of the worsted
and woollen yarn, or the proper arrangement of the warp and woof before
they are put into the loom; an operation which, pre-[390]vious to the
invention of those machines, must have been extremely tedious and troublesome. Thirdly, The employment of the fulling mill for thickening the
cloth, instead of treading it in water. Neither wind nor water mills of any
kind were known in England so early as the beginning of the sixteenth
century, nor, so far as I know, in any other part of Europe north of the
Alps.[7] They have been introduced into Italy some time before.

13   The consideration of these circumstances may, perhaps, in some measure
explain to us why the real price both of the coarse and of the fine manufacture, was so much higher in those antient, than it is in the present times. It
cost a greater quantity of labour to bring the goods to market. When they
were brought thither, therefore, they must have purchased or exchanged
for the price of a greater quantity.

14   The coarse manufacture probably was, in those antient times, carried on
in England, in the same manner as it always has been in countries where
arts and manufactures are in their infancy. It was probably a household
manufacture, in which every different part of the work was occasionally
performed by all the different members of almost every private family; but
so as to be their work only when they had nothing else to do, and not to be
the principal business from which any of them derived the greater part of
their subsistence. The work which is performed in this manner, it has
already been observed,[8] [391] comes always much cheaper to market
than that which is the principal or sole fund of the workman's subsistence.
The fine manufacture, on the other hand, was not in those times carried
on in England, but in the rich and commercial country of Flanders; and it
was probably conducted then, in the same manner as now, by people who
derived the whole, or the principal part of their subsistence from it. It was
besides a foreign manufacture, and must have paid some duty, the antient
custom of tonnage and poundage at least, to the king. This duty, indeed,

---

ᶜ⁻ᶜ *om.4, 5*

[6] Cf. I.i.8 where Smith declined to give examples of improved productivity arising
from the use of machines.
[7] See above, I.i.8 and note 15.   [8] See above, I.x.b.49.

would not probably be very great. It was not then the policy of Europe to restrain, by high duties, the importation of foreign manufactures, but rather to encourage it, in order that merchants might be enabled to supply, at as easy a rate as possible, the great men with the conveniences and luxuries which they wanted, and which the industry of their own country could not afford them.[9]

15   The consideration of these circumstances may perhaps in some measure explain to us why, in those antient times, the real price of the coarse manufacture was, in proportion to that of the fine, so much lower than in the present times.

[392]   CONCLUSION *of the* CHAPTER

1   I shall conclude this very long chapter with observing[1] that every improvement in the circumstances of the society tends either directly or indirectly to raise the real rent of land, to increase the real wealth of the landlord, his power of purchasing the labour, or the produce of the labour of other people.

2   The extension of improvement and cultivation tends to raise it directly. The landlord's share of the produce necessarily increases with the increase of the produce.[2]

3   That rise in the real price of those parts of the rude produce of land, which is first the effect of extended improvement and cultivation, and afterwards the cause of their being still further extended, the rise in the price of cattle, for example, tends too to raise the rent of land directly, and in a still greater proportion. The real value of the landlord's share, his real command of the labour of other people, not only rises with the real value of the produce, but the proportion of his share to the whole produce rises with it. That produce, after the rise in its real price, requires no more labour to collect it than before. A smaller proportion of it will, therefore, be sufficient to replace, with the ordinary profit, the stock which employs that labour. A greater proportion of it must, consequently, belong to the landlord.

4   [393] All those improvements in the productive powers of labour, which tend directly to reduce the real price of manufactures, tend indirectly to raise the real rent of land. The landlord exchanges that part of his rude produce, which is over and above his own consumption, or what comes to the same thing, the price of that part of it, for manufactured produce. Whatever reduces the real price of the latter, raises that of the former. An equal

---

[9] The significance of this point becomes apparent in Smith's account of the historical development of cities, in III.iii and iv.

[1] A similar expression is used at I.x.c.60.

[2] Cf. II.iii.9 where it is stated that rent increases in proportion to the extent, but diminishes in proportion to the produce, of land.

quantity of the former becomes thereby equivalent to a greater quantity of the latter; and the landlord is enabled to purchase a greater quantity of the conveniences, ornaments, or luxuries, which he has occasion for.

5   Every increase in the real wealth of the society, every increase in the quantity of useful labour employed within it, tends indirectly to raise the real rent of land. A certain proportion of this labour naturally goes to the land. A greater number of men and cattle are employed in its cultivation, the produce increases with the increase of the stock which is thus employed in raising it, and the rent increases with the produce.

6   The contrary circumstances, the neglect of cultivation and improvement, the fall in the real price of any part of the rude produce of land, the rise in the real price of manufactures from the decay of manufacturing art and industry, the declension of the real wealth of the society, all tend, on the other hand, to lower the real rent [394] of land, to reduce the real wealth of the landlord, to diminish his power of purchasing either the labour, or the produce of the labour of other people.

7   The whole annual produce of the land and labour of every country, or what comes to the same thing, the whole price of that annual produce, naturally divides itself, it has already been observed,[3] into three parts; the rent of land, the wages of labour, and the profits of stock; and constitutes a revenue to three different orders of people; to those who live by rent, to those who live by wages, and to those who live by profit. These are the three great, original and constituent orders of every civilized society, from whose revenue that of every other order is ultimately derived.

8   The interest of the first of those three great orders, it appears from what has been just now said, is strictly and inseparably connected with the general interest of the society. Whatever either promotes or obstructs the one, necessarily promotes or obstructs the other. When the publick deliberates concerning any regulation of commerce or police, the proprietors of land never can mislead it, with a view to promote the interest of their own particular order; at least, if they have any tolerable knowledge of that interest.[4] They are, indeed, too often defective in this tolerable knowledge. They are the only one of the three orders whose revenue costs them neither labour nor care, but comes to them, as [395] it were, of its own accord, and independent of any plan or project of their own.[5] That indolence, which is the natural effect of the ease and security of their situation, renders them too often, not only ignorant, but incapable of that application of mind which is necessary in order to foresee and understand the consequences of any publick regulation.[6]

[3] Above, I.vi.17. The same point is made at II.ii.1.   [4] Cf. IV.ii.21.
[5] Cf. below, V.ii.e.10.
[6] Smith comments on the ignorance of landlords at I.xi.a.1. It is perhaps interesting to note that Smith should have linked lack of mental application with indolence: cf. below, V.i.f.50, where the same phenomenon is linked with the effects of the division of labour.

9   The interest of the second order, that of those who live by wages, is as strictly connected with the interest of the society as that of the first. The wages of the labourer, it has already been shewn,[7] are never so high as when the demand for labour is continually rising, or when the quantity employed is every year increasing considerably. When this real wealth of the society becomes stationary, his wages are soon reduced to what is barely enough to enable him to bring up a family, or to continue the race of labourers.[8] When the society declines, they fall even below this. The order of proprietors may, perhaps, gain more by the prosperity of the society, than that of labourers: but there is no order that suffers so cruelly from its decline. But though the interest of the labourer is strictly connected with that of the society, he is incapable either of comprehending that interest, or of understanding its connection with his own. His condition leaves him no time to receive the necessary information, and his education and habits are commonly such as to render him unfit to judge even though he was fully informed.[9] In the [396] publick deliberations, therefore, his voice is little heard and less regarded, except upon some particular occasions, when his clamour is animated, set on, and supported by his employers, not for his, but their own particular purposes.

10   His employers constitute the third order, that of those who live by profit. It is the stock that is employed for the sake of profit, which puts into motion the greater part of the useful labour of every society. The plans and projects of the employers of stock regulate and direct all the most important operations of labour, and profit is the end proposed by all those plans and projects. But the rate of profit does not, like rent and wages, rise with the prosperity, and fall with the declension of the society. On the contrary, it is naturally low in rich, and high in poor countries, and it is always highest in the countries which are going fastest to ruin. The interest of this third order, therefore, has not the same connection with the general interest of the society as that of the other two.[10] Merchants and master manufacturers are, in this order, the two classes of people who commonly employ the largest capitals, and who by their wealth draw to themselves the greatest share of the publick consideration. As during their whole lives they are engaged in plans and projects, they have frequently more acuteness of understanding than the greater part of country gentlemen. As their thoughts, however, are commonly exercised rather about the interest of their own particular branch [397] of business, than about that of the society, their judgment, even when given with the greatest candour (which it has not been upon every occasion) is much more to be depended upon with regard to the former of those two objects, than with regard to the latter. Their superiority over the country gentleman is, not so much in

---

[7] Above, I.viii.22.   [8] See above, I.viii.15, 24.   [9] See below, V.i.f.50.
[10] See below, IV.iii.c.10.

their knowledge of the publick interest, as in their having a better knowledge of their own interest than he has of his. It is by this superior knowledge of their own interest that they have frequently imposed upon his generosity, and persuaded him to give up both his own interest and that of the publick, from a very simple but honest conviction, that their interest, and not his, was the interest of the publick.[11] The interest of the dealers, however, in any particular branch of trade or manufactures, is always in some respects different from, and even opposite to, that of the publick. To widen the market and to narrow the competition, is always the interest of the dealers. To widen the market may frequently be agreeable enough to the interest of the publick; but to narrow the competition must always be against it, and can serve only to enable the dealers, by raising their profits above what they naturally would be, to levy, for their own benefit, an absurd tax upon the rest of their fellow-citizens. The proposal of any new law or regulation of commerce which comes from this order, ought always to be listened to with great precaution, and ought never to be adopted [398] till after having been long and carefully examined, not only with the most scrupulous, but with the most suspicious attention. It comes from an order of men, whose interest is never exactly the same with that of the publick, who have generally an interest to deceive and even to oppress the publick, and who accordingly have, upon many occasions, both deceived and oppressed it.[12]

Years XII	Price of the Quarter of Wheat each Year.[13]		Average of the different Prices of the same Year.	The average Price of each Year in Money of the present Times.[14]
	£ s. d.		£ s. d.	£ s. d.
1202	– 12 –		– – –	1 16 –
1205	{ – 12 – – 13 4 – 15 – }		– 13 5	2 – 3

[11] See below, IV.ii.21.

[12] Smith often expressed concern over the role of sectional interests and typical examples of this concern occur, for example, at I.x.c.61, IV.ii.43, IV.vii.b.49, IV.viii.17, and V.i.e.4. It is perhaps worth noting that Smith distinguished between the role of private interest and that of national animosity at IV.iii.a.1. Book IV as a whole comments extensively on the role of the mercantile classes with regard to government policy, and especially IV.viii; a chapter which first appeared in the third edition. In Letter 248 addressed to Rochefoucauld, dated 1 November 1785, Smith remarked with reference to Great Britain that 'In a Country where Clamour always intimidates and faction often oppresses the Government, the regulations of Commerce are commonly dictated by those who are most interested to deceive and impose upon the Public.' He expressed similar sentiments in Letter 233 addressed to William Eden, dated 15 December 1783, in commenting that trade regulations 'may, I think, be demonstrated to be in every case a complete piece of dupery, by which the interest of the State and the nation is constantly sacrificed to that of some particular class of traders'. See below, IV.ii.44.

[13] The prices from 1202 to 1597 inclusive are from W. Fleetwood, *Chronicon Preciosum*, 74–124. The prices from 1598 to 1601 inclusive are from the Eton College accounts, quoted and explained below, 272, n.27.   [14] See above, I.xi.e.2.

Years XII	Price of the Quarter of Wheat each Year.			Average of the different Prices of the same Year.			The average Price of each Year in Money of the present Times.		
	£	s.	d.	£	s.	d.	£	s.	d.
1223	-	12	-	-	-	-	1	16	-
1237	-	3	4	-	-	-	-	10	-
1243	-	2	-	-	-	-	-	6	-
1244	-	2	-	-	-	-	-	6	-
1246	-	16	-	-	-	-	2	8	-
1247	.-	13	4	-	-	-	2	-	-
1257	1	4	-	-	-	-	3	12	-
1258	{ 1 - -, - 15 -, - 16 - }			-	17	-	2	11	-
1270	{ 4 16 -, 6 8 - }			5	12	-	16	16	-
1286	{ - 2 8, - 16 - }			-	9	4	1	8	-
						Total,	35	9	3
						Average Price,	2	19	1¼

Years	Price of the Quarter of Wheat each Year.			Average of the different Prices of the same Year.			The average Price of each Year in Money of the present Times.		
	£	s.	d.	£	s.	d.	£	s.	d.
1287	-	3	4	-	-	-	-	10	-
1288	{ - - 8, - 1 -, - 1 4, - 1 6, - 1 8, - 2 -, - 3 4, - 9 4 }			-	3	—¼ [15]	-	9	—¾
1289	{ - 12 -, - 6 -, - 2 -, - 10 8, 1 - - }			-	10	1¼	1	10	4¼ [16]
1290	-	16	—[17]	-	-	-	2	8	-
1294	-	16	-	-	-	-	2	8	-
1302	-	4	-	-	-	-	-	12	-

[15] The average for 1288 is 2s. 7¼d.
[16] Expressed thus in all editions, though strictly expressed, the fraction should be ⅔.
[17] 'And sometimes xxs. as H. Knighton' (W. Fleetwood, *Chronicon Preciosum*, 82).

Years XII	Price of the Quarter of Wheat each Year.			Average of the different Prices of the same Year.			The average Price of each Year in Money of the present Times.		
	£	s.	d.	£	s.	d.	£	s.	d.
1309	–	7	2	–	–	–	1	1	6
1315	1	–	–	–	–	–	3	–	–
1316	⎧1 ⎨1 10 ⎩1 12 2	– – – –	–⎫ –⎬ – –⎭	1	10	6	4	11	6
1317	⎧2 4 ⎪– 14 ⎨2 13 ⎪4 – ⎩– 6	– – –[18] – 8		1	19	6[19]	5	18	6
1336	–	2	–	–	–	–	–	6	–
1338	–	3	4	–	–	–	–	10	–
					Total,		23	4	11¼
					Average Price,		1	18	8

	£	s.	d.	£	s.	d.	£	s.	d.
1339	–	9	–	–	–	–	1	7	–
1349	–	2	–	–	–	–	–	5	2
1359	1	6	8	–	–	–	3	2	2
1361	–	2	–	–	–	–	–	4	8
1363	–	15	–	–	–	–	1	15	–
1369	⎧1 ⎨1 4	– –	–⎫ –⎬	1	2	–	2	9	4
1379	–	4	–	–	–	–	–	9	4
1387	–	2	–	–	–	–	–	4	8
1390	⎧– 13 ⎨– 14 ⎩– 16	4 – –[21]		–	14	5[20]	1	13	7
1401	–	16	–	–	–	–	1	17	4
1407	⎧– 4 ⎨– 3	4¾⎫ 4⎬		–	3	10[22]	–	8	11
1416	–	16	–	–	–	–	1	12	–
					Total,		15	9	4
					Average Price,		1	5	9⅓

[18] Miscopied; it is £2 13s. 4d. in Fleetwood, *Chronicon Preciosum*, 92.
[19] With the correct citation of prices, the average becomes £1 19s. 7d.
[20] With the correct citation of prices, the average becomes 14s. 8d.
[21] Miscopied; it is 16s. 8d. in Fleetwood, *Chronicon Preciosum*, 97.
[22] The average should be 3s. 10½d.

Years XII	Price of the Quarter of Wheat each Year.			Average of the different Prices of the same Year.			The average Price of each Year in Money of the present Times.		
	£	s.	d.	£	s.	d.	£	s.	d.
1423	-	8	-	-	-	-	-	16	-
1425	-	4	-	-	-	-	-	8	-
1434	1	6	8	-	-	-	2	13	4
1435	-	5	4	-	-	-	-	10	8
1439	{1 - - / 1 6 8}			1	3	4	2	6	8
1440	1	4	-	-	-	-	2	8	-
1444	{- 4 4 / - 4 -}			-	4	2	-	8	4
1445	-	4	6	-	-	-	-	9	-
1447	-	8	-	-	-	-	-	16	-
1448	-	6	8	-	-	-	-	13	4
1449	-	5	-	-	-	-	-	10	-
1451	-	8	-	-	-	-	-	16	-
					Total,		12	15	4
					Average Price,		1	1	$^{a}3\frac{1}{2}^{a}$

[401]

Years	Price of the Quarter of Wheat each Year.			Average of the different Prices of the same Year.			The average Price of each Year in Money of the present Times.		
	£	s.	d.	£	s.	d.	£	s.	d.
1453	-	5	4	-	-	-	-	10	8
1455	-	1	2	-	-	-	-	2	4
1457	-	7	8	-	-	-	-	15	4
1459	-	5	-	-	-	-	-	10	-
1460	-	8	-	-	-	-	-	16	-
1463	{- 2 - / - 1 8}			1	10	-	-	3	8
1464	-	6	8	-	-	-	-	10	-
1486	1	4	-	-	-	-	1	17	-
1491	-	14	8	-	-	-	1	2	-
1494	-	4	-	-	-	-	-	6	-
1495	-	3	4	-	-	-	-	5	-
1497	1	-	-[23]	-	-	-	1	11	-
					Total,		8	9	-
					Average Price,		-	14	1

$^{a-a}$ 3⅓ 1

23 £10 in Fleetwood, *Chronicon Preciosum*, 113, but obviously a misprint there, even though he refers to the price that year being 'very dear'.

Years XII	Price of the Quarter of Wheat each Year.			Average of the different Prices of the same Year.			The average Price of each Year in Money of the present Times.		
	£	s.	d.	£	s.	d.	£	s.	d.
1499	–	4	–	–	–	–	–	6	–
1504	–	5	8	–	–	–	–	8	6
1521	1	–	–	–	–	–	1	10	–
1551	–	8	–	–	–	–	–	2	–
1553	–	8	–	–	–	–	–	8	–
1554	–	8	–	–	–	–	–	8	–
1555	–	8	–	–	–	–	–	8	–
1556	–	8	–	–	–	–	–	8	–
1557	$\begin{cases} - & 4 & - \\ - & 5 & - \\ - & 8 & - \\ 2 & 13 & 4 \end{cases}$			$-^b 17$	$8\frac{1}{2}^b$ 24		$-^c 17$	$8\frac{1}{2}^c$	
1558	–	8	–	–	–	–	–	8	–
1559	–	8	–	–	–	–	–	8	–
1560	–	8	–	–	–	–	–	8	–

Total, $^d 6$ 0 $2\frac{1}{2}^d$

$-^e 10$ $-\frac{5}{12}^e$

Years	£	s.	d.	£	s.	d.	£	s.	d.
1561	–	8	–	–	–	–	–	8	–
1562	–	8	–	–	–	–	–	8	–
1574	$\begin{cases} 2 & 16 & - \\ 1 & 4 & - \end{cases}$			2	–	–	2	–	–
1587	3	4	–	–	–	–	3	4	–
1594	2	16	–	–	–	–	2	16	–
1595	2	13	–25	–	–	–	2	13	–
1596	4	–	–	–	–	–	4	–	–
1597	$\begin{cases} 5 & 4 & - \\ 4 & - & - \end{cases}$			4	12	–	4	12	–
1598	2	16	8	–	–	–	2	16	8
1599	1	19	2	–	–	–	1	19	2
1600	1	17	8	–	–	–	1	17	8
1601	1	14	10	–	–	–	1	14	10

Total, 28 9 4

Average Price, $^f 2$ 7 $5\frac{1}{3}^f$

$^{b-b}$ 12 7 *1–2* $^{c-c}$ 12 7 *1–2* $^{d-d}$ 6 5 1 *1–2* $^{e-e}$ 10 5 *1–2*
$^{f-f}$ 2 4 $9\frac{1}{3}$ *1–2*

24 The average for 1557 is 17s. 7d.
25 Miscopied; it is £2 13s. 4d. in Fleetwood, *Chronicon Preciosum*, 123.

[403] *Prices of the Quarter of nine Bushels of the best or highest priced Wheat at Windsor Market, on Lady-Day and Michaelmas, from 1595 to 1764, both inclusive; the Price of each Year being the medium between the highest Prices of those Two Market Days.*[26]

Years.		£	s.	d.	Years.		£	s.	d.
1595,	–	2	0	0	1621,	–	1	10	4
1596,	–	2	8	0	1622,	–	2	18	8
1597,	–	3	9	6	1623,	–	2	12	0
1598,	–	2	16	8	1624,	–	2	8	0
1599,	–	1	19	2	1625,	–	2	12	0
1600,	–	1	17	8	1626,	–	2	9	4
1601,	–	1	14	10	1627,	–	1	16	0
1602,	–	1	9	4	1628,	–	1	8	0
1603,	–	1	15	4	1629,	–	2	2	0
1604,	–	1	10	8	1630,	–	2	15	8
1605,	–	1	15	10	1631,	–	3	8	0
1606,	–	1	13	0	1632,	–	2	13	4
1607	–	1	16	8	1633,	–	2	18	0
1608,	–	2	16	8	1634,	–	2	16	0
1609,	–	2	10	0	1635,	–	2	16	0
1610,	–	1	15	10	1636,	–	2	16	8
1611,	–	1	18	8					
1612,	–	2	2	4	16)	40	0	0	
1613,	–	2	8	8					
1614,	–	2	1	8½			2	10	0
1615,	–	1	18	8					
1616,	–	2	0	4					
1617,	–	2	8	8					
1618,	–	2	6	8					
1619,	–	1	15	4					
1620,	–	1	10	4					

26) 54 0 6½

2 1 6$\frac{9}{13}$

---

[26] The prices are from the Audit Books of Eton College, quoted by Charles Smith, *Three Tracts on the Corn Trade* (London, 1766), 97. For an explanation of the measure of a quarter of nine bushels of the best wheat see above, I.xi.f.4.

404]

		Wheat per quarter.				Wheat per quarter.		
Years.		£	s.	d.	Years.		£	s.	d.
					Brought over,		79	14	10
1637,	–	2	13	0	1671,	–	2	2	0
1638,	–	2	17	4	1672,	–	2	1	0
1639,	–	2	4	10	1673,	–	2	6	8
1640,	–	2	4	8	1674,	–	3	8	8
1641,	–	2	8	0	1675,	–	3	4	8
1642,		0	0	0	1676,	–	1	18	0
					1677,	–	2	2	0
1643,		0	0	0	1678,	–	2	19	0
					1679,	–	3	0	0
1644,		0	0	0	1680,	–	2	5	0
					1681,	–	2	6	8
1645,		0	0	0	1682,	–	2	4	0
					1683,	–	2	0	0
1646,	–	2	8	0	1684,	–	2	4	0
1647,	–	3	13	8	1685,	–	2	6	8
1648,	–	4	5	0	1686,	–	1	14	0
1649,	–	4	0	0	1687,	–	1	5	2
1650,	–	3	16	8	1688,	–	2	6	0
1651,	–	3	13	4	1689,	–	1	10	0
1652,	–	2	9	6	1690,	–	1	14	8
1653,	–	1	15	6	1691,	–	1	14	0
1654,	–	1	6	0	1692,	–	2	6	8
1655,	–	1	13	4	1693,	–	3	7	8
1656,	–	2	3	0	1694,	–	3	4	0
1657,	–	2	6	8	1695,	–	2	13	0
1658,	–	3	5	0	1696,	–	3	11	0
1659,	–	3	6	0	1697,	–	3	0	0
1660,	–	2	16	6	1698,	–	3	8	4
1661,	–	3	10	0	1699,	–	3	4	0
1662,	–	3	14	0	1700,	–	2	0	0
1663,	–	2	17	0					
1664,	–	2	0	6	60)	153	1	8	
1665,	–	2	9	4					
1666,	–	1	16	0			2	11	0½
1667,	–	1	16	0					
1668,	–	2	0	0					
1669,	–	2	4	4					
1670,	–	2	1	8					

Wanting in the account. The year 1646 supplied by bishop Fleetwood.

Carry over,   79 14 10

[405]

Years.		Wheat per quarter. £ s. d.			Years.		Wheat per quarter. £ s. d.		
					Brought over		69	8	8
1701,	–	1	17	8	1734,	–	1	18	10
1702,	–	1	9	6	1735,	–	2	3	0
1703,	–	1	16	0	1736,	–	2	0	4
1704,	–	2	6	6	1737,	–	1	18	0
1705,	–	1	10	0	1738,	–	1	15	6
1706,	–	1	6	0	1739,	–	1	18	6
1707,	–	1	8	6	1740,	–	2	10	8
1708,	–	2	1	6	1741,	–	2	6	8
1709,	–	3	18	6	1742,	–	1	14	0
1710,	–	3	18	0	1743,	–	1	4	10
1711,	–	2	14	0	1744,	–	1	4	10
1712,	–	2	6	4	1745,	–	1	7	6
1713,	–	2	11	0	1746,	–	1	19	0
1714,	–	2	10	4	1747,	–	1	14	10
1715,	–	2	3	0	1748,	–	1	17	0
1716,	–	2	8	0	1749,	–	1	17	0
1717,	–	2	5	8	1750,	–	1	12	6
1718,	–	1	18	10	1751,	–	1	18	6
1719,	–	1	15	0	1752,	–	2	1	10
1720,	–	1	17	0	1753,	–	2	4	8
1721,	–	1	17	6	1754,	–	1	14	8
1722,	–	1	16	0	1755,	–	1	13	10
1723,	–	1	14	8	1756,	–	2	5	3
1724,	–	1	17	0	1757,	–	3	0	0
1725,	–	2	8	6	1758,	–	2	10	0
1726,	–	2	6	0	1759,	–	1	19	10
1727,	–	2	2	0	1760,	–	1	16	6
1728,	–	2	14	6	1761,	–	1	10	3
1729,	–	2	6	10	1762,	–	1	19	0
1730,	–	1	16	6	1763,	–	2	0	9
1731,	–	1	12	10	1764,	–	2	6	9
1732,	–	1	6	8					
1733,	–	1	8	4	64)	129	13	6	
Carry over,		69	8	8			2	0	$6\frac{10}{32}$ [27]

---

[27] The average is £2 0s. $6\frac{9}{32}d.$

[406]

Years.	Wheat per quarter. £ s. d.			Years.	Wheat per quarter. £ s. d.		
1731,	–	1 12	10	1741,	–	2 6	8
1732,	–	1 6	8	1742,	–	1 14	0
1733,	–	1 8	4	1743,	–	1 4	10
1734,	–	1 18	10	1744,	–	1 4	10
1735,	–	2 3	0	1745,	–	1 7	6
1736,	–	2 0	4	1746,	–	1 19	0
1737,	–	1 18	0	1747,	–	1 14	10
1738,	–	1 15	6	1748,	–	1 17	0
1739,	–	1 18	6	1749,	–	1 17	0
1740,	–	2 10	8	1750,	–	1 12	6

10) 18 12 8   10) 16 18 2

1 17 3$\frac{1}{5}$ 1 13 9$\frac{4}{5}$

BOOK II

Of the Nature, Accumulation, and Employment of Stock

INTRODUCTION

1   IN that rude state of society in which there is no division of labour, in which exchanges are seldom made, and in which every man provides every thing for himself, it is not necessary that any stock should be accumulated or stored up beforehand in order to carry on the business of the society. Every man endeavours to supply by his own industry his own occasional wants as they occur. When he is hungry, he goes to the forest to hunt; when his coat is worn out, he cloaths himself with the skin of the first large animal he kills: and when his hut begins to go to ruin, he repairs it, as well as he can, with the trees and the turf that are nearest it.

2   But when the division of labour has once been thoroughly introduced, the produce of a man's own labour can supply but a very small part of his occasional wants.[1] The far greater part of them are supplied by the produce of other mens labour, which he purchases with the produce, or, what is the same thing, with the price of the produce of his own. But this purchase [408] cannot be made till such time as the produce of his own labour has not only been compleated, but sold. A stock of goods of different kinds, therefore, must be stored up somewhere sufficient to maintain him, and to supply him with the materials and tools of his work till such time, at least, as both these events can be brought about.[2] A weaver cannot apply himself

---

[1] See above, I.i. and ii.

[2] Cf. LJ (A) vi. 93: 'The number of hands employed in business depends on the stored stock in the kingdom . . . Many goods produce nothing for a great while. The grower, the spinner, the dresser of flax, have no immediate profit . . . All these must be maintain'd by the stored stock of the manufacturer, as they gain nothing of themselves.' Similar points are made in LJ (B) 233, 287, ed. Cannan 181 and 223. Smith remarks in the latter place that: 'till some stock be produced there can be no division of labour, and before a division of labour take place there can be very little accumulation of stock.' This reference occurs in the course of a discussion of the causes of the slow progress of opulence and was designed to illustrate the difficulty faced by primitive societies in acquiring the limited amount of stock needed before a division of labour becomes possible. The same point is made in an interesting way in ED 5.2. Turgot also emphasized the importance of the prior accumulation of stock. See for example, *Reflections* LI and LIX. These sections introduce a discussion of 'advances' in agriculture and manufactures respectively.

entirely to his peculiar business, unless there is beforehand stored up some-where, either in his own possession or in that of some other person, a stock sufficient to maintain him, and to supply him with the materials and tools of his work, till he has not only compleated, but sold his web. This accumulation must, evidently, be previous to his applying his industry for so long a time to such a peculiar business.

3   As the accumulation of stock must, in the nature of things, be previous to the division of labour, so labour can be more and more subdivided *in proportion only* as stock is previously more and more accumulated. The quantity of materials which the same number of people can work up, increases in a great proportion as labour comes to be more and more sub-divided; and as the operations of each workman are gradually reduced to a greater degree of simplicity, a variety of new machines come to be invented for facilitating and abridging those operations. As the division of labour advances, therefore, in order to give constant employment to an equal number of workmen, an equal stock of provisions, and a greater stock of materials and tools [409] than what would have been necessary in a ruder state of things, must be accumulated beforehand. But the number of workmen in every branch of business generally increases with the division of labour in that branch, or rather it is the increase of their number which enables them to class and subdivide themselves in this manner.

4   As the accumulation of stock is previously necessary for carrying on this great improvement in the productive powers of labour, so that accumula-tion naturally leads to this improvement. The person who employs his stock in maintaining labour, necessarily wishes to employ it in such a manner as to produce as great a quantity of work as possible. He endeavours, therefore, both to make among his workmen the most proper distribution of employment, and to furnish them with the best machines which he can either invent or afford to purchase.[3] His abilities in both these respects are generally in proportion to the extent of his stock, or to the number of people whom it can employ. The quantity of industry, therefore, not only increases in every country with the increase of the stock which employs it, but, in consequence of that increase, the same quantity of industry pro-duces a much greater quantity of work.

5   Such are in general the effects of the increase of stock upon industry and its productive powers.

6   In the following book I have endeavoured to explain the nature of stock, the effects of its accumulation into capitals of different kinds, and the ef-fects of the different employments of [410] those capitals. This book is divided into five chapters. In the first chapter, I have endeavoured to show what are the different parts or branches into which the stock, either of an

a-a only in proportion *1–2*

[3] The same point is made at I.viii.57.

individual, or of a great society, naturally divides itself. In the second, I have endeavoured to explain the nature and operation of money considered as a particular branch of the general stock of the society. The stock which is accumulated into a capital, may either be employed by the person to whom it belongs, or it may be lent to some other person. In the third and fourth chapters, I have endeavoured to examine the manner in which it operates in both these situations. The fifth and last chapter treats of the different effects which the different employments of capital immediately produce upon the quantity both of national industry, and of the annual produce of land and labour.

CHAPTER I

Of the Division of Stock

1 WHEN the stock which a man possesses is no more than sufficient to maintain him for a few days or a few weeks, he seldom thinks of deriving any revenue from it. He consumes it as sparingly as he can, and endeavours by his labour to acquire something which may supply its place before it be consumed altogether. His [411] revenue is, in this case, derived from his labour only. This is the state of the greater part of the labouring poor in all countries.

2 But when he possesses stock sufficient to maintain him for months or years, he naturally endeavours to derive a revenue from the greater part of it; reserving only so much for his immediate consumption as may maintain him till this revenue begins to come in. His whole stock, therefore, is distinguished into two parts. That part which, he expects, is to afford him this revenue, is called his capital. The other is that which supplies his immediate consumption; and which consists either, first, in that portion of his whole stock which was originally reserved for this purpose; or, secondly, in his revenue, from whatever source derived, as it gradually comes in; or, thirdly, in such things as had been purchased by either of these in former years, and which are not yet entirely consumed; such as a stock of cloaths, household furniture, and the like. In one, or other, or all of these three articles, consists the stock which men commonly reserve for their own immediate consumption.

3 There are two different ways in which a capital may be employed so as to yield a revenue or profit to its employer.

4 First, it may be employed in raising, manufacturing, or purchasing goods, and selling them again with a profit. The capital employed in this manner yields no revenue or profit to its employer, while it either remains in his possession, or continues in the same shape. The goods of the [412] merchant yield him no revenue or profit till he sells them for money, and the money yields him as little till it is again exchanged for goods. His capital is continually going from him in one shape, and returning to him in another, and it is only by means of such circulation, or successive exchanges, that it can yield him any profit. Such capitals, therefore, may very properly be called circulating capitals.

5 Secondly, it may be employed in the improvement of land, in the purchase of useful machines and instruments of trade, or in suchlike things as yield a revenue or profit without changing masters, or circulating any further. Such capitals, therefore, may very properly be called fixed capitals.

6   Different occupations require very different proportions between the fixed and circulating capitals employed in them.

7   The capital of a merchant, for example, is altogether a circulating capital. He has occasion for no machines or instruments of trade, unless his shop, or warehouse, be considered as such.

8   Some part of the capital of every master artificer or manufacturer must be fixed in the instruments of his trade. This part, however, is very small in some, and very great in others. A master taylor requires no other instruments of trade but a parcel of needles. Those of the master shoemaker are a little, though but a very little, more expensive. Those of the weaver rise a good deal above those of the shoemaker. The far greater part of the capital of all such master [413] artificers, however, is circulated, either in the wages of their workmen, or in the price of their materials, and repaid with a profit by the price of the work.[1]

9   In other works a much greater fixed capital is required. In a great iron-work, for example, the furnace for melting the ore, the forge, the slitt-mill, are instruments of trade[2] which cannot be erected without a very great expence.[3] In coal-works and mines of every kind, the machinery necessary both for drawing out the water and for other purposes, is frequently still more expensive.

10   That part of the capital of the farmer which is employed in the instruments of agriculture is a fixed; that which is employed in the wages and maintenance of his labouring servants, is a circulating capital. He makes a profit of the one by keeping it in his own possession, and of the other by parting with it. The price or value of his labouring cattle is a fixed capital in the same manner as that of the instruments of husbandry: Their maintenance is a circulating capital in the same manner as that of the labouring servants. The farmer makes his profit by keeping the labouring cattle, and by parting with their maintenance. Both the price and the maintenance of the cattle which are bought in and fattened, not for labour, but for sale, are a circulating capital. The farmer makes his profit by parting with them. A flock of sheep or a herd of cattle that, in a breeding country, is bought in, neither for labour, nor for sale, [414] but in order to make a profit by their wool, by their milk, and by their increase, is a fixed capital. The profit is made by keeping them. Their maintenance is a circulating capital. The profit is made by parting with it; and it comes back with both its own profit, and the profit upon the whole price of the cattle, in the price of the wool,

---

[1] It is pointed out below, V. ii.k.43, that almost the whole capital of society circulates through the hands of the lower orders. See also II.v.11.

[2] Smith applies the term 'instrument' in a variety of contexts, referring for example to labour, materials, and fixed capital as 'instruments' of production. See for example below, IV.viii.1,38,42,44 and V.ii.k.12.

[3] See below, IV.vii.b.42, where Smith points out that the erection of slit-mills was prohibited in the American colonies.

the milk, and the increase. The whole value of the seed too is properly a fixed capital. Though it goes backwards and forwards between the ground and the granary, it never changes masters, and therefore does not properly circulate. The farmer makes his profit, not by its sale, but by its increase.

11   The general stock of any country or society is the same with that of all its inhabitants or members, and therefore naturally divides itself into the same three portions, each of which has a distinct function or office.

12   The First, is that portion which is reserved for immediate consumption, and of which the characteristick is, that it affords no revenue or profit. It consists in the stock of food, cloaths, household furniture, &c. which have been purchased by their proper consumers, but which are not yet entirely consumed. The whole stock of mere dwelling-houses too subsisting at any one time in the country, make a part of this first portion. The stock that is laid out in a house, if it is to be the dwelling-house of the proprietor, ceases from that moment to serve in the function of a capital, or to afford any revenue to its owner. A dwelling-house, as such, contributes nothing to the revenue of its inhabitant; and though it [415] is, no doubt, extremely useful to him, it is as his cloaths and household furniture are useful to him, which, however, make a part of his expence, and not of his revenue. If it is to be lett to a tenant for rent, as the house itself can produce nothing, the tenant must always pay the rent out of some other revenue which he derives either from labour, or stock, or land.[4] Though a house, therefore, may yield a revenue to its proprietor, and thereby serve in the function of a capital to him, it cannot yield any to the publick, nor serve in the function of a capital to it, and the revenue of the whole body of the people can never be in the smallest degree increased by it. Cloaths, and household furniture, in the same manner, sometimes yield a revenue, and thereby serve in the function of a capital to particular persons. In countries where masquerades are common, it is a trade to let out masquerade dresses for a night. Upholsterers frequently lett furniture by the month or by the year. Undertakers lett the furniture of funerals by the day and by the week. Many people lett furnished houses, and get a rent, not only for the use of the house, but for that of the furniture. The revenue, however, which is derived from such things, must always be ultimately drawn from some other source of revenue. Of all parts of the stock, either of an individual, or of a society, reserved for immediate consumption, what is laid out in houses is most slowly consumed.[5] A stock of cloaths may last several years: a stock of furniture half a century or a century: but a [416] stock of houses, well built and properly taken care of, may last many centuries. Though the period of their total consumption, however, is more distant, they are still

---

[4] This doctrine is applied below, V.ii.e.7.
[5] The point regarding the rate at which goods are used up is employed below, V.ii.k.16, in discussing taxes on consumable commodities.

as really a stock reserved for immediate consumption as either cloaths or household furniture.

13   The Second of the three portions into which the general stock of the society divides itself, is the fixed capital; of which the characteristick is, that it affords a revenue or profit without circulating or changing masters. It consists chiefly of the four following articles:

14   First, of all useful machines and instruments of trade which facilitate and abridge labour:

15   Secondly, of all those profitable buildings which are the means of procuring a revenue, not only to their proprietor who letts them for a rent, but to the person who possesses them and pays that rent for them; such as shops, warehouses, workhouses, farmhouses, with all their necessary buildings; stables, granaries, &c. These are very different from mere dwelling houses. They are a sort of instruments of trade, and may be considered in the same light:

16   Thirdly, of the improvements of land, of what has been profitably laid out in clearing, draining, enclosing, manuring, and reducing it into the condition most proper for tillage and culture. An improved farm may very justly be regarded in the same light as those useful machines which facilitate and abridge labour, and by means of which, an equal circulating capital can afford a much greater revenue to its em-[417]ployer. An improved farm is equally advantageous and more durable than any of those machines, frequently requiring no other repairs than the most profitable application of the farmer's capital employed in cultivating it:

17   Fourthly, of the acquired and useful abilities of all the inhabitants or members of the society. The acquisition of such talents, by the maintenance of the acquirer during his education, study, or apprenticeship, always costs a real expence, which is a capital fixed and realized, as it were, in his person.[6] Those talents, as they make a part of his fortune, so do they likewise of that of the society to which he belongs. The improved dexterity of a workman may be considered in the same light as a machine or instrument of trade which facilitates and abridges labour, and which, though it costs a certain expence, repays that expence with a profit.

18   The third and last of the three portions into which the general stock of the society naturally divides itself, is the circulating capital; of which the characteristick is, that it affords a revenue only by circulating or changing masters. It is composed likewise of four parts:

19   First, of the money by means of which all the other three are circulated and distributed to their proper *a* consumers:[7]

----

a users and *1*

[6] The artificer is described as a 'living instrument' of trade at IV.viii.44. The educated artificer is likened to an expensive machine at I.x.b.6.

[7] See below, II.i.26 and IV.i.17.

20   Secondly, of the stock of provisions which are in the possession of the butcher, the grazier, the farmer, the corn-merchant, the brewer, &c. and from the sale of which they expect to derive a profit:

21   [418] Thirdly, of the materials, whether altogether rude, or more or less manufactured, of cloaths, furniture, and building, which are not yet made up into any of those three shapes, but which remain in the hands of the growers, the manufacturers, the mercers and drapers, the timber-merchants, the carpenters and joiners, the brickmakers, &c.

22   Fourthly, and lastly, of the work which is made up and compleated, but which is still in the hands of the merchant ᵇorᵇ manufacturer, and not yet disposed of or distributed to the proper ᶜ consumers; such as the finished work which we frequently find ready-made in the shops of the smith, the cabinet-maker, the goldsmith, the jeweller, the china-merchant, &c. The circulating capital consists in this manner, of the provisions, materials, and finished work of all kinds that are in the hands of their respective dealers, and of the money that is necessary for circulating and distributing them to those who are finally to use, or to consume them.

23   Of these four parts three, provisions, materials, and finished work, are, either annually, or in a longer or shorter period, regularly withdrawn from it, and placed either in the fixed capital or in the stock reserved for immediate consumption.

24   Every fixed capital is both originally derived from, and requires to be continually supported by a circulating capital. All useful machines and instruments of trade are originally derived from a circulating capital, which furnishes the [419] materials of which they are made, and the maintenance of the workmen who make them. They require too a capital of the same kind to keep them in constant repair.

25   No fixed capital can yield any revenue but by means of a circulating capital. The most useful machines and instruments of trade will produce nothing without the circulating capital which affords the materials they are employed upon, and the maintenance of the workmen who employ them.[8] Land, however improved, will yield no revenue without a circulating capital, which maintains the labourers who cultivate and collect its produce.

26   To maintain and augment the stock which may be reserved for immediate consumption, is the sole end and purpose both of the fixed and circulating capitals. It is this stock which feeds, cloaths, and lodges the people. Their riches or poverty depends upon the abundant or sparing supplies which those two capitals can afford to the stock reserved for immediate consumption.

ᵇ⁻ᵇ and 6   ᶜ users and *1*

---

[8] It is pointed out at II.ii.64 that the return on fixed is generally slower than that on circulating capital.

27   So great a part of the circulating capital being continually withdrawn from it, in order to be placed in the other two branches of the general stock of the society; it must in its turn require continual supplies, without which it would soon cease to exist. These supplies are principally drawn from three sources, the produce of land, of mines, and of fisheries. These afford continual supplies of provisions and materials, of which part is afterwards wrought up [420] into finished work, and by which are replaced the provisions, materials, and finished work continually withdrawn from the circulating capital. From mines too is drawn what is necessary for maintaining and augmenting that part of it which consists in money. For though, in the ordinary course of business, this part is not, like the other three, necessarily withdrawn from it, in order to be placed in the other two branches of the general stock of the society, it must, however, like all other things, be wasted and worn out at last, and sometimes too be either lost or sent abroad, and must, therefore, require continual, though, no doubt, much smaller supplies.

28   Land, mines, and fisheries, require all both a fixed and a circulating capital to cultivate them; and their produce replaces with a profit, not only those capitals, but all the others in the society. Thus the farmer annually replaces to the manufacturer the provisions which he had consumed and the materials which he had wrought up the year before; and the manufacturer replaces to the farmer the finished work which he had wasted and worn out in the same time. This is the real exchange that is annually made between those two orders of people,[9] though it seldom happens that the rude produce of the one and the manufactured produce of the other, are directly bartered for one another; because it seldom happens that the farmer sells his corn and his cattle, his flax and his wool, to the very same person of whom he chuses to purchase the [421] cloaths, furniture, and instruments of trade which he wants. He sells, therefore, his rude produce for money, with which he can purchase, wherever it is to be had, the manufactured produce he has occasion for. Land even replaces, in part, at least, the capitals with which fisheries and mines are cultivated. It is the produce of land which draws the fish from the waters; and it is the produce of the surface of the earth which extracts the minerals from its bowels.

29   The produce of land, mines, and fisheries, when their natural fertility is equal, is in proportion to the extent and proper application of the capitals employed about them. When the capitals are equal and equally well applied, it is in proportion to their natural fertility.

30   In all countries where there is tolerable security,[10] every man of common

---

[9] See below, III.i.

[10] See below, III.iii.12, III.iv.4, and V.iii.7. Smith attributes England's relatively rapid rate of growth to the security enjoyed by her inhabitants. See for example IV.v.b.43, IV.vii.c.54, and II.iii.36.

understanding will endeavour to employ whatever stock he can command in procuring either present enjoyment or future profit. If it is employed in procuring present enjoyment, it is a stock reserved for immediate consumption. If it is employed in procuring future profit, it must procure this profit either by staying with him, or by going from him. In the one case it is a fixed, in the other it is a circulating capital. A man must be perfectly crazy who, where there is tolerable security, does not employ all the stock which he commands, whether it be his own or borrowed of other people, in some one or other of those three ways.[11]

31   [422] In those unfortunate countries, indeed, where men are continually afraid of the violence of their superiors, they frequently bury and conceal a great part of their stock, in order to have it always at hand to carry with them to some place of safety, in case of their being threatened with any of those disasters to which they consider themselves as at all times exposed. This is said to be a common practice in Turkey, in Indostan, and, I believe, in most other governments of Asia.[12] It seems to have been a common practice among our ancestors during the violence of the feudal government.[13] Treasure-trove was in those times considered as no contemptible part of the revenue of the greatest sovereigns in Europe. It consisted in such treasure as was found concealed in the earth, and to which no particular person could prove any right. This was regarded in those times as so important an object, that it was always considered as belonging to the sovereign, and neither to the finder nor to the proprietor of the land, unless the right to it had been conveyed to the latter by an express clause in his charter.[14] It was put upon the same footing with gold and silver mines, which, without a special clause in the charter, were never supposed to be comprehended in the general grant of the lands, though mines of lead, copper, tin, and coal were, as things of smaller consequence.

[11] See below, II.iii.18: 'What is annually saved is as regularly consumed as what is annually spent . . .'
[12] LJ (A) i.59 comments: 'At this day in Turky and the Moguls dominions every man almost has a treasure, and one of the last things he communicates to his heirs is the place where his treasure is to be found.'
[13] See below, III.iv.9 and V.iii.9. It is also pointed out at V.iii.1 that treasures were needed in primitive economies to meet the obligations of the sovereign. See also V.i.a.42.
[14] LJ (A) i.58–9 reads: 'unless the king had granted a proprietor of land the Franchise of treasure-troff, he could not take to himself the treasure found in his own ground, and far less what he found on anothers. These often make a good part of the king's revenues, for though they are now seldom met with, yet formerly in those confused periods when property was very insecure . . . nothing was more common than for a man to bury what he had got together.'

CHAPTER II

Of Money considered as a particular Branch of the general Stock of the Society, or of the Expence of maintaining the National Capital

1   IT has been shewn in the first Book, that the price of the greater part of commodities resolves itself into three parts, of which one pays the wages of the labour, another the profits of the stock, and a third the rent of the land which had been employed in producing and bringing them to market:[1] that there are, indeed, some commodities of which the price is made up of two of those parts only, the wages of labour, and the profits of stock:[2] and a very few in which it consists altogether in one, the wages of labour: but that the price of every commodity necessarily resolves itself into some one, or other, or all of these three parts; every part of it which goes neither to rent nor to wages, being necessarily profit to somebody.

2   Since this is the case, it has been observed, with regard to every particular commodity, taken separately; it must be so with regard to all the commodities which compose the whole annual produce of the land and labour of every country, taken complexly. The whole price or exchangeable value of that annual produce, must resolve itself into the same three parts, and be parcelled out among the different inhabitants of [424] the country, either as the wages of their labour, the profits of their stock, or the rent of their land.

3   But though the whole value of the annual produce of the land and labour of every country is thus divided among and constitutes a revenue to its different inhabitants, yet as in the rent of a private estate we distinguish between the gross rent and the neat rent, so may we likewise in the revenue of all the inhabitants of a great country.

4   The gross rent of a private estate comprehends whatever is paid by the farmer; the neat rent, what remains free to the landlord, after deducting the expence of management, of repairs, and all other necessary charges;[3] or what, without hurting his estate, he can afford to place in his stock reserved for immediate consumption, or to spend upon his table, equipage, the ornaments of his house and furniture, his private enjoyments and amusements. His real wealth is in proportion, not to his gross, but to his neat rent.

5   The gross revenue of all the inhabitants of a great country, comprehends the whole annual produce of their land and labour; the neat revenue, what remains free to them after deducting the expence of maintaining; first, their fixed; and, secondly, their circulating capital; or what, without encroaching upon their capital, they can place in their stock reserved for

---

[1] Above, I.vi.   [2] Above, I.vi.15.   [3] See above, I.xi.a.2.

immediate consumption, or spend upon their subsistence, conveniencies, and amusements. Their real wealth [425] too is in proportion, not to their gross, but to their neat revenue.

6   The whole expence of maintaining the fixed capital, must evidently be excluded from the neat revenue of the society. Neither the materials necessary for supporting their useful machines and instruments of trade, their profitable buildings, &c. nor the produce of the labour necessary for fashioning those materials into the proper form, can ever make any part of it. The price of that labour may indeed make a part of it; as the workmen so employed may place the whole value of their wages in their stock reserved for immediate consumption. But in other sorts of labour, both the price and the produce go to this stock, the price to that of the workmen, the produce to that of other people, whose subsistence, conveniencies, and amusements, are augmented by the labour of those workmen.

7   The intention of the fixed capital is to increase the productive powers of labour, or to enable the same number of labourers to perform a much greater quantity of work. In a farm where all the necessary buildings, fences, drains, communications, &c. are in the most perfect good order, the same number of labourers and labouring cattle will raise a much greater produce, than in one of equal extent and equally good ground, but not furnished with equal conveniencies. In manufactures the same number of hands, assisted with the best machinery, will work up a much greater quantity of goods than with more imperfect instruments of trade. The expence which is properly laid out upon a fixed [426] capital of any kind, is always repaid with great profit, and increases the annual produce by a much greater value than that of the support which such improvements require.[4] This support, however, still requires a certain portion of that produce. A certain quantity of materials, and the labour of a certain number of workmen, both of which might have been immediately employed to augment the food, cloathing and lodging, the subsistence and conveniencies of the society, are thus diverted to another employment, highly advantageous indeed, but still different from this one. It is upon this account that all such improvements in mechanicks, as enable the same number of workmen to perform an equal quantity of work, with cheaper and simpler machinery than had been usual before, are always regarded as advantageous to every society.[5] A certain quantity of materials, and the labour of a certain number of workmen, which had before been employed in supporting a more complex and expensive machinery, can afterwards be applied to augment the quantity of work which that or any other machinery is useful only for performing. The undertaker of some great manufactory who employs a thousand a-year in the maintenance of his machinery, if he can reduce this expence to five hundred, will naturally employ the other five hundred in purchasing an

---

[4] See above, I.x.b.6.   [5] See above, I.i.8, and below, II.iii.32, IV.ix.35.

additional quantity of materials to be wrought up by an additional number of workmen. The quantity of that work, therefore, which his machinery was useful only for performing, will naturally be augmented, and with [427] it all the advantage and conveniency which the society can derive from that work.

8   The expence of maintaining the fixed capital in a great country, may very properly be compared to that of repairs in a private estate. The expence of repairs may frequently be necessary for supporting the produce of the estate, and consequently both the gross and the neat rent of the landlord. When by a more proper direction, however, it can be diminished without occasioning any diminution of produce, the gross rent remains at least the same as before, and the neat rent is necessarily augmented.

9   But though the whole expence of maintaining the fixed capital is thus necessarily excluded from the neat revenue of the society, it is not the same case with that of maintaining the circulating capital. Of the four parts of which this latter capital is composed, money, provisions, materials, and finished work, the three last, it has already been observed, are regularly withdrawn from it, and placed either in the fixed capital of the society, or in their stock reserved for immediate consumption. Whatever portion of those consumable goods is not employed in maintaining the former, goes all to the latter, and makes a part of the neat revenue of the society. The maintenance of those three parts of the circulating capital, therefore, withdraws no portion of the annual produce from the neat revenue of the society, besides what is necessary for maintaining the fixed capital.

10   [428] The circulating capital of a society is in this respect different from that of an individual. That of an individual is totally excluded from making any part of his neat revenue, which must consist altogether in his profits. But though the circulating capital of every individual makes a part of that of the society to which he belongs, it is not upon that account totally excluded from making a part likewise of their neat revenue. Though the whole goods in a merchant's shop must by no means be placed in his own stock reserved for immediate consumption, they may in that of other people, who, from a revenue derived from other funds, may regularly replace their value to him, together with its profits, without occasioning any diminution either of his capital or of theirs.

11   Money, therefore, is the only part of the circulating capital of a society, of which the maintenance can occasion any diminution in their neat revenue.

12   The fixed capital, and that part of the circulating capital which consists in money, so far as they affect the revenue of the society, bear a very great resemblance to one another.

13   First, as those machines and instruments of trade, &c. require a certain expence, first to erect them, and afterwards to support them, both which

expences, though they make a part of the gross, are deductions from the neat revenue of the society; so the stock of money which circulates in any country must require a certain expence, first to collect it, and afterwards to sup-[429]port it, both which expences, though they make a part of the gross, are, in the same manner, deductions from the neat revenue of the society. A certain quantity of very valuable materials, gold and silver, and of very curious labour, instead of augmenting the stock reserved for immediate consumption, the subsistence, conveniences, and amusements of individuals, is employed in supporting that great but expensive instrument of commerce, by means of which every individual in the society has his subsistence, conveniencies, and amusements, regularly distributed to him in their proper ᵃproportionsᵃ.

14   Secondly, as the machines and instruments of trade, &c. which compose the fixed capital either of an individual or of a society, make no part either of the gross or of the neat revenue of either; so money, by means of which the whole revenue of the society is regularly distributed among all its different members, makes itself no part of that revenue. The great wheel of circulation is altogether different from the goods which are circulated by means of it.⁶ The revenue of the society consists altogether in those goods, and not in the wheel which circulates them. In computing either the gross or the neat revenue of any society, we must always, from their whole annual circulation of money and goods, deduct the whole value of the money, of which not a single farthing can ever make any part of either.

15   It is the ambiguity of language only which can make this proposition appear either doubtful [430] or paradoxical. When properly explained and understood, it is almost self-evident.

16   When we talk of any particular sum of money, we sometimes mean nothing but the metal pieces of which it is composed; and sometimes we include in our meaning some obscure reference to the goods which can be had in exchange for it, or to the power of purchasing which the possession of it conveys. Thus when we say, that the circulating money of England has been computed at eighteen millions, we mean only to express the amount of the metal pieces, which some writers have computed, or rather have supposed to circulate in that country. But when we say that a man is worth fifty or a hundred pounds a-year, we mean commonly to express not only the amount of the metal pieces which are annually paid to him, but the value of the goods which he can annually purchase or consume. We mean commonly to ascertain what is or ought to be his way of living, or the quantity and quality of the necessaries and conveniencies of life in which he can with propriety indulge himself.

ᵃ⁻ᵃ proportion 5–6

---

⁶ See below, II.ii.23.

17 When, by any particular sum of money, we mean not only to express the amount of the metal pieces of which it is composed, but to include in its signification some obscure reference to the goods which can be had in exchange for them, the wealth or revenue which it in this case denotes, is equal only to one of the two values which are thus intimated somewhat ambiguously by the same word, and to the latter more properly than to the former, to the money's worth more properly than to the money.

18 [431] Thus if a guinea be the weekly pension of a particular person, he can in the course of the week purchase with it a certain quantity of subsistence, conveniencies, and amusements. In proportion as this quantity is great or small, so are his real riches, his real weekly revenue. His weekly revenue is certainly not equal both to the guinea, and to what can be purchased with it, but only to one or other of those two equal values; and to the latter more properly than to the former, to the guinea's worth rather than to the guinea.

19 If the pension of such a person was paid to him, not in gold, but in a weekly bill for a guinea, his revenue surely would not so properly consist in the piece of paper, as in what he could get for it. A guinea may be considered as a bill for a certain quantity of necessaries and conveniencies upon all the tradesmen in the neighbourhood. The revenue of the person to whom it is paid, does not so properly consist in the piece of gold, as in what he can get for it, or in what he can exchange it for. If it could be exchanged for nothing, it would, like a bill upon a bankrupt, be of no more value than the most useless piece of paper.

20 Though the weekly, or yearly revenue of all the different inhabitants of any country, in the same manner, may be, and in reality frequently is paid to them in money, their real riches, however, the real weekly or yearly revenue of all of them taken together, must always be great or small in proportion to the quantity of con-[432]sumable goods which they can all of them purchase with this money. The whole revenue of all of them taken together is evidently not equal to both the money and the consumable goods; but only to one or other of those two values, and to the latter more properly than to the former.

21 Though we frequently, therefore, express a person's revenue by the metal pieces which are annually paid to him, it is because the amount of those pieces regulates the extent of his power of purchasing, or the value of the goods which he can annually afford to consume. We still consider his revenue as consisting in this power of purchasing or consuming, and not in the pieces which convey it.[7]

22 But if this is sufficiently evident even with regard to an individual, it is still more so with regard to a society. The amount of the metal pieces which are annually paid to an individual, is often precisely equal to his

[7] See above, I.v.

revenue, and is upon that account the shortest and best expression of its value. But the amount of the metal pieces which circulate in a society, can never be equal to the revenue of all its members. As the same guinea which pays the weekly pension of one man to-day, may pay that of another tomorrow, and that of a third the day thereafter, the amount of the metal pieces which annually circulate in any country, must always be of much less value than the whole money pensions annually paid with them.[8] But the power of purchasing, *or* the goods which can successively be bought with the whole of those money pensions as they are successively paid, must always [433] be precisely of the same value with those pensions; as must likewise be the revenue of the different persons to whom they are paid. That revenue, therefore, cannot consist in those metal pieces, of which the amount is so much inferior to its value, but in the power of purchasing, in the goods which can successively be bought with them as they circulate from hand to hand.

23   Money, therefore, the great wheel of circulation, the great instrument of commerce, like all other instruments of trade,[9] though it makes a part and a very valuable part of the capital, makes no part of the revenue of the society to which it belongs;[10] and though the metal pieces of which it is composed, in the course of their annual circulation, distribute to every man the revenue which properly belongs to him, they make themselves no part of that revenue.

24   Thirdly, and lastly, the machines and instruments of trade, &c. which compose the fixed capital, bear this further resemblance to that part of the circulating capital which consists in money; that as every saving in the expence of erecting and supporting those machines, which does not diminish the productive powers of labour, is an improvement of the neat revenue of the society; so every saving in the expence of collecting and supporting that part of the circulating capital which consists in money, is an improvement of exactly the same kind.

b–b 2–6

[8] See below, II.ii.88. Smith comments on the difficulty of establishing the quantity of money needed for circulation at II.ii.40. Cantillon also recognized the importance of velocity and the difficulty of its calculation: 'it is only conjectural when I say that "the real cash or money necessary to carry on the circulation and exchange in a State is about equal in value to one third of all the annual Rents of the proprietors of the said state".' (*Essai*, 172, ed. Higgs 131.)

[9] See above, § 14, and below, IV.i.18. It is stated at II.iii.23 that the 'sole use' of money is to circulate goods. In LJ (A) vi.127 Smith refers to 'money as an instrument of commerce'; ED 4.3: 'the sole use of money is to circulate commodities.' See also above, I.iv.11. In his essay 'Of Money' Hume remarked that: 'Money is not, properly speaking, one of the subjects of commerce; but only the instrument which men have agreed upon to facilitate the exchange of one commodity for another. It is none of the wheels of trade: It is the oil which renders the motion of the wheels more smooth and easy.' (*Essays Moral, Political and Literary*, ed. Green and Grose, i.309.)

[10] See II.i.19 and IV.i.17.

25   It is sufficiently obvious, and it has partly too been explained already, in what manner every saving in the expence of supporting the fixed [434] capital is an improvement of the neat revenue of the society.[11] The whole capital of the undertaker of every work is necessarily divided between his fixed and his circulating capital. While his whole capital remains the same, the smaller the one part, the greater must necessarily be the other. It is the circulating capital which furnishes the materials and wages of labour, and puts industry into motion. Every saving, therefore, in the expence of maintaining the fixed capital, which does not diminish the productive powers of labour, must increase the fund which puts industry into motion, and consequently the annual produce of land and labour, the real revenue of every society.

26   The substitution of paper in the room of gold and silver money, replaces a very expensive instrument of commerce with one much less costly, and sometimes equally convenient.[12] Circulation comes to be carried on by a new wheel, which it costs less both to erect and to maintain than the old one.[13] But in what manner this operation is performed, and in what manner it tends to increase either the gross or the neat revenue of the society, is not altogether so obvious, and may therefore require some further explication.

27   There are several different sorts of paper money; but the circulating notes of banks and bankers are the species which is best known, and which seems best adapted for this purpose.[14]

28   When the people of any particular country have such confidence in the fortune, probity, and prudence of a particular banker, as to be-[435]lieve that he is always ready to pay upon demand such of his promissory notes as are likely to be at any time presented to him; those notes come to have the same currency as gold and silver money, from the confidence that such money can at any time be had for them.

29   A particular banker lends among his customers his own promissory notes, to the extent, we shall suppose, of a hundred thousand pounds. As those notes serve all the purposes of money, his debtors pay him the same interest as if he had lent them so much money. This interest is the source of his gain. Though some of those notes are continually coming back upon him for payment, part of them continue to circulate for months and years together. Though he has generally in circulation, therefore, notes to the extent of a hundred thousand pounds, twenty thousand pounds in gold and

[11] Above, II.ii.8.

[12] The cost of coinage is stated to be £14,000 at IV.vi.31 and paper to be an acceptable substitute for coin, although less secure, at II.ii.86.

[13] Smith refers to the advantages accruing to America from the use of a cheaper instrument of exchange at V.iii.81.

[14] The following discussion of paper money would appear to be based on the analysis of the lectures. See for example, LJ (A) vi.127–46, LJ (B) 244–56, ed. Cannan 190–200.

silver may, frequently be a sufficient provision for answering occasional demands. By this operation, therefore, twenty thousand pounds in gold and silver perform all the functions which a hundred thousand could otherwise have performed. The same exchanges may be made, the same quantity of consumable goods may be circulated and distributed to their proper consumers, by means of his promissory notes, to the value of a hundred thousand pounds, as by an equal value of gold and silver money. Eighty thousand pounds of gold and silver, therefore, can, in this manner, be spared from the circulation of the country; and if different operations of the same kind [436] should, at the same time, be carried on by many different banks and bankers, the whole circulation may thus be conducted with a fifth part only of the gold and silver which would otherwise have been requisite.

30   Let us suppose, for example, that the whole circulating money of some particular country amounted, at a particular time, to one million sterling, that sum being then sufficient for circulating the whole annual produce of their land and labour. Let us suppose too, that some time thereafter, different banks and bankers issued promissory notes, payable to the bearer, to the extent of one million, reserving in their different coffers two hundred thousand pounds for answering occasional demands.[15] There would remain, therefore, in circulation, eight hundred thousand pounds in gold and silver, and a million of bank notes, or eighteen hundred thousand pounds of paper and money together. But the annual produce of the land and labour of the country had before required only one million to circulate and distribute it to its proper consumers, and that annual produce cannot be immediately augmented by those operations of banking. One million, therefore, will be sufficient to circulate it after them. The goods to be bought and sold being precisely the same as before, the same quantity of money will be sufficient for buying and selling them. The channel of circulation, if I may be allowed such an expression, will remain precisely the same as before. One million we have supposed sufficient [437] to fill that channel. Whatever, therefore, is poured into it beyond this sum, cannot run in it, but must overflow. One million eight hundred thousand pounds

[15] In his *Letter* (18–19) Pownall commented on this passage that:

many years experience in a country of paper money hath convinced me, that if any instrument of the exchange of commodities, other than that which, while it measures the correlative values in circulation, is founded on a DEPOSIT, equivalent at all times to the conversion of it into money, shall be introduced, it will be a source of fraud, which, leading by an unnatural influx of riches to luxury without bounds, and to enterprize without foundation, will derange all industry, and instead of substantial wealth end by bankruptcies in distress and poverty.

See below, II.ii.86 and 102. Pownall here approaches Hume's position and indeed refers to him as 'very clear-minded and ingenious' with regard to paper money (22).

are poured into it. Eight hundred thousand pounds, therefore, must over-flow, that sum being over and above what can be employed in the circulation of the country. But though this sum cannot be employed at home, it is too valuable to be allowed to lie idle.[16] It will, therefore, be sent abroad, in order to seek that profitable employment which it cannot find at home.[17] But the paper cannot go abroad; because at a distance from the banks which issue it, and from the country in which payment of it can be exacted by law, it will not be received in common payments.[18] Gold and silver, therefore, to the amount of eight hundred thousand pounds will be sent abroad, and the channel of home circulation will remain filled with a million of paper, instead of the million of those metals which filled it before.[19]

31   But though so great a quantity of gold and silver is thus sent abroad, we must not imagine it is sent abroad for nothing, or that its proprietors make a present of it to foreign nations. They will exchange it for foreign goods of some kind or another, in order to supply the consumption either of some other foreign country, or of their own.

32   If they employ it in purchasing goods in one foreign country in order to supply the consumption of another, or in what is called the carrying trade, whatever profit they make will be an ad-[438]dition to the neat revenue of their own country. It is like a new fund, created for carrying on a new trade; domestick business being now transacted by paper, and the gold and silver being converted into a fund for this new trade.

33   If they employ it in purchasing foreign goods for home consumption, they may either, first, purchase such goods as are likely to be consumed by idle people who produce nothing, such as foreign wines, foreign silks, &c.; or, secondly, they may purchase an additional stock of materials, tools, and provisions, in order to maintain and employ an additional number of industrious people, who re-produce, with a profit, the value of their annual consumption.

34   So far as it is employed in the first way, it promotes prodigality, in-creases expence and consumption without increasing production, or establishing any permanent fund for supporting that expence, and is in every respect hurtful to the society.

35   So far as it is employed in the second way, it promotes industry; and

----

[16] In commenting on this point Pownall added (*Letter*, 20) that paper money will 'not *pay taxes*, so far as those taxes are to *supply expences incurred or laid out abroad*'. This problem was regarded as acute in the case of America.

[17] See below, IV.i.19. The same point is made at II.ii.51 and at IV.v.a.18 the doctrine is applied to the case of Spain. Smith considers a related case at II.iii.23 where there is a redundancy of metals due to a fall in the level of output with the money supply constant.

[18] This argument is applied in the case of America at V.iii.81 and 82.

[19] A parallel argument may be found in LJ (A) vi.130–2 but with some difference in the figures used. See also LJ (B) 246 ed. Cannan 192: 'The only objection against paper money is that it drains the country of gold and silver, that bank notes will not circulate in a forreign mercat'.

though it increases the consumption of the society, it provides a permanent fund for supporting that consumption, the people who consume re-producing, with a profit, the whole value of their annual consumption. The gross revenue of the society, the annual produce of their land and labour, is increased by the whole value which the labour of those workmen adds to the materials upon which they are employed; and their neat revenue by what remains of this value, after deducting what is ne-[439]cessary for supporting the tools and instruments of their trade.

36   That the greater part of the gold and silver which, being forced abroad by those operations of banking, is employed in purchasing foreign goods for home consumption, is and must be employed in purchasing those of this second kind, seems not only probable but almost unavoidable. Though some particular men may sometimes increase their expence very considerably though their revenue does not increase at all, we may be assured that no class or order of men ever does so; because, though the principles of common prudence do not always govern the conduct of every individual, they always influence that of the majority of every class or order. But the revenue of idle people, considered as a class or order, cannot, in the smallest degree, be increased by those operations of banking. Their expence in general, therefore, cannot be much increased by them, though that of a few individuals among them may, and in reality sometimes is. The demand of idle people, therefore, for foreign goods, being the same, or very nearly the same, as before, a very small part of the money, which being forced abroad by those operations of banking, is employed in purchasing foreign goods for home consumption, is likely to be employed in purchasing those for their use. The greater part of it will naturally be destined for the employment of industry, and not for the maintenance of idleness.

37   [440] When we compute the quantity of industry which the circulating capital of any society can employ, we must always have regard to those parts of it only, which consist in provisions, materials, and finished work: the other, which consists in money, and which serves only to circulate those three, must always be deducted. In order to put industry into motion, three things are requisite; materials to work upon, tools to work with, and the wages or recompence for the sake of which the work is done. Money is neither a material to work upon, nor a tool to work with; and though the wages of the workman are commonly paid to him in money, his real revenue, like that of all other men, consists, not in the money, but in the money's worth; not in the metal pieces, but in what can be got for them.

38   The quantity of industry which any capital can employ, must, evidently, be equal to the number of workmen whom it can supply with materials, tools, and a maintenance suitable to the nature of the work. Money may be requisite for purchasing the materials and tools of the work, as well as the maintenance of the workmen. But the quantity of industry which the whole

capital can employ, is certainly not equal both to the money which purchases, and to the materials, tools, and maintenance, which are purchased with it; but only to one or other of those two values, and to the latter more properly than to the former.

39   [441] When paper is substituted in the room of gold and silver money, the quantity of the materials, tools, and maintenance, which the whole circulating capital can supply, may be increased by the whole value of gold and silver which used to be employed in purchasing them. The whole value of the great wheel of circulation and distribution, is added to the goods which are circulated and distributed by means of it. The operation, in some measure, resembles that of the undertaker of some great work, who, in consequence of some improvement in mechanicks, takes down his old machinery and adds the difference between its price and that of the new to his circulating capital, to the fund from which he furnishes materials and wages to his workmen.[20]

40   What is the proportion which the circulating money of any country bears to the whole value of the annual produce circulated by means of it, it is, perhaps, impossible to determine. It has been computed by different authors at a fifth, at a tenth, at a twentieth, and at a thirtieth part of that value.[21] But how small soever the proportion which the circulating money may bear to the whole value of the annual produce, as but a part, and frequently but a small part, of that produce, is ever destined for the maintenance of industry, it must always bear a very considerable proportion to that part. When, therefore, by the substitution of paper, the gold and silver necessary for circulation is reduced to, perhaps, a fifth part of the former quantity, if the value of only the greater part of the other four-fifths be added to [442] the funds which are destined for the maintenance of

[20] See above, II.ii.7. Smith elaborates on the advantage of paper money below, II.ii.86, in arguing that it contributes to convert a dead, into an active, stock.

[21] With regard to Britain, the figure of 30 millions is cited in LJ (B) 255, ed. Cannan 199, but with some doubts as to its accuracy. The same figure is cited in LJ (A) vi.136 although Smith thought that it would be nearer 25 millions (142–3). See below, IV.i.26, where 30 millions is cited as a 'most exaggerated computation'. Sir William Petty remarked, *Verbum Sapienti*, 13–14, in C. H. Hull, *The Economic Writings of Sir William Petty*, i.112–13):

It may be asked . . . whether the same 6 *Millions* . . . would suffice for such revolutions and circulations thereof as Trade requires? I answer yes; for the Expence being 40 Millions; if the revolutions were in such short Circles, *viz.* weekly, as happens among poorer artizans and labourers, who receive and pay every *Saturday*, then 40/52 parts of 1 Million of Money would answer those ends: But if the Circles be quarterly, according to our Custom of paying rent, and gathering Taxes, then 10 Millions were requisite. Wherefore supposing payments in general to be of a mixed Circle between One week and 13 then add 10 Millions to 40/52, the half of the which will be 5½, so as if we have 5½ Millions we have enough.

Gregory King estimated income in 1688 at £43,500,000 and coin at £8,500,000 gold and £3,000,000 silver. Gregory King, *State and Condition of England, 1688* in G. Chalmers *Comparative Strength of Great Britain to 1803*, 47 and 51.

industry, it must make a very considerable addition to the quantity of that industry, and, consequently, to the value of the annual produce of land and labour.[22]

41   An operation of this kind has, within these five-and-twenty or thirty years, been performed in Scotland, by the erection of new banking companies in almost every considerable town, and even in some country villages. The effects of it have been precisely those above described. The business of the country is almost entirely carried on by means of the paper of those different banking companies, with which purchases and payments of all kinds are commonly made. Silver very seldom appears except in the change of a twenty shillings bank note, and gold still seldomer. But though the conduct of all those different companies has not been unexceptionable,[23] and has accordingly required an act of parliament to regulate it;[24] the ᶜcountryᶜ, notwithstanding, has evidently derived great benefit from their trade. I have heard it asserted, that the trade of the city of Glasgow doubled in about fifteen years after the first erection of the banks there;[25] and that the trade of Scotland has more than quadrupled since the first erection of the two publick banks at Edinburgh,[26] of which the one, called The Bank of Scotland, was established by act of parliament in 1695;[27] the other, called The Royal Bank, by royal charter in 1727.[28] Whether the trade, either of Scotland in general, or of the city of Glasgow in particular, [443] has really increased in so great a proportion, during so short a period, I do not pretend to know. If either of them has increased in this proportion, it seems to be an effect too great to be accounted for by the sole operation of this cause. That the trade and industry of Scotland, however, have increased very considerably during this period, and that the banks have contributed a good deal to this increase, cannot be doubted.[29]

ᶜ⁻ᶜ contrary 5

---

[22] While expressing reservations about the use of paper money in his essay 'Of Money', Hume recognized in his essay 'Of the Balance of Trade' that 'there are certain lights, in which this subject may be placed, so as to represent the advantages of paper-credit and banks to be superior to their disadvantages'. Hume then proceeded to illustrate the point by reference to Scottish experience. *Essays Moral, Political, and Literary*, ed. Green and Grose, i.338–9.

[23] Smith discusses the difficulties faced by the Scottish banks at II.ii.65ff. See also II.ii.94, where he justifies regulation of the banking trade.

[24] Presumably 5 George III, c.49 (1765), which prohibited the issue of notes of a denomination smaller than £1 and required that all notes should be payable on demand. See below II.ii.89 and 98.

[25] Glasgow's first bank, the Ship Bank, was established as Colin Dunlop, Alexander Houston and Company, in 1750.

[26] The Edinburgh banks are described as being joint stock without exclusive privilege at V.i.e.33.

[27] *Acts of the Parliament of Scotland*, ix.494–5 (1695), Act for Erecting a Publick Bank.

[28] Sealed 8 July 1727.

[29] LJ (A) vi.130 refers to the '6 great banking companies in Scotland' and at 132 to the fact that 'since the institution of banks in Scotland the trade and manufactures have been gradually increasing'.

42   The value of the silver money which circulated in Scotland before the
union, in 1707, and which, immediately after it, was brought into the bank of
Scotland in order to be re-coined, amounted to 411,117*l.* 10*s.* 9*d.* sterling.
No account has been got of the gold coin; but it appears from the antient
accounts of the mint of Scotland, that the value of the gold annually
coined somewhat exceeded that of the silver.* There were a good many
people too upon this occasion, who, from a diffidence of repayment, did
not bring their silver into the bank of Scotland: and there was, besides,
some English coin, which was not called in. The whole value of the gold
and silver, therefore, which circulated in Scotland before the union, cannot
be estimated at less than a million sterling. It seems to have constituted
almost the whole circulation of that country; for though the circulation of
the bank of Scotland, which had then no rival, was considerable,[30] it seems
to have made but a very small part of the whole. In the present times the
[444] whole circulation of Scotland cannot be estimated at less than two
millions, of which that part which consists in gold and silver, most probably, does not amount to half a million. But though the circulating gold
and silver of Scotland have suffered so great a diminution during this period,
its real riches and prosperity do not appear to have suffered any. Its agriculture, manufactures, and trade, on the contrary, the annual produce of its
land and labour, have evidently been augmented.

43   It is chiefly by discounting bills of exchange, that is, by advancing money
upon them before they are due, that the greater part of banks and bankers
issue their promissory notes. They deduct always, upon whatever sum they
advance, the legal interest till the bill shall become due. The payment of
the bill, when it becomes due, replaces to the bank the value of what had
been advanced, together with a clear profit of the interest. The banker who
advances to the merchant whose bill he discounts, not gold and silver, but
his own promissory notes, has the advantage of being able to discount to a

---

* See Ruddiman's Preface to Anderson's Diplomata, &c. Scotiæ. [James Anderson,
Selectus diplomatum et numismatum Scotiæ thesaurus, ed. T. Ruddiman (Edinburgh, 1739),
84–5: '. . . this sum, no doubt, made up by far the greatest part of the silver coined money
current in Scotland at that time; but, it was not to be expected, that the whole money of
that kind, could be brought into the bank; for the folly of a few misers, or the fear that
people might have of losing their money, or various other dangers and accidents, prevented
very many of the old Scots coins from being brought in; . . . No certain rule can be found,
whereby to determine the precise quantity of gold coins in Scotland at that time; however,
there are a few which seem to convince us, that there was as great plenty of that, as of the
silver.' The statement is based on acts of the mint of Scotland from 16 December 1602
to 19 July 1606 and from 20 September 1611 to 14 April 1613. Translation of T. Ruddiman, *An Introduction to Mr. James Anderson's Diplomata Scotiae* (Edinburgh, 1782),
175–6.]

[30] In 1704 the Bank of Scotland suspended payment of notes, of which £50,847 were
then outstanding. A balance sheet struck on the day after the stoppage is in W. R. Scott,
Constitution and Finance of English, Scottish and Irish Joint Stock Companies to 1720
(Cambridge, 1912), iii.263.

greater amount, by the whole value of his promissory notes, which he finds
by experience, are commonly in circulation. He is thereby enabled to make
his clear gain of interest on so much a larger sum.

44   The commerce of Scotland, which at present is not very great, was still
more inconsiderable when the two first banking companies were established; and those companies would have had but little trade, had they
confined their business [445] to the discounting of bills of exchange. They
invented, therefore, another method of issuing their promissory notes;
by granting, what they called, cash accounts,[31] that is by giving credit to
the extent of a certain sum (two or three thousand pounds, for example),
to any individual who could procure two persons of undoubted credit and
good landed estate to become surety for him, that whatever money should
be advanced to him, within the sum for which the credit had been given,
should be repaid upon demand, together with the legal interest. Credits
of this kind are, I believe, commonly granted by banks and bankers in all
different parts of the world. But the easy terms upon which the Scotch
banking companies accept of re-payment are, so far as I know, peculiar to
them, and have, perhaps, been the principal cause, both of the great trade
of those companies, and of the benefit which the country has received from
it.

45   Whoever has a credit of this kind with one of those companies, and borrows a thousand pounds upon it, for example, may repay this sum piece-
meal, by twenty and thirty pounds at a time, the company discounting a
proportionable part of the interest of the great sum from the day on which
each of those small sums is paid in, till the whole be in this manner repaid. All merchants, therefore, and almost all men of business, find it convenient to keep such cash accounts with them, and are thereby interested
to promote the trade of those companies, by readily receiving their notes
in all payments, [446] and by encouraging all those with whom they have
any influence to do the same. The banks, when their customers apply to
them for money, generally advance it to them in their own promissory
notes. These the merchants pay away to the manufacturers for goods, the
manufacturers to the farmers for materials and provisions, the farmers to
their landlords for rent, the landlords repay them to the merchants for the
conveniencies and luxuries with which they supply them, and the merchants
again return them to the banks in order to balance their cash accounts, or
to replace what they may have borrowed of them; and thus almost the
whole money business of the country is transacted by means of them.
Hence, the great trade of those companies.

46   By means of those cash accounts every merchant can, without imprudence, carry on a greater trade than he otherwise could do. If there are two

[31] See David Hume, 'Of the Balance of Trade', *Essays Moral, Political, and Literary*, ed.
Green and Grose, i.338–40.

merchants, one in London, and the other in Edinburgh, who employ equal stocks in the same branch of trade, the Edinburgh merchant can, without imprudence, carry on a greater trade, and give employment to a greater number of people than the London merchant. The London merchant must always keep by him a considerable sum of money, either in his own coffers, or in those of his banker, who gives him no interest for it, in order to answer the demands continually coming upon him for payment of the goods which he purchases upon credit. Let the ordinary amount of this sum be supposed five [447] hundred pounds. The value of the goods in his warehouse must always be less by five hundred pounds than it would have been, had he not been obliged to keep such a sum unemployed. Let us suppose that he generally disposes of his whole stock upon hand, or of goods to the value of his whole stock upon hand, once in the year. By being obliged to keep so great a sum unemployed, he must sell in a year five hundred pounds worth less goods than he might otherwise have done. His annual profits must be less by all that he could have made by the sale of five hundred pounds worth more goods; and the number of people employed in preparing his goods for the market, must be less by all those that five hundred pounds more stock could have employed. The merchant in Edinburgh, on the other hand, keeps no money unemployed for answering such occasional demands. When they actually come upon him, he satisfies them from his cash account with the bank, and gradually replaces the sum borrowed with the money or paper which comes in from the occasional sales of his goods. With the same stock, therefore, he can, without imprudence, have at all times in his warehouse a larger quantity of goods than the London merchant; and can thereby both make a greater profit himself, and give constant employment to a greater number of industrious people who prepare those goods for the market. Hence the great benefit which the country has derived from this trade.

47 [448] The facility of discounting bills of exchange, it may be thought indeed, gives the English merchants a conveniency equivalent to the cash accounts of the Scotch merchants. But the Scotch merchants, it must be remembered, can discount their bills of exchange as easily as the English merchants; and have, besides, the additional conveniency of their cash accounts.

48 The whole paper money of every kind which can easily circulate in any country never can exceed the value of the gold and silver, of which it supplies the place, or which (the commerce being supposed the same) would circulate there, if there was no paper money. If twenty shilling notes, for example, are the lowest paper money current in Scotland, the whole of that currency which can easily circulate there cannot exceed the sum of gold and silver, which would be necessary for transacting the annual exchanges of twenty shillings value and upwards usually transacted within

that country. Should the circulating paper at any time exceed that sum, as the excess could neither be sent abroad nor be employed in the circulation of the country, it must immediately return upon the banks to be exchanged for gold and silver. Many people would immediately perceive that they had more of this paper than was necessary for transacting their business at home, and as they could not send it abroad, they would immediately demand payment of it from the banks. When this superfluous paper was converted into gold and silver, they could easily find a use for it by sending it [449] abroad; but they could find none while it remained in the shape of paper. There would immediately, therefore, be a run upon the banks to the whole extent of this superfluous paper, and, if they showed any difficulty or backwardness in payment, to a much greater extent; the alarm, which this would occasion, necessarily increasing the run.

49   Over and above the expences which are common to every branch of trade; such as the expence of house-rent, the wages of servants, clerks, accountants, &c.; the expences peculiar to a bank consist chiefly in two articles: First, in the expence of keeping at all times in its coffers, for answering the occasional demands of the holders of its notes, a large sum of money, of which it loses the interest:[32] And, secondly, in the expence of replenishing those coffers as fast as they are emptied by answering such occasional demands.

50   A banking company, which issues more paper than can be employed in the circulation of the country, and of which the excess is continually returning upon them for payment, ought to increase the quantity of gold and silver, which they keep at all times in their coffers, not only in proportion to this excessive increase of their circulation, but in a much greater proportion; their notes returning upon them much faster than in proportion to the excess of their quantity. Such a company, therefore, ought to increase the first article of their expence, not only [450] in proportion to this forced increase of their business, but in a much greater proportion.

51   The coffers of such a company too, though they ought to be filled much fuller, yet must empty themselves much faster than if their business was confined within more reasonable bounds, and must require, not only a more violent, but a more constant and uninterrupted exertion of expence in order to replenish them. The coin too, which is thus continually drawn in such large quantities from their coffers, cannot be employed in the circulation of the country. It comes in place of a paper which is over and above what can be employed in that circulation, and is therefore over and above what can be employed in it too. But as that coin will not be allowed to lie idle, it must, in one shape or another, be sent abroad, in order to find that

[32] Cf. LJ (B) 250, ed. Cannan 194, with regard to Great Britain: 'Here there is only about a sixth part of the stock kept in readiness for answering demands, and the rest is employed in trade.'

profitable employment which it cannot find at home;[33] and this continual exportation of gold and silver, by enhancing the difficulty, must necessarily enhance still further the expence of the bank, in finding new gold and silver in order to replenish those coffers, which empty themselves so very rapidly. Such a company, therefore, must, in proportion to this forced increase of their business, increase the second article of their expence still more than the first.

52   Let us suppose that all the paper of a particular bank, which the circulation of the country can easily absorb and employ, amounts exactly to forty thousand pounds; and that for answering [451] occasional demands, this bank is obliged to keep at all times in its coffers ten thousand pounds in gold and silver. Should this bank attempt to circulate forty-four thousand pounds, the four thousand pounds which are over and above what the circulation can easily absorb and employ, will return upon it almost as fast as they are issued. For answering occasional demands, therefore, this bank ought to keep at all times in its coffers, not eleven thousand pounds only, but fourteen thousand pounds. It will thus gain nothing by the interest of the four thousand pounds excessive circulation; and it will lose the whole expence of continually collecting four thousand pounds in gold and silver, which will be continually going out of its coffers as fast as they are brought into them.

53   Had every particular banking company always understood and attended to its own particular interest, the circulation never could have been overstocked with paper money. But every particular banking company has not always understood or attended to its own particular interest, and the circulation has frequently been overstocked with paper money.

54   By issuing too great a quantity of paper, of which the excess was continually returning, in order to be exchanged for gold and silver, the bank of England was for many years together obliged to coin gold to the extent of between eight hundred thousand pounds and a million a year; or at an average, about eight hundred and fifty thousand pounds.[34] For this great coin-[452]age the bank (in consequence of the worn and degraded state into which the gold coin had fallen a few years ago) was frequently obliged to purchase gold bullion at the high price of four pounds an ounce, which it soon after issued in coin at $3l.17s.10\frac{1}{2}d.$ an ounce, losing in this manner between two and a half and three per cent. upon the coinage of so very large a sum. Though the bank therefore paid no seignorage, though the government was properly at the expence of the coinage, this liberality of government did not prevent altogether the expence of the bank.[35]

[33] See above, II.ii.30.
[34] The same figure is cited at IV.vi.18 and 30. Between 1764 and 1772 the annual average of the gold coinage was valued at £788,000. B. R. Mitchell, *Abstract of British Historical Statistics* (Cambridge, 1962), 440.
[35] See above, I.v.31, and below, IV.vi.18. Smith appears to comment favourably on a government charge for coinage at V.i.d.3.

55   The Scotch banks, in consequence of an excess of the same kind, were all obliged to employ constantly agents at London to collect money for them, at an expence which was seldom below one a half or two per cent. This money was sent down by the waggon, and insured by the carriers at an additional expence of three quarters per cent. or fifteen shillings on the hundred pounds. Those agents were not always able to replenish the coffers of their employers so fast as they were emptied. In this case the resource of the banks was, to draw upon their correspondents in London bills of exchange to the extent of the sum which they wanted. When those correspondents afterwards drew upon them for the payment of this sum, together with the interest and a commission, some of those banks, from the distress into which their excessive circulation had thrown them, had sometimes no other means of satisfying this draught but by [453] drawing a second sett of bills either upon the same, or upon some other correspondents in London; and the same sum, or rather bills for the same sum, would in this manner make sometimes more than two or three journies; the debtor, bank, paying always the interest and commission upon the whole accumulated sum. Even those Scotch banks which never distinguished themselves by their extreme imprudence, were sometimes obliged to employ this ruinous resource.

56   The gold coin which was paid out either by the bank of England, or by the Scotch banks, in exchange for that part of their paper which was over and above what could be employed in the circulation of the country, being likewise over and above what could be employed in that circulation, was sometimes sent abroad in the shape of coin, sometimes melted down and sent abroad in the shape of bullion, and sometimes melted down and sold to the bank of England at the high price of four pounds an ounce. It was the newest, the heaviest, and the best pieces only which were carefully picked out of the whole coin, and either sent abroad or melted down. At home, and while they remained in the shape of coin, those heavy pieces were of no more value than the light: But they were of more value abroad, or when melted down into bullion, at home. The bank of England, notwithstanding their great annual coinage, found to their astonishment, that there was every year the same scarcity of coin as there had been the year be-[454]fore; and that notwithstanding the great quantity of good and new coin which was every year issued from the bank, the state of the coin, instead of growing better and better, became every year worse and worse. Every year they found themselves under the necessity of coining nearly the same quantity of gold as they had coined the year before, and from the continual rise in the price of gold bullion, in consequence of the continual wearing and clipping of the coin, the expence of this great annual coinage became every year greater and greater. The bank of England, it is to be observed, by supplying its own coffers with coin, is indirectly obliged to

supply the whole kingdom, into which coin is continually flowing from those coffers in a great variety of ways. Whatever coin therefore was wanted to support this excessive circulation both of Scotch and English paper money, whatever vacuities this excessive circulation occasioned in the necessary coin of the kingdom, the bank of England was obliged to supply them. The Scotch banks, no doubt, paid all of them very dearly for their own imprudence and inattention. But the bank of England paid very dearly, not only for its own imprudence; but for the much greater imprudence of almost all the Scotch banks.[36]

57   The over-trading of some bold projectors in both parts of the united kingdom, was the original cause of this excessive circulation of paper money.[37]

58   What a bank can with propriety advance to a merchant or undertaker of any kind, is not, [455] either the whole capital with which he trades, or even any considerable part of that capital; but that part of it only, which he would otherwise be obliged to keep by him unemployed, and in ready money for answering occasional demands. If the paper money which the bank advances never exceeds this value, it can never exceed the value of the gold and silver, which would necessarily circulate in the country if there was no paper money; it can never exceed the quantity which the circulation of the country can easily absorb and employ.

59   When a bank discounts to a merchant a real bill of exchange drawn by a real creditor upon a real debtor, and which, as soon as it becomes due, is really paid by that debtor; it only advances to him a part of the value which he would otherwise be obliged to keep by him unemployed, and in ready money for answering occasional demands. The payment of the bill, when it becomes due, replaces to the bank the value of what it had advanced, together with the interest. The coffers of the bank, so far as its dealings are confined to such customers, resemble a water pond, from which, though a stream is continually running out, yet another is continually running in, fully equal to that which runs out; so that, without any further care or attention, the pond keeps always equally, or very near equally full.[38] Little or no expence can ever be necessary for replenishing the coffers of such a bank.

60   [456] A merchant, without over-trading, may frequently have occasion for a sum of ready money, even when he has no bills to discount. When a

---

[36] For an example of the difficulties which emerged see Henry Hamilton, 'Scotland's Balance of Payments Problem in 1762', *Economic History Review* (second series), v (1953), 344–57.

[37] It is interesting to note that the role of the projector looms large in this chapter, and that Smith was willing to countenance regulation of the rate of interest in order to offset the consequences of speculative investment. See for example II.iv.15.

[38] The analogy of the water level is used in discussing the futility of Spanish and Portuguese policy regarding the export of gold at IV.v.a.19. See also II.ii.76.

bank, besides discounting his bills, advances him likewise upon such occasions, such sums upon his cash account, and accepts of a piece-meal repayment as the money comes in from the occasional sale of his goods, upon the easy terms of the banking companies of Scotland; it dispenses him entirely from the necessity of keeping any part of his stock by him unemployed, and in ready money for answering occasional demands. When such demands actually come upon him, he can answer them sufficiently from his cash account. The bank, however, in dealing with such customers, ought to observe with great attention, whether in the course of some short period (of four, five, six, or eight months, for example) the sum of the re-payments which it commonly receives from them, is, or is not, fully equal to that of the advances which it commonly makes to them. If, within the course of such short periods, the sum of the repayments from certain customers is, upon most occasions, fully equal to that of the advances, it may safely continue to deal with such customers. Though the stream which is in this case continually running out from its coffers may be very large, that which is continually running into them must be at least equally large; so that without any further care or attention those coffers are likely to be always equally or very near equally full; and [457] scarce ever to require any extraordinary expence to replenish them. If, on the contrary, the sum of the repayments from certain other customers falls commonly very much short of the advances which it makes to them, it cannot with any safety continue to deal with such customers, at least if they continue to deal with it in this manner. The stream which is in this case continually running out from its coffers in necessarily much larger than that which is continually running in; so that, unless they are replenished by some great and continual effort of expence, those coffers must soon be exhausted alto-gether.

61   The banking companies of Scotland, accordingly, were for a long time very careful to require frequent and regular repayments from all their customers, and did not care to deal with any person, whatever might be his fortune or credit, who did not make, what they called, frequent and regular operations with them. By this attention, besides saving almost entirely the extraordinary expence of replenishing their coffers, they gained two other very considerable advantages.

62   First, by this attention they were enabled to make some tolerable judg-ment concerning the thriving or declining circumstances of their debtors, without being obliged to look out for any other evidence besides what their own books afforded them; men being for the most part either regular or irregular in their repayments, according as their circumstances are either thriv-[458]ing or declining. A private man who lends out his money to perhaps half a dozen or a dozen of debtors, may, either by himself or his agents, observe and enquire both constantly and carefully into the conduct

and situation of each of them. But a banking company, which lends money to perhaps five hundred different people, and of which the attention is continually occupied by objects of a very different kind, can have no regular information concerning the conduct and circumstances of the greater part of its debtors beyond what its own books afford it. In requiring frequent and regular repayments from all their customers, the banking companies of Scotland had probably this advantage in view.

63   Secondly, by this attention they secured themselves from the possibility of issuing more paper money than what the circulation of the country could easily absorb and employ. When they observed, that within moderate periods of time the repayments of a particular customer were upon most occasions fully equal to the advances which they had made to him, they might be assured that the paper money which they had advanced to him, had not at any time exceeded the quantity of gold and silver which he would otherwise have been obliged to keep by him for answering occasional demands; and that, consequently the paper money, which they had circulated by his means, had not at any time exceeded the quantity of gold and silver which would have circulated in the country, had there been no paper money. The frequency, regula-[459]rity and amount of his repayments would sufficiently demonstrate that the amount of their advances had at no time exceeded that part of his capital which he would otherwise have been obliged to keep by him, unemployed and in ready money for answering occasional demands; that is, for the purpose of keeping the rest of his capital in constant employment. It is this part of his capital only which, within moderate periods of time, is continually returning to every dealer in the shape of money, whether paper or coin, and continually going from him in the same shape. If the advances of the bank had commonly exceeded this part of his capital, the ordinary amount of his repayments could not, within moderate periods of time, have equalled the ordinary amount of its advances. The stream which, by means of his dealings, was continually running into the coffers of the bank, could not have been equal to the stream which, by means of the same dealings, was continually running out. The advances of the bank paper, by exceeding the quantity of gold and silver which, had there been no such advances, he would have been obliged to keep by him for answering occasional demands, might soon come to exceed the whole quantity of gold and silver which (the commerce being supposed the same) would have circulated in the country had there been no paper money; and consequently to exceed the quantity which the circulation of the country could easily absorb and employ; and the excess of this paper money would immediately [460] have returned upon the bank in order to be exchanged for gold and silver. This second advantage, though equally real, was not perhaps so well understood by all the different banking companies of Scotland as the first.

64   When, partly by the conveniency of discounting bills, and partly by
that of cash accounts, the creditable traders of any country can be dis-
pensed from the necessity of keeping any part of their stock by them, unemployed and in ready money, for answering occasional demands, they can
reasonably expect no ^dfurther^d assistance from banks and bankers, who,
when they have gone thus far, cannot, consistently with their own interest
and safety, go farther. A bank cannot, consistently with its own interest,
advance to a trader the whole or even the greater part of the circulating
capital with which he trades; because, though that capital is continually
returning to him in the shape of money, and going from him in the same
shape, yet the whole of the returns is too distant from the whole of the
outgoings, and the sum of his repayments could not equal the sum of its
advances within such moderate periods of time as suit the conveniency of a
bank. Still less could a bank afford to advance him any considerable part
of his fixed capital; of the capital which the undertaker of an iron forge,
for example, employs in erecting his forge and smelting-house, his work-
houses and warehouses, the dwelling-houses of his workmen, &c.; of the
capital which the undertaker of a mine employs in sinking his shafts, in
erect-[461]ing engines for drawing out the water, in making roads and
waggon-ways, &c.; of the capital which the person who undertakes to
improve land employs in clearing, draining, enclosing, manuring and
ploughing waste and uncultivated fields, in building farm-houses, with all
their necessary appendages of stables, granaries, &c. The returns of the
fixed capital are in almost all cases much slower than those of the circulating capital; and such expences, even when laid out with the greatest prudence and judgment, very seldom return to the undertaker till after a
period of many years, a period by far too distant to suit the conveniency of
a bank. Traders and other undertakers may, no doubt, with great propriety,
carry on a very considerable part of their projects with borrowed money.
In justice to their creditors, however, their own capital ought, in this
case, to be sufficient to ensure, if I may say so, the capital of those creditors;
or to render it extremely improbable that those creditors should incur any
loss, even though the success of the project should fall very much short of
the expectation of the projectors. Even with this precaution too, the money
which is borrowed, and which it is meant should not be repaid till after a
period of several years, ought not to be borrowed of a bank, but ought to
be borrowed upon bond or mortgage, of such private people as propose to
live upon the interest of their money, without taking the trouble themselves
to employ the capital; and who are upon that account willing to lend that
capital to such [462] people of good credit as are likely to keep it for several
years. A bank, indeed, which lends its money without the expence of stampt
paper, or of attornies fees for drawing bonds and mortgages, and which

^{d-d} farther 4–6

accepts of repayment upon the easy terms of the banking companies of Scotland; would, no doubt, be a very convenient creditor to such traders and undertakers. But such traders and undertakers would, surely, be most inconvenient debtors to such a bank.

65   It is now more than five-and-twenty years since the paper money issued by the different banking companies of Scotland was fully equal, or rather was somewhat more than fully equal, to what the circulation of the country could easily absorb and employ.[39] Those companies, therefore, had so long ago given all the assistance to the traders and other undertakers of Scotland which it is possible for banks and bankers, consistently with their own interest, to give. They had even done somewhat more. They had over-traded a little, and had brought upon themselves that loss, or at least that diminution of profit, which in this particular business never fails to attend the smallest degree of over-trading. Those traders and other undertakers, having got so much assistance from banks and bankers, wished to get still more. The banks, they seem to have thought, could extend their credits to whatever sum might be wanted, without incurring any other expence besides that of a few reams of paper. They complained of the contracted views and dastardly spirit of the directors of those [463] banks, which did not, they said, extend their credits in proportion to the extension of the trade of the country; meaning, no doubt, by the extension of that trade the extension of their own projects beyond what they could carry on, either with their own capital, or with what they had credit to borrow of private people in the usual way of bond or mortgage. The banks, they seem to have thought, were in honour bound to supply the deficiency, and to provide them with all the capital which they wanted to trade with. The banks, however, were of a different opinion, and upon their refusing to extend their credits, some of those traders had recourse to an expedient which, for a time, served their purpose, though at a much greater expence, yet as effectually as the utmost extension of bank credits could have done. This expedient was no other than the well-known shift of drawing and redrawing; the shift to which unfortunate traders have sometimes recourse when they are upon the brink of bankruptcy. The practice of raising money in this manner had been long known in England, and during the course of the late war, when the high profits of trade afforded a great temptation to over-trading, is said to have been carried on to a very great extent. From England it was brought into Scotland, where, in proportion to the very limited commerce, and to the very moderate capital of the country, it was soon carried on to a much greater extent than it ever had been in England.

66   [464] The practice of drawing and re-drawing is so well known to all men of business, that it may perhaps be thought unnecessary to give

*e*any*e* account of it. But as this book may come into the hands of many people who are not men of business, and as the effects of this practice upon the banking trade are not perhaps generally understood even by men of business themselves, I shall endeavour to explain it as distinctly as I can.

67   The customs of merchants, which were established when the barbarous laws of Europe did not enforce the performance of their contracts, and which during the course of the two last centuries have been adopted into the laws of all European nations, have given such extraordinary privileges to bills of exchange, that money is more readily advanced upon them, than upon any other species of obligation; especially when they are made payable within so short a period as two or three months after their date.[40] If, when the bill comes due, the acceptor does not pay it as soon as it is presented, he becomes from that moment a bankrupt. The bill is protested, and returns upon the drawer, who, if he does not immediately pay it, becomes likewise a bankrupt. If, before it came to the person who presents it to the acceptor for payment, it had passed through the hands of several other persons, who had successively advanced to one another the contents of it either in money or goods, and who, to express that each of them had in his turn [465] received those contents, had all of them in their order endorsed, that is, written their names upon the back of the bill; each endorser becomes in his turn liable to the owner of the bill for those contents, and, if he fails to pay, he becomes too from that moment a bankrupt. Though the drawer, acceptor, and endorsers of the bill should, all of them, be persons of doubtful credit; yet still the shortness of the date gives some security to the owner of the bill. Though all of them may be very likely to become bankrupts; it is a chance if they all become so in so short a time. The house is crazy, says a weary traveller to himself, and will not stand very long; but it is a chance if it falls to-night, and I will venture, therefore, to sleep in it to-night.

68   The trader A in Edinburgh, we shall suppose, draws a bill upon B in London, payable two months after date. In reality B in London owes nothing to A in Edinburgh; but he agrees to accept of A's bill, upon condition that before the term of payment he shall redraw upon A in Edinburgh, for the same sum, together with the interest and a commission, another bill, payable likewise two months after date. B accordingly, before the expiration of the first two months, redraws this bill upon A in Edinburgh; who again, before the expiration of the second two months, draws a second bill upon B in London, payable likewise two months after date; and before the expiration of the third two months, B in London redraws upon A in Edinburgh another bill, payable also two months after

---

e-e an 5–6

[40] Smith discusses bills of exchange in LJ (B) 283–5, ed. Cannan 221–2, and the customs of merchants as a class at 326–7, ed. Cannan 253–4.

date. This prac-[466]tice has sometimes gone on, not only for several months, but for several years together, the bill always returning upon A in Edinburgh, with the accumulated interest and commission of all the former bills. The interest was five per cent. in the year, and the commission was never less than one half per cent. on each draught. This commission being repeated more than six times in the year, whatever money A might raise by this expedient must necessarily have cost him something more than eight per cent. in the year, and sometimes a great deal more; when either the price of the commission happened to rise, or when he was obliged to pay compound interest upon the interest and commission of former bills. This practice was called raising money by circulation.

69   In a country where the ordinary profits of stock in the greater part of mercantile projects are supposed to run between six and ten per cent.; it must have been a very fortunate speculation of which the returns could not only repay the enormous expence at which the money was thus borrowed for carrying it on; but afford, besides, a good surplus profit to the projector. Many vast and extensive projects, however, were undertaken, and for several years carried on without any other fund to support them besides what was raised at this enormous expence. The projectors, no doubt, had in their golden dreams the most distinct vision of this great profit. Upon their awaking, however, either at the end of their projects, or when they were no longer [467] able to carry them on, they very seldom, I believe, had the good fortune to find it*.

70   The bills which A in Edinburgh drew upon B in London, he regularly

ʲ* The method described in the text was by no means either the most common or the most expensive one in which those adventurers sometimes raised money by circulation. It frequently happened that A in Edinburgh would enable B in London to pay the first bill of exchange by drawing, a few days before it became due, a second bill at three months date upon the same B in London. This bill, being payable to his own order, A sold in Edinburgh at par; and with its contents purchased bills upon London payable at sight to the order of B, to whom he sent them by the post. Towards the end of the late war, the exchange between Edinburgh and London was frequently three per cent. against Edinburgh, and those bills at sight must frequently have cost A that premium. This transaction therefore being repeated at least four times in the year, and being loaded with a commission of at least one half per cent. upon each repetition, must at that period have cost A at least fourteen per cent. in the year. At other times A would enable B to discharge the first bill of exchange by drawing, a few days before it became due, a second bill at two months date; not upon B, but upon some third person, C, for ex-[468]ample, in London. This other bill was made payable to the order of B, who, upon its being accepted by C, discounted it with some banker in London; and A enabled C to discharge it by drawing, a few days before it became due, a third bill, likewise at two months date, sometimes upon his first corres- pondent B, and sometimes upon some fourth or fifth person, D or E, for example. This third bill was made payable to the order of C; who, as soon as it was accepted, discounted it in the same manner with some banker in London. Such operations being repeated at least six times in the year, and being loaded with a commission of at least one-half per cent. upon each repetition, together with the legal interest of five per cent. this method of raising money, in the same manner as that described in the text, must have cost A some- thing more than eight per cent. By saving, however, the exchange between Edinburgh and London it was less expensive than that mentioned in the foregoing part of this note; but discounted two months before they were due with some bank or banker in Edinburgh; and the bills which B in London re-drew upon A in Edinburgh, he as regularly discounted either with the bank of England, or with some other bankers in London. Whatever was advanced upon such circulating bills, was, in Edinburgh, advanced in the paper of the Scotch banks, and in London, when they were discounted at the bank of England, in the paper of that bank. Though the bills upon which this paper had been advanced, were all of them re-[468]paid in their turn as soon as they became due; yet the value which had been really advanced upon the first bill, was never really returned to the banks which advanced it; because, before each bill became due, another bill was always drawn to somewhat a greater amount than the bill which was soon to be paid; and the discounting of this other bill was essentially necessary towards the payment of that which was soon to be due. This payment, therefore, was altogether fictitious. The stream, which, by means of those circulating bills of exchange, had once been made to run out from the coffers of the banks, was never replaced by any stream which really run into them.

71   [469] The paper which was issued upon those circulating bills of exchange, amounted, upon many occasions, to the whole fund destined for carrying on some vast and extensive project of agriculture, commerce, or manufactures; and not merely to that part of it which, had there been no paper money, the projector would have been obliged to keep by him, unemployed and in ready money for answering occasional demands. The greater part of this paper was, consequently, over and above the value of the gold and silver which would have circulated in the country, had there been no paper money. It was over and above, therefore, what the circulation of the country could easily absorb and employ, and, upon that account, immediately returned upon the banks in order to be exchanged for gold and silver, which they were to find as they could. It was a capital which those projectors had very artfully contrived to draw from those banks, not only without their knowledge or deliberate consent, but for some time, perhaps, without their having the most distant suspicion that they had really advanced it.

72   When two people, who are continually drawing and re-drawing upon one another, discount their bills always with the same banker, he must immediately discover what they are about, and see clearly that they are trading, not with any capital of their own, but with the capital which he advances to them. But this discovery is not altogether so easy when they discount their bills sometimes with one banker, and sometimes with [470] another, and when the same two persons do not constantly draw and re-

then it required an established credit with more houses than one in London, an advantage which many of these adventurers could not always find it easy to procure.*

- 2–6

draw upon one another, but occasionally run the round of a great circle of projectors, who find it for their interest to assist one another in this method of raising money,[41] and to render it, upon that account, as difficult as possible to distinguish between a real and a fictitious bill of exchange; between a bill drawn by a real creditor upon a real debtor, and a bill for which there was properly no real creditor but the bank which discounted it; nor any real debtor but the projector who made use of the money. When a banker had even made this discovery, he might sometimes make it too late, and might find that he had already discounted the bills of those projectors to so great an extent, that, by refusing to discount any more, he would necessarily make them all bankrupts, and thus, by ruining them, might perhaps ruin himself. For his own interest and safety, therefore, he might find it necessary, in this very perilous situation, to go on for some time, endeavouring, however, to withdraw gradually, and upon that account making every day greater and greater difficulties about discounting, in order to force those projectors by degrees to have recourse, either to other bankers, or to other methods of raising money; so as that he himself might, as soon as possible, get out of the circle. The difficulties, accordingly, which the bank of England, which the principal bankers in London, and which even the more prudent Scotch banks began, after a certain time, and when all of them [471] had already gone too far, to make about discounting, not only alarmed, but enraged in the highest degree those projectors. Their own distress, of which this prudent and necessary reserve of the banks, was, no doubt, the immediate occasion, they called the distress of the country; and this distress of the country, they said, was altogether owing to the ignorance, pusillanimity, and bad conduct of the banks, which did not give a sufficiently liberal aid to the spirited undertakings of those who exerted themselves in order to beautify, improve, and enrich the country. It was the duty of the banks, they seemed to think, to lend for as long a time, and to as great an extent as they might wish to borrow. The banks, however, by refusing in this manner to give more credit to those, to whom they had already given a great deal too much, took the only method by which it was now possible to save either their own credit, or the publick credit of the country.[42]

[41] See below, II.iv.15, where Smith refers to the difficulties 'prodigals and projectors' face in borrowing.

[42] Hume provided a graphic account of the situation. In Letter 131 addressed to Smith, dated 27 June 1772 he wrote:

We are here in a very melancholy Situation: Continual Bankruptcies, universal Loss of Credit, and endless Suspicions ... even the Bank of England is not entirely free from Suspicion. Those of Newcastle, Norwich, and Bristol are said to be stopp'd: The Thistle Bank has been reported to be in the same Condition: The Carron Company is reeling, which is one of the greatest Calamities of the whole; as they gave Employment to near 10,000 people. Do these Events any-wise affect your Theory?

The only benefit which Hume saw in the current situation was that present experience

73   In the midst of this clamour and distress, a new bank was established
in Scotland[43] for the express purpose of relieving the distress of the country.
The design was generous; but the execution was imprudent, and the nature
and causes of the distress which it meant to relieve, were not, perhaps, well
understood. This bank was more liberal than any other had ever been,
both in granting cash accounts, and in discounting bills of exchange. With
regard to the latter, it seems to have made scarce any distinction between
real and circulating bills, but to have dis-[472]counted all equally. It was
the avowed principle of this bank to advance, upon any reasonable security,
the whole capital which was to be employed in ⁹those⁹ improvements of
which the returns are the most slow and distant, such as the improvements
of land. To promote such improvements was even said to be the chief of
the publick spirited purposes for which it was instituted. By its liberality
in granting cash accounts, and in discounting bills of exchange, it, no
doubt, issued great quantities of its bank-notes. But those bank-notes
being, the greater part of them, over and above what the circulation of the
country could easily absorb and employ, returned upon it, in order to be
exchanged for gold and silver, as fast as they were issued. Its coffers were
never well-filled. The capital which had been subscribed to this bank at two
different subscriptions, amounted to one hundred and sixty thousand
pounds, of which eighty per cent. only was paid up. This sum ought to
have been paid in at several different instalments. A great part of the proprietors, when they paid in their first instalment, opened a cash account
with the bank; and the directors, thinking themselves obliged to treat
their own proprietors with the same liberality with which they treated all
other men, allowed many of them to borrow upon this cash account what
they paid in upon all their subsequent instalments. Such payments, therefore, only put into one coffer, what had the moment before been taken
out of another. But had the coffers of this bank been filled ever so well,
[473] its excessive circulation must have emptied them faster than they
could have been replenished by any other expedient but the ruinous one of

---

⁹⁻⁹ 2–6

might induce people in the long run to concentrate on more conservative enterprizes 'and
at the same time introduce Frugality among the Merchants and Manufacturers'. Hume had
already expressed his doubts 'concerning the benefit of *banks* and *paper-credit*' in his essay
'Of Money' and again, with specific reference to Scottish experience, in that on 'The
Balance of Trade'. *Essays Moral, Political, and Literary*, ed. Green and Grose, i.311.

[43] Douglas, Heron and Company, commonly known as the Ayr Bank. For a contem-
porary account, of which Smith had a copy, see *The Precipitation and Fall of Messers.
Douglas, Heron and Company, late Bankers in Air, with the Causes of their Distress and
Ruin, investigated and considered by a Committee of Inquiry appointed by the Proprietors*
(Edinburgh, 1778). For a modern account see Henry Hamilton, 'The Failure of the Ayr
Bank, 1772', *Economic History Review* (2nd series), viii (1956), 405–17. A detailed example
of how it helped one firm already deeply involved in discounting bills is in R. H. Campbell,
Carron Company (Edinburgh, 1961), 131–6.

drawing upon London, and when the bill became due, paying it, together with interest and commission, by another draught upon the same place. Its coffers having been filled so very ill, it is said to have been driven to this resource within a very few months after it began to do business. The estates of the proprietors of this bank were worth several millions, and by their subscription to the original bond or contract of the bank, were really pledged for answering all its engagements. By means of the great credit which so great a pledge necessarily gave it, it was, notwithstanding its too liberal conduct, enabled to carry on business for more than two years. When it was obliged to stop, it had in the circulation about two hundred thousand pounds in bank-notes:[44] In order to support the circulation of those notes, which were continually returning upon it as fast as they were issued, it had been constantly in the practice of drawing bills of exchange upon London, of which the number and value were continually increasing, and, when it stopt, amounted to upwards of six hundred thousand pounds. This bank, therefore, had, in little more than the course of two years, advanced to different people upwards of eight hundred thousand pounds at five per cent. Upon the two hundred thousand pounds which it circulated in bank-notes, this five per cent. might, perhaps, be considered as clear gain, [474] without any other deduction besides the expence of management. But upon upwards of six hundred thousand pounds, for which it was continually drawing bills of exchange upon London, it was paying, in the way of interest and commission, upwards of eight per cent., and was consequently losing more than three per cent. upon more than three-fourths of all its dealings.

74   The operations of this bank seem to have produced effects quite opposite to those which were intended by the particular persons who planned and directed it. They seem to have intended to support the spirited undertakings, for as such they considered them, which were at that time carrying on in different parts of the country; and at the same time, by drawing the whole banking business to themselves, to supplant all the other

[44] In Letter 136 addressed to Smith, dated 10 April 1773, Hume reported that: 'To day News arriv'd in town that the Air Bank had shut up; and as many people think for ever.' In Letter 132 addressed to Pulteney, dated 3 September 1772, Smith had written that: 'Tho I have had no concern myself in the public calamities, some of the friends for whom I interest myself the most have been deeply concerned in them; and my attention has been a good deal occupied about the most proper method of extricating them.' Smith's efforts to help his friends (such as Buccleuch) may have contributed to delay the completion of the WN. In the same letter he went on to tell Pulteney that: 'My book would have been ready for the Press by the beginning of this winter; but the interruptions occasioned partly by bad health arising from want of amusement and from thinking too much upon one thing; and partly by the avocations above mentioned will oblige me to retard its publication for a few months longer.' It would appear that Smith's help took a fairly concrete form. In Letter 133 addressed to Smith, dated October 1772, Hume wrote that Sir William Forbes, the Edinburgh banker, had undertaken to take some Ayr Notes 'upon your Account', although he did not commonly do so.

Scotch banks; particularly those established at Edinburgh, whose backwardness in discounting bills of exchange had given some offence.[45]
This bank, no doubt, gave some temporary relief to those projectors, and
enabled them to carry on their projects for about two years longer than they
could otherwise have done. But it thereby only enabled them to get so
much deeper into debt, so that when ruin came, it fell so much the heavier
both upon them and upon their creditors. The operations of this bank,
therefore, instead of relieving, in reality aggravated in the long-run the
distress which those projectors had brought both upon themselves and upon
their country. It would have been [475] much better for themselves, their
creditors and their country, had the greater part of them been obliged to
stop two years sooner than they actually did. The temporary relief, however, which this bank afforded to those projectors, proved a real and permanent relief to the other Scotch banks. All the dealers in circulating bills
of exchange, which those other banks had become so backward in discounting, had recourse to this new bank, where they were received with
open arms. Those other banks, therefore, were enabled to get very easily
out of that fatal circle, from which they could not otherwise have dis-
engaged themselves without incurring a considerable loss, and perhaps
too even some degree of discredit.[46]

75   In the long-run, therefore, the operations of this bank increased the real
distress of the country which it meant to relieve; and effectually relieved
from a very great distress those rivals whom it meant to supplant.[47]

76   At the first setting out of this bank, it was the opinion of some people,
that how fast soever its coffers might be emptied, it might easily replenish
them by raising money upon the securities of those to whom it had advanced its paper. Experience, I believe, soon convinced them that this
method of raising money was by much too slow to answer their purpose;
and that coffers which originally were so ill filled, and which emptied themselves so very fast, could be replenished by no other expedient but the
ruinous one of drawing bills upon London, and when [476] they became
due, paying them by other draughts upon the same place with accumulated

---

[45] In Letter 133 addressed to Smith, dated October 1772, Hume commented: 'They do
not seem to have forseen, that it was the Interest of the two Banks here and of all the
Bankers to make a Run upon them; for which they ought to have been prepar'd.'
[46] It is remarked in LJ (B) 279, ed. Cannan 217–18, that in contrast to the position in
France, 'Brittain can never be much hurt by the breaking of a bank, because few people
keep notes by them to any value'.
[47] A later judgement adds qualifications: 'The fall of this Bank brought much calamity
on the country; but two things are remarkable in its history: First, that under its too
prodigal, yet beneficial influence, a fine county (that of Ayr) was converted from a desert
into a fertile land. Secondly, that, though at a distant interval, the Ayr Bank paid all its
engagements, and the loss only fell on the original stockholders.' (Sir Walter Scott, *Thoughts
on the Proposed Change of Currency . . . First Letter of Malachi Malagrowther* (1826), 24.)
Scott was supporting the retention of the £1 note; Smith was less sure of the wisdom of its
retention. See below, II.ii.91.

interest and commission. But though they had been able by this method to raise money as fast as they wanted it; yet, instead of making a profit, they must have suffered a loss by every such operation; so that in the long-run they must have ruined themselves as a mercantile company, though, perhaps, not so soon as by the more expensive practice of drawing and re-drawing. They could still have made nothing by the interest of the paper, which, being over and above what the circulation of the country could absorb and employ, returned upon them, in order to be exchanged for gold and silver, as fast as they issued it; and for the payment of which they were themselves continually obliged to borrow money. On the contrary, the whole expence of this borrowing, of employing agents to look out for people who had money to lend, of negociating with those people, and of drawing the proper bond or assignment, must have fallen upon them, and have been so much clear loss upon the balance of their accounts. The project of replenishing their coffers in this manner may be compared to that of a man who had a water-pond from which a stream was continually running out, and into which no stream was continually running, but who proposed to keep it always equally full by employing a number of people to go con-tinually with buckets to a well at some miles distance in order to bring water to replenish it.[48]

77   [477] But though this operation had proved, not only practicable, but profitable to the bank as a mercantile company; yet the country could have derived no benefit from it; but, on the contrary, must have suffered a very considerable loss by it. This operation could not augment in the smallest degree the quantity of money to be lent. It could only have erected this bank into a sort of general loan office for the whole country. Those who wanted to borrow, must have applied to this bank, instead of applying to the private persons who had lent it their money. But a bank which lends money, perhaps, to five hundred different people, the greater part of whom its directors can know very little about, is not likely to be more judicious in the choice of its debtors, than a private person who lends out his money among a few people whom he knows, and in whose sober and frugal con-duct he thinks he has good reason to confide. The debtors of such a bank, as that whose conduct I have been giving some account of, were likely, the greater part of them, to be chimerical projectors, the drawers and re-drawers of circulating bills of exchange, who would employ the money in extravagant undertakings, which, with all the assistance that could be given them, they would probably never be able to compleat, and which, if they should be compleated, would never repay the expence which they had really cost, would never afford a fund capable of maintaining a quantity of labour equal to that which had been employed about them. The sober and frugal debtors of pri-[478]vate persons, on the contrary, would be more

---

[48] A related analogy is used above, at II.ii.59, and below, IV.v.a.19.

likely to employ the money borrowed in sober undertakings which were proportioned to their capitals, and which, though they might have less of the grand and the marvellous, would have more of the solid and the profitable, which would repay with a large profit whatever had been laid out upon them, and which would thus afford a fund capable of maintaining a much greater quantity of labour than that which had been employed about them. The success of this operation, therefore, without increasing in the smallest degree the capital of the country, would only have transferred a great part of it from prudent and profitable, to imprudent and unprofitable undertakings.

78   That the industry in Scotland languished for want of money to employ it, was the opinion of the famous Mr. Law.[49] By establishing a bank of a particular kind, which he seems to have imagined, might issue paper to the amount of the whole value of all the lands in the country, he proposed to remedy this want of money. The parliament of Scotland, when he first proposed his project, did not think proper to adopt it. It was afterwards adopted, with some variations, by the duke of Orleans, at that time regent of France. The idea of the possibility of multiplying paper money to almost any extent, was the real foundation of what is called the Mississippi scheme,[50] the most extravagant project both of banking and stock-jobbing that, perhaps, the world ever saw.[51] The different opera-[479]tions of this scheme are explained so fully, so clearly, and with so much order and distinctness, by Mr. Du Verney, in his Examination of the Political Reflections upon Commerce and Finances of Mr. Du Tot,[52] that I shall not give any account of them.[53] The principles upon which it was founded are explained by Mr. Law himself, in a discourse concerning money and trade, which he published in Scotland when he first proposed his project.[54] The splendid, but visionary ideas which are set forth in that and some other works upon the same principles, still continue to make an impression upon many people, and have, perhaps, in part, contributed to that excess of

[49] 'Scotland has a very inconsiderable Trade, because she has but a very small part of the Money. There is a little Home Trade, but the Country is not improv'd, nor the Product Manufactur'd.' (John Law, *Money and Trade* (Edinburgh, 1705), 20.)

[50] See below, IV.vii.b.13 and 24.

[51] According to Douglass, 'never was such a bare-faced iniquitous scheme endeavoured to be put in execution' (*British Settlements in North America*, i.78n.).

[52] J. P. Duverney, *Examen du livre intitulé 'Réflexions politiques sur les finances et le commerce'* (La Haye, 1740) and Du Tot, *Réflexions politiques sur les finances et le commerce, ou l'on examine quelles ont été sur les revenues, les denrées, le change étranger et conséquemment sur notre commerce, les influences des augmentations et des diminutions des valeurs numéraires des monneyes* (La Haye, 1738). Sir James Steuart provided a long and often sympathetic account of Law's bank in the *Principles*, IV.2.xxiiiff.; an account which was rather more critical of authorities such as Du Tot than Smith seems to have thought necessary.

[53] However, Law's scheme was examined at some length in LJ (B) 270–81, ed. Cannan 211–19. At the time of writing the ED Smith evidently still intended to include this material in his book. See, for example, the conclusion to ED 4.

[54] J. Law, *Money and Trade* (Edinburgh, 1705).

banking, which has of late been complained of both in Scotland and in other places.

79   The bank of England is the greatest bank of circulation in Europe.[55] It was incorporated, in pursuance of an act of parliament,[56] by a charter under the great seal, dated the 27th ⁿofʰ July, 1694. It at that time advanced to government the sum of one million two hundred thousand pounds, for an annuity of one hundred thousand pounds; or for 96,000*l*. a year interest, at the rate of eight per cent., and 4,000*l*. a year for the expence of management. The credit of new government, established by the Revolution, we may believe, must have been very low, when it was obliged to borrow at so high an interest.[57]

80   In 1697 the bank was allowed to enlarge its capital stock by an engraftment of 1,001,171*l*. 10*s*.[58] Its whole capital stock, therefore, amounted at this time to 2,201,171*l*. 10*s*.[59] This engraftment is said to have been for the sup-[480]port of publick credit. In 1696, tallies had been at forty, and fifty, and sixty per cent. discount, and bank notes at twenty per cent.*.[60] During the great recoinage of the silver,[61] which was going on at this time, the bank had thought proper to discontinue the payment of its notes, which necessarily occasioned their discredit.

81   In pursuance of the 7th Anne, c. vii.[62] the bank advanced and paid into the exchequer, the sum of 400,000*l*.; making in all the sum of 1,600,000*l*. which it had advanced upon its original annuity of 96,000*l*. interest and

---

* James Postlethwaite's History of the Publick Revenue, page 301. [J. Postlethwayt, *History of the Public Revenue from 1688 to 1753, with an Appendix to 1758* (London, 1759), 301.]

ʰ⁻ʰ 3–6

[55] The following account of the Bank of England, and of its capital structure, relies heavily on James Postlethwayt, *History of the Public Revenue from 1688 to 1753, with an Appendix to 1758* (London, 1759), 301–10. The Bank of England is described as a joint stock company at V.i.e.33.

[56] 5 and 6 William and Mary, c.20 (1694).

[57] The effective rate to stockholders was higher because the subscription was not paid in full immediately. 'The effect of this operation was that the stockholders had found £720,000, and they were receiving interest on £1,200,000 at 8 per cent, so that the payment made by the government would have provided a dividend of 13⅓ per cent., subject to the cost of obtaining the half-million, not raised from share-capital.' (W. R. Scott, *Joint Stock Companies to 1720* (Cambridge, 1944), iii.206–7.)

[58] 8 and 9 William III, c.20 (1696).

[59] For details of adjustments to capital stock see J. H. Clapham, *The Bank of England* (Cambridge, 1944), i.48.

[60] See below, V.iii.11. The capital of the Bank was increased by permitting subscriptions to be four-fifths in tallies and one-fifth in bank notes. Both were so depreciated that, according to Scott, a subscriber was credited with £100 stock for about £65 worth of tallies and notes. W. R. Scott, *Joint Stock Companies to 1720*, iii.210–11, and J. H. Clapham, *The Bank of England*, i.48.

[61] See above, I.v.35.

[62] 7 Anne, c.30 (1708) in *Statutes of the Realm*, ix.113–32; 7 Anne, c.7 in Ruffhead's edition.

4,000*l.* for expence of management. In 1708,[63] therefore, the credit of
government was as good as that of private persons, since it could borrow
at six per cent. interest, the common legal and market rate of those times.
In pursuance of the same act, the bank cancelled exchequer bills to the
amount of 1,775,027*l.* 17*s.* 10½*d.* at six per cent. interest, and was at the
same time allowed to take in subscriptions for doubling its capital. In
1708, therefore, the capital of the bank amounted to 4,402,343*l.*; and it had
advanced to government the sum of 3,375,027*l.* 17*s.* 10½*d.*[64]

82   By a call of fifteen per cent. in 1709, there was paid in and made stock
656,204*l.* 1*s.* 9*d.*; and by another of ten per cent. in 1710, 501,448*l.* 12*s.* 11*d.*
In consequence of those two calls, therefore, the bank capital amounted to
5,559,995*l.* 14*s.* 8*d.*

83   [481] ¹In pursuance of the 3d George I.[65] c. 8. the bank delivered up
two millions of exchequer bills to be cancelled. It had at this time, therefore, advanced to government 5,375,027*l.* 17*s.* 10*d.*¹ In pursuance of the 8th
George I. c. 21.[66] the bank purchased of the South Sea Company, stock to
the amount of 4,000,000*l.*; and in 1722, in consequence of the subscriptions which it had taken in for enabling it to make this purchase, its capital
stock was increased by 3,400,000*l.* At this time, therefore, the bank had
advanced to the publick 9,375,027*l.* 17*s.* 10½*d.*; and its capital stock
amounted only to 8,959,995*l.* 14*s.* 8*d.* It was upon this occasion that the
sum which the bank had advanced to the publick, and for which it received
interest, began first to exceed its capital stock, or the sum for which it paid
a dividend to the proprietors of bank stock; or, in other words, that the
bank began to have an undivided capital, over and above its divided one.
It has continued to have an undivided capital of the same kind ever since.
In 1746, the bank had, upon different occasions, advanced to the publick
11,686,800*l.* and its divided capital had been raised by different calls and
subscriptions to 10,780,000*l.* The state of those two sums has continued to
be the same ever since. In pursuance of the 4th of George III. c. 25.[67] the
bank agreed to pay to government for the renewal of its charter 110,000*l.*
without interest or repayment.[68] This sum, therefore, did not increase
either of those two other sums.

84   [482] The dividend of the bank has varied according to the variations in
the rate of interest which it has, at different times, received for the money
it had advanced to the publick, as well as according to other circumstances.

---

¹⁻¹ 3–6

[63] The date of the additional advance to the government was 1709, though the proposals
had been discussed in 1708.
[64] See below, V.iii.22.   [65] 3 George I, c.8 (1716).
[66] 8 George I, c.21 (1721). For details see J. H. Clapham, *The Bank of England*, i.79–91.
[67] 4 George III, c.25 (1764).
[68] The Bank also agreed to advance £1,000,000 in Exchequer bills at 3 per cent. Clapham,
The Bank of England, i.101.

This rate of interest has gradually been reduced from eight to three per cent. For some years past the bank dividend has been at five and a half per cent.[69]

85   The stability of the bank of England is equal to that of the British government. All that it has advanced to the publick must be lost before its creditors can sustain any loss. No other banking company in England can be established by act of parliament, or can consist of more than six members. It acts, not only as an ordinary bank, but as a great engine of state. It receives and pays the greater part of the annuities which are due to the creditors of the publick, it circulates exchequer bills, and it advances to government the annual amount of the land and malt taxes, which are frequently not paid up till some years thereafter. In those different operations, its duty to the publick may sometimes have obliged it, without any fault of its directors, to overstock the circulation with paper money. It likewise discounts merchants bills, and has, upon several different occasions, supported the credit of the principal houses, not only of England, but of Hamburgh and Holland. Upon one occasion*ʲ*, in 1763,*ʲ* it is said to have advanced for this purpose, in one week, about 1,600,000*l.*; a great part of it [483] in bullion. I do not, however, pretend to warrant either the greatness of the sum, or the shortness of the time.[70] Upon other occasions, this great company has been reduced to the necessity of paying in sixpences.[71]

86   It is not by augmenting the capital of the country, but by rendering a greater part of that capital active and productive than would otherwise be so, that the most judicious operations of banking can increase the industry of the country. That part of his capital which a dealer is obliged to keep by him unemployed, and in ready money for answering occasional demands, is so much dead stock, which, so long as it remains in this situation, produces nothing either to him or to his country. The judicious operations of banking enable him to convert this dead stock into active and productive stock; into materials to work upon, into tools to work with, and into provisions and subsistence to work for; into stock which produces something both to *ᵏhimselfᵏ* and to his country. The gold and silver money which circulates in any country, and by means of which, the produce of its land and labour is annually circulated and distributed to the proper consumers, is, in the same manner as the ready money of the dealer, all dead stock. It is a

ʲ⁻ʲ 3–6   *ᵏ⁻ᵏ* him *1–2*

---

[69] The same figure is cited at V.ii.a.4. From 1768 to 1780 the rate was 5½ per cent; in 1781 it was 5¾ per cent; from 1782 to 1787 it was 6 per cent.

[70] Clapham quotes but does not confirm this story (*The Bank of England*, i.240).

[71] See above, I.v.37. Cantillon mentions the 'national Bank of London' as having to pay out in sixpences and shillings in order to gain time. *Essai*, 424–5, ed. Higgs 319 and 321. Magens held that in 1745 'perhaps the Reason for paying in small Silver might be a Suspicion, or something more, that much of the Money, so attempted to be drawn out, was to supply the Rebel Army; in which Case this Method rendered it in some Measure impracticable' (*The Universal Merchant*, ed. Horsley, 31, n.8).

very valuable part of the capital of the country, which produces nothing to the country. The judicious operations of banking, by substituting paper in the room of a great part of this gold and silver, enables the country to convert a [484] great part of this dead stock into active and productive stock; into stock which produces something to the country.[72] The gold and silver money which circulates in any country may very properly be compared to a highway, which, while it circulates and carries to market all the grass and corn of the country, produces itself not a single pile of either. The judicious operations of banking, by providing, if I may be allowed so violent a metaphor, a sort of waggon-way through the air;[73] enable the country to convert, as it were, a great part of its highways into good pastures and corn fields, and thereby to increase very considerably the annual produce of its land and labour. The commerce and industry of the country, however, it must be acknowledged, though they may be somewhat augmented, cannot be altogether so secure, when they are thus, as it were, suspended upon the Daedalian wings of paper money, as when they travel about upon the solid ground of gold and silver.[74] Over and above the accidents to which they are exposed from the unskilfulness of the conductors of this paper money, they are liable to several others, from which no prudence or skill of those conductors can guard them.

87   An unsuccessful war, for example, in which the enemy got possession of the capital, and consequently of that treasure which supported the credit of the paper money, would occasion a much greater confusion in a country where the whole circulation was carried on by paper, than [485] in one where the greater part of it was carried on by gold and silver. The usual instrument of commerce having lost its value, no exchanges could be made but either by barter or upon credit. All taxes having been usually paid in paper money, the prince would not have wherewithal either to pay his troops, or to furnish his magazines; and the state of the country would be much more irretrievable than if the greater part of its circulation had consisted in gold and silver. A prince, anxious to maintain his dominions at all times in the state in which he can most easily defend them, ought, upon this account, to guard, not only against that excessive multiplication of paper money which ruins the very banks which issue it; but even against that multiplication of it, which enables them to fill the greater part of the circulation of the country with it.

[72] See above, II.ii.40.

[73] A similar analogy is used in ED 4.4, LJ (A) vi.128–9. LJ (B) 245, ed. Cannan 191 reads: 'Money in this respect may be compared to the high roads of a country, which bear neither corn nor grass themselves but circulate all the corn and grass in the country. If we could find any way to save the ground taken up by highways, we would encrease considerably the quantity of commodities . . .'

[74] In this connection, Pownall made the point that while Smith reasons 'from the *abuse* . . . all these arguments do equally derive from the *defect* of this paper money'. *Letter*, 16 and 21; cf. above, II.ii.30.

88   The circulation of every country may be considered as divided into two different branches; the circulation of the dealers with one another, and the circulation between the dealers and the consumers. Though the same pieces of money, whether paper or metal, may be employed sometimes in the one circulation and sometimes in the other, yet as both are constantly going on at the same time, each requires a certain stock of money of one kind or another, to carry it on. The value of the goods circulated between the different dealers, never can exceed the value of those circulated between the dealers and the consum-[486]ers; whatever is bought by the dealers, being ultimately destined to be sold to the consumers. The circulation between the dealers, as it is carried on by wholesale, requires generally a pretty large sum for every particular transaction. That between the dealers and the consumers, on the contrary, as it is generally carried on by retail, frequently requires but very small ones, a shilling, or even a halfpenny, being often sufficient. But small sums circulate much faster than large ones. A shilling changes masters more frequently than a guinea, and a halfpenny more frequently than a shilling. Though the annual purchases of all the consumers, therefore, are at least equal in value to those of all the dealers, they can generally be transacted with a much smaller quantity of money; the same pieces, by a more rapid circulation, serving as the instrument of many more purchases of the one kind than of the other.

89   Paper money may be so regulated, as either to confine itself very much to the circulation between the different dealers, or to extend itself likewise to a great part of that between the dealers and the consumers. Where no bank notes are circulated under ten pounds value, as in London,[75] paper money confines itself very much to the circulation between the dealers. When a ten pound bank note comes into the hands of a consumer, he is generally obliged to change it at the first shop where he has occasion to purchase five shillings worth of goods, so that it often re-[487]turns into the hands of a dealer, before the consumer has spent the fortieth part of the money. Where bank notes are issued for so small sums as twenty shillings, as in Scotland, paper money extends itself to a considerable part of the circulation between dealers and consumers. Before the act of parliament,[76] which put a stop to the circulation of ten and five shilling notes, it filled a still greater part of that circulation. In the currencies of North America, paper was commonly issued for so small a sum as a shilling, and filled almost the whole of that circulation. In some paper currencies of Yorkshire, it was issued even for so small a sum as a sixpence.

[75] Initially notes were in multiples of £5. Clapham, citing A. Anderson *Origin of Commerce* (London, 1764), iii.308), comments: 'subsequently notes for less than £20 became so rare that when the Bank began a regular issue of £15 and £10 notes, in 1759, contemporaries referred to them as though they were a novelty' (*The Bank of England*, i.146).
[76] 5 George III, c. 49 (1765). See above, II.ii.41, and below, II.ii.98.

90   Where the issuing of bank notes for such very small sums is allowed and commonly practised, many mean people are both enabled and encouraged to become bankers. A person whose promissory note for five pounds, or even for twenty shillings, would be rejected by every body, will get it to be received without scruple when it is issued for so small a sum as a sixpence. But the frequent bankruptcies to which such beggarly bankers must be liable, may occasion a very considerable inconveniency, and sometimes even a very great calamity to many poor people who had received their notes in payment.

91   It were better, perhaps, that no bank notes were issued in any part of the kingdom for a smaller sum than five pounds. Paper money would then, probably, confine itself, in every part of the kingdom, to the circulation between [488] the different dealers, as much as it does at present in London, where no bank notes are issued under ten pounds value; five pounds being, in most parts of the kingdom, a sum which, though it will purchase, perhaps, little more than half the quantity of goods, is as much considered, and is as seldom spent all at once, as ten pounds are amidst the profuse expence of London.

92   Where paper money, it is to be observed, is pretty much confined to the circulation between dealers and dealers, as at London, there is always plenty of gold and silver. Where it extends itself to a considerable part of the circulation between dealers and consumers, as in Scotland, and still more in North America,[77] it banishes gold and silver almost entirely from the country; almost all the ordinary transactions of its interior commerce being thus carried on by paper. The suppression of ten and five shilling bank notes, somewhat relieved the scarcity of gold and silver in Scotland; and the suppression of twenty shilling notes, 'would' probably relieve it still more. Those metals are said to have become more abundant in America, since the suppression of some of their paper currencies. They are said, likewise, to have been more abundant before the institution of those currencies.

93   Though paper money should be pretty much confined to the circulation between dealers and dealers, yet banks and bankers might still be able to give nearly the same assistance to the in-[489]dustry and commerce of the country, as they had done when paper money filled almost the whole circulation. The ready money which a dealer is obliged to keep by him, for answering occasional demands, is destined altogether for the circulation between himself and other dealers, of whom he buys goods. He has no occasion to keep any by him for the circulation between himself and the consumers, who are his customers, and who bring ready money to him, instead of taking any from him. Though no paper money, therefore, was allowed to be issued, but for such sums as would confine it pretty much to

---

¹⁻¹ will 6

⁷⁷ American paper is mentioned in LJ (B) 247, ed. Cannan, 193. See also below, V.iii.83.

the circulation between dealers and dealers; yet, partly by discounting real bills of exchange, and partly by lending upon cash accounts, banks and bankers might still be able to relieve the greater part of those dealers from the necessity of keeping any considerable part of their stock by them, unemployed and in ready money, for answering occasional demands. They might still be able to give the utmost assistance which banks and bankers can, with propriety, give to traders of every kind.

94   To restrain private people, it may be said, from receiving in payment the promissory notes of a banker, for any sum whether great or small, when they themselves are willing to receive them; or, to restrain a banker from issuing such notes, when all his neighbours are willing to accept of them, is a manifest violation of that natural liberty which it is the proper business of [490] law, not to infringe, but to support. Such regulations may, no doubt, be considered as in some respect a violation of natural liberty. But those exertions of the natural liberty of a few individuals, which might endanger the security of the whole society, are, and ought to be, restrained by the laws of all governments; of the most free, as well as of the most despotical. The obligation of building party walls, in order to prevent the communication of fire, is a violation of natural liberty, exactly of the same kind with the regulations of the banking trade which are here proposed.

95   A paper money consisting in bank notes, issued by people of undoubted credit, payable upon demand without any condition, and in fact always readily paid as soon as presented, is, in every respect, equal in value to gold and silver money; since gold and silver money can at any time be had for it. Whatever is either bought or sold for such paper, must necessarily be bought or sold as cheap as it could have been for gold and silver.

96   The increase of paper money, it has been said, by augmenting the quantity, and consequently diminishing the value of the whole currency, necessarily augments the money price of commodities. But as the quantity of gold and silver, which is taken from the currency, is always equal to the quantity of paper which is added to it, paper money does not necessarily increase the quantity of the whole currency. From the be-[491]ginning of the last century to the present ᵐtimeᵐ, provisions never were cheaper in Scotland than in 1759,⁷⁸ though, from the circulation of ten and five shilling bank notes, there was then more paper money in the country than at present. The proportion between the price of provisions in Scotland and that in England, is the same now as before the great multiplication of banking companies in Scotland. Corn is, upon most occasions, fully as cheap in

---

ᵐ⁻ᵐ times *1*

⁷⁸ The fiars price of an imperial quarter of oats at Haddington in 1759 was 9s. 11¼d. The price was lower in twelve of the earlier years of the century and in only one (1760 at 9s. 10d.) in the later years.

England as in France; though there is a great deal of paper money in England, and scarce any in France. In 1751 and in 1752, when Mr. Hume published his Political Discourses, and soon after the great multiplication of paper money in Scotland, there was a very sensible rise in the price of provisions, owing, probably, to the badness of the seasons, and not to the multiplication of paper money.[79]

97   It would be otherwise, indeed, with a paper money consisting in promissory notes, of which the immediate payment depended, in any respect, either upon the good will of those who issued them; or upon a condition which the holder of the notes might not always have it in his power to fulfil; or of which the payment was not exigible till after a certain number of years, and which in the mean time bore no interest. Such a paper money would, no doubt, fall more or less below the value of gold and silver, according as the difficulty or uncertainty of obtaining immediate payment was supposed to be [492] greater or less; or according to the greater or less distance of time at which payment was exigible.

98   Some years ago the different banking companies of Scotland were in the practice of inserting into their bank notes, what they called an Optional Clause,[80] by which they promised payment to the bearer, either as soon as the note should be presented, or, in the option of the directors, six months after such presentment, together with the legal interest for the said six months. The directors of some of those banks sometimes took advantage of this optional clause, and sometimes threatened those who demanded gold and silver in exchange for a considerable number of their notes, that they would take advantage of it, unless such demanders would content themselves with a part of what they demanded. The promissory notes of those banking companies constituted at that time the far greater part of the currency of Scotland, which this uncertainty of payment necessarily degraded below the value of gold and silver money. During the continuance of this

---

[79] Hume's statement of the quantity theory of money is considered in LJ (B) 252–3, ed. Cannan 197. In his essays 'Of Money' and 'Of the Balance of Trade' Hume was critical of the alleged advantages of banks and paper credit, in Scotland in particular.'

I scarcely know any method of sinking money below its level, but those institutions of banks, funds, and paper-credit which are so much practised in this kingdom. These render paper equivalent to money, circulate it throughout the whole state, make it supply the place of gold and silver, raise proportionably the price of labour and commodities, and by that means either banish a great part of those precious metals, or prevent their farther encrease. What can be more short-sighted than our reasonings on this head?

(*Essays Moral, Political, and Literary*, ed. Green and Grose, i.337).

Smith's views are closer to those of Hume in the WN than in LJ (B) 253, ed. Cannan 197. He may have modified his views in light of the experience in Scotland in the financial crises of 1762, and especially in 1772.

[80] Steuart considers the optional clause in the *Principles*, IV.2.xiv. This section of the book gives a great deal of attention to the Scottish banking crisis of the 1760s; ed. Skinner, ii.521 and note.

abuse (which prevailed chiefly in 1762, 1763, and 1764), while the exchange between London and Carlisle was at par, that between London and Dumfries would sometimes be four per cent. against Dumfries, though this town is not thirty miles distant from Carlisle. But at Carlisle, bills were paid in gold and silver; whereas at Dumfries they were paid in Scotch bank notes, and the uncertainty of get-[493]ting those bank notes exchanged for gold and silver coin had thus degraded them four per cent. below the value of that coin. The same act of parliament[81] which suppressed ten and five shilling bank notes, suppressed likewise this optional clause, and thereby restored the exchange between England and Scotland to its natural rate, or to what the course of trade and remittances might happen to make it.

99   In the paper currencies of Yorkshire, the payment of so small a sum as a sixpence sometimes depended upon the condition that the holder of the note should bring the change of a guinea to the person who issued it; a condition, which the holders of such notes might frequently find it very difficult to fulfil, and which must have degraded this currency below the value of gold and silver money. An act of parliament, accordingly, declared all such clauses unlawful, and suppressed, in the same manner as in Scotland, all promissory notes, payable to the bearer, under twenty shillings value.[82]

100   The paper currencies of North America consisted, not in bank notes payable to the bearer on demand, but in a government paper, of which the payment was not exigible till several years after it was issued: And though the colony governments paid no interest to the holders of this paper, they declared it to be, and in fact rendered it, a legal tender of payment for the full value for which it was issued. But allowing the colony security to be perfectly good, a hundred [494] pounds payable fifteen years hence, for example, in a country where interest is at six per cent. is worth little more than forty pounds ready money. To oblige a creditor, therefore, to accept of this as full payment for a debt of a hundred pounds actually paid down in ready money, was an act of such violent injustice, as has scarce, perhaps, been attempted by the government of any other country which pretended to be free. It bears the evident marks of having originally been, what the honest and downright Doctor Douglas assures us it was, a scheme of fraudulent debtors to cheat their creditors.[83] The government of Pensylvania, indeed, pretended, upon their first emission of paper money, in 1722,[84] to render their paper of equal value with gold and silver, by enact-

[81] 5 George III, c.49 (1765). See above, II.ii.41 and 89.

[82] 15 George III, c.51 (1775).

[83] See W. Douglass (*British Settlements in North America*, i.310,n.): 'All our Paper-money making assemblies have been legislatures of debtors, the representatives of people who from incogitancy, idleness and profuseness, have been under a necessity of mortgaging their lands.' Douglass frequently condemns paper currency in uncompromising terms.

[84] For a modern interpretation see R. A. Lester, 'Currency Issues to overcome Depressions in Pennsylvania, 1723 and 1729', *Journal of Political Economy*, xlvi (1938), 324–75.

ing penalties against all those who made any difference in the price of their
goods when they sold them for a colony paper, and when they sold them
for gold and silver; a regulation equally tyrannical, but much less effectual
than that which it was meant to support. A positive law may render a
shilling a legal tender for a guinea; because it may direct the courts of
justice to discharge the debtor who has made that tender. But no positive
law can oblige a person who sells goods, and who is at liberty to sell
or not to sell, as he pleases, to accept of a shilling as equivalent to a guinea
in the price of them. Notwithstanding any regulation of this kind, it appeared by the course of exchange with Great Britain, that a hundred
pounds sterling was oc-[495]casionally considered as equivalent, in some of
the colonies, to a hundred and thirty pounds, and in others to so great a
sum as eleven hundred pounds currency; this difference in the value
arising from the difference in the quantity of paper emitted in the different
colonies, and in the distance and probability of the term of its final discharge and redemption.[85]

101   No law, therefore, could be more equitable than the act of parliament,
so unjustly complained of in the colonies, which declared that no paper
currency to be emitted there in time coming, should be a legal tender of
payment.[86]

102   Pensylvania was always more moderate in its emissions of paper money
than any other of our colonies.[87] Its paper currency accordingly is said
never to have sunk below the value of the gold and silver which was current
in the colony before the first emission of its paper money. Before that
emission, the colony had raised the denomination of its coin, and had, by
act of assembly, ordered five shillings sterling to pass in the colony for six
and three-pence, and afterwards for six and eight-pence. A pound colony
currency, therefore, even when that currency was gold and silver, was more
than thirty per cent. below the value of a pound sterling, and when that
currency was turned into paper, it was seldom much more than thirty
per cent. below that value. The pretence for raising the denomination of
the coin, was to prevent the exportation [496] of gold and silver, by making
equal quantities of those metals pass for greater sums in the colony than

[85] With regard to the high price of exchange prevailing between Virginia and Glasgow,
it is remarked in LJ (B) 284, ed. Cannan 221, that 'In the American colonies the currency
is paper, and their notes are 40 or 50 per cent below par because the funds are not sufficient.'
[86] 4 George III, c.34 (1764).
[87] Pownall compared the Bank of Amsterdam favourably with the Scottish banks, the
former being based on deposit and the latter on trust, and refers in the same context to
'the operations of that wise and prudent institution, the loan office of Pennsylvania'
(*Letter*, 22). Douglass merely commented that 'by the good management of their paper
loan office, the intrinsick value of their denominations has not been depreciated farther'
(*British Settlements in North America*, ii.335). See below, V.ii.a.11, where Smith describes
the operations of the office, and refers to the government of the state as 'frugal and orderly',
and also V.iii.81.

they did in the mother country. It was found, however, that the price of all goods from the mother country rose exactly in proportion as they raised the denomination of their coin, so that their gold and silver were exported as fast as ever.

103   The paper of each colony being received in the payment of the provincial taxes, for the full value for which it had been issued, it necessarily derived from this use some additional value, over and above what it would have had, from the real or supposed distance of the term of its final discharge and redemption. This additional value was greater or less, according as the quantity of paper issued was more or less above what could be employed in the payment of the taxes of the particular colony which issued it. It was in all the colonies very much above what could be employed in this manner.

104   A prince, who should enact that a certain proportion of his taxes should be paid in a paper money of a certain kind, might thereby give a certain value to this paper money; even though the term of its final discharge and redemption should depend altogether upon the will of the prince. If the bank which issued this paper was careful to keep the quantity of it always somewhat below what could easily be employed in this manner, the demand for it might be such as to make it even bear a premium, or sell for [497] somewhat more in the market than the quantity of gold or silver currency for which it was issued. Some people account in this manner for what is called the Agio of the bank of Amsterdam, or for the superiority of bank money over current money; though this bank money, as they pretend, cannot be taken out of the bank at the will of the owner.[88] The greater part of foreign bills of exchange must be paid in bank money, that is, by a transfer in the books of the bank; and the directors of the bank, they allege, are careful to keep the whole quantity of bank money always below what this use occasions a demand for. It is upon this account, they say, that bank money sells for a premium, or bears an agio of four or five per cent. above the same nominal sum of the gold and silver currency of the country.[89] This account of the bank of Amsterdam, however, *ⁿit will appear hereafter, is in a great measureⁿ* chimerical.[90]

105   A paper currency which falls below the value of gold and silver coin, does not thereby sink the value of *ᵒthose metalsᵒ*, or occasion equal quantities of *ᵖthemᵖ* to exchange for a smaller quantity of goods of any other kind. The proportion between the value of gold and silver and that of goods of any other kind, depends in all cases, not upon the nature or quantity of any particular paper money, which may be current in any particular

ⁿ⁻ⁿ I have reason to believe, is altogether *1*   *ᵒ⁻ᵒ* gold and silver *1*
ᵖ⁻ᵖ those metals *1*

---

[88] See below, IV.iii.b.6.   [89] The agio of the Bank is defined below, IV.iii.a.11.
[90] The Bank of Amsterdam is described below, IV.iii.b.

country, but upon the richness or poverty of the mines, which happen at any [498] particular time to supply the great market of the commercial world with those metals. It depends upon the proportion between the quantity of labour which is necessary in order to bring a certain quantity of gold and silver to market, and that which is necessary in order to bring thither a certain quantity of any other sort of goods.

106   If bankers are restrained from issuing any circulating bank notes, or notes payable to the bearer, for less than a certain sum; and if they are subjected to the obligation of an immediate and unconditional payment of such bank notes as soon as presented, their trade may, with safety to the publick, be rendered in all other respects perfectly free. The late multiplication of banking companies in both parts of the united kingdom, an event by which many people have been much alarmed, instead of diminishing, increases the security of the publick. It obliges all of them to be more circumspect in their conduct, and, by not extending their currency beyond its due proportion to their cash, to guard themselves against those malicious runs, which the rivalship of so many competitors is always ready to bring upon them. It restrains the circulation of each particular company within a narrower circle, and reduces their circulating notes to a smaller number. By dividing the whole circulation into a greater number of parts, the failure of any one company, an accident which, in the course of things, must sometimes [499] happen, becomes of less consequence to the publick. This free competition too obliges all bankers to be more liberal in their dealings with their customers, lest their rivals should carry them away. In general, if any branch of trade, or any division of labour, be advantageous to the publick, the freer and more general the competition, it will always be the more so.[91]

[91] The substance of this final paragraph appears in LJ (B) 251, ed. Cannan 195, which concludes: 'From all these considerations it is manifest that banks are beneficial to the commerce of a country, and that it is bad policy to restrain them.' The point is qualified to some extent in § 94 above.

CHAPTER III

*Of the Accumulation of Capital, or of productive and unproductive
Labour*

1   THERE is one sort of labour which adds to the value of the subject
upon which it is bestowed: There is another which has no such effect.
The former, as it produces a value, may be called productive; the
latter, unproductive* labour.¹ Thus the labour of a manufacturer adds,
generally, to the value of the materials which he works upon, that of
his own [2] maintenance, and of his master's profit. The labour of a menial
servant, on the contrary, adds to the value of nothing. Though the manufacturer has his wages advanced to him by his master, he, in reality, costs
him no expence, the value of those wages being generally restored, together with a profit, in the improved value of the subject upon which his
labour is bestowed. But the maintenance of a menial servant never is
restored. A man grows rich by employing a multitude of manufacturers:
He grows poor, by maintaining a multitude of menial servants. The labour
of the latter, however, has its value, and deserves its reward as well as that
of the former. But the labour of the manufacturer fixes and realizes itself in
some particular subject or vendible commodity, which lasts for some time at
least after that labour is past.² It is, as it were, a certain quantity of labour
stocked and stored up to be employed, if necessary, upon some other
occasion. That subject, or what is the same thing, the price of that subject,
can afterwards, if necessary, put into motion a quantity of labour equal to
that which had originally produced it.³ The labour of the menial servant,
on the contrary, does not fix or realize itself in any particular subject or
vendible commodity. His services generally perish in the very instant of
their performance, and seldom leave any trace or value behind them, for
which an equal quantity of service could afterwards be procured.⁴

2   The labour of some of the most respectable orders in the society is, like
that of menial ser-[3]vants, unproductive of any value, and does not fix or
realize itself in any permanent subject, or vendible commodity, which
endures after that labour is past, and for which an equal quantity of labour
could afterwards be procured. The sovereign, for example, with all the

* Some French authors of great learning and ingenuity have used those words in a
different sense. In the last chapter of the fourth book, I shall endeavour to show that their
sense is an improper one.

¹ The term 'unproductive' is described at IV.ix.5 as a 'humiliating appellation'. IV.ix may
acquire an added interest when read in conjunction with the present chapter.

² The activities of merchants are described as productive, e.g. at II.v.6. and 8.

³ This doctrine is related to that of 'labour commanded' as used in the discussion of
value in I.v.

⁴ Similar expressions to those used in the preceding two sentences occur at IV.ix.31.

officers both of justice and war who serve under him, the whole army and navy, are unproductive labourers.[5] They are the servants of the publick, and are maintained by a part of the annual produce of the industry of other people.[6] Their service, how honourable, how useful,[7] or how necessary soever, produces nothing for which an equal quantity of service can afterwards be procured. The protection, security, and defence of the commonwealth, the effect of their labour this year, will not purchase its protection, security, and defence, for the year to come. In the same class must be ranked, some both of the gravest and most important, and some of the most frivolous professions: churchmen, lawyers, physicians, men of letters of all kinds; players, buffoons, musicians, opera-singers, opera-dancers, &c.[8] The labour of the meanest of these has a certain value, regulated by the very same principles which regulate that of every other sort of labour;[9] and that of the noblest and most useful, produces nothing which could afterwards purchase or procure an equal quantity of labour. Like the declamation of the actor, the harangue of the orator, or the tune of the musician, the work of all of them perishes in the very instant of its production.[10]

[5] But see below, V.i.a.14 and V.ii.i.7.

[6] See below, IV.i.20 and V.i.a.11, where Smith discusses this point in relation to the costs of defence. In his essay 'Of Interest' Hume made the interesting point that 'lawyers and physicians beget no industry; and it is even at the expence of others they acquire their riches'. He went on, like Smith, to include merchants among the class who 'beget industry' by 'serving as canals to convey it through every corner of the state' (*Essays Moral, Political, and Literary*, ed. Green and Grose, i.326). Cantillon remarks, *Essai*, 61, ed. Higgs 47, that: 'As for those who exercise Professions which are not essential, like Dancers, Actors, Painters, Musicians, etc. they are only supported in the State for pleasure or for ornament, and their number is always very small in proportion to the other Inhabitants.'

[7] The term 'useful' appears to be equated with 'productive' in the Introduction, § 6.

[8] The rewards of opera singers etc are discussed in I.x.b.25. It is also suggested at V.i.g. 15 that the labour of those who provide public shows may be indirectly productive of benefit to the community.

[9] It is to be emphasized that Smith does not deny that the kinds of unproductive labour cited have a value. For example, it is pointed out in the Imitative Arts II.1 that after 'the gratification of the bodily appetites, there seem to be none more natural to man than Music and Dancing' and refers to the 'delicious pleasure' to be derived from such arts, including the opera, and to the 'pleasure and delight' to be derived from a concert of instrumental music. He also suggests that a very high intellectual pleasure may be derived from such a source, not unlike that to be derived from 'the contemplation of a great system in any other science' (ibid., II.30). See below. IV.ix.31.

[10] There is an interesting variant on the theme of this paragraph in Steuart's *Principles*, II.xxvi. Here Steuart draws a distinction between 'goods' which do, and those which do not, have an 'intrinsic substance' which is 'permanent and vendible'; i.e. a distinction between things which are 'corporeal' and those which are not.

The first species of things incorporeal, which may be purchased with money, is personal service; such as the attendance of a menial servant, the advice of a physician, of a lawyer, the assistance of skilful people in order to acquire knowledge, the service of those employed in the administration of public affairs at home and abroad, or for the defence of a kingdom by sea, or land; the residence of great men at court, who do honour to princes,

3   [4] Both productive and unproductive labourers, and those who do not
labour at all, are all equally maintained by the annual produce of the land
and labour of the country. This produce, how great soever, can never be
infinite, but must have certain limits. According, therefore, as a smaller
or greater proportion of it is in any one year employed in maintaining
unproductive hands, the more in the one case and the less in the other will
remain for the productive, and the next year's produce will be greater or
smaller accordingly; the whole annual produce, if we except the spontaneous productions of the earth, being the effect of productive labour.

4   Though the whole annual produce of the land and labour of every
country, is, no doubt, ultimately destined for supplying the consumption
of its inhabitants, and for procuring a revenue to them; yet when it first
comes either from the ground, or from the hands of the productive labourers, it naturally divides itself into two parts. One of them, and frequently the largest, is, in the first place, destined for replacing a capital, or
for renewing the provisions, materials, and finished work, which had been
withdrawn from a capital; the other for constituting a revenue either to the
owner of this capital, as the profit of his stock; or to some other person, as
the rent of his land. Thus, of the produce of land, one part replaces the
capital of the farmer; the other pays his profit and the rent of the landlord;
and thus constitutes a revenue both to the owner of this capital, as the
profits of his stock; [5] and to some other person, as the rent of his land.
Of the produce of a great manufactory, in the same manner, one part, and
that always the largest, replaces the capital of the undertaker of the work;
the other pays his profit, and thus constitutes a revenue to the owner of
ᵃthisᵃ capital.

5   That part of the annual produce of the land and labour of any country
which replaces a capital, never is immediately employed to maintain any
but productive hands. It pays the wages of productive labour only. That
which is immediately destined for constituting a revenue either as profit or
as rent, may maintain indifferently either productive or unproductive
hands.

6   Whatever part of his stock a man employs as a capital, he always expects
ᵇisᵇ to be replaced to him with a profit. He employs it, therefore, in maintaining productive hands only; and after having served in the function of a
capital to him, it constitutes a revenue to them. Whenever he employs any
part of it in maintaining unproductive hands of any kind, that part is, from
that moment, withdrawn from his capital, and placed in his stock reserved
for immediate consumption.

ᵃ⁻ᵃ his ⟨corrected *4e–6*⟩   ᵇ⁻ᵇ it 6

and make their authority respected; and even when money is given to procure amusement, pleasure, or dissipation, when no durable and transferable value is given in return.'
(*Principles*, i.369, ed. Skinner, i.318.)

7   Unproductive labourers, and those who do not labour at all, are all
     maintained by revenue; either, first, by that part of the annual produce
     which is originally destined for constituting a revenue to some particular
     persons, either as the rent of land or as the profits of stock; or, secondly,
     by that part which, though originally destined for replacing a capital and
     for maintaining productive labourers only, yet when it comes [6] into
     their hands, whatever part of it is over and above their necessary subsis-
     tence, may be employed in maintaining indifferently either productive or un-
     productive hands. Thus, not only the great landlord or the rich merchant,
     but even the common workman, if his wages are considerable, may maintain
     a menial servant; or he may sometimes go to a play or a puppet-show, and
     so contribute his share towards maintaining one set of unproductive labour-
     ers; or he may pay some taxes, and thus help to maintain another set, more
     honourable and useful, indeed, but equally unproductive. No part of the
     annual produce, however, which had been originally destined to replace a
     capital, is ever directed towards maintaining unproductive hands, till after
     it has put into motion its full complement of productive labour, or all that
     it could put into motion in the way in which it was employed.[11] The work-
     man must have earned his wages by work done, before he can employ any
     part of them in this manner. That part too is generally but a small one. It is
     his spare revenue only, of which productive labourers have seldom a great
     deal. They generally have some, however; and in the payment of taxes the
     greatness of their number may compensate, in some measure, the smallness
     of their contribution.[12] The rent of land and the profits of stock are every
     where, therefore, the principal sources from which unproductive hands
     derive their subsistence. These are the two sorts of revenue of which the
     owners have generally most to spare. They might both maintain indiffer-[7]
     ently either productive or unproductive hands. They seem, however, to
     have some predilection for the latter. The expence of a great lord feeds
     generally more idle than industrious people. The rich merchant, though
     with his capital he maintains industrious people only, yet by his expence,
     that is, by the employment of his revenue, he feeds commonly the very
     same sort as the great lord.[13]

8   The proportion, therefore, between the productive and unproductive

---

[11] This subject is discussed in the preceding chapter.
[12] See below, V.ii.k.43 and cf. II.1.8.
[13] The point made in this paragraph is that funds used as capital (savings) *directly* employ
productive labour, whereas funds used as revenue do not. Smith recognized, however, that
all forms of consumption expenditure, whether emanating directly from the productive
wage-earner, or from the expenditure of the player he pays, seem always ultimately to
support productive labour through the purchase of commodities. As Smith points out at
III.iv.11, the rich man who pays the price of a commodity 'indirectly contributes to the
maintenance of all the workmen and their employers'. See also the concluding paragraphs
of the present chapter where Smith comments on the different modes of *expense* and the
ways in which they contribute to public opulence.

hands, depends very much in every country upon the proportion between that part of the annual produce, which, as soon as it comes either from the ground or from the hands of the productive labourers, is destined for replacing a capital, and that which is destined for constituting a revenue, either as rent, or as profit. This proportion is very different in rich from what it is in poor countries.[14]

9   Thus, at present, in the opulent countries of Europe, a very large, frequently the largest portion of the produce of the land, is destined for replacing the capital of the rich and independent farmer; the other for paying his profits, and the rent of the landlord. But antiently, during the prevalency of the feudal government, a very small portion of the produce was sufficient to replace the capital employed in cultivation. It consisted commonly in a few wretched cattle, maintained altogether by the spontaneous produce of uncultivated land, and which might, therefore, be considered as a part of that spontaneous produce. It generally too belonged to the landlord, and [8] was by him advanced to the occupiers of the land. All the rest of the produce properly belonged to him too, either as rent for his land, or as profit upon this paultry capital. The occupiers of land were generally bondmen, whose persons and effects were equally his property. Those who were not bondmen were tenants at will, and though the rent which they paid was often nominally little more than a quit-rent, it really amounted to the whole produce of the land. Their lord could at all times command their labour in peace, and their service in war. Though they lived at a distance from his house, they were equally dependant upon him as his retainers who lived in it. But the whole produce of the land undoubtedly belongs to him, who can dispose of the labour and service of all those whom it maintains. In the present state of Europe, the share of the landlord seldom exceeds a third, sometimes not a fourth part of the whole produce of the land. The rent of land, however, in all the improved parts of the country, has been tripled and quadrupled since those antient times; and this third or fourth part of the annual produce is, it seems, three or four times greater than the whole had been before. In the progress of improvement, rent, though it increases in proportion to the extent, diminishes in proportion to the produce of the land.[15]

10   In the opulent countries of Europe, great capitals are at present employed in trade and manufactures. In the antient state, the little trade that was stirring, and the few homely and coarse [9] manufactures that were carried on, required but very small capitals. These, however, must have yielded very large profits. The rate of interest was no where less than ten per cent.

---

[14] Smith took account of a particular problem facing indebted countries at V.iii.47, where it is argued that investment in public funds may turn capital away from productive to unproductive uses.

[15] The figure of a third is cited at I.xi.c.20, II.v.12, and V.ii.a.17. Cf. above I.xi.p.2.

and their profits must have been sufficient to afford this great interest. At present the rate of interest, in the improved parts of Europe, is no where higher than six per cent. and in some of the most improved it is so low as four, three, and two per cent. Though that part of the revenue of the inhabitants which is derived from the profits of stock is always much greater in rich than in poor countries, it is because the stock is much greater: in proportion to the stock the profits are generally much less.

11   That part of the annual produce, therefore, which, as soon as it comes either from the ground, or from the hands of the productive labourers, is destined for replacing a capital, is not only much greater in rich than in poor countries, but bears a much greater proportion to that which is immediately destined for constituting a revenue either as rent or as profit. The funds destined for the maintenance of productive labour, are not only much greater in the former than in the latter, but bear a much greater proportion to those which, though they may be employed to maintain either productive or unproductive hands, have generally a predilection for the latter.

12   The proportion between those different funds necessarily determines in every country the general character of the inhabitants as to industry or idleness. We are more industrious than our [10] forefathers; because in the present times the funds destined for the maintenance of industry, are much greater in proportion to those which are likely to be employed in the maintenance of idleness, than they were two or three centuries ago. Our ancestors were idle for want of a sufficient encouragement to industry. It is better, says the proverb, to play for nothing, than to work for nothing. In mercantile and manufacturing towns, where the inferior ranks of people are chiefly maintained by the employment of capital, they are in general industrious, sober, and thriving; as in many English, and in most Dutch towns. In those towns which are principally supported by the constant or occasional residence of a court, and in which the inferior ranks of people are chiefly maintained by the spending of revenue, they are in general idle, dissolute, and poor; as at Rome, Versailles, Compiegne, and Fontainbleau. If you except Rouen and Bourdeaux, there is little trade or industry in any of the parliament towns of France;[16] and the inferior ranks of people, being chiefly maintained by the expence of the members of the courts of justice, and of those who come to plead before them, are in general idle and poor. The great trade of Rouen and Bourdeaux seems to be altogether the effect of their situation.[17] Rouen is necessarily the entrepôt of almost all the goods which are brought either from foreign countries, or from the

[16] In 1776 the thirteen Parlements of France, with dates of foundation were: Paris (1302), Toulouse (1443), Grenoble (1451), Bordeaux (1462), Dijon (1476) Rouen (1499), Aix-en-Provence (1501), Rennes (1553), Pau (1620), Metz (1633), Besançon (1674), Douai (1686), Nancy (1775). The *Encycopédie* (1765), xii.1, did not, of course, list Nancy.

[17] See above, I.iii.4, where Smith discusses the advantages of location on waterways

maritime provinces of France, for the consumption of the great city of Paris. Bourdeaux is in the same manner the entrepôt of the wines [11] which grow upon the banks of the Garonne, and of the rivers which run into it, one of the richest wine countries in the world, and which seems to produce the wine fittest for exportation, or best suited to the taste of foreign nations. Such advantageous situations necessarily attract a great capital by the great employment which they afford it; and the employment of this capital is the cause of the industry of those two cities. In the other parliament towns of France, very little more capital seems to be employed than what is necessary for supplying their own consumption; that is, little more than the smallest capital which can be employed in them. The same thing may be said of Paris, Madrid, and Vienna. Of those three cities, Paris is by far the most industrious; but Paris itself is the principal market of all the manufactures established at Paris, and its own consumption is the principal object of all the trade which it carries on. London, Lisbon, and Copenhagen, are, perhaps, the only three cities in Europe, which are both the constant residence of a court, and can at the same time be considered as trading cities, or as cities which trade not only for their own consumption, but for that of other cities and countries. The situation of all the three is extremely advantageous, and naturally fits them to be the entrepôts of a great part of the goods destined for the consumption of distant places. In a city where a great revenue is spent, to employ with advantage a capital for any other purpose than for supplying the consumption of that city, is [12] probably more difficult than in one in which the inferior ranks of people have no other maintenance but what they derive from the employment of such a capital. The idleness of the greater part of the people who are maintained by the expence of revenue, corrupts, it is probable, the industry of those who ought to be maintained by the employment of capital, and renders it less advantageous to employ a capital there than in other places. There was little trade or industry in Edinburgh before the union. When the Scotch parliament was no longer to be assembled in it, when it ceased to be the necessary residence of the principal nobility and gentry of Scotland, it became a city of some trade and industry. It still continues, however, to be the residence of the principal courts of justice in Scotland, of the boards of customs and excise, &c. A considerable revenue, therefore, still continues to be spent in it. In trade and industry it is much inferior to Glasgow, of which the inhabitants are chiefly maintained by the employment of capital. The inhabitants of a large village, it has sometimes been observed, after having made considerable progress in manufactures, have become idle and poor, in consequence of a great lord's having taken up his residence in their neighbourhood.[18]

[18] See LJ (B) 203–5, ed. Cannan 154–6. It is argued at 204, ed. Cannan 155, that the development of industry reduces idleness and thus crime and that 'Nothing tends so

13   The proportion between capital and revenue, therefore, seems every where to regulate the proportion between industry and idleness. Where-ever capital predominates, industry prevails: wherever revenue, idleness. Every increase or [13] diminution of capital, therefore, naturally tends to increase or diminish the real quantity of industry, the number of productive hands, and consequently the exchangeable value of the annual produce of the land and labour of the country, the real wealth and revenue of all its inhabitants.

14   Capitals are increased by parsimony, and diminished by prodigality and misconduct.

15   Whatever a person saves from his revenue he adds to his capital, and either employs it himself in maintaining an additional number of productive hands, or enables some other person to do so, by lending it to him for an interest, that is, for a share of the profits.[19] As the capital of an individual can be increased only by what he saves from his annual revenue or his annual gains, so the capital of a society, which is the same with that of all the individuals who compose it, can be increased only in the same manner.

16   Parsimony, and not industry, is the immediate cause of the increase of capital. Industry, indeed, provides the subject which parsimony accumulates. But whatever industry might acquire, if parsimony did not save and store up, the capital would never be the greater.[20]

17   Parsimony, by increasing the fund which is destined for the maintenance of productive hands, tends to increase the number of those hands whose labour adds to the value of the subject upon which it is bestowed. It tends therefore to increase the exchangeable value of the annual pro-[14]duce of the land and labour of the country. It puts into motion an additional quantity of industry, which gives an additional value to the annual produce.

18   What is annually saved is as regularly consumed as what is annually

much to corrupt mankind as dependencey, while independencey still encreases the honesty of the people.' Hence Smith suggested, 'In Glasgow where almost no body has more than one servant, there are fewer capital crimes than in Edinburgh.' Similar points are made at greater length in LJ (A) vi.1–6, and see below. III.iv.13–15.

[19] It is remarked at IV.vii.c.57 that capitals can be increased only through savings from revenue; see also IV.ix.33. Cf. Turgot (*Reflections*, LVIII): 'Anyone, who, whether in the form of revenue from his land, or of wages for his labour or his industry, receives each year more value than he needs to spend, can put this surplus into reserve and accumulate it: these accumulated values are what is called *a capital*.'

[20] Cf. Mandeville (*The Fable of the Bees*, pt. i. 105–6, ed. Kaye i.104–5): 'Frugality is like Honesty, a mean starving Virtue, that is only fit for small Societies of good peaceable Men, who are contented to be poor so they may be easy; but in a large stirring Nation you may have soon enough of it. 'Tis an idle dreaming Virtue that employs no Hands, and therefore very useless in a trading Country, where there are vast Numbers that one way or other must be all set to Work. Prodigality has a thousand Inventions to keep People from sitting still, that Frugality would never think of; and as this must consume a prodigious Wealth, so Avarice again knows innumerable Tricks to rake it together, which Frugality would scorn to make use of.'

spent, and nearly in the same time too; but it is consumed by a different set of people.[21] That portion of his revenue which a rich man annually spends, is in most cases consumed by idle guests, and menial servants, who leave nothing behind them in return for their consumption. That portion which he annually saves, as for the sake of the profit it is immediately employed as a capital, is consumed in the same manner, and nearly in the same time too, but by a different set of people, by labourers, manufacturers, and artificers, who re-produce with a profit the value of their annual consumption. His revenue, we shall suppose, is paid him in money. Had he spent the whole, the food, cloathing, and lodging which the whole could have purchased, would have been distributed among the former set of people. By saving a part of it, as that part is for the sake of the profit immediately employed as a capital either by himself or by some other person, the food, cloathing, and lodging, which may be purchased with it, are necessarily reserved for the latter. The consumption is the same, but the consumers are different.

19   By what a frugal man annually saves, he not only affords maintenance to an additional number of productive hands, for that or the ensuing [15] year, but, like the founder of a publick workhouse, he establishes as it were a perpetual fund for the maintenance of an equal number in all times to come. The perpetual allotment and destination of this fund, indeed, is not always guarded by any positive law, by any trust-right or deed of mortmain. It is always guarded, however, by a very powerful principle, the plain and evident interest of every individual to whom any share of it shall ever belong. No part of it can ever afterwards be employed to maintain any but productive hands, without an evident loss to the person who thus perverts it from its proper destination.[22]

[21] The necessary condition being 'tolerable security', II.i.30. See also, IV.iii.c.15 and IV.ii.8. Cf. Turgot (*Reflections*, CI): 'In fact almost all savings are made only in the form of money . . . but none of the entrepreneurs make any other use of it than to convert it immediately into the different kinds of effects upon which their enterprise depends.' In the Ashley edition of the *Reflections* (London, 1898) the word 'immediately' is italicized.

[22] TMS VI.i, which was added to the last edition of 1790, contains one of the most elaborate statements which Smith offered with regard to the psychology behind economic activity. Here Smith argued that if the pursuit of social status was the real objective of the drive to better our condition, then the means to this end are foresight and sacrifice—in short, prudence. He says also at VI.i.11 that such qualities attract general approval. Smith added that 'It is the consciousness of this merited approbation and esteem which is alone capable of supporting the agent in this tenour of conduct' (TMS IV.i.2.8). Cf. TMS VII.ii.3.16: 'The habits of œconomy, industry, discretion, attention, and application of thought, are generally supposed to be cultivated from self-interested motives, and at the same time are apprehended to be very praiseworthy qualities, which deserve the esteem and approbation of everybody.' See also TMS II.iii.3.3, where Smith emphasizes that we tend to approve of the actual achievement of fortune, not just the intention; of the end involved and not simply the means. Cf. Mandeville (*Fable of the Bees*. pt. 1.58, ed. Kaye i.68.) 'The Greediness we have after the Esteem of others, and the Raptures we enjoy in the Thoughts of being liked, and perhaps admired, are Equivalents that overpay the Conquest of the strongest Passions . . .'

20   The prodigal perverts it in this manner. By not confining his expence within his income, he encroaches upon his capital. Like him who perverts the revenues of some pious foundation to profane purposes, he pays the wages of idleness with those funds which the frugality of his forefathers had, as it were, consecrated to the maintenance of industry. By diminishing the funds destined for the employment of productive labour, he necessarily diminishes, so far as ᶜitᶜ depends upon him, the quantity of that labour which adds a value to the subject upon which it is bestowed, and, consequently, the value of the annual produce of the land and labour of the whole country, the real wealth and revenue of its inhabitants. If the prodigality of some was not compensated by the frugality of others, the conduct of every prodigal, by feeding the idle with the bread of the industrious, tends not only [16] to beggar himself, but to impoverish his country.

21   Though the expence of the prodigal should be altogether in home-made, and no part of it in foreign commodities, its effect upon the productive funds of the society would still be the same.[23] Every year there would still be a certain quantity of food and cloathing, which ought to have maintained productive, employed in maintaining unproductive hands. Every year, therefore, there would still be some diminution in what would otherwise have been the value of the annual produce of the land and labour of the country.

22   This expence, it may be said indeed, not being in foreign goods, and not occasioning any exportation of gold and silver, the same quantity of money would remain in the country as before. But if the quantity of food and cloathing, which were thus consumed by unproductive, had been distributed among productive hands, they would have reproduced, together with a profit, the full value of their consumption. The same quantity of money would in this case equally have remained in the country, and there would besides have been a reproduction of an equal value of consumable goods. There would have been two values instead of one.

23   The same quantity of money, besides, cannot long remain in any country, in which the value of the annual produce diminishes. The sole use of money is to circulate consumable goods.[24] By means of it, provisions, materials, and finished [17] work, are bought and sold, and distributed to their proper consumers. The quantity of money, therefore, which can be

ᶜ⁻ᶜ 2–6

---

[23] In LJ (B) 266–7, ed. Cannan 207–8, the view that 'no expence at home can be hurtful' is attributed to Mandeville and described as 'still another bad effect proceeding from that absurd notion that national opulence consists in money'. The same point is made in LJ (A) vi.169, where the authority of 'Dr John Mandeville' is cited. See below, IV.i. where Smith reviews the main doctrines of mercantilism.

[24] See for example, II.ii.23, IV.i.18, and IV.vi.27.

annually employed in any country must be determined by the value of the consumable goods annually circulated within it. These must consist either in the immediate produce of the land and labour of the country itself, or in something which had been purchased with some part of that produce. Their value, therefore, must diminish as the value of that produce diminishes, and along with it the quantity of money which can be employed in circulating them. But the money which by this annual diminution of produce is annually thrown out of domestick circulation will not be allowed to lie idle. The interest of whoever possesses it, requires that it should be employed. But having no employment at home, it will, in spite of all laws and prohibitions, be sent abroad, and employed in purchasing consumable goods which may be of some use at home.[25] Its annual exportation will in this manner continue for some time to add something to the annual consumption of the country beyond the value of its own annual produce. What in the days of its prosperity had been saved from that annual produce, and employed in purchasing gold and silver, will contribute for some little time to support its consumption in adversity. The exportation of gold and silver is, in this case, not the cause, but the effect of its declension, and may even, for some little time, alleviate the misery of that declension.

24   [18] The quantity of money, on the contrary, must in every country naturally increase as the value of the annual produce increases. The value of the consumable goods annually circulated within the society being greater, will require a greater quantity of money to circulate them. A part of the increased produce, therefore, will naturally be employed in purchasing, wherever it is to be had, the additional quantity of gold and silver necessary for circulating the rest. The increase of those metals will in this case be the effect, not the cause, of the publick prosperity. Gold and silver are purchased every where in the same manner.[26] The food, cloathing, and lodging, the revenue and maintenance of all those whose labour or stock is employed in bringing them from the mine to the market, is the price paid for them in Peru as well as in England. The country which has this price to pay, will never be long without the quantity of those metals which it has occasion for; and no country will ever long retain a quantity which it has no occasion for.

25   Whatever, therefore, we may imagine the real wealth and revenue of a country to consist in, whether in the value of the annual produce of its land and labour, as plain reason seems to dictate; or in the quantity of the precious metals which circulate within it, as vulgar prejudices suppose;[27] in either view of the matter, every prodigal appears to be a publick enemy, and every frugal man a publick benefactor.

26   [19] The effects of misconduct are often the same as those of prodigality.

[25] This point is made above, II.ii.30.   [26] See below, for example, IV.i.12.
[27] The 'vulgar prejudices' are discussed in IV.i and vii.

Every injudicious and unsuccessful project in agriculture, mines, fisheries, trade, or manufactures, tends in the same manner to diminish the funds destined for the maintenance of productive labour.[28] In every such project, though the capital is consumed by productive hands only, yet, as by the injudicious manner in which they are employed, they do not reproduce the full value of their consumption, there must always be some diminution in what would otherwise have been the productive funds of the society.

27   It can seldom happen, indeed, that the circumstances of a great nation can be much affected either by the prodigality or misconduct of individuals; the profusion or imprudence of some being always more than compensated by the frugality and good conduct of others.

28   With regard to profusion, the principle, which prompts to expence, is the passion for present enjoyment; which, though sometimes violent and very difficult to be restrained, is in general only momentary and occasional. But the principle which prompts to save, is the desire of bettering our condition,[29] a desire which, though generally calm and dispassionate, comes with us from the womb, and never leaves us till we go into the grave. In the whole interval which separates those two moments, there is scarce perhaps a single [d]instant[d] in which any man is so perfectly and completely satisfied with his situation, as to be without any wish of alteration or im-[20] provement, of any kind. An augmentation of fortune is the means by which the greater part of men propose and wish to better their condition.[30] It is

[d-d] instance 5-6

[28] See below, II.iv.15, where Smith justifies control of the rate of interest in terms of curtailing the activities of projectors; cf I.x.b.43. He was also prepared to curb prodigality through the use of taxation: see for example, V.ii.c.12 and cf. IV.vii.a.18.

[29] The general term 'bettering our condition' is often used in the course of the present chapter. See also I.viii.44, III.iii.12, IV.v.b.43, and IV.ix.28. In Mandeville's Third Dialogue, Cleo. remarks that 'The restless Industry of Man to supply his Wants, and his constant Endeavours to meliorate his Condition upon Earth, have produced and brought to Perfection many useful Arts and Sciences . . . ' (Fable of the Bees, pt. ii.132, ed. Kaye ii.128). A similar point occurs in the Fourth Dialogue where Horace inquires if the desire of 'meliorating our Condition' is so general that 'no Man is without it? Cleo. Not one that can be call'd a sociable Creature; and I believe this to be as much a Characteristick of our Species, as any can be named: For there is not a Man in the World, educated in Society, who, if he could compass it by wishing, would not have something added to, taken from, or alter'd in his Person, Possessions, Circumstances, or any part of the Society he belongs to. This is what is not to be perceiv'd in any Creature but Man'. (Ibid., pt. ii.200, ed. Kaye ii.181).

[30] In TMS I.iii.2.1 Smith inquires: 'what are the advantages which we propose by that great purpose of human life which we call bettering our condition? To be observed, to be attended to, to be taken notice of with sympathy, complacency, and approbation, are all the advantages which we can propose to derive from it.' Cf. TMS VI.i.3. Montesquieu also commented that 'It is pride that renders us polite; we are flattered with being taken notice of for behaviour that shows we are not of a mean condition'. (Esprit, IV.ii.12.) Mandeville made similar points several times. In 'An Enquiry into the Origin of Moral Virtue,' for example, he wrote: 'the great Recompence in view, for which the most exalted Minds have with so much Alacrity sacrificed their Quiet, Health, sensual Pleasures, and every Inch of themselves, has never been anything else but the Breath of Man, the Aerial Coin of

the means the most vulgar and the most obvious; and the most likely way of augmenting their fortune, is to save and accumulate some part of what they acquire, either regularly and annually, or upon some extraordinary occasions. Though the principle of expence, therefore, prevails in almost all men upon some occasions, and in some men upon almost all occasions, yet in the greater part of men, taking the whole course of their life at an average, the principle of frugality seems not only to predominate, but to predominate very greatly.

29   With regard to misconduct, the number of prudent and successful undertakings is every where much greater than that of injudicious and unsuccessful ones. After all our complaints of the frequency of bankruptcies, the unhappy men who fall into this misfortune make but a very small part of the whole number engaged in trade, and all other sorts of business; not much more perhaps than one in a thousand. Bankruptcy is perhaps the greatest and most humiliating calamity which can befal an innocent man. The greater part of men, therefore, are sufficiently careful to avoid it. Some, indeed, do not avoid it; as some do not avoid the gallows.

30   Great nations are never impoverished by private, though they sometimes are by publick prodigality and misconduct. The whole, or almost the whole publick revenue, is in most [21] countries employed in maintaining unproductive hands. Such are the people who compose a numerous and splendid court, a great ecclesiastical establishment, great fleets and armies, who in time of peace produce nothing, and in time of war acquire nothing which can compensate the expence of maintaining them, even while the war lasts. Such people, as they themselves produce nothing, are all maintained by the produce of other men's labour. When multiplied, therefore, to an unnecessary number, they may in a particular year consume so great a share of this produce, as not to leave a sufficiency for maintaining the productive labourers, who should reproduce it next year. The next year's produce, therefore, will be less than that of the foregoing, and if the same disorder should continue, that of the third year will be still less than that of the second. Those unproductive hands, who should be maintained by a part only of the spare revenue of the people, may consume so great a share of their whole revenue, and thereby oblige so great a number to encroach upon their capitals, upon the funds destined for the maintenance of productive labour, that all the frugality and good conduct of individuals may not be able to compensate the waste and degradation of produce occasioned by this violent and forced encroachment.

31   This frugality and good conduct, however, is upon most occasions, it

Praise.' (*Fable of the Bees*, pt. i.40, ed. Kaye i.54–5). In the Second Dialogue Cleo held: 'The true Object of Pride or Vain-glory is the Opinion of others; and the most superlative Wish, which a Man possess'd, and entirely fill'd with it can make, is, that he may be well thought of, applauded, and admired by the whole World...' (*Ibid.*, pt. ii.47, ed. Kaye ii.64.)

appears from experience, sufficient to compensate, not only the private prodigality and misconduct of indivi-[22]duals, but the publick extravagance of government. The uniform, constant, and uninterrupted effort of every man to better his condition, the principle from which publick and national, as well as private opulence is originally derived, is frequently powerful enough to maintain the natural progress of things toward improvement, in spite both of the extravagance of government, and of the greatest errors of administration.[31] Like the unknown principle of animal life, it frequently restores health and vigour to the constitution, in spite, not only of the disease, but of the absurd prescriptions of the doctor.

32   The annual produce of the land and labour of any nation can be increased in its value by no other means, but by increasing either the number of its productive labourers, or the productive powers of those labourers who had before been employed.[32] The number of its productive labourers, it is evident, can never be much increased, but in consequence of an increase of capital, or of the funds destined for maintaining them. The productive powers of the same number of labourers cannot be increased, but in consequence either of some addition and improvement to those machines and instruments which facilitate and abridge labour; or of a more proper division and distribution of employment.[33] In either case an additional capital is almost always required. It is by means of an additional capital only that the undertaker of any work can either provide his workmen with better machinery, or [23] make a more proper distribution of employment among them. When the work to be done consists of a number of parts, to keep every man constantly employed in one way, requires a much greater capital than where every man is occasionally employed in every different part of the work. When we compare, therefore, the state of a nation at two different periods, and find, that the annual produce of its land and labour is evidently greater at the latter than at the former, that its lands are better cultivated, its manufactures more numerous and more flourishing, and its trade more extensive, we may be assured that its capital must have increased during the interval between those two periods, and that more must have been added to it by the good conduct of some, than had been taken from it either by the private misconduct of others, or by the publick extravagance of government. But we shall find this to have been the case of almost all nations, in all tolerably quiet and peaceable times, even of those who have not enjoyed the most prudent and parsimonious governments. To form a right judgment of it, indeed, we must compare the state of the country at periods somewhat distant from one another. The progress is frequently so gradual, that, at near periods, the improvement is not only not sensible,

---

[31] Cf. V.iii.58. The extravagance of government is a recurring theme: see, for example, V.ii.a.4, V.iii.8 and 49.
[32] See IV.ix.34.   [33] See below, IV.ix.36.

but from the declension either of certain branches of industry, or of certain districts of the country, things which sometimes happen though the country in general ᵉbeᵉ in great prosperity, there frequently arises a [24] suspicion, that the riches and industry of the whole are decaying.

33   The annual produce of the land and labour of England, for example, is certainly much greater than it was, a little more than a century ago, at the restoration of Charles II. Though at present, few people, I believe, doubt of this, yet during this period, five years have seldom passed away in which some book or pamphlet has not been published, written too with such abilities as to gain some authority with the publick, and pretending to demonstrate that the wealth of the nation was fast declining, that the country was depopulated, agriculture neglected, manufactures decaying, and trade undone. Nor have these publications been all party pamphlets, the wretched offspring of falshood and venality. Many of them have been written by very candid and very intelligent people; who wrote nothing but what they believed, and for no other reason but because they believed it.

34   The annual produce of the land and labour of England again, was certainly much greater at the restoration, than we can suppose it to have been about an hundred years before, at the accession of Elizabeth. At this period too, we have all reason to believe, the country was much more advanced in improvement, than it had been about a century before, towards the close of the dissensions between the houses of York and Lancaster. Even then it was, probably, in a better condition than it had been at the Norman conquest, and at the Norman conquest, than during the confusion [25] of the Saxon Heptarchy. Even at this early period, it was certainly a more improved country than at the invasion of Julius Caesar, when its inhabitants were nearly in the same state with the savages in North America.³⁴

35   In each of those periods, however, there was, not only much private and publick profusion, many expensive and unnecessary wars, great perversion of the annual produce from maintaining productive to maintain unproductive hands; but sometimes, in the confusion of civil discord, such absolute waste and destruction of stock, as might be supposed, not only to retard, as it certainly did, the natural accumulation of riches, but to have left the country, at the end of the period, poorer than at the beginning. Thus, in the happiest and most fortunate period of them all, that which has passed since the restoration, how many disorders and misfortunes have occurred, which, could they have been foreseen, not only the impoverishment, but the total ruin of the country would have been expected from them? The fire and the plague of London, the two Dutch wars, the disorders of the revolution, the war in Ireland, the four expensive French

ᵉ⁻ᵉ is *1*

³⁴ The savage nations of North America are described as the 'lowest and rudest state of society' at V.i.a.2.

wars of 1688, *1702*, 1742, and 1756, together with the two rebellions of
1715 and 1745. In the course of the four French wars, the nation has
contracted more than a hundred and forty-five millions of debt, over and
above all the other extraordinary annual expence which they occasioned,
so that the whole cannot be computed at less than two hundred millions.[35]
So great a share of the annual [26] produce of the land and labour of the
country, has, since the revolution, been employed upon different occasions,
in maintaining an extraordinary number of unproductive hands. But had
not those wars given this particular direction to so large a capital, the greater
part of it would naturally have been employed in maintaining productive
hands, whose labour would have replaced, with a profit, the whole value of
their consumption. The value of the annual produce of the land and labour
of the country, would have been considerably increased by it every year,
and every year's increase would have augmented still more that of the
following year. More houses would have been built, more lands would
have been improved, and those which had been improved before would
have been better cultivated, more manufactures would have been established, and those which had been established before would have been
more extended; and to what height the real wealth and revenue of the
country might, by this time, have been raised, it is not perhaps very easy
even to imagine.[36]

36   But though the profusion of government must, undoubtedly, have
retarded the natural progress of England towards wealth and improvement,
it has not been able to stop it. The annual produce of its land and labour is,
undoubtedly, much greater at present than it was either at the restoration
or at the revolution. The capital, therefore, annually employed in cultivating this land, and in maintaining this labour, must likewise be much
greater. In the midst of all the [27] exactions of government, this capital
has been silently and gradually accumulated by the private frugality and
good conduct of individuals, by their universal, continual, and uninterrupted effort to better their own condition. It is this effort, protected by law
and allowed by liberty to exert itself in the manner that is most advantageous, which has maintained the progress of England towards opulence
and improvement in almost all former times, and which, it is to be hoped,
will do so in all future times.[37] England, however, as it has never been

f-f 1701 *1*   *g-g* next *1*

---

[35] It is stated at IV.i.26 that the last war with France cost over £90 millions and added
some £75 millions to the debt. See also IV.vii.c.64, IV.viii.53, and V.iii.92. The progress of
the British national debt is reviewed in V.iii. The highest total of the national debt before
1776 was £134·2 million in 1764.

[36] See below, V.iii.

[37] Smith discusses the link between industry and security, for example, at II.i.30 and
V.iii.7, and uses the point to explain the rapid progress of England at III.iii.12, IV. v.b.43,
and IV.vii.c.54.

blessed with a very parsimonious government, so parsimony has at no time been the characteristical virtue of its inhabitants. It is the highest impertinence and presumption, therefore, in kings and ministers, to pretend to watch over the œconomy of private people, and to restrain their expence either by sumptuary laws, or by prohibiting the importation of foreign luxuries.[38] They are themselves always, and without any exception, the greatest spendthrifts in the society. Let them look well after their own expence, and they may safely trust private people with theirs. If their own extravagance does not ruin the state, that of their subjects never will.

37   As frugality increases, and prodigality diminishes the publick capital, so the conduct of those, whose expence just equals their revenue, without either accumulating or encroaching, neither increases nor diminishes it. Some modes of expence, however, seem to contribute more to the growth of publick opulence than others.

38   [28] The revenue of an individual may be spent, either in things which are consumed immediately, and in which one day's expence can neither alleviate nor support that of another; or it may be spent in things more durable, which can therefore be accumulated, and in which every day's expence may, as he chuses, either alleviate or support and heighten the effect of that of the following day.[39] A man of fortune, for example, may either spend his revenue in a profuse and sumptuous table, and in maintaining a great number of menial servants, and a multitude of dogs and horses; or contenting himself with a frugal table and few attendants, he may lay out the greater part of it in adorning his house or his country villa, in useful or ornamental buildings, in useful or ornamental furniture, in collecting books, statues, pictures; or in things more frivolous, jewels, baubles, ingenious trinkets of different kinds; or, what is most trifling of all, in amassing a great wardrobe of fine cloaths, like the favourite and minister of a great prince who died a few years ago.[40] Were two men of equal fortune to spend their revenue, the one chiefly in the one way, the other in the other, the magnificence of the person whose expence had been chiefly in durable commodities, would be continually increasing, every day's expence contributing something to support and heighten the effect of that of the

---

[38] See below, IV.ix.51.

[39] In TMS V.i.1.4, 'Of the Influence of Custom and Fashion upon our notions of Beauty and Deformity', Smith made the point that the durability of goods, e.g. buildings as contrasted with articles of apparel, is often related to the nature and extent of their influence on fashion. Thus he suggests that styles of dress change more rapidly than styles of furniture, and the latter more rapidly than architectural styles. See above, I.xi.c.31.

[40] '. . . to what idol does that man offer incense, whom no less than three or four hundred suits of rich cloathes will satisfy? Count Bruhl has collected all the finest colours of all the finest cloths, velvets and silks of all the manufacturers, not to mention the different kinds of lace and embroideries, of EUROPE. He calls for his book of patterns, which are numbered, and chuses that suit which pleases his fancy for the day. They boast that he has boots and shoes in proportion to his cloathes.' (J. Hanway, *An Historical Account of the British Trade over the Caspian Sea* (London, 1753), ii.230.)

following day: that of the other, on the contrary, would be no greater at the end of the period than at the beginning. The former too would, at the end of the period, [29] be the richer man of the two. He would have a stock of goods of some kind or other, which, though it might not be worth all that it cost, would always be worth something. No trace or vestige of the expence of the latter would remain, and the effects of ten or twenty years profusion would be as completely annihilated as if they had never existed.

39   As the one mode of expence is more favourable than the other to the opulence of an individual, so is it likewise to that of a nation. The houses, the furniture, the cloathing of the rich, in a little time, become useful to the inferior and middling ranks of people.[41] They are able to purchase them when their superiors grow weary of them, and the general accommodation of the whole people is thus gradually improved, when this mode of expence becomes universal among men of fortune. In countries which have long been rich, you will frequently find the inferior ranks of people in possession both of houses and furniture perfectly good and entire, but of which neither the one could have been built, nor the other have been made for their use. What was formerly a seat of the family of Seymour, is now an inn upon the Bath road. The marriage-bed of James the First of Great Britain, which his Queen brought with her from Denmark, as a present fit for a sovereign to make to a sovereign, was, a few years ago, the ornament of an alehouse at Dunfermline. In some ancient cities, which either have been long stationary, or have gone somewhat to decay, you will sometimes [30] scarce find a single house which could have been built for its present inhabitants. If you go into those houses too, you will frequently find many excellent, though antiquated pieces of furniture, which are still very fit for use, and which could as little have been made for them. Noble palaces, magnificent villas, great collections of books, statues, pictures, and other curiosities, are frequently both an ornament and an honour, not only to the neighbourhood, but to the whole country to which they belong. Versailles is an ornament and a honour to France, Stowe and Wilton to England. Italy continues to command some sort of veneration by the number of monuments of this kind which it possesses, though the wealth which produced them has decayed, and ʰthoughʰ the genius which planned them seems to be extinguished, perhaps from not having the same employment.

40   The expence too, which is laid out in durable commodities, is favourable, not only to accumulation, but to frugality. If a person should at any time exceed in it, he can easily reform without exposing himself to the censure

ʰ⁻ʰ 2–6

---

[41] See above, I.xi.c.7.

of the publick.[42] To reduce very much the number of his servants, to reform his table from great profusion to great frugality, to lay down his equipage after he has once set it up, are changes which cannot escape the observation of his neighbours, and which are supposed to imply some acknowledgment of preceding bad conduct.[43] Few, therefore, of those who have once been so unfortunate as to launch out too far into this sort of expence, [31] have afterwards the courage to reform, till ruin and bankruptcy oblige them. But if a person has, at any time, been at too great an expence in building, in furniture, in books or pictures, no imprudence can be inferred from his changing his conduct. These are things in which further expence is frequently rendered unnecessary by former expence; and when a person stops short, he appears to do so, not because he has exceeded his fortune, but because he has satisfied his fancy.

41   The expence, besides, that is laid out in durable commodities, gives maintenance, commonly, to a greater number of people, than that which is employed in the most profuse hospitality. Of two or three hundred weight of provisions, which may sometimes be served up at a great festival, one-half, perhaps, is thrown to the dunghill, and there is always a great deal wasted and abused. But if the expence of this entertainment had been employed in setting to work, masons, carpenters, upholsterers, mechanicks, ⁱ&c.ⁱ a quantity of provisions, of equal value, would have been distributed

ⁱ⁻ⁱ 2–6

---

[42] Cf. TMS VI.i.3 'we cannot live long in the world without perceiving that the respect of our equals, our credit and rank in the society we live in, depend very much upon the degree in which we possess, or are supposed to possess, those advantages [of external fortune].' Cf. TMS I.iii.2.1.

[43] In TMS VI.iii.37 Smith ascribes this behaviour to the vain man who seeks to claim 'both a higher rank and a greater fortune than really belong to him' and who thereby reduces himself to 'poverty and distress'. In TMS III.i.3.18 it is argued that the person who has been guilty of such misconduct will often be supported by his friends so as to avoid the public degradation of poverty or reduced circumstances. Smith gave a good deal of attention to problems of this kind and commented at TMS VI.i.6 that we suffer more 'when we fall from a better to a worse situation, than we ever enjoy when we rise from a worse to a better.' Cf. LJ(A) i.24–5: 'One of the chief studies of a man's life is to obtain a good name, to rise above those about and render himself some way their superiors. When therefore one is thrown back not only to one level, but even degraded below the common sort of men, he receives one of the most affecting and atrocious injuries that possibly can be inflicted on him.'
    A related point is made in LJ (A) ii.22 in discussing pawnbroking: 'persons who enter into such agreements . . . are not inclined that their transactions should be known, . . . as it is an evident sign of their poverty and low circumstances.' It is pointed out at V.ii.k.3 that a 'creditable' labourer would be ashamed to appear in public without articles such as a linen shirt, the lack of which would be presumed to denote a degree of poverty caused by 'extreme bad conduct'. Smith also suggests at V.i.g.12 that the wealthy man 'is by his station the distinguished member of a great society, who attend to every part of his conduct'. This concern with the opinion of others also features in the discussion of net advantages, for example at I.x.b.25. The same idea was also applied to the political sphere, in the case of the American colonists, at IV.vii.c.74.

among a still greater number of people, who would have bought them in penny-worths and pound weights, and not have lost or thrown away a single ounce of them. In the one way, besides, this expence maintains productive, in the other unproductive hands. In the one way, therefore, it increases, in the other, it does not increase, the exchangeable value of the annual produce of the land and labour of the country.

42   [32] I would not, however, by all this be understood to mean, that the one species of expence always betokens a more liberal or generous spirit than the other. When a man of fortune spends his revenue chiefly in hospitality, he shares the greater part of it with his friends and companions; but when he employs it in purchasing such durable commodities, he often spends the whole upon his own person, and gives nothing to any body without an equivalent.[44] The latter species of expence, therefore, especially when directed towards frivolous objects, the little ornaments of dress and furniture, jewels, trinkets, gewgaws, frequently indicates, not only a trifling, but a base and selfish disposition. All that I mean is, that the one sort of expence, as it always occasions some accumulation of valuable commodities, as it is more favourable to private frugality, and, consequently, to the increase of the publick capital, and as it maintains productive, rather than unproductive hands, conduces more than the other to the growth of publick opulence.

[44] See below, III.iv.5, where Smith discusses the nature of feudal hospitality, linking it to the form of economy prevailing and with the self-interest of the great proprietors.

CHAPTER IV

Of Stock lent at Interest

1   THE stock which is lent at interest is always considered as a capital by the lender. He expects that in due time it is to be restored to him, and that in the mean time the borrower is to pay him a certain annual rent for the use of it. The borrower may use it either as a capital, or as a stock reserved for immediate consumption. If he uses it as a capital, he employs it in the maintenance of productive labourers, who reproduce the value with a profit. He can, in this case, both restore the capital and pay the interest without alienating or encroaching upon any other source of revenue. If he uses it as a stock reserved for immediate consumption, he acts the part of a prodigal, and dissipates in the maintenance of the idle, what was destined for the support of the industrious. He can, in this case, neither restore the capital nor pay the interest, without either alienating or encroaching upon some other source of revenue, such as the property or the rent of land.

2   The stock which is lent at interest is, no doubt, occasionally employed in both these ways, but in the former much more frequently than in the latter. The man who borrows in order to spend will soon be ruined, and he who lends to him will generally have occasion to repent of his [34] folly. To borrow or to lend for such a purpose, therefore, is in all cases, where gross usury is out of the question, contrary to the interest of both parties; and though it no doubt happens sometimes that people do both the one and the other; yet, from the regard that all men have for their own interest, we may be assured, that it cannot happen so very frequently as we are sometimes apt to imagine. Ask any rich man of common prudence, to which of the two sorts of people he has lent the greater part of his stock, to those who, he thinks, will employ it profitably, or to those who will spend it idly, and he will laugh at you for proposing the question. Even among borrowers, therefore, not the people in the world most famous for frugality, the number of the frugal and industrious surpasses considerably that of the prodigal and idle.

3   The only people to whom stock is commonly lent, without their being expected to make any very profitable use of it, are country gentlemen who borrow upon mortgage. Even they scarce ever borrow merely to spend. What they borrow, one may say, is commonly spent before they borrow it. They have generally consumed so great a quantity of goods, advanced to them upon credit by shopkeepers and tradesmen, that they find it necessary to borrow at interest in order to pay the debt. The capital borrowed replaces the capitals of those shopkeepers and tradesmen, which the country gentlemen could not have replaced from the rents of their estates.

It is not properly borrowed in order to be spent, but in [35] order to replace a capital which had been spent before.

4   Almost all loans at interest are made in money, either of paper, or of gold and silver. But what the borrower really wants, and what the lender really supplies him with, is, not the money, but the money's worth, or the goods which it can purchase.[1] If he wants it as a stock for immediate consumption, it is those goods only which he can place in that stock. If he wants it as a capital for employing industry, it is from those goods only that the industrious can be furnished with the tools, materials, and maintenance, necessary for carrying on their work. By means of the loan, the lender, as it were, assigns to the borrower his right to a certain portion of the annual produce of the land and labour of the country, to be employed as the borrower pleases.

5   The quantity of stock, therefore, or, as it is commonly expressed, of money which can be lent at interest in any country, is not regulated by the value of the money, whether paper or coin, which serves as the instrument of the different loans made in that country, but by the value of that part of the annual produce which, as soon as it comes either from the ground, or from the hands of the productive labourers, is destined not only for replacing a capital, but such a capital as the owner does not care to be at the trouble of employing himself. As such capitals are commonly lent out and paid back in money, they constitute what is called the monied interest. It is distinct, not only from the landed, but from the trading and [36] manufacturing interests, as in these last the owners themselves employ their own capitals.[2] Even in the monied interest, however, the money is, as it were, but the deed of assignment, which conveys from one hand to another those capitals which the owners do not care to employ themselves.[3] Those capitals may be greater in almost any proportion, than the amount of the money which serves as the instrument of their conveyance; the same pieces of money successively serving for many different loans, as well as for many different purchases. A, for example, lends to W a thousand pounds, with which W immediately purchases of B a thousand pounds worth of goods. B having no occasion for the money himself, lends the identical pieces to X, with which X immediately purchases of C another thousand pounds worth of goods. C in the same manner, and for

---

[1] The point that loans are in effect loans of goods rather than of money appears in LJ (B) 283, ed. Cannan 220.

[2] In his *Defence of Usury*, Bentham pointed out that a division of interest between borrower and lender reduced the possibility of purely speculative investment: 'there are, in this case, two wits, set to sift into the merits of the project . . . and of these two there is one, whose prejudices are certainly not most likely to be on the favourable side.' (*Economic Writings*, ed. W. Stark (London, 1952), i.181.)

[3] See above, I.vi.18 and below, V.iii.35, where it is pointed out that the great merchants are 'generally the people who advance money to government'. Hume also stresses the importance of the monied class in his essay 'Of Interest'.

the same reason, lends them to Y, who again purchases goods with them of D. In this manner the same pieces, either of coin or of paper, may, in the course of a few days, serve as the instrument of three different loans, and of three different purchases, each of which is, in value, equal to the whole amount of those pieces. What the three monied men A, B, and C, assign to the three borrowers, W, X, Y, is the power of making those purchases. In this power consist both the value and the use of the loans. The stock lent by the three monied men, is equal to the value of the goods which can be purchased with it, and is three times greater than that of the money with which the purchases are made. Those loans, however, may be all per-[37]fectly well secured, the goods purchased by the different debtors being so employed, as, in due time, to bring back, with a profit, an equal value either of coin or of paper. And as the same pieces of money can thus serve as the instrument of different loans to three, or, for the same reason, to thirty times their value, so they may likewise successively serve as the instrument of repayment.

6   A capital lent at interest may, in this manner, be considered as an assignment from the lender to the borrower of a certain considerable portion of the annual produce; upon condition that the borrower in return shall, during the continuance of the loan, annually assign to the lender a smaller portion, called the interest; and at the end of it a portion equally considerable with that which had originally been assigned to him, called the repayment. Though money, either coin or paper, serves generally as the deed of assignment both to the smaller, and to the more considerable portion, it is itself altogether different from what is assigned by it.

7   In proportion as that share of the annual produce which, as soon as it comes either from the ground, or from the hands of the productive labourers, is destined for replacing a capital, increases in any country, what is called the monied interest naturally increases with it. The increase of those particular capitals from which the owners wish to derive a revenue, without being at the trouble of employing them themselves, naturally accompanies the general increase of capitals; or, in other words, as stock increases, the quantity of [38] stock to be lent at interest grows gradually greater and greater.

8   As the quantity of stock to be lent at interest increases, the interest, or the price which must be paid for the use of that stock, necessarily diminishes, not only from those general causes which make the market price of things commonly diminish as their quantity increases, but from other causes which are peculiar to this particular case.[4] As capitals increase in any country, the profits which can be made by employing them necessarily diminish.[5] It becomes gradually more and more difficult to find within

---

[4] The relationship between profit and the rate of interest is considered above, I.ix.
[5] In his essay 'Of Interest' Hume remarked that 'when commerce has become extensive,

the country a profitable method of employing any new capital.[6] There
arises in consequence a competition between different capitals, the owner
of one endeavouring to get possession of that employment which is occupied by another. But upon most occasions he can hope to justle that
other out of this employment, by no other means but by dealing upon more
reasonable terms. He must not only sell what he deals in somewhat cheaper,
but in order to get it to sell, he must sometimes too buy it dearer. The
demand for productive labour, by the increase of the funds which are
destined for maintaining it, grows every day greater and greater. Labourers
easily find employment, but the owners of capitals find it difficult to get
labourers to employ. Their competition raises the wages of labour, and
sinks the profits of stock.[7] But when the profits which can be made by the
use of a capital are in this manner diminished, as it were, at both ends, the
price [39] which can be paid for the use of it,[8] that is, the rate of interest,
must necessarily be diminished with them.

9   Mr. Locke, Mr. Law, and Mr. Montesquieu,[9] as well as many other

and employs large stocks, there must arise rivalships among the merchants, which
diminish the profits of trade'. He added: 'An extensive commerce, by producing large
stocks, diminishes both interest and profits' and that 'if we consider the whole connexion
of causes and effects, interest is the barometer of the state, and its lowness is a sign almost
infallible of the flourishing condition of a people.' (*Essays Moral, Political, and Literary*,
ed. Green and Grose, i.327.) Cf. above I.ix.4. Cf. Hutcheson, *System*, ii.72: 'When many
hands and much wealth are employed in trade, as men can be supported by smaller gains
in proportion upon their large stocks, the profit made upon any given sum employed is
smaller, and the interest the trader can afford must be less.' Similar arguments appear in
the *Short Introduction*, 219.

   [6] See above, I.ix.2 and I.x.c.26.
   [7] The inverse relationship between profit and wages is considered in I.ix.
   [8] The phrase 'at both ends' is used in a similar context at I.ix.13.
   [9] John Locke, *Some Considerations of the Consequences of the Lowering of Interest, and
raising the Value of Money* (1691), *Works*, v.47:

   There being ten times as much silver now in the world (the discovery of the West
   Indies having made the plenty) as there was then [during the reign of Henry VII], it is
   nine-tenths less worth now than it was at that time; that is, it will exchange for nine-
   tenths less of any commodity now, which bears the same proportion to its vent, as it did
   200 years since.

J. Law, *Money and Trade*, 71–2:

   Silver having encreas'd more in Quantity than in Demand, and the Denomination
   being alter'd, Money is of less Value, and is to be had on easier terms. If the Demand
   had encreas'd in the same proportion with the Quantity, and the Money had not been
   rais'd, the same Interest would be given now as then, and the same Quantity of Victual
   to pay the Interest; for Money keeping its Value, *8sh* and 4 pence would be equal to a
   Chalder of Victual as it was then.

Montesquieu, *Esprit*, XXII.vi:

   A great quantity of specie being all of a sudden brought into Europe, much fewer
   persons had need of money. The price of all things increased, while the value of money
   diminished; the proportion was then broken, and all the old debts were discharged . . .
   In short, the course of exchange having rendered the conveying of specie from one
   country to another remarkably easy; money cannot be scarce in a place where they may
   be so readily supplied with it by those who have it in plenty.

writers, seem to have imagined that the increase of the quantity of gold and silver, in consequence of the discovery of the Spanish West Indies, was the real cause of the lowering of the rate of interest through the greater part of Europe.[10] Those metals, they say, having become of less value themselves, the use of any particular portion of them necessarily became of less value too, and consequently the price which could be paid for it. This notion, which at first sight seems so plausible, has been so fully exposed by Mr. Hume, that it is, perhaps, unnecessary to say any thing more about it.[11] The following very short and plain argument, however, may serve to explain more distinctly the fallacy which seems to have misled those gentlemen.

10   Before the discovery of the Spanish West Indies, ten per cent. seems to have been the common rate of interest through the greater part of Europe. It has since that time in different countries sunk to six, five, four, and three per cent.[12] Let us suppose that in every particular country the value of silver has sunk precisely in the same proportion as the rate of interest; and that in those countries, for example, where interest has been reduced from ten to five per cent., the same quantity of silver can now purchase just half the quantity of goods which it could have purchased [40] before. This supposition will not, I believe, be found any where agreeable to the truth, but it is the most favourable to the opinion which we are going to examine; and even upon this supposition it is utterly impossible that the lowering of the value of silver could have the smallest tendency to lower the rate of interest. If a hundred pounds are in those countries now of no more value than fifty pounds were then, ten pounds must now be of no

---

[10] Cf. LJ (B) 281–2, ed. Cannan 219–20: 'It is commonly supposed that the premium of interest depends upon the value of gold and silver . . . If we attend to it, however, we shall find that the premium of interest is regulated by the quantity of stock.'

Cantillon thought similarly (*Essai*, 282–3 and 285, ed. Higgs 213 and 215):

> It is a common idea, received of all those who have written on Trade, that the increased quantity of currency in a State brings down the price of Interest there, because when Money is plentiful it is more easy to find some to borrow. This idea is not always true or accurate.

> Plenty or Scarcity of Money in a State always raises or lowers the price of everything in bargaining without any necessary connection with the rate of interest.

[11] David Hume 'Of Interest', *Essays Moral, Political, and Literary*, ed. Green and Grose, i.321: 'Prices have risen near four times since the discovery of the INDIES; and it is probable gold and silver have multiplied much more: But interest has not fallen much above half. The rate of interest, therefore, is not derived from the quantity of the precious metals.' And, more positively, 'High interest arises from *three* circumstances: A great demand for borrowing; little riches to supply that demand; and great profits arising from commerce: And these circumstances are a clear proof of the small advance of commerce and industry, not of the scarcity of gold and silver.' (Ibid., 322.)

[12] 37 Henry VIII, c.9 (1545) legalized interest in England at a maximum of 10 per cent, reduced to 8 per cent by 21 James I, c.17 (1623), to 6 per cent by 12 Charles II, c.13 (1660), and to 5 per cent by 13 Anne, c.15 (1713). See above, I.ix.5 and below V.iii.27.

more value than five pounds were then. Whatever were the causes which lowered the value of the capital, the same must necessarily have lowered that of the interest, and exactly in the same proportion. The proportion between the value of the capital and that of the interest, must have remained the same, though the rate had never been altered. By altering the rate, on the contrary, the proportion between those two values is necessarily altered. If a hundred pounds now are worth no more than fifty were then, five pounds now can be worth no more than two pounds ten shillings were then. By reducing the rate of interest, therefore, from ten to five per cent., we give for the use of a capital, which is supposed to be equal to one-half of its former value, an interest which is equal to one-fourth only of the value of the former interest.

11   Any increase in the quantity of silver, while that of the commodities circulated by means of it remained the same, could have no other effect than to diminish the value of that metal. The nominal value of all sorts of goods would be greater, but their real value would be precisely [41] the same as before. They would be exchanged for a greater number of pieces of silver; but the quantity of labour which they could command, the number of people whom they could maintain and employ, would be precisely the same. The capital of the country would be the same, though a greater number of pieces might be requisite for conveying any equal portion of it from one hand to another. The deeds of assignment, like the conveyances of a verbose attorney,[13] would be more cumbersome, but the thing assigned would be precisely the same as before, and could produce only the same effects. The funds for maintaining productive labour being the same, the demand for it would be the same. Its price or wages, therefore, though nominally greater, would really be the same. They would be paid in a greater number of pieces of silver; but they would purchase only the same quantity of goods. The profits of stock would be the same both nominally and really. The wages of labour are commonly computed by the quantity of silver which is paid to the labourer. When that is increased, therefore, his wages appear to be increased, though they may sometimes be no greater than before. But the profits of stock are not computed by the number of pieces of silver with which they are paid, but by the proportion which those pieces bear to the whole capital employed. Thus in a particular country five shillings a week are said to be the common wages of labour, and ten per cent. the common profits of stock. But the whole capital of the country being the same [42] as before, the competition between the different capitals of individuals into which it was divided would likewise be the same. They would all trade with the same advantages and disadvantages. The common proportion between capital and profit, therefore, would be

---

13 The verbosity of the attorney is explained in V.i.b.22 as being due to the practice of setting fees in relation to the number of words used in legal documents.

the same, and consequently the common interest of money; what can commonly be given for the use of money being necessarily regulated by what can commonly be made by the use of it.

12   Any increase in the quantity of commodities annually circulated within the country, while that of the money which circulated them remained the same, would, on the contrary, produce many other important effects, besides that of raising the value of the money. The capital of the country, though it might nominally be the same, would really be augmented. It might continue to be expressed by the same quantity of money, but it would command a greater quantity of labour. The quantity of productive labour which it could maintain and employ would be increased, and consequently the demand for that labour. Its wages would naturally rise with the demand, and yet might appear to sink. They might be paid with a smaller quantity of money, but that smaller quantity might purchase a greater quantity of goods than a greater had done before. The profits of stock would be diminished both really and in appearance. The whole capital of the country being augmented, the competition between the different capitals of which it was composed, would naturally be augmented along with [43] it. The owners of those particular capitals would be obliged to content themselves with a smaller proportion of the produce of that labour which their respective capitals employed. The interest of money, keeping pace always with the profits of stock, might, in this manner, be greatly diminished, though the value of money, or the quantity of goods which any particular sum could purchase, was greatly augmented.

13   In some countries the interest of money has been prohibited by law. But as something can every where be made by the use of money, something ought every where to be paid for the use of it.[14] This regulation, instead of preventing, has been found from experience to increase the evil of usury; the debtor being obliged to pay, not only for the use of the money, but for the risk which his creditor runs by accepting a compensation for that use. He is obliged, if one may say so, to insure his creditor from the penalties of usury.

14   In countries where interest is permitted, the law, in order to prevent the extortion of usury, generally fixes the highest rate which can be taken without incurring a penalty. This rate ought always to be somewhat above the lowest market price, or the price which is commonly paid for the use of money by those who can give the most undoubted security. If this legal rate should be fixed below the lowest market rate, the effects of this fixation must be nearly the same as those of a total prohibition of interest.[15] The creditor will not lend his money for less than the use [44] of it is worth, and

[14] See above, I.ix.4.
[15] The relationship between the market and legal rate of interest is illustrated at I.ix.5.

the debtor must pay him for the risk which he runs by accepting the full value of that use. If it is fixed precisely at the lowest market price, it ruins with honest people, who respect the laws of their country, the credit of all those who cannot give the very best security, and obliges them to have recourse to exorbitant usurers. In a country, such as Great Britain, where money is lent to government at three per cent. and to private people upon good security at four, and four and a half, the present legal rate, five per cent., is, perhaps, as proper as any.

15   The legal rate, it is to be observed, though it ought to be somewhat above, ought not to be much above the lowest market rate.[16] If the legal rate of interest in Great Britain, for example, was fixed so high as eight or ten per cent., the greater part of the money which was to be lent, would be lent to prodigals and projectors, who alone would be willing to give this high interest. Sober people,[17] who will give for the use of money no more than a part of what they are likely to make by the use of it, would not venture into the competition. A great part of the capital of the country would thus be kept out of the hands which were most likely to make a profitable and advantageous use of it, and thrown into those which were most likely to waste and destroy it. Where the legal rate of interest, on the contrary, is fixed but a very little above the lowest market rate, sober people are universally preferred, as borrowers, to prodigals and projectors.[18] The person who lends money gets nearly as much [45] interest from the former as he dares to take from the latter, and his money is much safer in the hands of the one set of people, than in those of the other. A great part of the capital of the country is thus thrown into the hands in which it is most likely to be employed with advantage.[19]

16   No law can reduce the common rate of interest below the lowest ordinary

---

[16] See also Locke, *Some Considerations of the Consequences of lowering the Interest and raising the Value of Money* (1691), where the distinction is between the natural and the legal rates of interest. *Works*, v.9–10. Steuart makes a similar point in discussing the 'conventional' and legal rates, *Principles*, ii.128, ed. Skinner ii.460.

[17] By 'sober people', Smith means the 'prudent man' of the TMS, prudence being that virtue which is concerned with the fortune and rank of the individual. 'Security . . . is the first and principal object of prudence.' 'It is rather cautious than enterprising.' (TMS VI.i.6.) It is interesting to recall that Bentham objected to Smith's suggestion for regulation of the rate of interest, partly on the ground that such regulation was a violation of Smith's own principle of liberty, and partly on the ground that it would discourage those men of enterprize on whom the economic process depends. See especially, Letter XIII of the *Defence of Usury*, which is addressed to Smith and entitled 'On the Discouragement imposed by the above restraints to the progress of inventive industry.' Smith would appear to have had something of a bias against the projector largely because his failures constituted a loss of capital. See for example II.iii.26, but cf. I.x.b.43, where any new manufacture is described as being a speculation, and V.i.e.10, where it is stated that the activities of speculative traders would help to keep down the rate of profit.

[18] However, it is pointed out below, IV.i.16, that even sober men may face problems as a result of over-trading.

[19] Bentham's critique of Smith is founded on the argument of this passage. It is reported that Smith described the *Defence of Usury* as 'the work of a very superior man, and that tho'

market rate at the time when that law is made.[20] Notwithstanding the edict of 1766, by which the French king attempted to reduce the rate of interest from five to four per cent., money continued to be lent in France at five per cent., the law being evaded in several different ways.[21]

17   The ordinary market price of land, it is to be observed, depends every where upon the ordinary market rate of interest.[22] The person who has a capital from which he wishes to derive a revenue, without taking the trouble to employ it himself, deliberates whether he should buy land with it, or lend it out at interest. The superior security of land, together with some other advantages which almost every where attend upon this species of property, will generally dispose him to content himself with a smaller revenue from land, than what he might have by lending out his money at interest.[23] These advantages are sufficient to compensate a certain difference of revenue; but they will compensate a certain difference only; and if the rent of land should fall short of the interest of money by a greater difference, nobody would buy land, which would soon reduce its ordinary price.[24] On the contrary, if the ad-[46]vantages should much more than compensate

he had given him some hard knocks, it was done in so handsome a way that he could not complain'. The statement appears in Rae, *Life*, 423–4 on the authority of William Adam; it was suggested that Smith 'seemed to admit' that Bentham was right. In an addendum to Letter XIII of the *Defence* Bentham himself wrote: 'I have been flattered with the intelligence, that, upon the whole, your sentiments with respect to the points of difference are at present the same as mine', while stressing however that this information did not come directly from Smith. But the offending passage was not altered in subsequent editions.

[20] Cf. Cantillon, *Essai*, 292, ed. Higgs 221, where it is stated that regulation of the rate of interest must be 'fixed on the basis of the current market rate in the highest class, or thereabout'.

[21] Above, I.ix.9. Cf. M. Marion, *Dictionnaire des institutions de la France aux XVII et XVIII siècles* (Paris, 1923), 301: 'En réalité alors comme toujours, le taux de l'intérêt n'a jamais été réglé que par le plus ou moins d'abondance des capitaux et le plus ou moins de confiance qu'inspire l'emprunteur'.

[22] A similar argument appears in Hutcheson's *System*, ii.73. Cf. Cantillon (*Essai*, 294, ed Higgs 221): 'The current rate of Interest in a State seems to serve as a basis and measure for the purchase price of Land. If the current interest is 5 per cent. or one-twentieth part the price of Land should be the same.' But not so, according to Locke: 'The legal interest can never regulate the price of land, since it is plain, that the price of land has never changed with it, in the several changes . . . made in the rate of interest by law: nor now that the rate of interest is by law the same through all England, is the price of land every where the same, it being in some parts constantly sold for four or five years' purchase more than in others . . . this is plain demonstration against those who pretend to advance and regulate the price of land by a law concerning the interest of money.' (*Some Considerations of the Consequences of the Lowering of Interest, and raising the Value of Money, Works*, v.38.) Cf. Turgot, *Reflections*, LXXXV and LXXXIX.

[23] See below, IV.vii.c.58, where Smith comments further on the relationship between interest and rent, and V.ii.e.2, where he refers to the rate of interest and building rent.

[24] See above, I.x.b.34, and below, III.i.3, where Smith comments on the advantages of investment in land. Cf. Hutcheson, *System*, ii.72–3: 'As money grows plentier, and bears less interest in loans, more incline to purchases of lands than formerly; and this demand raises the rates of lands, so that smaller land rents can be obtained for any sum. Men are therefore contented with smaller interest than formerly when they could have

the difference, every body would buy land, which again would soon raise its ordinary price. When interest was at ten per cent., land was commonly sold for ten and twelve years purchase. As interest sunk to six, five, and four per cent., the price of land rose to twenty, five and twenty, and thirty years purchase. The market rate of interest is higher in France than in England; and the common price of land is lower. In England it commonly sells at thirty; in France at twenty years purchase.

got greater land-rents. They should be satisfied if it surpasses the annual profits of purchases, as much as compensates the greater troubles or hazards attending the loans.'

CHAPTER V

Of the different Employment of Capitals

1 THOUGH all capitals are destined for the maintenance of productive labour only, yet the quantity of that labour, which equal capitals are capable of putting into motion, varies extremely according to the diversity of their employment; as does likewise the value which that employment adds to the annual produce of the land and labour of the country.

2 A capital may be employed in four different ways: either, first, in procuring the rude produce annually required for the use and consumption of the society; or, secondly, in manufacturing and preparing that rude produce for immediate use and [47] consumption; or, thirdly, in transporting either the rude or manufactured produce from the places where they abound to those where they are wanted; or, lastly, in dividing particular portions of either into such small parcels as suit the occasional demands of those who want them. In the first way are employed the capitals of all those who undertake the improvement *or* cultivation of lands, mines, or fisheries; in the second, those of all master manufacturers; in the third, those of all wholesale merchants; and in the fourth, those of all retailers. It is difficult to conceive that a capital should be employed in any way which may not be classed under some one or other of those four.[1]

3 Each of those four methods of employing a capital is essentially necessary either to the existence or extension of the other three, or to the general conveniency of the society.

4 Unless a capital was employed in furnishing rude produce to a certain degree of abundance, neither manufactures nor trade of any kind could exist.

5 Unless a capital was employed in manufacturing that part of the rude produce which requires a good deal of preparation before it can be fit for

a-a of 4 ⟨corrected 4e–6⟩

[1] Cf. Turgot, *Reflections*, LXXXIII, where he summarizes the various employments of capital which he had examined in detail in previous sections:

'The first is to buy a landed estate which brings in a certain revenue.
The second is to invest one's money in agricultural enterprises, by taking a lease of land, the produce of which ought to yield, over and above the rent, the interest on the advances and the reward for the labour of the man who devotes both his wealth and his trouble to its cultivation.
The third is to invest one's capital in industrial or manufacturing enterprises.
The fourth is to invest it in commercial enterprises.
And the fifth is to lend it to those who are in need of it, at an annual interest.'

Turgot then continues to examine the interdependence which exists between the rates of return in different employments of capital, placing particular emphasis on differences in the labour and risk involved.

use and consumption, it either would never be produced, because there could be no demand for it; or if it was produced spontaneously, it would be of no value in exchange, and could add nothing to the wealth of the society.

6 [48] Unless a capital was employed in transporting, either the rude or manufactured produce, from the places where it abounds to those where it is wanted, no more of either could be produced than was necessary for the consumption of the neighbourhood. The capital of the merchant exchanges the surplus produce of one place for that of another, and thus encourages the industry and increases the enjoyments of both.

7 Unless a capital was employed in breaking and dividing certain portions either of the rude or manufactured produce, into such small parcels as suit the occasional demands of those who want them, every man would be obliged to purchase a greater quantity of the goods he wanted, than his immediate occasions required. If there was no such trade as a butcher, for example, every man would be obliged to purchase a whole ox or a whole sheep at a time. This would generally be inconvenient to the rich, and much more so to the poor. If a poor workman was obliged to purchase a month's or six months provisions at a time, a great part of the stock which he employs as a capital in the instruments of his trade, or in the furniture of his shop, and which yields him a revenue, he would be forced to place in that part of his stock which is reserved for immediate consumption, and which yields him no revenue. Nothing can be more convenient for such a person than to be able to purchase his subsistence from day to day, or even from hour to hour as he wants it. He is thereby enabled to employ almost his whole stock as a capital. He is thus enabled [49] to furnish work to a greater value, and the profit, which he makes by it in this way, much more than compensates the additional price which the profit of the retailer imposes upon the goods. The prejudices of some political writers against shopkeepers and tradesmen, are altogether without foundation.[2] So far is it from being necessary, either to tax them, or to restrict their numbers, that they can never be multiplied so as to hurt the publick, though they may so as to hurt one another. The quantity of grocery goods, for example, which can be sold in a particular town, is limited by the demand of that town and ᵇitsᵇ neighbourhood. The capital, therefore, which can be employed in the grocery trade cannot exceed what is sufficient to purchase that quantity. If this capital is divided between two different grocers, their competition will tend to make both of them sell cheaper, than if it were in the hands of one only; and if it were divided among twenty, their competition would be just so much the greater, and the chance of

ᵇ⁻ᵇ 2–6

---

[2] Smith discusses the physiocratic view that mercantile stock is sterile at IV.ix.11. The prejudices of shopkeepers are considered below, IV.vii.c.63.

their combining together, in order to raise the price, just so much the less. Their competition might perhaps ruin some of themselves; but to take care of this is the business of the parties concerned, and it may safely be trusted to their discretion. It can never hurt either the consumer, or the producer; on the contrary, it must tend to make the retailers both sell cheaper and buy dearer, than if the whole trade was monopolized by one or two persons. Some of them, perhaps, may sometimes decoy a weak customer to buy what [50] he has no occasion for. This evil, however, is of too little importance to deserve the publick attention, nor would it necessarily be prevented by restricting their numbers. It is not the multitude of ale-houses, to give the most suspicious example, that occasions a general disposition to drunkenness among the common people; but that disposition arising from other causes necessarily gives employment to a multitude of ale-houses.³

8   The persons whose capitals are employed in any of those four ways are themselves productive labourers. Their labour, when properly directed, fixes and realizes itself in the subject or vendible commodity upon which it is bestowed, and generally adds to its price the value at least of their own maintenance and consumption. The profits of the farmer, of the manufacturer, of the merchant, and retailer, are all drawn from the price of the goods which the two first produce, and the two last buy and sell. Equal capitals, however, employed in each of those four different ways, will ᶜimmediatelyᶜ put into motion very different quantities of productive labour, and augment too in very different proportions the value of the annual produce of the land and labour of the society to which they belong.⁴

9   The capital of the retailer replaces, together with its profits, that of the merchant of whom he purchases goods, and thereby enables him to continue his business. The retailer himself is the only productive labourer whom it ᵈimmediatelyᵈ employs. In his profits, consists the [51] whole value which its employment adds to the annual produce of the land and labour of the society.

10   The capital of the wholesale merchant replaces, together with their profits, the capitals of the farmers and manufacturers of whom he purchases the rude and manufactured produce which he deals in, and thereby enables them to continue their respective trades.⁵ It is by this service

ᶜ⁻ᶜ 2–6   ᵈ⁻ᵈ 2–6

---

³ See below, V.ii.g.2,4, where Smith discusses taxes on alehouses. Cf. also IV.iii.c.8.

⁴ Pownall (*Letter*, 22–48) suggested that Smith's thesis that different employments of capital set in motion different quantities of productive labour was deserving of attention, partly because he felt the point had not been fully demonstrated and partly because 'I find these propositions used in the second part of your work as data: whence you endeavour to prove, that the monopoly of the colony trade is a disadvantageous commercial institution.' (p. 23). See below, IV.vii.c.

⁵ One criticism of the laws which at one time governed the corn trade was that they

chiefly that he contributes indirectly to support the productive labour of the society, and to increase the value of its annual produce. His capital employs too the sailors and carriers who transport his goods from one place to another, and it augments the price of those goods by the value, not only of his profits, but of their wages. This is all the productive labour which it immediately puts into motion, and all the value which it immediately adds to the annual produce. Its operation in both these respects is a good deal superior to that of the capital of the retailer.

11   Part of the capital of the master manufacturer is employed as a fixed capital in the instruments of his trade, and replaces, together with its profits, that of some other artificer of whom he purchases them. Part of his circulating capital is employed in purchasing materials, and replaces, with their profits, the capitals of the farmers and miners of whom he purchases them. But a great part of it is always, either annually, or in a much shorter period, distributed among the different workmen whom he employs.[6] It augments the value of those materials by their wages, and by [52] their masters profits upon the whole stock of wages, materials, and instruments of trade employed in the business. It puts *ᵉimmediatelyᵉ* into motion, therefore, a much greater quantity of productive labour, and adds a much greater value to the annual produce of the land and labour of the society, than an equal capital in the hands of any wholesale merchant.

12   No equal capital puts into motion a greater quantity of productive labour than that of the farmer.[7] Not only his labouring servants, but his labouring cattle, are productive labourers. In agriculture too nature labours along with man; and though her labour costs no expence, its produce has its value, as well as that of the most expensive workmen. The most important operations of agriculture seem intended, not so much to increase, though they do that too, as to direct the fertility of nature towards the production of the plants most profitable to man. A field overgrown with briars and brambles may frequently produce as great a quantity of vegetables as the best cultivated vineyard or corn field. Planting and tillage frequently regulate more than they animate the active fertility of nature; and after all their labour, a great part of the work always remains to be done by her. The labourers and labouring cattle, therefore, employed in agriculture, not only occasion, like the workmen in manufactures, the reproduction of a value

---

ᵉ⁻ᵉ 2–6

discouraged middlemen, so that the farmers were obliged to exercise two trades, between which they had to divide their stock. See below, IV.v.b.16–21.

⁶ Cf. below, V.ii.k.43.

⁷ Cf. LJ (B) 289, ed. Cannan 224: 'Agriculture is of all other arts the most beneficent to society'. See also IV.vii.b.19, where Smith uses this point as part of his explanation of the relatively rapid rate of growth attained by new colonies. See also IV.ix.30, where the point is repeated in the course of an argument which rejects the physiocratic claim that agriculture alone is capable of producing a surplus.

equal to their own consumption, or to the capital which employs them, together with its owners profits; but of a much greater value. Over and above [53] the capital of the farmer and all its profits, they regularly occasion the reproduction of the rent of the landlord. This rent may be considered as the produce of those powers of nature, the use of which the landlord lends to the farmer.[8] It is greater or smaller according to the supposed extent of those powers, or in other words, according to the supposed natural or improved fertility of the land. It is the work of nature which remains after deducting or compensating every thing which can be regarded as the work of man. It is seldom less than a fourth, and frequently more than a third of the whole produce.[9] No equal quantity of productive labour employed in manufactures can ever occasion so great a reproduction. In them nature does nothing; man does all; and the reproduction must always be in proportion to the strength of the agents that occasion it. The capital employed in agriculture, therefore, not only puts into motion a greater quantity of productive labour than any equal capital employed in manufactures, but in proportion too to the quantity of productive labour which it employs, it adds a much greater value to the annual produce of the land and labour of the country, to the real wealth and revenue of its inhabitants. Of all the ways in which a capital can be employed, it is by far the most advantageous to the society.

13 The capitals employed in the agriculture and in the retail trade of any society, must always reside within that society. Their employment is confined almost to a precise spot, to the farm, [54] and to the shop of the retailer. They must generally too, though there are some exceptions to this, belong to resident members of the society.

14 The capital of a wholesale merchant, on the contrary, seems to have no fixed or necessary residence anywhere, but may wander about from place to place, according as it can either buy cheap or sell dear.[10]

15 The capital of the manufacturer must no doubt reside where the manufacture is carried on; but where this shall be is not always necessarily determined. It may frequently be at a great distance both from the place where the materials grow, and from that where the complete manufacture is consumed. Lyons is very distant both from the places which afford the materials of its manufactures, and from those which consume them.[11] The people of fashion in Sicily are cloathed in silks made in other countries,

---

[8] See below, V.ii.e.7, where it is argued that rent represents a payment for the use of a productive subject. The main determinants of rent are discussed above, I.xi.b.2–4.

[9] The same figure is cited at I.xi.c.20, II.iii.9, and V.ii.a.17.

[10] It is stated below, III.iv.24 that from the standpoint of the nation as a whole, the stock of a merchant is precarious until invested in land. The same point is made in discussing taxes on profits at V.ii.f.6 and V.iii.55. There is an interesting qualification to the view that merchants and manufacturers will be driven out of a country as a result of relatively low rates of return at V.ii.k.80.

[11] Smith comments on the introduction of silk manufactures in Lyons at III.iii.19.

from the materials which their own produces. Part of the wool of Spain is manufactured in Great Britain, and some part of that cloth is afterwards sent back to Spain.[12]

16   Whether the merchant whose capital exports the surplus produce of any society be a native or a foreigner, is of very little importance. If he is a foreigner, the number of their productive labourers is necessarily less than if he had been a native by one man only; and the value of their annual produce, by the profits of that one man. The sailors or carriers whom he employs may still belong indifferently either to his country, or to their country, or to some third country, in the [55] same manner as if he had been a native. The capital of a foreigner gives a value to their surplus produce equally with that of a native, by exchanging it for something for which there is a demand at home. It as effectually replaces the capital of the person who produces that surplus, and as effectually enables him to continue his business; the service by which the capital of a wholesale merchant chiefly contributes to support the productive labour, and to augment the value of the annual produce of the society to which he belongs.

17   It is of more consequence that the capital of the manufacturer should reside within the country. It necessarily puts into motion a greater quantity of productive labour, and adds a greater value to the annual produce of the land and labour of the society. It may, however, be very useful to the country, though it should not reside within it. The capitals of the British manufacturers who work up the flax and hemp annually imported from the coasts of the Baltic, are surely very useful to the countries which produce them. Those materials are a part of the surplus produce of those countries which, unless it was annually exchanged for something which is in demand there, would be of no value, and would soon cease to be produced. The merchants who export it, replace the capitals of the people who produce it, and thereby encourage them to continue the production; and the British manufacturers replace the capitals of those merchants.

18   [56] A particular country, in the same manner as a particular person, may frequently not have capital sufficient both to improve and cultivate all its lands, to manufacture and prepare their whole rude produce for immediate use and consumption, and to transport the surplus part either of the rude or manufactured produce to those distant markets where it can be exchanged for something for which there is a demand at home. The inhabitants of many different parts of Great Britain have not capital sufficient to improve and cultivate all their lands. The wool of the southern counties of Scotland is, a great part of it, after a long land carriage through very bad roads, manufactured in Yorkshire, for want of a capital to manufacture it at home.

---

[12] See below, III.iii.19, where it is pointed out that Spanish wool was the first material used in English manufactures of this kind which were fit for export.

There are many little manufacturing towns in Great Britain, of which the inhabitants have not capital sufficient to transport the produce of their own industry to those distant markets where there is demand and consumption for it. If there are any merchants among them, they are properly only the agents of wealthier merchants who reside in some of the greater commercial cities.

19   When the capital of any country is not sufficient for all those three purposes, in proportion as a greater share of it is employed in agriculture, the greater will be the quantity of productive labour which it puts into motion within the country; as will likewise be the value which its employment adds to the annual produce of the land and labour of the society. After agriculture, the capital employed in manufactures [57] puts into motion the greatest quantity of productive labour, and adds the greatest value to the annual produce. That which is employed in the trade of exportation, has the least effect of any of the three.

20   The country, indeed, which has not capital sufficient for all those three purposes, has not arrived at that degree of opulence for which it seems naturally destined. To attempt, however, prematurely and with an insufficient capital, to do all the three, is certainly not the shortest way for a society, no more than it would be for an individual, to acquire a sufficient one. The capital of all the individuals of a nation, has its limits in the same manner as that of a single individual, and is capable of executing only certain purposes. The capital of all the individuals of a nation is increased in the same manner as that of a single individual, by their continually accumulating and adding to it whatever they save out of their revenue. It is likely to increase the fastest, therefore, when it is employed in the way that affords the greatest revenue to all the inhabitants of the country, as they will thus be enabled to make the greatest savings. But the revenue of all the inhabitants of the country is necessarily in proportion to the value of the annual produce of their land and labour.

21   It has been the principal cause of the rapid progress of our American colonies towards wealth and greatness, that almost their whole capitals have hitherto been employed in agriculture.[13] They have no manufactures, those houshold and [58] coarser manufactures excepted which necessarily accompany the progress of agriculture, and which are the work of the women and children in every private family. The greater part both of the exportation and coasting trade of America, is carried on by the capitals of

[13] See above, I.ix.11 and below, III.iv.19 and IV.vii.b.2. It is stated at IV.vii.b.44 that America was still at a stage of development where capital was best employed in agriculture and at IV.vii.c.51 that agriculture was the 'proper business of all new colonies'. Smith remarked at IV.vii.b.17, however, that the British colonies were less well endowed than the Spanish or Portuguese with regard to land. He also remarks on the rapid progress of the American colonies at I.viii.23.

merchants who reside in Great Britain.[14] Even the stores and warehouses from which goods are retailed in some provinces, particularly in Virginia and Maryland, belong many of them to merchants who reside in the mother country, and afford one of the few instances of the retail trade of a society being carried on by the capitals of those who are not resident members of it. Were the Americans, either by combination or by any other sort of violence, to stop the importation of European manufactures,[15] and, by thus giving a monopoly to such of their own countrymen as could manufacture the like goods, divert any considerable part of their capital into this employment, they would retard instead of accelerating the further increase in the value of their annual produce, and would obstruct instead of promoting the progress of their country towards real wealth and greatness. This would be still more the case, were they to attempt, in the same manner, to monopolize to themselves their whole exportation trade.

22   The course of human prosperity, indeed, seems scarce ever to have been of so long continuance[16] as to enable any great country to acquire capital sufficient for all those three purposes; unless, perhaps, we give credit to the wonderful ac-[59]counts of the wealth and cultivation of China, of those of antient Egypt, and of the antient state of Indostan.[17] Even those three countries, the wealthiest, according to all accounts, that ever were in the world, are chiefly renowned for their superiority in agriculture and manufactures. They do not appear to have been eminent for foreign trade. The antient Egyptians had a superstitious antipathy to the sea;[18] a superstition nearly of the same kind prevails among the Indians;[19] and the Chinese have never excelled in foreign commerce.[20] The greater part of the surplus produce of all those three countries seems to have been always exported by foreigners, who gave in exchange for it something else for which they found a demand there, frequently gold and silver.

23   It is thus that the same capital will in any country put into motion a greater or smaller quantity of productive labour, and add a greater or smaller value to the annual produce of its land and labour, according to

[14] See below, IV.vii.b.56 and IV.vii.c.38. Smith considers the effect of the colony trade on the level of domestic profits at IV.vii.c.19 and comments on the favourable effects from a colonial point of view which had arisen from the use of foreign (British) capital.

[15] See below, IV.vii.c.43,44, where Smith comments on the expected rupture with the colonies and the current exclusion of British goods from the American market.

[16] It is stated at III.iv.20 that 200 years is a 'period as long as the course of human prosperity usually endures'.

[17] See above, I.ix.15, and below, V.i.d.17, where Smith comments on the 'wonderful' accounts brought back from China and Indostan by 'weak and wondering travellers; frequently by stupid and lying missionaries'.

[18] Montesquieu also refers to the fact that the Egyptians 'by their religion and their manners were averse to all communication with strangers'. He added that 'Their country was the Japan of those times; it possessed everything within itself.' (*Esprit*, XXI.vi.13.)

[19] See below, IV.ix.45.

[20] See above, I.iii.7, and below, III.i.7, IV.iii.c.11, IV.ix.40,41.

the different proportions in which it is employed in agriculture, manufactures, and wholesale trade. The difference too is very great, according to the different sorts of wholesale trade in which any part of it is
employed.

24   All wholesale trade, all buying in order to sell again by wholesale, may
be reduced to three different sorts. The home trade, the foreign trade of
consumption, and the carrying trade. The home trade is employed in
purchasing in one part of the same country, and selling in another, [60] the
produce of the industry of that country. It comprehends both the inland
and the coasting trade. The foreign trade of consumption is employed in
purchasing foreign goods for home consumption. The carrying trade is
employed in transacting the commerce of foreign countries, or in carrying
the surplus produce of one to another.

25   The capital which is employed in purchasing in one part of the country
in order to sell in another the produce of the industry of that country,
generally replaces by every such operation two distinct capitals that had
both been employed in the agriculture or manufactures of that country,
and thereby enables them to continue that employment. When it sends out
from the residence of the merchant a certain value of commodities, it
generally brings back in return at least an equal value of other commodities.
When both are the produce of domestick industry, it necessarily replaces
by every such operation two distinct capitals, which had both been employed in supporting productive labour, and thereby enables them to
continue that support. The capital which sends Scotch manufactures to
London and brings back English corn and manufactures to Edinburgh,
necessarily replaces, by every such operation, two British capitals which
had both been employed in the agriculture or manufactures of Great Britain.

26   The capital employed in purchasing foreign goods for home-consumption, when this purchase is made with the produce of domestick industry,
[61] replaces too, by every such operation, two distinct capitals; but one of
them only is employed in supporting domestick industry. The capital
which sends British goods to Portugal, and brings back Portuguese goods
to Great Britain, replaces by every such operation only one British capital.
The other is a Portuguese one. Though the returns, therefore, of the foreign
trade of consumption should be as quick as those of the home-trade, the
capital employed in it will give but one-half the encouragement to the
industry or productive labour of the country.

27   But the returns of the foreign trade of consumption are very seldom so
quick as those of the home-trade. The returns of the home-trade generally
come in before the end of the year, and sometimes three or four times in
the year. The returns of the foreign trade of consumption seldom come in
before the end of the year, and sometimes not till after two or three years.[21]

[21] The ability and willingness of merchants to lend to government is linked to the

A capital, therefore, employed in the home-trade will sometimes make twelve operations, or be sent out and returned twelve times, before a capital employed in the foreign trade of consumption has made one. If the capitals are equal, therefore, the one will give four and twenty times more encouragement and support to the industry of the country than the other.[22]

28　　The foreign goods for home-consumption may sometimes be purchased, not with the produce of domestick industry, but with some other foreign goods. These last, however, must have been purchased either immediately with the produce [62] of domestick industry, or with something else that had been purchased with it; for the case of war and conquest excepted, foreign goods can never be acquired, but in exchange for something that had been produced at home, either immediately, or after two or more different exchanges. The effects, therefore, of a capital employed in such a round-about foreign trade of consumption, are, in every respect, the same as those of one employed in the most direct trade of the same kind, except that the final returns are likely to be still more distant, as they must depend upon the returns of two or three distinct foreign trades. If the ᶠflax and hempᶠ of Riga are purchased with the tobacco of Virginia, which had been purchased with British manufactures, the merchant must wait for the returns of two distinct foreign trades before he can employ the same capital in re-purchasing a like quantity of British manufactures. If the tobacco of Virginia had been purchased, not with British manufactures, but with the sugar and rum of Jamaica which had been purchased with those manufactures, he must wait for the returns of three. If those two or three distinct foreign trades should happen to be carried on by two or three distinct merchants, of whom the second buys the goods imported by the first, and the third buys those imported by the second, in order to export them again, each merchant indeed will in this case receive the returns of his own capital more quickly; but the final returns of the whole capital employed in the trade will be just as slow as [63] ever. Whether the whole capital employed in such a round-about trade belong to one merchant or to three, can make no difference with regard to the country, though it may with regard to the particular merchants. Three times a greater capital must in both cases be employed, in order to exchange a certain value of British manufactures for a certain quantity of flax and hemp, than would have been necessary, had the manufactures and the flax and hemp been

---

ᶠ⁻ᶠ hemp and flax 6

---

rapidity of returns at V.iii.6. See also above, II.ii.64, where it is pointed out that the returns on fixed capital take many years.

[22] In a note to this passage, Cannan pointed out that 'If this doctrine as to the advantage of quick returns had been applied earlier in the chapter, it would have made havoc of the argument as to the superiority of agriculture'. Smith's analysis is applied in the critique of mercantile policy with regard to the colonial trade at IV.vii.c.35 ff; see also IV.iii.c.5,12.

directly exchanged for one another. The whole capital employed, therefore, in such a round-about foreign trade of consumption, will generally give less encouragement and support to the productive labour of the country, than an equal capital employed in a more direct trade of the same kind.[23]

29 Whatever be the foreign commodity with which the foreign goods for home-consumption are purchased, it can occasion no essential difference either in the nature of the trade, or in the encouragement and support which it can give to the productive labour of the country from which it is carried on. If they are purchased with the gold of Brazil, for example, or with the silver of Peru, this gold and silver, like the tobacco of Virginia, must have been purchased with something that either was the produce of the industry of the country, or that had been purchased with something else that was so. So far, therefore, as the productive labour of the country is concerned, the foreign trade of consumption which is carried on by means of gold and silver, has all [64] the advantages and all the inconveniencies of any other equally round-about foreign trade of consumption, and will replace just as fast or just as slow the capital which is immediately employed in supporting that productive labour. It seems even to have one advantage over any other equally round-about foreign trade. The transportation of those metals from one place to another, on account of their small bulk and great value, is less expensive than that of almost any other foreign goods of equal value. Their freight is much less, and their insurance not greater[g]; and no goods, besides, are less liable to suffer by the carriage[g].[24] An equal quantity of foreign goods, therefore, may frequently be purchased with a smaller quantity of the produce of domestick industry, by the intervention of gold and silver, than by that of any other foreign goods. The demand of the country may frequently, in this manner, be supplied more completely and at a smaller expence than in any other. Whether, by the continual exportation of those metals, a trade of this kind is likely to impoverish the country from which it is carried on, in any other way, I shall have occasion to examine at great length hereafter.[25]

30 That part of the capital of any country which is employed in the carrying trade, is altogether withdrawn from supporting the productive labour of that particular country, to support that of some foreign countries. Though it may replace by every operation two distinct capitals, yet neither of them [h]belongs[h] to that particular [65] country. The capital of the Dutch mer-

[g-g] 2–6   [h-h] belong 1

---

[23] Pownall distinguished between a 'circuitous commerce' and a round-about trade, and argued that Smith had confused the two. By the former, Pownall meant a trade which involved a complex number of transactions in each of which the returns could be quite rapid; by the latter, a trade which 'sends to market some commodity (as the proverb well expresses it), by *Tom-Long the carrier*' (*Letter*, 24).

[24] See below, IV.i.12, IV.v.a.18, and IV.vi.15.   [25] In Book IV.

chant, which carries the corn of Poland to Portugal, and brings back the fruits and wines of Portugal to Poland, replaces by every such operation two capitals, neither of which had been employed in supporting the productive labour of Holland; but one of them in supporting that of Poland, and the other that of Portugal. The profits only return regularly to Holland, and constitute the whole addition which this trade necessarily makes to the annual produce of the land and labour of that country. When, indeed, the carrying trade of any particular country is carried on with the ships and sailors of that country, that part of the capital employed in it which pays the freight, is distributed among, and puts into motion, a certain number of productive labourers of that country. Almost all nations that have had any considerable share of the carrying trade have, in fact, carried it on in this manner. The trade itself has probably derived its name from it, the people of such countries being the carriers to other countries. It does not, however, seem essential to the nature of the trade that it should be so. A Dutch merchant may, for example, employ his capital in transacting the commerce of Poland and Portugal, by carrying part of the surplus produce of the one to the other, not in Dutch, but in British bottoms. It may be presumed, that he actually does so upon some particular occasions. It is upon this account, however, that the carrying trade has been supposed peculiarly advantageous to such a country as Great [66] Britain, of which the defence and security depend upon the number of its sailors and shipping.[26] But the same capital may employ as many sailors and shipping, either in the foreign trade of consumption, or even in the home-trade, when carried on by coasting vessels, as it could in the carrying trade. The number of sailors and shipping which any particular capital can employ, does not depend upon the nature of the trade, but partly upon the bulk of the goods in proportion to their value, and partly upon the distance of the ports between which they are to be carried; chiefly upon the former of those two circumstances. The coal-trade from Newcastle to London, for example, employs more shipping than all the carrying trade of England, though the ports are at no great distance. To force, therefore, by extraordinary encouragements, a larger share of the capital of any country into the carrying trade, than what would naturally go to it, will not always necessarily increase the shipping of that country.

31   The capital, therefore, employed in the home-trade of any country will generally give encouragement and support to a greater quantity of productive labour in that country, and increase the value of its annual produce more than an equal capital employed in the foreign trade of consumption: and the capital employed in this latter trade has in both these

---

[26] See below, IV.ii.24,30. In the latter reference, the Navigation Acts are defended on the ground that defence is of more importance than opulence. See also IV.v.a.27, IV.vii.b. 30, and IV.vii.c.23.

respects a still greater advantage over an equal capital employed in the carrying trade. The riches, and so far as power depends upon riches, the power of every country,[27] [67] must always be in proportion to the value of its annual produce, the fund from which all taxes must ultimately be paid. But the great object of the political œconomy of every country, is to encrease the riches and power of that country.[28] It ought, therefore, to give no preference nor superior encouragement to the foreign trade of consumption above the home-trade, nor to the carrying trade above either of the other two. It ought neither to force nor to allure into either of those two channels, a greater share of the capital of the country than what would naturally flow into them of its own accord.[29]

32   Each of those different branches of trade, however, is not only advantageous, but necessary and unavoidable, when the course of things, without any constraint or violence, naturally introduces it.

33   When the produce of any particular branch of industry exceeds what the demand of the country requires, the surplus must be sent abroad, and exchanged for something for which there is a demand at home. Without such exportation, a part of the productive labour of the country must cease, and the value of its annual produce diminish. The land and labour of Great Britain produce generally more corn, woollens, and hard ware, than the demand of the home-market requires. The surplus part of them, therefore, must be sent abroad, and exchanged for something for which there is a demand at home.[30] It is only by means of such exportation, that this surplus can acquire a value sufficient to [68] compensate the labour and expence of producing it. The neighbourhood of the sea coast, and the banks of all navigable rivers, are advantageous situations for industry, only because they facilitate the exportation and exchange of such surplus produce for something else which is more in demand there.[31]

34   When the foreign goods which are thus purchased with the surplus produce of domestick industry exceed the demand of the home-market, the surplus part of them must be sent abroad again, and exchanged for something more in demand at home. About ninety-six thousand hogsheads of tobacco are annually purchased in Virginia and Maryland, with a part of the surplus produce of British industry.[32] But the demand of Great

[27] See above I.v.3.
[28] The objects of political economy are defined below, in the introduction to Book IV. See also IV.ix.38. The term is also used, for example, at Intro. 8, I.xi.n.1, and IV.i.35.
[29] Smith made much of the point that intervention with the use of capital gave an 'artificial direction' to industry which was unlikely to be advantageous. See, for example, IV.ii.3 and note.
[30] The gains from trade are examined below, for example, at IV.i.31 and IV.iii.c.4.
[31] See above, I.iii. with regard to the importance of water carriage, and below, III.iii.13 where the point is elaborated in connection with the historical development of cities.
[32] The same figures are cited below, IV.iv.5 and IV.vii.c.40. A modern authority states the quantities and values of British tobacco imports as: [*continues*]

Britain does not require, perhaps, more than fourteen thousand. If the remaining eighty-two thousand, therefore, could not be sent abroad and exchanged for something more in demand at home, the importation of them must cease immediately, and with it the productive labour of all those inhabitants of Great Britain, who are at present employed in preparing the goods with which these eighty-two thousand hogsheads are annually purchased. Those goods, which are part of the produce of the land and labour of Great Britain, having no market at home, and being deprived of that which they had abroad, must cease to be produced. The most round-about foreign trade of consumption, therefore, may, upon some occasions, be as necessary for supporting the produc-[69]tive labour of the country, and the value of its annual produce, as the most direct.[33]

35   When the capital stock of any country is increased to such a degree, that it cannot be all employed in supplying the consumption, and supporting the productive labour of that particular country, the surplus part of it naturally disgorges itself into the carrying trade, and is employed in performing the same offices to other countries.[34] The carrying trade is the natural effect and symptom of great national wealth: but it does not seem to be the natural cause of it. Those statesmen who have been disposed to favour it with particular encouragements, seem to have mistaken the effect and symptom for the cause. Holland, in proportion to the extent of the land and the number of its inhabitants, by far the richest country in Europe, has, accordingly, the greatest share of the carrying trade of Europe. England, perhaps the second richest country of Europe, is likewise supposed to have a considerable share of it; though what commonly passes for the carrying trade of England, will frequently, perhaps, be found to be no more than a round-about foreign trade of consumption. Such are, in a great measure, the trades which carry the goods of the East and West Indies, and of America, to different European markets. Those goods are generally purchased either immediately with the produce of British industry, or with something else which had been purchased with that produce, and the final returns of those trades are generally used or con-[70]sumed in Great Britain. The trade which is carried on in British bottoms between the different ports of the Mediterranean, and some trade of the same kind

	Quantity (*pounds*)	Value (£)
1774	56,056,796	526,294
1775	55,969,208	525,562
1776	7,279,160	68,215
1777	295,725	8,528

E. B. Schumpeter, *English Overseas Trade Statistics 1697–1808*, (Oxford, 1960), 56.

[33] A similar point is made at IV.vii.c.87.

[34] Cf. IV.iv.12 and IV.vii.c.96.

carried on by British merchants between the different ports of India, make, perhaps, the principal branches of what is properly the carrying trade of Great Britain.

36   The extent of the home-trade and of the capital which can be employed in it, is necessarily limited by the value of the surplus produce of all those distant places within the country which have occasion to exchange their respective productions with one another. That of the foreign trade of consumption, by the value of the surplus produce of the whole country and of what can be purchased with it. That of the carrying trade, by the value of the surplus produce of all the different countries in the world. Its possible extent, therefore, is in a manner infinite in comparison of that of the other two, and is capable of absorbing the greatest capitals.

37   The consideration of his own private profit, is the sole motive which determines the owner of any capital to employ it either in agriculture, in manufactures, or in some particular branch of the wholesale or retail trade. The different quantities of productive labour which it may put into motion, and the different values which it may add to the annual produce of the land and labour of the society, according as it is employed in one or other of those different ways, never enter into his thoughts. In countries, therefore, where agriculture is the most profitable of [71] all employments, and farming and improving the most direct roads to a splendid fortune, the capitals of individuals will naturally be employed in the manner most advantageous to the whole society. The profits of agriculture, however, seem to have no superiority over those of other employments in any part of Europe. Projectors, indeed, in every corner of it, have within these few years amused the public with most magnificent accounts of the profits to be made by the cultivation and improvement of land. Without entering into any particular discussion of their calculations, a very simple observation may satisfy us that the result of them must be false. We see every day the most splendid fortunes that have been acquired in the course of a single life by trade and manufactures, frequently from a very small capital, sometimes from no capital. A single instance of such a fortune acquired by agriculture in the same time, and from such a capital, has not, perhaps, occurred in Europe during the course of the present century. In all the great countries of Europe, however, much good land still remains uncultivated, and the greater part of what is cultivated is far from being improved to the degree of which it is capable. Agriculture, therefore, is almost every where capable of absorbing a much greater capital than has ever yet been employed in it.[35] What circumstances in the policy of Europe have given the trades which are carried on in towns so great an advantage over that which is carried on in the [72] country, that private persons frequently find it more for their

[35] See above, I.x.c.21, and below, IV.v.b.20.

advantage to employ their capitals in the most distant carrying trades of Asia and America, than in the improvement and cultivation of the most fertile fields in their own neighbourhood, I shall endeavour to explain at full length in the two following books.

BOOK III

Of the different Progress of Opulence in different Nations

CHAPTER I

Of the natural Progress of Opulence

1 THE great commerce of every civilized society, is that carried on between the inhabitants of the town and those of the country.[1] It consists in the exchange of rude for manufactured produce, either immediately, or by the intervention of money, or of some sort of paper which represents money. The country supplies the town with the means of subsistence, and the materials of manufacture. The town repays this supply by sending back a part of the manufactured produce to the inhabitants of the country. The town, in which there neither is nor can be any reproduction of substances, may very properly be said to gain its whole wealth and subsistence from the country. We must not, however, upon this account, imagine that the gain of the town is the loss of the country. The gains of both are mutual and reciprocal, and the division of labour is in this, as in all other cases, advantageous to all the different persons employed in the various occupations into which it is [74] subdivided. The inhabitants of the country purchase of the town a greater quantity of manufactured goods, with the produce of a much smaller quantity of their own labour, than they must have employed had they attempted to prepare them themselves. The town affords a market for the surplus produce of the country, or what is over and above the maintenance of the cultivators, and it is there that the inhabitants of the country exchange it for something else which is in demand among them.[2] The greater the number and revenue of the inhabitants of the town, the more extensive is the market which it affords to those of the country; and the more extensive that market, it is always the more advantageous to a great number. The corn which grows within a mile of the town, sells there for the same price with that which comes from twenty miles distance. But the price of the latter must generally, not only pay the

---

[1] See above, I.x.c.19, II.i.28, IV.ix.37 and 48.
[2] The gains from trade are described in similar terms at IV.i.31 and IV.iii.c.4. Cf. I.xi.c.4.

expence of raising and bringing it to market, but afford too the ordinary profits of agriculture to the farmer.[3] The proprietors and cultivators of the country, therefore, which lies in the neighbourhood of the town, over and above the ordinary profits of agriculture, gain, in the price of what they sell, the whole value of the carriage of the like produce that is brought from more distant parts, and they save, besides, the whole value of this carriage in the price of what they buy. Compare the cultivation of the lands in the neighbourhood of any considerable town, with that of those which lie at some distance [75] from it, and you will easily satisfy yourself how much the country is benefited by the commerce of the town. Among all the absurd speculations that have been propagated concerning the balance of trade,[4] it has never been pretended that either the country loses by its commerce with the town, or the town by that with the country which maintains it.

2   As subsistence is, in the nature of things, prior to conveniency and luxury, so the industry which procures the former, must necessarily be prior to that which ministers to the latter. The cultivation and improvement of the country, therefore, which affords subsistence, must, necessarily, be prior to the increase of the town, which furnishes only the means of conveniency and luxury. It is the surplus produce of the country only, or what is over and above the maintenance of the cultivators, that constitutes the subsistence of the town, which can therefore increase only with the increase of this surplus produce. The town, indeed, may not always derive its whole subsistence from the country in its neighbourhood, or even from the territory to which it belongs, but from very distant countries; and this, though it forms no exception from the general rule, has occasioned considerable variations in the progress of opulence in different ages and nations.

3   That order of things which necessity imposes in general, though not in every particular country, is, in every particular country, promoted by the natural inclinations of man. If human insti-[76]tutions had never thwarted those natural inclinations, the towns could no-where have increased beyond what the improvement and cultivation of the territory in which they were situated could support; till such time, at least, as the whole of that territory was compleatly cultivated and improved. Upon equal, or nearly equal profits, most men will chuse to employ their capitals rather in the improvement and cultivation of land, than either in manufactures or in foreign trade. The man who employs his capital in land, has it more under his view and command, and his fortune is much less liable to accidents than that of the trader, who is obliged frequently to commit it, not only

[3] See above, I.xi.b.4, regarding the costs of transport.
[4] It is stated at IV.iii.c.2 that 'nothing . . . can be more absurd' than this whole doctrine of the balance of trade. Cf. IV.i.8.

to the winds and the waves, but to the more uncertain elements of human folly and injustice, by giving great credits in distant countries to men, with whose character and situation he can seldom be thoroughly acquainted. The capital of the landlord, on the contrary, which is fixed in the improvement of his land, seems to be as well secured as the nature of human affairs can admit of. The beauty of the country besides, the pleasures of a country life, the tranquillity of mind which it promises, and wherever the injustice of human laws does not disturb it, the independency which it really affords, have charms that more or less attract every body; and as to cultivate the ground was the original destination of man, so in every stage of his existence he seems to retain a predilection for this primitive employment.[5]

4   [77] Without the assistance of some artificers, indeed, the cultivation of land cannot be carried on, but with great inconveniency and continual interruption. Smiths, carpenters, wheel-wrights, and plough-wrights, masons, and bricklayers, tanners, shoemakers, and taylors, are people, whose service the farmer has frequent occasion for. Such artificers too stand, occasionally, in need of the assistance of one another; and as their residence is not, like that of the farmer, necessarily tied down to a precise spot, they naturally settle in the neighbourhood of one another, and thus form a small town or village. The butcher, the brewer, and the baker, soon join them, together with many other artificers and retailers, necessary or useful for supplying their occasional wants, and who contribute still further to augment the town. The inhabitants of the town and those of the country are mutually the servants of one another. The town is a continual fair or market, to which the inhabitants of the country resort, in order to exchange their rude for manufactured produce. It is this commerce which supplies the inhabitants of the town both with the materials of their work, and the means of their subsistence. The quantity of the finished work which they sell to the inhabitants of the country, necessarily regulates the quantity of the materials and provisions which they buy. Neither their employment nor subsistence, therefore, can augment, but in proportion to the augmentation of the demand from the country for finished work; and this demand can augment [78] only in proportion to the extension of improvement and cultivation. Had human institutions, therefore, never disturbed the natural course of things, the progressive wealth and increase of the towns would, in every political society, be consequential, and in proportion to the improvement and cultivation of the territory or country.

5   In our North American colonies, where uncultivated land is still to be had upon easy terms, no manufactures for distant sale have ever yet been established in any of their towns.[6] When an artificer has acquired a little

---

[5] See above, II.iv.17.

[6] It is stated at IV.vii.43–44 that the lack of manufactures for distant sale in America

more stock than is necessary for carrying on his own business in supplying the neighbouring country, he does not, in North America, attempt to establish with it a manufacture for more distant sale, but employs it in the purchase and improvement of uncultivated land.[7] From artificer he becomes planter, and neither the large wages nor the easy subsistence which that country affords to artificers, can bribe him rather to work for other people than for himself. He feels that an artificer is the servant of his customers, from whom he derives his subsistence;[8] but that a planter who cultivates his own land, and derives his necessary subsistence from the labour of his own family, is really a master, and independent of all the world.

6   In countries, on the contrary, where there is either no uncultivated land, or none that can be had upon easy terms, every artificer who has acquired more stock than he can employ in the occasional jobs of the neighbourhood, endeavours to [79] prepare work for more distant sale. The smith erects some sort of iron, the weaver some sort of linen or woollen manufactory. Those different manufactures come, in process of time, to be gradually subdivided, and thereby improved and refined in a great variety of ways, which may easily be conceived, and which it is therefore unnecessary to explain any further.

7   In seeking for employment to a capital, manufactures are, upon equal or nearly equal profits, naturally preferred to foreign commerce, for the same reason that agriculture is naturally preferred to manufactures. As the capital of the landlord or farmer is more secure than that of the manufacturer, so the capital of the manufacturer, being at all times more within his view and command, is more secure than that of the foreign merchant. In every period, indeed, of every society, the surplus part both of the rude and manufactured produce, or that for which there is no demand at home, must be sent abroad in order to be exchanged for something for which there is some demand at home. But whether the capital, which carries this surplus produce abroad, be a foreign or a domestick one, is of very little importance. If the society has not acquired sufficient capital both to cultivate all its lands, and to manufacture in the compleatest manner the whole of *a*its*a* rude produce, there is even a considerable advantage that *b*that rude produce*b* should be exported by a foreign capital, in order that the whole stock of the society may be employed in more useful purposes. The [80] wealth of antient Egypt, that of China and Indostan, sufficiently demonstrate that a nation may attain a very high degree of opulence,

---

a-a their *1*   *b-b* it *1*

was the consequence of mercantile policy with regard to the colonies, although it is also pointed out that their state of improvement was such as to preclude them.

[7] See IV.vii.b.2 and 19. Cf. I.ix.11.

[8] See below, III.iv.11 where Smith describes the nature of this kind of dependence.

though the greater part of its exportation trade be carried on by foreigners.[9] The progress of our North American and West Indian colonies would have been much less rapid, had no capital but what belonged to themselves been employed in exporting their surplus produce.[10]

8   According to the natural course of things, therefore, the greater part of the capital of every growing society is, first, directed to agriculture, afterwards to manufactures, and last of all to foreign commerce. This order of things is so very natural, that in every society that had any territory, it has always, I believe, been in some degree observed. Some of their lands must have been cultivated before any considerable towns could be established, and some sort of coarse industry of the manufacturing kind must have been carried on in those towns, before they could well think of employing themselves in foreign commerce.

9   But though this natural order of things must have taken place in some degree in every such society, it has, in all the modern states of Europe, been, in many respects, entirely inverted. The foreign commerce of some of their cities has introduced all their finer manufactures, or such as were fit for distant sale; and manufactures and foreign commerce together, have given birth to the principal improvements of agriculture.[11] The manners and customs which the nature of [81] their original government introduced, and which remained after that government was greatly altered,
√   necessarily forced them into this unnatural and retrograde order.

[9] See, for example, I.iii.7, II.v.22 and IV.ix.40.
[10] See above, II.v.21, and below, IV.vii.b.56, IV.vii.c.38, and V.iii.83.
[11] This argument is a feature of III.iii.

CHAPTER II

Of the Discouragement of Agriculture in the antient State of Europe after the Fall of the Roman Empire[1]

1 WHEN the German and Scythian nations over-ran the western provinces of the Roman empire, the confusions which followed so great a revolution lasted for several centuries.[2] The rapine and violence which the barbarians exercised against the antient inhabitants, interrupted the commerce between the towns and the country.[3] The towns were deserted, and the country was left uncultivated, and the western provinces of Europe, which

[1] In both LJ (A) and LJ (B) Smith dealt at some length with the rise, progress, and decline, of Greece and Rome. The argument then offered a version of the events outlined in the following chapters of this Book, treating these events as parts of a single historical argument ranging from the foundation of Greek civilization to the English Revolution Settlement. See generally, LJ (A) iv. and LJ (B) 5–99, ed. Cannan 9–72. It would appear that when Smith came to write this section of the WN, he decided to divide the historical argument by starting from the fall of Rome, and placing much of the material which was concerned with earlier classical experience in V.i.a and b.

The subjects of this particular chapter are covered in LJ (B) 285–99, ed. Cannan 222–31, where Smith in effect continued the critique of the mercantile system as established in previous lectures, by examining the causes of the slow progress of opulence. In the case of *agriculture*, Smith reviewed the natural impediments to growth, such as lack of stock, before going on to consider the influence of 'oppresive measures' such as the feudal services, the laws of entail, and other factors which had contributed to slow down the rate of growth in this field. ED 5 provides a similar argument. The only major point of contrast between these references and WN is that the former discuss forms of lease *before* proceeding to examine the laws of primogeniture and entail. In LJ (B) 299–307, ed. Cannan 231–6, the discussion continues from this point to consider the causes of the slow progress of *manufactures*. These passages do not occur in ED or in LJ (A).

One possible reason for Smith's decision to separate the discussion from the general critique of mercantilism in this way, may be that in the historical period examined in this Book, dealing as it does with the transition from the feudal to the 'commercial' stage, Smith was concerned with a socio-economic *system* as distinct from a system of *police* or government policy. Moreover, in the period examined, the development of foreign trade is shown to be a major force contributing to socio-economic change, and the point is made at I.xi.o.14 that this development was *not* marked by a restrictive (mercantile) policy on the part of governments with regard to trade.

[2] The causes of the decline of Rome are considered below, V.i.a.36. Smith also refers, at V.i.b.16, to 'our German and Scythian ancestors' as having just emerged from the shepherd state. Smith refers to the savage nations 'issuing out from Scandinavia and other Northern countries' in LJ (A) iii.12; LJ (A) ii.97 records that among the nations which invaded Rome, 'society was a step further advanced than amongst the Americans at this day' in that they had arrived at 'the state of shepherds, and had even some little agriculture'. Cf. below, V.i.a.2, and LJ (B) 184, ed. Cannan 137, where it is stated that the 'Germans were much further advanced than the Americans at this day'. Smith also comments on the confusions following the collapse of Rome, Astronomy, IV.21, in explaining the 'entire neglect' of the sciences for several centuries thereafter.

[3] LJ (A) iv.117: 'the country was infested by robbers and banditti, so that the cities soon became deserted, for unless there be a free communication betwixt the country and the town to carry out the manufactures and import provisions, no town can subsist.' See also LJ (B) 50, ed. Cannan 35.

had enjoyed a considerable degree of opulence under the Roman empire, sunk into the lowest state of poverty and barbarism. During the continuance of those confusions, the chiefs and principal leaders of those nations, acquired or usurped to themselves the greater part of the lands of those countries. A great part of them was uncultivated; but no part of them, whether cultivated or uncultivated, was left without a proprietor. All of them were en-[82]grossed, and the greater part by a few great proprietors.⁴

2   This original engrossing of uncultivated lands, though a great, might have been but a transitory evil. They might soon have been divided again, and broke into small parcels either by succession or by alienation. The law of primogeniture hindered them from being divided by succession: the introduction of entails prevented their being broke into small parcels by alienation.⁵

3   When land, like moveables, is considered as the means only of subsistence and enjoyment, the natural law of succession divides it, like them, among all the children of the family; of all of whom the subsistence and enjoyment may be supposed equally dear to the father. This natural law of succession accordingly took place among the Romans, who made no more distinction between elder and younger, between male and female, in the inheritance of lands, than we do in the distribution of moveables.⁶ But

⁴ ED 5.5 comments that 'the chiefs of an independent nation which settles in any country, either by conquest or otherwise, as soon as the idea of private property in land is introduced never leave any part of the Land vacant, but constantly, from that greediness which is natural to man, seize much greater tracts of it to themselves than they have, either strength or stock to cultivate.' See also LJ (B) 289–90, ed. Cannan 224–5; 50, ed. Cannan 35. In LJ (A) iv.114 it is stated that the Germans had a knowledge of 'agriculture and of property in land' and that 'The first thing therefore which they set about after they had got possession of any kingdom, as Britain, France, etc., was to make a division of the lands.' The form of government thus introduced by such peoples as the Saxons, Franks, Visigoths, and Burgundians, is described in LJ (A) iv.114-24 and stated to be 'allodial properly so called'.

Montesquieu also commented on the form of government found among the German nations which overran the Western empire, and added that the 'corruption' of the form of government which they introduced had, in the long run, the surprising effect of giving 'birth to the best species of constitution that could possibly be imagined by man!' (*Esprit*, XI.viii.3). See especially Books XXX and XXXI, where Montesquieu traces the progress of institutions in France from the period of German dominance with its allodial form of government, until the advent of the feudal system. Elsewhere he remarked: 'No doubt but these barbarians retained in their respective conquests the manners, inclinations, and usages of their own country; for no nation can change in an instant their manner of thinking and acting.' (*Esprit*, XXX.vi.2).

⁵ It is pointed out at III.iv.19 that such institutions impede the sale of land and thus the flow of capital to agriculture. Smith attributed the rapid rate of growth attained in America, at least in part, to the absence of such laws, IV.vii.b.19. Cf. Montesquieu '. . . The laws ought to abolish the right of primogeniture among the nobles, to the end that by a continual division of the inheritances their fortunes be always upon a level.' (*Esprit*, V.viii. 20):

⁶ The law of succession among the Romans is described in LJ (A) i.94-104, where it is stated that 'all children shared equally in the estate of the father or master of the family'. Smith also commented that wealth was divided equally in the shepherd states of Greece

[*continues*]

when land was considered as the means, not of subsistence merely, but of ✓ power and protection, it was thought better that it should descend undivided to one. In those disorderly times, every great landlord was a sort of petty prince. His tenants were his subjects. He was their judge, and in some respects their legislator in peace, and their leader in war. He made war according to his own discretion, frequently against his neighbours, and sometimes against his sovereign. The security of a landed estate, therefore, the protection [83] which its owner could afford to those who dwelt on it, depended upon its greatness. To divide it was to ruin it, and to expose every part of it to be oppressed and swallowed up by the incursions of its neighbours.[7] The law of primogeniture, therefore, came to take place, not immediately, indeed, but in process of time, in the succession of landed estates, for the same reason that it has generally taken place in that of monarchies, though not always at their first institution. That the power, and consequently the security of the monarchy, may not be weakened by division, it must descend entire to one of the children. To which of them so important a preference shall be given, must be determined by some general rule, founded not upon the doubtful distinctions of personal merit, but upon some plain and evident difference which can admit of no dispute. Among the children of the same family, there can be no indisputable difference but that of sex, and that of age. The male sex is universally preferred to the female; and when all other things are equal, the elder everywhere takes place of the younger. Hence the origin of the right of primogeniture, and of what is called lineal succession.[8]

4   Laws frequently continue in force long after the circumstances, which first gave occasion to them, and which could alone render them reasonable, are no more.[9] In the present state of Europe, the proprietor of a single

at the time of the Trojan War in LJ (A) iv.11. Speaking of modern countries in LJ (A) i.104 he states that the succession to moveables was founded 'on precisely the same principles' as in Rome and that 'during the allodiall government of Europe, the succession to land estates was directed in the same manner'. It is stated in LJ (A) i.115–16 that the Goths, Huns and Vandals originally used the natural law of succession and that the law of primogeniture was 'contrary to nature, to reason, and to justice', being occasioned by the nature of the feudal government. The laws of succession among the Romans are considered at some length by Montesquieu (*Esprit*, XXVII.i). See below, IV.vii.a.3.

[7] Lord Stair justified primogeniture as the means for 'the preservation of the memory and dignity of families, which by frequent divisions of the inheritance would become despicable or forgotten'. (*Institutions of the Law of Scotland*, III.iv.22).

[8] Cf. LJ (A) iv.46: 'We see that there is in man a great propensity to continue his regard towards those which are nearly connected with him whom we have formerly respected. The sons and particularly the eldest son commonly attract this regard, as they seem most naturally to come in the place of their father; and accordingly in most nations have been continu'd in their father's dignity.' See also LJ (B) 161, ed. Cannan 118, and LJ (A) i.133: 'it was not the introduction of the feudal government and military fiefs that brought in the right of primogeniture; but the independency of the great allodiall estates, and the inconveniences attending divisions of such estates.'

[9] A similar phrase is used below, V.i.f.20, in discussing religious observances. Smith gave a good deal of attention to these issues, and provides examples of institutions which

acre of land is as perfectly secure of his possession as the proprietor of a hundred thousand. The right of primoge-[84]niture, however, still continues to be respected, and as of all institutions it is the fittest to support the pride of family distinctions, it is still likely to endure for many centuries. In every other respect, nothing can be more contrary to the real interest of a numerous family, than a right which, in order to enrich one, beggars all the rest of the children.

5   Entails are the natural consequences of the law of primogeniture. They were introduced to preserve a certain lineal succession, of which the law of primogeniture first gave the idea, and to hinder any part of the original estate from being carried out of the proposed line either by gift, or devise, or alienation; either by the folly, or by the misfortune of any of its successive owners. They were altogether unknown to the Romans.[10] Neither their substitutions nor fideicommisses bear any resemblance to entails, though some French lawyers have thought proper to dress the modern institution in the language and ᵃgarbᵃ of those antient ones.

6   When great landed estates were a sort of principalities, entails might not be unreasonable.[11] Like what are called the fundamental laws of some monarchies, they might frequently hinder the security of thousands from being endangered by the caprice or extravagance of one man. But in the present state of Europe, when small as well as great estates derive their security from the laws of their country, nothing can be more completely absurd. They are founded upon the most absurd of all suppositions, the supposition [85] that every successive generation of men have not an equal right to the earth, and to all that it possesses; but that the property of the present generation should be restrained and regulated according to the fancy of those who died perhaps five hundred years ago. Entails, however, are still respected through the greater part of Europe, in those countries particularly in which noble birth is a necessary qualification for the enjoyment either of civil or military honours. Entails are thought necessary for

ᵃ⁻ᵃ form *1*

had once been useful but were now outdated in LJ (B) 304, ed. Cannan 235, and LJ (A) i.96, LJ (A) ii.38–41. In the latter place he argued that thirlage, i.e. that rule which obliged a number of farms to grind their corn at a certain mill, while justified at its first inception, was 'one of those old constitutions which had much better be removed; and of this sort there are many.'

[10] LJ (B) 167, ed. Cannan 123, states that 'Entails were first introduced into the modern law by the ecclesiastics, whose education made them acquainted with the Roman customs.' It is also stated at LJ (A) i.155 that 'In time however entails were introduced among the Romans, and . . . this was brought about by means of fideicommisses.'

[11] Smith makes this point at some length in LJ (A) i.130 and suggests that the great allodial lords were 'in much the same state as the greater and lesser princes of Germany at this day'. He also pointed out that the problem of power made the division of lands undesirable, using the homely example of the Gordon, Douglas, and Fraser families in Scotland (133).

maintaining this exclusive privilege of the nobility to the great offices and
honours of their country; and that order having usurped one unjust advantage over the rest of their fellow-citizens, lest their poverty should
render it ridiculous, it is thought reasonable that they should have another.
The common law of England, indeed, is said to abhor perpetuities, and
they are accordingly more restricted there than in any other European
monarchy; though even England is not altogether without them.[12] In
Scotland more than one-fifth, perhaps more than one-third part of the
whole lands of the country, are at present *supposed to be* under strict
entail.[13]

7   Great tracts of uncultivated land were, in this manner, not only engrossed by particular families, but the possibility of their being divided
again was as much as possible precluded for ever. It seldom happens, however, that a great proprietor is a great improver.[14] In the disorderly times
which gave birth to those barbarous institutions, the great proprietor was
sufficiently em-[86]ployed in defending his own territories, or in extending
his jurisdiction and authority over those of his neighbours. He had no
leisure to attend to the cultivation and improvement of land. When the
establishment of law and order afforded him this leisure, he often wanted
the inclination, and almost always the requisite abilities.[15] If the expence
of his house and person either equalled or exceeded his revenue, as it did
very frequently, he had no stock to employ in this manner. If he was an
œconomist, he generally found it more profitable to employ his annual
savings in new purchases, than in the improvement of his old estate. To
improve land with profit, like all other commercial projects, requires an
exact attention to small savings and small gains, of which a man born to a
great fortune, even though naturally frugal, is very seldom capable. The
situation of such a person naturally disposes him to attend rather to ornament which pleases his fancy, than to profit for which he has so little
occasion. The elegance of his dress, of his equipage, of his house, and
houshold furniture, are objects which from his infancy he has been

b–b 3–6

---

[12] Hume makes the interesting comment: 'the most important law in its consequences,
which was enacted during the reign of Henry [4 Henry 7, c.24] was that by which the nobility and gentry acquired a power of breaking the ancient entails, and of alienating their
estates.' (*The History of England* (1778) iii.400.) See also v.490.

[13] The figure might not be unreasonable. It was estimated that about one-half of the land
of Scotland was entailed early in the nineteenth century. H. H. Monteath, 'Heritable
Rights', in G. C. H. Paton, ed., *An Introduction to Scottish Legal History* (Edinburgh,
1958), 177.

[14] It is stated in LJ (B) 163, ed. Cannan 120, that the right of primogeniture 'hinders
agriculture' and at 168, ed. Cannan 124, that entails are 'absurd'. Similar points are made
in LJ (B) 295, ed. Cannan 228, and ED 5.9. It is argued in LJ (A) i.164 that it is 'altogether
absurd to suppose that our ancestors who lived 500 years ago should have had the power of
disposing of all lands at this time'. See below, III.iv.3.

[15] See below, III.iv.13.

accustomed to have some anxiety about. The turn of mind which this habit naturally forms, follows him when he comes to think of the improvement of land. He embellishes perhaps four or five hundred acres in the neighbourhood of his house, at ten times the expence which the land is worth after all his improvements; and finds that if he was to improve his whole estate in the same manner, [87] and he has little taste for any other, he would be a bankrupt before he had finished the tenth part of it.[16] There still remain in both parts of the united kingdom some great estates which have continued without interruption in the hands of the same family since the times of feudal anarchy.[17] Compare the present condition of those estates with the possessions of the small proprietors in their neighbourhood, and you will require no other argument to convince you how unfavourable such extensive property is to improvement.

8   If little improvement was to be expected from such great proprietors, still less was to be hoped for from those who occupied the land under them. In the antient state of Europe, the occupiers of land were all tenants at will.[18] They were all or almost all slaves; but their slavery was of a milder kind than that known among the antient Greeks and Romans, or even in our West Indian colonies. They were supposed to belong more directly to the land than to their master. They could, therefore, be sold with it, but not separately. They could marry, provided it was with the consent of their master; and he could not afterwards dissolve the marriage by selling the man and wife to different persons. If he maimed or murdered any of them, he was liable to some penalty, though generally but to a small one. They were not, however, capable of acquiring property.[19] Whatever they acquired was acquired to their master, and he could take it from them at pleasure.

---

[16] In Letter 30 addressed to Lord Shelburne, dated 4 April 1759, Smith wrote that: 'We have in Scotland some noblemen whose estates extend from the east to the west sea, who called themselves improvers, & are called so by their countrymen, when they cultivate two or three hundred acres round their own family seat, while they allow all the rest of their country to lie waste, almost uninhabited & entirely unimproved, not worth a shilling the hundred acres, without thinking themselves answerable to God, their country & their Posterity for so shameful as well as so foolish a neglect.'

[17] Smith refers to the 'disorderly state' of Europe at the time of the feudal government at V.ii.g.6, III.iv.9, and comments at I.xi.e.23 on the 'disorderly state' of England under the Plantagenets ands its economic consequences. See also V.iii.1, where Smith mentions the problem of hoarding in a 'rude state of society', and cf. II.i.31.

[18] Cf. LJ (B) 282, ed. Cannan 220: 'The peasants had leases which depended upon the caprice of their masters . . . As little could the landlords increase their wealth as they lived so indolent a life and were involved in perpetual wars.' LJ (A) iii.112 comments: 'The reason of the loss in cultivating land in this manner other than by free tenants will be very evident. The slave or villain who cultivated the land cultivated it entirely for his master; whatever it produced over and above his maintenance belonged to the landlord.' Cf. I.viii.44 and I.x.b.15.

[19] These points are also made in LJ (A) iv.142, where Smith also adds that the tenants at will were secured in the benefit of marriage by the clergy: 'It was also a rule that if the lord used him unjustly, or did not plead his cause and appear for him in court when he was accused, and it was found that he was innocent in this case, he was free.' In the same place,

Whatever cultivation and improvement could be [88] carried on by means of such slaves, was properly carried on by their master. It was at his expence. The seed, the cattle, and the instruments of husbandry were all his. It was for his benefit. Such slaves could acquire nothing but their daily maintenance. It was properly the proprietor himself, therefore, that, in this case, occupied his own lands, and cultivated them by his own bondmen. This species of slavery still subsists in Russia,[20] Poland, Hungary, Bohemia, Moravia, and other parts of Germany.[21] It is only in the western and southwestern provinces of Europe, that it has gradually been abolished altogether.[22]

9   But if great improvements are seldom to be expected from great proprietors, they are least of all to be expected when they employ slaves for their workmen. The experience of all ages and nations, I believe, demonstrates that the work done by slaves, though it appears to cost only their maintenance, is in the end the dearest of any.[23] A person who can acquire no property, can have no other interest but to eat as much, and to labour as little as possible. Whatever work he does beyond what is sufficient to purchase his own maintenance, can be squeezed out of him by violence only,

Smith described the villeins as the first of the ignoble classes, and the inhabitants of cities as the second. See below, III.iii, and LJ (B) 56–7, ed. Cannan 39–40.

[20] See below, V.ii.g.11.

[21] Montesquieu cites as the most imperfect form of its type, the aristocratic government of Poland where 'the peasants are slaves to the nobility' (*Esprit*, II.iii.11). He also states that 'real' (as distinct from 'personal') slavery still subsisted in Hungary, Bohemia, and 'several parts of Lower Germany (*Esprit*, XV.ix.1).

[22] See LJ (B) 134, ed. Cannan 96 and ED 5.6–7. Cf. LJ (A) iii. 101–2:

We are apt to imagine that slavery is entirely abolished at this time, without considering that this is the case in only a small part of Europe; not remembering that all over Muscovy and all the eastern parts of Europe, and the whole of Asia, that is, from Bohemia to the Indian Ocean, all over Africa, and the greatest part of America, it is still in use. It is indeed allmost impossible that it should ever be totally or generally abolished. In a republican government it will scarcely ever happen that it should be abolished. The persons who make all the laws in that country are persons who have slaves themselves.

A similar point is made in LJ (A) iii.114. In LJ (B) 138, ed. Cannan 99, colliers and salters are cited as examples of slave labour in modern times 'in our own country' and ED 5.6 also refers to 'those who work in the coal and salt works of Scotland'. In LJ (A) iii.126 such people are described as the 'only vestiges of slavery which remain amongst us' and their condition, as 'far more easy in many points than . . . antient slaves'. Smith pointed out, however, that the colliers and salters were sold along with their place of work: 'They in this respect resemble the villani or adscripti glebae in Germany, which always go along with the land they cultivate but can not be sold separate. The colliers in the same manner are adscripti operi they are sold allong with the work, but cannot be sold or given away singly.' (LJ (A) iii.127.) See also LJ (A) iii.96, where he refers to 'legall slaves at this time'.

[23] Smith comments on the poor productivity of slave labour at I.viii.41 and IV.ix.47. See also LJ (A) iii.112, ED 5.6, and LJ (B) 138, 290, 299, ed. Cannan 99, 225, 231. He also remarked in LJ (A) iii.131 that slavery was detrimental to population growth. For alternative views, though in a different context, see A. H. Conrad and J. R. Meyer, *Studies in Econometric History* (London, 1965), 43–114.

and not by any interest of his own. In antient Italy, how much the cultivation of corn degenerated, how unprofitable it became to the master when it fell under the management of slaves, is remarked by both Pliny and Columella.[24] In the time of Aristotle it had not been much better in antient Greece. Speaking of the ideal republick described in the [89] laws of Plato, to maintain five thousand idle men (the number of warriors supposed necessary for its defence) together with their women and servants, would require, he says, a territory of boundless extent and fertility, like the plains of Babylon.[25]

10   The pride of man makes him love to domineer, and nothing mortifies him so much as to be obliged to condescend to persuade his inferiors.[26] Wherever the law allows it, and the nature of the work can afford it, therefore, he will generally prefer the service of slaves to that of freemen. The planting of sugar and tobacco can afford the expence of slave-cultivation.[27] The raising of corn, it seems, in the present times, cannot. In the English colonies, of which the principal produce is corn, the far greater part of the work is done by freemen. The late resolution of the Quakers in Pennsylvania to set at liberty all their negro slaves, may satisfy us that their number cannot be very great. Had they made any considerable part of their property, such a resolution could never have been agreed to.[28] In our sugar

[24] 'And we forsooth are surprised that we do not get the same profits from the labour of slave-gangs as used to be obtained from that of generals.' (Pliny, *Natural History*, XVIII. iv, translated by H. Rackham in Loeb Classical Library (1950), v.203. Columella, *De Re Rustica*, i (preface), 11–12, translated by H. B. Ash in Loeb Classical Library (1941), i.9–11.)

[25] 'All the discourses of Socrates are masterly, noble, new, and inquisitive; but that they are all true it may probably be too much to say. For now with respect to the number just spoken of, it must be acknowledged that he would want the country of Babylonia for them, or some one like it, of an immeasurable extent, to support five thousand idle persons, besides a much greater number of women and children.' (Aristotle, *Politics*, 1265a, translated by William Ellis in Everyman edn. (1912), 38–9.)

[26] LJ (B) 134, ed. Cannan 96, comments: 'It is to be observed that slavery takes place in all societies at their beginning, and proceeds from that tyranic disposition which may almost be said to be natural to mankind.' In LJ (A) i.54 Smith refers to the tyranny of the feudal government and the inclination which men have to extort all they can from their inferiors. In a similar vein he refers to man's love of domination and authority in discussing slavery in LJ (A) iii.114 and again at 130. Mandeville also refers to 'the love of Dominion and that usurping Temper all Mankind are born with' (*The Fable of the Bees*, pt. i.319, ed. Kaye, i.281).

[27] In ED 5.6 Smith argued that the colonies dealing in sugar and tobacco could only afford slave labour because of the 'exhorbitancy of their profites' arising from the monopoly of the two trades. He added that: 'the planters in the more northern colonies, cultivating chiefly wheat and Indian corn, by which they can expect no such exhorbitant returns, find it not for their interest to employ many slaves, and yet Pennsilvania, the Jerseys and some of the Provinces of New England are much richer and more populous than Virginia, notwithstanding that tobacco is, by its ordinary high price a more profitable cultivation.' The high profits of sugar cultivation are also mentioned in LJ (B) 291, ed. Cannan 225; See below, IV.vii.b.54, regarding the use of slave labour in the colonies.

[28] In commenting on the use of slaves in modern times John Millar also referred to Russia, Poland, Hungary, etc., together with the American colonies. He went on to note

colonies, on the contrary, the whole work is done by slaves, and in our tobacco colonies a very great part of it. The profits of a sugar-plantation in any of our West Indian colonies are generally much greater than those of any other cultivation that is known either in Europe or America: And the profits of a tobacco plantation, though inferior to those of sugar, are superior to those of corn, as has already been observed.[29] Both can afford the ex-[90]pence of slave-cultivation, but sugar can afford it still better than tobacco. The number of negroes accordingly is much greater, in proportion to that of whites, in our sugar than in our tobacco colonies.

11   To the slave cultivators of antient times, gradually succeeded a species of farmers known at present in France by the name of Metayers. They are called in Latin, Coloni Partiarii.[30] They have been so long in disuse in England that at present I know no English name for them. The proprietor furnished them with the seed, cattle, and instruments of husbandry, the whole stock, in short, necessary for cultivating the farm. The produce was divided equally between the proprietor and the farmer, after setting aside what was judged necessary for keeping up the stock, which was restored to the proprietor when the farmer either quitted, or was turned out of the farm.[31]

12   Land occupied by such tenants is properly cultivated at the expence of the proprietor, as much as that occupied by slaves. There is, however, one very essential difference between them. Such tenants, being freemen, are capable of acquiring property, and having a certain proportion of the produce of the land, they have a plain interest that the whole produce should be as great as possible, in order that their own proportion may be so. A slave, on the contrary, who can acquire nothing but his maintenance, consults his own ease by making the land produce as little as possible over and above that [91] maintenance. It is probable that it was partly upon account of this advantage, and partly upon account of the encroachments which the sovereign, always jealous of the great lords, gradually encouraged their villains to make upon their authority, and which seem at last to have been such as rendered this species of servitude altogether inconvenient, that tenure in villanage gradually wore out through the greater part of Europe. The time and manner, however, in which so important a revolution was brought about, is one of the most obscure points in modern history.

that: 'The Quakers of Pennsylvania, are the first body of men in those countries, who have discovered any scruples upon that account, and who seem to have thought that the abolition of this practice is a duty they owe to religion and humanity.' (*The Origin of the Distinction of Ranks* (1771), VI.iii, ed. W. C. Lehmann (Cambridge 1960), 311.)

[29] See above, I.xi.b.32.

[30] LJ (A) ii.26, states that 'The lands in Italy were . . . cultivated either by servi, slaves which were the property of the landlord, or by coloni, which were in much the same condition as the holders by steel-bow.' The metayer system is discussed in ED 5.7. In LJ (B) 292, ed. Cannan 226, the French system is described as 'steel-bow'.

[31] Smith examines the causes of change in the form of leases in III.iv.

The church of Rome claims great merit in it; and it is certain that so early as the twelfth century, Alexander III. published a bull for the general emancipation of slaves. It seems, however, to have been rather a pious exhortation, than a law to which exact obedience was required from the faithful.³² Slavery continued to take place almost universally for several centuries afterwards, till it was gradually abolished by the joint operation of the two interests above mentioned, that of the proprietor on the one hand, and that of the sovereign on the other.³³ A villain enfranchised, and at the same time allowed to continue in possession of the land, having no stock of his own, could cultivate it only by means of what the landlord advanced to him, and must, therefore, have been what the French call a Metayer.

13   It could never, however, be the interest even of this last species of cultivators to lay out, in the further improvement of the land, any part of the [92] little stock which they might save from their own share of the produce, because the lord, who laid out nothing, was to get one-half of whatever it produced. The tithe, which is but a tenth of the produce, is found to be a very great hindrance to improvement.³⁴ A tax, therefore, which amounted to one half, must have been an effectual bar to it. It might be the interest of a metayer to make the land produce as much as could be brought out of it by means of the stock furnished by the proprietor; but it could never be

---

³² LJ (A) iii.127–8 comments that 'we are not to imagine the temper of the Christian religion is necessarily contrary to slavery, . . . There are . . . many Christian countries where slavery is tollerated at this time.' See above, III.ii.8. In LJ (B) 141–2, ed. Cannan 101–2, it was suggested that 'Another cause of the abolition of slavery was the influence of the clergy, but by no means the spirit of Christianity, for our planters are all Christians'. Smith here cites Pope Innocent III, rather than Alexander III, as having given support to the emancipation of slaves.

³³ It is argued in LJ (A) iii.118–19 that the emancipation of slaves reflected the political interest of both King and Clergy, both of whom wished to reduce the power of the great barons. The clergy 'therefore promoted greatly the emancipation of villains, and discouraged as much as lay in their power the authority of the great men over them. The king's interest tended also to promote the same thing . . . The king's courts, on this account, were very favourable to all claims of the villains, and on every occasion endeavoured to lessen the authority of the landlord over them.' Smith added at iii.121–2 that the power of the Church, taken in conjunction with that of the King, helped to set the slaves at liberty, while commenting that 'it was absolutely necessary' that the authority of both should be great. Where this condition was satisfied, he argued, slavery had been successfully eliminated—for example, in Scotland, England, France, and Spain. Where it was not, as in Poland, Germany, Bohemia, and Russia, slavery continued to survive (see above, III.iii.8). With regard to Russia Smith remarked that: 'tho the Tsars of Muscovy have very great power, yet slavery is still in use, as the authority of the Greek Church tho' very considerable, has never been nearly so great as that of the Romish Church was in the other countries of Europe; as we see from the accounts of that country even before the time of Peter the Great.' (LJ (A) iii.122.) Smith comments on the political problems presented by a powerful Church in this period at V.i.g.24.

³⁴ Tithes are stated to be inimical to improvement at V.ii.d.3. The disincentive effects here described are also cited as an objection to a variable land tax at V.ii.c.18; see also V.ii.d.2.

his interest to mix any part of his own with it. In France, where five parts out of six of the whole kingdom are said to be still occupied by this species of cultivators,[35] the proprietors complain that their metayers take every opportunity of employing the masters cattle rather in carriage than in cultivation; because in the one case they get the whole profits to themselves, in the other they share them with their landlord. This species of tenants still subsists in some parts of Scotland. They are called steel-bow tenants.[36] Those antient English tenants, who are said by Chief Baron Gilbert[37] and Doctor Blackstone[38] to have been rather bailiffs of the landlord than farmers properly so called, were probably of the same kind.

14   To this species of tenancy succeeded, though by very slow degrees, farmers properly so called, who cultivated the land with their own stock, paying a rent certain to the landlord.[39] When such farmers have a lease for a term of years, they may sometimes find it for their interest to [93] lay out

[35] This figure is also cited in ED 5.7, LJ (A) ii.25. Quesnay remarks: 'Les terres sont communément cultivées par des *fermiers* avec des chevaux, ou par des métayers avec des bœufs.' Quesnay calculated that the lands of France were cultivated by these two methods in the ratio of 6 to 30. (*Œuvres Economiques et Philosophiques*, ed. A. Oncken (Paris, 1888), 160 and 171.) See also *Encyclopédie*, vi.527f. Turgot describes the metayer system in France in section XXV of the *Reflections* before going on to consider what Smith later describes as 'farmers properly so called'. Turgot added that: 'In Picardy, Normandy, the environs of Paris, and in the majority of the Provinces of the North of France, the land is cultivated by farmers. In the Provinces of the South they are cultivated by *Metayers*; therefore the Provinces of the North of France are incomparably more wealthy and better cultivated than those of the South.' See also LXIV.

[36] Steelbow tenants are discussed in ED 5.7 and LJ (B) 140, 174, 292, ed. Cannan 100–1, 129, 226 where it is stated that they still exist in Scotland. In LJ (A) ii.25 this form of let is described as 'one of the worst that have ever been in use' and in LJ (A) iii.123 the method is said to be 'the worst of any by free tenants . . . yet greatly preferable to that by slaves'.

[37] 'A lease is a covenant real, that binds the possession of lands into whose hands soever afterwards they come, if the lands be not evicted by a superior title; but the termor has not the freehold in him, but holds possession, as bailiff of the freeholder, *nomine alieno*, by virtue of the obligation of the covenant.' (G. Gilbert, *A Treatise of Tenures* (London, 1757), 34.)

[38] 'These estates [let for years] were originally granted to mere farmers or husbandmen, who every year rendered some equivalent in money, provisions, or other rent, to the lessors or landlords; but, in order to encourage them to manure and cultivate the ground, they had a permanent interest granted them, not determinable at the will of the lord. And yet their possession was esteemed of so little consequence, that they were rather considered as the bailiffs or servants of the lord, who were to receive and account for the profits at a settled price, than as having any property of their own.' (W. Blackstone, *Commentaries on the Laws of England* (Oxford, 1765–9), ii.141–2.)

[39] Cf. LJ (A) iii.124–5: 'When these farmers by steel-bow had by hard labour and great parsimony got together in 10 or 20 years as much as would enable them to stock a farm, they would then make an offer to their master that they should stock the farm themselves and maintain this stock, and instead of his having the uncertain produce of the harvest, which might vary with the season, he should have a yearly gratuity, on condition that he should not be removed at pleasure, but should hold his farm for a term of years. This proposall would not only be agreable to the farmer but also to the landlord.' The term 'farmers properly so called' is used in ED 5.8. In LJ (B) 292, ed. Cannan 226, they are simply described as 'tenants, such as we have at present'.

part of their capital in the further improvement of the farm; because they may sometimes expect to recover it, with a large profit, before the expiration of the lease.[40] The possession even of such farmers, however, was long extremely precarious, and still is so in many parts of Europe.[41] They could before the expiration of their term be legally outed of their lease, by a new purchaser; in England, even by the fictitious action of a common recovery. If they were turned out illegally by the violence of their master, the action by which they obtained redress was extremely imperfect. It did not always re-instate them in the possession of the land, but gave them damages which never amounted to the real loss. Even in England, the country perhaps of Europe where the yeomanry has always been most respected, it was not till about the 14th of Henry the VIIth that the action of ejectment was invented,[42] by which the tenant recovers, not damages only but possession, and in which his claim is not necessarily concluded by the uncertain decision of a single assize. This action has been found so effectual a remedy that, in the modern practice, when the landlord has occasion to sue for the possession of the land, he seldom makes use of the actions which properly belong to him as landlord, the writ of right or the writ of entry, but sues in the name of his tenant, by the writ of ejectment. In England, therefore, the security of the tenant is equal to that of the proprietor. In England besides a lease for life of forty shillings a year value is a [94] freehold, and entitles the lessee to vote for a member of parliament; and as a great part of the yeomanry have freeholds of this kind, the whole order becomes respectable to their landlords on account of the political consideration which this gives them.[43] There is, I believe, nowhere in Europe, except in England, any instance of the tenant building upon the land of which he had no lease, and trusting that the honour of his landlord would take no advantage of so important an improvement. Those laws and customs so favourable to the yeomanry, have perhaps contributed more to the present grandeur of England than all their boasted regulations of commerce taken together.[44]

15   The law which secures the longest leases against successors of every kind

[40] LJ (A) i.167 comments: 'Farms let out for long leases . . . are those which tend most to the improvement of the country. Short ones, as leases at pleasure, can never induce the tenant to improve, as what he lays out will not be on his own account, but on an other's.'
[41] For a modern interpretation see G. E. Mingay, *English Landed Society in the Eighteenth Century* (London, 1963), 167–71.
[42] This writ is also mentioned at V.i.b.21 and discussed in ED 5.8, LJ (B) 293, ed. Cannan 227.
[43] Smith makes a similar point in LJ (B) 294, ed. Cannan 227–8. In ED 5.8 he refers to 'the advantage which agriculture derives in England from the law which gives certain lease holders a right of voting for Members of Parliament, which thereby establishes a mutual dependance between the landlord and the tenant, and makes the former, if he has any regard to his interest in the county, very cautious of attempting to raise his rents, or of demanding any other oppressive exactions of the latter.'
[44] Smith comments on the security of the English yeomanry at III.iv.20.

is, so far as I know, peculiar to Great Britain. It was introduced into Scotland so early as 1449, by a law of James the IId.[45] Its beneficial influence, however, has been much obstructed by entails; the heirs of entail being generally restrained from letting leases for any long term of years, frequently for more than one year. A late act of parliament has,[46] in this respect, somewhat slackened their fetters, though they are still by much too strait. In Scotland, besides, as no leasehold gives a vote for a member of parliament, the yeomanry are upon this account less respectable to their landlords than in England.[47]

16   In other parts of Europe, after it was found convenient to secure tenants both against heirs and purchasers, the term of their security was [95] still limited to a very short period; in France, for example, to nine years from the commencement of the lease. It has in that country, indeed, been lately extended to twenty-seven,[48] a period still too short to encourage the tenant to make the most important improvements. The proprietors of land were antiently the legislators of every part of Europe. The laws relating to land, therefore, were all calculated for what they supposed the interest of the proprietor. It was for his interest, they had imagined, that no lease granted by any of his predecessors should hinder him from enjoying, during a long term of years, the full value of his land. Avarice and injustice are always short-sighted, and they did not foresee how much this regulation must obstruct improvement, and thereby hurt in the long-run the real interest of the landlord.

17   The farmers too, besides paying the rent, were antiently, it was supposed, bound to perform a great number of services to the landlord, which were seldom either specified in the lease, or regulated by any precise rule, but by the use and wont of the manor or barony. These services, therefore, being almost entirely arbitrary, subjected the tenant to many vexations. In Scotland the abolition of all services, not precisely stipulated in the lease,[49] has in the course of a few years very much altered for the better the condition of the yeomanry of that country.

18   The public services to which the yeomanry were bound, were not less arbitrary than the private ones. To make and maintain the high [96] roads,[50] a servitude which still subsists,[51] I believe, every where, though with different degrees of oppression in different countries, was not the only one.

---

[45] *Acts of the Parliament of Scotland*, ii.35 (1449).

[46] 10 George III, c.51 (1770). The longer leases were granted on condition that the tenant effected improvements.

[47] Though only freeholders could vote in Scotland, a landowner could use his estate for electoral purposes by means of trust dispositions. Scottish politics were notoriously corrupt in the eighteenth century, perhaps no more so than in the general election of 1768. C. E. Adam (ed.), *View of the Political State of Scotland in 1788* (Edinburgh, 1887). See also below, III.iv.20.

[48] See below, IV.ix.38.   [49] 20 George II, c.50 (1746).   [50] See below, V.i.d.19.

[51] Most of the provisions for the maintenance of roads in Scotland, including 'statute

When the king's troops, when his household or his officers of any kind passed through any part of the country, the yeomanry were bound to provide them with horses, carriages, and provisions, at a price regulated by the purveyor. Great Britain is, I believe, the only monarchy in Europe where the oppression of purveyance has been entirely abolished. It still subsists in France and Germany.

19   The publick taxes to which they were subject were as irregular and oppressive as the services. The antient lords, though extremely unwilling to grant themselves any pecuniary aid to their sovereign, easily allowed him to tallage,[52] as they called it, their tenants, and had not knowledge enough to foresee how much this must in the end affect their own revenue.[53] The taille, as it still subsists in France, may serve as an example of those antient tallages. It is a tax upon the supposed profits of the farmer, which they estimate by the stock that he has upon the farm. It is his interest, therefore, to appear to have as little as possible, and consequently to employ as little as possible in its cultivation, and none in its improvement. Should any stock happen to accumulate in the hands of a French farmer, the taille is almost equal to a prohibition of its ever being employed upon the land.[54] This tax besides is supposed to dishonour whoever is subject to it, and to degrade him below, not only the rank of [97] a gentleman, but that of a burgher, and whoever rents the lands of another becomes subject to it. No gentleman, nor even any burgher ᶜwhoᶜ has stock, will submit to this degradation. This tax, therefore, not only hinders the stock which accumulates upon the land from being employed in its improvement, but drives away all other stock from it. The antient tenths and fifteenths,[55] so

ᶜ⁻ᶜ that *r*

---

labour' were reiterated by 5 George I, c.30 (1718). Statute labour was commuted for a money payment and the turnpike acts enabled additional funds to be obtained through tolls. The first Scottish turnpike act was for the county of Edinburgh in 1713, but improvements were significant only in the last quarter of the eighteenth century.

[52] See below, V.ii.g.6 and V.ii.k.20.

[53] Cf. LJ (B) 294, ed. Cannan 227: 'Another embarrassment was that the feudal lords sometimes allowed the king to levy subsidies from their tenants, which greatly discouraged their industry.' ED 5.8 also refers to the 'arbitrary and exorbitant tallages' to which tenants were liable.

[54] The taille is described more extensively below, V.ii.g.5 f.

[55] 'Subsidies and fifteenths are frequently mentioned by historians; but neither the amount of these taxes, nor the method of imposing them have been well explained. It appears, that the fifteenths formerly corresponded to the name, and were that proportionable part of the moveables. But a valuation being made, during the reign of Edward III that valuation was always adhered to, and each town payed unalterably a particular sum, which they themselves assessed upon the inhabitants. The same tax in corporate towns was called a tenth; probably, because there it was, at first, a tenth of the moveables. The whole amount of a tenth and fifteenth thro' the kingdom, or a fifteenth, as it is often more concisely called, was about 29,000 pound.' (Hume, *History of England* (1778), vi.174.) See also R. Brady, *An Historical Treatise of Cities and Burghs or Boroughs* (London, 1711), 39.

usual in England in former times, seem, so far as they affected the land, to have been taxes of the same nature with the taille.

20   Under all these discouragements, little improvement could be expected from the occupiers of land. That order of people, with all the liberty and security which law can give, must always improve under great disadvantages. The farmer compared with the proprietor, is as a merchant who trades with borrowed money compared with one who trades with his own. The stock of both may improve, but that of the one, with only equal good conduct, must always improve more slowly than that of the other, on account of the large share of the profits which is consumed by the interest of the loan. The lands cultivated by the farmer must, in the same manner, with only equal good conduct, be improved more slowly than those cultivated by the proprietor; on account of the large share of the produce which is consumed in the rent,[56] and which, had the farmer been proprietor, he might have employed in the further improvement of the land.[57] The station of a farmer besides is, from the nature of things, inferior to that of a pro-[98]prietor. Through the greater part of Europe the yeomanry are regarded as an inferior rank of people, even to the better sort of tradesmen and mechanicks, and in all parts of Europe to the great merchants and master manufacturers. It can seldom happen, therefore, that a man of any considerable stock should quit the superior, in order to place himself in an inferior station. Even in the present state of Europe, therefore, little stock is likely to go from any other profession to the improvement of land in the way of farming. More does perhaps in Great Britain than in any other country, though even there the great stocks which are, in some places, employed in farming, have generally been acquired by farming, the trade, perhaps, in which of all others stock is commonly acquired most slowly. After small proprietors, however, rich and great farmers are, in every country, the principal improvers. There are more such perhaps in England than in any other European monarchy. In the republican governments of Holland and of Berne in Switzerland, the farmers are said to be not inferior to those of England.[58]

---

[56] See below, IV.vii.b.2 where Smith comments on the absence of rent payments in the American colonies.

[57] A similar point is made in LJ (B) 291, ed. Cannan 226.

[58] After discussing the agriculture of Holland and Berne, Harte continues: 'That republics are better calculated than monarchies, for the advancement of agriculture, is partly true; for most republics (from natural reasons, rather than any strange concurrence of circumstances) are generally situated in a neglected barren soil: And there it is that art and industry make the most shining improvements in husbandry. Add to this, that the common-wealth we are now speaking of, and others of Switzerland in a lesser proportion, are living proofs, that there is, in such sorts of government, something analagous to the advancement of agriculture. The inhabitants are free from ambition (at least for a considerable time after the first establishment of their community;) Liberty gives them scope to exercise their industry, and equality excites emulation: For suddenly acquired fortunes out-strip, over-shade, and starve the lesser ones; whilst luxury keeps always in proportion

21 The antient policy of Europe was, over and above all this, unfavourable to the improvement and cultivation of land, whether carried on by the proprietor or by the farmer; first, by the general prohibition of the exportation of corn without a special licence, which seems to have been a very universal regulation;[59] and secondly, by the restraints which were laid upon the inland commerce, not only of corn but of almost every [99] other part of the produce of the farm, by the absurd laws against engrossers, regrators, and forestallers, and by the privileges of fairs and markets.[60] It has already been observed in what manner the prohibition of the exportation of corn, together with some encouragement given to the importation of foreign corn, obstructed the cultivation of antient Italy, naturally the most fertile country in Europe, and at that time the seat of the greatest empire in the world.[61] To what degree such restraints upon the inland commerce of this commodity, joined to the general prohibition of exportation, must have discouraged the cultivation of countries less fertile, and less favourably circumstanced, it is not perhaps very easy to imagine.

to the inequality of fortunes—Besides, small shares of property are better distinguished, secured, and bounded: And, at the same time, more capable of admitting a correct and accurate husbandry.' (*Essays on Husbandry* (London, 1764), 79.)

[59] The prohibition on the export of corn in ancient times is mentioned in ED 5.10 and in LJ (B) 296–7, ed. Cannan 229.

[60] See IV.v.b.10, 26 and generally IV.v.b.

[61] See above, I.xi.b.12. The distribution of foreign corn is also mentioned at V.iii.61.

CHAPTER III

Of the Rise and Progress of Cities and Towns, after the Fall of the Roman Empire

1 THE inhabitants of cities and towns were, after the fall of the Roman empire, not more favoured than those of the country. They consisted, indeed, of a very different order of people from the first inhabitants of the antient republicks of Greece and Italy. These last were composed chiefly of the proprietors of lands, among whom the publick territory was originally divided, and who found it convenient to build [100] their houses in the neighbourhood of one another, and to surround them with a wall, for the sake of common defence.¹ After the fall of the Roman empire, on the contrary, the proprietors of land seem generally to have lived in fortified castles on their own estates, and in the midst of their own tenants and dependants. The towns were chiefly inhabited by tradesmen and mechanicks, who seem in those days to have been of servile, or very nearly of servile condition. The privileges which we find granted by antient charters to the inhabitants of some of the principal towns in Europe, sufficiently shew what they were before those grants.² The people to whom it is granted as a privilege, that they might give away their own daughters in marriage without the consent of their lord, that upon their death their own children, and not their lord, should succeed to their goods, and that they might dispose of their own effects by will, must, before those grants, have been either altogether, or very nearly in the same state of villanage with the occupiers of land in the country.

2 They seem, indeed, to have been a very poor, mean sett of people, who used to travel about with their goods from place to place, and from fair to fair, like the hawkers and pedlars of the present times.³ In all the different countries of Europe then, in the same manner as in several of the Tartar governments of Asia at present, taxes used to be levied upon the persons and goods of travellers, when they passed through certain manors, when they went over certain bridges, when [101] they carried about their goods from place to place in a fair, when they erected in it a booth or stall to sell them in. These different taxes were known in England by the names of passage,

---

¹ Smith considers the origins of cities in ancient Greece in LJ (B) 32–3, ed. Cannan 23.
² In LJ (A) i.112, Smith comments on the servile condition of those living on the land and adds: 'It is . . . certain, tho' not equally known, that the burghers and traders in towns, tho' they might have some greater liberties, were also in a state of villainage. This is evident from the charters granted them in the earliest times . . .' Smith then went on to make similar points to those cited in the text, with regard to the rights of marriage, succession, etc.
³ Smith refers to taxes on hawkers and pedlars at V.ii.g.2.

pontage, lastage, and stallage.[4] Sometimes the king, sometimes a great lord, who had, it seems, upon some occasions, authority to do this, would grant to particular traders, to such particularly as lived in their own demesnes, a general exemption from such taxes. Such traders, though in other respects of servile, or very nearly of servile condition, were upon this account called Free-traders.[5] They in return usually paid to their protector a sort of annual poll-tax. In those days protection was seldom granted without a valuable consideration, and this tax might, perhaps, be considered as compensation for what their patrons might lose by their exemption from other taxes. At first, both those poll-taxes and those exemptions seem to have been altogether personal, and to have affected only particular individuals, during either their lives, or the pleasure of their protectors. In the very imperfect accounts which have been published from Domesday-book, of several of the towns of England, mention is frequently made, sometimes of the tax which particular burghers paid, each of them, either to the king, or to some other great lord, for this sort of protection;[6] and sometimes of the general amount only of all those taxes*.

[a]* See Brady's historical treatise of Cities and Burroughs, p. 3, &c.[a] [For example: '. . . the Kings of England kept this Burg [Yarmouth] in their own Hands, and received by their Officers the Profits of the Port, until the time of King John, who in the 9th year of his Reign Granted the Burg in Fee-Farm to the Burgesses for ever, at the Rent of Fifty Five Pounds by the Year to be paid by the Provost or Bayliff of Yarmouth, and Granted they should yearly chuse a Bayliff amongst themselves, fit both to serve him, and themselves.' After a number of similar instances from Domesday Brady continued, 'By these instances we find the Burgesses or Tradesmen in great Towns, had in those times their Patrons under whose Protection they Traded, and paid an acknowledgement therefor, or else were in a more Servile Condition, as being in Dominio Regis vel aliorum, altogether under the power of the King, or other Lords, and it seems to me that then they Traded not, as being in any Merchant-Gild, Society and Community, but meerly under the Liberty and Protection given them by their Lords and Patrons, who probably might have Power from the King to Licence such a number in this or that Port, or Trading Town . . .' (R. Brady, *Cities and Boroughs*, 3 and 16.)

[a-a] 2–6

[4] Duties of passage are considered below, V.ii.k.56.

[5] See below, V.ii.k.20, where Smith comments on the position of merchants at this period.

[6] Cf. Hume (*History of England* (1778), i.205–6): 'we find, by the extracts which Dr. Brady has given us from Domesday, that almost all the inhabitants even of towns, had placed themselves under the clientship of some particular nobleman, whose patronage they purchased by annual payments, and whom they were obliged to consider as their sovereign, more than the king himself, or even the legislature.' The Domesday Book is also cited at V.ii.c.21 and LJ (B) 301, ed. Cannan 232–3. In LJ (A) iv.143 it is stated that at the time of William the Conqueror, towns such as York were very small:

The lawless and disorderly state of the country rendered communication dangerous, and besides there was little demand for any of the produce of the mechanick. There were therefore but few of them in the country and very small towns. The tradesman or merchant in a country in that state would be altogether helpless. They were generally slaves of some lord, or if they were poor freemen they became dependents either on the king or on some great lord, according as their lands lay most contiguous and were best

3   [102] But how servile soever may have been originally the condition of the inhabitants of ᵇtheᵇ towns, it appears evidently, that they arrived at liberty and independency much earlier than the occupiers of land in the country. That part of the king's revenue which arose from such poll-taxes in any particular town, used commonly to be lett in farm, during a term of years for a rent certain, sometimes to the sheriff of the county, and sometimes to other persons. The burghers themselves frequently got credit enough to be admitted to farm the revenues of this sort which arose out of their own town, they becoming jointly and severally answerable for the whole rent*. To lett a farm in this manner was quite agreeable to the usual œconomy of, I believe, the sovereigns of all the different countries of Europe;[7] who used

ᶜ* See Madox Firma Burgi, p. 18, also History of the Exchequer, chap. 10. Sect. v. p. 223, first edition.ᶜ ['The yearly profit which the King made of his Cities Towns or Burghs was commonly raised and paid to Him in a sundry manner . . . sometimes the King was pleased to demise or let his Town to the Townsmen thereof at Ferm, that is to say, either in Fee-ferm, or at Ferm for Years.' But Madox does not suggest the development came necessarily from the farming of the poll tax. 'The yearly Ferme of Towns arose out of certain locata or demised things that yielded Issues or profit. Insomuch that when a Town was committed to a Sherif Fermer or *Custos*, such Fermer or *Custos* well knew how to raise the Ferme out of the ordinary issues of the Towns, with an overplus of profit to himself.' (T. Madox, *Firma Burgi* 18 and 251.) 'From the reign of K. William I, down to the succeeding times, the King . . . used to let-out the several Counties of England upon a yearly Ferm or Rent concerted between the Crown and the Fermer, or else to commit them to Custody.' (Madox, *The History and Antiquities of the Exchequer* (London, 1711), 223.) In Letter 115 addressed to Lord Hailes, dated 15 January 1769 Smith also described Madox's work as the *History of the Exchequer*.]

ᵇ⁻ᵇ 2–6   ᶜ⁻ᶜ 2–6

able to afford them protection and liberty. By this means they were very little better than villains or slaves of these great men.

In LJ (B) 302, ed. Cannan 233, Smith commented on the impediment to economic progress represented by the 'mean and despicable idea' which men had of merchants at this time. He added:

when merchants were so despicable and laid under so great taxations for liberty of trade, they could never amass that degree of stock which is necessary for making the division of labour and improving manufactures.
    The only persons in those days who made any money by trade were the Jews, who, as they were considered as vagabonds, had no liberty of purchasing lands, and had no other way to dispose of themselves but by becoming mechanics or merchants. Their character could not be spoiled by the merchandize, because they could not be more odious than their religion made them. Even they were grievously oppressed and consequently the progress of opulence was greatly retarded.

See below, V.iii.1 where Smith comments that at one time to trade was 'disgraceful to a gentleman' and the lending of money at interest even more so. Very similar ideas with regard to the mean condition of merchants and the persecution of the Jews are stated by Montesquieu, *Esprit*, XXI.xx, in a section entitled 'How Commerce broke through the Barbarism of Europe'.
    [7] 'Then the King if he pleased demised his Towns to the Townsmen or others, in like manner as he demised any of his Manors to the Tenants thereof.' (T. Madox, *Firma Burgi*, 21.) Wotton-under-Edge in Gloucestershire is cited as an example.

frequently to lett whole manors to all the tenants of those manors, they becoming jointly and severally answerable for the whole rent; but in return being allowed to collect it in their own way, and to pay it into the king's exchequer by the hands of their own bailiff, and being thus altogether freed from the insolence of the king's officers; a circumstance in those days regarded as of the greatest importance.[8]

4   At first, the farm of the town was probably lett to the burghers, in the same manner as it had been to other farmers, for a term of years only. In process of time, however, it seems to [103] have become the general practice to grant it to them in fee, that is for ever, reserving a rent certain never afterwards to be augmented. The payment having thus become perpetual, the exemptions, in return for which it was made, naturally became perpetual too. Those exemptions, therefore, ceased to be personal, and could not afterwards be considered as belonging to individuals as individuals, but as burghers of a particular burgh, which, upon this account, was called a Free-burgh, for the same reason that they had been called Free-burghers or Free-traders.[9]

5   Along with this grant, the important privileges above mentioned, that they might give away their own daughters in marriage, that their children should succeed to them, and that they might dispose of their own effects by will, were generally bestowed upon the burghers of the town to whom it was given. Whether such privileges had before been usually granted along with the freedom of trade, to particular burghers, as individuals, I know not. I reckon it not improbable that they were, though I cannot produce any direct evidence of it. But however this may have been, the principal attributes of villanage and slavery being thus taken away from them, they now, at least, became really free in our present sense of the word Freedom.

6   Nor was this all. They were generally at the same time erected into a commonality or corporation,[10] with the privilege of having magistrates and

[8] In LJ (A) iv.144 Smith explained the origins of the cities as part of a general drive to reduce the power of the nobles. He went on to remark that the units thus created: 'were afterwards formed into corporations holding in capite of the king, having a jurisdiction and territory for which they paid a certain rent. At first this was taken up from every individual, but afterwards the community farmed it, which made the burthen much easier than when it was exacted without distinction by the king's officers.' See also LJ (A) iv.151-2, and LJ (B) 57, ed. Cannan 40.

[9] Brady (*Cities and Boroughs*, 17) explained the development: 'How long in most Burghs, very many Burgesses remained in this *Servile State*, or others in a Middle or Neutral State of between Servitude and Freedom; I cannot say certainly, but do suppose, until our Ancient Norman Kings granted by their Charters, there should be Merchant or Trading-Gilds, Communities and Societies, in Burghs, and gave them Free Liberty of Trade, without paying Toll or Custom anywhere, other than their Fee-Farm-Rent in Lieu of them, where that was Reserved; or to Raise and Multiply such Payments by Incouragement of Trade, which by the Grants of such Liberties did mightily Increase, where the Kings Bayliffs collected them.'

[10] See I.x.c.17.

a town-council of their own, of making [104] bye-laws for their own government, of building walls for their own defence, and of reducing all their inhabitants under a sort of military discipline, by obliging them to watch and ward; that is, as antiently understood, to guard and defend those walls against all attacks and surprises by night as well as by day.[11] In England they were generally exempted from suit to the hundred and county courts; and all such pleas as should arise among them, the pleas of the crown excepted, were left to the decision of their own magistrates. In other countries much greater and more extensive jurisdictions were frequently granted to them*.

7   It might, probably, be necessary to grant to such towns as were admitted to farm their own revenues, some sort of compulsive jurisdiction to oblige their own citizens to make payment. In those disorderly times it might have been extremely inconvenient to have left them to seek this sort of justice from any other tribunal. But it must seem extraordinary that the sovereigns of all the different countries of Europe, should have exchanged in this manner for a rent certain, never more to be augmented, that branch of their revenue, which was, perhaps, of all others the most likely to be improved by the natural course of things, without either expence or attention of their own: and that they should, be-[105]sides, have in this manner voluntarily erected a sort of independent republicks in the heart of their own dominions.[12]

8   In order to understand this, it must be remembered, that in those days the sovereign of perhaps no country in Europe, was able to protect, through the whole extent of his dominions, the weaker part of his subjects from the oppression of the great lords.[13] Those whom the law could not protect, and who were not strong enough to defend themselves, were obliged either to have recourse to the protection of some great lord, and in order to obtain it to become either his slaves or vassals; or to enter into a league of mutual defence for the common protection of one another. The inhabitants of cities and burghs, considered as single individuals, had no power to defend themselves: but by entering into a league of mutual

---

d* See Madox Firma Burgi: See also Pfeffel in the remarkable events under Frederick II. and his successors of the house of Suabia.d [The heading 'evénements remarquables sous Frédéric II' is used by Pfeffel for several similar chapters. C. F. Pfeffel von Kriegelstein, *Nouvel Abrégé chronologique de l'histoire et du droit publique d'Allemagne* (Paris, 1766), i.284–307.]

---

d–d 2–6

---

11 In LJ (A) ii.39 Smith found the origins of corporations in the need to ensure that the inhabitants of cities had the means of defending themselves, while pointing out that they also gave a degree of security to individuals working in particular trades, encouraging by this means the division of labour. See above I.ii.1.

12 Hume also noted that 'The government of cities . . ., even under absolute monarchies, is commonly republican.' (*History of England* (1778), vi.295.)

13 This point is elaborated in the following chapter, III.iv. especially 8 and 9.

defence with their neighbours, they were capable of making no contemptible resistance. The lords despised the burghers, whom they considered not only as of a different order, but as a parcel of emancipated slaves, almost of a different species from themselves.[14] The wealth of the burghers never failed to provoke their envy and indignation, and they plundered them upon every occasion without mercy or remorse. The burghers naturally hated and feared the lords. The king hated and feared them too; but though perhaps he might despise, he had no reason either to hate or fear the burghers.[15] Mutual interest, therefore, disposed them to support the king, and the king to support [106] them against the lords. They were the enemies of his enemies, and it was his interest to render them as secure and independent of those enemies as he could. By granting them magistrates of their own, the privilege of making bye-laws for their own government, that of building walls for their own defence, and that of reducing all their inhabitants under a sort of military discipline, he gave them all the means of security and independency of the barons which it was in his power to bestow. Without the establishment of some regular government of this kind, without some authority to compel their inhabitants to act according to some certain plan or system, no voluntary league of mutual defence could either have afforded them any permanent security, or have enabled them to give the king any considerable support. By granting them the farm of their town in fee, he took away from those whom he wished to have for his friends, and, if one may say so, for his allies, all ground of jealousy and suspicion that he was ever afterwards to oppress them, either by raising the farm rent of their town, or by granting it to some other farmer.

9   The princes who lived upon the worst terms with their barons, seem accordingly to have been the most liberal in grants of this kind to their burghs. King John of England,[16] for example, appears to have been a most munificent benefactor to his towns*. Philip the First of France lost all

---

ᵉ See Madox.*ᵉ* ['King John granted some of his Towns in Normandy, to wit, to Falaise, Danfront, and Caen, that they might have a *Communa* during his pleasure.' (T. Madox, *Firma Burgi*, 35.)]

ᵉ⁻ᵉ 2–6

---

[14] That did not prevent medieval lords from trying to set up 'towns' on their lands. M. W. Beresford, *The New Towns of the Middle Ages: Town Plantations in England, Wales and Gascony* (1967).

[15] The additional problem which was presented by the power of the Church is considered below, V.i.g.17.

[16] The king is identified as John in LJ (A) iii.74. It is also pointed out in LJ (A) iv.154 that the feudal emoluments tended to decline at the very time that the needs of government increased, and that in consequence the reigns most favourable to liberty were 'those of martiall, conquering, military kings. Edward the 1st and Henry the 4th, the two most warlike of the English kings, granted greater immunities to the people than any others.' Two reasons are suggested: first, that such kings became dependent on the people for funds, and, secondly, that 'it soon became a rule with the people that they should grant no subsidies till their requests were first granted'.

authority over his barons. Towards the [107] end of his reign, his son Lewis, known afterwards by the name of Lewis the Fat, consulted, according to Father Daniel,[17] with the bishops of the royal demesnes, concerning the most proper means of restraining the violence of the great lords. Their advice consisted of two different proposals. One was to erect a new order of jurisdiction, by establishing magistrates and a town council in every considerable town of his demesnes. The other was to form a new militia, by making the inhabitants of those towns, under the command of their own magistrates, march out upon proper occasions to the assistance of the king. It is from this period, according to the French antiquarians, that we are to date the institution of the magistrates and councils of cities in France.[18] It was during the unprosperous reigns of the princes of the house of Suabia that the greater part of the free towns of Germany received the first grants of their privileges, and that the famous Hanseatic[19] league first became formidable*.

10   The militia of the cities seems, in those times, not to have been inferior to that of the country, and as they could be more readily assembled upon any sudden occasion, they frequently had the advantage in their disputes with the neighbouring lords. In countries, such as Italy and Switzerland, in which, on account either of their distance from the principal seat of government, of the natural strength of the country [108] itself, or of some other reason, the sovereign came to lose the whole of his authority, the cities generally became independent republicks, and conquered all the nobility in their neighbourhood; obliging them to pull down their castles in the country, and to live, like other peaceable inhabitants, in the city.[20] This is the short history of the republick of Berne, as well as of several other cities in Switzerland. If you except Venice, for of that city the history

ʃ See Pfeffel.ʃ

ʃ-ʃ 2–6

[17] G. Daniel, *Histoire de France* (Amsterdam 1720) was a work which Smith ordered for Glasgow University Library. His Quaestor's accounts are printed in Scott, 178–9.

[18] C. Du Fresne, Sieur du Cange, *Glossarium* (1688) s.v. *Commune* (Paris, 1842 edn., ii.482). Brady, quoting du Fresne, states 'The Kings of France erected these Communities to cheque the Insolencies of their great Vassals, and to protect them from their over-grown Dominion and Extravagant Power over them, that they reputed such Cities and Towns their own, where there were such Communities; and truley, for that the Inhabitants were in a manner Freed from the Dominion of their Lords thereby, and became immediately Subject to their Kings.' (*Cities and Boroughs*, 17.) Hume, citing the same source, held that 'the erecting of these communities was an invention of Lewis the Gross, in order to free the people from slavery under the lords, and to give them protection, by means of certain privileges and a separate jurisdiction.' (*History of England* (1778), ii.118.)

[19] See above, III.iii.7.

[20] Smith comments on Italian, Swiss, and German experience in LJ (A) v.46–50 and LJ (B) 77, ed. Cannan 54.

is somewhat different, it is the history of all the considerable Italian republicks, of which so great a number arose and perished, between the end
of the twelfth and the beginning of the sixteenth century.

11   In countries such as France or England, where the authority of the
sovereign, though frequently very low, never was destroyed altogether, the
cities had no opportunity of becoming entirely independent.[21] They became, however, so considerable that the sovereign could impose no tax
upon them, besides the stated farm-rent of the town, without their own
consent. They were, therefore, called upon to send deputies to the general
assembly of the states of the kingdom, where they might join with the
clergy and the barons in granting, upon urgent occasions, some extraordinary aid to the king. Being generally too more favourable to his power,
their deputies seem, sometimes, to have been employed by him as a counter-
balance *g*in those assemblies*g* to the authority of the great lords *h*. Hence the
origin [109] of the representation of burghs in the states general of all the
great monarchies in Europe.[22]

g–g 2–6
h in those assemblies *1*

---

[21] See above, III.iii.6.
[22] The origins and development of the British House of Commons are considered in
LJ (A) iv.134–57, and rather more briefly in LJ(B) 58–9, ed. Cannan 40–1. Smith argues in
LJ (B) 60–1, ed. Cannan 42, that the initial result of the rising importance of the Commons
was the *absolutist* state, the point being that 'the power of the nobility was diminished, and
that too before the House of Commons had established its authority'. The same point is
made in LJ (A) iv.159–60, with regard to the emergence of absolutism in Scotland and
England, while in addition the examples of France, Spain, and Portugal are cited at pp. 162
and 167. In LJ (A) iv.167–8, it is emphasized that 'In England alone a different government
has been established from the naturall course of things', partly no doubt as a consequence
of her pattern of economic development, but also as a result of factors of a more 'accidental'
kind. For example, Smith cited a number of forces which militated against the preservation
of the absolute power of kings, including:
(1) Ease of defence by sea which minimized the danger of foreign invasion, together with
the political solution to the Scottish problem through union—both of which reduced the
need for a standing army as a potential instrument of oppression.
(2) The need of the King to summon Parliament on any extraordinary contingency,
allied to the dependence of the Crown on the Commons for supplies—a trend which had
been accelerated by the sale of Crown lands by Elizabeth I.
(3) The gradual growth in the significance of the Commons who were eventually enabled
to look upon themselves as in power 'equall or perhaps greater' than the nobles.
(4) The dissipation of the civil list through the 'extravagant and luxurious turn of Charles'
who chose to employ it in the pursuit of his pleasures so that 'he became as necessitous and
dependent on Parliament as any of the preceding monarchs had been'.
(5) The fact that once a standing army had been formed, it became a source of security
rather than of oppression owing to the fact that 'Many of the persons of chief rank and
station in the army have also large estates of their own and are members of the House of
Commons.' LJ (A) iv.168–79 (and see below, V.i.a.41). Similar points are made in LJ (A)
v.1–15 where Bolingbroke's authority is cited with regard to the conduct of Elizabeth,
whose willingness to sell Crown lands was linked with her lack of a direct heir. Smith also
adverts to the role of the Courts as a security for English liberties in LJ (B) 63–4, ed.
Cannan 45–6. See generally, LJ (B) 60–4, ed. Cannan 42–6, and below, V.i.b.25.

12   Order and good government, and along with them the liberty and security of individuals, were, in this manner, established in cities at a time when
the occupiers of land in the country were exposed to every sort of violence.
But men in this defenceless state naturally content themselves with their
necessary subsistence; because to acquire more might only tempt the
injustice of their oppressors. On the contrary, when they are secure of
enjoying the fruits of their industry, they naturally exert it to better their
condition,[23] and to acquire not only the necessaries, but the conveniencies
and elegancies of life.[24] That industry, therefore, which aims at something
more than necessary subsistence, was established in cities long before it
was commonly practised by the occupiers of land in the country. If in the
hands of a poor cultivator, oppressed with the servitude of villanage, some
little stock should accumulate, he would naturally conceal it with great
care from his master, to whom it would otherwise have belonged, and take
the first opportunity of running away to a town. The law was at that time
so indulgent to the inhabitants of towns, and so desirous of diminishing
the authority of the lords over those of the country, that if he could conceal
himself there from the pursuit of his lord for a year, he was free for ever.[25]
Whatever stock, therefore, accumulated in the hands of the industrious
part of the inhabitants of the country, naturally took refuge in [110] cities,
as the only sanctuaries in which it could be secure to the person that
acquired it.

13   The inhabitants of a city, it is true, must always ultimately derive their
subsistence, and the whole materials and means of their industry from the
country. But those of a city, situated near either the sea-coast or the banks
of a navigable river, are not necessarily confined to derive them from the
country in their neighbourhood.[26] They have a much wider range, and
may draw them from the most remote corners of the world, either in
exchange for the manufactured produce of their own industry, or by
performing the office of carriers between distant countries, and exchanging
the produce of one for that of another.[27] A city might in this manner grow
up to great wealth and splendor, while not only the country in its neighbourhood, but all those to which it traded, were in poverty and wretched-
ness.[28] Each of those countries, perhaps, taken singly, could afford it but

[23] This term is used, for example, at II.iii.28, IV.v.b.43, and IV.ix.28.

[24] See above, II.i.30 and II.iii.36, where Smith elaborates on the importance of security
for industry; and see also III.iv.4 and IV.v.b.43.

[25] The fact that slaves could receive their freedom after a residence of one year is mentioned in LJ (A) iv.144 and LJ (B) 57, ed. Cannan 40.

[26] Cantillon, *Essai*, 22–3, ed. Higgs 19, also noted that 'Great Cities are usually built on
the seacoast or on the banks of large Rivers for the convenience of transport; because water-
carriage of the produce and merchandise necessary for the subsistence and comfort of the
inhabitants is much cheaper than Carriages and Land Transport.' See also *Essai*, 202–3,
ed. Higgs 153.

[27] The importance of water carriage is emphasized in I.iii, and see also II.v.33.

[28] See above, I.xi.o.14, where it is pointed out that 'It was not then the policy of Europe

a small part, either of its subsistence, or of its employment; but all of them taken together could afford it both a great subsistence and a great employment. There were, however, within the narrow circle of the commerce of those times, some countries that were opulent and industrious. Such was the Greek empire as long as it subsisted, and that of the Saracens during the reigns of the Abassides. Such too was Egypt till it was conquered by the Turks, some part of the coast of Barbary, and all those provinces of Spain which were under the government of the Moors.[29]

14   [111] The cities of Italy seem to have been the first in Europe which were raised by commerce to any considerable degree of opulence. Italy lay in the center of what was at that time the improved and civilized part of the world.[30] The cruzades too, though by the great waste of stock and destruction of inhabitants which they occasioned, they must necessarily have retarded the progress of the greater part of Europe, were extremely favourable to that of some Italian cities. The great armies which marched from all parts to the conquest of the Holy Land, gave extraordinary encouragement to the shipping of Venice, Genoa, and Pisa,[31] sometimes in transporting them thither, and always in supplying them with provisions. They were the commissaries, if one may say so, of those armies; and the most destructive frenzy that ever befel the European nations, was a source of opulence to those republicks.[32]

15   The inhabitants of trading cities, by importing the improved manufactures and expensive luxuries of richer countries, afforded some food to

to restrain, by high duties, the importation of foreign manufactures, but rather to encourage it.'

[29] In Astronomy, IV.22, Smith refers to the development of science and the translation of classical works on astronomy into Arabic as a result of the 'munificence of the Abassides, the second race of the Califfs'. He also remarked at § 23 that the 'victorious arms of the Saracens carried into Spain the learning, as well as the gallantry, of the East; and along with it, . . . the Arabian translations of Ptolemy and Aristotle'.

[30] See LJ (A) iv.111: 'The Italian republicks had in their hands at that time the most profitable branches of trade. They had the whole of the silk manufacture, a very profitable one, and the greatest part of the linnen trade. Their situation also gave them an opportunity of having the whole of the East Indian trade that came into Europe pass thro their hands. The Cape of Good Hope was not then discovered; the goods brought from the East Indies were conveyed up the Red Sea, from thence into the Nile, and by that means to Alexandria, where they were bought up by the Venetian and Genoese merchants chiefly, and by them dispersed thro Europe. Milan, too, tho no sea port, had great commerce. It was the centre of the trade betwixt the other towns, and had besides the greatest share of the silk trade, which all centered in it.' Cf. LJ (B) 49, ed. Cannan 34, and below, IV.vii.a.5.

[31] In LJ (A) iv.68 Smith cites Genoa, Milan, and Venice as examples of democracies in former times, while pointing out that in these cases the power of the state was now in the hands of the nobility. Cf. LJ (A) v.48 and LJ (B) 34, ed. Cannan 24.

[32] In LJ (B) 347–8, ed. Cannan 272, the Holy War is also associated with an improvement in military manners. Smith suggested that as the European princes 'had all been on one side in that common cause, and as they thought that Christians should not be treated in the same manner with infidels, a greater degree of humanity was introduced. From those causes, moderns behave differently from the ancients with regard to the persons of prisoners . . .' Cf. V.i.g.21.

the vanity of the great proprietors, who eagerly purchased them with great quantities of the rude produce of their own lands. The commerce of a great part of Europe in those times accordingly, consisted chiefly in the exchange of their own rude, for the manufactured produce of more civilized nations. Thus the wool of England used to be exchanged for the wines of France, and the fine cloths of Flanders, in the same manner as the corn ⁱofⁱ Poland is at this [112] day exchanged for the wines and brandies of France, and for the silks and velvets of France and Italy.

16   A taste for the finer and more improved manufactures, was in this manner introduced by foreign commerce into countries where no such works were carried on. But when this taste became so general as to occasion a considerable demand, the merchants, in order to save the expence of carriage, naturally endeavoured to establish some manufactures of the same ✓ kind in their own country. Hence the origin of the first manufactures for distant sale that seem to have been established in the western provinces of Europe, after the fall of the Roman empire.

17   No large country, it must be observed, ever did or could subsist without some sort of manufactures being carried on in it; and when it is said of any such country that it has no manufactures, it must always be understood of the finer and more improved, or of such as are fit for distant sale. In every large country, both the cloathing and houshold furniture of the far greater part of the people, are the produce of their own industry. This is even more universally the case in those poor countries which are commonly said to have no manufactures, than in those rich ones that are said to abound in them. In the latter, you will generally find, both in the cloaths and houshold furniture of the lowest rank of people, a much greater proportion of foreign productions than in the former.

18   [113] Those manufactures which are fit for distant sale, seem to have been introduced into different countries in two different ways.

19   Sometimes they have been introduced, in the manner above mentioned, by the violent operation, if one may say so, of the stocks of particular merchants and undertakers, who established them in imitation of some foreign manufactures of the same kind. Such manufactures, therefore, are the offspring of foreign commerce, and such seem to have been the antient manufactures of silks, velvets, and brocadesʲ, which flourished in Lucca duringʲ the thirteenth century. ᵏThey were banished from thence by the tyranny of one of Machiavel's heroes, Castruccio Castracani. In 1310, nine hundred families were driven out of Lucca, of whom thirty-one retired to Venice, and offered to introduce there the silk manufacture*. Their offer

ˡ* See Sandi Istoria Civile de Vinezia, Part 2. vol. 1. page 247, and 256.ˡ [V. Sandi, *Principj di Storia Civile della Republica de Venezia* (Venice, 1755), part 2, i.258.]

ⁱ⁻ⁱ in 4–6   ʲ⁻ʲ that were introduced into Venice in the beginning of *1*
ᵏ⁻ᵏ 2–6 [includes the following 3 sentences]   ˡ⁻ˡ 2–6

was accepted; many privileges were conferred upon them, and they began the manufacture with three hundred workmen.[k] Such too seem to have been the manufactures of fine cloths that antiently flourished in Flanders, and which were introduced into England in the beginning of the reign of Elizabeth; and such are the present silk manufactures of Lyons and Spital-fields.[33] Manufactures introduced in this manner are generally employed upon foreign materials, being [m]imitations of foreign manufactures. When the Venetian manu-[114]facture [n]was first established the materials were all brought from Sicily and the Levant. The more antient manufacture of Lucca was likewise carried on with foreign materials. The cultivation of mulberry trees, and the breeding of silk worms, seem not to have been common in the northern parts of Italy before the sixteenth century. Those arts were not introduced into France till the reign of Charles IX.[n] The manufactures of Flanders were carried on chiefly with Spanish and English wool. Spanish wool was the material, not of the first woollen manufacture of England, but of the first that was fit for distant sale.[34] More than one half the materials of the Lyons manufacture is at this day foreign silk; when it was first established, the whole or very nearly the whole was so. No part of the materials of the Spital-fields manufacture is ever likely to be the produce of England. The seat of such manufactures, as they are generally introduced by the scheme and project of a few individuals, is sometimes established in a maritime city, and sometimes in an inland town, according as their interest, judgment or caprice happen to determine.

20   At other times manufactures for distant sale grow up naturally, and as it were of their own accord, by the gradual refinement of those houshold and coarser manufactures which must at all times be carried on even in the poorest and rudest countries.[35] Such manufactures are generally employed upon the materials which the country produces, and they seem frequently to [115] have been first refined and improved in such inland countries as were, not indeed at a very great, but at a considerable distance from the sea coast, and sometimes even from all water carriage. An inland country naturally fertile and easily cultivated, produces a great surplus of provisions beyond what is necessary for maintaining the cultivators, and on

---

[m] in *I*

[n-n] flourished, there was not a mulberry tree, nor consequencely a silkworm in all Lombardy. They brought the materials from Sicily and from the Levant, the manufacture itself being in imitation of those carried on in the Greek empire. Mulberry trees were first planted in Lombard in the beginning of the sixteenth century, by the encouragement of Ludovico Sforza Duke of Milan. *I*

[33] The manufactures of Lyons are mentioned at II.v.15. It is stated at IV.ii.1 that the British manufacturers of completed goods based on silk had been successful in prohibiting the import of foreign commodities.
[34] See above, II.v.15.
[35] See below, V.i.a.6.

account of the expence of land carriage, and inconveniency of river navigation, it may frequently be difficult to send this surplus abroad. Abundance,
therefore, renders provisions cheap, and encourages a great number of
workmen to settle in the neighbourhood, who find that their industry can
there procure them more of the necessaries and conveniencies of life than in
other places.[36] They work up the materials of manufacture which the land
produces, and exchange their finished work, or what is the same thing the
price of it, for more materials and provisions. They give a new value to the
surplus part of the rude produce, by saving the expence of carrying it to the
water side, or to some distant market; and they furnish the cultivators with
something in exchange for it that is either useful or agreeable to them, upon
easier terms than they could have obtained it before. The cultivators get a
better price for their surplus produce, and can purchase cheaper other
conveniencies which they have occasion for. They are thus both encouraged
and enabled to increase this surplus produce by a further improvement and
better cultivation of the land; and as the fertility of the land had given
birth [116] to the manufacture, so the progress of the manufacture re-acts
upon the land, and increases still further its fertility. The manufacturers
first supply the neighbourhood, and afterwards, as their work improves and
refines, more distant markets. For though neither the rude produce, nor
even the coarse manufacture, could, without the greatest difficulty, support
the expence of a considerable land carriage, the refined and improved
manufacture easily may. In a small bulk it frequently contains the price of a
great quantity of rude produce. A piece of fine cloth, for example, which
weighs only eighty pounds, contains in it, the price, not only of eighty
pounds weight of wool, but sometimes of several thousand weight of corn,
the maintenance of the different working people, and of their immediate
employers. The corn, which could with difficulty have been carried abroad
in its own shape, is in this manner virtually exported in that of the complete manufacture, and may easily be sent to the remotest corners of the
world.[37] In this manner have grown up naturally, and as it were of their
own accord, the manufactures of Leeds, Halifax, Sheffield, Birmingham,
and Wolverhampton. Such manufactures are the offspring of agriculture.[38]

[36] See above, I.xi.c.3. In discussing the location of industry, Steuart argued that the
situation of manufactures which did not depend on the residence of the consumer would
tend to be dictated by the conveniency of transportation, the cheapness of subsistence, and:
'Relative to the place and situation of the establishment, which gives a preference to the
sides of rivers and rivulets, when machines wrought by water are necessary; to the proximity of forests and collieries when fire is employed; to the place which produces the substance of the manufacture; as in mines, collieries, brick-works, &c.' (*Principles*, i.49, ed.
Skinner, i.58.) See especially, I.ix.

[37] See below, IV.i.29 and IV.ix.41, where the finer manufactures are stated to be the
basis of foreign trade.

[38] The manufactures of Birmingham and Sheffield are mentioned at I.x.b.42, where
the former are said to be based on fashion, and the latter on necessity.

In the modern history of Europe, their extension and improvement have generally been posterior to those which were the offspring of foreign commerce.[39] England was noted for the manufacture of fine cloths made of Spanish wool, more than a century before any of those which now flourish in the places above [117] mentioned were fit for foreign sale. The extension and improvement of these last could not take place but in consequence of the extension and improvement of agriculture, the last and greatest effect of foreign commerce, and of the manufactures immediately introduced by it, and which I shall now proceed to explain.

[39] In his essay 'Of Commerce' Hume took a rather similar view to Smith's, emphasizing the role of imitation and emulation of foreign manufactures and stating that 'If we consult history, we shall find, that, in most nations, foreign trade has preceded any refinement in home manufactures, and given birth to domestic luxury.' (*Essays Moral, Political, and Literary*, ed. Green and Grose, i.295.) A similar point is made in the essay 'Of the Jealousy of Trade' where it is stated that every improvement made in the last two hundred years in Great Britain had 'arisen from our imitation of foreigners' (ibid. i.346).

CHAPTER IV

How the Commerce of the Towns contributed to the Improvement of the Country

1 THE increase and riches of commercial and manufacturing towns, contributed to the improvement and cultivation of the countries to which they belonged, in three different ways.

2 First, by affording a great and ready market for the rude produce of the country, they gave encouragement to its cultivation and further improvement. This benefit was not even confined to the countries in which they were situated, but extended more or less to all those with which they had any dealings. To all of them they afforded a market for some part either of their rude or manufactured produce, and consequently gave some encouragement to the industry and improvement of all. Their own country, however, on account of its neighbourhood, necessarily derived the greatest benefit from this market. [118] Its rude produce being charged with less carriage, the traders could pay the growers a better price for it, and yet afford it as cheap to the consumers as that of more distant countries.

3 Secondly, the wealth acquired by the inhabitants of cities was frequently employed in purchasing such lands as were to be sold, of which a great part would frequently be uncultivated.[1] Merchants are commonly ambitious of becoming country gentlemen, and when they do, they are generally the best of all improvers.[2] A merchant is accustomed to employ his money chiefly in profitable projects; whereas a mere country gentleman is accustomed to employ it chiefly in expence. The one often sees his money go from him and return to him again with a profit: the other, when once he parts with it, very seldom expects to see any more of it. Those different habits naturally affect their temper and disposition in every sort of business. A merchant is commonly a bold; a country gentleman, a timid undertaker. The one is not afraid to lay out at once a large capital upon the improvement of his land, when he has a probable prospect of raising the value of it in proportion to the expence. The other, if he has any capital, which is not always the case, seldom ventures to employ it in this manner. If he improves at all, it is commonly not with a capital, but with what he can save out of his annual revenue. Whoever has had the fortune to live in a mercantile town situated in an unimproved country, must have frequently observed how much more spirited [119] the operations of merchants were in this way, than those of

---

[1] See above, I.x.c.26.

[2] The merchant improver is contrasted with the country gentleman in LJ (B) 295, ed. Cannan 228. See below, V.ii.a.18 where Smith advocates the sale of Crown lands to those who might improve them, and cf. III.ii.7.

mere country gentlemen. The habits, besides, of order, œconomy and attention, to which mercantile business naturally forms a merchant, render him much fitter to execute, with profit and success, any project of improvement.[3]

4   Thirdly, and lastly, commerce and manufactures gradually introduced order and good government,[4] and with them, the liberty and security of individuals, among the inhabitants of the country, who had before lived almost in a continual state of war with their neighbours, and of servile dependency upon their superiors.[5] This, though it has been the least observed, is by far the most important of all their effects. Mr. Hume is the only writer who, so far as I know, has hitherto taken notice of it.[6]

5   In a country which has neither foreign commerce, nor any of the finer

---

[3] For an example of such activities, see T. M. Devine, 'Glasgow Colonial Merchants and Land, 1770–1815', in J. T. Ward and R. G. Wilson (eds.), *Land and Industry* (Newton Abbot, 1971), chapter 6.

[4] However, it is pointed out in the concluding sentence of I.xi.n.1 that the abolition of the feudal government in the case of Spain and Portugal had not produced anything better.

[5] See above, I.xi.n.1, where the fall of the feudal system is linked with the establishment of a form of government which gives industry the only encouragement which it requires, namely liberty.

[6] Hume remarked, for example, that 'If we consider the matter in a proper light, we shall find, that a progress in the arts is rather favourable to liberty, and has a natural tendency to preserve, if not produce a free government.' He then described the state of disorder found in 'rude unpolished nations' and went on to argue that the development of commerce had the effect of drawing 'authority and consideration to that middling rank of men, who are the best and firmest basis of public liberty.' *Essays Moral, Political, and Literary*, ed. Green and Grose, i.306. He also concluded in the essay 'Of Commerce' that 'The greatness of the sovereign and the happiness of the state are, in a great measure, united with regard to trade and manufactures.' (Ibid. i.294.) Another close student of Hume's *History*, Sir James Steuart, also drew attention to the link between commerce and liberty, and having drawn attention to the changing patterns of dependence, together with changes in the balance of power, made the further comment that 'When once a state begins to subsist by the consequences of industry, there is less danger to be apprehended from the power of the sovereign. The mechanism of his administration becomes more complex, and . . . he finds himself so bound up by the laws of his political œconomy, that every transgression of them runs him into new difficulties.' (*Principles*, i.249, ed. Skinner 217; see especially, II.xiii.) Apart from Steuart, Smith's comment that Hume was the only writer to have noticed a link between commerce and liberty seems a little odd when it is recalled that a number of works by people known to Smith had included comment on this issue: for example, Adam Ferguson's *History of Civil Society* (1767) and Kames's *Sketches of the History of Man* (1774). In addition John Millar's *Origin of the Distinction of Ranks* (1771), chapter v, provides a close parallel with the argument of the present section. However, of the works written prior to 1776, perhaps William Robertson's introduction to the *History of Charles V* (1769) provides the closest parallel to the argument of this book taken as a whole, where he traced the progress of society in Europe from the fall of the Roman empire. It has even been suggested that Robertson owed a good deal to lectures which Smith had delivered in *Edinburgh*, which, if true, is an interesting commentary on the age of this part of Smith's work. See, for example, Scott, 55. Smith's citation of Hume alone among the writers above mentioned may itself be a reflection of the age of this part of his work, and of the fact that Hume was the first author known to Smith to have commented on the subjects of this chapter.

manufactures, a great proprietor, having nothing for which he can exchange the greater part of the produce of his lands which is over and above the maintenance of the cultivators, consumes the whole in rustick hospitality at home.[7] If this surplus produce is sufficient to maintain a hundred or a thousand men, he can make use of it in no other way than by maintaining a hundred or a thousand men. He is at all times, therefore, surrounded with a multitude of retainers and dependants, who having no equivalent to give in return for their maintenance, but being fed entirely by his bounty, must obey him, for the same reason that sol-[120]diers must obey the prince who pays them. Therefore the extension of commerce and manufactures in Europe, the hospitality of the rich and the great, from the sovereign down to the smallest baron, exceeded every thing which in the present times we can easily form a notion of. Westminster-hall was the dining-room of William Rufus, and might frequently, perhaps, not be too large for his company.[8] It was reckoned a piece of magnificence in Thomas Becket, that he strowed the floor of his hall with clean hay or rushes in the season, in order that the knights and squires, who could not get seats, might not spoil their fine cloaths when they sat down on the floor to eat their dinner.[9] The great earl of Warwick is said to have entertained every day at his different manors, thirty thousand people; and though the number here may have been exaggerated, it must, however, have been very great to admit of such exaggeration.[10] A hospitality nearly of the same kind was exercised not many years ago in many different parts of the highlands of Scotland. It seems to be common in all nations to whom commerce and manufactures are little known. I have seen, says Doctor Pocock,[11] an

[7] With regard to the relationship between dependence and the power of a superior, see below V.i.b.7. See also LJ (B) 21, 51, 159, ed. Cannan 16, 35, 116, where it is remarked that: 'As the great had no way of spending their fortunes but by hospitality, they necessarily acquired prodigious influence over their vassals.'

[8] Smith comments on the hospitality (and enforced frugality) of sovereigns in this situation at IV.i.30 See also V.i.g.22, where he comments on the hospitality of the clergy. Hume describes the rustic hospitality of the great and the general conditions of the economy found in the 'first and more uncultivated ages of any state' in his essay 'Of Money' *Essays Moral, Political and Literary*, ed. Green and Grose, i.317.

[9] Hume cites the same example in *The History of England* (1778), i.384.

[10] This figure is cited in LJ (A) i.120. Smith also cites the examples of Becket, Warwick, and Rufus, pointing out in the latter case that his hall, 'now called Westminster Hall, is three hundred feet long and proportionably wide, and was not reckoned too large for a dining room to him and the nobles who attended his court'. In LJ (B) 59, ed. Cannan 42, the number dined by Warwick is given as 40,000 rather than the 30,000 also cited in LJ (A) iv.158. Hume gives the figure of 30,000 in *The History of England* (1778), iii.182.

[11] '... an Arab Prince will often dine in the street, before his door, and call to all that pass, even beggars, in the usual expression, Bismillah, that is, In the name of God; who come and sit down, and when they have done, give their Hamdellilah, that is, God be praised. For the Arabs are great levellers, put everybody on a footing with them; and it is by such generosity and hospitality that they maintain their interest; but the middling people among them, and the Coptis, live but poorly.' (R. Pococke, *A Description of the East and some other Countries* (London, 1743), i.183.)

Arabian chief dine in the streets of a town where he had come to sell his cattle, and invite all passengers, even common beggars, to sit down with him and partake of his banquet.[12]

6   The occupiers of land were in every respect as dependent upon the great proprietor as his retainers.[13] Even such of them as were not in a state of villanage, were tenants at will, who paid [121] a rent in no respect equivalent to the subsistence which the land afforded them.[14] A crown, half a crown, a sheep, a lamb, was some years ago in the highlands of Scotland a common rent for lands which maintained a family. In some places it is so at this day; nor will money at present purchase a greater quantity of commodities there than in other places. In a country where the surplus produce of a large estate must be consumed upon the estate itself, it will frequently be more convenient for the proprietor, that part of it be consumed at a distance from his own house, provided they who consume it are as dependent upon him as either his retainers or his menial servants. He is thereby saved from the embarrassment of either too large a company or too large a family. A tenant at will, who possesses land sufficient to maintain his family for little more than a quit-rent, is as dependent upon the proprietor as any servant or retainer whatever, and must obey him with as little reserve. Such a proprietor, as he feeds his servants and retainers

[12] In Letter 116 addressed to Lord Hailes, dated 5 March 1769, Smith mentioned an additional problem found in barbarous countries, namely the dependence of travellers on the hospitality of private families, and added that 'the danger too, of travelling either alone or with few attendants, made all men of any consequence carry along with them a numerous suite of retainers which rendered this Hospitality still more oppressive.' Smith added that 'Travelling, from the disorders of the Country, must have been extremely dangerous, & consequently very rare.'

[13] In LJ (A) iv.118–19 Smith used the distinction between tenants and retainers to explain a source of disorder within the individual estate. The lord's 'tenants naturally hated these idle fellows who eat up the fruits of their labours at their ease, and were allways ready to give their assistance to curb the insolence of his retainers; they again were no less ready to give their assistance to bring the tenants into proper order.' The same point is made in LJ (B) 51, 204, ed. Cannan 35, 155, where Smith remarked that 'great numbers of retainers were kept idle about the noblemen's houses' as late as the reign of Queen Elizabeth I. Similar points are made in LJ (A) vi.3–7 where Hume's authority is cited, and see above, II.iii.12.

[14] Cf. Steuart: 'I deduce the origin of the great subordination under the feudal government from the necessary dependence of the lower classes for their subsistence. They consumed the produce of the land, as the price of their subordination, not as the reward of their industry in making it produce.' (*Principles*, i.240, ed. Skinner i.208.) Steuart comments extensively on the relation between the degree of dependence and the mode of earning subsistence in II.xiii. LJ (A) i. 119 reads:

The possessors of these farms pay'd a small rent to the possessor rather as an acknowledgment of their dependence than as the value of the land. This rent again he could dispose of no other way than by bestowing it on those who came to his table. The rent of the land was accordingly paid in victualls, and the term Farm signifies properly lands which paid victualls for their rent; the world Farm signifying in the old Saxon or German language victualls.'

See above, I.iv.8. Similar points are made in LJ (A) iv. 135.

at his own house, so he feeds his tenants at their houses. The subsistence of both is derived from his bounty, and its continuance depends upon his good pleasure.

7   Upon the authority which the great proprietors necessarily had in such a state of things over their tenants and retainers, was founded the power of the antient barons.[15] They necessarily became the judges in peace, and the leaders in war, of all who dwelt upon their estates.[16] They could maintain order and execute the law within their [122] respective demesnes, because each of them could there turn the whole force of all the inhabitants against the injustice of any one. No other person had sufficient authority to do this. The king in particular had not.[17] In those antient times he was little more than the greatest proprietor in his dominions, to whom, for the sake of common defence against their common enemies, the other great proprietors paid certain respects. To have enforced payment of a small debt within the lands of a great proprietor, where all the inhabitants were armed and accustomed to stand by one another, would have cost the king, had he attempted it by his own authority, almost the same effort as to extinguish a civil war.[18] He was, therefore, obliged to abandon the administration of justice through the greater part of the country, to those who were capable of administering it; and for the same reason to leave the command of the country militia to those whom that militia would obey.

8   It is a mistake to imagine that those territorial jurisdictions took their origin from the feudal law. Not only the highest jurisdictions both civil and criminal, but the power of levying troops, of coining money, and even

[15] By implication Smith recognizes the strategic benefits of maintaining a large number of retainers.

[16] Cf. LRBL ii.198–9: 'In the early periods the same persons generally exercise the duties of Judge, General, and Legislator: at least the two former are very commonly conjoined . . . When men, especially in a barbarous state, are accustomed to submit themselves in some points, they naturally do it in others. The same persons therefore who judged them in peace, lead them also to battle.' (ed. Lothian, 168) See also LJ (B) 141, ed. Cannan 101: 'By the feudal law, the lord had an absolute sway over his vassals. In peace he was the administrator of justice, and they were obliged to follow him in war.'

[17] The inability of the king to enforce payment and to administer justice in the feudal period is mentioned in LJ (A) i.128 and LJ (B) 51, ed. Cannan 36. Hume remarked with reference to Scotland that: 'Amidst the contentions of such powerful vassals, who may be considered as petty princes rather than eminent nobles, the authority of the king, which was the same with that of the laws, was very uncertain and precarious. Like the Roman pontiff in the ages of superstition, the Scottish monarch, tho' possessed of extensive claims, enjoyed but little power; and when provoked by the rebellion of any potent baron, his usual resource was to animate some hostile clans against him, and to arm them with legal authority.' (*History of England* (1754), i.60–1.)

[18] A similar point is made above, III.iii.8. Hume highlights the weak position of the monarch when considering the case of the Earl of Warwick: 'The military men, allured by his munificence and hospitality, as well as by his bravery, were zealously attached to his interests: His numerous retainers were more devoted to his will, than to the prince or to the laws: And he was the greatest, as well as the last, of those mighty barons, who formerly overawed the crown, and rendered the people incapable of any regular system of civil government.' (*History of England* (1778), iii.182.)

that of making bye-laws for the government of their own people, were all rights possessed allodially by the great proprietors of land several centuries before even the name of the feudal law was known in Europe. The authority and jurisdiction of the Saxon lords in England, *appear* to have been as great before the conquest,[19] as that of any of the Norman [123] lords after it. But the feudal law is not supposed to have become the common law of England till after the conquest.[20] That the most extensive authority and jurisdictions were possessed by the great lords in France allodially, long before the feudal law was introduced into that country, is a matter of fact that admits of no doubt.[21] That authority and those jurisdictions all necessarily flowed from the state of property and manners just now described.[22] Without remounting to the remote antiquities of either the French or English monarchies, we may find in much later times many proofs that such effects must always flow from such causes. It is not thirty years ago since Mr. Cameron of Lochiel, a gentleman of Lochabar in Scotland, without any legal warrant whatever, not being what was then called a lord of regality, nor even a tenant in chief, but a vassal of the duke of Argyle, and without being so much as a justice of peace, used, notwithstanding, to exercise the highest criminal jurisdiction over his own people. He is said to

a-a appears *1-2*

[19] According to Hume 'The great influence of the lords over their slaves and tenants, the clientship of the burghers, the total want of a middling rank of men, the extent of the monarchy, the loose execution of the laws, the continued disorders and convulsions of the state; all these circumstances evince, that the Anglo-Saxon government became at last extremely aristocratical.' *The History of England* (1778), i.214-15.

[20] Smith states that the allodial system preceded the feudal in LJ (A) i.122 and argues that there 'is no mention of the word feodum in the English law till a few years after the Norman conquest, nor in the French till after the time of 50 or 60 years after Conrad.' A similar point is made in LJ (B) 54-5, ed. Cannan 38, and the argument is elaborated in LJ (A) iv where Smith cites the authority of Spelman, 'tho he does not seem to have understood it', and that of Bouquet who is said to have 'explaind it extremely well'. (132). Smith suggests at p. 134 that the change from allodial to feudal 'happend in the whole of Europe about the 9th, 10th and 11th centuries'. The contrast between the two forms of constitution is explained in LJ (A) i.67 where Smith refers to countries where lands were 'what we call allodial, i.e. held of no one, but were intirely the property of the proprietor, so that the state could not limit the use he was to make of any part of his estate. But in the feudal governments, the king was considered as the dominus directus, which had then a considerable benefit attending on it.' The allodial system is described in LJ (B) 49-52, ed. Cannan 34-6, and in LJ (A) iv.121-4, where the popular courts which feature in this system are also mentioned. It is stated in LJ (A) iv.137 that the feudal government 'took away every thing which was popular in the allodial form'. The transition from allodial to feudal is also described in LJ (B) 52-7, ed. Cannan 36-40. The distinction between allodial and feudal would also appear to have been grasped also by Montesquieu. See for example, *Esprit*, XXXI.viii. Hume also remarked that the Saxons 'found no occasion for the feudal institutions', and that William I 'introduced into England the feudal law, which he found established in France and Normandy' (*History of England* (1778), i.225 and 253).

[21] See below, V.i.a.7, where Smith refers to 'what is properly called the feudal law'.

[22] A similar argument appears at V.i.b.7, where Smith considers the great authority enjoyed by the Tartar (shepherd) chiefs.

have done so with great equity, though without any of the formalities of justice; and it is not improbable that the state of that part of the country at that time made it necessary for him to assume this authority in order to maintain the publick peace.[23] That gentleman, whose rent never exceeded five hundred pounds a year, carried, in 1745, eight hundred of his own people into the rebellion with him.[24]

9   [124] The introduction of the feudal law, so far from extending, may be regarded as an attempt to moderate the authority of the great allodial lords.[25] It established a regular subordination, accompanied with a long train of services and duties, from the king down to the smallest proprietor. During the minority of the proprietor, the rent, together with the management of his lands, fell into the hands of his immediate superior, and, consequently, those of all great proprietors into the hands of the king, who was charged with the maintenance and education of the pupil, and who, from his authority as guardian, was supposed to have a right of disposing of him in marriage, provided it was in a manner not unsuitable to his rank.[26] But though this institution necessarily tended to strengthen the authority of the king, and to weaken that of the great proprietors, it could not do either sufficiently for establishing order and good government among the inhabitants of the country; because it could not alter sufficiently that state of property and manners from which the disorders arose. The authority

---

[23] Lochiel's situation was not necessarily so devoid of legal authority as Smith implies. Lochiel, and others, could possess baronial rights, derived from their subject superior, in Lochiel's case from Argyll. No written charter need exist, so long as the rights were customarily recognized. The judicial functions of Cameron of Lochiel are mentioned in LJ (A) i.129. In LJ (B) 159, ed. Cannan 116, Smith notes that 'So lately as in the year 1745 this power remained in the Highlands of Scotland, and some gentlemen could bring several hundreds of men into the field', and he remarks at 171, ed. Cannan 126, that in general the 'duty of vassals to their lords continued longer in Scotland than in England'. In an interesting comment on Scottish affairs, Smith stated in LJ (A) ii.174 that Lochiel's relative, Dr. Cameron, was 'executed in the year '50 or '51 on the sentence passed on him in the year 1745. The government were then not altogether free from the fear of another rebellion, and thought it necessary to take that precaution. But had he kept out of the way for some years longer he would probably have been altogether safe.' See also LJ (B) 200, ed. Cannan 152.

[24] The Highlanders are described at V.i.a.26 as 'stationary shepherds' unwilling to stay in arms for long periods, or to travel great distances from home—as the events of the '45 Rebellion had proved.

[25] It is remarked in LJ (B) 55, ed Cannan 38–9, that 'these historians who give an account of the origin of feudal laws from the usurpation of the nobility are quite mistaken' since 'it required great influence in the king to make the lords hold their land feudally'. The same point is made in LJ (A) iv.133–4, where Smith also dates the beginning of orderly government from the introduction of the feudal system, remarking that 'the times after the conquest seem clear and enlightend compared with those of the Saxon race'. Smith argues in the same way that in France comparative order was to be found in the times of Hugh Capet as contrasted with the situation under the 'Merovingian and Carlovingian races'. An account of the introduction of feudal law is given by Montesquieu, *Esprit*, XXXI.xxx.

[26] The burdens of wardship and marriage are mentioned in LJ (A) i.125–7, ii.17–18, and iv.128; LJ (B) 160, ed. Cannan 117. See below, V.ii.h.5, 6.

of government still continued to be, as before, too weak in the head and too strong in the inferior members, and the excessive strength of the inferior members was the cause of the weakness of the head. After the institution of feudal subordination, the king was as incapable of restraining the violence of the great lords as before. They still continued to make war according to their own discretion, al-[125]most continually upon one another, and very frequently upon the king; and the open country still continued to be a scene of violence, rapine, and disorder.[27]

10   But what all the violence of the feudal institutions could never have effected, the silent and insensible operation of foreign commerce and manufactures gradually brought about.[28] These gradually furnished the great proprietors with something for which they could exchange the whole surplus produce of their lands, and which they could consume themselves without sharing it either with tenants or retainers.[29] All for ourselves, and nothing for other people, seems, in every age of the world, to have been the vile maxim of the masters of mankind. As soon, therefore, as they could find a method of consuming the whole value of their rents themselves, they had no disposition to share them with any other persons.[30] For a pair of

[27] Cf. LJ (A) i.127–8: 'It is to be observed that this government was not at all cut out for maintaining civill government, or Police. The king had property in the land superior indeed to what the others had, but not so greatly superior as that they had any considerable power over them. The only person who had any command in the remoter parts of the kingdom was the superior or lord.' A similar point is made in LJ (A) iv.119. See above, I.xi.e.23. Smith also refers to 'feudal anarchy' at III.ii.7. He comments on the superior power of the clergy as compared to the temporal lords at V.i.g.22, attributing this to their unity of interest.

[28] Cf. LJ (A) iv.157: 'the power of the nobles . . . declin'd in the feudall governments from the same causes as everywhere else, viz, from the introduction of arts, commerce, and luxury.' Cf. LJ (B) 36, ed. Cannan 25. In referring to the transition from the feudal state, Kames remarked that 'after the Arts of Peace began to be cultivated, Manufactures and Trade to revive in *Europe*, and Riches to encrease, this institution behoved to turn extreme burdensome. It first tottered, and then fell by its own Weight, as wanting a solid Foundation.' (*Essays upon several Subjects Concerning British Antiquities* (Edinburgh, 1747), 155.)

[29] By contrast, Montesquieu remarks that in Poland, despite the introduction of foreign commerce, some of the lords 'possess entire provinces; they oppress the husbandmen, in order to have greater quantities of corn, which they send to strangers, to procure the superfluous demands of luxury. If Poland had no foreign trade, its inhabitants would be happier.' Montesquieu seems to attribute the fact that the riches of the great had done little or nothing, directly or indirectly, to encourage domestic manufactures to the sheer size of their land holdings. Montesquieu, *Esprit*, XX.xxiii.4. See below, n. 38.

[30] Cf. LJ (A) i.117: 'men are so selfish that when they have an opportunity of laying out on their own persons what they possess, tho on things of no value, they will never think of giving it to be bestowed on the best purposes by those who stand in need of it.' It is also stated in LJ (A) vi.7 that commerce gives the rich 'an opportunity of spending their fortunes with fewer servants, which they never fail of embracing'. Smith comments in this context on the improvement of manners which arises as a result of reducing the number of retainers. See also LJ (B) 205–6, ed. Cannan 155–6 and cf. II.iii.12. The same theme is developed in Hume's *History of England* (1778), iii.400:

The encrease of the arts, more effectually than all the severities of law, put an end to the pernicious practice [of maintaining armies of retainers]. The nobility, instead of

diamond buckles perhaps, or for something as frivolous and useless, they exchanged the maintenance, or what is the same thing, the price of the maintenance of a thousand men for a year, and with it the whole weight and authority which it could give them.[31] The buckles, however, were to be all their own, and no other human creature was to have any share of them; whereas in the more antient method of expence they must have shared with at least a thousand people. With the judges that were to determine the preference, this difference was perfectly decisive; and thus, for the gratification of the most childish, the meanest and [126] the most sordid of all vanities, they gradually bartered their whole power and authority.[32]

11   In a country where there is no foreign commerce, nor any of the finer manufactures, a man of ten thousand a year cannot well employ his revenue in any other way than in maintaining, perhaps, a thousand families, who are all of them necessarily at his command.[33] In the present state of Europe, a man of ten thousand a year can spend his whole revenue, and he generally does so, without directly maintaining twenty people, or being able to

vying with each other, in the number and boldness of their retainers, acquired by degrees a more civilized species of emulation, and endeavoured to excel in the splendour and elegance of their equipage, houses, and tables. The common people, no longer maintained in vicious idleness by their superiors, were obliged to learn some calling or industry, and became useful both to themselves and to others . . .

Hume also noted in his essay 'Of Refinement in the Arts' (*Essays Moral, Political, and Literary*, ed. Green and Grose, i.301), that:

Another advantage of industry and of refinements in the mechanical arts, is, that they commonly produce some refinements in the liberal; nor can one be carried to perfection, without being accompanied, in some degree, with the other. The same age, which produces great philosophers and politicians, renowned generals and poets, usually abounds with skilful weavers, and ship-carpenters.

[31] LJ (A) i.117–18 comments on the limited dependence of the tradesman and adds: 'This manner of laying out ones money is the chief cause that the balance of property conferrs so small a superiority of power in modern times. A tradesman to retain your custom, may perhaps vote for you in an election, but you need not expect that he will attend you to battle.' In LRBL ii.144, ed. Lothian 144, the same point is made with reference to Greek experience; commerce and luxury 'gave the lowest an opportunity of raising themselves to an equality with the nobles, and the nobles an easy way of reducing themselves to the state of the meanest citizen'. See especially lectures 25 and 26. Cf. LJ (B) 36, ed. Cannan 25: 'When a man becomes capable of spending on domestic luxury what formerly supported an hundred retainers, his power and influence naturaly decrease.' See also LJ (B) 59, ed. Cannan 42, and below, V.iii.3.

[32] Smith examines the breakdown in the power of the clergy at V.i.g.24, 25, and attributes it to the same process. He suggests, however, that this decline took place more rapidly than in the case of the lords. See also IV.i.30.

[33] Cf. LJ (A) iii.135: 'A man who consumes 10,000 pounds appears to destroy what ought to give maintenance to 1000 men. He therefore appears to be the most destructive member of society we can possibly conceive. But if we observe this man we will find that he is in no way prejudiciall to society, but rather of advantage to it.' A similar example occurs in LJ (A) i.119.

command more than ten footmen not worth the commanding.[34] Indirectly, perhaps, he maintains as great or even a greater number of people than he could have done by the antient method of expence. For though the quantity of precious productions for which he exchanges his whole revenue be very small, the number of workmen employed in collecting and preparing it, must necessarily have been very great. Its great price generally arises from the wages of their labour, and the profits of all their immediate employers. By paying that price he indirectly pays all those wages and profits, and thus indirectly contributes to the maintenance of all the workmen and their employers.[35] He generally contributes, however, but a very small proportion to that of each, to very few perhaps a tenth, to many not a hundredth, and to some not a thousandth, nor even a ten thousandth part of their whole annual maintenance. Though he contributes, therefore, to the maintenance of them all, they are all more or less independent [127] of him, because generally they can all be maintained without him.[36]

12   When the great proprietors of land spend their rents in maintaining their tenants and retainers, each of them maintains entirely all his own tenants and all his own retainers. But when they spend them in maintaining tradesmen and artificers, they may, all of them taken together, perhaps, maintain as great, or, on account of the waste which attends rustick hospitality, a greater number of people than before. Each of them, however, taken singly, contributes often but a very small share to the maintenance of any individual of this greater number. Each tradesman or artificer derives his subsistence from the employment, not of one, but of a hundred or a thousand different customers. Though in some measure obliged to them all, therefore, he is not absolutely dependent upon any one of them.

13   The personal expence of the great proprietors having in this manner gradually increased, it was impossible that the number of their retainers should not as gradually diminish, till they were at last dismissed altogether. The same cause gradually led them to dismiss the unnecessary part of their tenants. Farms were enlarged, and the occupiers of land, notwithstanding the complaints of depopulation, reduced to the number necessary for cultivating it, according to the imperfect state of cultivation and improvement in those times. By the removal of the unnecessary mouths, and by exacting from the farmer the full value of the farm, a greater surplus, or what [128] is the same thing, the price of a greater surplus, was obtained for the proprietor, which the merchants and manufacturers soon furnished

[34] A similar point is made at V.i.b.7 where it is stated that the power of the landlord in an opulent state must be diminished, since 'as he gives scarce any thing to any body but in exchange for an equivalent, there is scarce any body who considers himself as entirely dependent upon him'.

[35] See above, I.xi.c.7.

[36] Cf. III.i.5, where Smith comments on the attitude of the American colonists to even this degree of dependence.

him with a method of spending upon his own person in the same manner as he had done the rest. The same cause continuing to operate, he was desirous to raise his rents above what his lands, in the actual state of their improvement, could afford. His tenants could agree to this upon one condition only, that they should be secured in their possession, for such a term of years as might give them time to recover with profit whatever they should lay out in the further improvement of the land. The expensive vanity of the landlord made him willing to accept of this condition; and hence the origin of long leases.[37]

14   Even a tenant at will, who pays the full value of the land, is not altogether dependent upon the landlord. The pecuniary advantages which they receive from one another, are mutual and equal, and such a tenant will expose neither his life nor his fortune in the service of the proprietor. But if he has a lease for a long term of years, he is altogether independent; and his landlord must not expect from him even the most trifling service beyond what is either expressly stipulated in the lease, or imposed upon him by the common and known law of the country.

15   The tenants having in this manner become independent, and the retainers being dismissed, the great proprietors were no longer capable of interrupting the regular execution of justice, or [129] of disturbing the peace of the country. Having sold their birth-right, not like Esau for a mess of pottage in time of hunger and necessity, but in the wantonness of plenty, for trinkets and baubles, fitter to be the play-things of children than the serious pursuits of men, they became as insignificant as any substantial burgher or tradesman in a city. A regular government was established in the country as well as in the city, nobody having sufficient power to disturb its operations in the one, any more than in the other.[38]

16   It does not, perhaps, relate to the present subject, but I cannot help remarking it, that very old families, such as have possessed some considerable estate from father to son for many successive generations, are very rare in commercial countries. In countries which have little commerce, on the contrary, such as Wales or the highlands of Scotland, they are very common.[39] The Arabian histories seem to be all full of genealogies, and

---

[37] The same point is made with regard to the clergy as landowners at V.i.g.25.

[38] This general statement is further qualified in LJ (A) iv.166: 'The ruin of the feudall government which followed on arts and luxury had a very different effect in Germany: it occasioned the increase of the power and absolute authority of the great nobles or princes of the empire, and not of the emperor.' This is explained as being due to the sheer size of the country and the extent of the fortunes held by the nobility. See LJ (A) iv.161–4, LJ (B) 60, ed. Cannan 43, and above, n. 29. Smith comments on the military consequences of this situation, and of the decay of the feudal militia, at V.i.a.37.

[39] In TMS VI.ii.1.12 Smith commented on the importance of family in another sense, with regard to pastoral communities: an 'extensive regard to kindred is said to take place among the Tartars, the Arabs, the Turkomans and, I believe, among all other nations who are nearly in the same state of society in which the Scots Highlanders were about the

there is a history written by a Tartar Khan, which has been translated into several European languages, and which contains scarce any thing else;[40] a proof that antient families are very common among those nations. In countries where a rich man can spend his revenue in no other way than by maintaining as many people as it can maintain, he is not apt to run out, and his benevolence it seems is seldom so violent as to attempt to maintain more than he can afford. But where he can spend the greatest revenue upon his own person, he frequently has [130] no bounds to his expence, because he frequently has no bounds to his vanity, or to his affection for his own person. In commercial countries, therefore, riches, in spite of the most violent regulations of law to prevent their dissipation, very seldom remain long in the same family. Among simple nations, on the contrary, they frequently do without any regulations of law; for among nations of shepherds, such as the Tartars and Arabs, the consumable nature of their property necessarily renders all such regulations impossible.

17   A revolution of the greatest importance to the publick happiness, was in this manner brought about by two different orders of people, who had not the least intention to serve the publick. To gratify the most childish vanity was the sole motive of the great proprietors. The merchants and artificers, much less ridiculous, acted merely from a view to their own interest, and in pursuit of their own pedlar principle of turning a penny wherever a penny was to be got. Neither of them had either knowledge or foresight of that great revolution which the folly of the one, and the industry of the other, was gradually bringing about.[41]

18   It is thus that through the greater part of Europe the commerce and manufactures of cities, instead of being the effect, have been the cause and occasion of the improvement and cultivation of the country.

19   This order, however, being contrary to the natural course of things, is necessarily both slow and uncertain. Compare the slow progress of [131] those European countries of which the wealth depends very much upon their commerce and manufactures, with the rapid advances of our North

beginning of the present century.' Smith contrasts this situation with that prevailing in commercial countries.

[40] It is remarked in LJ (B) 28, ed. Cannan 20, that 'In no age is antiquity of family more respected than in this', and in LJ (A) iv.44, with regard to the respect shown for antiquity and family at certain stages of society, Smith refers to a history recently translated from the French (in turn translated from the Swedish) of a man taken prisoner while with Charles XII of Sweden, and carried into Russia. Smith refers to this history as providing 'just such an account as we should expect to meet with in the history of one of the clans in the remoter parts of this country'. In the same place, Smith points out that 'the Jews, who were originally a tribe of Arabs, paid the greatest respect to genealogies and were at great pains to preserve them.' It is stated at V.i.b.10 with regard to the shepherd state that there are 'no nations . . . who abound more in families revered and honoured on account of their descent . . .'

[41] A similar form of argument is used below when speaking of the collapse in the temporal power of the clergy. V.i.g.24.

American colonies, of which the wealth is founded altogether in agriculture.[42] Through the greater part of Europe, the number of inhabitants is not supposed to double in less than five hundred years. In several of our North American colonies, it is found to double in twenty or five-and-twenty years.[43] In Europe, the law of primogeniture, and perpetuities of different kinds, prevent the division of great estates, and thereby hinder the multiplication of small proprietors.[44] A small proprietor, however, who knows every part of his little territory, *who* views it *with all* the affection which property, especially small property, naturally inspires, and who upon that account takes pleasure not only in cultivating but in adorning it, is generally of all improvers the most industrious, the most intelligent, and the most successful.[45] The same regulations, besides, keep so much land out of the market, that there are always more capitals to buy than there is land to sell, so that what is sold always sells at a monopoly price. The rent never pays the interest of the purchase-money, and is besides burdened with repairs and other occasional charges, to which the interest of money is not liable. To purchase land is every where in Europe a most unprofitable employment of a small capital. For the sake of the superior security, indeed, a man of moderate circumstances, when he retires from business, will sometimes [132] chuse to lay out his little capital in land. A man of profession too, whose revenue is derived from another source, often loves to secure his savings in the same way. But a young man, who, instead of applying to trade or to some profession, should employ a capital of two or three thousand pounds in the purchase and cultivation of a small piece of land, might indeed expect to live very happily, and very independently, but must bid adieu, for ever, to all hope of either great fortune or great illustration, which by a different employment of his stock he might have had the same chance of acquiring with other people. Such a person too, though he cannot aspire at being a proprietor, will often disdain to be a farmer. The small quantity of land, therefore, which is brought to market, and the high price of what is brought *thither*, prevents a great number of capitals from being employed in its cultivation and improvement which would otherwise have taken that direction. In North America, on the contrary, fifty or sixty pounds is often found a sufficient stock to begin a plantation with. The purchase and improvement of uncultivated land, is there the most profitable employment of the smallest as well as of the

b-b om. 5-6   *c-c* all with *1*   *d-d 2-6*

[42] See above, II.v.21 and IV.vii.b.17.
[43] The same figures are cited above, I.viii.23.
[44] See above, III.ii.2, and below, IV.vii.b.19.
[45] See above, III.ii.7, where Smith comments that great proprietors are seldom great improvers, and III.iv.3, where it is stated that merchants are the best of all. Smith also recommends the sale of crown lands to accelerate improvement at V.ii.a.18.

greatest capitals, and the most direct road to all the fortune and illustration which can be acquired in that country. Such land, indeed, is in North America to be had almost for nothing, or at a price much below the value of the natural produce; a thing impossible in Europe, or, indeed, in any country where all lands have long been [133] private property.[46] If landed estates, however, were divided equally among all the children, upon the death of any proprietor who left a numerous family, the estate would generally be sold. So much land would come to market, that it could no longer sell at a monopoly price. The free rent of the land would go nearer to pay the interest of the purchase-money, and a small capital might be employed in purchasing land as profitably as in any other way.

20   England, on account of the natural fertility of the soil, of the great extent of ᵉtheᵉ sea-coast in proportion to that of the whole country, and of the many navigable rivers which run through it, and afford the conveniency of water carriage to some of the most inland parts of it, is perhaps as well fitted by nature as any large country in Europe, to be the seat of foreign commerce, of manufactures for distant sale, and of all the improvements which these can occasion. From the beginning of the reign of Elizabeth too, the English legislature has been peculiarly attentive to the interests of commerce and manufactures, and in reality there is no country in Europe, Holland itself not excepted, of which the law is, upon the whole, more favourable to this sort of industry. Commerce and manufactures have accordingly been continually advancing during all this period. The cultivation and improvement of the country has, no doubt, been gradually advancing too: But it seems to have followed slowly, and at a distance, the more rapid progress of commerce and manufactures. The greater [134] part of the country must probably have been cultivated before the reign of Elizabeth; and a very great part of it still remains uncultivated, and the cultivation of the far greater part, much inferior to what it might be. The law of England, however, favours agriculture not only indirectly by the protection of commerce, but by several direct encouragements. Except in times of scarcity, the exportation of corn is not only free, but encouraged by a bounty.[47] In times of moderate plenty, the importation of foreign corn is loaded with duties that amount to a prohibition.[48] The importation of live cattle, except from Ireland, is prohibited at all times,[49] and it is but

ᵉ⁻ᵉ 2–6

---

[46] See below, IV.vii.b.2.

[47] See above, I.xi.g.4, and below, IV.v.a.5, IV.v.b.37, V.ii.k.13.

[48] 22 Charles II, c.13 (1670). See below, IV.ii.1, IV.ii.16, IV.v.a.23, IV.v.b.33 and 37, IV.vii.b.33, V.ii.k.13.

[49] 18 and 19 Charles II, c.2 (1666) in *Statutes of the Realm*, v.597; 18 Charles II, c.2 in Ruffhead's edition declared that from 2 February 1666 the importation of cattle is a 'publique and common Nusance'. Earlier 15 Charles II, c.7 (1663) had imposed a levy on any cattle imported: 20s. for each head to the King; 10s to the informer; 10s. to the poor of

of late that it was permitted from thence.[50] Those who cultivate the land, therefore, have a monopoly against their countrymen for the two greatest and most important articles of land produce, bread and butcher's meat. These encouragements, though at bottom, perhaps, as I shall endeavour to show hereafter,[51] altogether illusory, sufficiently demonstrate at least the good intention of the legislature to favour agriculture. But what is of much more importance than all of them, the yeomanry of England are rendered as secure, as independent, and as respectable as law can make them.[52] No country, therefore, in which the right of primogeniture takes place, which pays tithes, and where perpetuities, though contrary to the spirit of the law, are admitted in some cases, can give more encouragement to agriculture than England. Such, however, notwithstanding, is the state of its cultivation. [135] What would it have been, had the law given no direct encouragement to agriculture besides what arises indirectly from the progress of commerce, and had left the yeomanry in the same condition as in most other countries of Europe? It is now more than two hundred years since the beginning of the reign of Elizabeth, a period as long as the course of human prosperity usually endures.[53]

21   France seems to have had a considerable share of foreign commerce near a century before England was distinguished as a commercial country. The marine of France was considerable, according to the notions of the times, before the expedition of Charles the VIIIth to Naples. The cultivation and improvement of France, however, is, upon the whole, inferior to that of England. The law of the country has never given the same direct encouragement to agriculture.

22   The foreign commerce of Spain and Portugal to the other parts of Europe, though chiefly carried on in foreign ships, is very considerable. That to

---

the parish where the information was laid. See also 32 Charles II, c.2 (1680). See below, IV.ii.1, 16 and V.ii.k.13.

[50] 32 George II, c.11 (1758), extended by 5 George III, c.10 (1765) and 12 George III, c.2 (1772). See also IV.ii.17 and V.ii.k.13. Salt provisions from Ireland were allowed on payment of duty by 4 George III, c.1 (1763), later extended and without duty by 8 George III, c.9 (1768) and 12 George III, c.2 (1772).

[51] See below, IV.ii.16–22, and generally IV.v.b.

[52] See above, III.ii.14 and 15.

[53] See above, II.v.22. Cantillon, *Essai*, 244, ed. Higgs 185, also remarked that 'When a State has arrived at the highest point of wealth . . . it will inevitably fall into poverty by the ordinary course of things.' He cites as examples the fate of Venice, the Hanseatic Towns, etc. at 246–7, ed. Higgs 187. It is also stated at 312, ed. Higgs 235, that 'States who rise by trade do not fail to sink afterwards.' The thesis of 'growth and decay' also features in Hume's essay 'Of Money' and in a letter to Lord Kames, dated 4 March 1758, where he says that 'Great empires, great cities, great commerce, all of them receive a check, not from accidental events, but necessary principles.' (J. Y. T. Greig, *The Letters of David Hume* (Oxford, 1932), i.270–2.) The same thesis appears in Hutcheson, *System*, ii.377, where it is stated that states 'have within them the seeds of death and destruction'. Sir James Steuart also uses the argument, *Principles*, i.224–5, ed. Skinner i.195–6, and see also Kame's *Sketches of the History of Man* (Edinburgh, 1774), II.iv.

their colonies is carried on in their own, and is much greater, on account of the great riches and extent of those colonies. But it has never introduced any considerable manufactures for distant sale into either of those countries, and the greater part of both still remains uncultivated. The foreign commerce of Portugal is of older standing than that of any great country in Europe, except Italy.[54]

23   Italy is the only great country of Europe which seems to have been cultivated and im-[136]proved in every part, by means of foreign commerce and manufactures for distant sale. Before the invasion of Charles the VIIIth, Italy, according to Guicciardin,[55] was cultivated not less in the most mountainous and barren parts of the country, than in the plainest and most fertile. The advantageous situation of the country, and the great number of independent states which at that time subsisted in it, probably contributed not a little to this general cultivation. It is not impossible too, notwithstanding this general expression of one of the most judicious and reserved of modern historians, that Italy was not at that time better cultivated than England is at present.

24   The capital, however, that is acquired to any country by commerce and manufactures, is all a very precarious and uncertain possession, till some part of it has been secured and realized in the cultivation and improvement of its lands. A merchant, it has been said very properly, is not necessarily the citizen of any particular country. It is in a great measure indifferent to him from what place he carries on his trade; and a very trifling disgust will make him remove his capital, and together with it all the industry which it supports, from one country to another. No part of it can be said to belong to any particular country, till it has been spread as it were over the face of that country, either in buildings, or in the lasting improvement of lands.[56] No vestige now remains of the great wealth, said to have been possessed by the greater part of the Hans towns, [137] except in the obscure histories of the thirteenth and fourteenth centuries. It is even uncertain where some of them were situated, or to what towns in Europe the Latin names given to some of them belong. But though the misfortunes of Italy in the end of the fifteenth and beginning of the sixteenth centuries greatly diminished the commerce and manufactures of the cities of Lombardy and Tuscany, those countries still continue to be among the most

[54] See above, I.xi.n.1, where Spain and Portugal are described as the 'two most beggarly countries in Europe'. It is suggested at IV.vii.c.82 that the colonies of these two countries may give more encouragement to the industry of others than to their own domestic output.

[55] Guicciardini, *Della Istoria d'Italia* (Venice, 1738), i.2. In LRBL ii.69–70, ed. Lothian 110, Guicciardini and Machiavelli are described as 'the two most famous modern Italian historians'. Machiavelli was especially admired, being 'of all modern Historians the only one who has contented himself with that which is the chief purpose of History, to relate events and connect them with their causes, without becoming a party on either side.'

[56] See above, II.v.14, and below, V.ii.f.6.

populous and best cultivated in Europe. The civil wars of Flanders, and the Spanish government which succeeded them, chased away the great commerce of Antwerp, Ghent, and Bruges. But Flanders still continues to be one of the richest, best cultivated, and most populous provinces of Europe. The ordinary revolutions of war and government easily dry up the sources of that wealth which arises from commerce only. That which arises from the more solid improvements of agriculture, is much more durable, and cannot be destroyed but by those more violent convulsions occasioned by the depredations of hostile and barbarous nations continued for a century or two together; such as those that happened for some time before and after the fall of the Roman empire in the western provinces of Europe.

BOOK IV

Of Systems of political Oeconomy

INTRODUCTION

1 POLITICAL œconomy, considered as a branch of the science of a statesman or legislator, proposes two distinct objects; first, to provide a plentiful revenue or subsistence for the people, or more properly to enable them to provide such a revenue or subsistence for themselves; and secondly, to supply the state or commonwealth with a revenue sufficient for the publick services. It proposes to enrich both the people and the sovereign.

2 The different progress of opulence in different ages and nations, has given occasion to two different systems of political œconomy, with regard to enriching the people. The one may be called the system of commerce, the other that of agriculture. I shall endeavour to explain both as fully and distinctly as I can, and shall begin with the system of commerce. It is the modern system, and is best understood in our own country and in our own times.

CHAPTER I

Of the Principle of the commercial, or mercantile System[1]

1 THAT wealth consists in money, or in gold and silver, is a popular notion which naturally arises from the double function of money, as the instrument of commerce, and as the measure of value.[2] In consequence of its being the instrument of commerce, when we have money we can more readily obtain whatever else we have occasion for, than by means of any other commodity. The great affair, we always find, is to get money. When that is obtained, there is no difficulty in making any subsequent purchase. In consequence of its being the measure of value, we estimate that of all other commodities by the quantity of money which they will exchange for. We say of a rich man that he is worth a great deal, and of a poor man that he is worth very little money. A frugal man, or a man eager to be rich, is said to love money; and a careless, a generous, or a profuse man, is said to be indifferent about it. To grow rich is to get money; and wealth and money, in short, are, in common language, considered as in every respect synonymous.[3]

2 A rich country, in the same manner as a rich man, is supposed to be a country abounding in money; and to heap up gold and silver in any [140] country is supposed to be the readiest way to enrich it. For some time after the discovery of America, the first enquiry of the Spaniards, when they arrived upon any unknown coast, used to be, if there was any gold or silver to be found in the neighbourhood? By the information which they received, they judged whether it was worth while to make a settlement there, or if the country was worth the conquering. Plano Carpino, a monk sent ambassador from the king of France to one of the sons of the famous Gengis Khan, says that the Tartars used frequently to ask him, if there was plenty of sheep and oxen in the kingdom of France?[4] Their enquiry had the

---

[1] The thesis that opulence does not consist in money is examined in LJ (A) vi.127–71, LJ (B) 244–70, ed. Cannan 190–211, and ED 4.6–10. While there are differences of detail, all three versions follow a similar plan: The statement of the mercantile fallacy is followed by an appreciation of paper money (see above, II.ii) before proceeding to review the errors of the system in practice, e.g. the prohibition of the export of bullion, the doctrine of the balance of trade, the thesis that intervention will upset the natural balance of industry (see for example, IV.ii.3). In each case, Smith also emphasized the benefits of free trade and highlighted the problems of national animosity, in a manner which is reminiscent of Hume. In both ED and LJ (B) the critique of Law's Mississippi Scheme is included as a part of the general critique of the mercantile system, i.e. treated as one of the errors to which it had given occasion. See above, II.ii.78. The subjects of this particular chapter are considered in LJ (A) vi.127–46 and LJ (B) 244–56, ed. Cannan 190–200.

[2] See below, IV.i.1.   [3] This is explained above, I.v.6.

[4] Cannan has noted that there may be a confusion between Plano Carpini, sent as a legate by Pope Innocent IV in 1246, and Guillaume de Rubruquis, sent as ambassador by Louis IX in 1253. Cannan also observes that both are mentioned in N. Bergeron's *Voyages faits principalement en Asie dans les xii., xiii., xiv., et xv. siècles* (La Haye, 1735).

same object with that of the Spaniards.[5] They wanted to know if the country was rich enough to be worth the conquering. Among the Tartars, as among all other nations of shepherds, who are generally ignorant of the use of money, cattle are the instruments of commerce and the measures of value. Wealth, therefore, according to them, consisted in cattle, as according to the Spaniards it consisted in gold and silver. Of the two, the Tartar notion, perhaps, was the nearest to the truth.[6]

3   Mr. Locke remarks a distinction between money and other moveable goods.[7] All other moveable goods, he says, are of so consumable a nature that the wealth which consists in them cannot be much depended on, and a nation which abounds in them one year may, without any exportation, but merely by their own waste and extravagance, be in great want of them the [141] next. Money, on the contrary, is a steady friend, which, though it may travel about from hand to hand, yet if it can be kept from going out of the country, is not very liable to be wasted and consumed. Gold and silver, therefore, are, according to him, the most solid and substantial part of the moveable wealth of a nation, and to multiply those metals ought, he thinks, upon that account, to be the great object of its political œconomy.

4   Others admit that if a nation could be separated from all the world, it would be of no consequence how much, or how little money circulated in it.[8] The consumable goods which were circulated by means of this money, would only be exchanged for a greater or a smaller number of pieces; but the real wealth or poverty of the country, they allow, would depend

---

[5] The Spanish attitude to colonization is mentioned at I.xi.c.36 and IV.vii.a.17.

[6] See above, I.iv.3, where it is mentioned that cattle were used as instruments of commerce in the 'rude ages of society'.

[7] It is difficult to find a parallel passage in Locke. The nearest probably are: 'Money has a value, as it is capable, by exchange, to procure us the necessaries or conveniences of life, and in this it has the nature of a commodity; only with this difference, that it serves us commonly by its exchange, never almost by its consumption.' (*Some Considerations of the Consequences of the Lowering of Interest, and raising the Value of Money, Works* (1823), v.34.) 'Thus came in the use of money, some lasting thing that men might keep without spoiling, and that by mutual consent men would take it in exchange for the truly useful, but perishable supports of life.' (*Essay on Civil Government, Works* (1823), v.365.) In LJ (A) vi.135, Locke is referred to as a follower of the mercantile system, and one who had given it 'somewhat more of a philosophicall air and the appearance of probability by some amendments'. In this connection, Smith cited the allowance which Locke is said to have made for the fact that cattle and corn could be regarded as part of a nation's wealth, albeit less significant than money. Cf. LJ (B) 254, ed. Cannan 198–9.

[8] Harris admitted: 'In a country having no foreign commerce, any quantity of money will, in a manner, be sufficient for all purposes; and any increase or diminution of the original stock, if it be but gradual and slow, will scarce be attended with any consequence of moment.' But later he wrote: 'In the days of prosperity . . . it would be prudent to lay up a kind of dead stock of the precious metals, against any emergencies that might happen . . . He that is ready armed, is less liable to be assailed; and silver and gold are keen and destructive weapons.' (*Essay*, i.80 and 99–100.) Hume argued in his essay 'Of Money' that 'If we consider any one kingdom by itself, it is evident, that the greater or less plenty of money is of no consequence.' (*Essays Moral, Political, and Literary*, ed. Green and Grose, i.309.)

altogether upon the abundance or scarcity of those consumable goods. But it is otherwise, they think, with countries which have connections with sovereign nations, and which are obliged to carry on foreign wars, and to maintain fleets and armies in distant countries. This, they say, cannot be done, but by sending abroad money to pay them with; and a nation cannot send much money abroad, unless it has a good deal at home. Every such nation, therefore, must endeavour in time of peace to accumulate gold and silver, that, when occasion requires, it may have wherewithal to carry on foreign wars.

5   In consequence of these popular notions, all the different nations of Europe have studied, though to little purpose, every possible means of accu-[142]mulating gold and silver in their respective countries. Spain and Portugal, the proprietors of the principal mines which supply Europe with those metals, have either prohibited their exportation under the severest penalties, or subjected it to a considerable duty.[9] The like prohibition seems antiently to have made a part of the policy of most other European nations. It is even to be found, where we should ᵃleast of all expectᵃ to find it, in some old Scotch acts of parliament, which forbid under heavy penalties the carrying gold or silver *forth of the kingdom.*[10] The like policy antiently took place both in France and England.

6   When those countries became commercial, the merchants found this prohibition, upon many occasions, extremely inconvenient. They could frequently buy more advantageously with gold and silver than with any other commodity, the foreign goods which they wanted, either to import into their own, or to carry to some other foreign country. They remonstrated, therefore, against this prohibition as hurtful to trade.[11]

7   They represented, first, that the exportation of gold and silver in order to purchase foreign goods, did not always diminish the quantity of those metals in the kingdom. That, on the contrary, it might frequently increase ᵇthat quantityᵇ; because, if the consumption of foreign goods was not thereby increased in the country, those goods might be re-exported to foreign countries, and being there sold for a large profit, might bring back much more treasure [143] than was originally sent out to purchase them.[12] Mr. Mun compares this operation of foreign trade to the seed-time and harvest of agriculture. "If we only behold," says he, "the actions of the husbandman in the seed-time, when he casteth away much good corn into the ground, we shall account him rather a madman than a husbandman.

ᵃ⁻ᵃ expect least of all *r*   ᵇ⁻ᵇ it *r*

⁹ The point is elaborated below, IV.v.a.19.
¹⁰ Act anent the having of the money furth of the Realme (1487). *Acts of the Parliament of Scotland*, ii.183.
¹¹ The subjects of this and the preceding paragraph follow the argument of LJ (A) vi.147–8; cf. LJ (B) 257–8, ed. Cannan 200–1.
¹² See below, IV.iii.a.3.

But when we consider his labours in the harvest, which is the end of his endeavours, we shall find the worth and plentiful increase of his actions."[13]

8   They represented, secondly, that this prohibition could not hinder the exportation of gold and silver, which, on account of the smallness of their bulk in proportion to their value, could easily be smuggled abroad. That this exportation could only be prevented by a proper attention to, what they called, the balance of trade.[14] That when the country exported to a greater value than it imported, a balance became due to it from foreign nations, which was necessarily paid to it in gold and silver, and thereby increased the quantity of those metals in the kingdom. But that when it imported to a greater value than it exported, a contrary balance became due to foreign nations, which was necessarily paid to them in the same manner, and thereby diminished that quantity. That in this case to prohibit the exportation of those metals could not prevent it, but only, by making it more dangerous, render it more expensive. That the exchange was thereby turned more against the country which owed the balance, than it [144] otherwise might have been; the merchant who purchased a bill upon the foreign country being obliged to pay the banker who sold it, not only for the natural risk, trouble and expence of sending the money thither, but for the extraordinary risk arising from the prohibition. But that the more the

[13] Thomas Mun, *England's Treasure by Forraign Trade* (London, 1664, reprinted Oxford, 1967), 19, which reads 'we will rather accompt him a mad man'. Smith comments on the prohibition on the exportation of bullion in LJ (A) v.75-6 where he states that it was based on a mistaken notion. He added:

> The wealth of a kingdom has by allmost all authors after Mun been considered as consisting in the gold and silver in it. In his book called England's [treasure] by foreign trade, he endeavours to shew the balance of trade is the only thing which can support England, as by this means gold and silver are brought into the kingdom, and in these allone he says the wealth of the kingdom can consist, as they alone are not perishable. On this doctrine of his, which however foolish has been adopted by all succeding writers, these laws [of felony] have been founded.'

Smith added that the exportation of bullion was first allowed by King William 'on the importunities of the merchants'. A similar point is made in LJ (B) 256–7, ed. Cannan 200–201, and see also LJ (B) 83, ed. Cannan 59, LJ (A) vi.147. LJ (A) vi.135 remarks, with regard to mercantilism, that 'Mr. Mun was the first who formed it into a regular system' and in ED 4.5 he states that confusion of wealth with money 'has given occasion to the systems of Mun and Gee; of Mandeville who built upon them; and of Mr Hume who endeavoured to refute them'. On the subject of felony, see below, IV.viii.19.

[14] See III.i.1. and IV.iii.c.2, where it is stated that nothing can be 'more absurd' than this doctrine. Mandeville held in Remark L that good politicians will 'keep a watchful Eye over the Balance of Trade in general, and never suffer that all the Foreign Commodities together, that are imported in one Year, shall exceed in Value what their own Growth or Manufacture is in the same exported to others . . . If what I urg'd last be but diligently look'd after, and the Imports are never allow'd to be superior to the Exports, no Nation can ever be impoverish'd by Foreign Luxury.' (*The Fable of the Bees*, pt.i.115, ed. Kaye, i.116.) Cantillon also held that 'To revive a State it is needful to have a care to bring about the influx of an annual, a constant and a real balance of Trade.' (*Essai*, 256, ed. Higgs 193.) See also, J. Child, *New Discourse of Trade* (1694), 152.

exchange was against any country, the more the balance of trade became necessarily against it; the money of that country becoming necessarily of so much less value, in comparison with that of the country to which the balance was due. That if the exchange between England and Holland, for example, was five per cent. against England, it would require a hundred and five ounces of silver in England to purchase a bill for a hundred ounces of silver in Holland: that a hundred and five ounces of silver in England, therefore, would be worth only a hundred ounces of silver in Holland, and would purchase only a proportionable quantity of Dutch goods: but that a hundred ounces of silver in Holland, on the contrary, would be worth a hundred and five ounces in England, and would purchase a proportionable quantity of English goods: That the English goods which were sold to Holland would be sold so much cheaper; and the Dutch goods which were sold to England, so much dearer, by the difference of the exchange; that the one would draw so much less Dutch money to England, and the other so much more English money to Holland as this difference amounted to: and that the balance of trade, therefore, would necessarily be [145] so much more against England, and would require a greater balance of gold and silver to be exported to Holland.

9   Those arguments were partly solid and partly sophistical. They were solid so far as they asserted that the exportation of gold and silver in trade might frequently be advantageous to the country. They were solid too in asserting that no prohibition could prevent their exportation, when private people found any advantage in exporting them.[15] But they were sophistical in supposing, that either to preserve or to augment the quantity of those metals required more the attention of government, than to preserve or to augment the quantity of any other useful commodities, which the freedom of trade, without any such attention, never fails to supply in the proper quantity. They were sophistical too, perhaps, in asserting that the high price of exchange necessarily increased, what they called, the unfavourable balance of trade, or occasioned the exportation of a greater quantity of gold and silver. That high price, indeed, was extremely disadvantageous to the merchants who had any money to pay in foreign countries. They paid so much dearer for the bills which their bankers granted them upon those countries. But though the risk arising from the prohibition might occasion some extraordinary expence to the bankers, it would not necessarily carry any more money out of the country. This expence would generally be all laid out in the country, in smuggling the money out of it, and could seldom occasion [146] the exportation of a single six-pence beyond the precise sum drawn for. The high price of exchange too would naturally dispose the merchants to endeavour to make their exports nearly balance their imports, in order that they might have this high exchange to pay upon

[15] See IV.v.a.19 and above, II.ii.30.

as small a sum as possible. The high price of exchange, ᶜbesides, must necessarily have operated as a tax, in raising the price of foreign goods, and thereby diminishing their consumption. It would tend, therefore,ᶜ not to increase, but to diminish, what they called, the unfavourable balance of trade, and consequently the exportation of gold and silver.¹⁶

10   Such as they were, however, those arguments convinced the people to whom they were addressed. They were addressed by merchants to parliaments, and to the councils of princes, to nobles and to country gentlemen; by those who were supposed to understand trade, to those who were conscious to themselves that they knew nothing about the matter.¹⁷ That foreign trade enriched the country, experience demonstrated to the nobles and country gentlemen, as well as to the merchants; but how, or in what manner, none of them well knew. The merchants knew perfectly in what manner it enriched themselves. It was their business to know it. But to know in what manner it enriched the country, was no part of their business. ᵈThisᵈ subject never came into their consideration, but when they had occasion to apply to their country for some change in the laws relating to foreign trade. It then be-[147]came necessary to say something about the beneficial effects of foreign trade, and the manner in which those effects were obstructed by the laws as they then stood. To the judges who were to decide the business, it appeared a most satisfactory account of the matter, when they were told that foreign trade brought money into the country, but that the laws in question hindered it from bringing so much as it otherwise would do. Those arguments therefore produced the wished-for effect. The prohibition of exporting gold and silver was in France and England confined to the coin of those respective countries. The exportation of foreign coin and of bullion was made free. In Holland, and in some other places, this liberty was extended even to the coin of the country. The attention of government was turned away from guarding against the exportation of gold and silver, to watch over the balance of trade, as the only cause which could occasion any augmentation or diminution of those metals.¹⁸ From one fruitless care it was turned away to another care much more intricate, much more embarrassing, and just equally fruitless. The title of Mun's book, England's Treasure in Foreign Trade,¹⁹ became a fundamental maxim in the political œconomy, not of England only, but of

---

ᶜ⁻ᶜ therefore, would tend, *1*   ᵈ⁻ᵈ The *6*

---

¹⁶ Compare Mun's comment that 'the undervaluing of our money in exchange, will not carry it out of the Kingdom, as some men have supposed, but rather is a means to make a less quantity thereof to be exported, than would be done at the *Par pro pari*.' (*England's Treasure by Forraign Trade* (reprinted 1967), 41–2.)

¹⁷ See below, IV.ii.21.

¹⁸ In LJ (B) 252, ed. Cannan 196 Smith also quotes Joshua Gee on the problems of an adverse balance, and John Locke at 254, ed. Cannan 198. Gee is also cited in LJ (A) vi.167.

¹⁹ 'By' not 'in'.

all other commercial countries. The inland or home trade, the most important of all, the trade in which an equal capital affords the greatest revenue, and creates the greatest employment to the people of the country,[20] was considered as subsidiary only to foreign trade. It [148] neither brought money into the country, it was said, nor carried any out of it. The country therefore could never become either richer or poorer by means of it, except so far as its prosperity or decay might indirectly influence the state of foreign trade.

11   A country that has no mines of its own must undoubtedly draw its gold and silver from foreign countries, in the same manner as one that has no vineyards of its own must draw its wines. It does not seem necessary, however, that the attention of government should be more turned towards the one than towards the other object. A country that has wherewithal to buy wine, will always get the wine which it has occasion for; and a country that has wherewithal to buy gold and silver, will never be in want of those metals.[21] They are to be bought for a certain price like all other commodities, and as they are the price of all other commodities, so all other commodities are the price of those metals. We trust with perfect security that the freedom of trade, without any attention of government, will always supply us with the wine which we have occasion for: and we may trust with equal security that it will always supply us with all the gold and silver which we can afford to purchase or to employ, either in circulating our commodities, or in other uses.[22]

12   The quantity of every commodity which human industry can either purchase or produce, naturally regulates itself in every country according to the effectual demand, or according to the [149] demand of those who are willing to pay the whole rent, labour and profits which must be paid in order to prepare and bring it to market. But no commodities regulate themselves more easily or more exactly according to this effectual demand[23] than gold and silver; because on account of the small bulk and great value of those metals, no commodities can be more easily transported from one place to another, from the places where they are cheap, to those where they are dear, from the places where they exceed, to those where they fall short of this effectual demand. If there *was* in England, for example, an effectual demand for an additional quantity of gold; a packet-boat could bring from Lisbon, or from wherever else it was to be had, fifty tuns of gold,

e-e were 4–6

----

[20] See above, II.v.25, for an elaboration of this point.

[21] Hume develops this theme in his essay 'Of the Balance of Trade', *Essays Moral, Political, and Literary*, ed. Green and Grose i.330–45.

[22] LJ (B) 247, ed. Cannan 192: 'Goods will always bring in money, and as long as the stock of commodities in any nation encreases, they have it in their power to augment the quantity of coin.'

[23] This term is explained above, I.vii.8, and below, IV.vi.13.

which could be coined into more than five millions of guineas.²⁴ But if there ᶠwasᶠ an effectual demand for grain to the same value, to import it would require, at five guineas a tun, a million of tuns of shipping, or a thousand ships of a thousand tuns each. The navy of England would not be sufficient.

13   When the quantity of gold and silver imported into any country exceeds the effectual demand, no vigilance of government can prevent their exportation. All the sanguinary laws of Spain and Portugal are not able to keep their gold and silver at home.²⁵ The continual importations from Peru and Brazil exceed the effectual demand of those countries, and sink the price of those metals there below that in the neighbouring countries.²⁶ If, on the contrary, in any particular country their quantity fell short of the effectual [150] demand, so as to raise their price above that ᵍofᵍ the neighbouring countries, the government would have no occasion to take any pains to import them. If it ʰwasʰ even to take pains to prevent their importation, it would not be able to effectuate it. Those metals, when the Spartans had got wherewithal to purchase them, broke through all the barriers which the laws of Lycurgus opposed to their entrance into Lacedemon.²⁷ All the sanguinary laws of the customs are not able to prevent the importation of the teas of the Dutch and Gottenburgh East India companies; because somewhat cheaper than those of the British company. A pound of tea, however, is about a hundred times the bulk of one of the highest prices, sixteen shillings, that is commonly paid for it in silver, and more than two thousand times the bulk of the same price in gold, and consequently just so many times more difficult to smuggle.

ᶠ⁻ᶠ were 4–6   ᵍ⁻ᵍ in ₁   ʰ⁻ʰ were 4–6

²⁴ See below, IV.vi.8, where it is stated on the authority of Joseph Baretti that the packet boat from Lisbon brings more than £50,000 in gold into England. Smith also comments on the ease with which gold may be transported at II.v.29, IV.v.a.18, and IV.vi.15.

²⁵ See below, IV.v.a.19, where Smith applies the analogy of the dam-head in this case. The Spanish and Portuguese prohibition on the export of gold is discussed in LJ (B) 258–9, ed. Cannan 202. Hume made a similar point in his essay 'Of the Balance of Trade' in inquiring: 'Can one imagine, that it had ever been possible, by any laws, or even by any art or industry, to have kept all the money in SPAIN, which the galleons have brought from the INDIES?' (*Essays Moral, Political and Literary*, ed. Green and Grose, i.334.)

²⁶ It is stated at IV.vii.c.53 that the degradation of the value of gold and silver is one of the causes which nearly overbalanced the 'natural good effects of the colony trade' in the case of Spain and Portugal. See also I.xi.n.1.

²⁷ 'In the reign of Agis, gold and silver money first flowed into Sparta, and with money, greed and a desire for wealth prevailed through the agency of Lysander, who, though incorruptible himself, filled his country with the love of riches and with luxury, by bringing home gold and silver from the war, and thus subverting the laws of Lycurgus.' (Plutarch *Life of Lycurgus*, xxx, translated by B. Perrin, *Plutarch's Lives* (1914), i.297.) in Loeb Classical Library. Cantillon and Hume both refer to this aspect of the Lycurgan Laws. Cantillon, *Essai*, 143–4, ed. Higgs 109, and Hume 'On the Balance of Trade', *Essays Moral, Political, and Literary*, ed. Green and Grose, i.338. Sir James Steuart described the republic of Lycurgus as 'the most perfect plan of political œconomy' in *Principles of Political Oeconomy*, II.xiv.

14   It is partly owing to the easy transportation of gold and silver from the places where they abound to those where they are wanted, that the price of those metals does not fluctuate continually like that of the greater part ⎯ of other commodities, which are hindered by their bulk from shifting their situation, when the market happens to be either over or under-stocked with them.[28] The price of those metals, indeed, is not altogether exempted from variation, but the changes to which it is liable are generally slow, gradual, and uniform. In Europe, for example, it is supposed, without much foundation, perhaps, [151] that, during the course of the present and preceding century, they have been constantly, but gradually, sinking in their value, on the account of the continual importations from the Spanish West Indies.[29] But to make any sudden change in the price of gold and silver, so as to raise or lower at once, sensibly and remarkably, the money price of all other commodities, requires such a revolution in commerce as that occasioned by the discovery of America.

15   If, notwithstanding all this, gold and silver should at any time fall short in a country which has wherewithal to purchase them, there are more expedients for supplying their place, than that of almost any other commodity. If the materials of manufacture are wanted, industry must stop. If provisions are wanted, the people must starve. But if money is wanted, barter will supply its place, though with a good deal of inconveniency. Buying and selling upon credit, and the different dealers compensating their credits with one another, once a month or once a year, will supply it with less inconveniency. A well regulated paper money will supply it, not only without any inconveniency, but[i], in some cases, with some[i] advantages.[30] Upon every account, therefore, the attention of government never was so unnecessarily employed, as when directed to watch over the preservation or increase of the quantity of money in any country.

16   No complaint, however, is more common than that of a scarcity of money. Money, like wine, must always be scarce with those who have nei-[152]ther wherewithal to buy it, nor credit to borrow it. Those who have either, will seldom be in want either of the money, or of the wine which they have occasion for. This complaint, however, of the scarcity of money, is not always confined to improvident spendthrifts. It is sometimes general through a whole mercantile town, and the country in its neighbourhood. Overtrading is the common cause of it. Sober men, whose projects have

---

[i-i] with very great *1*

[28] See above, I.vii.17.
[29] See above, I.xi.g.16–37, where Smith discusses the trends in the value of the metals, and IV.v.a.5, where he refers to a 'gradual and insensible rise' in the value of silver during the present century.
[30] See above, II.ii.26. The use of paper as a substitute for gold is considered in LJ (A) vi.130.

been disproportioned to their capitals, are as likely to have neither wherewithal to buy money, nor credit to borrow it, as prodigals whose expence
has been disproportioned to their revenue.[31] Before their projects can be
brought to bear, their stock is gone, and their credit with it. They run
about every where to borrow money, and every body tells them that they
have none to lend. Even such general complaints of the scarcity of money
do not always prove that the usual number of gold and silver pieces are
not circulating in the country, but that many people want those pieces
who have nothing to give for them. When the profits of trade happen to
be greater than ordinary, overtrading becomes a general error both among
great and small dealers. They do not always send more money abroad than
usual, but they buy upon credit both at home and abroad, an unusual
quantity of goods, which they send to some distant market, in hopes that
the returns will come in before the demand for payment. The demand
comes before the returns, and they have nothing at hand, with which they
can either [153] purchase money, or give solid security for borrowing. It is
not any scarcity of gold and silver, but the difficulty which such people
find in borrowing, and which their creditors find in getting payment, that
occasions the general complaint of the scarcity of money.

17   It would be too ridiculous to go about seriously to prove, that wealth
does not consist in money, or in gold and silver; but in what money purchases, and is valuable only for purchasing.[32] Money, no doubt, makes
always a part of the national capital; but it has already been shown that it
generally makes but a small part, and always the most unprofitable part
of it.[33]

18   It is not because wealth consists more essentially in money than in
goods, that the merchant finds it generally more easy to buy goods with
money, than to buy money with goods; but because money is the known
and established instrument of commerce, for which every thing is readily
given in exchange, but which is not always with equal readiness to be
got in exchange for every thing. The greater part of goods besides are more
perishable than money, and he may frequently sustain a much greater loss
by keeping them.[34] When his goods are upon hand too, he is more liable to
such demands for money as he may not be able to answer, than when
he has got their price in his coffers. Over and above all this, his profit
arises more directly from selling than from buying, and he is upon all these
accounts generally much more anxious to exchange his goods for money,

[31] Cf. II.iv.15.
[32] See above, I.v.
[33] See above, II.i.19, where money is stated to be a part of the circulating capital of
society. It is remarked at II.ii.23 that this part of capital does not contribute to revenue.
See generally II.ii and especially §1–23.
[34] Smith comments on the problem of perishable commodities in discussing price
determination at I.vii.10.

than his mo-[154]ney for goods. But though a particular merchant, with abundance of goods in his warehouse, may sometimes be ruined by not being able to sell them in time, a nation or country is not liable to the same accident. The whole capital of a merchant frequently consists in perishable goods destined for purchasing money. But it is but a very small part of the annual produce of the land and labour of a country which can ever be destined for purchasing gold and silver from their neighbours. The far greater part is circulated and consumed among themselves; and even of the surplus which is sent abroad, the greater part is generally destined for the purchase of other foreign goods. Though gold and silver, therefore, could not be had in exchange for the goods destined to purchase them, the nation would not be ruined. It might, indeed, suffer some loss and inconveniency, and be forced upon some of those expedients which are. necessary for supplying the place of money. The annual produce of its land and labour, however, would be the same, or very nearly the same, as usual, because the same, or very nearly the same consumable capital would be employed in maintaining it. And though goods do not always draw money so readily as money draws goods, in the long-run they draw it more necessarily than even it draws them. Goods can serve many other purposes besides purchasing money, but money can serve no other purpose besides purchasing goods. Money, therefore, necessarily runs after goods, but goods do not always or necessarily run after money. [155] The man who buys, does not always mean to sell again, but frequently to use or to consume; whereas he who sells, always means to buy again. The one may frequently have done the whole, but the other can never have done more than the one-half of his business. It is not for its own sake that men desire money, but for the sake of what they can purchase with it.[35]

19   Consumable commodities, it is said, are soon destroyed; whereas gold and silver are of a more durable nature, and, were it not for this continual exportation, might be accumulated for ages together, to the incredible augmentation of the real wealth of the country. Nothing, therefore, it is pretended, can be more disadvantageous to any country, than the trade which consists in the exchange of such lasting for such perishable commodities. We do not, however, reckon that trade disadvantageous which consists in the exchange of the hardware of England for the wines of France; and yet hardware is a very durable commodity, and *ʲwasʲ* it not for this continual exportation, might too be accumulated for ages together, to the incredible augmentation of the pots and pans of the country. But it readily occurs that the number of such utensils is in every country necessarily limited by the use which there is for them; that it would be absurd to have

----

ʲ⁻ʲ were *4–6*

[35] Money is described as 'the great wheel of circulation' at II.ii.23; see also IV.vi.27, where money is described as a commodity with regard to which every man is a merchant.

more pots and pans than were necessary for cooking the victuals usually consumed there; and that if the quantity of victuals were to increase, the number of pots and pans would readily increase along with it,[36] a part of the increased quantity of victuals being employed in [156] purchasing them, or in maintaining an additional number of workmen whose business it was to make them. It should as readily occur that the quantity of gold and silver is in every country limited by the use which there is for those metals; that their use consists in circulating commodities as coin, and in affording a species of houshold furniture as plate; that the quantity of coin in every country is regulated by the value of the commodities which are to be circulated by it: increase that value, and immediately a part of it will be sent abroad to purchase, wherever it is to be had, the additional quantity of coin requisite for circulating them: that the quantity of plate is regulated by the number and wealth of those private families who chuse to indulge themselves in that sort of magnificence: increase the number and wealth of such families, and a part of this increased wealth will most probably be employed in purchasing, wherever it is to be found, an additional quantity of plate: that to attempt to increase the wealth of any country, either by introducing or by detaining in it an unnecessary quantity of gold and silver, is as absurd as it would be to attempt to increase the good cheer of private families, by obliging them to keep an unnecessary number of kitchen utensils. As the expence of purchasing those unnecessary utensils would diminish instead of increasing either the quantity or goodness of the family provisions; so the expence of purchasing an unnecessary quantity of gold and silver must, in every country, as necessarily diminish the wealth which feeds, cloaths, and [157] lodges, which maintains and employs the people. Gold and silver, whether in the shape of coin or of plate, are utensils, it must be remembered, as much as the furniture of the kitchen. Increase the use for them, increase the consumable commodities which are to be circulated, managed, and prepared by means of them, and you will infallibly increase the quantity; but if you attempt, by extraordinary means, to increase the quantity, you will as infallibly diminish the use and even the quantity too, which in those metals can never be greater than what the use requires. Were they ever to be accumulated beyond this quantity, their transportation is so easy, and the loss which attends their lying idle and unemployed so great, that no law could prevent their being immediately sent out of the country.

20   It is not always necessary to accumulate gold and silver, in order to enable a country to carry on foreign wars, and to maintain fleets and armies in distant countries. Fleets and armies are maintained, not with gold and silver, but with consumable goods.[37] The nation which, from the annual

[36] See above, II.ii.30, for an elaboration of this point.
[37] See above, II.iii.2.

produce of its domestick industry, from the annual revenue arising out of its lands, labour, and consumable stock, has wherewithal to purchase those consumable goods in distant countries, can maintain foreign wars there.

21   A nation may purchase the pay and provisions of an army in a distant country three different ways; by sending abroad either, first, some part of its accumulated gold and silver; or, se-[158]condly, some part of the annual produce of its manufactures; or last of all, some part of its annual rude produce.

22   The gold and silver which can properly be considered as accumulated or stored up in any country, may be distinguished into three parts; first, the circulating money; secondly, the plate of private families; and last of all, the money which may have been collected by many years parsimony, and laid up in the treasury of the prince.

23   It can seldom happen that much can be spared from the circulating money of the country; because in that there can seldom be much redundancy. The value of goods annually bought and sold in any country requires a certain quantity of money to circulate and distribute them to their proper consumers, and can give employment to no more. The channel of circulation necessarily draws to itself a sum sufficient to fill it, and never admits any more. Something, however, is generally withdrawn from this channel in the case of foreign war. By the great number of people who are maintained abroad, fewer are maintained at home. Fewer goods are circulated there, and less money becomes necessary to circulate them. An extraordinary quantity of paper money, of some sort or other too, such as exchequer notes, navy bills, and bank bills in England, is generally issued upon such occasions, and by supplying the place of circulating gold and silver, gives an opportunity of sending a greater quantity of it abroad. All [159] this, however, could afford but a poor resource for maintaining a foreign war, of great expence and several years duration.

24   The melting down the plate of private families, has upon every occasion been found a still more insignificant one. The French, in the beginning of the last war, did not derive so much advantage from this expedient as to compensate the loss of the fashion.

25   The accumulated treasures of the prince have, in former times, afforded a much greater and more lasting resource. In the present times, if you except the king of Prussia, to accumulate treasure seems to be no part of the policy of European princes.[38]

26   The funds which maintained the foreign wars of the present century, the most expensive perhaps which history records, seem to have had little dependency upon the exportation either of the circulating money, or of the plate of private families, or of the treasure of the prince. The last French

---

[38] See below, §30. Smith comments on accumulated treasures of modern times at V.i.g.41, V.ii.a.8, and V.iii.3.

war cost Great Britain upwards of ninety millions, including not only the seventy-five millions of new debt that was contracted,[39] but the additional two shillings in the pound land tax, and what was annually borrowed of the sinking fund. More than two-thirds of this expence ᵏwasᵏ laid out in distant countries; in Germany, Portugal, America, in the ports of the Mediterranean, in the East and West Indies. The kings of England had no accumulated treasure. We never heard of any extraordinary quantity of plate being melted down. The cir-[160]culating gold and silver of the country had not been supposed to exceed eighteen millions. Since the late recoinage of the gold, however, it is believed to have been a good deal under-rated.[40] Let us suppose, therefore, according to the ˡmostˡ exaggerated computation ᵐwhich I remember to have either seen or heard of,ᵐ that, gold and silver together, it amounted to thirty millions.[41] Had the war been carried on, by means of our money, the whole of it must, even according to this computation, have been sent out and returned again at least twice, in a period of between six and seven years. Should this be supposed, it would afford the most decisive argument to demonstrate how unnecessary it is for government to watch over the preservation of money, since upon this supposition the whole money of the country must have gone from it and returned to it again, two different times in so short a period, without any body's knowing any thing of the matter. The channel of circulation, however, never appeared more empty than usual during any part of this period. Few people wanted money who had wherewithal to pay for it. The profits of foreign trade, indeed, were greater than usual during the whole war; but especially towards the end of it. This occasioned, what it always occasions, a general overtrading in all the ports of Great Britain; and this again occasioned the usual complaint of the scarcity of money, which always follows overtrading. Many people wanted it, who had neither wherewithal to buy it, nor credit to borrow it; and because the debtors [161] found it difficult to borrow, the creditors found it difficult to get

---

ᵏ⁻ᵏ were *4–6*   ˡ⁻ˡ *2–6*   ᵐ⁻ᵐ of Mr. Horsely, *1* [See index, s.v. Magens]

[39] Smith comments on the cost of the conflict with France at II.iii.35 and cites the same figures at IV.vii.c.64 and V.iii.92; cf. also IV.viii.53. See *The Present State of the Nation*, attributed to W. Knox (1768), 27, and cf. Sir John Sinclair, *The History of the Public Revenue of the British Empire* (London, 1803), i.465, especially n.2.

[40] The 'late reformation' of the coinage is discussed extensively at I.v.29 ff. and IV.vi.18 ff.

[41] Cf. LJ (A) vi.136–7: 'The highest computation of the cash in Great Britain makes it not above 30 mills; it is probably less, but can not be more, by no computation.' Smith endeavours to justify this statement in the remaining part of the lecture and in the course of his argument suggests that 'The only method we have to judge of the quantity of money requisite to carry on the circulation is the amount of the rent of land estates. This according to the computation of the land tax is but 12½ mills. in the half year. The landholders in fact pay all the others . . . So that the land rent circulates thro the country and pays all the nation.' (LJ (A) vi.142–3.) In LJ (B) 289, ed. Cannan 224, the annual rents in England are valued at 24 millions; cf. Cantillon, *Essai* ᵗI.iv.

payment. Gold and silver, however, were generally to be had for their value, by those who had that value to give for them.

27   The enormous expence of the late war, therefore, must have been chiefly defrayed, not by the exportation of gold and silver, but by that of British commodities of some kind or other. When the government, or those who acted under them, contracted with a merchant for a remittance to some foreign country, he would naturally endeavour to pay his foreign correspondent, upon whom he had granted a bill, by sending abroad rather commodities than gold and silver. If the commodities of Great Britain were not in demand in that country, he would endeavour to send them to some other country, in which he could purchase a bill upon that country. The transportation of commodities, when properly suited to the market, is always attended with a considerable profit; whereas that of gold and silver is scarce ever attended with any. When those metals are sent abroad in order to purchase foreign commodities, the merchant's profit arises, not from the purchase, but from the sale of the returns. But when they are sent abroad merely to pay a debt, he gets no returns, and consequently no profit. He naturally, therefore, exerts his invention to find out a way of paying his foreign debts, rather by the exportation of commodities than by that of gold and silver. The great quantity of British goods exported [162] during the course of the late war, without bringing back any returns, is accordingly remarked by the author of The Present State of the Nation.[42]

28   Besides the three sorts of gold and silver above mentioned, there is in all great commercial countries a good deal of bullion alternately imported and exported for the purposes of foreign trade. This bullion, as it circulates among different commercial countries in the same manner as the national coin circulates in every particular country, may be considered as the money of the great mercantile republick. The national coin receives its movement and direction from the commodities circulated within the precincts of each particular country: the money of the mercantile republick, from those circulated between different countries. Both are employed in facilitating exchanges, the one between different individuals of the same, the other between those of different nations. Part of this money of the great mercantile republick may have been, and probably was, employed in carrying on the late war. In time of a general war, it is natural to suppose that a movement and direction should be impressed upon it, different from what it usually follows in profound peace; that it should circulate more about the seat of the war, and be more employed in purchasing there, and in the neighbouring countries, the pay and provisions of the different armies.

---

[42] 'The increase in the exports was found to have been occasioned chiefly by the demands of our own fleets and armies, and, instead of bringing wealth to the nation, were to be paid for by oppressive taxes upon the people of England.' (*The Present State of the Nation*, attributed to W. Knox, 8.)

But whatever part of this money of the mercantile republick, Great Britain may have annually employed in this [163] manner, it must have been annually purchased, either with British commodities, or with something else that had been purchased with them; which still ⁿbringsⁿ us back to commodities, to the annual produce of the land and labour of the country, as the ultimate resources which enabled us to carry on the war. It is natural indeed to suppose, that so great an annual expence must have been defrayed from a great annual produce. The expence of 1761, for example, amounted to more than nineteen millions.[43] No accumulation could have supported so great an annual profusion. There is no annual produce even of gold and silver which could have supported it. The whole gold and silver annually imported into both Spain and Portugal, according to the best accounts, does not commonly much exceed six millions sterling,[44] which, in some years, would scarce have paid four months expence of the late war.

29   The commodities most proper for being transported to distant countries, in order to purchase there, either the pay and provisions of an army, or some part of the money of the mercantile republick to be employed in purchasing them, seem to be the finer and more improved manufactures; such as contain a great value in a small bulk, and can, therefore, be exported to a great distance at little expence. A country whose industry produces a great annual surplus of such manufactures, which are usually exported to foreign countries, may carry on for many years a very expensive foreign war, without either ex-[164]porting any considerable quantity of gold and silver, or even having any such quantity to export. A considerable part of the annual surplus of its manufactures must, indeed, in this case be exported, without bringing back any returns ᵒto the country, though it does to the merchant; the government purchasing of the merchant his bills upon foreign countries, in order to purchase there the pay and provisions of an armyᵒ. Some part of ᵖthis surplusᵖ, however, may still continue to bring back a return. The manufacturers, during the war, will have a double demand upon them, and be called upon, first, to work up goods to be sent abroad, for paying the bills drawn upon foreign countries for the pay and provisions of the army; and, secondly, to work up such as are necessary for purchasing the common returns that had usually been consumed in the country. In the midst of the most destructive foreign war,

---

ⁿ⁻ⁿ bring 6   ᵒ⁻ᵒ 3–6   ᵖ⁻ᵖ it 1–2

[43] 'During the year which ended with the dissolution of Parliament on 19 March 1761 supplies of £18,816,019—19—19¾ had been granted for the year, and of that sum £13,948,700—2—3½ was for sea and land service. A sum should be added as a share of the total civil list expenditure of £800,000, fixed for a year from 25 October 1760.' (A. Anderson, *Origin of Commerce* (1764), ii.420–1.)

[44] These figures are cited at I.xi.g.32,33 on the authority of Raynal and Magens; and see below, IV.v.b.45.

therefore, the greater part of manufactures may frequently flourish greatly; and, on the contrary, they may decline on the return of the peace. They may flourish amidst the ruin of their country, and begin to decay upon the return of its prosperity. The different state of many different branches of the British manufactures during the late war, and for some time after the peace, may serve as an illustration of what has been just now said.

30   No foreign war of great expence or duration could conveniently be carried on by the exportation of the rude produce of the soil. The expence of sending such a quantity of it to a fo-[165]reign country as might purchase the pay and provisions of an army, would be too great. Few countries too produce much more rude produce than what is sufficient for the subsistence of their own inhabitants. To send abroad any great quantity of it, therefore, would be to send abroad a part of the necessary subsistence of the people. It is otherwise with the exportation of manufactures. The maintenance of the people employed in them is kept at home, and only the surplus part of their work is exported. Mr. Hume frequently takes notice of the inability of the ancient kings of England to carry on, without interruption, any foreign war of long duration.[45] The English, in those days, had nothing wherewithal to purchase the pay and provisions of their armies in foreign countries, but either the rude produce of the soil, of which no considerable part could be spared from the home consumption, or a few manufactures of the coarsest kind, of which, as well as of the rude produce, the transportation was too expensive. This inability did not arise from the want of money, but of the finer and more improved manufactures. Buying and selling was transacted by means of money in England then, as well as now. The quantity of circulating money must have borne the same proportion to the number and value of purchases and sales usually transacted at that time, which it does to those transacted at present; or rather it must have borne a greater proportion because there was then no paper, which now occupies a great part of the employment of gold [166] and silver. Among nations to whom commerce and manufactures are little known, the sovereign, upon extraordinary occasions, can seldom draw any considerable aid from his subjects, for reasons which shall be explained hereafter.[46] It is in such countries, therefore, that he generally endeavours to accumulate a treasure, as the only resource against such emergencies. Independent of this necessity, he is in such a situation naturally disposed to the parsimony requisite for accumulation. In that simple state, the

---

[45] Hume commented on the war between England and France in 1415: 'The poverty of all the European princes, and the small resources of their kingdoms, were of cause of these continual interruptions in their hostilities; and though the maxims of war were in general destructive, their military operations were mere incursions, which, without any settled plan, they carried on against each other.' (*History of England* (1778), iii.103–4.)

[46] See below, V.iii.9.

expence even of a sovereign is not directed by the vanity which delights in the gaudy finery of a court, but is employed in bounty to his tenants, and hospitality to his retainers.[47] But bounty and hospitality very seldom lead to extravagance; though vanity almost always does. Every Tartar chief, accordingly, has a treasure.[48] The treasures of Mazepa, chief of the Cossacks in the Ukraine, the famous ally of Charles the XIIth, are said to have been very great. The French kings of the Merovingian race had all treasures. When they divided their kingdom among their different children, they divided their treasure too. The Saxon princes, and the first kings after the conquest, seem likewise to have accumulated treasures. The first exploit of every new reign was commonly to seize the treasure of the preceding king, as the most essential measure for securing the succession.[49] The sovereigns of improved and commercial countries are not under the same necessity of accumulating treasures, because they can generally draw from their subjects extraordi-[167]nary aids upon extraordinary occasions. They are likewise less disposed to do so.[50] They naturally, perhaps necessarily, follow the mode of the times, and their expence comes to be regulated by the same extravagant vanity which directs that of all the other great proprietors in their dominions.[51] The insignificant pageantry of their court becomes every day more brilliant, and the expence of it not only prevents accumulation, but frequently encroaches upon the funds destined for more necessary expences. What Dercyllidas said of the court of Persia, may be applied to that of several European princes, that he saw there much splendor but little strength, and many servants but few soldiers.[52]

31   The importation of gold and silver is not the principal, much less the sole benefit which a nation derives from its foreign trade. Between whatever places foreign trade is carried on, they all of them derive two distinct benefits from it. It carries out that surplus part of the produce of their land and labour for which there is no demand among them, and brings back in return for it something else for which there is a demand. It gives a value to their superfluities, by exchanging them for something else, which may satisfy a part of their wants, and increase their enjoyments.[53] By means of

[47] See above, III.iv.5, and below, V.iii.2.

[48] The military organization of the Tartars is described in V.i.a.3–5.

[49] See above, II.i.31.

[50] It is remarked at V.iii.8 that modern governments, in contrast to more primitive forms, foresee 'the facility of borrowing' and therefore dispense with the duty of saving.

[51] See above, III.iv, and especially § 10.

[52] 'Antiochus [not Dercyllidas] reported back to the Ten Thousand [The Arcadian Assembly] that the King [of the Persians] had bakers, and cooks, and wine-pourers, and door-keepers in vast numbers, but as for men who could fight with Greeks, he said that though he sought diligently he could not see any.' (Xenophon, *Hellenica*, VII.i.38, translated by C. L. Brownson in Loeb Classical Library (1921), 142–3.)

[53] The doctrine of 'vent for surplus' was widely applied: see, for example, II.v.33, III.i.1, and IV.iii.c.4.

it, the narrowness of the home market does not hinder the division of labour in any particular branch of art or manufacture from being carried to the highest perfection.[54] By opening a more extensive market for whatever part of the produce of their labour [168] may exceed the home consumption, it encourages them to improve its productive powers, and to augment its annual produce to the utmost, and thereby 9to9 increase the real revenue and wealth of the society. These great and important services foreign trade is continually occupied in performing, to all the different countries between which it is carried on.[55] They all derive great benefit from it, though that in which the merchant resides generally derives the greatest, as he is generally more employed in supplying the wants, and carrying out the superfluities of his own, than of any other particular country. To import the gold and silver which may be wanted, into the countries which have no mines, is, no doubt, a part of the business of foreign commerce. It is, however, a most insignificant part of it. A country which carried on foreign trade merely upon this account, could scarce have occasion to freight a ship in a century.

32   It is not by the importation of gold and silver, that the discovery of America has enriched Europe. By the abundance of the American mines, those metals have become cheaper.[56] A service of plate can now be purchased for about a third part of the corn, or a third part of the labour, which it would have cost in the fifteenth century. With the same annual expence of labour and commodities, Europe can annually purchase about three times the quantity of plate which it could have purchased at that time. But when a commodity comes to be sold for a third part of what had been its usual price, not [169] only those who purchased it before can purchase three times their former quantity, but it is brought down to the level of a much greater number of purchasers; perhaps to more than ten, perhaps to more than twenty times the former number. So that there may be in Europe at present not only more than three times, but more than twenty or thirty times the quantity of plate which would have been in it, even in its present state of improvement, had the discovery of the American mines never been made. So far Europe has, no doubt, gained a real

9–9 3–6

---

[54] The basic principle is discussed in I.iii.

[55] Smith comments on the fact that trade is mutually advantageous to the parties involved in LJ (B) 261–2, ed. Cannan 204, and goes on to suggest that 'It were happy, therefore, both for this country and for France, that all national prejudices were rooted out, and a free and uninterrupted commerce established.' (LJ (B) 265, ed. Cannan 206.) The same point is made at 269, ed. Cannan 209, and in LJ (A) vi.160–7, where the advantages involved are explicitly linked to the division of labour: 'It is on the power of this exchange that the division of labour depends, which as has been shown to the satisfaction of the whole of you is the great foundation of opulence, as it occasions the production of a greater quantity of the severall things wrought in.' (161–2.)

[56] See above, I.xi.f.3 and V.ii.c.5.

conveniency, though surely a very trifling one. The cheapness of gold and silver renders those metals rather less fit for the purposes of money than they were before. In order to make the same purchases, we must load ourselves with a greater quantity of them, and carry about a shilling in our pocket where a groat would have done before. It is difficult to say which is most trifling, this inconveniency, or the opposite conveniency. Neither the one nor the other could have made any very essential change in the state of Europe. The discovery of America, however, certainly made a most essential one.[57] By opening a new and inexhaustible market to all the commodities of Europe, it gave occasion to new divisions of labour and improvements of art, which, in the narrow circle of the antient commerce, could never have taken place for want of a market to take off the greater part of their produce. The productive powers of labour were improved, and its produce increased in all the different coun-[170]tries of Europe, and together with it the real revenue and wealth of the inhabitants. The commodities of Europe were almost all new to America, and many of those of America were new to Europe. A new sett of exchanges, therefore, began to take place which had never been thought of before, and which should naturally have proved as advantageous to the new, as it certainly did to the old continent. The savage injustice of the Europeans rendered an event, which ought to have been beneficial to all, ruinous and destructive to several of those unfortunate countries.[58]

33   The discovery of a passage to the East Indies, by the Cape of Good Hope, which happened much about the same time, opened, perhaps, a still more extensive range to foreign commerce than even that of America, notwithstanding the greater distance.[59] There were but two nations in America, in any respect superior to savages, and these were destroyed almost as soon as discovered. The rest were mere savages. But the empires of China, Indostan, Japan, as well as several others in the East Indies, without having richer mines of gold or silver, were in every other respect much richer, better cultivated, and more advanced in all arts and manufactures than either Mexico or Peru, even though we should credit, what plainly deserves no credit, the exaggerated accounts of the Spanish writers, concerning the antient state of those empires. But rich and civilized nations can always exchange to a much greater value with one another, than [171] with savages and barbarians. Europe, however, has hitherto derived much less advantage from its commerce with the East Indies, than from that

[57] See generally, IV.vii.c, where Smith discusses the advantages acquired by Europe from the discovery of America.
[58] Smith comments at IV.vii.c.80 and 100 on the injustices inflicted by the Europeans on the original peoples of the colonies.
[59] The discovery of America, and of the passage to India via the Cape of Good Hope are cited at IV.vii.c.80 as the 'two greatest and most important events recorded in the history of mankind'.

with America. The Portuguese monopolized the East India trade to themselves for about a century, and it was only indirectly and through them,
that the other nations of Europe could either send out or receive any goods
from that country. When the Dutch, in the beginning of the last century,
began to encroach upon them, they vested their whole East India commerce
in an exclusive company. The English, French, Swedes, and Danes, have
all followed their example, so that no great nation in Europe has ever yet
had the benefit of a free commerce to the East Indies. No other reason need
be assigned why it has never been so advantageous as the trade to America,
which, between almost every nation of Europe and its own colonies, is free
to all its subjects. The exclusive privileges of those East India companies,
their great riches, the great favour and protection which these have procured them from their respective governments, have excited much envy
against them. This envy has frequently represented their trade as altogether pernicious, on account of the great quantities of silver, which it
every year exports from the countries from which it is carried on. The
parties concerned have replied, that their trade, by this continual exportation of silver, might, indeed, tend to impoverish Europe in general, but not
the particular country from which it was carried on; because, by the export-
[172]ation of a part of the returns to other European countries, it annually
brought home a much greater quantity of that metal than it carried out.
Both the objection and the reply are founded in the popular notion which I
have been just now examining. It is, therefore, unnecessary to say any
thing further about either. By the annual exportation of silver to the
East Indies, plate is probably somewhat dearer in Europe than it otherwise might have been; and coined silver probably purchases a larger quantity both of labour and commodities. The former of these two effects is a
a very small loss, the latter a very small advantage; both too insignificant
to deserve any part of the publick attention. The trade to the East Indies,
by opening a market to the commodities of Europe, or, what comes nearly
to the same thing, to the gold and silver which is purchased with those
commodities, must necessarily tend to increase the annual production of
European commodities, and consequently the real wealth and revenue of
Europe. That it has hitherto increased them so little, is probably owing to
the restraints which it every where labours under.

34   I thought it necessary, though at the hazard of being tedious, to examine
at full length this popular notion that wealth consists in money, or in gold
and silver. Money in common language, as I have already observed, frequently signifies wealth;[60] and this ambiguity of expression has rendered
this popular notion so familiar to us, that even they, who are convinced of
its ab-[173]surdity, are very apt to forget their own principles, and in the
course of their reasonings to take it for granted as a certain and undeniable

[60] See generally, IV.i.

truth. Some of the best English writers upon commerce set out with observing, that the wealth of a country consists, not in its gold and silver only, but in its lands, houses, and consumable goods of all different kinds. In the course of their reasonings, however, the lands, houses, and consumable goods seem to slip out of their memory, and the strain of their argument frequently supposes that all wealth consists in gold and silver, and that to multiply those metals is the great object of national industry and commerce.

35   The two principles being established, however, that wealth consisted in gold and silver, and that those metals could be brought into a country which had no mines only by the balance of trade, or by exporting to a greater value than it imported; it necessarily became the great object of political œconomy to diminish as much as possible the importation of foreign goods for home-consumption, and to increase as much as possible the exportation of the produce of domestick industry. Its two great engines for enriching the country, therefore, were restraints upon importation, and encouragements to exportation.[61]

36   The restraints upon importation were of two kinds.

37   First, Restraints upon the importation of such foreign goods for home-consumption as [174] could be produced at home, from whatever country they were imported.

38   Secondly, Restraints upon the importation of goods of almost all kinds from those particular countries with which the balance of trade was supposed to be disadvantageous.

39   Those different restraints consisted sometimes in high duties, and sometimes in absolute prohibitions.

40   Exportation was encouraged sometimes by drawbacks, sometimes by bounties, sometimes by advantageous treaties of commerce with foreign states, and sometimes by the establishment of colonies in distant countries.

41   Drawbacks were given upon two different occasions. When the home-manufactures were subject to any duty or excise, either the whole or a part of it was frequently drawn back upon their exportation; and when foreign goods liable to a duty were imported in order to be exported again, either the whole or a part of this duty was sometimes given back upon such exportation.

42   Bounties were given for the encouragement either of some beginning manufactures, or of such sorts of industry of other kinds as were supposed to deserve particular favour.

----

[61] Similar sentiments are expressed below, IV.viii.1, where Smith also drew attention to types of policy designed to *encourage* certain kinds of import and to discourage some exports, e.g. the materials of manufacture and 'instruments' of trade. Smith also refers to monopoly 'of one kind or another' as the 'sole engine of the mercantile system' at IV.vii.c.89.

43   By advantageous treaties of commerce, particular privileges were procured in some foreign state for the goods and merchants of the country,
beyond what were granted to those of other countries.

44   [175] By the establishment of colonies in distant countries, not only particular privileges, but a monopoly was frequently procured for the goods
and merchants of the country which established them.

45   The two sorts of restraints upon importation above-mentioned, together
with these four encouragements to exportation, constitute the six principal
means by which the commercial system proposes to increase the quantity
of gold and silver in any country by turning the balance of trade in its
favour. I shall consider each of them in a particular chapter, and without
taking much further notice of their supposed tendency to bring money into
the country, I shall examine chiefly what are likely to be the effects of each
of them upon the annual produce of its industry. According as they tend
either to increase or diminish the value of this annual produce, they must
evidently tend either to increase or diminish the real wealth and revenue
of the country.

CHAPTER II

Of Restraints upon the Importation ᵃfrom foreign Countries of such Goodsᵃ as can be produced at Home

1 BY restraining, either by high duties, or by absolute prohibitions, the importation of such goods from foreign countries as can be produced at home, the monopoly of the home-market is more or less secured to the domestick industry employed in producing them. Thus the prohibition[1] of importing either live cattle or salt provisions from foreign countries secures to the graziers of Great Britain the monopoly of the home-market for butchers-meat. The high duties upon the importation of corn, which in times of moderate plenty amount to a prohibition, give a like advantage to the growers of that commodity.[2] The prohibiton of the importation of foreign woollens is equally favourable to the woollen manufacturers.[3] The silk manufacture, though altogether employed upon foreign materials, has lately obtained the same advantage.[4] The linen manufacture has not yet obtained it, but is making great strides towards it.[5] Many other sorts of manufacturers have, in the same manner, obtained in Great Britain, either altogether, or very nearly a monopoly against their countrymen. ᵇThe variety of goods of which the importation into Great Britain is prohibited, [177] either absolutely, or under certain circumstances, greatly exceeds what can easily be suspected by those who are not well acquainted with the laws of the customs.ᵇ [6]

ᵃ⁻ᵃ *of such Goods from Foreign Countries* 1   ᵇ⁻ᵇ *3–6*

---

[1] By 18 and 19 Charles II, c. 2 (1666) in *Statutes of the Realm*, v.597; 18 Charles II, c. 2 in Ruffhead's edition. Imports from Ireland were allowed from 1759 by 32 George II, c. 11 (1758). See above, III.iv.20, and below, IV.ii.16 and V.ii.k.13.

[2] 22 Charles II, c. 13 (1670). See above, III.iv.20, and below, IV.ii.16, IV.v.a.23, IV.v.b.33 and 37, IV.vii.b.33, V.ii.k.13.

[3] By 4 Edward IV, c. 1 (1464). Controls over the import and export of wool are discussed at IV.viii.17, where it is pointed out that the manufacturers of woollen products had been more successful than others in persuading the legislature to meet their special needs. Cf. Pownall, *Letter*, 29–31. In Letter 203 addressed to William Eden, dated 3 January 1780, Smith called for a repeal of all prohibitions on importation, and that on the exportation of wool.

[4] 6 George III, c. 28 (1766), extended by 11 George III, c. 49 (1771). See below, IV.iv.7. See also above, II.v.15 and III.iii.19, where Smith comments on the fact that the silk manufacture was based on foreign materials.

[5] Additional duties were imposed from 25 May 1767 by 7 George III, c. 28 (1766).

[6] In the letter (203) to Eden just cited, Smith commented on the ineffectiveness of absolute prohibitions on importation, and added that:

About a week after I was made a Commissioner of the Customs, upon looking over the list of prohibited goods, (which is hung up in every Customhouse and which is well worth your considering) and upon examining my own wearing apparel, I found, to my great astonishment, that I had scarce a stock, a cravat, a pair of ruffles, or a pocket

2   That this monopoly of the home-market frequently gives great encouragement to that particular species of industry which enjoys it, and frequently turns towards that employment a greater share of both the labour and stock of the society than would otherwise have gone to it, cannot be doubted. But whether it tends either to increase the general industry of the society, or to give it the most advantageous direction, is not, perhaps, altogether so ^cevident^c.[7]

3   The general industry of the society never can exceed what the capital of the society can employ. As the number of workmen that can be kept in employment by any particular person must bear a certain proportion to his capital, so the number of those that can be continually employed by all the members of a great society, must bear a certain proportion to the whole capital of that society, and never can exceed that proportion. No regulation of commerce can increase the quantity of industry in any society beyond what its capital can maintain. It can only divert a part of it into a direction into which it might not otherwise have gone; and it is by no means certain that this artificial direction is likely to be more advantageous to the society than that into which it would have gone of its own accord.[8]

^{c-c} certain *I*

---

handkerchief which was not prohibited to be worn or used in G. Britain. I wished to set an example and burnt them all. I will not advise you to examine either your own or Mrs Eden's apparal or household furniture, least you be brought into a scrape of the same kind.

See below, V.ii.k.64: 'to pretend to have any scruple about buying smuggled goods . . . would in most countries be regarded as one of those pedantic pieces of hypocrisy which . . . serve only to expose the person who affects to practice them, to the suspicion of being a greater knave than most of his neighbours.' Smith's appointment afforded Edward Gibbon an opportunity for some heavy humour; In Letter 187 addressed to Smith, dated 26 November 1777 he wrote that:

Among the strange reports, which are every day circulated in this wide town, I heard one to-day so very extraordinary, that I know not how to give credit to it. I was informed that a place of Commissioner of the Customs in Scotland had been given to a Philosopher who for his own glory and for the benefit of mankind had enlightened the world by the most profound and systematic treatise on the great objects of trade and revenue which had ever been published in any age or in any Country.

[7] See above, II.v.31. Smith comments frequently on the 'natural balance of industry' in this chapter and throughout Book IV. See, for example, IV.ii.12,31, IV.iv.14, and IV.v.a.39. The claim that an artificial direction regarding the use of resources is less satisfactory than a 'natural' one is made at IV.v.a.3,24, IV.vii.c.43,97, and cf. IV.ix.51. The idea is applied in the analysis of taxation, for example, at V.ii.k.63. It will be observed that in making this point, the reference is to the dynamic analysis of II.v. and III.i rather than to the treatment of the static allocative mechanism offered in Book I.

[8] In LJ (B) 233-4, ed. Cannan 180-1, Smith refers to 'a natural balance of industry' and to the 'natural connection of all trades', and makes the point that regulation will break the 'balance of industry'. A similar point is made in LJ (A) vi.92. The doctrine is succinctly stated in ED 3.5.: *[continues]*

4   Every individual is continually exerting himself to find out the most advantageous employ-[178]ment for whatever capital he can command. It is his own advantage, indeed, and not that of the society, which he has in view. But the study of his own advantage naturally, or rather necessarily leads him to prefer that employment which is most advantageous to the society.

5   First, every individual endeavours to employ his capital as near home as he can, and consequently as much as he can in the support of domestick industry; provided always that he can thereby obtain the ordinary, or not a great deal less than the ordinary profits of stock.

6   Thus upon equal or nearly equal profits, every wholesale merchant naturally prefers the home-trade to the foreign trade of consumption, and the foreign trade of consumption to the carrying trade. In the home-trade his capital is never so long out of his sight as it frequently is in the foreign trade of consumption. He can know better the character and situation of the persons whom he trusts, and if he should happen to be deceived, he knows better the laws of the country from which he must seek redress. In the carrying trade, the capital of the merchant is, as it were, divided between two foreign countries, and no part of it is ever necessarily brought home, or placed under his own immediate view and command. The capital which an Amsterdam merchant employs in carrying corn from Konnigsberg to Lisbon, and fruit and wine from Lisbon to Konnigsberg, must generally be the one-half of it at Konnigsberg and the other half at Lisbon. No part of it need ever [179] come to Amsterdam. The natural residence of such a merchant should either be at Konnigsberg or Lisbon, and it can only be some very particular circumstances which can make him prefer the residence of Amsterdam. The uneasiness, however, which he feels at being separated so far from his capital, generally determines him to bring part both of the Konnigsberg goods which he destines for the market of Lisbon, and of the Lisbon goods which he destines for that of Konnigsberg, to Amsterdam: and though this necessarily subjects him to a double charge of loading and unloading, as well as to the payment of some duties and customs, yet for the sake of having some part of his capital always under his

there is in every country what may be called a natural balance of industry, or a disposition in the people to apply to each species of work precisely in proportion to the demand for that work. That whatever tends to break this balance tends to hurt national or public opulence; whether it be by giving extraordinary discouragement to some sorts of industry or extraordinary encouragement to others.

In this context, the criticism is extended to bounties (see below, IV.v.) and occurs in the discussion of policies which prevent the coincidence of market and natural price. See especially, LJ (B) 232–5, ed. Cannan 180–1, and above, I.vii. Compare Mandeville's comment in the Sixth Dialogue: 'we may learn, how the short-sighted Wisdom, of perhaps well-meaning People, may rob us of a Felicity, that would flow spontaneously from the Nature of every large Society, if none were to divert or interrupt the Stream.' (*The Fable of the Bees*, pt. ii. 425, ed. Kaye ii.353.)

own view and command, he willingly submits to this extraordinary charge; and it is in this manner that every country which has any considerable share of the carrying trade, becomes always the emporium, or general market, for the goods of all the different countries whose trade it carries on. The merchant, in order to save a second loading and unloading, endeavours always to sell in the home-market as much of the goods of all those different countries as he can, and thus, so far as he can, to convert his carrying trade into a foreign trade of consumption. A merchant, in the same manner, who is engaged in the foreign trade of consumption, when he collects goods for foreign markets, will always be glad, upon equal or nearly equal profits, to sell as great a part of them at home as he can. He saves himself the risk and trouble of exportation, [180] when, so far as he can, he thus converts his foreign trade of consumption into a home-trade. Home is in this manner the center, if I may say so, round which the capitals of the inhabitants of every country are continually circulating, and towards which they are always tending, though by particular causes they may sometimes be driven off and repelled from it towards more distant employments.[9] But a capital employed in the home-trade, it has already been shown,[10] necessarily puts into motion a greater quantity of domestic industry, and gives revenue and employment to a greater number of the inhabitants of the country, than an equal capital employed in the foreign trade of consumption: and one employed in the foreign trade of consumption has the same advantage over an equal capital employed in the carrying trade. Upon equal, or only nearly equal profits, therefore, every individual naturally inclines to employ his capital in the manner in which it is likely to afford the greatest support to domestick industry, and to give revenue and employment to the greatest number of [d] people of his own country.

7   Secondly, every individual who employs his capital in the support of domestick industry, necessarily endeavours so to direct that industry, that its produce may be of the greatest possible value.

8   The produce of industry is what it adds to the subject or materials upon which it is employed. In proportion as the value of this produce is great or small, so will likewise be the profits of the employer. But it is only for the sake of profit [181] that any man employs a capital in the support of industry; and he will always, therefore, endeavour to employ it in the support of that industry of which the produce is likely to be of the greatest value, or to exchange for the greatest quantity either of money or of other goods.[11]

9   But the annual revenue of every society is always precisely equal to the exchangeable value of the whole annual produce of its industry, or rather is

[d] the *1*

---

[9] Rather similar terms are used in the discussion of equilibrium price, in I.vii.15.
[10] Above, II.v.27.   [11] See above, II.iii.6.

precisely the same thing with that exchangeable value.[12] As every individual, therefore, endeavours as much as he can both to employ his capital in the support of domestick industry, and so to direct that industry that its produce may be of the greatest value; every individual necessarily labours to render the annual revenue of the society as great as he can.[13] He generally, indeed, neither intends to promote the publick interest, nor knows how much he is promoting it. By preferring the support of domestick to that of foreign industry, he intends only his own security; and by directing that industry in such a manner as its produce may be of the greatest value, he intends only his own gain, and he is in this, as in many other cases, led by an invisible hand to promote an end which was no part of his intention.[14] Nor is it always the worse for the society that it was no part of it. By pursuing his own interest he frequently promotes that of the society more effectually than when he really intends to promote it. I have never known much good done by those who affected to trade for the publick good. It is an [182] affectation, indeed, not very common among merchants, and very few words need be employed in dissuading them from it.[15]

10   What is the species of domestick industry which his capital can employ, and of which the produce is likely to be of the greatest value, every individual, it is evident, can, in his local situation, judge much better than any statesman or lawgiver can do for him. The stateman, who should attempt to direct private people in what manner they ought to employ their capitals, would not only load himself with a most unnecessary attention, but assume an authority which could safely be trusted, not only to no single person, but to no council or senate whatever, and which would nowhere be so dangerous as in the hands of a man who had folly and presumption enough to fancy himself fit to exercise it.[16]

11   To give the monopoly of the home-market to the produce of domestick industry, in any particular art or manufacture, is in some measure to direct private people in what manner they ought to employ their capitals, and must, in almost all cases, be either a useless or a hurtful regulation. If the produce of domestick can be brought there as cheap as that of foreign industry, the regulation is evidently useless. If it cannot, it must generally be hurtful. It is the maxim of every prudent master of a family, never to attempt to make at home what it will cost him more to make than to buy. The taylor does not attempt to make his own shoes, but buys them of the

---

[12] A similar point is made at I.vi.17, I.xi.p.7, and II.ii.1.

[13] See below, IV.vii.c.88.

[14] Cf. TMS IV.i.1.10, where Smith also uses the concept of the 'invisible hand' in an economic context.

[15] There is an interesting variation on this theme in Steuart's *Principles*, i.165, ed. Skinner i.143–4.

[16] Similar sentiments are expressed in IV.v.b.16 and IV.ix.51, where intervention is said to be presumptuous and impolitic, not to mention unjust. The argument is also applied at I.x.c.12.

shoemaker. The shoemaker does not attempt to [183] make his own cloaths, but employs a taylor. The farmer attempts to make neither the one nor the other, but employs those different artificers. All of them find it for their interest to employ their whole industry in a way in which they have some advantage over their neighbours, and to purchase with a part of its produce, or what is the same thing, with the price of a part of it, whatever else they have occasion for.[17]

12   What is prudence in the conduct of every private family, can scarce be folly in that of a great kingdom. If a foreign country can supply us with a commodity cheaper than we ourselves can make it, better buy it of them with some part of the produce of our own industry, employed in a way in which we have some advantage.[18] The general industry of the country, being always in proportion to the capital which employs it, will not thereby be diminished, no more than that of the above-mentioned artificers; but only left to find out the way in which it can be employed with the greatest advantage. It is certainly not employed to the greatest advantage, when it is thus directed towards an object which it can buy cheaper than it can make. The value of its annual produce is certainly more or less diminished, when it is thus turned away from producing commodities evidently of more value than the commodity which it is directed to produce. According to the supposition, that commodity could be purchased from foreign countries cheaper than it can be made at home. It could, therefore, have been purchased with a [184] part only of the commodities, or, what is the same thing, with a part only of the price of the commodities, which the industry employed by an equal capital, would have produced at home, had it been left to follow its natural course. The industry of the country, therefore, is thus turned away from a more, to a less advantageous employment, and the exchangeable value of its annual produce, instead of being increased, according to the intention of the lawgiver, must necessarily be diminished by every such regulation.[19]

[17] See above, I.ii.5.

[18] Cf. LJ (B) 261–2, ed. Cannan 204: 'All commerce that is carried on betwixt any two countries must necessarily be advantageous to both. The very intention of commerce is to exchange your own commodities for others which you think will be more convenient for you. When two men trade between themselves it is undoubtedly for the advantage of both ... The case is exactly the same betwixt any two nations.' See also ED 4.9. The same example is provided in LJ (A) vi.159–60, with the qualification that exchange between individuals will always be beneficial only where they are 'prudent'. See above, 447 n. 55.

[19] See below, IV.ix.50, where it is pointed out that intervention with the use of capital is 'in reality subversive of the great purpose which it means to promote'. Without questioning this argument, Pownall adverted to the infant industry case as justifying protection on the ground that trades so protected might in the long run become competitive—citing as examples, the woollen and hardware manufactures. However, Pownall did not extend his argument to cases where manufactures were based on foreign materials, such as flax and silk: 'Against such your principle, in the full force of its arguments, stands unanswerable.' (*Letter*, 28–9.) Smith's main qualifications to the doctrine of free trade appear below, IV.ii.22f. See also III.iii.19 and IV.viii.4.

13   By means of such regulations, indeed, a particular manufacture may sometimes be acquired sooner than it could have been otherwise, and after a certain time may be made at home as cheap or cheaper than in the foreign country. But through the industry of the society may be thus carried with advantage into a particular channel sooner than it could have been otherwise, it will by no means follow that the sum total, either of its industry, or of its revenue, can ever be augmented by any such regulation. The industry of the society can augment only in proportion as its capital augments, and its capital can augment only in proportion to what can be gradually saved out of its revenue. But the immediate effect of every such regulation is to diminish its revenue, and what diminishes its revenue, is certainly not very likely to augment its capital faster than it would have augmented of its own accord, had both capital and industry been left to find out their natural employments.

14   [185] Though for want of such regulations the society should never acquire the proposed manufacture, it would not, upon that account, necessarily be the poorer in any one period of its duration. In every period of its duration its whole capital and industry might still have been employed, though upon different objects, in the manner that was most advantageous at the time. In every period its revenue might have been the greatest which its capital could afford, and both capital and revenue might have been *augmented* with the greatest possible rapidity.

15   The natural advantages which one country has over another in producing particular commodities are sometimes so great, that it is acknowledged by all the world to be in vain to struggle with them.[20] By means of glasses, hotbeds, and hotwalls, very good grapes can be raised in Scotland, and very good wine too can be made of them at about thirty times the expence for which at least equally good can be brought from foreign countries. Would it be a reasonable law to prohibit the importation of all foreign wines, merely to encourage the making of claret and burgundy in Scotland? But if there would be a manifest absurdity in turning towards any employment, thirty times more of the capital and industry of the country, than would be necessary to purchase from foreign countries an equal quantity of the commodities wanted, there must be an absurdity, though not altogether so glaring, yet exactly of the same kind, in turning [186] towards any such employment a thirtieth, or even a three hundredth part more of either. Whether the advantages which one country has over another, be natural or acquired, is in this respect of no consequence. As long as the one country has those advantages, and the other wants them, it will always be more advantageous for the latter, rather to buy of the former than to make. It is

e–e augmenting *1*

[20] See above, I.vii.24.

an acquired advantage only, which one artificer has over his neighbour, who exercises another trade; and yet they both find it more advantageous to buy of one another, than to make what does not belong to their particular trades.[21]

16   Merchants and manufacturers are the people who derive the greatest advantage from this monopoly of the home market. The prohibition[22] of the importation of foreign cattle, and of salt provisions, together with the high duties upon foreign corn, which in times of moderate plenty amount to a prohibition,[23] are not near so advantageous to the graziers and farmers of Great Britain, as other regulations of the same kind are to its merchants and manufacturers. Manufactures, those of the finer kind especially, are more easily transported from one country to another than corn or cattle. It is in the fetching and carrying manufactures, accordingly, that foreign trade is chiefly employed.[24] In manufactures, a very small advantage will enable foreigners to undersell our own workmen, even in the home market. It will require a very great one to enable them to do so in the rude produce [187] of the soil. If the free importation of foreign manufactures ʲwasʲ permitted, several of the home manufactures would probably suffer, and some of them, perhaps, go to ruin altogether, and a considerable part of the stock and industry at present employed in them, would be forced to find out some other employment. But the freest importation of the rude produce of the soil could have no such effect upon the agriculture of the country.

17   If the importation of foreign cattle, for example, ᵍwasᵍ made ever so free, so few could be imported, that the grazing trade of Great Britain could be little affected by it. Live cattle are, perhaps, the only commodity of which the transportation is more expensive by sea than by land.[25] By land they carry themselves to market. By sea, not only the cattle, but their food and their water too must be carried at no small expence and inconveniency. The short sea between Ireland and Great Britain, indeed, renders the importation of Irish cattle more easy. But though the free importation of them, which was lately permitted only for a limited time,[26] were rendered perpetual, it should have no considerable effect upon the interest of the graziers of Great Britain. Those parts of Great Britain which border upon

---

[21] See above, I.ii.4.

[22] 18 and 19 Charles II, c. 2 (1666) in *Statutes of the Realm*, v.597; 18 Charles II, c. 2 in Ruffhead's edition. See above, III.iv.20, IV.ii.1, and below, V.ii.k.13.

[23] 22 Charles II, c. 13 (1670). See above, III.iv.20 and IV.ii.1, and below, IV.v.a.23, IV.v.b.33 and 37, IV.vii.b.33, V.ii.k.13.

[24] See above, IV.i.29, and generally, III.iii.17–20.

[25] See above, I.iii.3, where Smith comments on the cheapness of water-carriage.

[26] 32 George II, c. 11 (1758), continued by 5 George III, c. 10 (1765) and 12 George III, c. 2 (1772). See above, III.iv.20, and below, V.ii.k.13.

the Irish sea are all grazing countries. Irish cattle could never be imported for their use, but must be drove through those very extensive countries, at no small expence and inconveniency, before they could arrive at their proper market. Fat cattle could be drove [188] so far. Lean cattle, therefore, only could be imported, and such importation could interfere, not with the interest of the feeding or fattening countries, to which, by reducing the price of lean cattle, it would rather be advantageous, but with that of the breeding countries only. The small number of Irish cattle imported since their importation was permitted, together with the good price at which lean cattle still continue to sell, seem to demonstrate that even the breeding countries of Great Britain are never likely to be much affected by the free importation of Irish cattle. The common people of Ireland, indeed, are said to have sometimes opposed with violence the exportation of their cattle. But if the exporters had found any great advantage in continuing the trade, they could easily, when the law was on their side, have conquered this mobbish opposition.

18   Feeding and fattening countries, besides, must always be highly improved, whereas breeding countries are generally uncultivated. The high price of lean cattle, by augmenting the value of uncultivated land, is like a bounty against improvement. To any country which was highly improved throughout, it would be more advantageous to import its lean cattle than to breed them. The province of Holland, accordingly, is said to follow this maxim at present. The mountains of Scotland, Wales, and Northumberland, indeed, are countries not capable of much improvement, and seem destined by nature to be the breeding countries of Great Britain. [189] The freest importation of foreign cattle could have no other effect than to hinder those breeding countries from taking advantage of the increasing population and improvement of the rest of the kingdom, from raising their price to an exorbitant height, and from laying a real tax upon all the more improved and cultivated parts of the country.[27]

19   The freest importation of salt provisions, in the same manner, could have as little effect upon the interest of the graziers of Great Britain as that of live cattle. Salt provisions are not only a very bulky commodity, but when compared with fresh meat, they are a commodity both of worse quality, and as they cost more labour and expence, of higher price. They could never, therefore, come into competition with the fresh meat, though they might with the salt provisions of the country. They might be used for victualling ships for distant voyages, and such like uses, but could never make any considerable part of the food of the people. The small quantity of salt provisions imported from Ireland since their importation was rendered free, is an experimental proof that our graziers have nothing to apprehend

[27] See above, I.xi.l.1–7.

from it. It does not appear that the price of butcher's-meat has ever been sensibly affected by it.

20 		Even the free importation of foreign corn could very little affect the interest of the farmers of Great Britain. Corn is a much more bulky commodity than butcher's-meat.[28] A pound of wheat at a penny is as dear as a pound of but-[190]cher's-meat at fourpence. The small quantity of foreign corn imported even in times of the greatest scarcity, may satisfy our farmers that they can have nothing to fear from the freest importation. The average quantity imported, one year with another, amounts only, according to the very well informed author of the tracts upon the corn trade,[29] to twenty-three thousand seven hundred and twenty-eight quarters of all sorts of grain, and does not exceed the five hundredth and seventy-first part of the annual consumption.[30] But as the bounty upon corn occasions a greater exportation in years of plenty, so it must of consequence occasion a greater importation in years of scarcity, than *ʰin the actual state of tillage,ʰ* would otherwise take place. By means of it, the plenty of one year does not compensate the scarcity of another,[31] and as the average quantity exported is necessarily augmented by it, so must likewise, in the actual state of tillage, the average quantity imported. If there ⁱwasⁱ no bounty, as less corn would be exported, so it is probable that, one year with another, less would be imported than at present. The corn merchants, the fetchers and carriers of corn, between Great Britain and foreign countries, would have much less employment, and might suffer considerably; but the country gentlemen and farmers could suffer very little. It is in the corn merchants accordingly, rather than in the country gentlemen and farmers, that I have observed the greatest anxiety for the renewal and continuation of the bounty.[32]

21 		[191] Country gentlemen and farmers are, to their great honour, of all people, the least subject to the wretched spirit of monopoly.[33] The under-taker of a great manufactory is sometimes alarmed if another work of the same kind is established within twenty miles of him. The Dutch undertaker of the woollen manufacture at Abbeville, stipulated that no work of the

ʰ⁻ʰ 2–6 		ⁱ⁻ⁱ were 4–6

---

[28] Cf. I.xi.b.12.

[29] Charles Smith, *Three Tracts on the Corn Trade and Corn Laws*, 144–5. Charles Smith is described as 'ingenious and well-informed' at IV.v.a.4. See also IV.v.a.8 and IV.v.b.28. There is a long discussion of the bounty in IV.v.a.

[30] The same figure is quoted at IV.v.b.28. Pownall, *Letter*, 30, disputed these figures: 'It is not the ratio of the quantity of corn exported or imported, and the quantity of the whole stock raised, but the ratio between the *surplus* and this quantity exported or imported, which creates the effect: it is not a ratio of 1/571, but a ratio of 1/15, which acts and operates on the market; it is not the 1/571 part but the 1/15 part which would operate to the depression of the market and the oppression of the farmer'.

[31] See above, I.xi.g.4, and below, IV.v.a.22.

[32] See below, IV.v.a.22, where it is stated that corn merchants are the only set of men to whom the bounty could be 'essentially serviceable'.

[33] Cf. I.xi.a, where Smith discusses the determinants of rent.

same kind should be established within thirty leagues of that city.[34] Farmers and country gentlemen, on the contrary, are generally disposed rather to promote than to obstruct the cultivation and improvement of their neighbours farms and estates. They have no secrets, such as those of the greater part of manufacturers, but are generally rather fond of communicating to their neighbours, and of extending as far as possible any new practice which they have found to be advantageous. *Pius Questus*, says old Cato, *stabilissimusque, minimeque invidiosus; minimeque male cogitantes sunt, qui in eo studio occupati sunt.*[35] Country gentlemen and farmers, dispersed in different parts of the country, cannot so easily combine[36] as merchants and manufacturers, who being collected into towns, and accustomed to that exclusive corporation spirit which prevails in them, naturally endeavour to obtain against all their countrymen, the same exclusive privilege which they generally possess against the inhabitants of their respective towns. They accordingly seem to have been the original inventors of those restraints upon the importation of foreign goods, which secure to them the monopoly of the home-market. It [192] was probably in imitation of them, and to put themselves upon a level with those who, they found, were disposed to oppress them, that the country gentlemen and farmers of Great Britain so far forgot the generosity which is natural to their station, as to demand the exclusive privilege of supplying their countrymen with corn and butcher's-meat.[37] They did not perhaps take time to consider, how much less their interest could be affected by the freedom of trade, than that of the people whose example they followed.

[34] The authority for the extreme statement is not clear. King stated: 'In 1665, He [the King of France] settled Mr. Josas van Robay, a foreign Protestant, at Abbeville in Picardy, and by Letters Patent granted to him and his Workmen the free Exercise of their Religion, and several other very considerable Privileges, which their Families enjoy to this Day. This Clothier fixed the Manufacture of all sorts of *Spanish* Cloth in that City, and the King lent him by Agreement 2,000 Livres for every Loom he set up, until he had 40 Looms at work; so that he received 80,000 Livres. And at last it was found, he had so well established that Manufacture, that by degrees the Payment of the whole was remitted.' (Charles King, *The British Merchant* (London 1743), ii.82.)

[35] 'At ex agricolis et viri fortissimi et milites strenuissimi gignuntur, maximeque pius quaestus stabilissimusque consequitur minimeque invidiosus, minimeque male cogitantes sunt qui in eo studio occupati sunt. . . . On the other hand, it is from the farming class that the bravest men and the sturdiest soldiers come, their calling is most highly respected, their livelihood is most assured and is looked on with the least hostility, and those who are engaged in that pursuit are least inclined to be disaffected.' (Cato, *De Re Rustica*, introduction, translated by W. D. Hooper, revised by H. B. Ash in Loeb Classical Library (1934), 2–3.)

[36] Smith makes much of the point regarding ease of combination in discussing positions of economic power. See, for example, I.x.c.19, IV.v.b.4,24, IV.viii.34; and cf. I.viii.12, where the point is brought into the discussion of wages. See also IV.viii.4, where Smith discusses the poor bargaining position of those people who were engaged in the production of linen on an outwork basis; and cf. I.x.b.50, where it is remarked that the low rates of return for such workers were partly due to the fact that this was not their sole employment.

[37] See above, IV.i.10. Smith comments on the generosity of country gentlemen at I.xi.p.10.

22   To prohibit by a perpetual law the importation of foreign corn and cattle, is in reality to enact, that the population and industry of the country shall at no time exceed what the rude produce of its own soil can maintain.

23   There seem, however, to be two cases in which it will generally be advantageous to lay some burden upon foreign, for the encouragement of domestick industry.

24   The first is when some particular sort of industry is necessary for the defence of the country. The defence of Great Britain, for example, depends very much upon the number of its sailors and shipping. The act of navigation,[38] therefore, very properly endeavours to give the sailors and shipping of Great Britain the monopoly of the trade of their own country, in some cases, by absolute prohibitions, and in others by heavy burdens upon the shipping of foreign countries. The following are the principal dispositions of this act.

25   [193] First, all ships, of which the owners, masters, and three-fourths of the mariners are not British subjects, are prohibited, upon pain of forfeiting ship and cargo, from trading to the British settlements and plantations, or from being employed in the coasting trade of Great Britain.

26   Secondly, a great variety of the most bulky articles of importation can be brought into Great Britain only, either in such ships as are above described, or in ships of the country where those goods are produced, and of which the owners, masters, and three-fourths of the mariners, are of that particular country; and when imported even in ships of this latter kind, they are subject to double aliens duty. If imported in ships of any other country, the penalty is forfeiture of ship and *goods*. When this act was made, the Dutch were, what they still are, the great carriers of Europe, and by this regulation they were entirely excluded from being the carriers to Great Britain, or from importing to us the goods of any other European country.

27   Thirdly, a great variety of the most bulky articles of importation are prohibited[39] from being imported, even in British ships, from any country but that in which they are produced; under pain of forfeiting ship and cargo. This regulation too was probably intended against the Dutch. Holland was then, as now, the great emporium for all European goods, and by this regulation, British ships were hindered from [194] loading in Holland the goods of any other European country.

28   Fourthly, salt fish of all kinds, whale-fins, whale-bone, oil, and blubber,

ʲ⁻ʲ cargo *1–2*

---

[38] 12 Charles II, c. 18 (1660). The provisions of the Navigation Acts are discussed at IV.vii.b.25–35. It is stated at IV.vii.c.19 that the restrictions thus imposed on trade with the colonies had the effect of raising the rate of profit in Great Britain. Smith remarks at IV.vii.c.23 that the provisions of the acts were not strictly enforced for several years after enactment. See also IV.vii.c.97.

[39] The prohibition applied to all foreign goods which could not be imported except in British ships, not only to 'bulky articles of importation'.

464 The Nature and Causes of [IV.ii

not caught by and cured on board British vessels, when imported into Great Britain, are subjected to double aliens duty. The Dutch, as they are still the principal, were then the only fishers in Europe that attempted to supply foreign nations with fish. By this regulation, a very heavy burden was laid upon their supplying Great Britain.

29   When the act of navigation was made, though England and Holland were not actually at war, the most violent animosity subsisted between the two nations. It had begun during the government of the long parliament, which first framed this act,[40] and it broke out soon after in the Dutch wars during that of the Protector and of Charles the Second. It is not impossible, therefore, that some of the regulations of this famous act may have proceeded from national animosity.[41] They are as wise, however, as if they had all been dictated by the most deliberate wisdom. National animosity at that particular time aimed at the very same object which the most deliberate wisdom would have recommended, the diminution of the naval power of Holland, the only naval power which could endanger the security of England.

30   The act of navigation is not favourable to foreign commerce, or to the growth of that opulence which can arise from it. The interest of a nation in its commercial relations to foreign [195] nations is, like that of a merchant with regard to the different people with whom he deals, to buy as cheap and to sell as dear as possible. But it will be most likely to buy cheap, when by the most perfect freedom of trade it encourages all nations to bring to it the goods which it has occasion to purchase; and, for the same reason, it will be most likely to sell dear, when its markets are thus filled with the greatest number of buyers. The act of navigation, it is true, lays no burden upon foreign ships that come to export the produce of British industry. Even the antient aliens duty, which used to be paid upon all goods exported as well as imported, has, by several subsequent acts, been taken off from the greater part of the articles of exportation.[42] But if foreigners, either by prohibitions or high duties, are hindered from coming to sell, they cannot always afford to come to buy; because coming without a cargo, they must lose the freight from their own country to Great Britain. By diminishing the number of sellers, therefore, we necessarily diminish that of buyers, and are thus likely not only to buy foreign goods dearer, but to sell our own cheaper, than if there was a more perfect freedom of trade.[43] As defence, however, is

[40] An Act for increase of Shipping, and Encouragement of the Navigation of this Nation (1651). *Acts and Ordinances of the Interregnum*, ed. C. H. Firth and R. S. Rait, ii.559–62.

[41] At IV.iii.a.1 Smith draws a distinction between policies based on partial interests and those which reflect national animosity.

[42] From all except coal by 25 Charles II, c. 6 (1672). The aliens duty is frequently mentioned, for example, at I.x.c.25, IV.iii.c.10, IV.iv.3, and V.ii.k.21.

[43] Cf. 'Buying is Bartering, and no Nation can buy Goods of others that has none of her own to purchase them with. . . . We know that we could not continue long to purchase

of much more importance than opulence, the act of navigation is, perhaps, the wisest of all the commercial regulations of England.[44]

31   The second case, in which it will generally be advantageous to lay some burden upon foreign for the encouragement of domestick industry, is, when some tax is imposed at home upon the pro-[196]duce of the latter. In this case, it seems reasonable that an equal tax should be imposed upon the like produce of the former. This would not give the monopoly of the home market to domestick industry, nor turn towards a particular employment a greater share of the stock and labour of the country, than what would naturally go to it. It would only hinder any part of what would naturally go to it from being turned away by the tax, into a less natural direction,[45] and would leave the competition between foreign and domestick industry, after the tax, as nearly as possible upon the same footing as before it. In Great Britain, when any such tax is laid upon the produce of domestick industry, it is usual at the same time, in order to stop the clamorous complaints of our merchants and manufacturers, that they will be undersold at home, to lay a much heavier duty upon the importation of all foreign goods of the same kind.

32   This second limitation of the freedom of trade according to some people should, upon some occasions, be extended much *further* than to the precise foreign commodities which could come into competition with those which had been taxed at home. When the necessaries of life have been taxed in any country, it becomes proper, they pretend, to tax not only the like necessaries of life imported from other countries, but all sorts of foreign goods which can come into competition with any thing that is the produce of domestick industry. Subsistence, they say, becomes necessarily dearer in consequence [197] of such taxes; and the price of labour must always rise with the price of the labourers subsistence.[46] Every commodity, therefore, which is the produce of domestick industry, though not immediately taxed itself, becomes dearer in consequence of such taxes, because the labour which produces it becomes so. Such taxes, therefore, are really equivalent, they say, to a tax upon every particular commodity produced at home. In order to put domestick upon the same footing with

k-k farther 4–6

---

the Goods of other Nations, if they would not take our Manufactures in Payment for them; and why should we judge otherwise of other Nations.' (Mandeville, *The Fable of the Bees*, pt. i. 111, ed. Kaye i.111.)

[44] It is stated at II.v.30 that the security of Great Britain depends on the 'number of its sailors and shipping'. Smith also comments on the contribution to national defence which was made by the fishing bounty at IV.v.a. 27. The needs of defence are also cited at IV.v.a.36 as justification for granting bounties on the *exportation* of strategic materials such as gunpowder, in order to encourage their (domestic) manufacture.

[45] See above, IV.ii.3, where Smith distinguishes between the natural and 'artificial' uses of stock.

[46] See above, I.viii.52.

foreign industry, therefore, it becomes necessary, they think, to lay some duty upon every foreign commodity, equal to this enhancement of the price of the home commodities with which it can come into competition.

33   Whether taxes upon the necessaries of life, such as those in Great Britain upon [1] soap, salt, leather, candles, &c. necessarily raise the price of labour, and consequently that of all other commodities, I shall consider hereafter, when I come to treat of taxes.[47] Supposing, however, in the mean time, that they have this effect, and they have it undoubtedly, this general enhancement of the price of all commodities, in consequence of that of labour, is a case which differs in the two following respects from that of a particular commodity, of which the price was enhanced by a particular tax immediately imposed upon it.

34   First, it might always be known with great exactness how far the price of such a commodity could be enhanced by such a tax: but how far the general enhancement of the price of labour [198] might affect that of every different commodity, about which labour was employed, could never be known with any tolerable exactness. It would be impossible, therefore, to proportion with any tolerable exactness the tax upon every foreign, to this enhancement of the price of every home commodity.

35   Secondly, taxes upon the necessaries of life have nearly the same effect upon the circumstances of the people as a poor soil and a bad climate. Provisions are thereby rendered dearer in the same manner as if it required extraordinary labour and expence to raise them. As in the natural scarcity arising from soil and climate, it would be absurd to direct the people in what manner they ought to employ their capitals and industry, so *is it* likewise in the artificial scarcity arising from such taxes. To be left to accommodate, as well as they could, their industry to their situation, and to find out those employments in which, notwithstanding their unfavourable circumstances, they might have some advantage either in the home or in the foreign market, is what in both cases would evidently be most for their advantage. To lay a new tax upon them, because they are already over-burdened with taxes, and because they already pay too dear for the necessaries of life, to make them likewise pay too dear for the greater part of other commodities, is certainly a most absurd way of making amends.

36   Such taxes, when they have grown up to a certain height, are a curse equal to the barren-[199]ness of the earth and the inclemency of the heavens; and yet it is in the richest and most industrious countries that they have been most generally imposed. No other countries could support so great a disorder. As the strongest bodies only can live and enjoy health, under an unwholesome regimen; so the nations only, that in every sort of

---

[1] malt, beer; *1*   *m-m* it is *1*

---

[47] See above, I.viii.35, and below, V.ii.k.1–12.

industry have the greatest natural and acquired advantages, can subsist and prosper under such taxes. Holland is the country in Europe in which they abound most, and which from peculiar circumstances continues to prosper, not by means of them, as has been most absurdly supposed, but in spite of them.[48]

37   As there are two cases in which it will generally be advantageous to lay some burden upon foreign, for the encouragement of domestick industry; so there are two others in which it may sometimes be a matter of deliberation; in the one, how far it is proper to continue the free importation of certain foreign goods; and in the other, how far, or in what manner it may be proper to restore that free importation after it has been for some time interrupted.

38   The case in which it may sometimes be a matter of deliberation how far it is proper to continue the free importation of certain foreign goods, is, when some foreign nation restrains by high duties or prohibitions the importation of some of our manufactures into their country. Revenge in this case naturally dictates retaliation, and that we should impose the like duties and prohibitions upon the importation of some [200] or all of their manufactures into ours. Nations, accordingly seldom fail to retaliate in this manner. The French have been particularly forward to favour their own manufactures by restraining the importation of such foreign goods as could come into competition with them. In this consisted a great part of the policy of Mr. Colbert,[49] who, notwithstanding his great abilities, seems in this case to have been imposed upon by the sophistry of merchants and manufacturers, who are always demanding a monopoly against their countrymen. It is at present the opinion of the most intelligent men in France that his operations of this kind have not been beneficial to his country.[50] That minister, by the tarif of 1667, imposed very high duties upon a great number of foreign manufactures. Upon his refusing to moderate them in favour of the Dutch, they in 1671 prohibited the importation of the wines, brandies, and manufactures of France. The war of 1672 seems to have been in part occasioned by this commercial dispute. The peace of Nimeguen put an end to it in 1678, by moderating some of those duties in favour of the Dutch, who in consequence took off their prohibition. It was about the same time that the French and English began mutually to oppress each other's industry, by the like duties and prohibitions, of which

---

[48] See below, V.ii.k.14, 79–80, for comment on this point. It is stated at IV.ix.28 that Quesnay was mistaken in imagining that a country could prosper only 'under a certain precise regimen, the exact regimen of perfect liberty and perfect justice'.

[49] Colbert is mentioned below, IV.ix.3,4, as a man of great industry and acuteness, who had 'unfortunately embraced all the prejudices of the mercantile system'.

[50] Presumably this is a reference to the physiocrats, whose doctrines are reviewed in IV.ix. Cf. IV.ix.49, where it is stated that from one point of view the inconsistencies of physiocratic policy were more marked than those of the mercantile system.

the French, however, seem to have set the first example. The spirit of hostility which has subsisted between the two nations ever since, has hitherto hindered them from being moderated on either [201] side. In 1697 the English prohibited the importation of bonelace, the manufacture of Flanders.[51] The government of that country, at that time under the dominion of Spain, prohibited in return the importation of English woollens. In 1700, the prohibition of importing bonelace into England, was taken off upon condition that the importation of English woollens into Flanders should be put on the same footing as before.[52]

39   There may be good policy in retaliations of this kind, when there is a probability that they will procure the repeal of the high duties or pro- hibitions complained of. The recovery of a great foreign market will generally more than compensate the transitory inconveniency of paying dearer during a short time for some sorts of goods. To judge whether such retaliations are likely to produce such an effect, does not, perhaps, belong so much to the science of a legislator, whose deliberations ought to be governed by general principles which are always the same, as to the skill of that insidious and crafty animal, vulgarly called a statesman or politician,[53] whose councils are directed by the momentary fluctuations of affairs. When there is no probability that any such repeal can be procured, it seems a bad method of compensating the injury done to certain classes of our people, to do another injury ourselves[n], not only to those classes, but[n] to almost all the other classes of them. When our neighbours prohibit some manufacture of ours, we generally prohibit, not only the same, for that alone would seldom affect them consider-[202]ably, but some other manufacture of theirs. This may no doubt give encouragement to some particular class of workmen among ourselves, and by excluding some of their rivals, may enable them to raise their price in the home-market. Those workmen, however, who suffered by our neighbours prohibition will not be benefited by ours. On the contrary, they and almost all the other classes of our citizens will thereby be obliged to pay dearer than before for certain goods. Every such law, therefore, imposes a real tax upon the whole country, not in favour of that particular class of workmen who were injured by our neighbours prohibition, but of some other class.

40   The case in which it may sometimes be a matter of deliberation, how far,

---

[n-n] both to those classes and *I*

[51] 14 Charles II, c. 13 (1662) in *Statutes of the Realm*, v.405–6; 13 and 14 Charles II, c. 13 in Ruffhead's edition, and 9 William III, c. 9 (1697) in *Statutes of the Realm*, vii. 304–6; 9 and 10 William III, c. 9 in Ruffhead's edition.
[52] 11 William III, c. 11 (1698) in *Statutes of the Realm*, vii.600; 11 and 12 William III, c. 11 in Ruffhead's edition, to become effective 'three months after the prohibition of the Woollen manufactures in Flanders shall be taken off'.
[53] Cf. LJ (B) 327, ed. Cannan 254: 'They whom we call politicians are not the most remarkable men in the world for probity and punctuality.'

or in what manner it is proper to restore the free importation of foreign goods, after it has been for some time interrupted, is, when particular manufactures, by means of high duties or prohibitions upon all foreign goods which can come into competition with them, have been so far extended as to employ a great multitude of hands.[54] Humanity may in this case require that the freedom of trade should be restored only by slow gradations, and with a good deal of reserve and circumspection. Were those high duties and prohibitions taken away all at once, cheaper foreign goods of the same kind might be poured so fast into the home market, as to deprive all at once many thousands of our people of their ordinary employment and means of subsistence. The dis-[203]order which this would occasion might no doubt be very considerable. It would in all probability, however, be much less than is commonly imagined, for the two following reasons:

41   First, all those manufactures, of which any part is commonly exported to other European countries without a bounty, could be very little affected by the freest importation of foreign goods. Such manufactures must be sold as cheap abroad as any other foreign goods of the same quality and kind, and consequently must be sold cheaper at home. They would still, therefore, keep possession of the home market, and though a capricious man of fashion might sometimes prefer foreign wares, merely because they were foreign, to cheaper and better goods of the same kind that were made at home, this folly could, from the nature of things, extend to so few, that it could make no sensible impression upon the general employment of the people. But a great part of all the different branches of our woollen manufacture, of our tanned leather, and of our hardware, are annually exported to other European countries without any bounty, and these are the manufactures which employ the greatest number of hands. The silk, perhaps, is the manufacture which would suffer the most by this freedom of trade, and after it the linen, though the latter much less than the former.

42   Secondly, though a great number of people should, by thus restoring the freedom of trade, be thrown all at once out of their ordinary employment and common method of subsistence, it [204] would by no means follow that they would thereby be deprived either of employment or subsistence. By the reduction of the army and navy at the end of the late war more than a hundred thousand soldiers and seamen, a number equal to what is employed in the greatest manufactures, were all at once thrown out of their ordinary employment; but, though they no doubt suffered some inconveniency, they were not thereby deprived of all employment and subsistence. The greater

[54] Smith discusses another problem of dislocation in IV.vii.c.44,45, arising from the likely loss of the American trade. He also introduces a qualification to the doctrine of free trade at IV.v.b.39, where he points out that the policy of one country may hinder another from establishing 'what would otherwise be the best policy'.

part of the seamen, it is probable, gradually betook themselves to the merchant-service as they could find occasion, and in the mean time both they and the soldiers were absorbed in the great mass of the people, and employed in a great variety of occupations. Not only no great convulsion, but no sensible disorder arose from so great a change in the situation of more than a hundred thousand men, all accustomed to the use of arms, and many of them to rapine and plunder. The number of vagrants was scarce anywhere sensibly increased by it, even the wages of labour were not reduced by it in any occupation, so far as I have been able to learn, except in that of seamen in the merchant-service.[55] But if we compare together the habits of a soldier and of any sort of manufacturer, we shall find that those of the latter do not tend so much to disqualify him from being employed in a new trade, as those of the former from being employed in any. The manufacturer has always been accustomed to look for his subsistence from his labour only: the soldier to expect it from his pay. [205] Application and industry have been familiar to the one; idleness and dissipation to the other. But it is surely much easier to change the direction of industry from one sort of labour to another, than to turn idleness and dissipation to any. To the greater part of manufactures besides, it has already been observed,[56] there are other collateral manufactures of so similar a nature, that a workman can easily transfer his industry from one of them to another. The greater part of such workmen too are occasionally employed in country labour. The stock which employed them in a particular manufacture before, will still remain in the country to employ an equal number of people in some other way. The capital of the country remaining the same, the demand for labour will likewise be the same, or very nearly the same, though it may be exerted in different places and for different occupations. Soldiers and seamen, indeed, when discharged from the king's service, are at liberty to exercise any trade, within any town or place of Great Britain or Ireland.[57] Let the same natural liberty of exercising what species of industry they please be restored to all his majesty's subjects, in the same manner as to soldiers and seamen; that is, break down the exclusive privileges of corporations, and repeal the statute of apprenticeship, both which are real encroachments upon natural liberty, and add to these the repeal of the law of settlements, so that a poor workman, when thrown out of employment either in one trade or in one place, may seek for it in [206] another trade or in another place, without the fear either of a prosecution or of a removal, and neither the publick nor the individuals will suffer much more from the occasional disbanding some particular classes of manufacturers, than from

[55] See above, I.x.b.45.   [56] Above, I.x.c.43.
[57] The privilege was given after particular wars by 12 Charles II, c. 16 (1660); 12 Anne, c. 14, (1712) in *Statutes of the Realm*, ix.791–3; 12 Anne, st.1, c. 13 in Ruffhead's edition, and 3 George III, c. 8 (1762). See above, I.x.c.9.

that of soldiers.[58] Our manufacturers have no doubt great merit with their country, but they cannot have more than those who defend it with their blood, nor deserve to be treated with more delicacy.

43   To expect, indeed, that the freedom of trade should ever be entirely restored in Great Britain, is as absurd as to expect that an Oceana or Utopia should ever be established in it. Not only the prejudices of the publick, but what is much more unconquerable, the private interests of many individuals, irresistibly oppose it. Were the officers of the army to oppose with the same zeal and unanimity any reduction in the number of forces, with which master manufacturers set themselves against every law that is likely to increase the number of their rivals in the home market; were the former to animate their soldiers, in the same manner as the latter enflame their workmen, to attack with violence and outrage the proposers of any such regulation; to attempt to reduce the army would be as dangerous as it has now become to attempt to diminish in any respect the monopoly which our manufacturers have obtained against us. This monopoly has so much increased the number of some particular tribes of them, that, like an overgrown standing army, they have become formid-[207]able to the government, and upon many occasions intimidate the legislature.[59] The member of parliament who supports every proposal for strengthening this monopoly, is sure to acquire not only the reputation of understanding trade, but great popularity and influence with an order of men whose numbers and wealth render them of great importance. If he opposes them, on the contrary, and still more if he has authority enough to be able to thwart them, neither the most acknowledged probity, nor the highest rank, nor the greatest publick services can protect him from the most infamous abuse and detraction, from personal insults, nor sometimes from real danger, arising from the insolent outrage of furious and disappointed monopolists.

44   The undertaker of a great manufacture who, by the home markets being suddenly laid open to the competition of foreigners, should be obliged to abandon his trade, would no doubt suffer very considerably. That part of his capital which had usually been employed in purchasing materials and in paying his workmen, might, without much difficulty, perhaps, find another employment. But that part of it which was fixed in workhouses, and in the instruments of trade, could scarce be disposed of without considerable loss. The equitable regard, therefore, to his interest requires that changes of this kind should never be introduced suddenly, but slowly, gradually, and after a very long warning. The legislature, were it possible

---

[58] The obstructions caused by the corporation laws and the Poor Laws are discussed above, I.x.c.

[59] See above, I.xi.p.10, where Smith points out that mercantile groups may influence the legislature. Cf. I.viii.13, I.x.c.61, IV.vii.b.49, IV.viii.17, and V.i.e.4.

that its deliberations could be always directed, not by the clamorous [208] importunity of partial interests, but by an extensive view of the general good, ought upon this very account, perhaps, to be particularly careful neither to establish any new monopolies of this kind, nor to extend further those which are already established. Every such regulation introduces some degree of real disorder into the constitution of the state,[60] which it will be difficult afterwards to cure without occasioning another disorder.

45   How far it may be proper to impose taxes upon the importation of foreign goods, in order, not to prevent their importation, but to raise a revenue for government, I shall consider hereafter when I come to treat of taxes.[61] Taxes imposed with a view to prevent, or even to diminish importation, are evidently as destructive of the revenue of the customs as of the freedom of trade.

[60] TMS VI.ii.2.8 states that: 'Upon the manner in which any state is divided into the different orders and societies which compose it . . . depends what is called the constitution of that particular state.' For a more conventional use of the term, see below, IV.vii.c.77. In the chapter of the TMS above cited, Smith spends a good deal of time in describing the 'subaltern' societies which comprise the state and the loyalties which they attract; an interesting emphasis when we recall that Part VI was the last major piece of work which Smith completed, together with the emphasis given to economic pressure groups, especially in WN IV.

[61] Below, V.ii.k.57–65.

CHAPTER III

Of the extraordinary Restraints upon the Importation of Goods of almost all Kinds, from those Countries with which the Balance is supposed to be disadvantageous

^aPART I
Of the Unreasonableness of those Restraints even upon the Principles of the Commercial System^a

1 To lay extraordinary restraints upon the importation of goods of almost all kinds, from those particular countries with which the balance of trade is supposed to be disadvantageous, is the second expedient by which the commercial system proposes to increase the quantity of gold and silver. ^bThus in Great Britain Silesia lawns may be imported for home consumption, upon paying certain duties. But French cambricks and lawns are prohibited to be imported, except into the port of London, there to be warehoused for exportation.[1] Higher duties are imposed upon the wines of France than upon those of Portugal, or indeed of any other country. By what is called the impost 1692, a duty of five and twenty per cent., of the rate or value, was laid upon all French goods;[2] while the goods of other nations were, the greater part of them, subjected to much lighter duties, seldom exceed-[210]ing five per cent. The wine, brandy, salt and vinegar of France were indeed excepted; these commodities being subjected to other heavy duties, either by other laws, or by particular clauses of the same law. In 1696, a second duty of twenty-five per cent., the first not having been thought a sufficient discouragement, was imposed upon all French goods, except brandy; together with a new duty of five and twenty pounds upon the ton of French wine, and another of fifteen pounds upon the ton of French vinegar.[3] French goods have never been omitted in any of those general subsidies, or duties of five per cent., which have been imposed upon all, or the greater part of the goods enumerated in the book of rates. If we count the one third and two third subsidies[4] as making a

---

^{a-a} 2A–6
^{b-b} [to 3rd last sentence of § 1] Thus in Great Britain higher duties are laid upon the wines of France than upon those of Portugal. German linen may be imported upon paying certain duties; but French linen is altogether prohibited. *1–2* text *2A–6*

---

[1] 18 George II, c.36 (1744); 21 George II, c.26 (1747); 32 George II, c.32 (1758); 7 George III, c.43 (1766). See below, IV.iv.7 and IV.viii.4.
[2] 4 William and Mary, c.5 (1692). See below, IV.iv.9.
[3] 7 and 8 William III, c.20 (1695). Wine and vinegar, as well as brandy, were not subject to the general increase of 25 per cent. The additional duties on brandy were £30 a tun on single proof and £60 a tun on double proof. See below, IV.iv.8,9 and IV.viii.43.
[4] See below, IV.iv.9 and V.ii.k.23.

compleat subsidy between them, there have been five of these general subsidies; so that before the commencement of the present war seventy-five per cent. may be considered as the lowest duty, to which the greater part of the goods of the growth, produce, or manufacture of France were liable. But upon the greater part of goods, those duties are equivalent to a prohibition. The French in their turn have, I believe, treated our goods and manufactures just as hardly; though I am not so well acquainted with the particular hardships which they have imposed upon them. Those mutual restraints have put an end to almost all fair commerce between the two nations, and smugglers are now the principal importers, either of British goods into France, or of French goods [211] into Great Britain.[b5] The principles which I have been examining ᶜin the foregoing chapterᶜ took their origin from private interest and the spirit of monopoly; those which I am going to examine ᵈin thisᵈ, from national prejudice and animosity.[6] They are, accordingly, as might well be expected, still more unreasonable. They are so, even upon the principles of the commercial system.[7]

2   First, though it were certain that in the case of a free trade between France and England, for example, the balance would be in favour of

ᶜ⁻ᶜ *om.* I   ᵈ⁻ᵈ 2–6

---

[5] See V.ii.b.6. The relationship between smuggling and taxes is frequently mentioned: see for example, IV.vi.27, V.ii.k.27,49,75.

[6] Hume developed this theme in his essay 'Of the Jealousy of Trade'. Montesquieu also implied that jealousy may be a natural concomitant of an extended trade in stating that a trading nation (like England) 'has a prodigious number of little particular interests; it may then injure or be injured in an infinite number of ways. Thus it becomes immoderately jealous, and is more afflicted at the prosperity of others than it rejoices at its own.' (*Esprit*, XIX.xxvii.32.) In TMS IV.i.1.11, however, Smith added love of system as a motive for policy, quite apart from sectional or national interest:

> When the Legislature establishes premiums and other encouragements to advance the linen or woollen manufactures, its conduct seldom proceeds from pure sympathy with the wearer of cheap or fine cloth, and much less from that with the manufacturer or merchant. The perfection of police, the extension of trade and manufactures, are noble and magnificent objects. The contemplation of them pleases us, and we are interested in whatever can tend to advance them. They make part of the great system of government, and the wheels of the political machine seem to move with more harmony and ease by means of them. We take pleasure in beholding the perfection of so beautiful and grand a system, and we are uneasy till we remove any obstruction that can in the least disturb or encumber the regularity of its motions.

Cf. TMS VII.iii.1.2.

[7] Cf. LJ (A) vi.164–5: 'All these national jealousies which prompt them to spite and ill-will each other, and refuse to be supplied by them in any convenience of life, must lessen the exchange of commodities, hurt the division of labour, and diminish the opulence of both.' Cf. LJ (B) 264, ed. Cannan 206, and TMS VI.ii.2,3, where Smith also points out that 'the mean principle of national prejudice is often founded upon the noble one of the love of our own country'. However, Smith went on to state that while France and England may each have reason to fear the military power of the other, their riches are 'proper objects of national emulation, not of national prejudice or envy'. Cf. Hume, 'Of the Balance of Trade', *Essays Moral, Political, and Literary*, ed. Green and Grose, i.335–6.

France, it would by no means follow that such a trade would be disadvantageous to England, or that the general balance of its whole trade would thereby be turned more against it. If the wines of France are better and cheaper than those of Portugal, or its linens than those of Germany, it would be more advantageous for Great Britain to purchase both the wine and the foreign linen which it had occasion for of France, than of Portugal and Germany. Though the value of the annual importations from France would thereby be greatly augmented, the value of the whole annual importations would be diminished, in proportion as the French goods of the same quality were cheaper than those of the other two countries. This would be the case, even upon the supposition that the whole French goods imported were to be consumed in Great Britain.

3   But, secondly, a great part of them might be re-exported to other countries, where, being sold with profit, they might bring back a return equal [212] in value, perhaps, to the prime cost of the whole French goods imported. What has frequently been said of the East India trade might possibly be true of the French; that though the greater part of East India goods were bought with gold and silver, the re-exportation of a part of them to other countries, brought back more gold and silver to that which carried on the trade than the prime cost of the whole amounted to.[8] One of the most important branches of the Dutch trade, at present, consists in the carriage of French goods to other European countries. *Some* part even of the French wine drank in Great Britain is clandestinely imported from Holland and Zealand. If there was either a free trade between France and England, or if French goods could be imported upon paying only the same duties as those of other European nations, to be drawn back upon exportation, England might have some share of a trade which is found so advantageous to Holland.

4   Thirdly, and lastly, there is no certain criterion by which we can determine on which side what is called the balance between any two countries lies, or which of them exports to the greatest value. National prejudice and animosity, prompted always by the private interest of particular traders, are the principles which generally direct our judgment upon all questions concerning it. There are two criterions, however, which have frequently been appealed to upon such occasions, the custom-house books and the course of exchange. The custom-house books, [213] I think, it is now

---

e–e A great *1*

---

[8] Anderson commented:

Objections, and answers to the East India trade . . . I. Its exhausting our Treasure. Answered, We may, by this Trade, draw as much Silver from other Countries as we send to India.

Origin of Commerce (1764), ii.452. See above, IV.i.7–8.

generally acknowledged, are a very uncertain criterion, on account of the inaccuracy of the valuation at which the greater part of goods are rated in them.⁹ The course of exchange ᶠ is, perhaps, almost equally so.

5   When the exchange between two places, such as London and Paris, is at par, it is said to be a sign that the debts due from London to Paris are compensated by those due from Paris to London. On the contrary, when a premium is paid at London for a bill upon Paris, it is said to be a sign that the debts due from London to Paris are not compensated by those due from Paris to London, but that a balance in money must be sent out from the latter place; for the risk, trouble, and expence of exporting which, the premium is both demanded and given. But the ordinary state of debt and credit between those two cities must necessarily be regulated, it is said, by the ordinary course of their dealings with one another. When neither of them imports from the other to a greater amount than it exports to ᵍthat otherᵍ, the debts and credits of each may compensate one another. But when one of them imports from the other to a greater value than it exports to ʰthat otherʰ, the former necessarily becomes indebted to the latter in a greater sum than the latter becomes indebted to it: the debts and credits of each do not compensate one another, and money must be sent out from that place of which the debts over-balance the credits. The ⁱordinaryⁱ course of exchange, therefore, being an indication of the ordinary [214] state of debt and credit between two places, must likewise be an indication of the ordinary course of their exports and imports, as these necessarily regulate that state.

6   But though ʲthe ordinary course of exchange ᵏshouldᵏ be allowed to be a sufficient indication of the ordinary state of debt and credit between any two places, it would not from thence follow, that the balance of trade was in favour of that place which had the ordinary state of debt and credit in its favour.¹⁰ The ordinary state of debt and credit between any two

---

ᶠ, at least, as it has hitherto been estimated, *1*   ᵍ⁻ᵍ it *1–2*   ʰ⁻ʰ it *1–2*
ⁱ⁻ⁱ common *1*
ʲ⁻ʲ [to end of §7] this doctrine, of which some part is, perhaps, not a little doubtful, were supposed ever so certain, the manner in which the par of exchange has hitherto been computed, renders uncertain every conclusion that has ever yet been drawn from it. *1*
ᵏ⁻ᵏ shall *6*

---

⁹ 'It is a matter of great difficulty to know the true balance of trade; some expect the custom house accounts will set us to rights, but there may be a great many fallacies in those accounts; a great many goods exported may be over-rated, and a great many imported under-rated: besides, it is possible to run-in vast quantities of goods that we can have no account of; and some merchants have entered double the quantity of woollens they intend to ship off, to discourage others from sending to the same market.' (J. Gee, *The Trade and Navigation of Great Britain Considered* (Glasgow, 1760), 127–8.) The rates at which commodities were valued were fixed, though it is possible to use the figures as a volume index. E. B. Schumpeter, *English Overseas Trade Statistics, 1697–1808* (Oxford, 1960).
¹⁰ '. . . the course of exchange betwixt different countries, is not so critical and exact a

places is not always entirely regulated by the ordinary course of their dealings with one another; but is often influenced by that of the dealings of either with many other places. If it is usual, for example, for the merchants of England to pay for the goods which they buy of Hamburgh, Dantzic, Riga, &c. by bills upon Holland, the ordinary state of debt and credit between England and Holland will not be regulated entirely by the ordinary course of the dealings of those two countries with one another, but will be influenced by that of the dealings of England with those other places.[11] England may be obliged to send out every year money to Holland, though its annual exports to that country may exceed very much the annual value of its imports from thence; and though what is called the balance of trade may be very much in favour of England.

7   In the way besides in which the par of exchange has hitherto been computed, the ordinary course of exchange can afford no sufficient indi-[215]cation that the ordinary state of debt and credit is in favour of that country which seems to have, or which is supposed to have, the ordinary course of exchange in its favour: or, in other words, the real exchange may be, and, in fact, often is so very different from the computed one, that from the course of the latter no certain conclusion can, upon many occasions, be drawn concerning that of the former.[j]

8   When for a sum of money paid in England, containing, according to the standard of the English mint, a certain number of ounces of pure silver, you receive a bill for a sum of money to be paid in France, containing, according to the standard of the French mint, an equal number of ounces of pure silver, exchange is said to be at par between England and France. When you pay more, you are supposed to give a premium, and exchange is said to be against England, and in favour of France. When you pay less, you are supposed to get a premium, and exchange is said to be against France, and in favour of England.

9   But, first we cannot always judge of the value of the current money of different countries by the ¹standard¹ of their respective mints. In some it is more, in others it is less worn, clipt, and otherwise degenerated from that standard. But the value of the current coin of every country, compared with that of any other country, is in proportion not to the quantity of pure

---

¹⁻¹ standards *I*

rule for measuring the ballance of trade, as is commonly imagined; since it is hardly possible to ascertain what is the *true par*.' (J. Harris, *Essay*, i.118.)

[11] Harris provided an example (*Essay*, i.125.): 'The business of exchange between *England* and *Germany*, and the northern countries, is chiefly transacted at *London* and *Amsterdam*. The course of exchange then between us and *Holland*, indicates how the state of accounts stands between us and all those countries in general, but not in respect of any one in particular. The ballance of our trade to *Holland* may be greatly in our favour, and yet the exchange to *Amsterdam* be generally against us; both which are supposed to be matters of fact.'

silver which it ought to contain, but to that which it actually does contain. Before the reformation of [216] the silver coin in king William's time, exchange between England and Holland, computed, in the usual manner, according to the ᵐstandardᵐ of their respective mints, was five and twenty per cent. against England. But the value of the current coin of England, as we learn from Mr Lowndes, was at that time rather more than five and twenty per cent. below its standard value.[12] The real exchange, therefore, may even at that time have been in favour of England, notwithstanding the computed exchange was so much against it; a smaller number of ounces of pure silver, actually paid in England, may have purchased a bill for a greater number of ounces of pure silver to be paid in Holland, and the man who was supposed to give, may in reality have got the premium. The French coin was, before the late reformation of the English gold coin,[13] much less worn than the English, and was, perhaps, two or three per cent. nearer its standard. If the computed exchange with France, therefore, was not more than two or three per cent. against England, the real exchange might have been in its favour. Since the reformation of the gold coin, the exchange has been constantly in favour of England, and against France.

10   Secondly, in some countries, the expence of coinage is defrayed by the government; in others, it is defrayed by the private people who carry their bullion to the mint, and the government even derives some revenue from the coinage. In England, it is defrayed by the government, and if you carry a pound weight of standard silver to [217] the mint, you get back sixty-two shillings, containing a pound weight of the like standard silver. In France, a duty of eight per cent. is deducted for the coinage, which not only defrays the expence of it, but affords a small revenue to the government.[14] In England, as the coinage costs nothing, the current coin can never be much more valuable than the quantity of bullion which it actually contains.[15] In France, the workmanship as you pay for it, adds to the value, in the same manner as to that of wrought plate. A sum of French money, therefore, containing a certain weight of pure silver, is more valuable than a sum of English money containing an equal weight of pure silver, and must require more bullion, or other commodities to purchase it. Though the current coin of the two countries, therefore, were equally near the standards of their respective mints, a sum of English money could not well purchase a sum of French money, containing an equal number of ounces of pure silver, nor consequently a bill upon France for such a sum. If for such a bill no

ᵐ⁻ᵐ standards *I*

[12] The same point, quoting the same authority, is mentioned above, I.xi.g.5.

[13] In 1774. See above, I.v.32 and I.xi.g.6.

[14] The seignorage was 3 per cent. See above, I.v.39, and below, IV.vi.19.

[15] See below, IV.vi.18. It is pointed out at I.v.38 that any delay in converting bullion into coin is equivalent to a small duty.

more additional money was paid than what was sufficient to compensate the expence of the French coinage, the real exchange might be at par between the two countries, their debts and credits might mutually compensate one another, while the computed exchange was considerably in favour of France. If less than this was paid, the real exchange might be in favour of England, while the computed was in favour of France.

11   [218] Thirdly, and lastly, in some places, as at Amsterdam, Hamburgh, Venice, &c. foreign bills of exchange are paid in what they call bank money; while in others, as at London, Lisbon, Antwerp, Leghorn, &c. they are paid in the common currency of the country. What is called bank money is always of more value than the same nominal sum of common currency. A thousand guilders in the bank of Amsterdam, for example, are of more value than a thousand guilders of Amsterdam currency. The difference between them is called the agio of the bank,[16] which, at Amsterdam, is generally about five per cent. Supposing the current money of ⁿtheⁿ two countries equally near to the standard of their respective mints, and that the one pays foreign bills in this common currency, while the other pays them in bank money, it is evident that the computed exchange may be in favour of that which pays in bank money, though the real exchange should be in favour of that which pays in current money; for the same reason that the computed exchange may be in favour of that which pays in better money, or in money nearer to its own standard, though the real exchange should be in favour of that which pays in worse. The computed exchange, before the late reformation of the gold coin, was generally against London with Amsterdam, Hamburgh, Venice, and, I believe, with all other places which pay in what is called bank money. It will by no means follow, however, that the real exchange was against it. Since the reformation of the gold [219] coin, it has been in favour of London even with those places. The computed exchange has generally been in favour of London with Lisbon, Antwerp, Leghorn, and, if you except France, I believe, with most other parts of Europe that pay in common currency; and it is not improbable that the real exchange was so too.

Digression concerning Banks of Deposit, particularly concerning that of Amsterdam[1]

1   The currency of a great state, such as France or England, generally consists almost entirely of its own coin. Should this currency, therefore, be at any time worn, clipt, or otherwise degraded below its standard value,

ⁿ⁻ⁿ *2–6*

---

16 The agio is mentioned above, II.ii.104.

1 It is stated in the preface of the 4th edition, that 'I find myself at liberty to acknowledge my very great obligations to Mr. Henry Hope of Amsterdam' with regard to information on the bank. cf. Steuart, *Principles*, ii.300, and generally, IV.2.xxxvii–xxxix.

the state by a reformation of its coin can effectually re-establish its currency. But the currency of a small state, such as Genoa or Hamburgh, can seldom consist altogether in its own coin, but must be made up, in a great measure, of the coins of all the neighbouring states with which its inhabitants have a continual intercourse. Such a state, therefore, by reforming its coin, will not always be able to reform its currency. If foreign bills of exchange are paid in this currency, the uncertain value of any sum, of what is in its own nature so uncertain, must render the exchange always very much against such a state, its currency being, in all foreign states, necessarily valued even below what it is worth.

2   [220] In order to remedy the inconvenience to which this disadvantageous exchange must have subjected their merchants, such small states, when they began to attend to the interest of trade, have frequently enacted, that foreign bills of exchange of a certain value should be paid, not in common currency, but by an order upon, or by a transfer in the books of a certain bank, established upon the credit, and under the protection of the state; this bank being always obliged to pay, in good and true money, exactly according to the standard of the state. The banks of Venice, Genoa, Amsterdam, Hamburgh, and Nuremberg, seem to have been all originally established with this view,[2] though some of them may have afterwards been made subservient to other purposes. The money of such banks being better than the common currency of the country, necessarily bore an agio, which was greater or smaller, according as the currency was supposed to be more or less degraded below the standard of the state. The agio of the bank of Hamburgh, for example, which is said to be commonly about fourteen per cent. is the supposed difference between the good standard money of the state, and the clipt, worn, and diminished currency poured into it from all the neighbouring states.

3   Before 1609 the great quantity of clipt and worn foreign coin, which the extensive trade of Amsterdam brought from all parts of Europe, reduced the value of its currency about nine per cent. below that of good money fresh from [221] the mint. Such money no sooner appeared than it was melted down or carried away, as it always is in such circumstances. The merchants, with plenty of currency, could not always find a sufficient quantity of good money to pay their bills of exchange; and the value of those bills, in spite of several regulations which were made to prevent it, became in a great measure uncertain.

4   In order to remedy these inconveniencies, a bank was established in 1609 under the guarantee of the city. This bank received both foreign coin, and the light and worn coin of the country at its real intrinsic value in the good

---

²'...the main if not the sole design of erecting these banks [Venice, Amsterdam, Hamburg, Nuremberg], was for the fixing of a kind of an indelible standard of money.' (J. Harris, *Essay*, i.102.)

standard money of the country, deducting only so much as was necessary for defraying the expence of coinage, and the other necessary expence of management. For the value which remained, after this small deduction was made, it gave a credit in its books. This credit was called bank money, which, as it represented money exactly according to the standard of the mint, was always of the same real value, and intrinsically worth more than current money. It was at the same time enacted, that all bills drawn upon or negociated at Amsterdam of the value of six hundred guilders and up-wards should be paid in bank money, which at once took away all uncer-tainty in the value of those bills. Every merchant, in consequence of this regulation, was obliged to keep an account with the bank in order to pay his foreign bills of exchange, which necessarily occasioned a certain demand for bank money.

5   [222] Bank money, over and above both its intrinsic superiority to currency, and the additional value which this demand necessarily gives it, has likewise some other advantages. It is secure from fire, robbery, and other accidents;[3] the city of Amsterdam is bound for it; it can be paid away by a simple transfer, without the trouble of counting, or the risk of transporting it from one place to another. In consequence of those dif-ferent advantages, it seems from the beginning to have borne an agio, and it is generally believed that all the money originally deposited in the bank was allowed to remain there, nobody caring to demand payment of a debt which he could sell for a premium in the market. By demanding payment of the bank, the owner of a bank credit would lose this premium. As a shilling fresh from the mint will buy no more goods in the market than one of our common worn shillings, so the good and true money which might be brought from the coffers of the bank into those of a private person, being mixed and confounded with the common currency of the country, would be of no more value than that currency, from which it could no longer be readily distinguished. While it remained in the coffers of the bank, its superiority was known and ascertained. When it had come into those of a private person, its superiority could not well be ascertained without more trouble than perhaps the difference was worth. By being brought from the coffers of the bank, besides, it lost all the other advantages of bank money; its secu-[223]rity, its easy and safe transferability, its use in paying foreign bills of exchange. Over and above all this, it could not be brought from those coffers, as it will appear by and by, without previously paying for the keeping.

6   Those deposits of coin, *or those deposits* which the bank was bound to restore in coin, constituted the original capital of the bank, or the whole

---

a–a 2–6

[3] See below, IV.iii.b.15

value of what was represented by what is called bank money. At present they are supposed to constitute but a very small part of it. In order to facilitate the trade in bullion, the bank has been for these many years in the practice of giving credit in its books upon deposits of gold and silver bullion. This credit is generally about five per cent. below the mint price of such bullion. The bank grants at the same time what is called a recipice or receipt, intitling the person who makes the deposit, or the bearer, to take out the bullion again at any time within six months, upon re-transfering to the bank a quantity of bank money equal to that for which credit had been given in its books when the deposit was made, and upon paying one-fourth per cent. for the keeping, if the deposit was in silver; and one-half per cent. if it was in gold; but at the same time declaring, that in default of such payment, and upon the expiration of this term, the deposit should belong to the bank at the price at which it had been received, or for which credit had been given in the transfer books. What is thus paid for the keeping of the deposit may be considered as a sort of ware-[224]house rent; and why this warehouse rent should be so much dearer for gold than for silver, several different reasons have been assigned. The fineness of gold, it has been said, is more difficult to be ascertained than that of silver. Frauds are more easily practised, and occasion a greater loss in the more precious metal. Silver, besides, being the standard metal, the state, it has been said, wishes to encourage more the making of deposits of silver than ᵇofᵇ those of gold.

7   Deposits of bullion are most commonly made when the price is somewhat lower than ordinary; and they are taken out again when it happens to rise. In Holland the market price of bullion is generally above the mint price, for the same reason that it was so in England before the late reformation of the gold coin.[4] The difference is said to be commonly from about six to sixteen stivers upon the mark, or eight ounces of silver of eleven parts fine, and one part alloy. The bank price, or the credit which the bank gives for deposits of such silver (when made in foreign coin, of which the fineness is well known and ascertained, such as Mexico dollars) is twenty-two guilders the mark; the mint price is about twenty-three guilders, and the market price is from twenty-three guilders six, to twenty-three guilders sixteen stivers, or from two to three per cent. above the mint price.* The propor-[225]tions between the bank price, the mint price, and the market price

* The following are the prices at which the bank of Amsterdam at present (September, 1775) receives bullion and coin of different kinds: [225]

SILVER

Mexico dollars ⎫	Guilders
French crowns ⎬	B-22 per mark. [*continues*]
English silver coin ⎭	

ᵇ⁻ᵇ *om. 4–6*

[4] In 1774. See above, I.v.32 and I.xi.g.6.

of gold bullion, are nearly the same. A person can generally sell his receipt for the difference between the mint price of bullion and the market price. A receipt for bullion is almost always worth something, and it very seldom happens, therefore, that any body suffers his receipt to expire, or allows his bullion to fall to the bank at the price at which it had been received, either by not taking it out before the end of the six months, or by neglecting to pay the one-fourth or one-half per cent. in order [226] to obtain a new receipt for another six months. This, however, though it happens seldom, is said to happen sometimes, and more frequently with regard to gold, than with regard to silver, on account of the higher warehouse-rent which is paid for the keeping of the more precious metal.

8   The person who by making a deposit of bullion obtains both a bank credit and a receipt, pays his bills of exchange as they become due with his bank credit; and either sells or keeps his receipt according as he judges that the price of bullion is likely to rise or to fall. The receipt and the bank credit seldom keep long together, and there is no occasion that they should. The person who has a receipt, and who wants to take out bullion, finds always plenty of bank credits, or bank money to buy at the ordinary price; and the person who has bank money, and wants to take out bullion, finds receipts always in equal abundance.

9   The owners of bank credits, and the holders of receipts, constitute two different sorts of creditors against the bank. The holder of a receipt cannot draw out the bullion for which it is granted, without re-assigning to the bank a sum of bank money equal to the price at which the bullion had been received. If he has no bank money of his own, he must purchase it of those who have it. The owner of bank money cannot draw out bullion without producing to the bank receipts for the quantity which he wants. If he has none of his own, he must buy them of those [227] who have them. The holder of a receipt, when he purchases bank money, purchases the power of taking out a quantity of bullion, of which the mint price is five per cent.

> Mexico dollars new coin 21 10
> Ducatoons   3
> Rix dollars   2   8

Bar silver containing $\frac{11}{12}$ fine silver 21 per mark, and in this proportion down to $\frac{1}{4}$ fine, on which 5 guilders are given.

> Fine bars, 23 per mark.

GOLD

> Portugal coin ⎫
> Guineas   ⎬ B-310 per mark.
> Louis d'ors new ⎭
> Ditto old   300
> New ducats   4 19 8 per ducat.

Bar or ingot gold is received in proportion to its fineness compared with the above foreign gold coin. Upon fine bars the bank gives 340 per mark. In general, however, something more is given upon coin of a known fineness, than upon gold and silver bars, of which the fineness cannot be ascertained but by a process of melting and assaying.

above the bank price. The agio of five per cent. therefore, which he commonly pays for it, is paid, not for an imaginary, but for a real value. The owner of bank money, when he purchases a receipt, purchases the power of taking out a quantity of bullion of which the market price is commonly from two to three per cent. above the mint price. The price which he pays for it, therefore, is paid likewise for a real value. The price of the receipt, and the price of the bank money, compound or make up between them the full value or price of the bullion.

10   Upon deposits of the coin current in the country, the bank grants receipts likewise as well as bank credits; but those receipts are frequently of no value, and will bring no price in the market. Upon ducatoons, for example, which in the currency pass for three guilders three stivers each, the bank gives a credit of three guilders only, or five per cent. below their current value. It grants a receipt likewise intitling the bearer to take out the number of ducatoons deposited at any time within six months, upon paying one-fourth per cent. for the keeping. This receipt will frequently bring no price in the market. Three guilders bank money generally sell in the market for three guilders three stivers, the full value of the ducatoons, if they were taken out of the bank; and before they can be taken out, [228] one-fourth per cent. must be paid for the keeping, which would be mere loss to the holder of the receipt. If the agio of the bank, however, should at any time fall to three per cent. such receipts might bring some price in the market, and might sell for one and three-fourths per cent. But the agio of the bank being now generally about five per cent. such receipts are frequently allowed to expire, or as they express it, to fall to the bank. The receipts which are given for deposits of gold ducats fall to it yet more frequently, because a higher warehouse-rent, or one-half per cent. must be paid for the keeping of them before they can be taken out again. The five per cent. which the bank gains, when deposits either of coin or bullion are allowed to fall to it, may be considered as the warehouse-rent for the perpetual keeping of such deposits.

11   The sum of bank money for which the receipts are expired must be very considerable. It must comprehend the whole original capital of the bank, which, it is generally supposed, has been allowed to remain there from the time it was first deposited, nobody caring either to renew his receipt or to take out his deposit, as, for the reasons already assigned, neither the one nor the other could be done without loss. But whatever may be the amount of this sum, the proportion which it bears to the whole mass of bank money is supposed to be very small. The bank of Amsterdam has for these many years past been the great warehouse of Europe for bul-[229]lion, for which the receipts are very seldom allowed to expire, or, as they express it, to fall to the bank. The far greater part of the bank money, or of the credits upon the books of the bank, is supposed to have been created, for these many

years past, by such deposits which the dealers in bullion are continually both making and withdrawing.

12   No demand can be made upon the bank but by means of a recipice or receipt. The smaller mass of bank money, for which the receipts are expired, is mixed and confounded with the much greater mass for which they are still in force; so that, though there may be a considerable sum of bank money, for which there are no receipts, there is no specific sum or portion of it, which may not at any time be demanded by one. The bank cannot be debtor to two persons for the same thing; and the owner of bank money who has no receipt, cannot demand payment of the bank till he buys one. In ordinary and quiet times, he can find no difficulty in getting one to buy at the market price, which generally corresponds with the price at which he can sell the coin or bullion it intitles him to take out of the bank.

13   It might be otherwise during a publick calamity; an invasion, for example, such as that of the French in 1672. The owners of bank money being then all eager to draw it out of the bank, in order to have it in their own keeping, the demand for receipts might raise their price to an exorbitant height. The holders of them [230] might form extravagant expectations, and, instead of two or three per cent. demand half the bank money for which credit had been given upon the deposits that the receipts had respectively been granted for. The enemy, informed of the constitution of the bank, might even buy them up in order to prevent the carrying away of the treasure. In such emergencies, the bank, it is supposed, would break through its ordinary rule of making payment only to the holders of receipts. The holders of receipts, who had no bank money, must have received within two or three per cent. of the value of the deposit for which their respective receipts had been granted. The bank, therefore, it is said, would in this case make no scruple of paying, either with money or bullion, the full value of what the owners of bank money who could get no receipts, were credited for in its books; paying at the same time two or three per cent. to such holders of receipts as had no bank money, that being the whole value which in this state of things could justly be supposed due to them.

14   Even in ordinary and quiet times it is the interest of the holders of receipts to depress the agio, in order either to buy bank money (and consequently the bullion, which their receipts would then enable them to take out of the bank) so much cheaper, or to sell their receipts to those who have bank money, and who want to take out bullion, so much dearer; the price of a receipt being generally equal to the difference between the market price of bank money, and [231] that of the coin or bullion for which the receipt had been granted. It is the interest of the owners of bank money, on the contrary, to raise the agio, in order either to sell their bank money so much

dearer, or to buy a receipt so much cheaper. To prevent the stock-jobbing tricks which those opposite interests might sometimes occasion, the bank has of late years come to the resolution to sell at all times bank money for currency, at five per cent. agio, and to buy it in again at four per cent. agio. In consequence of this resolution, the agio can never either rise above five, or sink below four per cent. and the proportion between the market price of bank and that of current money, is kept at all times very near to the proportion between their intrinsick values. Before this resolution was taken, the market price of bank money used sometimes to rise so high as nine per cent. agio, and sometimes to sink so low as par, according as opposite interests happened to influence the market.

15   The bank of Amsterdam professes to lend out no part of what is deposited with it, but, for every guilder for which it gives credit in its books, to keep in its repositories the value of a guilder either in money or bullion. That it keeps in its repositories all the money or bullion for which there are receipts in force, for which it is at all times liable to be called upon, and which, in reality, is continually going from it and returning to it again, cannot well be doubted. But whether it does so likewise with regard to that part of its capital, for which the receipts [232] are long ago expired, for which in ordinary and quiet times it cannot be called upon, and which in reality is very likely to remain with it for ever, or as long as the States of the United Provinces subsist, may perhaps appear more uncertain. At Amsterdam, however, no point of faith is better established than that for every guilder, circulated as bank money, there is a correspondent guilder in gold or silver to be found in the treasure of the bank. The city is guarantee that it should be so. The bank is under the direction of the four reigning burgomasters, who are changed every year. Each new sett of burgomasters visits the treasure, compares it with the books, receives it upon oath, and delivers it over, with the same awful solemnity, to the sett which succeeds [c] ; and in that sober and religious country oaths are not yet disregarded. A rotation of this kind seems alone a sufficient security against any practices which cannot be avowed. Amidst all the revolutions which faction has ever occasioned in the government of Amsterdam, the prevailing party has at no time accused their predecessors of infidelity in the administration of the bank. No accusation could have affected more deeply the reputation and fortune of the disgraced party, and if such an accusation could have been supported, we may be assured that it would have been brought. In 1672, when the French king was at Utrecht, the bank of Amsterdam paid so readily as left no doubt of the fidelity with which it had observed its engagements. Some of the pieces which were then [233] brought from its repositories appeared to have been scorched with the fire which happened

in the town-house soon after the bank was established.[5] Those pieces, therefore, must have lain there from that time.[6]

16   What may be the amount of the treasure in the bank, is a question which has long employed the speculations of the curious. Nothing but conjecture can be offered concerning it. It is generally reckoned that there are about two thousand people who keep accounts with the bank, and allowing them to have, one with another, the value of fifteen hundred pounds sterling lying upon their respective accounts (a very large allowance), the whole quantity of bank money, and consequently of treasure in the bank, will amount to about three millions sterling, or, at eleven guilders the pound sterling, thirty-three millions of guilders; a great sum, and sufficient to carry on a very extensive circulation; but vastly below the extravagant ideas which some people have formed of this treasure.[7]

17   The city of Amsterdam derives a considerable revenue from the bank. Besides what may be called the warehouse-rent above mentioned, each person, upon first opening an account with the bank, pays a fee of ten guilders; and for every new account three guilders three stivers; for every transfer two stivers; and if the transfer is for less than three hundred guilders, six stivers, in order to discourage the multiplicity of small transactions. The person who neglects to balance his account twice in the year forfeits [234] twenty-five guilders. The person who orders a transfer for more than is upon his account, is obliged to pay three per cent. for the sum over-drawn, and his order is set aside into the bargain. The bank is supposed too to make a considerable profit by the sale of the foreign coin or bullion which sometimes falls to it by the expiring of receipts, and which is always kept till it can be sold with advantage. It makes a profit likewise by selling bank money at five per cent. agio, and buying it in at four. These different emoluments amount to a good deal more than what is necessary for paying the salaries of officers, and defraying the expence of management. What is paid for the keeping of bullion upon receipts, is alone supposed to

---

[5] Voltaire, *Siècle de Louis XIV*, in *Oeuvres* (Paris, 1878), i.258, quoted by A. Anderson, *Origin of Commerce* (1764), ii.153.

[6] In LJ (B) 249, ed. Cannan 193, the date is given incorrectly as 1701; Smith then proceeds to show that the 'constitution' of the Bank of England differed from that of Amsterdam. This material does not figure in either LJ (A) or ED. See above. §5.

[7] Cf. LJ (B) 249, ed. Cannan 194: 'It has been affirmed by some that the bank of Amsterdam has always money in its stores to the ammount of 80 or 90 millions. But this has lately been shown by an ingenious gentleman to be false, from a comparison of the trade of London and Amsterdam.' The authority is probably that of Magens, who wrote: 'The Bank of Amsterdam has the Fame of more Treasure than any other; the *French* Author of The Essay on Commerce says its Capital is 400,000,000 of Gilders; and the *Amsterdam* Edition of that Book is noted in the Margin 8, or 900,000,000, which amounts to 80,000,000 Sterling. *Davenant* seems assured that it is 36,000,000 Sterling, effectual Money Gold and Silver in Bank, and that their Transactions are not with Money, but by Assignments.' (*The Universal Merchant*, ed. Horsley, 32.) Magens suggests maxima of 3,000 accounts and 60,000,000 guilders of treasure.

amount to a neat annual revenue of between one hundred and fifty thousand and two hundred thousand guilders. Public utility, however, and not revenue, was the original object of this institution. Its object was to relieve the merchants from the inconvenience of a disadvantageous exchange. The revenue which has arisen from it was unforeseen, and may be considered as accidental. But it is now time to return from this long digression, into which I have been insensibly led in endeavouring to explain the reasons why the exchange between the countries which pay in what is called bank money, and those which pay in common currency, should generally appear to be in favour of the former, and against the latter. The former pay in a species of money of which the intrinsic value is always the same, and exactly [235] agreeable to the standard of their respective mints; the latter in a species of money of which the intrinsic value is continually varying, and is almost always more or less below that standard.[d]

^aPART II

Of the Unreasonableness of those extraordinary Restraints upon other Principles[a]

1   [b]In the foregoing Part of this Chapter I have endeavoured to[b] shew, even upon the principles of the commercial system, how unnecessary it is to lay extraordinary restraints upon the importation of goods from those countries with which the balance of trade is supposed to be disadvantageous.

2   Nothing, however, can be more absurd than this whole doctrine of the balance of trade,[1] upon which, not only these restraints, but almost all the other regulations of commerce are founded. When two places trade with

----

[d] But though the computed exchange must generally be in favour of the former, the real exchange may frequently be in favour of the latter. *1*

[a-a] *End of the Digression concerning Banks of Deposit. 1*

[b-b] Though the computed exchange between any two places were in every respect the same with the real, it would not always follow that what is called the balance of trade was in favour of that place which had the ordinary course of exchange in its favour. The ordinary course of exchange might, indeed, in this case, be a tolerable indication of the ordinary state of debt and credit between them, and show which of the two countries usually had occasion to send out money to the other. But the ordinary state of debt and credit between any two places is not always entirely regulated by the ordinary course of their dealings with one another, but is influenced by that of the dealings of both with many other countries. If it was usual, for example, for the merchants of England to pay the goods which they buy from Hamburgh, Dantzick, Riga, &c. by bills upon Holland, the ordinary state of debt and credit between England and Holland would not be entirely regulated by the ordinary course of the dealings of those two countries with one another, but would be influenced by that of England with those other places. England might, in this case, be annually obliged to send out money to Holland, though its annual exports to that country exceeded the annual value of its imports from it, and though what is called the balance of trade was very much in favour of England.

Hitherto I have been endeavouring to *1*

----

[1] Smith refers to 'absurd speculations' regarding the balance of trade at III.i.1, and see generally, IV.i.

one another, this doctrine supposes that, if the balance be even, neither of them either loses or gains; but if it leans in any degree to one side, that one of them loses, and the other gains in proportion to its declension from the exact equilibrium. Both suppositions are false. A trade which is forced by means of bounties and monopolies, may be, and commonly is disadvantageous to the country in whose favour it is meant to be established, as I shall endeavour to shew hereafter.[2] But that [236] trade which, without force or constraint, is naturally and regularly carried on between any two places, is always advantageous, though not always equally so, to both.

3   By advantage or gain, I understand, not the increase of the quantity of gold and silver, but that of the exchangeable value of the annual produce of the land and labour of the country, or the increase of the annual revenue of its inhabitants.

4   If the balance be even, and if the trade between the two places consist altogether in the exchange of their native commodities, they will, upon most occasions, not only both gain, but they will gain equally, or very near equally; each will in this case afford a market for a part of the surplus produce of the other: each will replace a capital which had been employed in raising ^{c}and preparing for the market^{c3} this part of the surplus produce of the other, and which had been distributed among, and given revenue and maintenance to a certain number of its inhabitants. Some part of the inhabitants of each, therefore, will indirectly derive their revenue and maintenance from the other. As the commodities exchanged too are supposed to be of equal value, so the two capitals employed in the trade will, upon most occasions, be equal, or very nearly equal; and both being employed in raising the native commodities of the two countries, the revenue and maintenance which their distribution will afford to the inhabitants of each will be equal, or very nearly equal. This revenue [237] and maintenance, thus mutually afforded, will be greater or smaller in proportion to the extent of their dealings. If these should annually amount to an hundred thousand pounds, for example, or to a million on each side, each of them ^{d}would^d afford an annual revenue, in the one case, of an hundred thousand pounds, in the other, of a million, to the inhabitants of the other.

5   If their trade should be of such a nature that one of them exported to the other nothing but native commodities, while the returns of that other consisted altogether in foreign goods; the balance, in this case, would still be supposed even, commodities being paid for with commodities. They would, in this case too, both gain, but they would not gain equally; and the inhabitants of the country which exported nothing but native commodities would derive the greatest revenue from the trade. If England,

$^{c-c}$ 2–6 $^{d-d}$ will 6

---

[2] See below, IV.v.a.1–3; cf. IV.viii.51.   [3] See above, IV.i.31 and III.i.1.

for example, should import from France nothing but the native commodities of that country, and, not having such commodities of its own as were in demand there, should annually repay them by sending thither a large quantity of foreign goods, tobacco, we shall suppose, and East India goods; this trade, though it would give some revenue to the inhabitants of both countries, would give more to those of France than to those of England. The whole French capital annually employed in it would annually be distributed among the people of France. But that part of the English capital only which was employed in producing the English commodities with which those [238] foreign goods were purchased, would be annually distributed among the people of England. The greater part of it would replace the capitals which had been employed in Virginia, Indostan, and China, and which had given revenue and maintenance to the inhabitants of those distant countries. If the capitals were equal, or nearly equal, therefore, this employment of the French capital would augment much more the revenue of the people of France, than that of the English capital would the revenue of the people of England. France would in this case carry on a direct foreign trade of consumption with England; whereas England would carry on a round-about trade of the same kind with France. The different effects of a capital employed in the direct, and of one employed in the round-about foreign trade of consumption, have already been fully explained.[4]

6   There is not, probably, between any two countries, a trade which consists altogether in the exchange either of native commodities on both sides, or of native commodities on one side and of foreign goods on the other. Almost all countries exchange with one another partly native and partly foreign goods. That country, however, in whose cargoes there is the greatest proportion of native, and the least of foreign goods, will always be the principal gainer.

7   [e]If it was not with tobacco and East India goods, but with gold and silver, that England paid for the commodities annually imported from France, the balance, in this case, would be sup-[239]posed uneven, commodities not being paid for with commodities, but with gold and silver. The trade, however, would, in this case, as in the foregoing, give some revenue to the inhabitants of both countries, but more to those of France than to those of England. It would give some revenue to those of England. The capital which had been employed in producing the English goods that purchased this gold and silver, the capital which had been distributed among, and given revenue to certain inhabitants of England, would thereby be replaced, and enabled to continue that employment. The whole capital of

[e] no ¶ *1*

---

[4] See above, II.v.28.

England would no more be diminished by this exportation of gold and silver, than by the exportation of an equal value of any other goods. On the contrary, it would, in most cases, be augmented. No goods are sent abroad but those for which the demand is supposed to be greater abroad than at home, and of which the returns consequently, it is expected, will be of more value at home than the commodities exported. If the tobacco which, in England, is worth only a hundred thousand pounds, when sent to France will purchase wine which is, in England, worth a hundred and ten thousand pounds, the exchange will augment the capital of England by ten thousand pounds. If a hundred thousand pounds of English gold, in the same manner, purchase French wine, which, in England, is worth a hundred and ten thousand, this exchange will equally augment the capital of England by ten thousand pounds. As a merchant who has [240] a hundred and ten thousand pounds worth of wine in his cellar, is a richer man than he who has only a hundred thousand pounds worth of tobacco in his warehouse, so is he likewise a richer man than he who has only a hundred thousand pounds worth of gold in his coffers. He can put into motion a greater quantity of industry, and give revenue, maintenance, and employment, to a greater number of people than either of the other two. But the capital of the country is equal to the capitals of all its different inhabitants, and the quantity of industry which can be annually maintained in it, is equal to what all those different capitals can maintain. Both the capital of the country, therefore, and the quantity of industry which can be annually maintained in it, must generally be augmented by this exchange. It would, indeed, be more advantageous for England that it could purchase the wines of France with its own hardware and broad-cloth, than with either the tobacco of Virginia, or the gold and silver of Brazil and Peru. A direct foreign trade of consumption is always more advantageous than a round-about one. But a round-about foreign trade of consumption, which is carried on with gold and silver, does not seem to be less advantageous than any other equally round-about one. Neither is a country which has no mines more likely to be exhausted of gold and silver by this annual exportation of those metals, than one which does not grow tobacco by the like annual exportation of that plant. As a country which has where-[241]withal to buy tobacco will never be long in want of it, so neither will one be long in want of gold and silver which has wherewithal to purchase those metals.[5]

8   It is a losing trade, it is said, which a workman carries on with the alehouse; and the trade which a manufacturing nation would naturally carry on with a wine country, may be considered as a trade of the same nature. I answer, that the trade with the alehouse is not necessarily a losing trade. In its own nature it is just as advantageous as any other, though, perhaps,

---

[5] See above, II.iii.24, and below, IV.vi.12.

somewhat more liable to be abused.[6] The employment of a brewer, and even that of a retailer of fermented liquors, are as necessary divisions of labour as any other. It will generally be more advantageous for a workman to buy of the brewer the quantity he has occasion for, than to 'brew' it himself, and if he is a poor workman, it will generally be more advantageous for him to buy it, by little and little of the retailer, than a large quantity of the brewer. He may no doubt buy too much of either, as he may of any other dealers in his neighbourhood, of the butcher, if he is a glutton, or of the draper, if he affects to be a beau among his companions. It is advantageous to the great body of workmen, notwithstanding, that all these trades should be free, though this freedom may be abused in all of them, and is more likely to be so, perhaps, in some than in others. Though individuals, besides, may sometimes ruin their fortunes by an excessive consumption of fermented liquors, there [242] seems to be no risk that a nation should do so. Though in every country there are many people who spend upon such liquors more than they can afford, there are always many more who spend less. It deserves to be remarked too that, if we consult experience, the cheapness of wine seems to be a cause, not of drunkenness, but of sobriety. The inhabitants of the wine countries are in general the soberest people in Europe; witness the Spaniards, the Italians, and the inhabitants of the southern provinces of France. People are seldom guilty of excess in what is their daily fare. Nobody affects the character of liberality and good fellowship, by being profuse of a liquor which is as cheap as small beer. On the contrary, in the countries which, ⁹either from⁹ excessive heat or cold, produce no grapes, and where wine consequently is dear and a rarity, drunkenness is a common vice, as among the northern nations, and all those who live between the tropics, the negroes, for example, on the coast of Guinea. When a French regiment comes from some of the northern provinces of France, where wine is somewhat dear, to be quartered in the southern, where it is very cheap, the soldiers, I have frequently heard it observed, are at first debauched by the cheapness and novelty of good wine; but after a few months residence, the greater part of them become as sober as the rest of the inhabitants. Were the duties upon foreign wines, and the excises upon malt, beer, and ale, to be taken away all at once, it might, in the same manner, occasion in Great [243] Britain a pretty general and temporary drunkenness among the middling and inferior ranks of people, which would probably be soon followed by a permanent and almost universal sobriety.[7] At present drunkenness is by no

ᶠ⁻ᶠ make *I–2*   ⁹⁻⁹ from either *I*

---

[6] See above, II.v.7.

[7] It is pointed out at V.ii.k.50 that current British policy was to discourage the consumption of spirituous liquors on account of their tendency to 'ruin the health and to corrupt the morals of the common people'.

means the vice of people of fashion, or of those who can easily afford the most expensive liquors. A gentleman drunk with ale, has scarce ever been seen among us.[8] The restraints upon the wine trade in Great Britain, besides, do not so much seem calculated to hinder the people from going, if I may say so, to the alehouse, as from going where they can buy the best and cheapest liquor. They favour the wine trade of Portugal, and discourage that of France. The Portuguese, it is said, indeed, are better customers for our manufactures than the French, and should therefore be encouraged in preference to them. As they give us their custom, it is pretended, we should give them ours. The sneaking arts of underling tradesmen are thus erected into political maxims for the conduct of a great empire: for it is the most underling tradesmen only who make it a rule to employ chiefly their own customers. A great trader purchases his goods always where they are cheapest and best, without regard to any little interest of this kind.

9   By such maxims as these, however, nations have been taught that their interest consisted in beggaring all their neighbours. Each nation has been made to look with an invidious eye upon the prosperity of all the nations with which it trades, and to consider their gain as its own [244] loss. Commerce, which ought naturally to be, among nations, as among individuals, a bond of union and friendship, has become the most fertile source of discord and animosity. The capricious ambition of kings and ministers has not, during the present and the preceding century, been more fatal to the repose of Europe, than the impertinent jealousy of merchants and manufacturers. The violence and injustice of the rulers of mankind is an ancient evil, for which, I am afraid, the nature of human affairs can scarce admit of a remedy. But the mean rapacity, the monopolizing spirit of merchants and manufacturers, who neither are, nor ought to be the rulers of mankind, though it cannot perhaps be corrected, may very easily be prevented from disturbing the tranquillity of any body but themselves.

10   That it was the spirit of monopoly which originally both invented and propagated this doctrine, cannot be doubted; and they who first taught it were by no means such fools as they who believed it. In every country it always is and must be the interest of the great body of the people to buy whatever they want of those who sell it cheapest. The proposition is so very

---

[8] In LJ (A) vi.86 Smith attacked the view that an increase in the price of some liquors was likely to have the effect of reducing drunkenness:

> By raising their price they make them an object of their desire, and such as good fellowship requires them to press on their guests. We see accordingly that in Spain and France, where all liquors are very cheap, there is less drunkenness than in this country. We may also see that this is the case here. A gentleman drunk with ale is a sight never to be seen, whereas one drunk with wine is not so uncommon. One will never press his friend to drink a glass of ale, as he never imagines he will scruple him that. But good fellowship requires that he should press him to drink wine, which costs him all he can well afford.

A similar point is made in LJ (B) 231, ed. Cannan 179, and see below, V.ii.k.50.

manifest, that it seems ridiculous to take any pains to prove it; nor could it ever have been called in question, had not the interested sophistry of merchants and manufacturers confounded the common sense of mankind. Their interest is, in this respect, directly opposite to that of the great body of the people.[9] As it is the interest of the freemen [245] of a corporation to hinder the rest of the inhabitants from employing any workmen but themselves, so it is the interest of the merchants and manufacturers of every country to secure to themselves the monopoly of the home market. Hence in Great Britain, and in most other European countries, the extra-ordinary duties upon almost all goods imported by alien merchants.[10] Hence the high duties and prohibitions upon all those foreign manufactures which can come into competition with our own. Hence too the extraordinary restraints upon the importation of almost all sorts of goods from those countries with which the balance of trade is supposed to be disadvantageous; that is, from those against whom national animosity happens to be most violently inflamed.

11   The wealth of a neighbouring nation, however, though dangerous in war and politicks, is certainly advantageous in trade. In a state of hostility it may enable our enemies to maintain fleets and armies superior to our own; but in a state of peace and commerce it must likewise enable them to exchange with us to a greater value, and to afford a better market, either for the immediate produce of our own industry, or for whatever is purchased with that produce. As a rich man is likely to be a better customer to the industrious people in his neighbourhood, than a poor, so is likewise a rich nation. A rich man, indeed, who is himself a manufacturer, is a very dangerous neighbour to all those who deal in the same way. All the rest of the neigh-[246]bourhood, however, by far the greatest number, profit by the good market which his expence affords them. They even profit by his under-selling the poorer workmen who deal in the same way with him. The manufacturers of a rich nation, in the same manner, may no doubt be very dangerous rivals to those of their neighbours. This very competition, however, is advantageous to the great body of the people, who profit greatly besides by the good market which the great expence of such a nation affords them in every other way. Private people who want to make a fortune, never think of retiring to the remote and poor provinces of the country, but resort either to the capital or to some of the great commercial towns. They know, that, where little wealth circulates, there is little to be got, but that where a great deal is in motion, some share of it may fall to them. The same maxims which would in this manner direct the common sense of one, or ten, or twenty individuals, should regulate the judgment of one, or ten, or twenty millions, and should make a whole nation regard

[9] The same point is made at I.xi.p.10.
[10] The alien duties are frequently mentioned, e.g. at IV.ii.30, IV.iv.3, and V.ii.k.21.

the riches of its neighbours, as a probable cause and occasion for itself to acquire riches. A nation that would enrich itself by foreign trade is certainly most likely to do so when its neighbours are all rich, industrious, and commercial nations. A great nation surrounded on all sides by wandering savages and poor barbarians might, no doubt, acquire riches by the cultivation of its own lands, and by its own interior commerce, but not by foreign trade. It seems to have been [247] in this manner that the antient Egyptians and the modern Chinese acquired their great wealth. The antient Egyptians, it is said, neglected foreign commerce, and the modern Chinese, it is known, hold it in the utmost contempt, and scarce deign to afford it the decent protection of the laws. The modern maxims of foreign commerce, by aiming at the impoverishment of all our neighbours, so far as they are capable of producing their intended effect, tend to render that very commerce insignificant and contemptible.[11]

12   ʰIt is in consequence of these maxims that the commerce between France and England has in both countries been subjected to so many discouragements and restraints. If those two countries, however, were to consider their real interest, without either mercantile jealousy or national animosity, the commerce of France might be more advantageous to Great Britain than that of any other country, and for the same reason that of Great Britain to France. France is the nearest neighbour to Great Britain. In the trade between the southern coast of England and the northern and north-western coasts of France, the returns might be expected, in the same manner as in the inland trade, four, five, or six times in the year. The capital, therefore, employed in this trade, could in each of the two countries keep in motion four, five, or six times the quantity of industry, and afford employment and subsistence to four, five, or six times the number of people, which an equal capital could do in the [248] greater part of the other branches of foreign trade. Between the parts of France and Great Britain most remote from one another, the returns might be expected, at least, once in the year, and even this trade would so far be at least equally advantageous as the greater part of the other branches of our foreign European trade. It would be, at least, three times more advantageous, than the boasted trade with our North American colonies, in which the returns were seldom made in less than three years, frequently not in less than four or five years.[12] France, besides, is supposed to contain twenty-four millions of inhabitants.[13] Our North American colonies were never supposed to contain

ʰ⁻ʰ [to end of §13] *om.* 1–2 text 2A–6

[11] The attitude of the Chinese and ancient Egyptians to foreign trade is mentioned for example, at I.iii.7, I.ix.15, II.v.22, III.i.7, IV.ix.40 and 41.

[12] See below, IV.vii.c.35.

[13] See below, V.ii.k.78, where the population of France is stated to be 23 or 24 millions, and that of Britain, less than 8. Rickman estimated the population of England and Wales at less than 8 millions in the 1770s; Webster estimated the population of Scotland at 1¼

more than three millions:[14] And France is a much richer country than North America; though, on account of the more unequal distribution of riches, there is much more poverty and beggary in the one country, than in the other. France, therefore, could afford a market at least eight times more extensive, and, on account of the superior frequency of the returns, four and twenty times more advantageous, than that which our North American colonies ever afforded. The trade of Great Britain would be just as advantageous to France, and, in proportion to the wealth, population and proximity of the respective countries, would have the same superiority over that which France carries on with her own colonies.[15] Such is the very great difference between that trade which the wisdom of both nations has thought [249] proper to discourage, and that which it has favoured the most.

13   But the very same circumstances which would have rendered an open and free commerce between the two countries so advantageous to both, have occasioned the principal obstructions to that commerce. Being neighbours, they are necessarily enemies, and the wealth and power of each becomes, upon that account, more formidable to the other; and what would increase the advantage of national friendship, serves only to inflame the violence of national animosity. They are both rich and industrious nations; and the merchants and manufacturers of each, dread the competition of the skill and activity of those of the other. Mercantile jealousy is excited, and both inflames, and is itself inflamed, by the violence of national animosity: And the traders of both countries have announced, with all the passionate confidence of interested falsehood, the certain ruin of each, in consequence of that unfavourable balance of trade, which, they pretend, would be the infallible effect of an unrestrained commerce with the other.[h]

14   There is no commercial country in Europe of which the approaching ruin has not frequently been foretold by the pretended doctors of this system, from an unfavourable balance of trade.[16] After all the anxiety, however, which they have excited about this, after all the vain attempts of almost all trading nations to turn that balance in their own favour and against their neighbours, it does not appear that any one nation in Europe

million in 1755. For details see B. R. Mitchell, *Abstract of British Historical Statistics*. For various estimates of French population, including Expilly and Necker, see M. Marion, *Dictionnaire des institutions de la France aux XVII et XVIII siècles* (Paris, 1923), 445.

[14] The same figure is cited at V.iii.76. Smith comments on the rapid rate of growth of population in America at I.viii.23.

[15] Smith makes a rather similar point in LJ (B) 264–5, ed. Cannan 206, in discussing the limitations imposed on trade with France and Spain, pointing out the superior advantages of trade with a country of some 20 millions as compared to another society consisting of only 'two or three millions'. The argument also features in LJ (A) vi.166, where the population of France is stated to be about 20 millions and that of Portugal about 2 millions.

[16] Smith examines the doctrine of the balance of trade in LJ (A) vi.167–8, and LJ (B) 261–6, ed. Cannan 204–7. The 'pretended doctors' of the system whom he cites include Mun, Gee, Swift, Locke, and Mandeville.

[250] has been in any respect impoverished by this cause. Every town and country, on the contrary, in proportion as they have opened their ports to all nations; instead of being ruined by this free trade, as the principles of the commercial system would lead us to expect, have been enriched by it.[17] Though there are in Europe, indeed, a few towns which in some respects deserve the name of free ports, there is no country which does so. Holland, perhaps, approaches the nearest to this character of any, though still very remote from it; and Holland, it is acknowledged, not only derives its whole wealth, but a great part of its necessary subsistence, from foreign trade.

15   There is another balance, indeed, which has already been explained, very different from the balance of trade, and which, according as it happens to be either favourable or unfavourable, necessarily occasions the prosperity or decay of every nation. This is the balance of the annual produce and consumption. If the exchangeable value of the annual produce, it has already been observed, exceeds that of the annual consumption, the capital of the society must annually increase in proportion to this excess. The society in this case lives within its revenue, and what is annually saved out of its revenue, is naturally added to its capital, and employed so as to increase still further the annual produce.[18] If the exchangeable value of the annual produce, on the contrary, fall short of the annual consumption, the capital of the society must an-[251]nually decay in proportion to this deficiency. The expence of the society in this case exceeds its revenue, and necessarily encroaches upon its capital. Its capital, therefore, must necessarily decay, and, together with it, the exchangeable value of the annual produce of its industry.

16   This balance of produce and consumption is entirely different from, what is called, the balance of trade. It might take place in a nation which had no foreign trade, but which was entirely separated from all the world. It may take place in the whole globe of the earth, of which the wealth, population, and improvement may be either gradually increasing or gradually decaying.

17   The balance of produce and consumption may be constantly in favour of a nation, though what is called the balance of trade be generally against it. A nation may import to a greater value than it exports for half a century, perhaps, together; the gold and silver which comes into it during all this time may be all immediately sent out of it; its circulating coin may gradually decay, different sorts of paper money being substituted in its place,

[17] Cf. LJ (B) 269, ed. Cannan 209: 'From the above considerations it appears that Brittain should by all means be made a free port, that there should be no interruptions of any kind made to forreign trade, that if it were possible to defray the expences of government by any other method, all duties, customs, and excise should be abolished, and that free commerce and liberty of exchange should be allowed with all nations and for all things.'

[18] See above, II.iii.14–18.

and even the debts too which it contracts in the principal nations with whom it deals, may be gradually increasing; and yet its real wealth, the exchangeable value of the annual produce of its lands and labour, may, during the same period, have been increasing in a much greater proportion. The state of our North American colonies, and *of* the trade which they carried on with Great Britain, before [252] the commencement of the *present* disturbances*, may serve as a proof that this is by no means an impossible supposition.

*** This paragraph was written in the year 1775.*

$^{i-i}$ 2–6 $^{j-j}$ late *I* $^{k-k}$ 3–6

CHAPTER IV
Of Drawbacks

1 MERCHANTS and manufacturers are not contented with the monopoly of the home market, but desire likewise the most extensive foreign sale for their goods. Their country has no jurisdiction in foreign nations, and therefore can seldom procure them any monopoly there. They are generally obliged, therefore, to content themselves with petitioning for certain encouragements to exportation.

2 Of these encouragements what are called Drawbacks seem to be the most reasonable. To allow the merchant to draw back upon exportation, either the whole or a part of whatever excise or inland duty is imposed upon domestick industry, can never occasion the exportation of a greater quantity of goods than what would have been exported had no duty been imposed. Such encouragements do not tend to turn towards any particular employment a greater share of the capital of the country, than what would go to ^athat employment^a of its own accord, but only to hinder the duty from driving away any part of [253] that share to other employments. They tend not to overturn that balance which naturally establishes itself among all the various employments of the society; but to hinder it from being overturned by the duty. They tend not to destroy, but to preserve, what it is in most cases advantageous to preserve, the natural division and distribution of labour in the society.

3 The same thing may be said of the drawbacks upon the re-exportation of foreign goods imported; which in Great Britain generally amount to by much the largest part of the duty upon importation. ^bBy the second of the rules, annexed to the act of parliament,[1] which imposed, what is now called, the old subsidy, every merchant, whether English or alien, was allowed to draw back half that duty upon exportation; the English merchant, provided the exportation took place within twelve months; the alien, provided it took place within nine months. Wines, currants, and wrought silks were the only goods which did not fall within this rule, having other and more advantageous allowances. The duties imposed by this act of parliament were, at that time, the only duties upon the importation of foreign goods. The term within which this, and all other drawbacks, could be claimed,

---

^{a–a} it *1–2*
^{b–b} [to end of § 11] Half the duties imposed by what is called the old subsidy, are drawn back universally, except upon goods exported to the British plantations; and frequently the whole, almost always a part of those imposed by later subisidies and imposts. *1–2* text *2A–6*

---

[1] 12 Charles II, c. 4 (1660). See below, IV.v.b.37, IV.viii.41, V.ii.k.23–24.

was afterwards (by 7 Geo. I. chap. 21. sect. 10.) extended to three years.[2]

4 The duties which have been imposed since the old subsidy, are, the greater part of them, wholly drawn back upon exportation. This general rule, however, is liable to a great number [254] of exceptions, and the doctrine of drawbacks has become a much less simple matter, than it was at their first institution.

5 Upon the exportation of some foreign goods, of which it was expected that the importation would greatly exceed what was necessary for the home consumption, the whole duties are drawn back, without retaining even half the old subsidy. Before the revolt of our North American colonies, we had the monopoly of the tobacco of Maryland and Virginia. We imported about ninety-six thousand hogsheads, and the home consumption was not supposed to exceed fourteen thousand.[3] To facilitate the great exportation which was necessary, in order to rid us of the rest, the whole duties were drawn back, provided the exportation took place within three years.

6 We still have, though not altogether, yet very nearly, the monopoly of the sugars of our West Indian Islands. If sugars are exported within a year, therefore, all the duties upon importation are drawn back, and if exported within three years, all the duties, except half the old subsidy, which still continues to be retained upon the exportation of the greater part of goods. Though the importation of sugar exceeds, a good deal, what is necessary for the home consumption, the excess is inconsiderable, in comparison of what it used to be in tobacco.

7 Some goods, the particular objects of the jealousy of our own manufacturers, are prohibited to be imported for home consumption. They [255] may, however, upon paying certain duties, be imported and warehoused for exportation. But upon such exportation, no part of these duties ᶜareᶜ drawn back. Our manufacturers are unwilling, it seems, that even this restricted importation should be encouraged, and are afraid lest some part of these goods should be stolen out of the warehouse, and thus come into competition with their own. It is under these regulations only that we can import wrought silks,[4] French cambricks and lawns,[5] callicoes painted, printed, stained, or dyed, &c.

8 We are unwilling even to be the carriers of French goods, and choose rather to forego a profit to ourselves, than to suffer those, whom we consider as our enemies, to make any profit by our means. Not only half the old

---

ᶜ⁻ᶜ is 6

[2] 4 William and Mary, c. 5 (1692) allowed drawbacks on certain goods if re-exported in three years. Other statutes set different periods. By 7 George I, st. 1, c. 21 (1720) the term was made three years for all. See below, V.ii.k.24.
[3] The same figures are used above, II v.34 and below, IV.vii.c.40.
[4] and [5] Footnotes on next page.

subsidy, but the second twenty-five per cent., is retained upon the exportation of all French goods.⁶

9   By the fourth of the rules annexed to the old subsidy,⁷ the drawback allowed upon the exportation of all wines amounted to a great deal more than half the duties which were, at that time, paid upon their importation; and it seems, at that time, to have been the object of the legislature to give somewhat more than ordinary encouragement to the carrying trade in wine. Several of the other duties too, which were imposed, either at the same time, or subsequent to the old subsidy; what is called the additional duty, the new subsidy,⁸ the one-third⁹ and two-thirds subsidies,¹⁰ the impost 1692,¹¹ the coinage on wine,¹² were allowed to be wholly drawn back [256] upon exportation.¹³ All those duties, however, except the additional duty and impost 1692, being paid down in ready money, upon importation, the interest of so large a sum occasioned an expence, which made it unreasonable to expect any profitable carrying trade in this article. Only a part, therefore, of the duty called the impost on wine,¹⁴ and no part of the twenty-five pounds the ton upon French wines,¹⁵ or of the duties imposed

⁴ 26 George II, c. 21 (1753) (An Act for encouraging the Silk Manufactures of this Kingdom) made provision for the release of imported velvets, silks, and silks mixed with other materials and for the payment of the drawback on proper notice being given. H. Saxby, *The British Customs* (1757), 596, notes the drawback given under that Act. As Smith recognizes above, IV.ii.1, the regulations became even more stringent. 6 George III, c. 28 (1766) prohibited the importation of foreign silks and made provision for the seizure and subsequent sale of any commodities so imported. 11 George III, c. 49 (1771) continued the prohibition.

⁵ 18 George II, c. 36 (1744); 21 George II, c. 26 (1747); 32 George II, c. 32 (1758); 7 George III, c. 43 (1766). See above, IV.iii.a.1, and below, IV.viii.4.

⁶ 7 and 8 William III, c. 20 (1695) and 1 George I, st. 2, c. 12 (1714). See above, IV.iii.a.1, and below, IV.viii.43.

⁷ The fourth rule stated that: 'Every Merchant as well English as Stranger that shall ship and export any kind of Wines which formerlie have paid all the dutyes of the Tonnage inwarde shall have repaid . . . to them all the dutyes of Tonnage paid inwards except to the Englishman twenty shillinge the Tonne, and except to the stranger five and twenty shillinge the Tonne . . .' (12 Charles II, c. 4 (1660)).

⁸ 9 William III, c. 23 (1697) in *Statutes of the Realm*, vii.382–5; 9 and 10 William III, c. 23 in Ruffhead's edition. See also below, V.ii.k.23.

⁹ 2 and 3 Anne, c. 18 (1703) in *Statutes of the Realm*, viii.295–300; 2 and 3 Anne, c. 9 in Ruffhead's edition. See below, V.ii.k.23.

¹⁰ 3 and 4 Anne, c. 3 (1704) in *Statutes of the Realm*, viii.332–6; 3 and 4 Anne, c. 5 in Ruffhead's edition. See below, V.ii.k.23.

¹¹ 4 William and Mary, c. 5 (1692). See above, IV.iii.a.1.

¹² The coinage on wine was a duty of 10s. a tun on imported wine, vinegar, cider, and beer, and 20s. a tun on brandy and strong wines to enable the cost of coinage at the mint to take place duty free. For details of the coinage see below, IV.vi.22.

¹³ For details of the various duties see H. Saxby, *The British Customs*, 13–16—additional duty; 18–21—new subsidy; 21–2—one-third duty; 22—two-thirds duty; 35–9—impost of 1692; 46—coinage on wine.

¹⁴ Of 1 James II, c. 3 (1685) and subsequent acts. £8 a tun on French wine and £12 a tun on Spanish and other wine.

¹⁵ 7 and 8 William III, c. 20 (1695) and 1 George I, c. 12 (1714).

in 1745,[16] in 1763,[17] and in 1778,[18] were allowed to be drawn back upon exportation. The two imposts of five per cent., imposed in 1779[19] and 1781,[20] upon all the former duties of customs, being allowed to be wholly drawn back upon the exportation of all other goods, were likewise allowed to be drawn back upon that of wine. The last duty that has been particularly imposed upon wine, that of 1780,[21] is allowed to be wholly drawn back, an indulgence, which, when so many heavy duties are retained, most probably could never occasion the exportation of a single ton of wine. These rules take place with regard to all places of lawful exportation, except the British colonies in America.

10   The 15th Charles II. chap. 7.[22] called an act for the encouragement of trade, had given Great Britain the monopoly of supplying the colonies with all the commodities of the growth or manufacture of Europe; and consequently with wines. In a country of so extensive a coast as our North American and West Indian colonies, where our authority was always so very [257] slender, and where the inhabitants were allowed to carry out, in their own ships, their non-enumerated commodities, at first, to all parts of Europe, and afterwards, to all parts of Europe South of Cape Finisterre,[23] it is not very probable that this monopoly could ever be much respected; and they probably, at all times, found means of bringing back some cargo from the countries to which they were allowed to carry out one. They seem, however, to have found some difficulty in importing European wines from the places of their growth, and they could not well import them from Great Britain, where they were loaded with many heavy duties, of which a considerable part was not drawn back upon exportation. Madeira wine, not being a European commodity,[24] could be imported directly into America and the West Indies, countries which, in all their non-enumerated commodities, enjoyed a free trade to the island of Madeira. These circumstances had probably introduced that general taste for Madeira wine, which our officers found established in all our colonies at the commencement of the war, which began in 1755, and which they brought

---

[16] 18 Geoerge II, c. 9 (1744): £8 a tun on French wine and vinegar, £4 a tun on other wine.

[17] 3 George III, c. 12 (1762): additional duty from 31 March 1763 of £8 a tun on French wine and vinegar and £4 a tun on other wine.

[18] 18 George III, c. 27 (1778): additional duties of £8. 8s. a tun on French wine and vinegar and £4. 4s. a tun on other wine.

[19] 19 George III, c. 25 (1779).

[20] 22 George III, c. 66 (1782), imposed from 25 July 1782.

[21] 20 George III, c. 30 (1780): £8 a tun on French wine and vinegar and £4 a tun on others.

[22] 15 Charles II, c. 7 (1663).

[23] See below, IV.vii.b.25–35 and IV.vii.c.15.

[24] Imports of Madeira wine were permitted because its European status was uncertain. Scottish servants and horses could also be imported by the same section of 15 Charles II, c. 7 (1663).

back with them to the mother country, where that wine had not been much in fashion before. Upon the conclusion of that war, in 1763 (by the 4th Geo. III. Chap. 15. Sect. 12.),[25] all the duties, except 3*l.* 10*s.* were allowed to be drawn back, upon the exportation to the colonies of all wines, except French wines, to the commerce and consumption of which, na-[258]tional prejudice would allow no sort of encouragement. The period between the granting of this indulgence and the revolt of our North American colonies was probably too short to admit of any considerable change in the customs of those countries.

11   The same act, which, in the drawback upon all wines, except French wines, thus favoured the colonies so much more than other countries; in those, upon the greater part of other commodities, favoured them much less. Upon the exportation of the greater part of commodities to other countries, half the old subsidy was drawn back. But this law enacted, that no part of that duty should be drawn back upon the exportation to the colonies of any commodities, of the growth or manufacture either of Europe or the East Indies, except wines, white callicoes and muslins.[b]

12   Drawbacks were, perhaps, originally granted for the encouragement of the carrying trade, which, as the freight of the ships is frequently paid by foreigners in money, was supposed to be peculiarly fitted for bringing gold and silver into the country. But though the carrying trade certainly deserves no peculiar encouragement, though the motive of the institution was, perhaps abundantly foolish, the institution itself seems reasonable enough. Such drawbacks cannot force into this trade a greater share of the capital of the country than what would have gone to it of its own accord, had there been no duties upon importation. They only prevent [259] its being excluded altogether by those duties. The carrying trade, though it deserves no preference, ought not to be precluded, but to be left free like all other trades. It is a necessary resource [d]for[d] those capitals which cannot find employment either in the agriculture or in the manufactures of the country, either in its home trade or in its foreign trade of consumption.[26]

13   The revenue of the customs, instead of suffering, profits from such drawbacks, by that part of the duty which is retained. If the whole duties had been retained, the foreign goods upon which they are paid, could seldom have been exported, nor consequently imported, for want of a market. The duties, therefore, of which a part is retained, would never have been paid.

14   These reasons seem sufficiently to justify drawbacks, and would justify them, though the whole duties, whether upon the produce of domestick

[d-d] to 6

---

[25] 4 George III, c. 15 (1764). See below, IV.vii.b.48.
[26] See above, II.v.35, and below, IV.vii.c.96, where Smith discusses the case of Holland.

industry, or upon foreign goods, were always drawn back upon exportation. The revenue of excise would in this case, indeed, suffer a little, and that of the customs a good deal more; but the natural balance of industry,[27] the natural division and distribution of labour, which is always more or less disturbed by such duties, would be more nearly re-established by such a regulation.

15   These reasons, however, will justify drawbacks only upon exporting goods to those countries which are altogether foreign and independent, not to those in which our merchants [260] and manufacturers enjoy a monopoly. A drawback, for example, upon the exportation of European goods to our American colonies, will not always occasion a greater exportation than what would have taken place without it. By means of the monopoly which our merchants and manufacturers enjoy there, the same quantity might frequently, perhaps, be sent thither, though the whole duties were retained. The drawback, therefore, may frequently be pure loss to the revenue of excise and customs, without altering the state of the trade, or rendering it in any respect more extensive. How far such drawbacks can be justified, as a proper encouragement to the industry of our colonies, or how far it is advantageous to the mother country, that they should be exempted from taxes which are paid by all the rest of their fellow-subjects, will appear hereafter when I come to treat of colonies.[28]

16   Drawbacks, however, it must always be understood, are useful only in those cases in which the goods for the exportation of which they are given, are really exported to some foreign country; and not clandestinely re-imported into our own. That some drawbacks, particularly those upon tobacco, have frequently been abused in this manner, and have given occasion to many frauds equally hurtful both to the revenue and to the fair trader, is well known.

[27] A similar expression is used at IV.v.a.39 and IV.vii.c.43. See above, IV.ii.3 and note, and cf. LJ (A) vi. 92, LJ (B) 233–4, ed. Cannan 181.
[28] The nature of the colonial relationship is described below, chiefly in IV.vii.b.24–50.

CHAPTER V

Of Bounties

1 BOUNTIES upon exportation are, in Great Britain, frequently petitioned for, and sometimes granted to the produce of particular branches of domestick industry.[1] By means of them our merchants and manufacturers, it is pretended, will be enabled to sell their goods as cheap, or cheaper than their rivals in the foreign market. A greater quantity, it is said, will thus be exported, and the balance of trade consequently turned more in favour of our own country. We cannot give our workmen a monopoly in the foreign, as we have done in the home market. We cannot force foreigners to buy their goods, as we have done our own countrymen. The next best expedient, it has been thought, therefore, is to pay them for buying. It is in this manner that the mercantile system proposes to enrich the whole country, and to put money into all our pockets by means of the balance of trade.[2]

2 Bounties, it is allowed, ought to be given to those branches of trade only which cannot be carried on without them. But every branch of trade in which the merchant can sell his goods for a price which replaces to him, with the ordinary profits of stock, the whole capital employed in preparing and sending them to market, can be [262] carried on without a bounty. Every such branch is evidently upon a level with all the other branches of trade which are carried on without bounties, and cannot therefore require one more than they. Those trades only require bounties in which the merchant is obliged to sell his goods for a price which does not replace to him his capital, together with the ordinary profit; or in which he is obliged to sell them for less than it really costs him to send them to market. The bounty is given in order to make up this loss, and to encourage him to continue, or perhaps to begin, a trade of which the expence is supposed to be greater than the returns, of which every operation eats up a part of the capital employed in it, and which is of such a nature, that, if all other trades resembled it, there would soon be no capital left in the country.

3 The trades, it is to be observed, which are carried on by means of boun-ties, are the only ones which can be carried on between two nations for any considerable time together, in such a manner as that one of them shall always and regularly lose, or sell its goods for less than it really costs to send them to market.[3] But if the bounty did not repay to the merchant what

---

[1] Bounties on *importation* are discussed in IV.viii.

[2] Cantillon argued: 'It will always be found by examining particular cases that the exportation of all Manufactured articles is advantageous to the State, because in this case the Foreigner always pays and supports Workmen useful to the State.' (*Essai*, 308, ed. Higgs 233.)

[3] See below, § 24, IV.iii.c.2, and IV.viii.51.

he would otherwise lose upon the price of his goods, his own interest would soon oblige him to employ his stock in another way, or to find out a trade in which the price of the goods would replace to him, with the ordinary profit, the capital employed in sending them to market. The effect of bounties, like that of all the other ex-[263]pedients of the mercantile system, can only be to force the trade of a country into a channel much less advantageous than that in which it would naturally run of its own accord.[4]

4   The ingenious and well-informed author of the tracts upon the corn trade has shown very clearly,[5] that since the bounty upon the exportation of corn was first established,[6] the price of the corn exported, valued moderately enough, has exceeded that of the corn imported, valued very high, by a much greater sum than the amount of the whole bounties which have been paid during that period. This, he imagines, upon the true principles of the mercantile system, is a clear proof that this forced corn trade is beneficial to the nation; the value of the exportation exceeding that of the importation by a much greater sum than the whole extraordinary expence which the publick has been at in order to get it exported. He does not consider that this extraordinary expence, or the bounty, is the smallest part of the expence which the exportation of corn really costs the society. The capital which the farmer employed in raising it must likewise be taken into the account. Unless the price of the corn when sold in the foreign markets replaces, not only the bounty, but this capital, together with the ordinary profits of stock, the society is a loser by the difference, or the national stock is so much diminished. But the very reason for which it has been thought necessary to grant a bounty, is the supposed insufficiency of the price to do this.

5   [264] The average price of corn, it has been said, has fallen considerably since the establishment of the bounty.[7] That the average price of corn began to fall somewhat towards the end of the last century, and has continued to do so during the course of the sixty-four first years of the present, I have

---

[4] Smith examines the bounties on corn and coarse linen in LJ (A) vi.91–7, and LJ (B) 232–5, ed. Cannan 180–2, arguing that they must break the natural balance of industry and thus diminish opulence. Smith thus concluded, in LJ (A) vi.97, that 'the best police would be to leave everything to its naturall course, without bounty or any discouragement'. See above, IV.ii.3.

[5] Charles Smith, *Three Tracts on the Corn Trade and Corn Laws* (1766), 133–7. Charles Smith is described as 'very well informed' at IV.ii.20 and below, § 8.

[6] 1 William and Mary, c. 12 (1688). See above, I.xi.g.4, III.iv.20, and below, IV.v.b.37, V.ii.k.13.

[7] In this chapter Smith argues against the view which had been stated in the lectures, to the effect that the bounty had reduced the price of corn. See for example, LJ (A) vi.95–6, LJ (B) 234, ed. Cannan 181–2, and ED 3.5. Cf. LJ (B) 298, ed. Cannan 230: 'It is easy to shew that the free export and import of corn is favourable to agriculture. In England the country has been better stored with corn, and the price of it has gradualy sunk, since the exportation of it was permitted. The bounty on exportation does harm in other respects, but it increases the quantity of corn.'

already endeavoured to show. But this event, supposing it to be as real as I believe it to be, must have happened in spite of the bounty, and cannot possibly have happened in consequence of it. ᵃIt has happened in France, as well as in England, though in France there was, not only no bounty, but, till 1764, the exportation of corn was subjected to a general prohibition.⁸ This gradual fall in the average price of grain, it is probable, therefore, is ultimately owing neither to the one regulation nor to the other, but to that gradual and insensible rise in the real value of silver, which, in the first book of this discourse, I have endeavoured to show has taken place in the general market of Europe, during the course of the present century.⁹ It seems to be altogether impossible that the bounty could ever contribute to lower the price of grain.ᵃ

6   In years of plenty, it has already been observed,¹⁰ the bounty, by occasioning an extraordinary exportation, necessarily keeps up the price of corn in the home market above what it would naturally fall to. To do so was the avowed purpose of the institution. In years of scarcity, though the bounty is frequently suspended, yet the great exportation which it occasions in years [265] of plenty, must frequently hinder more or less the plenty of one year from relieving the scarcity of another. Both in years of plenty, and in years of scarcity, therefore, the bounty necessarily tends to raise the money price of corn somewhat higher than it otherwise would be in the home market.

7   That, in the actual state of tillage, the bounty must necessarily have this tendency, will not, I apprehend, be disputed by any reasonable person. But it has been thought by many people that ᵇit tends to encourage tillage¹¹, and that in two different ways; first, by opening a more extensive foreign market to the corn of the farmer, it tends, they imagine, to increase the demand for, and consequently the production of that commodity; and secondly, by securing to himᵇ a better price than he could otherwise expect in the actual state of tillage, it ᶜtends, they suppose, to encourage tillage. This double encouragement must, they imagine, in a long period of years,

---

ᵃ⁻ᵃ 2A–6   ᵇ⁻ᵇ by securing to the farmer *1–2*
ᶜ⁻ᶜ to encourage tillage; and that the consequent increase of corn may, in a long period of years, lower its price *1–2*

---

⁸ See above, I.xi.g.15, and cf. IV.ix.38, where the existing degree of liberty in the corn trade of France is ascribed to physiocratic influence. In commenting on Smith's critique of the bounty, Pownall remarked (*Letter*, 31–7) on the similarity between Smith and Necker, and suggested that Smith had copied the latter's 'decisive proof' that the bounty on corn had not lowered prices. Necker's proof was that a general fall in the price of corn had taken place in France despite a prohibition on its export. Smith quotes Necker's *Sur la legislation et le commerce des grains* (1775), below, V.ii.k.78.

⁹ See above, I.xi.f, and cf. IV.i.14, where Smith refers to the more common view that the value of the precious metals had been falling in the present and preceding centuries owing to importation from the Spanish West Indies.

¹⁰ See above, I.xi.g.12, and cf. V.ii.k.13.

¹¹ See above, I.xi.g.4, 15.

occasion such an increase in the production of corn, as may lower its price in the home market, much^c more than the bounty can raise it, in the actual state which tillage may, at the end of that period, happen to be in.

8   ^dI answer, that whatever extension of the foreign market can be occasioned by the bounty, must, in every particular year, be altogether at the expence of the home market; as every bushel of corn which is exported by means of the bounty, and which would not have been exported without the bounty, would have remained in the [266] home market to increase the consumption, and to lower the price of that commodity. The corn bounty, it is to be observed, as well as every other bounty upon exportation, imposes two different taxes upon the people; first, the tax which they are obliged to contribute, in order to pay the bounty; and secondly, the tax which arises from the advanced price of the commodity in the home-market, and which, as the whole body of the people are purchasers of corn, must, in this particular commodity, be paid by the whole body of the people. In this particular commodity, therefore, this second tax, is by much the heaviest of the two. Let us suppose that, taking one year with another, the bounty of five shillings upon the exportation of the quarter of wheat, raises the price of that commodity in the home-market, only sixpence the bushel, or four shillings the quarter, higher than it ^eotherways^e would have been in the actual state of the crop. Even upon this very moderate supposition, the great body of the people, over and above contributing the tax which pays the bounty of five shillings upon every quarter of wheat exported, must pay another of four shillings upon every quarter which they themselves consume. But, according to the very well informed author of the tracts upon the corn-trade,[12] the average proportion of the corn exported to that consumed at home, is not more than that of one to thirty-one.[13] For every five shillings, therefore, which they contribute to the payment of the first tax, they must contribute six [267] pounds four shillings to the payment of the second. So very heavy a tax upon the first necessary of life, must either reduce the subsistence[14] of the labouring poor, or it must occasion some augmentation in their pecuniary wages, proportionable to that in the pecuniary price of their subsistence. So far as it operates in the one way, it must reduce the ability of the labouring poor to educate and bring up their children, and must, so far, tend to restrain the population of the country. So far as it operates in the other, it must reduce the ability of the employers of the poor, to employ so great a number as they otherwise might do, and must, so far, tend to restrain the industry of the country. The

---

^d-d [to end of § 9] 2A–6   ^e-e otherwise 2A

[12] Charles Smith, *Three Tracts on the Corn Trade and Corn Laws,* 144. Charles Smith is similarly described at IV.ii.20.

[13] The same figures are cited at IV.v.b.29.

[14] See below, V.ii.k.3f where Smith discusses taxes on necessaries.

extraordinary exportation of corn, therefore, occasioned by the bounty, not only, in every particular year, diminishes the home, just as much as it extends the foreign market and consumption, but, by restraining the population and industry of the country, its final tendency is to stunt and restrain the gradual extension of the home-market; and thereby, in the long run, rather to diminish, than to augment, the whole market and consumption of corn.

9   This enhancement of the money price of corn, however, it has been thought, by rendering that commodity more profitable to the farmer, must necessarily encourage its production.*d*

10   I answer, that this might be the case if the effect of the bounty was to raise the real price of corn, or to enable the farmer, with an equal quantity of it, to maintain a greater number [268] of labourers in the same manner, whether liberal, moderate, or scanty, that other labourers are commonly maintained in his neighbourhood. But neither the bounty, it is evident, nor any other human institution, can have any such effect. It is not the real, but the nominal price of corn*f*, which can in any considerable degree be*f* affected by the bounty.[15] *g*And though the tax which that institution imposes upon the whole body of the people, may be very burdensome to those who pay it, it is of very little advantage to those who receive it.*g*

11   The real effect of the bounty is not so much to raise the real value of corn, as to degrade the real value of silver; or to make an equal quantity of it exchange for a smaller quantity, not only of corn, but of all other *h*home-made*h* commodities: for the money price of corn regulates that of all other *i*home-made*i* commodities.

12   It regulates the money price of labour, which must always be such as to enable the labourer to purchase a quantity of corn sufficient to maintain him and his family either in the liberal, moderate, or scanty manner in which the advancing, stationary or declining circumstances of the society oblige his employers to maintain him.[16]

13   It regulates the money price of all the other parts of the rude produce of land, which, in every period of improvement, must bear a certain proportion to that of corn, though this proportion is different in different periods. It regulates, for example, the money price of grass [269] and hay, of butcher's meat, of horses, and the maintenance of horses, of land carriage consequently, or of the greater part of the inland commerce of the country.[17]

---

f-f only, which can be at all *1-2*   *g-g* 2A–6   *h-h* 3–6   *i-i* 3–6

[15] See below, § 23. The distinction between real and nominal price is discussed in I.v
[16] See above, I.viii.52.
[17] Cf. LJ (B) 234, ed. Cannan 181–2: 'tho the effects of the bounty encourageing agriculture brought down the price of corn, yet it raised the grass-farms, for the more corn the less grass. The price of grass being raised, butchers meat, in consequence of its dependance upon it, must be raised also. So that if the price of corn is diminished, the price of other commodities is necessarily raised.' A similar point is made in LJ (A) vi.96.

14 By regulating the money price of all the other parts of the rude produce of land, it regulates that of the materials of ʲalmostʲ all manufactures. By regulating the money price of labour, it regulates that of manufacturing art and industry. And by regulating both, it regulates that of the compleat manufacture. The money price of labour, and of every thing that is the produce either of land or labour, must necessarily either rise or fall in proportion to the money price of corn.

15 Though in consequence of the bounty, therefore, the farmer should be enabled to sell his corn for four shillings the bushel instead of three and sixpence, and to pay his landlord a money rent proportionable to this rise in the money price of his produce; yet if, in consequence of this rise in the price of corn, four shillings will purchase no more ᵏhome-madeᵏ goods of any other kind than three and sixpence would have done before, neither the circumstances of the farmer, nor those of the landlord, will be ˡmuchˡ mended by this change. The farmer will not be able to cultivate ᵐmuchᵐ better: the landlord will not be able to live ⁿmuchⁿ better. ᵒIn the purchase of foreign commodities this enhancement in the price of corn may give them some little advantage. In that of home-made commodities it can give them none at all. And almost the whole expence of [270] the farmer, and the far greater part, ᵖeven ofᵖ that of the landlord, is in home-made commodities.ᵒ

16 That degradation in the value of silver which is the effect of the fertility of the mines, and which operates equally, or very near equally, through the greater part of the commercial world, is a matter of very little consequence to any particular country. The consequent rise of all money prices, though it does not make those who receive them really richer, does not make them really poorer. A service of plate becomes really cheaper, and every thing else remains precisely of the same real value as before.

17 But that degradation in the value of silver which, being the effect either of the peculiar situation, or of the political institutions of a particular country, takes place only in that country, is a matter of very great consequence, which, far from tending to make any body really richer, tends to make every body really poorer. The rise in the money price of all commodities, which is in this case peculiar to that country, tends to discourage more or less every sort of industry which is carried on within it, and to enable foreign nations, by furnishing almost all sorts of goods for a smaller quantity of silver than its own workmen can afford to do, to undersell them, not only in the foreign, but even in the home market.

18 It is the peculiar situation of Spain and Portugal as proprietors of the mines, to be the distributors of gold and silver to all the other countries of Europe. Those metals ought na-[271]turally, therefore, to be somewhat cheaper in Spain and Portugal than in any other part of Europe. The

ʲ⁻ʲ 3–6   ᵏ⁻ᵏ 3–6   ˡ⁻ˡ in the smallest degree 1–2   ᵐ⁻ᵐ 3–6   ⁿ⁻ⁿ 3–6
ᵒ⁻ᵒ 2A–6   ᵖ⁻ᵖ of even 2A

difference, however, should be no more than the amount of the freight and insurance; and, on account of the great value and small bulk of those metals, their freight is no great matter, and their insurance is the same as that of any other goods of equal value. Spain and Portugal, therefore, could suffer very little from their peculiar situation, if they did not aggravate its disadvantages by their political institutions.

19   Spain by taxing, and Portugal by prohibiting the exportation of gold and silver, load that exportation with the expence of smuggling, and raise the value of those metals in other countries so much more above what it is in their own, by the whole amount of this expence.[18] When you dam up a stream of water, as soon as the dam is full, as much water must run over the dam-head as if there was no dam at all.[19] The prohibition of exportation cannot detain a greater quantity of gold and silver in Spain and Portugal than what they can afford to employ, than what the annual produce of their land and labour will allow them to employ, in coin, plate, gilding, and other ornaments of gold and silver.[20] When they have got this quantity the dam

[18] G. T. F. Raynal, *Histoire philosophique* iii.267–8, trans. Justamond, ii.352–3:

[Spain] prohibited, upon pain of capital punishment, the exportation of gold and silver; as if the Spaniards were not obliged to pay for what they wanted to buy . . . The prohibition of exporting gold and silver was to so little purpose, that though a prodigious quantity came over every year from America, there was very little seen in the kingdom . . . Spain has only agreed of late years, that the foreign trade should have all the profit of the goods it should send to America, only paying three *per cent*. The money was to be transmitted by bankers, settled for that purpose in the principal cities of Europe . . . Every private man is now at liberty to draw his money from Spain, upon paying the accustomed duties, which, in the year 1768, were advanced from three to four *per cent*. If they were more moderate, government would derive greater advantages from them. There are certain times, when the Spanish smugglers can bring the piastres on board the ships, for a price· below the stated value; and it may easily be imagined those opportunities are eagerly seized.

Cf. G. de Uztariz, *The Theory and Practice of Commerce*, trans. by John Kippax (London, 1751), ii.70: 'Spain . . . which for some years has had, and still continues the like rigorous prohibition, and for a long time has had great and vigilant princes and zealous ministers, that have done their utmost to have them punctually observed, but without success.'

[19] Hume uses this analogy in his essay 'Of the Balance of Trade', *Essays Moral, Political, and Literary*, ed. Green and Grose, i.333. The analogy of the stream is used at II.ii.76, and cf. IV.vii.c.43.

[20] See above, IV.i.5, 12, 13, where Smith mentions the ease with which the precious metals can be transported and the futility of Spanish and Portuguese policy with regard to their export; It is also stated at IV.v.b.45 that the system of government in the two countries would ensure their poverty irrespective of policy with regard to gold. See also IV.vii.c.53 and I.xi.n.1, where the paragraph concludes with the remark that 'though the feudal system has been abolished in Spain and Portugal, it has not been succeeded by a much better.' LJ (A) vi.151 reads: 'Portugall has little or nothing else to give in exchange for our corn and other goods but money. If therefore the exportation of it be prohibited by high penalties, the Portugese merchant who byes any commodities must pay not only the naturall price and what is requisite for the expense of transportation, but must also give a price on account of the risque the English merchant runns in getting it out of the country.' Cf. LJ (A) vi.156.

The case of Spain, where the problems of prohibiting the export of coin are explained

is full, and the whole stream which flows in afterwards must run over. The annual exportation of gold and silver from Spain and Portugal accordingly is, by all accounts, notwithstanding these restraints, very near equal to [272] the whole annual importation. As the water, however, must always be deeper behind the dam-head than before it, so the quantity of gold and silver which these restraints detain in Spain and Portugal must, in proportion to the annual produce of their land and labour, be greater ᑫthanᑫ what is to be found in other countries. The higher and stronger the dam-head, the greater must be the difference in the depth of water behind and before it. The higher the tax, the higher the penalties with which the prohibition is guarded, the more vigilant and severe the police which looks after the execution of the law, the greater must be the difference in the proportion of gold and silver to the annual produce of the land and labour of Spain and Portugal, and to that of other countries. It is said accordingly to be very considerable, and that you frequently find there a profusion of plate in houses, where there is nothing else which would, in other countries, be thought suitable or correspondent to this sort of magnificence. The cheapness of gold and silver, or what is the same thing, the dearness of all commodities, which is the necessary effect of this redundancy of the precious metals, discourages both the agriculture and manufactures of Spain and Portugal, and enables foreign nations to supply them with many sorts of rude, and with almost all sorts of manufactured produce, for a smaller quantity of gold and silver than what they themselves can either raise or make them for at home.[21] The tax and prohibition operate in two different

---

ᑫ⁻ᑫ that *1*

in terms of the analogy of the water level and the dam-head, is cited in LJ (A) vi.153 and LJ (B) 258–9, ed. Cannan 202. Harris makes a similar point, *Essay*, i.90, with regard to Spain and Portugal. However, it is pointed out at i.99 that money could be effectively hoarded provided that steps were taken to keep the excess quantity out of circulation. Cantillon also makes a similar point, *Essai*, 220–1, ed. Higgs 167. See generally, II.vi.

Mandeville (*Fable of the Bees*, pt. i.215, ed. Kaye, i.196–7) also remarked on the adverse effects which had followed from Spain's acquisition of gold-producing colonies: from '*too much Money*, the making of Colonies and other Mismanagements, of which it was the occasion, *Spain* is from a fruitful and well-peopled Country, with all its mighty Titles and Possessions, made a barren and empty Thoroughfare, thro' which Gold and Silver pass from *America* to the rest of the World; and the Nation, from a rich, acute, diligent and laborious, become a slow, idle, proud and beggarly People; so much for *Spain*. The next Country where Money may be called the Product is *Portugal*, and the Figure which that Kingdom with all its Gold makes in *Europe*, I think is not much to be envied.'

[21] LJ (A) vi.157–8 comments: 'Nothing was ever seen in any country which came from Spain but what was the naturall produce of the country . . . They have wool without which no broad cloth can be made in Europe, and yet no one ever saw Spanish broad cloth in the market; nor is any other thing else to be met with. The only things to be met with of Spanish growth are their fruits and their wines, which are allmost the only naturall productions of that fine country. The only other production we meet with is Spanish steel, which is of a peculiarily excellent quality, but the quantity of it is but very inconsiderable.' See also LJ (B) 259–60, ed. Cannan 203, and below, IV.viii.24. The Spanish attitude to

ways. They [273] not only lower very much the value of the precious metals in Spain and Portugal, but by detaining there a certain quantity of those metals which would otherwise flow over other countries, they keep up their value in those other countries somewhat above what it otherwise would be, and thereby give those countries a double advantage in their commerce with Spain and Portugal. Open the flood-gates, and there will presently be less water above, and more below, the dam-head, and it will soon come to a level in both places. Remove the tax and the prohibition, and as the quantity of gold and silver will diminish considerably in Spain and Portugal, so it will increase somewhat in other countries, and the value of those metals, their proportion to the annual produce of land and labour, will soon come to a level, or very near to a level, in all. The loss which Spain and Portugal could sustain by this exportation of their gold and silver would be altogether nominal and imaginary. The nominal value of their goods, and of the annual produce of their land and labour, would fall, and would be expressed or represented by a smaller quantity of silver than before: but their real value would be the same as before, and would be sufficient to maintain, command, and employ, the same quantity of labour. As the nominal value of their goods would fall, the real value of what remained of their gold and silver would rise, and a smaller quantity of those metals would answer all the same purposes of commerce and circulation which had employed a [274] greater quantity before. The gold and silver which would go abroad would not go abroad for nothing, but would bring back an equal value of goods of some kind or another.[22] Those goods too would not be all matters of mere luxury and expence, to be consumed by idle people who produce nothing in return for their consumption. As the real wealth and revenue of idle people would not be augmented by this extraordinary exportation of gold and silver, so neither would their consumption be much augmented by it. Those goods would, probably, the greater part of them, and certainly some part of them, consist in materials, tools, and provisions, for the employment and maintenance of industrious people, who would reproduce, with a profit, the full value of their consumption. A part of the dead stock of the society would thus be turned into active stock, and would put into motion a greater quantity of industry than had been employed before. The annual produce of their land and labour would immediately be augmented a little, and in a few years would, probably, be augmented a great deal; their industry being thus relieved from one of the most oppressive burdens which it at present labours under.

20   The bounty upon the exportation of corn necessarily operates exactly in

colonization and the consequences which followed from a considerable inflow of the precious metals are considered by Montesquieu, *Esprit*, XXI.xxii, 'Of the Riches which Spain drew from America'.
    [22] See above, II.ii.30.

the same way as this absurd policy of Spain and Portugal. Whatever be the actual state of tillage, it renders our corn somewhat dearer in the home market than it otherwise would be in that state, and [275] somewhat cheaper in the foreign; and as the average money price of corn regulates more or less that of all other commodities, it lowers the value of silver considerably in the one, and tends to raise it a little in the other. It enables foreigners, the Dutch in particular, not only to eat our corn cheaper than they otherwise could do, but sometimes to eat it cheaper than even our own people can do upon the same occasions; as we are assured by an excellent authority, that of Sir Matthew Decker.[23] It hinders our own workmen from furnishing their goods for so small a quantity of silver as they otherwise might do; and enables the Dutch to furnish their's for a smaller. It tends to render our manufactures somewhat dearer in every market, and their's somewhat cheaper than they otherwise would be, and consequently to give their industry a double advantage over our own.

21   The bounty, as it raises in the home market, not ʳso muchʳ the real, ˢasˢ the nominal price of our corn, as it augments, not the quantity of labour which a certain quantity of corn can maintain and employ, but only the quantity of silver which it will exchange for, it discourages our manufactures, without rendering ᵗany considerableᵗ service either to our farmers or country gentlemen. It puts, indeed, a little more money into the pockets of both, and it will perhaps be somewhat difficult to persuade the greater part of them that this is not rendering them a very ᵘconsiderableᵘ service. But if this money sinks in its value, in the quantity of labour, provisions, [276] and ᵛhome-madeᵛ commodities of all different kinds which it is capable of purchasing, as much as it rises in its quantity, the service will be ʷlittle more thanʷ nominal and imaginary.

22   There is, perhaps, but one set of men in the whole commonwealth to whom the bounty either was or could be ˣessentiallyˣ serviceable. These were the corn merchants, the exporters and importers of corn. In years of plenty the bounty necessarily occasioned a greater exportation than would otherwise have taken place; and by hindering the plenty of one year from relieving the scarcity of another, it occasioned in years of scarcity a greater importation than would otherwise have been necessary.[24] It increased the business of the corn merchant in both; and in years of scarcity, it not only enabled him to import a greater quantity, but to sell it for a better price, and consequently with a greater profit than he could otherwise have made,

---

ʳ⁻ʳ 3–6   ˢ⁻ˢ but only 1–2   ᵗ⁻ᵗ the smallest real 1–2   ᵘ⁻ᵘ real 1–2
ᵛ⁻ᵛ 3–6   ʷ⁻ʷ merely 1–2   ˣ⁻ˣ really 1–2

---

[23] '. . . bounties on exported corn, fish and flesh serve to feed the French cheaper than our own people.' (M. Decker, *Essay on the Causes of the Decline of Foreign Trade* (London, 1740), 45.) Decker is also mentioned at IV.vii.c.22, V.ii.k.9, 18, and V.iii.74.
[24] The same point is made above, I.xi.g.4 and IV.ii.20.

if the plenty of one year had not been more or less hindered from relieving the scarcity of another. It is in this set of men, accordingly, that I have observed the greatest zeal for the continuance or renewal of the bounty.

23   Our country gentlemen, when they imposed the high duties upon the importation of foreign corn, which in times of moderate plenty amount to a prohibition,[25] and when they established the bounty, seem to have imitated the conduct of our manufacturers.[26] By the one institution, they secured to themselves the monopoly of the home-market, and by the other they endeavoured [277] to prevent that market from ever being over-stocked with their commodity. By both they endeavoured to raise its real value, in the same manner as our manufacturers had, by the like institutions, raised the real value of many different sorts of manufactured goods. They did not perhaps attend to the great and essential difference which nature has established between corn and almost every other sort of goods. When either by the monopoly of the home-market, or by a bounty upon exportation, you enable our woollen or linen manufacturers to sell their goods for somewhat a better price than they otherwise could get for them, you raise, not only the nominal, but the real price of those goods. You render them equivalent to a greater quantity of labour and subsistence, you encrease not only the nominal, but the real profit, the real wealth and revenue of those ʸmanufacturersʸ, and you enable them either to live better themselves, or to employ a greater quantity of labour in those particular manufactures. You really encourage those manufactures, and direct towards them a greater quantity of the industry of the country, than what would probably go to them of its own accord.[27] But when by the like institutions you raise the nominal or money-price of corn, you do not raise its real value. You do not increase the real wealth, the real revenue either of our farmers or country gentlemen. You do not encourage the growth of corn, because you do not enable them to maintain and employ more labourers in raising it. The nature [278] of things has stamped upon corn a real value which ᶻcannot be altered by merely altering its money priceᶻ.[28]

ʸ⁻ʸ manufactures 4 ⟨corrected 4e–6⟩   ᶻ⁻ᶻ no human institution can alter 1

[25] 22 Charles II, c. 13 (1670). See also III.iv.20, IV.ii.1, IV.ii.16, IV.v.b.33, IV.v.b.37–8, IV.vii.b.33, V.ii.k.13.

[26] See above, I.xi.g.10, where it is pointed out that in 1688, when the bounty was first granted, the country gentlemen 'then composed a still greater proportion of the legislature than they do at present'. See also IV.ii.21.

[27] See above, IV.ii.2, for an elaboration of this point, and cf. IV.ix.49.

[28] In the original formulation of this passage, Smith referred to corn as having a 'real value which no human institution can alter'. Pownall objected to this doctrine, (*Letter*, 13) but it would appear that Smith altered the passage as a result of criticism from James Anderson, author of *Observations on the Means of Exciting a Spirit of National Industry* (1777). In Letter 208 addressed to Andreas Holt, dated October 1780, Smith referred to Anderson as 'A very diligent, laborious, honest Man' and added that in the first edition of the WN:

I happened to say that the nature of things had stamped a real value upon Corn which

No bounty upon exportation, no monopoly of the home market, can raise ᵃthat valueᵃ.²⁹ The freest competition cannot lower it. Through the world in general that value is equal to the quantity of labour which it can maintain, and in every particular place it is equal to the quantity of labour which it can maintain in the way, whether liberal, moderate, or scanty, in which labour is commonly maintained in that place. Woollen or linen cloth are not the regulating commodities by which the real value of all other commodities must be finally measured and determined. Corn is. The real value of every other commodity is finally measured and determined by the proportion which its average money price bears to the average money price of corn. The real value of corn does not vary with those variations in its average money price, which sometimes occur from one century to another. It is the real value of silver which varies with them.

24   Bounties upon the exportation of any home-made commodity are liable, first, to that general objection which may be made to all the different expedients of the mercantile system; the objection of forcing some part of the industry of the country into a channel less advantageous than that in which it would run of its own accord:³⁰ and, secondly, to the particular objection of forcing it, not only into a channel that is less advantageous, but into one that is actually dis-[279]advantageous; the trade which cannot be carried on but by means of a bounty being necessarily a losing trade. The bounty upon the exportation of corn is liable to this further objection, that it can in no respect promote the raising of that particular commodity of which it was meant to encourage the production. When our country gentlemen, therefore, demanded the establishment of the bounty, though they acted in imitation of our merchants and manufacturers, they did not act with that compleat comprehension of their own interest which commonly directs the conduct of those two other orders of people.³¹ They

---

ᵃ⁻ᵃ it *1*

no human institution can alter. The expression was certainly too strong, and had escaped me in the heat of Writing. I ought to have said that the nature of things had stamped upon corn a real value which could not be altered merely by altering its Money price. This was all that the argument required, and all that I really meant.

Anderson quotes the disputed passage at p. 355 and considers Smith's position as a whole in his postscript to Letter XIII entitled 'On the Nature and Influence of the Bounty on Corn, and the other Corn Laws of Great Britain'. In this section Anderson argued that the 'general system of corn laws in England' was calculated to prevent the fluctuation of the price of grain', and as such 'extremely wise legislation' (310). He did, however, accept Smith's argument 'with regard to the very great utility of an unlimited freedom . . . to the internal police of grain', since otherwise 'the bounty can produce but a very limited and partial effect in regulating the price of grain' (370).

²⁹ See above, § 10.
³⁰ A similar phrase occurs above, at § 3.
³¹ See above, I.xi.p.10. Smith points out below, V.ii.k.12, that if a bounty could 'in any case be reasonable', it might be applied to the transportation of coal.

loaded the publick revenue with a very considerable expence;[32] *b*they imposed a very heavy tax upon the whole body of the people;*b* but they did not, in any *c*sensible degree,*c* increase the real value of their own commodity; and by lowering somewhat the real value of silver, they discouraged, in some degree, the general industry of the country, and, instead of advancing, retarded more or less the improvement of their own lands, which necessarily depends upon the general industry of the country.

25   To encourage the production of any commodity, a bounty upon production, one should imagine, would have a more direct operation, than one upon exportation.[33] It *d*would, besides, impose only one tax upon the people, that which they must contribute in order to pay the bounty.[34] Instead of raising, it would tend to lower the price of the commodity in the home market; and thereby, instead of imposing a second tax [280] upon the people, it might, at least, in part, repay them for what they had contributed to the first. Bounties upon production, however, have been very*d* rarely granted. The prejudices established by the commercial system have taught us to believe, that national wealth arises more immediately from exportation than from production. It has been more favoured accordingly, as the more immediate means of bringing money into the country. Bounties upon production, it has been said too, have been found by experience more liable to frauds than those upon exportation. How far this is true, I know not. That bounties upon exportation have been abused to many fraudulent purposes, is very well known. But it is not the interest of merchants and manufacturers, the great inventors of all these expedients, that the home market should be overstocked with their goods, an event which a bounty upon production might sometimes occasion. A bounty upon exportation, by enabling them to send abroad the surplus part, and to keep up the price of what remains in the home market, effectually prevents this. Of all the expedients of the mercantile system, accordingly, it is the one of which they are the fondest. I have known the different undertakers of some particular works agree privately among themselves to give a bounty out of their own pockets upon the exportation of a certain proportion of the goods which they dealt in. This expedient succeeded so well, that it more than doubled the price of their goods in the home market, not-[281]withstanding a very considerable increase in the produce. The operation of the bounty upon corn must have been wonderfully different, if it has lowered the money price of that commodity.

b–b *2A–6*   *c–c* respect *1–2*   *d–d* has, however, been more *1–2* text *2A–6*

[32] The same sentiments are expressed below, V.ii.k.13. Estimates of the cost of the bounty are provided at I.xi.g.18 and V.ii.k.28.
[33] Bounties on production are mentioned at IV.viii.15.
[34] See below, IV.viii.51, where it is pointed out that bounties involve in effect a double tax on the consumer.

26   Something like a bounty upon production, however, has been granted
upon some particular occasions. The ᵉtonnage bountiesᵉ given to the white-
herring and whale-fisheries³⁵ may, perhaps, be considered as somewhat of
this nature. They tend directlyᶠ, it may be supposed,ᶠ to render the goods
cheaper in the home market than they otherwise would beᵍ. In other
respects their effectsʰ, it must be acknowledged,ʰ are the same as those of
bounties upon exportation. By means of them a part of the capital of the
country is employed in bringing goods to market, of which the price does
not repay the cost, together with the ordinary profits of stock.

27   ⁱBut though the ʲtonnageʲ bounties to those fisheries do not contribute
to the opulence of the nation, ᵏitᵏ may perhaps be ˡthought, that they
contributeˡ to its defence, by augmenting the number of its sailors and
shipping.³⁶ Thisᵐ, it may be alleged, may sometimesᵐ be done by means
of such bounties at a much smaller expence, than by keeping up a great
standing navy, if I may use such an expression,ⁿ in the same ᵒwayᵒ as a
standing army.

28   ᵖNotwithstanding these favourable allegations, however, the following
considerations dispose me to believe, that in granting at least one of these
bounties, the legislature has been very grossly imposed upon.³⁷

ᵉ⁻ᵉ encouragements *1–2*   ᶠ⁻ᶠ *2A–6*   ᵍ in the actual state of production *1–2*
ʰ⁻ʰ *2A–6*   ⁱ No ¶ *1–2* ʲ⁻ʲ *2A–6*   ᵏ⁻ᵏ they *1–2*   ˡ⁻ˡ defended as conducing *1–2*
ᵐ⁻ᵐ may frequently *1–2*   ⁿ in time of peace, *1–2*   ᵒ⁻ᵒ manner *1–2*
ᵖ⁻ᵖ [to end of § 37] Some other bounties may be vindicated perhaps upon the same
principle. It is of importance that the kingdom should depend as little as possible upon its
neighbours for the manufactures necessary for its defence; and if these cannot otherwise
be maintained at home, it is reasonable that all other branches of industry should be taxed in
order to support them. The bounties upon the importation of naval stores from America,
upon British made sail-cloth, and upon British made gunpowder, may perhaps all three be
vindicated upon this principle. The first is a bounty upon the production of America, for
the use of Great Britain. The two others are bounties upon exportation. *1–2* text *2A–6.*
[The added passages may have been responsible for some delay in the publication of the
third edition. In Letter 227 addressed to Strahan, dated 22 May 1783, Smith wrote that
he awaited 'some accounts which my friend Sir Grey Cooper was so good as to promise
                                                                                    [*continues*]

---

³⁵ By 23 George II, c. 24 (1749) a bounty of 30s. a ton was to be paid on vessels of
between 20 and 80 tons, and a bounty of 2s. 8d. per barrel on herring exported. The Act
made other and less permanent provision for encouraging fisheries, notably the flotation
of the Society of the Free British Fishery. See below, IV.v.a.35. The bounty was raised to
50s. per ton in 1757 but payment became irregular. When the charter of the Society was
not renewed, the bounty was fixed at 30s. a ton and payment guaranteed by being charged
on the revenue from customs and excise duties. See also 11 George III, c.31 (1771). 11
George III, c.38 (1771) fixed the whale fishing bounty at 40s. a ton from 1771 to 1776;
30s. a ton from 1776 to 1781; 20s. a ton from 1781 to 1786. See below, IV.vii.b.30. In
Letter 299 addressed to Sir John Sinclair (undated), Smith wrote that: 'I could write a
volume upon the folly and bad effects of all the legal encouragements that have been given
either to the linen manufacture or to the fisheries.'
³⁶ See above, IV.ii.30, II.v.30. Smith refers to the need to protect strategically important industries below, § 36, and makes a related point at IV.vii.b.36.
³⁷ For a modern discussion see A. J. Youngson, *After the Forty-Five* (Edinburgh, 1973),
101–9.

29   First, the herring buss bounty seems too large.

30   [282] From the commencement of the winter fishing 1771 to the end of the winter fishing 1781, the tonnage bounty upon the herring buss fishery has been at thirty shillings the ton. During these eleven years the whole number of barrels caught by the herring buss fishery of Scotland amounted to 378,347. The herrings caught and cured at sea, are called ^qsea sticks^q. In order to render them what are called merchantable herrings, it is necessary to repack them with an additional quantity of salt; and in this case, it is reckoned, that three barrels of ʳsea sticksʳ, are usually repacked into two barrels of merchantable herrings. The number of barrels of merchantable herrings, therefore, caught during these eleven years, will amount only, according to this account, to 252,231⅓. During these eleven years the tonnage bounties paid amounted to 155,463*l*. 11*s*. or to 8*s*.2¼*d*. upon every barrel of ˢsea sticksˢ, and to 12*s*. 3¾*d*. upon every barrel of merchantable herrings.

31   The salt with which these herrings are cured, is sometimes Scotch, and sometimes foreign salt; both which are delivered free of all excise duty to the fish-curers. The excise duty upon Scotch salt is at present 1*s*. 6*d*. that upon foreign salt 10*s*. the bushel. A barrel of herrings is supposed to require about one bushel and one-fourth of a bushel foreign salt. Two bushels are the supposed average of Scotch salt. If the herrings are entered for exportation, no part of this duty is paid up; if entered for home consumption, whether the herrings were cured with foreign or with Scotch salt, only one shilling the [283] barrel is paid up.[38] It was the old Scotch duty upon a bushel of salt, the quantity which, at a low estimation, had been supposed necessary for curing a barrel of herrings. In Scotland, foreign salt is very little used for any other purpose but the curing of fish. But from the 5th April 1771, to the 5th April 1782, the quantity of foreign salt imported amounted to 936,974 bushels, at eighty-four pounds the bushel: the quantity of Scotch salt, delivered from the works to the fish-curers, to no more than 168,226, at fifty-six pounds the bushel only. It would appear, therefore, that it is principally foreign salt that is used in the fisheries.

me from the treasury, in order to compleat all the Additions which I propose to make to my third edition.' Writing again on 6 October (Letter 231) Smith indicated that while his proposed changes were virtually complete, he still awaited the accounts and the point is repeated in another letter (232) to Strahan dated 20 November. In letter 231 Smith told Strahan that he had hoped to get four months' leave of absence in order to see the new edition through the press: 'But a Welch Nephew of mine tells me that unless I advance him two hundred pounds he must sell his commission in the army. This robs me of the money with which I intended to defray the expence of my edition.' However Smith was successful in obtaining a similar period of leave some five years later, when working on the final edition of the TMS. Letter 276 addressed to Thomas Cadell, dated 15 March 1788.]

^{q–q} seasteeks 2*A*   ^{r–r} seasteeks 2*A*   ^{s–s} seasteeks 2*A*

[38] The amount paid in drawbacks may often have been less in many cases. The difficulties of notification were particularly acute in the Highlands, which were ill supplied with customs houses. Similar difficulties of collection applied to the bounties.

Upon every barrel of herrings exported there is, besides, a bounty of 2*s*. 8*d*. and more than two-thirds of the buss caught herrings are exported. Put all these things together and you will find, that, during these eleven years, every barrel of buss caught herrings, cured with Scotch salt when exported, has cost government 17*s*. 11¾*d*.; and when entered for home consumption 14*s*. 3¾*d*: and that every barrel cured with foreign salt, when exported, has cost government 1*l*. 7*s*. 5¾*d*; and when entered for home consumption 1*l*. 3*s*. 9¾*d*. The price of a barrel of good merchantable herrings runs from seventeen and eighteen to four and five and twenty shillings;[39] about a guinea at an average*.

32   Secondly, the bounty to the white herring fishery is a tonnage bounty; and is proportioned to the burden of the ship, not to her diligence [284] or success in the fishery; and it has, I am afraid, been too common for vessels to fit out for the sole purpose of catching, not the fish, but the bounty.[40] In the year 1759, when the bounty was at fifty shillings the ton, the whole buss fishery of Scotland brought in only four barrels of sea sticks. In that year each barrel of sea sticks cost government in bounties alone 113*l*. 15*s*.; each barrel of merchantable herrings 159*l*. 7*s*. 6*d*.

33   Thirdly, the mode of fishing for which this tonnage bounty in the white herring fishery has been given (by busses or decked vessels from twenty to eighty tons burthen), seems not so well adapted to the situation of Scotland as to that of Holland; from the practice of which country it appears to have been borrowed. Holland lies at a great distance from the seas to which herrings are known principally to resort; and can, therefore, carry on that fishery only in decked vessels, which can carry water and provisions sufficient for a voyage to a distant sea. But the Hebrides or western islands, the islands of Shetland, and the northern and north-western coasts of Scotland, the countries in whose neighbourhood the herring fishery is principally carried on, are every where intersected by arms of the sea which run up a considerable way into the land, and which, in the language of the country,

---

ᵗ See the accounts at the end of the volume.*ᵗ*

ᵗ⁻ᵗ om. 2A. In 2A the accounts are printed in the text.

[39] In Letter 203 addressed to William Eden, dated 3 January 1780, Smith discusses the desirability of repealing the prohibitions on imports and the abolition of bounties. In this connection, he mentioned that the selling price of British and Dutch cured herrings was 'about a guinea' per barrel, despite the fact that the latter were so vastly superior to British cured that 'you can scarce imagine the difference'. By putting a tax of half a guinea on Dutch herrings, thus confining them to the 'tables of the better sort'. Smith thought that British manufacturers might be encouraged to sell in a dearer market and thus raise the quality of their product: 'in five or six years time raise the manufacture to a degree of improvement, which at present I despair of its attaining to in fifty or Sixty years.'

[40] Cf. LJ (A) vi.92: 'When any branch of trade has a bounty on it all croud into it, and work not so much with expectation of answering a great demand but from a desire of making a fortune by this bounty, and proportion their work to it rather than to the demand.'

are called sea-lochs. It is to these sea-lochs that the herrings principally resort, during the seasons in which they visit those seas; for the visits of this, and, I am assured, of many other sorts of fish, are not quite regular and constant. A [285] boat fishery, therefore, seems to be the mode of fishing best adapted to the peculiar situation of Scotland; the fishers carrying the herrings on shore, as fast as they are taken, to be either cured or consumed fresh. But the great encouragement, which a bounty of thirty shillings the ton gives to the buss fishery, is necessarily a discouragement to the boat fishery; which, having no such bounty, cannot bring its cured fish to market upon the same terms as the buss fishery.[41] The boat-fishery, accordingly, which, before the establishment of the buss bounty, was very considerable, and is said to have employed a number of seamen, not inferior to what the buss fishery employs at present, is now gone almost entirely to decay. Of the former extent, however, of this now ruined and abandoned fishery, I must acknowledge, that I cannot pretend to speak with much precision. As no bounty was paid upon the outfit of the boat-fishery, no account was taken of it by the officers of the customs or salt duties.

34   Fourthly, in many parts of Scotland, during certain seasons of the year, herrings make no inconsiderable part of the food of the common people. A bounty, which tended to lower their price in the home market, might contribute a good deal to the relief of a great number of our fellow-subjects, whose circumstances are by no means affluent. But the herring buss bounty contributes to no such good purpose. It has ruined the boat fishery, which is, by far, the best adapted for the supply of the home market, [286] and the additional bounty of 2s. 8d. the barrel upon exportation, carries the greater part, more than two thirds, of the produce of the buss fishery abroad. Between thirty and forty years ago, before the establishment of the buss bounty, sixteen shillings the barrel, I have been assured, was the common price of white herrings. Between ten and fifteen years ago, before the boat fishery was entirely ruined, the price is said to have run from seventeen to twenty shillings the barrel. For these last five years, it has, at an average, been at twenty-five shillings the barrel. This high price, however, may have been owing to the real scarcity of the herrings upon the coast of Scotland. I must observe too, that the cask or barrel, which is usually sold with the herrings, and of which the price is included in all the foregoing prices, has, since the commencement of the American war, risen to about double its former price, or from about three shillings, to about six shillings. I must likewise observe, that the accounts I have received of the prices of former times, have been by no means quite uniform and consistent; and an old man of great accuracy and experience has assured me, that more than fifty years ago, a guinea was the usual price of a barrel of good

---

[41] Catches of the boat fishery were sometimes sold to the buss fishery, though the practice was illegal until 1787.

merchantable herrings; and this, I imagine, may still be looked upon as the average price. All accounts, however, I think, agree, that the price has not been lowered in the home market, in consequence of the buss bounty.

35   [287] When the undertakers of fisheries, after such liberal bounties have been bestowed upon them, continue to sell their commodity at the same, or even at a higher price than they were accustomed to do before, it might be expected that their profits should be very great; and it is not improbable that those of some individuals may have been so. In general, however, I have every reason to believe, they have been quite otherwise. The usual effect of such bounties is to encourage rash undertakers to adventure in a business, which they do not understand, and what they lose by their own negligence and ignorance, more than compensates all that they can gain by the utmost liberality of government. In 1750, by the same act, which first gave the bounty of thirty shillings the ton for the encouragement of the white herring fishery, (the 23 Geo. II. chap. 24.) a joint stock company was erected,[42] with a capital of five hundred thousand pounds, to which the subscribers (over and above all other encouragements, the tonnage bounty just now mentioned, the exportation bounty of two shillings and eight pence the barrel, the delivery of both British and foreign salt duty free) were, during the space of fourteen years, for every hundred pounds which they subscribed and paid in to the stock of the society, entitled to three pounds a year, to be paid by the receiver-general of the customs in equal half yearly payments. Besides this great company, the residence of whose governor and directors was to be in London, it was declared [288] lawful to erect different fishing-chambers, in all the different out-ports of the kingdom, provided a sum not less than ten thousand pounds was subscribed into the capital of each, to be managed at its own risk, and for its own profit and loss. The same annuity, and the same ᵘencouragementsᵘ of all kinds, were given to the trade of those inferior chambers, as to that of the great company. The subscription of the great company was soon filled up, and several different fishing-chambers were erected in the different out-ports of the kingdom. In spite of all these encouragements, almost all those different companies, both great and small, lost either the whole, or the greater part of their capitals; scarce a vestige now remains of any of them, and the white herring fishery is now entirely, or almost entirely, carried on by private adventurers.

36   If any particular manufacture was necessary, indeed, for the defence of the society, it might not always be prudent to depend upon our neighbours for the supply; and if such manufacture could not otherways be supported at home, it might not be unreasonable that all the other branches

---

ᵘ⁻ᵘ encouragement 2*A*

[42] The Society of the Free British Fishery.

of industry should be taxed in order to support it. The bounties upon the exportation of British-made sail-cloth,[43] and British-made gun-powder,[44] may, perhaps, both be vindicated upon this principle.

37   But though it can very seldom be reasonable to tax the industry of the great body of the people, in order to support that of some par-[289]ticular class of manufacturers; yet in the wantonness of great prosperity, when the publick enjoys a greater revenue than it knows well what to do with, to give such bounties to favourite manufactures, may, perhaps, be as natural, as to incur any other idle expence. In publick, as well as in private expences, great wealth may, perhaps, frequently be admitted as an apology for great folly. But there must surely be something more than ordinary absurdity, in continuing such profusion in times of general difficulty and distress.

38   What is called a bounty is sometimes no more than a drawback, and consequently is not liable to the same objections as what is properly a bounty. The bounty, for example, upon refined sugar exported, may be considered as a drawback of the duties upon the brown and muscovado sugars, from which it is made.[45] The bounty upon wrought silk exported, a drawback of the duties upon raw and thrown silk imported.[46] The bounty upon gunpowder exported, a drawback of the duties upon brimstone and saltpetre imported.[47] In the language of the customs those allowances only are called drawbacks, which are given upon goods exported in the same form in which they are imported. When that form has been ᵛsoᵛ altered by manufacture of any kind, ʷas to come under a new denomination,ʷ they are called bounties.

39   Premiums given by the publick to artists and manufacturers who excel in their particular occupations, are not liable to the same objections [290] as bounties.[48] By encouraging extraordinary dexterity and ingenuity, they serve to keep up the emulation of the workmen actually employed in those respective occupations, and are not considerable enough to turn towards any one of them a greater share of the capital of the country than what would go to it of its own accord. Their tendency is not to overturn the natural balance of employments,[49] but to render the work which is done in each as perfect and compleat as possible. The expence of premiums, besides, is very trifling; that of bounties very great. The bounty upon corn alone has sometimes cost the publick in one year, more than three hundred thousand pounds.[50]

ᵛ⁻ᵛ 3–6   ʷ⁻ʷ 3–6

---

[43] 12 Anne, c. 12 (1712) in *Statutes of the Realm*, ix.781–2; 12 Anne, st. 1, c. 16 in Ruffhead's edition.

[44] 4 George II, c. 29 (1730) and subsequent acts.   [45] 21 George II, c. 2 (1747).

[46] 8 George I, c. 15 (1721).   [47] 4 George II, c. 29 (1730).

[48] Smith also defends the use of premiums in order to encourage elementary education, at V.i.f. 56.

[49] A similar expression is used, for example, at IV.iv.14 and IV.vii.c.43.

[50] In Letter 203 addressed to William Eden, dated 3 January 1780, Smith made the

40 Bounties are sometimes called premiums, as drawbacks are sometimes called bounties. But we must in all cases attend to the nature of the thing, without paying any regard to the word.

ªDigression concerning the Corn Trade and Corn Lawsª

1 I cannot conclude this chapter concerning bounties, without observing that the praises which have been bestowed upon the law which establishes the bounty upon the exportation of corn, and upon that system of regulations which is connected with it, are altogether unmerited. A particular examination of the nature of the corn trade, and of the principal British laws which relate to it, will sufficiently demonstrate [291] the truth of this assertion. The great importance of this subject must justify the length of the digression.

2 The trade of the corn merchant is composed of four different branches, which, though they may sometimes be all carried on by the same person, are in their own nature four separate and distinct trades. These are, first, the trade of the inland dealer; secondly, that of the merchant importer for home consumption; thirdly, that of the merchant exporter of home produce for foreign consumption; and, fourthly, that of the merchant carrier, or of the importer of corn in order to export it again.

3 I. The interest of the inland dealer, and that of the great body of the people, how opposite soever they may at first sight appear, are, even in years of the greatest scarcity, exactly the same. It is his interest to raise the price of his corn as high as the real scarcity of the season requires, and it can never be his interest to raise it higher. By raising the price he discourages the consumption, and puts every body more or less, but particularly the inferior ranks of people, upon thrift and good management. If, by raising it too high, he discourages the consumption so much that the supply of the season is likely to go beyond the consumption of the season, and to last for some time after the next crop begins to come in, he runs the hazard, not only of losing a considerable part of his corn by natural causes, but of being obliged to sell what remains of it for much less than what he might have had [292] for it several months before. If by not raising the price high enough he discourages the consumption so little, that the supply of the season is likely to fall short of the consumption of the season, he not only loses a part of the profit which he might otherwise have made, but he exposes the people to suffer before the end of the season, instead of the hardships of a dearth, the dreadful horrors of a famine. It is the interest of

---

ª⁻ª 2–6

following reference to bounties on exportation: 'These in Scotland and England together amount to about £300,000 a year; exclusive of the Bounty upon Corn which in some years has amounted to a sum equal to all the other bounties.' See above, I.xi.g.18.

the people that their daily, weekly, and monthly consumption, should be proportioned as exactly as possible to the supply of the season. The interest of the inland corn dealer is the same. By supplying them, as nearly as he can judge, in this proportion, he is likely to sell all his corn for the highest price, and with the greatest profit; and his knowledge of the state of the crop, and of his daily, weekly, and monthly sales, enable him to judge, with more or less accuracy, how far they really are supplied in this manner. Without intending the interest of the people, he is necessarily led, by a regard to his own interest, to treat them, even in years of scarcity, pretty much in the same manner as the prudent master of a vessel is sometimes obliged to treat his crew. When he foresees that provisions are likely to run short, he puts them upon short allowance. Though from excess of caution he should sometimes do this without any real necessity, yet all the inconveniencies which his crew can thereby suffer are inconsiderable in comparison of the danger, misery, and ruin, to which they might sometimes be exposed by a less [293] provident conduct. Though from excess of avarice, in the same manner, the inland corn merchant should sometimes raise the price of his corn somewhat higher than the scarcity of the season requires, yet all the inconveniencies which the people can suffer from this conduct, which effectually secures them from a famine in the end of the season, are inconsiderable in comparison of what they might have been exposed to by a more liberal way of dealing in the beginning of it. The corn merchant himself is likely to suffer the most by this excess of avarice; not only from the indignation which it generally excites against him, but, though he should escape the effects of this indignation, from the quantity of corn which it necessarily leaves upon his hands in the end of the season, and which, if the next season happens to prove favourable, he must always sell for a much lower price than he might otherwise have had.

4   Were it possible, indeed, for one great company of merchants to possess themselves of the whole crop of an extensive country, it might, perhaps, be their interest to deal with it as the Dutch are said to do with the spiceries of the Molluccas,[1] to destroy or throw away a considerable part of it, in order to keep up the price of the rest. But it is scarce possible, even by the violence of law, to establish such an extensive monopoly with regard to corn; and, wherever the law leaves the trade free, it is of all commodities the least liable to be engrossed or monopolized by the force of a few large capitals, [294] which buy up the greater part of it. Not only its value far exceeds what the capitals of a few private men are capable of purchasing, but, supposing they were capable of purchasing it, the manner in which it is produced renders this purchase altogether impracticable. As in every civilized country it is the commodity of which the annual consumption is the greatest, so a greater quantity of industry is annually employed in producing

¹ The same point is made at I.xi.b.33 and IV.vii.c.101.

corn than in producing any other commodity. When it first comes from the
ground too, it is necessarily divided among a greater number of owners
than any other commodity; and these owners can never be collected into
one place like a number of independent manufacturers, but are necessarily scattered through all the different corners of the country. These first
owners either immediately supply the consumers in their own neighbourhood, or they supply other inland dealers who supply those consumers. The
inland dealers in corn, therefore, including both the farmer and the baker,
are necessarily more numerous than the dealers in any other commodity,
and their dispersed situation renders it altogether impossible for them to
enter into any general combination.[2] If in a year of scarcity therefore, any
of them should find that he had a good deal more corn upon hand than, at
the current price, he could hope to dispose of before the end of the season,
he would never think of keeping up this price to his own loss, and to the
sole benefit of his rivals and competitors, but would immediately lower
[295] it, in order to get rid of his corn before the new crop began to come in.
The same motives, the same interests, which would thus regulate the
conduct of any one dealer, would regulate that of every other, and oblige
them all in general to sell their corn at the price which, according to the
best of their judgment, was most suitable to the scarcity or plenty of the
season.

5   Whoever examines, with attention, the history of the dearths and famines
which have afflicted any part of Europe, during either the course of the
present or that of the two preceding centuries, of several of which we have
pretty exact accounts, will find, I believe, that a dearth never has arisen
from any combination among the inland dealers in corn, nor from any
other cause but a real scarcity, occasioned sometimes, perhaps, and in some
particular places, by the waste of war, but in by far the greatest number of
cases, by the fault of the seasons; and that a famine has never arisen from
any other cause but the violence of government attempting, by improper
means, to remedy the inconveniencies of a dearth.

6   In an extensive corn country, between all the different parts of which
there is a free commerce and communication, the scarcity occasioned by the
most unfavourable seasons can never be so great as to produce a famine;
and the scantiest crop, if managed with frugality and œconomy, will
maintain, through the year, the same number of people that are commonly
fed in a more affluent manner by one of moderate plenty. [296] The
seasons most unfavourable to the crop are those of excessive drought or
excessive rain. But, as corn grows equally upon high and low lands, upon
grounds that are disposed to be too wet, and upon those that are disposed to
be too dry, either the drought or the rain which is hurtful to one part of the

---

[2] The problem of dispersed situation is frequently mentioned in the discussion of
economic power. See, for example, IV.ii.21, IV.vii.b.24, and IV.viii.4, 34.

country is favourable to another; and though both in the wet and in the dry season the crop is a good deal less than in one more properly tempered, yet in both what is lost in one part of the country is in some measure compensated by what is gained in the other. In rice countries, where the crop not only requires a very moist soil, but where in a certain period of its growing it must be laid under water, the effects of a drought are much more dismal. Even in such countries, however, the drought is, perhaps, scarce ever so universal as necessarily to occasion a famine, if the government would allow a free trade. The drought in Bengal, a few years ago, might probably have occasioned a very great dearth. Some improper regulations, some injudicious restraints imposed by the servants of the East India Company upon the rice trade, contributed, perhaps, to turn that dearth into a famine.[3]

7   When the government, in order to remedy the inconveniencies of a dearth, orders all the dealers to sell their corn at what it supposes a reasonable price, it either hinders them from bringing it to market, which may sometimes produce a famine even in the beginning of the season; or if they bring it thither, it enables [297] the people, and thereby encourages them to consume it so fast, as must necessarily produce a famine before the end of the season. The unlimited, unrestrained freedom of the corn trade, as it is the only effectual preventative of the miseries of a famine, so it is the best palliative of the inconveniencies of a dearth; for the inconveniencies of a real scarcity cannot be remedied; they can only be palliated. No trade deserves more the full protection of the law, and no trade requires it so much; because no trade is so much exposed to popular odium.

8   In years of scarcity the inferior ranks of people impute their distress to the avarice of the corn merchant, who becomes the object of their hatred and indignation. Instead of making profit upon such occasions, therefore, he is often in danger of being utterly ruined, and of having his magazines plundered and destroyed by their violence. It is in years of scarcity, however, when prices are high, that the corn merchant expects to make his principal profit. He is generally in contract with some farmers to furnish him for a certain number of years with a certain quantity of corn at a certain price. This contract price is settled according to what is supposed to be the moderate and reasonable, that is, the ordinary or average price, which, before the late years of scarcity, was commonly about eight-and-twenty-shillings for the quarter of wheat, and for that of other grain in proportion. In years of scarcity, therefore, the corn merchant buys a great part of his corn for the ordinary [298] price, and sells it for a much higher. That this extraordinary profit, however, is no more than sufficient to put his trade upon a fair level with other trades, and to compensate the many losses which he sustains upon other occasions, both from the perishable

[3] See below, IV.vii.c.101.

nature of the commodity itself, and from the frequent and unforeseen fluctuations of its price, seems evident enough, from this single circumstance, that great fortunes are as seldom made in this as in any other trade. The popular odium, however, which attends it in years of scarcity, the only years in which it can be very profitable, renders people of character and fortune averse to enter into it.[4] It is abandoned to an inferior set of dealers; and millers, bakers, mealmen, and meal factors, together with a number of wretched hucksters, are almost the only middle people that, in the home market, come between the grower and the consumer.

9   The ancient policy of Europe, instead of discountenancing this popular odium against a trade so beneficial to the publick, seems, on the contrary, to have authorised and encouraged it.

10   By the 5th and 6th of Edward VI. cap. 14.[5] it was enacted, That whoever should buy any corn or grain with intent to sell it again, should be reputed an unlawful engrosser, and should, for the first fault, suffer two months imprisonment, and forfeit the value of the corn; for the second, suffer six months imprisonment, and forfeit double the value; and for the third, be set in the pillory, suffer imprisonment during the [299] king's pleasure, and forfeit all his goods and chattels.[6] The ancient policy of most other parts of Europe was no better than that of England.

11   Our ancestors seem to have imagined that the people would buy their corn cheaper of the farmer than of the corn merchant, who, they were afraid, would require, over and above the price which he paid to the farmer, an exorbitant profit to himself. They endeavoured, therefore, to annihilate his trade altogether. They even endeavoured to hinder as much as possible any middle man of any kind from coming in between the grower and the consumer; and this was the meaning of the many restraints which they imposed upon the trade of those whom they called kidders or carriers of corn, a trade which nobody was allowed to exercise without a licence ascertaining his qualifications as a man of probity and fair dealing. The authority of three justices of the peace was, by the statute of Edward VI. necessary, in order to grant this licence.[7] But even this restraint was afterwards thought insufficient, and by a statute of Elizabeth, the privilege of granting it was confined to the quarter-sessions.[8]

---

[4] It is remarked above, I.x.b.34, in the discussion of 'net advantages', that of the five circumstances which affect wages, only two are relevant in the determination of profits, the agreeableness of the business and the risk involved.

[5] 5 and 6 Edward VI, c. 14 (1551).

[6] See above, III.ii.21, and below, IV.v.b.26, where Smith compares the popular fear of engrossing and forestalling with the terrors of witchcraft.

[7] 5 and 6 Edward VI, c. 14, s. 5 (1551) allowed for licensing and so made the act less rather than more stringent. But in general the Act was aimed against regrators, forestallers, and engrossers.

[8] 5 Elizabeth I, c. 12 (1562), by transferring the power of licensing to quarter sessions, confirmed the impression of stringency in the provision for concessions.

12   The antient policy of Europe endeavoured in this manner to regulate
agriculture, the great trade of the country, by maxims quite different from
those which it established with regard to manufactures, the great trade of
the towns. By leaving the farmer no other customers but either the
ᵇconsumersᵇ or ᶜtheirᶜ immediate factors, the kidders and carriers of corn,
it endeavoured to [300] force him to exercise the trade, not only of a farmer,
but of a corn merchant or corn retailer. On the contrary, it in many cases
prohibited the manufacturer from exercising the trade of a shop-keeper, or
from selling his own goods by retail. It meant by the one law to promote the
general interest of the country, or to render corn cheap, without, perhaps,
its being well understood how this was to be done. By the other it meant to
promote that of a particular order of men, the shopkeepers, who would be
so much undersold by the manufacturer, it was supposed, that their trade
would be ruined if he was allowed to retail at all.

13   The manufacturer, however, though he had been allowed to keep a
shop, and to sell his own goods by retail, could not have undersold the
common shopkeeper. Whatever part of his capital he might have placed in
his shop, he must have withdrawn it from his manufacture. In order to
carry on his business on a level with that of other people, as he must have
had the profit of a manufacturer on the one part, so he must have had that
of a shopkeeper upon the other. Let us suppose, for example, that in the
particular town where he lived, ten per cent. was the ordinary profit both of
manufacturing and shopkeeping stock; he must in this case have charged
upon every piece of his own goods which he sold in his shop, a profit of
twenty per cent. When he carried them from his workhouse to his shop, he
must have valued them at the price for which he could have sold them to a
[301] dealer or shopkeeper, who would have bought them by wholesale.
If he valued them lower, he lost a part of the profit of his manufacturing
capital. When again he sold them from his shop, unless he got the same
price at which a shopkeeper would have sold them, he lost a part of the
profit of his shopkeeping capital. Though he might appear, therefore, to
make a double profit upon the same piece of goods, yet as these goods made
successively a part of two distinct capitals, he made but a single profit
upon the whole capital employed about them; and if he made less than this
profit, he was a loser, or did not employ his whole capital with the same
advantage as the greater part of his neighbours.

14   What the manufacturer was prohibited to do, the farmer was in some
measure enjoined to do; to divide his capital between two different employments; to keep one part of it in his granaries and stack yard, for supplying
the occasional demands of the market; and to employ the other in the
cultivation of his land. But as he could not afford to employ the latter for
less than the ordinary profits of farming stock, so he could as little afford to

ᵇ⁻ᵇ consumer *1*   ᶜ⁻ᶜ his *1*

employ the former for less than the ordinary profits of mercantile stock. Whether the stock which really carried on the business of the corn merchant belonged to the person who was called a farmer, or to the person who was called a corn merchant, an equal profit was in both cases requisite, in order to indemnify its owner for employing it in this manner; in order to put his business upon a level with other [302] trades, and in order to hinder him from having an interest to change it as soon as possible for some other. The farmer, therefore, who was thus forced to exercise the trade of a corn merchant, could not afford to sell his corn cheaper than any other corn merchant would have been obliged to do in the case of a free competition.

15   The dealer who can employ his whole stock in one single branch of business, has an advantage of the same kind with the workman who can employ his whole labour in one single operation.[9] As the latter acquires a dexterity which enables him, with the same two hands, to perform a much greater quantity of work; so the former acquires so easy and ready a method of transacting his business, of buying and disposing of his goods, that with the same capital he can transact a much greater quantity of business. As the one can commonly afford his work a good deal cheaper, so the other can commonly afford his goods somewhat cheaper than if his stock and attention were both employed about a greater variety of objects. The greater part of manufacturers could not afford to retail their own goods so cheap as a vigilant and active shop-keeper, whose sole business it was to buy them by wholesale, and to retail them again. The greater part of farmers could still less afford to retail their own corn, [d]or[d] to supply the inhabitants of a town, at perhaps four or five miles distance from the greater part of them, so cheap as a vigilant and active corn merchant, whose [303] sole business it was to purchase corn by wholesale, to collect it into a great magazine, and to retail it again.

16   The law which prohibited the manufacturer from exercising the trade of a shopkeeper, endeavoured to force this division in the employment of stock to go on faster than it might otherwise have done. The law which obliged the farmer to exercise the trade of a corn merchant, endeavoured to hinder it from going on so fast. Both laws were evident violations of natural liberty, and therefore unjust; and they were both too as impolitick as they were unjust. It is the interest of every society, that things of this kind should never either be forced or obstructed. The man who employs either his labour or his stock in a greater variety of ways than his situation renders necessary, can never hurt his neighbour by underselling him. He may hurt himself, and he generally does so. Jack of all trades will never be rich, says

[d-d] *om. 4–6*

[9] Smith comments on the advantages accruing to the London merchant dealing in a single type of linen, as compared to his counterpart in Glasgow or Aberdeen who might handle goods from Scotland, Ireland and Hamburg. See above, 32 n. 6.

the proverb. But the law ought always to trust people with the care of their own interest, as in their local situations they must generally be able to judge better of it than the legislator can do.[10] The law, however, which obliged the farmer to exercise the trade of a corn merchant, was by far the most pernicious of the two.

17   It obstructed, not only that division in the employment of stock which is so advantageous to every society, but it obstructed likewise the improvement and cultivation of the land. By obliging the farmer to carry on two trades in-[304]stead of one, it forced him to divide his capital into two parts, of which one only could be employed in cultivation. But if he had been at liberty to sell his whole crop to a corn merchant as fast as he could thresh it out, his whole capital might have returned immediately to the land, and have been employed in buying more cattle, and hiring more servants, in order to improve and cultivate it better. But by being obliged to sell his corn by retail, he was obliged to keep a great part of his capital in his granaries and stack yard through the year, and could not, therefore, cultivate so well as with the same capital he might otherwise have done. This law, therefore, necessarily obstructed the improvement of the land, and, instead of tending to render corn cheaper, must have tended to render it scarcer, and therefore dearer, than it would otherwise have been.

18   After the business of the farmer, that of the corn merchant is in reality the trade which, if properly protected and encouraged, would contribute the most to the raising of corn. It would support the trade of the farmer in the same manner as the trade of the wholesale dealer supports that of the manufacturer.

19   The wholesale dealer, by affording a ready market to the manufacturer, by taking his goods off his hand as fast as he can make them, and by sometimes even advancing their price to him before he has made them, enables him to keep his whole capital, and sometimes even more than his whole capital, constantly employed in manu-[305]facturing, and consequently to manufacture a much greater quantity of goods than if he was obliged to dispose of them himself to the immediate consumers, or even to the retailers. As the capital of the wholesale merchant too is generally sufficient to replace that of many manufacturers, this intercourse between him and them interests the owner of a large capital to support the owners of a great number of small ones, and to assist them in those losses and misfortunes which might otherwise prove ruinous to them.

20   An intercourse of the same kind universally established between the farmers and the corn merchants, would be attended with effects equally beneficial to the farmer. They would be enabled to keep their whole capitals, and even more than their whole capitals, constantly employed in cultivation. In case of any of those accidents, to which no trade is more

[10] Similar sentiments are expressed, for example, at IV.ii.10, IV.v.b.43, and IV.ix.51.

liable than theirs, they would find in their ordinary customer, the wealthy corn merchant, a person who had both an interest to support them, and the ability to do it, and they would not, as at present, be entirely dependent upon the forbearance of their landlord, or the mercy of his steward. Were it possible, as perhaps it is not, to establish this intercourse universally, and all at once, were it possible to turn all at once the whole farming stock of the kingdom to its proper business, the cultivation of land, withdrawing it from every other employment into which any part of it may be at present diverted,[11] and were it possible, in order to support and assist upon occasion the [306] operations of this great stock, to provide all at once another stock almost equally great, it is not perhaps very easy to imagine how great, how extensive, and how sudden would be the improvement which this change of circumstances would alone produce upon the whole face of the country.

21   The statute of Edward VI.,[12] therefore, by prohibiting as much as possible any middle man from coming in between the grower and the consumer, endeavoured to annihilate a trade, of which the free exercise is not only the best palliative of the inconveniencies of a dearth, but the best preventative of that calamity: after the trade of the farmer, no trade contributing so much to the growing of corn as that of the corn merchant.

22   The rigour of this law was afterwards softened by several subsequent statutes, which successively permitted the engrossing of corn when the price of wheat should not exceed twenty, twenty-four, thirty-two, and forty shillings the quarter. At last, by the 15th of Charles II. c. 7. the engrossing or buying of corn in order to sell it again, as long as the price of wheat did not exceed forty-eight shillings the quarter, and that of other grain in proportion, was declared lawful to all persons not being fore-stallers, that is, not selling again in the same market within three months.[13] All the freedom which the trade of the inland corn dealer has ever yet enjoyed, was bestowed upon it by this statute.[14] The statute of the twelfth

---

[11] It is pointed out at II.v.37 that agriculture was 'almost every where capable of absorbing a much greater capital than has ever yet been employed in it'.

[12] 5 and 6 Edward VI, c. 14 (1551).

[13] See above, II.v.10, where the productive role of the merchant is explained.

[14] Smith's use of statutes in support of his argument in this paragraph is confusing. 5 and 6 Edward VI, c. 14 (1551) held 'it shall be lawful to every person or persons not fore-stalling, to buy engross and keep in his or their garners or houses such corn of the kind aforesaid': wheat at 6s. 8d. a quarter and other grain at related prices. The distinction was thus made clear, and was confirmed by 5 Elizabeth I, c. 12 (1562); between a forestaller as someone who bought or tried to influence the price of commodities on their way to market, a regrator who bought and sold grain in a market within a radius of four miles, and engrossers who bought growing corn. In 15 Charles II, c. 7 (1663) the provisions of 5 and 6 Edward VI, c. 14 were repeated but in a way which led to the confusion in the text between forestallers and regrators: 'It shall be lawfull for all and every person and persons (not forestalling nor selling the same in the same Market within three Months after the buying thereof) to buy in open Market, and to lay up and keep in his and their Graineries or Houses.'

[continues]

of the present king, which repeals almost [307] all the other ancient laws against engrossers and forestallers, does not repeal the restrictions of this particular statute, which therefore still continue in force.[15]

23   This statute, however, authorises in some measure two very absurd popular prejudices.

24   First, it supposes that when the price of wheat has risen so high as forty-eight shillings the quarter, and that of other grain in proportion, corn is likely to be so engrossed as to hurt the people. But from what has been already said, it seems evident enough that corn can at no price be so engrossed by the inland dealers as to hurt the people: and forty-eight shillings the quarter besides, though it may be considered as a very high price, yet in years of scarcity it is a price which frequently takes place immediately after harvest, when scarce any part of the new crop can be sold off, and when it is impossible even for ignorance to suppose that any part of it can be so engrossed as to hurt the people.

25   Secondly, it supposes that there is a certain price at which corn is likely to be forestalled, that is, bought up in order to be sold again soon after in the same market, so as to hurt the people. But if a merchant ever buys up corn, either going to a particular market or in a particular market, in order to sell it again soon after in the same market, it must be because he judges that the market cannot be so liberally supplied through the whole season as upon that particular occasion, and that the price, therefore, must [308] soon rise. If he judges wrong in this, and if the price does not rise, he not only loses the whole profit of the stock which he employs in this manner, but a part of the stock itself, by the expence and loss which necessarily *attend* the storing and keeping of corn. He hurts himself, therefore, much more essentially than he can hurt even the particular people whom he may hinder from supplying themselves upon that particular market day, because they may afterwards supply themselves just as cheap upon any other market day. If he judges right, instead of hurting the great body of the people, he renders them a most important service. By making them feel the inconveniencies of a dearth somewhat earlier than they otherwise might do, he prevents their feeling them afterwards so severely as they certainly would do, if the cheapness of price encouraged them to consume faster than suited the real scarcity of the season. When the scarcity is real,

e-e attends *1-2*

The various statutes determining the prices at which engrossing was permitted are difficult to trace. Smith may have been thinking of statutes which permitted exportation at certain prices. He refers to these statutes at IV.v.b.37, 38.

[15] It is doubtful if Smith's interpretation of 12 George III, c. 71 (1772) is wholly valid. The Act was a general statute repealing several laws against engrossers. 15 Charles II, c. 7 (1663) was not repealed until 10 Edward 7 and 1 George V, c. 8, s. 96 (1910), but the effectiveness of its restrictions on forestallers after the enactment of 12 George III, c. 71 is difficult to see.

the best thing that can be done for the people is to divide the inconveniencies of it as equally as possible through all the different months, and weeks, and days of the year. The interest of the corn merchant makes him study to do this as exactly as he can; and as no other person can have either the same interest, or the same knowledge, or the same abilities to do it so exactly as he, this most important operation of commerce ought to be trusted entirely to him; or, in other words, the corn trade, so far at least as concerns the supply of the home-market, ought to be left perfectly free.

26   [309] The popular fear of engrossing and forestalling may be compared to the popular terrors and suspicions of witchcraft.[16] The unfortunate wretches accused of this latter crime were not more innocent of the misfortunes imputed to them, than those who have been accused of the former. The law which put an end to all prosecutions against witchcraft, which put it out of any man's power to gratify his own malice by accusing his neighbour of that imaginary crime, seems effectually to have put an end to those fears and suspicions, by taking away the great cause which encouraged and supported them. The law which should restore entire freedom to the inland trade of corn, would probably prove as effectual to put an end to the popular fears of engrossing and forestalling.

27   The 15th of Charles II. c. 7. however, with all its imperfections, has perhaps contributed more both to the plentiful supply of the home market, and to the increase of tillage, than any other law in the statute book. It is from this law that the inland corn trade has derived all the liberty and protection which it has ever yet enjoyed; and both the supply of the home market, and the interest of tillage, are much more effectually promoted by the inland, than either by the importation or exportation trade.

28   The proportion of the average quantity of all sorts of grain imported into Great Britain to that of all sorts of grain consumed, it has been computed by the author of the tracts upon the corn trade, does not exceed that of one to five hun-[310]dred and seventy.[17] For supplying the home market, therefore, the importance of the inland trade must be to that of the importation trade as five hundred and seventy to one.

29   The average quantity of all sorts of grain exported from Great Britain does not, according to the same author, exceed the one-and-thirtieth part of the annual produce.[18] For the encouragement of tillage, therefore, by providing a market for the home produce, the importance of the inland trade must be to that of the exportation trade as thirty to one.

30   I have no great faith in political arithmetick, and I mean not to warrant

[16] See above, § 10, and also III.ii.21, where the laws affecting engrossing are described as 'absurd'.

[17] Charles Smith, *Three Tracts on the Corn Trade and Corn Laws* (1766), 145. See above, IV.ii.20, and IV.v.a.8.

[18] Ibid. 144. See above, IV.ii.20 and IV.v.a.8.

the exactness of either of these computations[19]. I mention them only in order to show of how much less consequence, in the opinion of the most judicious and experienced persons, the foreign trade of corn is than the home trade. The great cheapness of corn in the years immediately preceding the establishment of the bounty, may perhaps, with reason, be ascribed in some measure to the operation of this statute of Charles II., which had been enacted about five-and-twenty years before, and which had therefore full time to produce its effect.

31   A very few words will sufficiently explain all that I have to say concerning the other three branches of the corn trade.

32   II. The trade of the merchant importer of foreign corn for home consumption, evidently contributes to the immediate supply of the home market, and must so far be immediately bene-[311]ficial to the great body of the people. It tends, indeed, to lower somewhat the average money price of corn, but not to diminish its real value, or the quantity of labour which it is capable of maintaining. If importation was at all times free, our farmers and country gentlemen would, probably, one year with another, get less money for their corn than they do at present, when importation is at most times in effect prohibited; but the money which they got would be of more value, would buy more goods of all other kinds, and would employ more labour. Their real wealth, their real revenue, therefore, would be the same as at present, though it might be expressed by a smaller quantity of silver; and they would neither be disabled nor discouraged from cultivating corn as much as they do at present. On the contrary, as the rise in the real value of silver, in consequence of lowering the money price of corn, lowers somewhat the money price of all other commodities, it gives the industry of the country, where it takes place, some advantage in all foreign markets, and thereby tends to encourage and increase that industry. But the extent of the home market for corn must be in proportion to the general industry of the country where it grows, or to the number of those who produce something else, and therefore have something else, or what comes to the same thing, the price of something else, to give in exchange for corn. But in

---

[19] Cantillon remarked: 'There is no branch of knowledge in which one is more subject to error than Statistics when they are left to imagination, and none more demonstrable when they are based upon detailed facts.' (*Essai*, 175, ed. Higgs 133.) In Letter 249 addressed to George Chalmers, dated 10 November 1785, Smith commented that he had 'little faith in Political Arithmetic' and cited as an example the difficulties which had encumbered Alexander Webster's attempt to offer an accurate account of the population of Scotland. Webster (1707–84) had prepared *An Account of the Numbers of People in Scotland in the year 1755* (1755; reprinted in J. G. Kyd, *Scottish Population Statistics*, Scottish Historical Society Publication, 3rd series, xliii (Edinburgh, 1952)). In the same letter, Smith referred to Webster as 'of all the men I have ever known, the most skilful in Politic Arithmetic'. Despite his reservations about political arithmetic Smith was able to refer to the 'ever honoured' Sir William Petty, in Letter 30 addressed to Lord Shelburne, dated 4 April 1759.

every country the home market, as it is the nearest and most convenient, so is it likewise the greatest and most important market for corn. That rise in the [312] real value of silver, therefore, which is the effect of lowering the average money price of corn, tends to enlarge the greatest and most important market for corn, and thereby to encourage, instead of discouraging, its growth.

33   By the 22d of Charles II. c. 13. the importation of wheat, whenever the price in the home market did not exceed fifty-three shillings and four pence the quarter, was subjected to a duty of sixteen shillings the quarter; and to a duty of eight shillings whenever the price did not exceed four pounds.[20] The former of these two prices has, for more than a century past, taken place only in times of very great scarcity; and the latter has, so far as I know, not taken place at all. Yet, till wheat had risen above this latter price, it was by this statute subjected to a very high duty; and, till it had risen above the former, to a duty which amounted to a prohibition. The importation of other sorts of grain was restrained *at rates, and* by duties*g*, in proportion to the value of the grain, almost equally*g* high*. [313] *Subsequent laws still further increased those duties.*i

34   The distress which, in years of scarcity, the strict execution of *those laws* might have brought upon the people, would probably have been very great. But, upon such occasions, its execution was generally suspended by temporary statutes, which permitted, for a limited time, the importation of foreign corn.[21] The necessity of these temporary statutes sufficiently demonstrates the impropriety of this general one.

h* Before the 13th of the present king, the following were the duties payable upon the importation of the different sorts of grain:

Grain.	Duties.		Duties.	Duties.
Beans to 28s. per qr.	19s. 10d. after till 40s.	—	16s. 8d. then 12d.	
Barley to 28s.	19s. 10d.	32s.	— 16s.	12d.
Malt is prohibited by the annual Malt-tax Bill.				
Oats to 16s.	5s. 10d. after			9½d.
Pease to 40s.	16s. 0d. after			9¾d.
Rye to 36s.	19s. 10d. till	40s.	— 16s. 8d. then 12d.	
Wheat to 44s.	21s. 9d. till	53s. 4d. —	17s.	then 8s.
till 4 *l.* and after that about 1s. 4d.				

Buck wheat to 32s. per qr. to pay 16s.

These different duties were imposed, partly by the 22d of Charles II. in place of the Old Subsidy, partly by the New Subsidy, by the One-third and Two-thirds Subsidy, and by the Subsidy 1747.*h* [Smith has apparently taken his table from Charles Smith, *Three Tracts on the Corn Trade and Corn Laws*, 83. Charles Smith claims to have taken his from H. Saxby, *The British Customs*, but, apart from some inconsistencies in the rounding off of some very unwieldy fractions, Charles Smith miscopied some items from Saxby. The table is dervied from Saxby, 111–14.]

f-f 2–6   *g-g* proportionably *1*   *h-h* 2–6   *i-i* 3–6   *j-j* this statute *1–2*

[20] See above, III.iv.20, IV.ii.1, IV.ii.16, IV.v.a.23, and below, IV.v.b.37–8, IV.vii.b.33, V.ii.k.13.
[21] See below, § 38.

35   These restraints upon importation, though prior to the establishment
of the bounty, were dictated by the same spirit, by the same principles,
which afterwards enacted that regulation. How hurtful soever in themselves, these or some other restraints upon importation became necessary
in consequence of that regulation. If, when wheat was either below forty-
eight shillings the quarter, or not much above it, foreign corn could have
been imported either duty free, or upon paying only a small duty, it might
have been exported again, with the benefit of the bounty, to the great loss of
the publick revenue, and to the entire perversion of the institution, of
which the object was to extend the market for the home growth, not that
for the growth of foreign countries.

36   III. The trade of the merchant exporter of corn for foreign consumption,
certainly does not contribute directly to the plentiful supply of the home
market. It does so, however, indirectly. From whatever source this supply
may be usually [314] drawn, whether from home growth or from foreign
importation, unless more corn is either usually grown, or usually imported
into the country, than what is usually consumed in it, the supply of the
home market can never be very plentiful. But, unless the surplus can, in all
ordinary cases, be exported, the growers will be careful never to grow more,
and the importers never to import more, than what the bare consumption
of the home market requires. That market will very seldom be overstocked;
but it will generally be understocked, the people, whose business it is to
supply it, being generally afraid lest their goods should be left upon their
hands. The prohibition of exportation limits the improvement and cultivation of the country to what the supply of its own inhabitants requires.
The freedom of exportation enables it to extend *k* cultivation for the supply
of foreign nations.

37   By the 12th of Charles II. c. 4.[22] the exportation of corn was permitted
whenever the price of wheat did not exceed forty shillings the quarter, and
that of other grain in proportion. By the 15th of the same prince,[23] this
liberty was extended till the price of wheat exceeded forty-eight shillings
the quarter; and by the 22d,[24] to all higher prices. A poundage, indeed, was
to be paid to the king upon such exportation. But all grain was rated so low
in the book of rates, that this poundage amounted only upon wheat to a
shilling, upon oats to four-pence, and upon all other grain to six-pence the
quarter. By the 1st of William and Mary,[25] the act which established [315]
the bounty, this small duty was virtually taken off whenever the price of

---

k its *1–2*

[22] See above, IV.iv.3, and below, IV.viii.41 and V.ii.k.23–4.
[23] 15 Charles II, c. 7 (1663). See above, IV.v.b.22.,
[24] 22 Charles II, c. 13 (1670). See above, III.iv.20, IV.ii.1, IV.ii.16, IV.v.a.23, IV.v.b.33;
and below, IV.vii.b.33 and V.ii.k.13.
[25] 1 William and Mary, c. 12 (1688). See also I.xi.g.4, III.iv.20, IV.v.a.8, V.ii.k.13.

wheat did not exceed forty-eight shillings the quarter; and by the 11th and 12th of William III. c. 20. it was expressly taken off at all higher prices.[26]

38   The trade of the merchant exporter was, in this manner, not only encouraged by a bounty, but rendered much more free than that of the inland dealer. By the last of these statutes, corn could be engrossed at any price for exportation; but it could not be engrossed for inland sale, except when the price did not exceed forty-eight shillings the quarter.[27] The interest of the inland dealer, however, it has already been shown, can never be opposite to that of the great body of the people. That of the merchant exporter may, and in fact sometimes is. If, while his own country labours under a dearth, a neighbouring country should be afflicted with a famine, it might be his interest to carry corn to the latter country in such quantities as might very much aggravate the calamities of the dearth. The plentiful supply of the home market was not the direct object of those statutes;[28] but, under the pretence of encouraging agriculture, to raise the money price of corn as high as possible, and thereby to occasion, as much as possible, a constant dearth in the home market. By the discouragement of importation, the supply of that market, even in times of great scarcity, was confined to the home growth; and by the encouragement of exportation, when the price was so high as forty-eight shillings the quarter, that [316] market was not, even in times of considerable scarcity, allowed to enjoy the whole of that growth. The temporary laws, prohibiting for a limited time the exportation of corn, and taking off for a limited time the duties upon its importation, expedients to which Great Britain has been obliged so frequently to have recourse,[29] sufficiently demonstrate the impropriety of her general system. Had that system been good, she would not so frequently have been reduced to the necessity of departing from it.

39   Were all nations to follow the liberal system of free exportation and free importation, the different states into which a great continent was divided would so far resemble the different provinces of a great empire. As among the different provinces of a great empire the freedom of the inland trade appears, both from reason and experience, not only the best palliative of a dearth, but the most effectual preventative of a famine; so would the freedom of the exportation and importation trade be among the different states into which a great continent was divided. The larger the continent,

---

[26] 11 William III, c. 20 (1698) in *Statutes of the Realm*, vii.610–11; 11 and 12 William III, c. 20 in Ruffhead's edition.

[27] Because of 15 Charles II, c. 7 (1663). See above, IV.v.b.22 and 37.

[28] See above, III.iv.20, IV.ii.1,16, IV.v.a.23, IV.v.b.33; and below, IV.vii.b.33 and V.ii.k.13.

[29] In his *Three Tracts on the Corn Trade*, 44–5, C. Smith lists the major statutes about corn from 1534 to 1766 and then comments that 'although the Bounty hath been before suspended, and the Exportation prohibited, yet, till 1757, the Importation was never allowed duty free' (46). The statute to which he refers is 30 George II, c. 7 (1757), which allowed imports duty free until 25 August 1757.

the easier the communication through all the different parts of it, both by land and by water, the less would any one particular part of it ever be exposed to either of these calamities, the scarcity of any one country being more likely to be relieved by the plenty of some other. But very few countries have entirely adopted this liberal system. The freedom of the corn trade is almost every where more or less restrained, and, [317] in many countries, is confined by such absurd regulations, as frequently aggravate the unavoidable misfortune of a dearth, into the dreadful calamity of a famine. The demand of such countries for corn may frequently become so great and so urgent, that a small state in their neighbourhood, which happened at the same time to be labouring under some degree of dearth, could not venture to supply them without exposing itself to the like dreadful calamity. The very bad policy of one country may thus render it in some measure dangerous and imprudent to establish what would otherwise be the best policy in another. The unlimited freedom of exportation, however, would be much less dangerous in great states, in which the growth being much greater, the supply could seldom be much affected by any quantity of corn that was likely to be exported. In a Swiss canton, or in some of the little states of Italy, it may, perhaps, sometimes be necessary to restrain the exportation of corn. In such great countries as France or England it scarce ever can. To hinder, besides, the farmer from sending his goods at all times to the best market, is evidently to sacrifice the ordinary laws of justice to an idea of publick utility, to a sort of reasons of state; an act of legislative authority which ought to be exercised only, which can be pardoned only in cases of the most urgent necessity. The price at which the exportation of corn is prohibited, if it is ever to be prohibited, ought always to be a very high price.

40   [318] The laws concerning corn may every where be compared to the laws concerning religion. The people feel themselves so much interested in what relates either to their subsistence in this life, or to their happiness in a life to come, that government must yield to their prejudices, and, in order to preserve the publick tranquillity, establish that system which they approve of. It is upon this account, perhaps, that we so seldom find a reasonable system established with regard to either of those two capital objects.[30]

41   IV. The trade of the merchant carrier, or of the importer of foreign corn in order to export it again, contributes to the plentiful supply of the home market. It is not indeed the direct purpose of his trade to sell his corn there. But he will generally be willing to do so, and even for a good deal less money than he might expect in a foreign market; because he saves in this manner the expence of loading and unloading, of freight and insurance. The inhabitants of the country which, by means of the carrying trade,

---

[30] It is pointed out below, V.i.g.8, that positive law with regard to religion will always be 'more or less influenced by popular superstition and enthusiasm'.

becomes the magazine and storehouse for the supply of other countries, can very seldom be in want themselves. Though the carrying trade 'might' thus contribute to reduce the average money price of corn in the home market, it would not thereby lower its real value. It would only raise somewhat the real value of silver.

42   The carrying trade was in effect prohibited in Great Britain, upon all ordinary occasions, by the high duties upon the importation of foreign [319] corn*m*, of the greater part of which there was no drawback*m*; and upon extraordinary occasions, when a scarcity made it necessary to suspend those duties by temporary statutes, exportation was always prohibited. By this system of laws, therefore, the carrying trade was in effect prohibited upon all occasions.

43   That system of laws, therefore, which is connected with the establishment of the bounty, seems to deserve no part of the praise which has been bestowed upon it. The improvement and prosperity of Great Britain, which has been so often ascribed to those laws, may very easily be accounted for by other causes. That security which the laws in Great Britain give to every man that he shall enjoy the fruits of his own labour, is alone sufficient to make any country flourish, notwithstanding these and twenty other absurd regulations of commerce; and this security was perfected by the revolution, much about the same time that the bounty was established.[31] The natural effort of every individual to better his own condition,[32] when suffered to exert itself with freedom and security, is so powerful a principle, that it is alone, and without any assistance, not only capable of carrying on the society to wealth and prosperity, but of surmounting a hundred impertinent obstructions with which the folly of human laws too often incumbers its operations; though the effect of these obstructions is always more or less either to encroach upon its freedom, or to diminish its security. In Great Britain industry is perfectly secure; and though [320] it is far from being perfectly free, it is as free or freer than in any other part of Europe.

'–' must 6   *m–m* 2–6

[31] The link between personal security and economic growth is mentioned at II.i.30, and applied in explaining the rapid rate of growth attained in England, for example, at II.iii.36 and IV.vii.c.54. The same point is made with reference to the English colonies at IV.vii.b. 51ff.

[32] The term 'bettering our condition' occurs frequently, for example, at II.iii.28, III.iii.12, and IV.ix.28. Hume in his essay, 'Of Commerce', provides a rather interesting contrast with this passage: 'The poverty of the common people is a natural, if not an infallible effect of absolute monarchy; though I doubt, whether it be always true, on the other hand, that their riches are an infallible result of liberty. Liberty must be attended with particular accidents, and a certain turn of thinking, in order to produce that effect.' He continues: 'Where the labourers and artisans are accustomed to work for low wages, and to retain but a small part of the fruits of their labour, it is difficult for them, even in a free government, to better their condition . . .' (*Essays Moral, Political, and Literary*, ed. Green and Grose, i.297.)

44 Though the period of the greatest prosperity and improvement of Great Britain, has been posterior to that system of laws which is connected with the bounty, we must not upon that account impute it to those laws. It has been posterior likewise to the national debt. But the national debt has most assuredly not been the cause of it.[33]

45 Though the system of laws which is connected with the bounty, has exactly the same tendency with the police of Spain and Portugal; to lower somewhat the value of the precious metals in the country where it takes place; yet Great Britain is certainly one of the richest countries in Europe, while Spain and Portugal are perhaps among the most beggarly. This difference of situation, however, may easily be accounted for from two different causes. First, the tax in Spain, the prohibition in Portugal of exporting gold and silver,[34] and the vigilant police which watches over the execution of those laws, must, in two very poor countries, which between them import annually upwards of six millions sterling,[35] operate, not only more directly, but much more forcibly in reducing the value of those metals there, than the corn laws can do in Great Britain. And, secondly, this bad policy is not in those countries counter-balanced by the general liberty and security of the people. Industry is there neither free nor secure, and the civil and ecclesiastical governments of both Spain [321] and Portugal, are such as would alone be sufficient to perpetuate their present state of poverty, even though their regulations of commerce were as wise as the greater part of them are absurd and foolish.

46 The 13th of the present king, c. 43.[36] seems to have established a new system with regard to the corn laws, in many respects better than the ancient one, but in one [n]or two respects[n] perhaps not quite so good.

47 By this statute the high duties upon importation for home consumption are taken off [o]so[o] soon as the price of [p]middling wheat rises to[p] forty-eight shillings the quarter; [q]that of middling rye, pease or beans, to thirty-two shillings; that of barley to twenty-four shillings; and that of oats to sixteen shillings;[q] and instead of them a small duty is imposed of only six-pence upon the quarter of wheat, and upon that of other grain in proportion. [r]With regard to all these different sorts of grain, but particularly with regard to wheat, the home market is thus opened to foreign supplies at prices considerably lower than[r] before.

48 By the same statute the old bounty of five shillings upon the [s]exportation[s] of wheat ceases [t]so soon as the price rises to forty-four shillings the quarter,

[n–n] respect *1* [o–o] as *1* [p–p] wheat is so high as *1* [q–q] *2–6*
[r–r] The home market is in this manner not so totally excluded from foreign supplies as it was *1* [s–s] quarter *1*
[t–t] when the price rises so high as forty-four shillings, and upon that of other grain in

[33] Smith discusses the impact of a large and growing national debt on economic growth in V.iii.
[34] See above, IV.v.a.19. [35] See above, I.xi.g.33. [36] 13 George III, c. 43 (1772).

instead of forty-eight, the price at which it ceased before; that of two shillings and six-pence upon the exportation of barley ceases so soon as the price rises to twenty-two shillings, instead of twenty-four, the price at which it [322] ceased before; that of two shillings and sixpence upon the exportation of oatmeal ceases so soon as the price rises to fourteen shillings, instead of fifteen, the price at which it ceased before. The bounty upon rye is reduced from three shillings and sixpence to three shillings, and it ceases so soon as the price rises to twenty-eight shillings, instead of thirty-two, the price at which it ceased before.^{t} If bounties are as improper as I have endeavoured to prove them to be, the sooner they cease, and the lower they are, so much the better.

49   The same statute permits, at ^{u}the lowest^u prices, the importation of corn, in order to be exported again, duty free, provided it is in the mean time lodged in ^{v}a warehouse under the joint locks of the king and the importer^v. This liberty, indeed, extends to no more than twenty-five of the different ports of Great Britain. They are, however, the principal ones, and there may not, perhaps, be warehouses proper for this purpose in the greater part of the others.^{w}

50   So far this law seems evidently an improvement upon the antient system.

51   ^{x}But by the same law a bounty of two shillings the quarter is given for the exportation of oats whenever the price does not exceed fourteen shillings. No bounty had ever been given before for the exportation of this grain, no more than for that of peas or beans.^{x}

52   ^{y}By the same law too, the exportation of wheat is prohibited so soon as the price rises to forty-[323]four shillings the quarter; that of rye so soon as it rises to twenty-eight shillings; that of barley so soon as it rises to twenty-two shillings; and that of oats so soon as they rise to fourteen shillings. Those several prices seem all of them a good deal too low, and there seems to be an impropriety, besides, in prohibiting exportation altogether at those precise prices^y at which that bounty, which was given in order to force it, is withdrawn. The bounty ought certainly either to have been withdrawn at a much lower price, or exportation ought to have been allowed at a much higher.

53   So far, therefore, this law seems to be inferior to the antient system.

proportion. The bounties too upon the coarser sorts of grain are reduced somewhat lower than they were before, even at the prices at which they take place *1*
      $^{u-u}$ all *1* $^{v-v}$ king's warehouse *1*
      ^{w} Some provision is thus made for the establishment of the carrying trade. *1*
      $^{x-x}$ 2–6
      $^{y-y}$ But by the same law exportation is prohibited as soon as the price of wheat rises to forty-four shillings the quarter, and that of other grain in proportion. The price seems to be a good deal too low, and there seems to be an impropriety besides in stopping exportation altogether, at the very same price *1*

²With all its imperfections, however, we may perhaps say of it what was said of the laws of Solon, that, though not the best in itself, it is the best which the interests, prejudices, and temper of the times would admit of. It may perhaps in due time prepare the way for a better.²³⁷

---

²⁻² 2–6

---

³⁷ TMS VI.ii.2.18 makes an interesting point: 'Some general, and even systematical, idea of the perfection of policy and law, may no doubt be necessary for directing the views of the statesman. But to insist upon establishing, and upon establishing all at once, and in spite of all opposition, every thing which that idea may seem to require, must often be the highest degree of arrogance. It is to erect his own judgment into the supreme standard of right and wrong.' The example of Solon is cited in § 16.

Value between labor
interest } in free market
stock

TJ   farmer / manufacture
primogeniture
Cutvil